Selected Spiritual Writings of Anne Dutton:

Eighteenth Century, British-Baptist, Woman Theologian

Volume 7: Words of Grace

MERCER
UNIVERSITY PRESS

Endowed by
Tom Watson Brown
and
The Watson-Brown Foundation, Inc.

Selected Spiritual Writings of Anne Dutton

Eighteenth Century, British-Baptist, Woman Theologian

Volume 7: Words of Grace

Compiled and with an Introduction

by JoAnn Ford Watson

MERCER UNIVERSITY PRESS | *Macon, Georgia*

The James N. Griffith Series in Baptist Studies

This series on Baptist life and thought explores and investigates Baptist history, offers analyses of Baptist theologies, provides studies in hymnody, and examines the role of Baptists in societies and cultures around the world. The series also includes classics of Baptist literature, letters, diaries, and other writings.
—C. Douglas Weaver, Series Editor

MUP/ H889

Published by Mercer University Press
1400 Coleman Avenue
Macon, Georgia 31207

9 8 7 6 5 4 3 2 1

Books published by Mercer University Press are printed on acid-free paper that meets the requirements of the American National Standard for Information Sciences—Permanence of Paper for Printed Library Materials.

ISBN 978-0-88146-498-6

Cataloging-in-Publication Data is available from the Library of Congress

Contents

ANNE DUTTON
from the frontispiece to
Selections from Letters on Spiritual Subjects /etc./ (1884)

Preface

I want to thank Ms. Sylvia Locher, Head Librarian of Ashland Theological Seminary, for help in acquiring the manuscripts between these covers. I also wish to thank Mr. Kenneth Henke, Reference Archivist, and Dr. Clifford Anderson, Special Collections Curator, both of Princeton Theological Seminary Library, for permission to publish in rekeyed format the following manuscripts from the Luce Special Collection of Rare Books and Manuscripts of their library. These manuscripts were made available on the Theological Commons digital library project of the 2012 Bicentennial of Princeton Theological Seminary. These manuscripts are:

Letters On Spiritual Subjects, And Divers Occasions, Sent to the Reverend Mr. George Whitefield, And others of his Friends and Acquaintance. To which is added, *A Letter on the Being and Working of Sin, in the Soul of a justify'd Man, as consistent with his State of Justification in Christ, and Sanctification through Him: With the Nature of his Obedience, and of his Comfort, consider'd: As the one is from God, and the other to Him; notwithstanding his Corruptions may be great, and his Graces small in his own Sight.* As also, *A Letter on the Duty and Privilege of a Believer, To live by Faith, and to improve his Faith unto Holiness.* By One who has tasted that the Lord is Gracious. London: Printed by J. Hart, in Popping's-Court, Fleetstreet: And Sold by J. Lewis, in Bartholomew-Close, near West-Smithfield; and E. Gardner, at Milton's-Head, near Aldgate. 1745.

Letters On Spiritual Subjects, And Divers Occasions; Sent To Relations and Friends. By One who has tasted that the Lord is Gracious. London: Printed; and Sold by John Oswald, at the Rose and Crown in the Poultry, near the Mansion-house; and Ebenezer Gardner, at Milton's Head in Grace-church-street. 1740.

Letters On Spiritual Subjects, And Divers Occasions; Sent To Relations and Friends. By One who has tasted that the Lord is Gracious. London: Printed by J. Hart, in Popping's-Court, Fleet-street: And sold by J. Lewis, in Bartholomew Close, near West-Smithfield; and E. Gardner, at Milton's-Head, near Aldgate. 1746. Volume IV.

Letters On Spiritual Subjects, And Divers Occasions; Sent To Relations and Friends. By One who has tasted that the Lord is Gracious. London: Printed by

J. Hart, in Popping's-Court, Fleet-Street: And sold by J. Lewis, in Pater-noster Row; and G. Keith, at Mercers-Chapel, Cheapside. 1750. Volume VIII.

A huge thank you to Ms. Kathleen Slusser for typing and preparing the manuscript. My appreciation goes also to Mercer University Press for undertaking this seven-volume series.

The manuscripts have been rekeyed, but the original spelling has been retained, except for the Old and Middle English "f" routinely becomes "s," and the long "s" (B) becomes "ss." Page references to Anne Dutton's works in the introduction refer to the original manuscripts, not as reprinted in this volume.

Thanks to my husband, Dr. Duane F. Watson for editorial assistance, and my daughter, Christina, for love and encouragement. Thanks to my mother, Dr. Lucille Ford, for her support.

Introduction

Letters to George Whitefield and His Friends and Acquaintances

The first work by Anne Dutton offered here is:

Letters On Spiritual Subjects, And Divers Occasions, Sent to the Reverend Mr. George Whitefield, And others of his Friends and Acquaintance. To which is added, *A Letter on the Being and Working of Sin, in the Soul of a justify'd Man, as consistent with his State of Justification in Christ, and Sanctification through Him: With the Nature of his Obedience, and of his Comfort, consider'd: As the one is from God, and the other to Him; notwithstanding his Corruptions may be great, and his Graces small in his own Sight.* As also, *A Letter on the Duty and Privilege of a Believer, To live by Faith, and to improve his Faith unto Holiness.* By One who has tasted that the Lord is Gracious. London: Printed by J. Hart, in Popping's-Court, Fleetstreet: And Sold by J. Lewis, in Bartholomew-Close, near West-Smithfield; and E. Gardner, at Milton's-Head, near Aldgate. 1745.[1]

Dutton corresponded frequently with George Whitefield and was on favorable terms with him, probably due to his Calvinist sympathies. One of Dutton's letters to Whitefield is already included in volume 1, *Letters*, of this series. It is entitled, *A Letter from Mrs. Anne Dutton to the Reverend Mr. G. Whitefield,* and was published in Philadelphia and printed and sold by William Bradford, 1743.[2] This letter shows her influence in the American colonies and the Evangelical revival at the time.

Dutton wrote seventeen letters to Whitefield and his friends. The corpus of her correspondence is entitled, *Letters On Spiritual Subjects, And Divers Occasions, Sent to the Reverend Mr. George Whitefield, And others of his Friends and Acquaintance.* Letters 1–7 and 17 are addressed to Whitefield, and letters 7–16 are addressed to his friends. Whitefield has been called Dutton's "patron and

---

[1] Princeton Theological Seminary Library has the complete edition of the letters that are used here. The Pitts Theological Library of Emory University has an incomplete copy.

[2] *Selected Spiritual Writings of Anne Dutton*, 7 vols., ed. JoAnn Ford Watson (Macon GA: Mercer University Press, 2003) 1:1–4.

spiritual advisor."[3] Five of Whitefield's own letters are clearly addressed to Dutton. These are published in volume 1 of the 1771–1772 edition of Whitefield's *Works*.[4] Whitebrook's bibliography of Dutton's works mentions a collection of *Letters on Spiritual Subjects, sent to Relations and Friends* in which the third volume includes letters 1–6 and 17 addressed to Whitefield, and letters 7–16 addressed to Whitefield's friends. This refers to the collection published here.[5] Also, Dutton's *Occasional Letters on Spiritual Subjects*[6] contains various letters to Whitefield in volume 3 published between 1743–1744.[7] It is uncertain if this is the same as the volume 3 just mentioned or another volume of published letters to Whitefield. These letters to Whitefield are mentioned in the bibliography of Dutton's works by William Thomas Whitley,[8] and the bibliography edited by Edward C. Starr.[9]

This much-sought-after collection of letters to Whitefield is a rare treasure of correspondence between Dutton and Whitefield. Dutton penned the letters in 1745 and they include not only letters 1–6 and letter 17 to Whitefield ("W...d"),[10] but also letters 7–16 to acquaintances and friends of Whitefield. Notables are addressed such as Welsh revivalist Howell Harris (letter 7).[11] Letter

---

[3] Stephen Stein, "A Note on Anne Dutton, Eighteenth-Century Evangelical," *Church History* 44 (1975): 488.

[4] For a discussion of these, see Watson, ed., *Selected Spiritual Writings of Anne Dutton*, 1:xxiii–xxxvi. We are uncertain if other letters written by Whitefield to Dutton in volumes 2 and 3 of his *Works* are addressed to Dutton. See Watson, ed., *Selected Spiritual Writings of Anne Dutton*,1:xxv–xxvi.

[5] John Cudworth Whitebrook, *Ann Dutton: A Life and Bibliography* (London: A. W. Cannon and Co., 1921) 19n.50.

[6] 7 volumes. Popping's Court: J. Hart and Bartholomew Close. J. Lewis, 1740–1749.

[7] Whitebrook, *Ann Dutton*, 16n.5.

[8] *A Baptist Bibliography: Being a Register of the Chief Materials for Baptist History, whether in Manuscript or in Print, preserved in Great Britain, Ireland and the Colonies*, 2 vols. (London: Kingsgate Press, 1916, 1922; repr., 1 vol. [Hildesheim: Georg Olms, 1984] 213).

[9] *A Baptist Bibliography* (Rochester NY: American Baptist Historical Society, 1959), sect. D, p. 202.

[10] *Letters on Spiritual Subjects, and Divers Occasions, Sent to the Reverend Mr. George Whitefield, And others of his Friends and Acquaintance*, letters 1–6, pp. 3, 5, 8, 14, 17, 23; letter 17, p. 103.

[11] *Letters on Spiritual Subjects*, letter 7, p. 28.

9 mentions Whitefield's ministry in Georgia at Bethesda.[12] Letter 8 mentions Whitefield's ministry of preaching to the "Negroes"[13] and Whitefield's ministry in London at the Tabernacle.[14]

Of note is letter 16 addressed to the "Family at Bethesda," dated 28 February 1743. This letter which mentions the defeat of the Spaniards by the British.[15] It highlights the great victory of the British defeat of the Spanish invasion in the colony of Georgia in 1742. Dutton gives God glory for preserving Whitefield's Bethesda orphanage in Georgia in the "Battle of Bloody Marsh," 7 July 1742.[16]

Also included with the Whitefield corpus of letters is Dutton's letter on sin and the comfort of grace in Christ. It is entitled, *A Letter on the Being and Working of Sin, in the Soul of a justify'd Man, as consistent with his State of Justification in Christ, and Sanctificaton through Him: With the Nature of his Obedience, and of his Comfort, consider'd: As the one is from God, and the other to Him; notwithstanding his Corruptions may be great, and his Graces small in his own Sight.* This letter includes a brief epistle to the reader written by William Collins who recognized the great contribution of spiritual writing by the author as a woman, "wrote by a woman."[17] Her great blessing of grace was her writing for him and for the reader. He comments on her spiritual work to benefit the reader.[18]

Another of Dutton's letters included with the Whitefield letters is entitled, *A Letter on the Duty and Privilege of a Believer, To live by Faith, and to improve his Faith unto Holiness* (1745). This letter is addressed to Whitefield's "Society at the Tabernacle in London." Dutton describes herself as their "Friend and Servant."[19] Whitefield began the Tabernacle in 1741 in Moorfields in London.

---

[12] *Letters on Spiritual Subjects,* letter 9, p. 52.

[13] *Letters on Spiritual Subjects,* letter 8, p. 36.

[14] *Letters on Spiritual Subjects,* letter 8. p. 41.

[15] *Letters on Spiritual Subjects,* letter 16, p. 91.

[16] See a similar reference to this event in Dutton's letter 17 in Watson, ed., *Selected Spiritual Writings of Anne Dutton,*1:129–30. See also Edward J. Cashin, *Beloved Bethesda: A History of George Whitefield's Home for Boys, 1740–2000* (Macon GA: Mercer University Press, 2001).

[17] *A Letter on the Being and Working of Sin,* 109.

[18] *A Letter on the Being and Working of Sin,* 110. William Collins was a minister who had left Whitefield's Tabernacle in London as well as other places. See Whitebrook, *Ann Dutton,* 19n.48.

[19] *A Letter on the Duty and Privilege of a Believer,* 144.

By 1742, he had about 1100 members. John Cennick (1718–1755), a lay evangelist, was Whitefield's assistant at the Tabernacle. Howell Harris, a Welsh revivalist and associate of Whitefield, later took charge of Whitefield's work at the Tabernacle. Harris had warned that many of Whitefield's followers would leave and become Moravian Brethren due to their heavy influence there. Not surprisingly, in 20 November 1745, Cennick asked to become Moravian Brethren and many followed him. By 1746, Whitefield stated he had lost 400 of his approximately 1100 members to the Moravians.[20] Dutton later wrote a postscript to this letter to the Tabernacle addressing the Moravian Brethren controversy there. The *Postscript* was written in 1746, a year after this letter and is included in volume 6 of this series.[21] Dutton writes at the crucial time when the Moravian Brethren influence is heavy and is dividing the Tabernacle. She calls for obedience to faith and holiness among Whitefield's flock at the Tabernacle at this controversial time.

Dutton's correspondence with Whitefield demonstrates her great support of and encouragement for his work and ministry. In letter 1, Dutton encourages Whitefield to endure any trial the Lord asks of him and to offer the Lord whatever he asks. She admonishes that God asked Abraham to give up his son, Isaac, so Whitefield should have the same willing attitude.[22] In letter 2, Dutton writes of Whitefield's great revival work in England and Wales, and the "wonders of love" shown to him in Wales and Gloucester.[23] She speaks of God's great mercy and grace being poured out on Whitefield in London where he was

---

[20] Watson, ed., *Selected Spiritual Writings of Anne Dutton*, 4:xi–xii. See also Colin Podmore, *The Moravian Church in England, 1728–1760* (Oxford Historical Monographs; Oxford: Clarendon Press, 1998), 88–94.

[21] The postscript is entitled, *A Postscript to a Letter lately published on the Duty and Privilege of a Believer, To live by Faith, and to improve his Faith unto Holiness. Directed To the Society at the Tabernacle in London. To Make the Author's Sense of some Words and Phrases in that Letter, more plain to the Persons to whom That was sent, and This is addressed. To which is added A Caution against Error, when it springs up Together with Truth. In a Letter to a friend. As Also, Some of the Mistakes of the Moravian Brethren. In a Letter to another Friend with Postscripts to the Letters added. By One who has tasted that the Lord is Gracious.* London: Printed by J. Hart in Popping's-Court, Fleet- Street, 1746. This work is published in Watson, ed., *Selected Spiritual Writings of Anne Dutton*, 6:156–228. See the discussion in the introduction to volume 6, xiii-xvi.

[22] *Letters On Spiritual Subjects,* letter 1, p. 4.

[23] *Letters On Spiritual Subjects,* letter 2, p. 5.

working at the time this letter was written.[24] In letter 4, Dutton shows compassion for Whitefield and his well-being in ministry. She comments that she has not heard from him in some time: "It's an Age since I heard from you."[25] She encourages him to remain faithful in service to Christ and that Christ will refresh his soul. She is convinced of his faithfulness and that he will complete his work.[26]

Dutton opens letter 5 with great thanksgiving for Whitefield's kindness in writing to her, noting his labor for the Lord, which will be rewarded. Dutton encourages him, "CHRIST will lose nothing, none of your Service, but a full Reward shall be given you of the Prince of Love, according to his abundant Grace." [27] She also writes of the communion of love in the blood of the Lamb, and asserts that there will be no more discord or distance in the eternal Glory to come.[28] In letter 6, Dutton gives thanks for a letter recently received from Whitefield.[29] She affirms the all sufficiency of the grace of Christ for the Master's work against all of Whitefield's adversaries.[30]

Letters 7–16 are addressed to Whitefield's acquaintances and friends. Letter 7 is addressed to "Mr. H__ll H__s, Mr. R__d, and the rest of the Brethren that help with them and labour in the Gospel of Christ in Wales."[31] This letter is addressed to Howell Harris, the Welsh revivalist (1714–1773). Dutton is praising these revivalists for their success in preaching the gospel in Wales. She writes, "Oh my Brethren, what a bright Display of glorious Grace is *this*, That God is come down to dwell in poor *Wales*?"[32]

Letter 9 concerns Whitefield's various ministries in the American colony of Georgia. Dutton comments that Whitefield mentions that he might leave the ministry at Bethesda's orphan house. Dutton says she will pray for his sheep and leadership there.[33] She also refers to a woman who had read her *Letter to the*

---

[24] *Letters On Spiritual Subjects,* letter, 2, p. 5.
[25] *Letters On Spiritual Subjects,* letter 4, p. 14.
[26] *Letters On Spiritual Subjects,* letter, 4, p. 16.
[27] *Letters On Spiritual Subjects,* letter 5, p. 17.
[28] *Letters On Spiritual Subjects,* letter 5, p. 18.
[29] *Letters On Spiritual Subjects,* letter 5, p. 23.
[30] *Letters On Spiritual Subjects,* letter 5, p. 24.
[31] *Letters On Spiritual Subjects,* letter 7, p. 28.
[32] *Letters On Spiritual Subjects,* letter 7, p. 28.
[33] *Letters On Spiritual Subjects,* letter 7, p. 52.

Negroes and was moved by it.[34] This letter was occasioned by the conversion of twelve black slaves in 1741 in Jonathan Bryan's plantation in South Carolina. Bryan was a wealthy planter converted by Whitefield who became a benefactor of Whitefield's orphan house at Bethesda. Dutton comments on this letter, "Some Months ago, a dear young Woman told me, 'That in Reading my Letter to the *Negroes*, the Lord overcome her soul with the Love of Christ to poor Sinners....'"[35] This reference demonstrates that this letter was significant and had a readership and an evangelical influence in reaching out to African Americans in Georgia in the American colonies in the 1740s.[36]

Letter 16, dated 28 February 1743, is addressed to Whitefield's orphan house in Bethesda, to the "dear Family at Bethesda; assembled by the Father of Mercies, to be his Care, his Delight, his Habitation."[37] The letter has a note attached to it about the Spanish invasion in Georgia in 1742 and their defeat by the British. Dutton speaks of the power of God to deliver them from cruel enemies.[38]

Letter 17 is addressed to Whitefield, to "Mr. W__d." Dutton thanks Whitefield for his kind letter to her from Biddiford.[39] She speaks of God's deliverance of him from danger and assault as he risked his life to testify to the gospel and grace of God and spread the gospel in England. Dutton writes, "I rejoice and give Thanks; for that marvelous Deliverance which God wrought for you, when your Life was in such imminent Danger; and that the cruel Assault was over-rul'd for the Furtherance of the Gospel."[40]

---

[34] *Letters On Spiritual Subjects,* letter 7, p. 42. The full reference for this letter is, *A Letter to the Negroes Lately Converted to Christ in America. And Particularly to Those, lately Called out of Darkness, into God's Marvellous Light, at Mr. Jonathan Bryan's in South Carolina or A Welcome to the Believing Negroes, into the Household of God. By a Friend and Servant of Theirs in England.* Printed by J. Hart, in Poppings-Court, Fleet-Street: And Sold by J. Lewis, in Bartholomew-Close, near West-Smithfield; and E. Gardner, at Milton's-Head, in Grace Church-Street, MDCCXLIII.

[35] *Letters on Spiritual Subjects and Divers Occasions, Sent to the Reverend Mr. Whitefield*, letter 7, p. 42.

[36] This letter is published in Watson, ed., *Selected Spiritual Writings of Anne Dutton*, 5:363–79. See discussion of this letter in the same volume, xlii–xlvii.

[37] *Letters On Spiritual Subjects,* letter 16, p. 91.

[38] *Letters on Spiritual Subjects,* letter 16, p. 91.

[39] *Letters On Spiritual Subjects,* letter 17, p. 103.

[40] *Letters On Spiritual Subjects,* letter 17, p. 104.

Two further letters of Dutton are published with the corpus of the Whitefield letters. The first addresses the being and working of sin. It is entitled, *A Letter on the Being and Working of Sin, in the Soul of a justify'd Man, as consistent with his State of Justification in Christ, and Sanctification through Him: With the Nature of his Obedience, and of his Comfort, consider'd: As the one is from God, and the other to Him; notwithstanding his Corruptions may be great, and his Graces small in his own Sight.* She addresses justification in Christ and sanctification through him and his grace. Dutton is answering a letter referred to her by a friend concerning sin. She desires to answer his request for further clarification.[41] Dutton is a spiritual director and offers advice.[42] She writes that she will consider his complaints about the being and working of sin. She supports his desire for filial obedience and for comfort in Christ. She writes that humans are corrupt in their sin, but are regenerate in the grace of Christ.[43] The Holy Ghost is a comforting and sanctifying influence on the soul.[44]

Dutton writes that God furthers his grace in believers' souls. God gives consolations and fruits of holiness to the soul.[45] Dutton writes of the growth of holiness in the soul by the graces and fruits of the Holy Spirit: "And under further and greater consolations, you shall see further and greater Fruits unto Holiness. Your *old Heart*, your Iniquities, shall be *subdu'd*, and your *new Heart*, your Graces, shall be strengthened."[46] Dutton tells the recipient to make Christ his all in life, and look to Christ for all in life. She calls him to abide by faith in Christ and to come to him daily.[47] Christ will supply all human needs by his grace, which is like a fountain in plenty and abundance.[48]

In her second additional letter, Dutton writes as a friend to admonish the brethren at Whitefield's Society of the Tabernacle in London. The letter is entitled *A Letter on the Duty and Privilege of a Believer, To live by Faith, and to improve his Faith unto Holiness*. She calls the believers to live by faith as God commands, to faithfully believe in the name of Jesus.[49] She writes, "*First*, That it is the Duty and Privilege of a *Believer*, to live by *Faith*, is evident; in that *this is*

---

[41] *A Letter on the Being and Working of Sin*, 111.

[42] *A Letter on the Being and Working of Sin*, 112.

[43] *A Letter on the Being and Working of Sin*, 122.

[44] *A Letter on the Being and Working of Sin*, 130.

[45] *A Letter on the Being and Working of Sin*, 135.

[46] *A Letter on the Being and Working of Sin*, 135.

[47] *A Letter on the Being and Working of Sin*, 135.

[48] *A Letter on the Being and Working of Sin*, 138.

[49] *A Letter on the Duty and Privilege of a Believer*, 145.

God's Commandment, that we should believe on the Name of his Son Jesus Christ, I Joh. iii.23. That we should believe his infinite All-sufficiency, his Ability and Willingness to save...."[50]

Dutton continues to drive home the point to live by faith and to be filled with peace and joy.[51] She writes that God teaches his children to trust in him and his grace.[52] God calls believers to live a life of pure faith and holiness, resting in the promises of his grace.[53] She thus emphasizes, "*Secondly*, That it is the Duty and Privilege of a *Believer* to improve his Faith, unto *Holiness*."[54] Dutton states, "Believing our Interest in JESUS, it is our Duty to go out of our empty needy Selves, unto the Fulness of Christ by Faith, to derive Life and Strength from Him continually to maintain and increase our Graces, and to enable us for all holy Duties."[55] She calls believers to improve their faith unto holiness.[56] She states that it is the duty and privilege of believers to grow their faith and to use their faith for holy works in Christ Jesus.[57]

Letters on Spiritual Subjects

Three more works of Anne Dutton offered here are from a series of Dutton's letters published between 1740 and 1750, and all bearing the same title *Letters On Spiritual Subjects*. These include the following:[58]

Letters On Spiritual Subjects, And Divers Occasions; Sent To Relations and Friends. By One who has tasted that the Lord is Gracious. Printed; and Sold by John Oswald, at the Rose and Crown in the Poultry, near the Mansion-house; and Ebenezer Gardner, at Milton's Head in Grace-church-street. 1740.

Letters On Spiritual Subjects, And Divers Occasions; Sent To Relations and Friends. By One who has tasted that the Lord is Gracious. Volume IV. Printed by J. Hart, in Popping's-Court, Fleet-street: And sold by J. Lewis, in Bartholomew

---

[50] *A Letter on the Duty and Privilege of a Believer*, 145.

[51] *A Letter on the Duty and Privilege of a Believer*, 147.

[52] *A Letter on the Duty and Privilege of a Believer*, 158.

[53] *A Letter on the Duty and Privilege of a Believer*, 158.

[54] *A Letter on the Duty and Privilege of a Believer*, 163.

[55] *A Letter on the Duty and Privilege of a Believer*, 163.

[56] *A Letter on the Duty and Privilege of a Believer*, 163.

[57] *A Letter on the Duty and Privilege of a Believer*, 166.

[58] Princeton Theological Seminary Library has the complete editions of the letters that are used here.

Close near West Smithfield; and E. Gardner, at Milton's-Head, near Aldgate, 1746. Volume 4.

Letters On Spiritual Subjects, And Divers Occasions; Sent To Relations and Friends By One who has tasted that the Lord is Gracious. Volume VIII. Printed by J. Hart, in Popping's-Court, Fleet-Street: And sold by J. Lewis, in Pater-noster Row; and G. Keith, at Mercers-Chapel, Cheapside. 1750. Volume 8.

These volumes are held in the Princeton Theological Seminary Library in the Luce Special Collection, along with what is volume 4 (1748), which is included already in our current series.[59] The 1740 volume, as referenced first above, has no volume number, but is assumed to be volume 1 of its series. It contains Dutton's thirty-six letters of spiritual encouragement, quite a number of which are addressed to women. Volume 4 (1746) contains Dutton's forty-five letters of spiritual wisdom and advice addressed to a variety of people. Volume 8 (1750) includes Dutton's sixty-six letters giving spiritual direction.[60]

The series that includes these three volumes is not to be confused with the *Letters on Spiritual Subjects; Sent to Relations and Friends. By the Late Mrs. Anne Dutton.* Parts I and II, edited by Christopher Goulding (1823–1824), which is already included in our current series,[61] nor with the *Selections from Letters on*

---

[59] *Letters On Spiritual Subjects, And Divers Occasions; Sent To Relations and Friends. By One who has tasted that the Lord is Gracious.* London: Printed by J. Hart in Popping's-Court, Fleet Street: And Sold by J. Lewis, in Bartholomew-Close, near West-Smithfield, 1748. In Watson, ed., *Selected Spiritual Writings of Anne Dutton*, 5:103–288. See the discussion, xxi.

[60] Published with it is a document by another author that is not included here, entitled, *A Sermon Occasioned by the Sudden Death Of The Reverend and Learned Zephaniah Marryat, D.D. Preached In Southwark, September the 22d. By Thomas Hall. To which is added, The Funeral Oration at his Interment, By Thomas Towle.* Both Published at the People's Request. London: Printed for J. Buckland, in Pater-noster-Row; T. Field, in Cheapside; E. Dilly, in the Poultry; and A. Mason, in Fore-Street. MDCCLIV.

[61] *Letters On Spiritual Subjects; Sent To Relations and Friends. By The Late Mrs. Anne Dutton.* Edited by Christopher Goulding. Part I. Second Edition Revised. London: Printed For The Editor, By T. Bensley; And Sold By R. Baynes, 25 Ivy-Lane; John Eedes, 58 High-Street, Borough; And Other Booksellers, 1823 and Part II. Second Edition Revised. London: Printed For The Editor, By T. Bensley; And Sold By R. Baynes, 28, Paternoster-Row; J. Eedes, 2, Newgate-Street, And Other Booksellers, 1824. In Watson, ed., *Selected Spiritual Writings of Anne Dutton*, 6:57–155. See the discussion, ix.

Spiritual Subjects Addressed to Relatives and Friends edited by James Knight (1884), which is also already included in our current series.[62] These may or may not overlap with the seven-volume set of 1740–1749 bearing the title *Occasional Letters upon Spiritual Subjects*,[63] and the G. Keith edition entitled the *Letters On Spiritual Subjects and Divers Occasions* (1749).[64] There is also a compilation of Dutton's letters entitled, *Spiritual Subjects and Divers Occasions; Sent to Relations and Friends…to Which Are Prefixed, Memoirs of the Dealings of God with Her, in Her Last Sickness* (2 volumes in 1; London: G. Keith, 1769) in the Beinecke Rare Book and Manuscript Library of the Yale University Library.[65]

In volume I of *Letters On Spiritual Subjects, And Divers Occasions; Sent To Relations and Friends* (1740), Dutton addresses "My dear Friends'" and gives her letters as tokens of love for public reading to strengthen and encourage faith unto salvation. She now offers to have these letters printed for the public. They are useful for others to strengthen their faith for God's glory.[66] For example, letter 4 addressed to "Mr. H. T." is to encourage him to walk in the vocation to which he has been called. Dutton encourages him to walk in the love and grace in Jesus Christ.[67] Dutton addresses letter 18 to "Mrs. L" because Dutton does not have the ability to come to her for a visit.[68] She speaks to her of the grace of God for the sinner and the mercy of God poured out in Christ alone for salvation. Dutton writes that Christ saves a sinner "*with* his *whole Heart, and* his *whole* Soul…."[69]

Letter 24 is addressed to another woman, "Mrs. E.D."[70] Dutton speaks of Christ as the woman's husband in the relationship of faith and love. She

---

[62] *Selections From Letters On Spiritual Subjects Addressed To Relatives and Friends. By Mrs. Anne Dutton*, comp. James Knight, Southport (London, 1884). In Watson, ed., *Selected Spiritual Writings of Anne Dutton*, 1:85–402. See the discussion, xxxv.

[63] Whitebrook, *Ann Dutton*, 16n.5.

[64] Whitebrook, *Ann Dutton*, 18n.29.

[65] See the discussion in Watson, ed., *Selected Spiritual Writings of Anne Dutton*, 5:xxi.

[66] *Letters On Spiritual Subjects, And Divers Occasions; Sent To Relations and Friends. By One who has tasted that the Lord is Gracious.* Printed; and Sold by John Oswald, at the Rose and Crown in the Poultry, near the Mansion-house; and Ebenezer Gardner, at Milton's Head in Grace-church-street. 1740. Letter 1, pp. 3–4.

[67] *Letters On Spiritual Subjects*, letter 1, p. 11.

[68] *Letters On Spiritual Subjects*, letter 1, p. 126.

[69] *Letters On Spiritual Subjects*, letter 1, p. 129.

[70] *Letters On Spiritual Subjects*, letter 1, p. 162.

employs a marriage metaphor, writing to her of the sweetness of the woman's union with Christ as her husband. She writes, "that he should give himself to thee, to be thy Husband, and betroth thee unto himself for ever, while thousands are passed by!"[71]

In letter 29 to "Mrs. E. G.," Dutton offers spiritual comfort and hope against the distress of atheistic thoughts and the attacks of Satan.[72] She exhorts Mrs. E.G. to flee for refuge in Christ. She encourages her to hope in him against temptation and sin, for Christ is our "Hiding-Place from the Wind of Satan's Temptations."[73] Letter 31 is addressed to "Mr. W. and E. C." as "*Dear Brother and Sister*" and speaks of hearing of their troubles. Dutton is seeking a holy use for their troubles and hopes for a happy deliverance for them.[74]

Volume 4 of *Letters On Spiritual Subjects, And Divers Occasions; Sent To Relations and Friends* (1746) comprises forty-five letters. Letter 1 is addressed to "Mr. and Mrs. W__s" and "*My Dear and Honour'd Parents.*"[75] These are Dutton's parents. Her maiden name was Williams and she was born in Northampton, England, probably in 1692.[76] She writes, "We are *Heirs of Promise*, my dear Parents: And therefore our Inheritance is secure."[77] She speaks of their union of love in Christ, and that they are all chosen in Him for salvation and eternity by grace.[78] Their salvation is secure. She ends the letter with the words, "*The Grace of Christ be with your Spirit*—I am, my honour'd Parents, *Your most dutiful Child,...*"[79]

Letter 3 is addressed to two women, "Mrs. A. and Mrs. M. W__s." Dutton speaks of the help of Jesus for sinners caught in the wages of sin.[80]

---

[71] *Letters On Spiritual Subjects*, letter 1, p. 165.

[72] *Letters On Spiritual Subjects*, letter 1, pp. 192–93.

[73] *Letters On Spiritual Subjects*, letter 1, p. 195.

[74] *Letters On Spiritual Subjects*, letter 1, p. 214.

[75] *Letters On Spiritual Subjects, And Divers Occasions; Sent To Relations and Friends. By One who has tasted that the Lord is Gracious.* Volume IV. Printed by J. Hart, in Popping's-Court, Fleet-street: And sold by J. Lewis, in Bartholomew Close near West Smithfield; and E. Gardner, at Milton's-Head, near Aldgate, 1746. Letter 4, p. 3.

[76] For bibliographical information on Dutton's life, see Watson, ed., *Selected Spiritual Writings of Anne Dutton*, 1:xiii.

[77] *Letters On Spiritual Subjects*, letter 4, p. 3.

[78] *Letters On Spiritual Subjects*, letter 4, pp. 3–4.

[79] *Letters On Spiritual Subjects*, letter 4, p. 4. Letter 4 (pp. 11–12) and letter 9 (pp. 22–23) are also addressed to "My Dear and Honour'd Parents."

[80] *Letters On Spiritual Subjects*, letter 4, p. 9.

Letter 5 to "Mr. F__o" describes Jesus as a "loving, tender *Friend*, an omnipotent, faithful *Friend*, the only, and everlasting *Friend* of Sinners."[81] In letter 27, addressed to "Mr. L__s," Dutton thanks him for his letter and rejoices with him that his hope in God is strengthened. She is glad that her letters to him are a means of comfort to his soul.[82] She writes, "The Account you gave me, of the Lord's making my poor Letters of such Use to you, melted me into Tears of Joy and Thanksfulness. The Lord thereby enlarg'd my Heart to praise Him, and fill'd me with vast Desires to serve Him."[83]

Letter 39 is addressed to "Mrs. L__n." Dutton is concerned that this woman will perish by her ignorance and sin, but recognizes that the woman sees her need for Jesus, the Physician. Dutton emphasizes that Jesus is a remedy for her sin, offering salvation rather than eternal death. She writes, "Now you are sick, you have *need of the Physician.* Now you see your Sickness as a Sinner, the Savior will be desired by you."[84]

Letter 43 addressed to "Mr. B__m" is a letter of spiritual encouragement during the sharp winter season of faith. Dutton is a fervent spiritual encourager and guide through this season of darkness. She offers safety and hope in Christ. By Christ's grace, our life is preserved under opposition. For Dutton, we are, nevertheless perfected in glory through Christ in times of darkness and trial. She writes encouraging words of the power of Christ's grace, telling this gentleman that Christ's grace in him can never be extinguished by the dark circumstances of life or by Satan. She pens, "I Hope you experience that *Christ lives in you.* That your Life as a Branch in him your living Root, as a Union to him, as having Communion with him, is secretly maintain'd in the darkest and sharpest Winter-Seasons.[85]

In volume 8 of *Letters On Spiritual Subjects, And Divers Occasions; Sent To Relations and Friends* (1750) there are sixty-six letters addressed to people offering spiritual direction. Letters 1 and 2 are addressed to "Mr. W., *Ever Dear and Honour'd Father*,"[86] are addressed to Dutton's own father, for her maiden

---

[81] *Letters On Spiritual Subjects,* letter 4, p. 13. Letter 19 (pp. 41–42) is also addressed to "Mr. F___O."

[82] *Letters On Spiritual Subjects,* letter 4, p. 61.

[83] *Letters On Spiritual Subjects,* letter 4, p. 61.

[84] *Letters On Spiritual Subjects,* letter 4, p. 93.

[85] *Letters On Spiritual Subjects,* letter 4, p. 102.

[86] *Letters On Spiritual Subjects, and Divers Occasions; Sent To Relations and Friends By One who has tasted that the Lord is Gracious.* Volume VIII. Printed by J. Hart, in

name was Williams. A lot of the letters in this last volume of this series are addressed to men. Letter 4 is addressed to "Mr. T., *My very Dear and Honour'd Brother*."[87] She prays for the return of his health. She also prays for continued blessing in his service to his Church.[88]

Letter 13 addressed to "Mr. L.,"[89] concerns the salvation of his soul. Dutton writes to him to call him to salvation. She states that "*Jesus Christ came into the World to save lost Sinners*."[90] In letter 21 to "Mr. F.,"[91] Dutton speaks eschatologically. She believes the time of Christ's return is imminent. She advocates expectancy of Christ's parousia; to be waiting and watching for him is her admonition. She writes, "It is indeed, Sir, the *last Time*, the Signs of our *Lord's Coming* are upon us. Happy will it be for those Servants of his, who shall be found *watching*."[92] She also warns of coming judgment, citing recent events as evidence: "Two late Shocks of *Earthquakes* felt in *London*, are eminently such."[93]

Dutton does address some letters to women. For example, she corresponds with "Mrs. K" in letter 39.[94] Dutton thanks her for her letter. She rejoices that the Lord is doing the work of good obedience in her soul. She writes, "I rejoyce that the Lord is carrying on his good Work in your dear Soul."[95] She calls this sister to continue following Jesus for good work. Letter 46 is addressed to two women, "Mrs. A. and Mrs. G." who are addressed as "*My Dear Sisters in Christ*."[96] Dutton writes, "*JESUS loves you: Believe it*; and your Hearts will be *full of Joy*."[97]

Letter 48 is addressed to "Mr. and Mrs. W." with the words, "*Ever Dear and Honour'd Parents*."[98] Again, these are Dutton's own parents. She asks her parents to pray for her. She writes, "Oh pray, that I may love my Dear Lord

---

Popping's-Court, Fleet-Street: And sold by J. Lewis, in Pater-noster Row; and G. Keith, at Mercers-Chapel, Cheapside. 1750, letter 8, pp. 3–5.

[87] *Letters On Spiritual Subjects*, letter 8, p. 10.

[88] *Letters On Spiritual Subjects*, letter 8, p. 23.

[89] *Letters On Spiritual Subjects*, letter 8, p. 35.

[90] *Letters On Spiritual Subjects*, letter 8, p. 35.

[91] *Letters On Spiritual Subjects*, letter 8, p. 54.

[92] *Letters On Spiritual Subjects*, letter 8, p. 55.

[93] *Letters On Spiritual Subjects*, letter 8, p. 55.

[94] *Letters On Spiritual Subjects*, letter 8, p. 115.

[95] *Letters On Spiritual Subjects*, letter 8, p. 115.

[96] *Letters On Spiritual Subjects*, letter 8, p. 129.

[97] *Letters On Spiritual Subjects*, letter 8, p. 129.

[98] *Letters On Spiritual Subjects*, letter 8, p. 132.

greatly, in every *little Thing* I aim to do for Him."[99] Letter 45 is addressed to "Mr. F." Dutton opens with joy that her writings have benefited him and others. She writes, "It gives me Joy, that my last, with the Books sent, were acceptable and useful unto you and others."[100]

Dutton offers spiritual comfort in this gentleman's season of trouble and darkness with words from Hosea 14:7–8. The Lord has given her these words for his spiritual darkness. She speaks of the comfort of the Holy Ghost. She highlights God's call for renewal in him. The man is to be like Israel and return to the Lord.[101] Dutton further expounds on this text. She speaks of reviving of the soul by the grace of Jesus Christ. She writes, "You shall *grow as the Vine*: Which after a piercing cold Winter, by the reviving Summer-Sun speedily casts abroad its Branches, and with its tender *Grapes*, gives a *good Smell.* Yea, so fragrant shall you be in your full Fruits of Righteousness, which are by Jesus Christ…"[102]

Dutton writes all these letters as words of grace addressed to uplift the recipients in their life of faith, pursuit of holiness, and growth into Christlikeness. She writes out of the great abundance of grace she feels she has received. Through these letters, Dutton freely offers the fruits of Christ's light and love. Her words of encouragement and spiritual direction are offered to souls to fill them with Christ's grace.

---

[99] *Letters On Spiritual Subjects,* letter 8, p. 132.

[100] *Letters On Spiritual Subjects,* letter 8, p. 185.

[101] *Letters On Spiritual Subjects,* letter 8, p. 185.

[102] *Letters On Spiritual Subjects,* letter 8, p. 189.

1
LETTERS
ON
SPIRITUAL SUBJECTS,
AND
Divers Occasions,
Sent to the Reverend
Mr. *George Whitefield*,
And others of his
Friends and Acquaintance.
To which is added,

A LETTER on the Being and Working of SIN, in the Soul of a *justify'd Man*, as consistent with his State of Justification in CHRIST, and Sanctification through HIM: With the Nature of his OBEDIENCE, and of his COMFORT, consider'd: As the one is *from* GOD, and the other *to* HIM; notwithstanding his Corruptions may be *great*, and his Graces *small* in his own Sight.

As also,

A LETTER on the DUTY and PRIVILEGE of a *Believer*, To live by FAITH, and to improve his Faith unto HOLINESS.

By ONE who has tasted that the LORD is GRACIOUS.

Wherefore comfort yourselves together, and edify one another, even as also ye do, I Thes. v. 11.

LONDON:

Printed by J. HART, in *Popping's-Court, Fleetstreet:* And Sold by J. LEWIS, in *Bartholomew-Close,* near *West-Smithfield;* and E. GARDNER, at *Milton's-Head,* near *Aldgate.* 1745. [Price stitch'd One Shilling and Three-pence]

LETTERS

ON

Spiritual Subjects, &c.

LETTER I

To Mr. W_______d.

Very dear and reverend Sir,

YOUR last sweet Letter was very savoury to my Taste. It brought GOD to my Soul. I feel much Heart-Union with you. I thank you for all the kind Expressions of your increasing Love. May the Lord *reward you an Hundred-fold in this World, and in that to come!* Oh what a blessed Instrument of much Good, has the Lord made you to my poor soul!

My dearest Brother, you was on the *Mount,* when you wrote last. Don't wonder, if your wise and gracious Leader, should again bring you into the *Valley.* The Lord prepares us by *great Comforts,* for *great Trials:* And by *sore Trials,* for *strong Consolations.* Which Way soever he deals with us, it is in infinite Love and Wisdom. – I rejoice in your Joy; and that under the Apprehension of an approaching Trial, your Spirit flow'd sweetly into the Will of GOD: Not only with humble Submission, but with joyful Acquiescence. With Pleasure I saw, how the Love of GOD, drew your Soul to love Him; and I long'd to be Like-minded. When the Lord winds up the Love of his Children to an *high Pitch,* He delights to *try it.* And try us he will in our *Isaacs,* in that which is most near and dear to us. And if thus the Lord should *try you,* my dear Brother, give him *Leave* to do what *He pleaseth.* Call nothing *your own*, but GOD'S *Great* SELF! Have no *Will* but *His;* and then *your Will* cannot be *crost.* God call'd *Abraham* to *offer up his Son, his only Son* Isaac, *whom he loved.* He readily *obey'd; and he was called, The Friend of GOD.* And the Lord grant *you Grace,* to offer up all that HE calls for, in a Flame of Love to Him! And He will record your Kindness, what a *Friend* you was to Him: And bring it forth *unto Praise, and Honour, and Glory at Christ's Appearing!* – Into the Arms of JESUS, I commit you, and am with the dearest Love,

Reverend Sir,

Your humble Servant in the LORD,

LETTER II.

To Mr. W________d.

Reverend and very dear Sir,

GLAD should I be of a Line from you. But dear, very dear are you to me for JESU'S Sake, whether you have Time to write to worthless me, or not. I hope our dear LORD will still give me a Place in your Heart, and that you will not forget me before HIM; if thro' your abundant Work, you must forget me in Letter. – I remember you at the Throne of Grace, and do all I can to hold up your Hands in your great MASTER'S Work. Much I rejoice with you, for the rich abundant Grace, which is constantly extended towards you. Oh my dear dear Brother, how good is your MASTER CHRIST unto *you!* How doth HE honour you with his Service, spirit you for it, and own you in it! I know you give HIM all the Glory. That you feel your Insufficiency, rejoice in CHRIST'S All-sufficiency, and go on in his Work, as able to do all Things thro' CHRIST strengthening you.—Greatly I rejoice in the Wonders of Love shewn you in *Wales, Gloucester,* &c. May *London* feel the happy Influence of boundless Grace, pour'd out through CHRIST, upon and by *you,* during this your present Stay in it more than ever!—Oh my dear Brother, *now* is your Salvation nearer than when you first believed. A little more Labour, a few more Trials; and then comes on your eternal Rest, your incorruptible Crown! The Bosom of CHRIST awaits you. Yet a little while, and you shall see him HIM Face to Face! Without a Veil between, without an intervening Cloud, to the Days of ETERNITY!—Oh love and work for JESUS now, this little Moment of Time! Glad you will be to have *done much* for CHRIST in your Day, when the Night comes, and you can do *no more* for HIM.—Oh my Brother, I tell you of a *Night,* wherein you can do no more for CHRIST: Methinks I hear you say, 'Then 'twill be DAY, eternal DAY, in which I shall serve HIM more than ever! I long for Immortality, to drop weak, sinful Flesh, that in perfect Praises, and ceaseless Songs, I may adore GOD and the LAMB for ever!' True, my Brother, when the Night of Death approaches, then comes on the DAY of eternal Life: The DAY you have so long desir'd; wherein you shall know, love and serve the LORD *perfectly*, among the *flaming Glories* of the *upper World*, the Saints and Seraphs round the Throne! But then, you cannot serve CHRIST on *the Earth*. Wherefore prize your Time for *that* Service *now*.—A Thought of that Eternity of Glory which awaits me with my LORD, when the happy Prospect strikes my Eyes, sets my Soul on Fire, to *do something* for his Glory in the present Time.—And is it not thus with *you*, my Brother? Would you not be *glad* to spend your *Life* in *Telling out the Glories of CHRIST*, whose GLORY can never be *told!* Are you not *willing* to woo and win a few more Souls to CHRIST, aye, many Thousands and Tens of Thousands, to be the Bride the LAMB'S Wife, and your Companions in the heavenly World, before you leave this earthly Globe?—Oh why do I *ask*, I see you spend your Life, your Strength, your All, your Body, your Soul in this *blessed Work!*—Only then, dear Sir, permit me to *stir up your pure Mind by way of Remembrance*, and to say, *O dear Man of GOD!* Continue to make *full Proof* of your Ministry. That to the last Moment of your Life, for *you* to *live*, may be CHRIST: And then to *die*, will be your *Ineffable Gain!*

My Soul rejoiceth in the LORD, and with you magnifies GOD our SAVIOUR, for his late kind Visit to your dear Family, for that rich Distillation of the heavenly Dew, which has fallen upon them, in *Georgia's* desart Land. I doubt not, it is an Answer of your, and your Brethren's Prayers. And truly I can say, it is an answer of mine. Many a Time have I intreated the LORD to visit them *Himself*, and make their Hearts glad, under the present Trial of *your* being detain'd from them, by the Work HE has assign'd you in *England* and *Wales*. And now, to my Joy, I see HE is *come* to dwell in the midst of them. Oh happy Family, where GOD *dwells!* LORD let thy Reign be glorious *there!* Thy Subjects *increase!* Thy Servants supply'd with all *Good*, and defended from all *Evil! Amen, and Amen!*—Into the Arms of JESUS I commit you: and am,

Reverend Sir,

Yours most affectionately in HIM,

LETTER III.

To Mr. W_______d.

Reverend and very dear Brother,

I Humbly thank you for your kind Present of the Books. Your Sermons have been made very sweet and precious to my soul. I rejoice for the Grace bestow'd on *you;* for that abundant Growth which the Lord hath given you, and that brave Testimony which He hath enabled you to bear for the precious Truths of his glorious Gospel.—May the Blessing of Heaven rest upon you, and all your Labours for the Advancement of the Redeemer's Glory, and the Good of his dear Children!—I long to hear from you, and to know your State.—I doubt not our Lord is with you, and makes your Heart glad in Him and his Work.

I know you must have *Trials*, from within and without. Much Difficulty, will many Times be cast in the Way of your serving the dear Lord Jesus.—But, my dear Brother, press thro' all. The Strength of Christ shall be made perfect in your Weakness; and *to him that overcometh,* our Lord will *grant to sit with Him in his Throne, even as he also overcame, and is set down with the Father in his Throne.* If we were not to meet with Difficulties, Discouragements and Oppositions, in the Course of our walking with GOD, and working for CHRIST; how could we be crown'd as Overcomers?—Let us therefore press forward, when our Hearts are weak, and our Burdens great, for thro' the Power of CHRIST resting upon us, we shall surmount all Difficulties, *Run and not be weary, walk and not faint,* yea, *go from Strength to Strength, until we appear before GOD in Zion.*—If now and then our dear Lord calls us to walk, to run with *Loads* upon our Backs; He will not *always* try us thus.—He will take *off* our Burdens, make us *leap for Joy,* and *as light of Foot as a wild Roe* in his Service.—For He is a GOD of boundless Compassions! *He knows our Frame, and remembers that we are Dust.*—Our dear Lord Jesus, was *tempted in all Points like unto us,* that He might *be able to succour them that are tempted.* That from his own Experience, as having been in the same Trials, He might have an Ability of Sympathy with us in all our Distresses; and that from an inward Fellow-feeling, and inexpressible Tenderness towards us, He might send us suitable, and seasonable Relief, in all the Times and Cases of our Need. We have a SAVIOUR, that is our *Brother,* that hath a Brother's *Heart* towards us.—This was the Will of our heavenly *Father.* He well knew, that we should be such *miserable Children*, that we should need Abundance of *Sympathy*; and therefore He gave his *Son,* his *own* Son, to take our *Nature,* to become our *Brother,* our *near Kinsman*; that so the infinite Bowels of the Son of GOD, clothed with the Compassions of our Nature, might become an inexhaustible, eternal *Flow,* of kindly Sympathy with us, and Salvation to us. And such was the infinite Love of GOD our Father, that HE gave his Son, not only to take our Nature, but to take it in all its sinless *Infirmities,* to be made in the *Likeness* of sinful Flesh! And such was the boundless Grace of the LORD our Redeemer, that he humbled himself, and became *like* unto his Brethren in all Things, Sin only excepted!

Our Lord *was* to be try'd, would be try'd, with all the Temptations which attend us in our present State. With the World, the Flesh, and the Devil, was our JESUS *tried*; yea, with the most severe Trials from his own God and Father, was he exercis'd. Our Lord, our Lover, for us was try'd with the *Weakness* of our Nature, and with the *Sinfulness* of it too. For tho' He had no Sin of his *own,* yet was He try'd with the Sins of *others.* He was infinitely more try'd with the Being and Power, with the Guilt and Filth of Sin in *others,* than any of *us* are, with all these in *ourselves:* By reason of the spotless Purity, and infinite Holiness of his Person, when he condescended to dwell among us, in the midst of our Uncleanness. He was try'd with the Sins of his Brethren, and with the Sins of the World, with the Sins of Friends, and with the Sins of Enemies. And oh, *how* was our JESUS try'd with *Sin,* and all the woful *Effects* of it, when the LORD *laid upon him the Iniquity of us all!* when his own God and Father, *made him, who knew no Sin, to be Sin for us,* that we Sinners, might be *made the Righteousness of God in Him!* Oh how *near* did the Spotless LAMB of GOD, come unto us *Sinners,* when HE by Imputation, became all *that,* which *we* were by Perpetration! When He took all our Uncleanness upon him, and to *sanctify us with his own Blood, suffer'd without the Gate!*—Oh my dear Brother, our glorious LOVER JESUS, was made so *like* unto us Sinners, in his Trial of *imputed Sin,* that HE well knows how to sympathize with us, in our Trial of *inherent Sin:* and from an Infinity of Bowels, will He succour us in it, and save us from it! Our merciful High Priest, well knows how to pity us, under all that Weakness, and Indisposedness for divine Service, which we at any time feel, by reason of Sin; and He can have Compassion according to the *Measure* of our Distress.—He well knows what it is to be tempted in all Respects by *Satan,* to be both flatter'd and reproach'd by the *World,* revil'd by *Professors,* slighted by *Countrymen,* despis'd by *Relations,* betray'd by *professed Friends,* oppos'd and disregarded by *real Ones,* yea, and to be try'd by GOD Himself!—And having gone thro' *all* our Trials, He hath took away the *Curse* of them, *sanctify'd* them to us, is well prepar'd in all Respects to *succour* us, and *ever liveth to save us to the uttermost.*

Let us therefore hope in Him, wait for Him, and in the Way of our Duty, press forward to serve and glorify Him; being fully perswaded, that the Grace of CHRIST is sufficient for us. Sufficient to *strengthen* us for our Work, to *pity* our Weakness therein, to *pardon* the Sin that cleaves to us in it, to *accept* our imperfect Services, to *present* them in his own Perfections, a Sacrifice well-pleasing to his and our Father, to *bless* our weak Labours for the Good of his People here, and to *crown* them with endless Glory hereafter!

And oh the suitable, seasonable, sufficient Help, that our compassionate High Priest above, sends down to his labouring, sorrowing, suffering People below? Great is our *Help,* and full is our *Joy,* when kind *Succours* come from our dear Lord's Hand! And our Joy would be *full* indeed, if in all the Succour afforded by our Lord's *Hand,* we believ'd the infinite Grace of his *Heart,* and the kind *Offices of Love,* which He performs for us, in his all-prevailing Advocacy, and Intercession with the Father; whence every Kind and Degree of our Help cometh!

Oh what a *compassionate* SAVIOUR, is our JESUS! Oh what a *gracious* MASTER do we serve! How *easy* is his Yoke, all overspread with his *infinite Love!* How *light* is his Burden, all-supported by his *Omnipotent Arm!*—Oh *who* would not love and serve the Prince of Grace; *who hath loved us, and washed us from our Sins in his own Blood, and hath made us Kings and Priests unto God and his Father! To HIM be Glory and Dominion, for ever and ever. AMEN!*

That the Grace of CHRIST may be with your Spirit, and his Hand with you in all the Work He calls you to; that your Stay in *England* may be a rich Blessing to Thousands; a Joy to your own Soul, and to all the Saints; and to the Glory of our renowned Prince EMANUEL: is the hearty Desire of,

Reverend Sir,

Your most Affectionate Humble Servant,

In our own LORD JESUS,

________ ________.

LETTER IV.

To Mr. W_______d.

My very Dear Reverend Brother,

Methinks, it's an Age since I heard from you. Has my dear Brother quite forgot me? I confess, I am unworthy you should ever spend a Thought upon, or send a Line to me. Yet will I persuade myself you love me, for the Sake of my worthy Lord, and as a Fellow-Member with *you,* of that Body, of which HE is the Head. Our Communion here, is imperfect, interrupted, inconstant. In Heaven, it will be perfect, uninterrupted, and eternal. We shall soon *see* JESUS, and be both with him for ever.—Oh to do a little more *Work*, for HIM that liv'd and dy'd for *us!* And then, *come*, *Lord Jesus,* and take us into thy own Bosom! I doubt not, my dear Brother, you love your Master's Service as much as ever, and labour in it to your uttermost. Go on, sweet Soul! 'tis *Heaven* to *work* for CHRIST, as well as *rest* with Him. Oh, the ineffable Sweets of serving the LORD the LAMB! Well doth your dear Soul know, what a Heaven *this* is: And shortly you shall be taken up to your Heaven of *Rest,* in the immediate Vision of GOD and the LAMB for ever. But oh, the infinite Glories of that Feast, your LORD will make for you, when your Labours for him are finished! Oh, the inconceivable Joys of *that Heaven* which awaits you! One Hour's Rest at GOD'S *Right-Hand,* will infinitely reward all the Toil and Labour you have been at, in your *Way thither.* To deny one's self for CHRIST, to cross the Interest of sinful Self, and wear out natural Self for JESUS, hath a peculiar *Sweetness* in it, a *Joy which a Stranger intermeddles not with.* And if the *Cross* is so *sweet,* has such a Sweetness cast into it by our Lord's own Hand, what will the *Crown* be, when HE sets it upon our Heads! Oh! *worthy is the* LAMB, to be lov'd, ador'd, and served for ever. Such is the infinite Glory of his Person, the Excellency of his Work, and the Immensity of his Love to us; that had we *ten thousand Souls,* they would all be due to HIM, and well employ'd in *his* most glorious Service. And had we *ten thousand Lives* to praise EMANUEL in, they would all be but as a *Drop of Duty,* cast into the boundless, bottomless Ocean, of *his Love and Glory!* Oh how *happy,* how ineffably *happy,* are those blessed Souls, that love and serve JESUS here! And if the *Service* of CHRIST is so *sweet,* oh, what will the *Enjoyment* of him be! If now and then a *Glimpse* of our Lord's Love and Glory, is so *transporting,* while he shews himself thro' the Lattess; Oh, what Raptures shall we *feel,* when we shall *see* HIM *as* HE is, without a Vail between!—Oh! my Brother, JESUS, the Son of GOD, *loves you.* He lov'd you antiently, he loves you infinitely and unchangeably, and will love you eternally. He gave himself *for you,* he gives himself *to you,* and lives to *serve you* at his Father's Right-Hand.—Oh! give him yourself in Love, and all the Service you are capable of. I know you *do,* I know you *will,* and think all *too little,* far, far *too little,* for your *loving, lovely, worthy* LORD. But suffer me to say, *love* JESUS. Oh my Brother, little do you think how *kindly* he will take it, and how *much* he will make of it. Did you know how much your Service glads CHRIST'S Heart *now,* your Soul would be refresh'd as with new Wine, and nimbly would you spring thro' your Work, as a Giant to run a Race. And think, my dear Brother, when CHRIST and *you meet,* and he recounts all your Service, what an inconceivable Joy it will be to hear him say, *I was an hungred, and you gave me Meat: Thirsty, and you gave me Drink: Naked, and you clothed me: Sick and in Prison, and you ministred unto me.—Come, you blessed of my Father, inherit the Kingdom prepared for you from the Foundation of the World!* Then, dear sir, as CHRIST'S *good and faithful Servant,* he will bid you, *enter into the Joy of your Lord.* And what the Greatness of that Glory will *be,* is yet to be *reveal'd.—Great Grace be with you and yours!* I am,

Dear Sir,
Your most Affectionate humble Servant,

LETTER V.

To Mr. W________d.

My very dear, and reverend Brother,

THE acceptable Favour of your *last,* gave me much Pleasure; for which I give humble Thanks. Indeed I long'd to hear from you; but I knew your Work too well, to conceive any Offence given on that you wrote no sooner. I am exceeding unworthy of your Notice, and esteem it a peculiar Favour, that God puts it into your Heart ever to remember *me.* CHRIST takes it kindly, my dear Brother, that you now and then cast a Glance of Favour upon the least of his. He well knows, with what Difficulty you redeem Time for that Service. He knows, not only your *Love* to him and his, but the *Labour* of it also; and not only your *Works,* but the *Labour* you are at to perform them. And none of your labour of Love, even to the least Part of it, shall in any wise lose its Reward. CHRIST will lose nothing, none of your Service, but a full Reward shall be given you of the Prince of Love, according to his abundant Grace.—It much delights our dear Lord, to see us *love one another.* He sees with Pleasure, the Union and Communion of Saints, as the Fruit of his Blood. He dy'd to make us *one* with himself, and with each other. And if we are *Twain,* if we don't love as Brethren, as united in the LAMB'S Blood, we don't walk as the *Redeem'd of the Lord.* Oh, the Glory of that Unity, we shall one Day enjoy, when we are made perfectly *one* with the innumerable Multitude of the *saved ones,* and *one* in the *Son,* and in the *Father,* by *one and the Self same Spirit!* No more Discord then among the Saints, no more seperate Interest, no more Diversity of Worship, nor Distance of Place. But all the vast Number of the whole Elect, gather'd together from the four Winds, brought up in the *Unity of the Faith, and the Knowledge of the Son of God, unto a perfect Man;* shall together in one august Assembly, in one living Temple, under one and the same Display of Divine Glory, with one Heart, Soul and Voice, worship one GOD, as their ALL IN ALL, unto Ages without End!

"They all are *one,* in one they all *agree:* ONE is their ALL, which makes all one to *be.*"

Lord, hasten that Glory-Day! It *comes,* it *comes,* my Brother! Don't you *see* the Day dawn? The Morning-Star appear? What labour you so hard for in CHRIST'S *Gospel?* Is it not *to make ready a People prepared for the Lord?* Is it not to *espouse many unto one Husband? Whom you may present as a chaste Virgin unto Christ?* Oh glorious Work! And don't you *see* how the Bridegroom cometh? What Haste he makes? What mighty Steps he takes?—*Behold, he comes quickly! Leaping on the Mountains, and skipping on the Hills! He sheweth himself thro' the Lattess:* By and by we shall see his Face, and be blest with the full, and eternal Vision of his Glory!

Mean Time, Labour hard in the Lord's Work; do all you can, according to his Working, to get the Bride ready for the Marriage-Glory with her Royal Bridegroom. *Oh dear Man of God!* The Attendance you give to this Work, and the Diligence you shew in it, doth as it were forbid me to press you forward, to bid a winged Flame, *fly!* But CHRIST *flies,* and YOU *must fly.* The winged Flame of his Love, brings him sweetly, swiftly, gloriously to save his Bride! Enkindled then with this Fire of GOD, this Flame of JEHOVAH, fly after him; *the* LORD *is gone out before you;* wing the Way; run through Opposition; lick up the Waters of Affliction, and *always abound in the Work of the* LORD; *forasmuch as you know, that your Labour is not in vain in the* LORD. Amongst his Children, he has chosen *you,* that Multitudes by your Mouth should *hear the Word of the Gospel,* and *believe.* I know you say, why *me,* LORD! Indeed it is ALL of *Grace.* And, *behold how he loved you!* He lov'd you antiently, freely, richly, and will love you eternally!

The Wonders of God's Love, which daily open to your View, with a new amazing Glory, are no *new Things* unto GOD, but the *new Fruits* of his *old Love,* or the *new Displays* of his *everlasting Thoughts of Grace towards you in* CHRIST! The GOD of all Grace, call'd a Council in

HIMSELF before the World was, how he might lay out his Grace upon *you,* to the Glory of its exceeding Riches. And according to the Infinity of his Wisdom, he then resolv'd to be *thus* and *thus* gracious unto *you!* When therefore, you see GOD, even your Father, pouring out new Blessings upon you daily *thro' Christ;* Oh, trace the Streams unto the Fountain-Head, to that ALL of *spiritual Blessings,* wherewith he *blest you in Christ, before the Foundation of the World,* and, to that eternal, boundless *Love,* which is the *Source* of all your Bliss! For God's Dispensations of Grace in *Time* towards the Heirs of Salvation, are but the Transcript of his *eternal Decrees,* the opening, or unfolding of his manifold Wisdom and Grace, in the eternal Counsel of his Will concerning them. And *think,* my dear Brother, when the eternal, omniscient GOD, with one View beheld all the Creatures he resolv'd to make, in the Glass of his own Decrees; how *freely* he lov'd *you,* in that he chose *you* unto eternal Life, and to such eminent Service, while *thousands* were passed by! This was *Free-love* indeed! And behold, it is as *rich* as it's *free!* Oh, can you count up a thousandth Part of those *exceeding Riches of Grace,* which God's free Love has laid out upon you thro' *Jesus Christ!* Are not Love's Riches, *unsearchable!* Oh how great is that Goodness which He has *laid out upon you!* And yet, behold, He has goodness, an Immensity, and an Eternity of Goodness *laid up for you!* GOD'S LOVE, like HIMSELF, knows no Decay, Change or End! And this LOVE of God, this GOD of Love, thro' the once-bleeding LAMB, will be an exuberant, inexhaustible, and eternal SEA of Bliss unto *you!* Oh, *Love the LORD* therefore! You have nothing else to *do,* but to love Him. Love him in *doing,* love him in *suffering.* You *see* He loves *you* into, and thro' both; and every Way crowns you with Loving-kindness! How *goodly is your Heritage?* How *pleasant is your Place?* How *extensive is your Border?* how doth it pass on from one Place to another? from Privilege to Privilege? And oh, the Immensity of that *Love,* which drew the *Line* of it! Verily your Time-Lot, is exceeding large! And your eternal Lot, INEFFABLE!

O Man greatly beloved! My Heart rejoiceth with you in all your Joy. I rejoice to *hear,* while you *see* such glorious Days of the Son of Man. Oh may you pass on from Glory to Glory, and still *see greater Things than these!*—And since you are so *highly favoured,* don't think it a strange Thing, to meet *Opposition* from every Quarter. If you are for CHRIST, you must have Earth and Hell *against* you. Never was any great Work done for GOD, but *it,* and its *Instruments* met with great *Opposition:* Which only serv'd as a Foil, to illustrate the Glory of that Power, which bears down all before it. *In vain the Heathen rage, the Kings of the Earth, set themselves, and the Rulers take Counsel together against the LORD, and against his Anointed.* For yet *He has set his King upon his holy Hill of Zion.* Since the Strength of JESUS is *yours;* fear no adverse Power. None of the Power of Darkness, are a *Match* for *Omnipotence.* The LORD is on your side: Live in Him, and to Him; and fear not what Men, or Devils can do unto you. *The LORD on high is mightier than the Noise of many Waters, than the mighty Waves fo the Sea.*—Since you have *glorious Consolations,* you must have *close Trials.* They are needful and advantageous. *The LORD maketh the Weight for the Winds, and weigheth the Waters by Measure.* You must have Trials to poize you. *A Thorn in the Flesh is given you, the Messenger of Satan to buffet you; lest you should be exalted above Measure.* But the Grace of CHRIST is *sufficient* for you, and his Power shall *rest* upon you.—Into his Arms I commit you. Forget me not before him. In HIM, dear Sir, I am

Your most affectionate,

Humble Servant,

______ ___________.

LETTER VI.

To Mr. W_______d.

Reverend and very dear Sir,

YOUR last very kind Letter, I thankfully receiv'd, and embrace the first Opportunity to answer it. Your abundant Love exprest in your *last,* your Heart-union with me, and especially your Prayers for a Blessing upon my weak Endeavours, to lispe out the Praises of the *Strong* JAH, refresh'd and delighted me much. The Lord reward all your Kindness to worthless *me,* an *Hundred-fold!*—I have just now been reading the Letter with Pleasure. But when I came to that Clause, *I think our dear Lord will employ "you more and more:"* Being pressed with a Sense of my own Vileness, I had some Fears that He *would not.* But sweetly He spoke to my Heart in that Word, *I know the Thoughts which I think towards you, Thoughts of Peace, and not of Evil, to give you an expected End.* Which revived, humbled, and melted me. Oh my Brother, I wonder at the infinite Grace and Long-suffering of my God, that He should not *cast me off!* That He should have *Thoughts of Peace towards me still!* Indeed, my Brother, I have multiplied my Transgressions against Him. As Figures in *Arithmetick* increase the Number, so have I have multiply'd to Sin, *added Sin to Sin.* Oh *lamentable!*—But behold, my gracious GOD, the God of Peace, thro' the Blood of JESUS, multiplies to pardon, *abundantly pardons! Grace and Peace, is multiplied* towards me daily: Extended like a *River,* a full, free, flowing River, that prevails over all my Sins!

I rejoice before God, for His astonishing Kindness towards *you,* continually. For the Light of his Countenance, and the Joy of his Salvation, with which your Soul is bless'd; and for the Wonders of his Love, in your abundant Usefulness. Oh how great, free, and distinguishing has God's Loving-kindness been unto you, my dear Brother! The Lord continue and increase it! And make you more and more humble, that you may give Him the Glory of all his Grace.—Sin, Satan, and the World will shoot at you, that you may fall. The Lord hold you up continually, by his Almighty Hand! And make you an *Iron Pillar,* and a Brasen Wall, that they which fight against you may never prevail! Your Enemies are very potent, and *your* Strength, mere Weakness; but the Grace of CHRIST is sufficient for you, *His* Power shall rest upon you, and the *Arms of your Hands be made strong, by the mighty* God *of Jacob.* Go on, dear Sir, in your Great MASTER's Work, in His great Strength, fearless of all your Adversaries, tho' ten Thousand should set themselves against you round about. For, *stronger is He that is in you, than he which is in them. The* LORD *your* GOD, *will not fail you, nor forsake you.* Wherefore, *be strong, and of a good Courage.*—I bear you on my Heart before the Lord. He enables me to pray for you. And I believe, as you say, "That the Lord will hear, and bless me therein." The LORD is with them that help you, and will bless those that bless you, and curse the Wicked that curse you. And severely rebuke his own Children, that oppose or slight you. Your Name is exceeding precious to your dear MASTER; none can *touch you* therein, but they *touch the Apple of his Eye.* He takes all the Affronts you meet with, as given to Himself. And from his infinite Love to your Person, and Zeal for your Honour, as a dear Servant of his, called to eminent Service, He will *plead your Cause,* and *execute Judgment for you.* I know your loving Soul, like your LORD, says, *Father, forgive them, for they know not what they do.* And so go on to shew the Meekness and Gentleness of Christ towards all Men, *committing yourself* and Cause *unto Him that judgeth righteously:* And the End will be glorious!—

And now, sir, as your glorious MASTER is calling you from *us*, to proclaim his Gospel, and serve his Cause and People in *other* Parts of the World; I *must* for myself, and I think *may* for Thousands more say, we are grieved to *part with you.* And yet we cheerfully *resign you up* to the LORD and his Work. Praying his Presence may be with, and his Blessing upon you. That He will make you a begetting, and a nursing Father unto Thousands, while absent from *us;* and in his good Time return you to his People *here*, as a greater Blessing than ever. O dear Man of GOD! *What great Things hath the LORD done for you,* since you visited us last! How richly has he crown'd you with Loving-kindness in these Lands! What a Reaping-time, what a glorious Harvest of Souls have you had in *England* and *Scotland,* who shall be your *Joy and Crown in the Day of the Lord Jesus!* Blessed be GOD, *who always causeth you to triumph in CHRIST! And maketh manifest by you the Savour of his Knowledge in every Place!*—Go then, thrice happy Soul! With the Lord, and for Him; visit *America,* visit *Georgia, and see how your Brethren do.* Go over the Places again where you have been preaching the Word, give the Brethren much Exhortation, and confirm the Souls of the Disciples, by telling them, that *through much Tribulation we must enter into the Kingdom.* Yea, Go in your great Lord's Name, *seek up his lost Sheep,* and bring them to his Fold. And tho' you should go forth *weeping,* in Labours, Sorrows and Trials of all Kinds, yet, *bearing precious Seed,* the immortal Seed of Christ's Gospel; you shall doubtless come again *rejoicing,* bringing your *Sheaves* with you. We shall wait and pray, dear Sir, for your happy Return to *England,* and hope to rejoice with you in the glorious Fruits of your distant Labours.—But with what *Joy* will you return to your Great MASTER, when the whole Course of your ministerial Service, and Sufferings are finish'd! And what a glorious Number of *Sheaves* will you have to rejoice in at our Lord's Appearing? What a Multitude of precious Souls, will you have the Honour in that Day, to *present as a chaste Virgin to CHRIST!* And how great, how exceeding great will be your Joy, while *you* with them, and *they* with you, together with the whole Number of *GOD's Elect,* in one complete Body, one glorious Church, a meet Bride for the LORD the LAMB, shall by him as such, be *presented faultless before the Presence of his FATHER's Glory!*—This glorious Day *hasten.* The intervening Time is *short:* And therefore we *weep,* as tho' we wept *not.* We meet and part *now.* But *then* we shall meet, never to part *more!*—At present, dear Sir, committing you into the Hands of CHRIST, I most heartily bid you *Farewel in the LORD!* Pray for,

Reverend Sir,

Yours most Affectionately in our

Sweet JESUS,

______ ____________.

LETTER VII.

To Mr. H_______ll H_________s, *Mr.* R____________d, *and the rest of the Brethren that help with them and labour in the* Gospel of CHRIST, in *Wales.*

Much Honoured and Beloved Brethren,

Permit the least of your Father's House, unknown to you in the Flesh, to rejoice with you in the Spirit, and to congratulate your Happiness, in that Fulness of Work which the Lord of the Harvest hath call'd you to, that rich Assistance HE hath given you, and that glorious Success with which HE crowns your Labours. Oh my Brethren, what a bright Display of glorious Grace is *this,* That GOD is come down to dwell in poor *Wales?* That KING JESUS erects his Throne *there!* And that HE hath chosen *you* to be his Servants, and each of *you* to your particular Employment, in a Work that is surpassingly glorious!—*Some* of you, my Brethren, I doubt not, have long pray'd for these blessed Days of the REDEEMER's Kingdom in *Wales.* And now it comes with Power and great Glory, for *you* his People that have *sought* HIM. Your Prayer-hearing GOD, has made your *Wilderness like Eden,* and your *Desart like the Garden of the LORD!* Thus richly doth your heavenly Father *reward you openly,* that have pray'd in *Secret* for these *Days of the Son of Man!*—And perhaps there are *others* of you, my Brethren, that have been sweetly surpriz'd by unthought of, and unsought for Grace. The LORD has been found of *you* that sought him not. The Kingdom of GOD has come into your dear Souls, and unto and among your People, with an irresistible Power, and ineffable Sweetness, and an all-enlightning Glory, ere you were *aware!*—Which Way soever it be, my Brethren, whether you have *sought the LORD,* or *not,* in the Exuberance of his Grace, HE is *come,* HE is *come* to dwell in the midst of *you!* Wherefore, *Rejoice greatly* in your happy Lot.—We in *England* will join the Joy, and assist the Praise, together with all the Saints in every Place, unto whom these joyful Tidings, this blessed News shall come. *We,* my Brethren, are Partakers of *your Joy, we* join *your Hosanna's;* and with you pray, That the REDEEMER's Kingdom may rise and shine in *Wales,* and the Glories of his Reign *fill the whole Earth!* To which all the Friends of the Bridegroom will say, *Even so come* LORD JESUS, *Amen, and Amen!*

My dear and honour'd Brethren, will you suffer one that is less than the least of all Saints, to point your Eye to the *Glories* of your KING, the Glories of his *Work,* and the Glories of his *Reward?*—CHRIST, my Brethren, your Royal MASTER CHRIST, hath all the Glories of the GODHEAD in Him! HE hath all the Glories of the MEDIATOR and SAVIOUR of Sinners in Him! Oh what a *fit,* what an *able,* what a *glorious* SAVIOUR is your Prince EMANUEL! With regard to his great *Person,* in which both the Divine and Human Natures, are hypostatically united! With regard to his glorious *Offices,* as Prophet, Priest and King! With regard to his infinite *Fulness of the Spirit,* and all Grace and Glory! With regard to his *Authority,* as having the Broad Seal of Heaven! And with regard to the *Eternity of his Life,* to save Sinners to the uttermost!—How great then is your *Honour,* my Brethren, as call'd of GOD, to be *Ambassadors* to this *mighty Prince!* As sent with an Ambassy of Peace to poor rebellious Sinners, to pray them in CHRIST's stead to be *reconciled unto GOD!* How great are the Glories of this *Work,* which are put upon Mortal, sinful Worms!—And how great, my Brethren, are the Glories of your LORD's *Reward,* of that present Reward, which he makes your very *Work* to be, to your dear Souls! Of that Reward, which He gives you in the glorious *Success* of your happy Labours! And oh the Fulness, the Glory of that exceeding great Reward, which awaits you at CHRIST's *Appearing!*—Wherefore, my dear Brethren, go on with an holy Boldness, and heavenly Greatness of Spirit, to proclaim the Glories of your LORD before all; always abound in his glorious *Work;* and frequently look to his glorious *Reward.* That exceeding great Reward of all your Labours, which the Prince of Love will confer upon you, of the freest Grace, both in this World, and in that to come. So shall your Hands be strong, and your hearts rejoice in the LORD and his Work.

And tho' you must expect that the Powers of Darkness will be in a *Rage* against you, yet fear not: For your great MASTER, the Prince of Light, arising in his Glory, will put them all to *Flight.* CHRIST will maintain the *Field.* Cover your *Heads* on the Day of Battle. And *ride on* in the Victories of his *Love,* to save his People, and in the Triumphs of his *Power,* to destroy his Enemies.

And you his dear Servants, that are at *work* for your LORD now, shall ere long be call'd to enter into his *Rest,* to *sit down to Meat, to eat and drink with HIM, at his Table in his Kingdom. And such* are the Glories of that Feast, my Brethren, which your royal MASTER will make for you, when your Work is done, that *Eye hath not seen, nor Ear heard, nor have they entred into the Heart of Man,* of any spiritual Man, to conceive a *thousandth Part* of them! CHRIST will make A *Feast* for you, my Brethren, according to his own Greatness, his State, his Majesty, as the LORD and KING of GLORY! Think then, how *great,* how *glorious,* your *everlasting Feast,* your *eternal Rest* will be! And like *nimble Flames,* fir'd with the *Love,* and fill'd with the *Strength* of JESUS, *run* thro' your *present Labours,* rejoicing in *Hope of the Glory of GOD.* For to *you,* my Brethren, to you as *Overcomers,* as victorious Princes, thro' the LAMB's Love, Blood and Strength, will HE *grant, to sit with HIM in his Throne, even as HE also overcame, and is set down with his FATHER in his Throne.* A wonderful *Grant,* my Brethren! Oh, *who* would not love and serve *the*

Prince of Grace, who thus loves, rewards, and exalts *his Servants! The Poor from the Dust, and the Beggars from the Dunghil, to set them among Princes, to make them inherit the Throne of Glory.* Yea, to *sit with HIM the* KING of GLORY, even in *his Throne!*—That *great Grace may be upon you all, the Lord's Hand with you in your Work, many believe, and turn unto the Lord, and all Opposition fall before him; while CHRIST glorifies himself in you, and you in HIM:* is the hearty Prayer of, my dear and honoured Brethren,

Yours most Humbly and Affectoinately,
In our own LORD JESUS,

__________ __________.

LETTER VIII.

To Mr. C_______r.

Reverend and very dear Brother,

I Rejoice, that the Spirit of Grace and of Supplication, is pour'd down upon you, that you lament after the LORD, earnestly seek the Good of *Sion,* and the Advancement of the Redeemer's Kingdom, in the Increase of his willing Subjects in *Carolina. Blessed are they that* so *mourn: for they shall be comforted.* I am perswaded, that the Lord *will turn your Mourning into Joy, will comfort you, and make you rejoice from your Sorrow.* Yea, satisfy you with his great Goodness. Leave the Way and Time, wholly with GOD: Who will work in both Respects, as shall be most for his Glory. It is God's ordinary Way, to set his People a crying for those Mercies, which He designs to bestow upon them. And therefore prize the Spirit of Supplication which is given you, and improve it to the utmost. *Open your Mouth wide;* for God will *fill it:* Your Prayers shall be fully answer'd, to your Satisfaction and Admiration. *Jacob*'s God, hath not said unto the Seed of *Jacob, seek ye ME in vain.* Expect an Answer of your Prayers, either immediate, or remote.

First, Immediate. Look for the Lord's Appearance with *you.* Perhaps He will surprize you with his Kindness; and pour you out a Blessing, that there shall not be Room enough to receive it. It is GOD'S Way to do for his People, *exceeding abundantly above all that we ask or think.* We ask for

Tens; He gives us *Hundreds.* We ask according to our own *Littleness,* our narrow, shallow Apprehensions: Our GOD gives us according to his own infinite *Greatness,* and the deep, extensive Thoughts of his boundless, bottomless Love. Our GOD, gives like HIMSELF; and according to the great, the innumerable Thoughts of his Heart, which have been ever of old. To make a *Shew,* a bright, a soul-affecting, and soul-attracting Display, of *the exceeding Riches of his Grace, in his Kindness towards us thro' Christ Jesus.* To work *Wonders,* to do *Marvels;* is GOD's Covenant with his People. He hath wrought Wonders of Love for *me,* my Brother, for *you,* for *all* that call upon his Name. And still He will shew us *greater Things than these.* Wait you therefore for your own GOD; you shall not be ashamed.—And if for his Glory, and your Good, He should try your Faith, by deferring, or not granting that immediate Answer of your Requests which you desire; then look for an Answer, which will be,

Secondly, Remote. If you should not see at present, the Glory of Christ's Kingdom with *you,* as your Soul desires; your Prayers shall bring on the Glory of the Church *elsewhere,* and upon *your Part* of *Sion*'s Wilderness, in the Lord's Time. Yet a little while, and GOD will have his universal Church glorious. All *Sion*'s waste Places shall be comforted: *Her Wilderness shall be as* Eden, *and her Desart like the Garden of the LORD.* And the Prayers of the Saints for the Glory of the Church, in general, or particular, in their Prevalency with GOD, are cast into the general Treasury of the Church's Glory. And those Prayers of the Glory of *Sion* in her particular Apartments, which are not immediately and directly *granted;* shall be fully *answer'd* in the general Glory of the universal Church. When the Glory of the Church in some particular Places, and under some particular Dispensations, is reduc'd to so low an Ebb, that it seems to be almost quite *destroy'd:* Yet shall it *live,* as the Plant in its Seed, in those few that *seek* GOD, and again take Root, revive and flourish, in other Places, or in the same Places, under other Dispensations. GOD will have the Glory, the Excellency of *Sharon,* and the Verdure and Greenness of the Valley of *Achor* come unto his Church. "And *Sharon,* shall be a Fold of Flocks, and the Valley of *Achor* a Place for the Herds to lie down in, for his People that have *sought Him.*" Oh, in no wise, will the Lord forget, or neglect to hear the Prayers of his People. He may defer, or transpose his Answers. *Defer* his Answers to their Requests for the Glory of *Sion,* in particular Places and Times; or *transpose* his Answers unto other Places or Times; or *cast* his Answers into the general Glory of the Church, at the Times of refreshing promis'd: But in no wise, shall *the Seed of* Jacob, for the Glory of *Sion, seek their GOD in vain.*

Let this then, my dear Brother, be the Confidence that we have in HIM, *That if we ask any Thing according to his Will,* (as we always do, when we pray for the Advancement of our Lord's Kingdom and Glory) *that we* have *the Petitions that we asked of Him.* That we *have* the Answers of our Requests for *Sion*'s Glory, in the Grant, and shall have the Enjoyment of them, in that Way, Time and Measure, which shall be most for the Glory of GOD, the Good of his Church, and our own Joy. And accordingly, let is *go on,* to pour out our Hearts before the LORD, and say with the Psalmist, for the Glory of GOD, and the Good of the Church, in general and particular, *Peace be within thy Walls; and Prosperity within thy Palaces. For my Brethren and Companions Sakes, I will now say, Peace be within Thee. Because of the House of the LORD our God, I will seek thy Good.*

I rejoice, dear Sir, that the Lord gives you such Bowels for Souls, and spirits you to preach the Gospel to the poor *Negroes.* May the *Hand of the Lord be with you, and many believe and turn unto the Lord!* May the Lord make you a Father of many Children, who shall be your *Joy and Crown, in the Day of the Lord Jesus!* Oh my Brother, do your utmost in the Service of your *dear* MASTER. His Work is exceeding sweet; and his Reward, is and will be ineffably glorious! Little do you think, how kindly Jesus Christ will take every Word you say of, or for Him, to poor Sinners, to win them to his Obedience. Nor how much He will commend your Service, in gathering, and feeding his Household, when He comes to take *Account of his Servants,* and to give them *Rewards according to their Works.* I know my Brother, that *the Love of Christ,* his great, free, and unchangeable Live to you, *constrains you* to serve Him. And that your ministerial Work, is cast upon you, as a rich Donation of infinite Grace. Nevertheless, that same Grace, which chose you to eternal

Life, and unto this Service, which assists you in, and accepts every Part of it; will richly reward all your Obedience, with immortal Glory! CHRIST doth *all,* in us and by us; worketh in us, both to will, and to do of his own good Pleasure, and succeeds our Labours with his own Hand. And then he says, *We* have done *this* and *that* Piece of Service. That *we* have fed his Hungry, cloth'd his Naked, minister'd to his sick and imprison'd Brethren. *&c.* And as the blessed of his Father, as his obedient Children, as his good and faithful Servants, will call us to inherit that Kingdom of Glory, which was prepared for us, by free, infinite Grace, from the Foundation of the World. Oh never was such a MASTER, as JESUS CHRIST! Never was such a LOVER, as the Son of GOD! Come my Brother, let us go on to *love* and *serve* Him. In his Strength, wash'd in his Blood, cloth'd with his righteousness, accepted in his Perfections, and looking for his Glory, which shall be revealed in us; let us *go on,* in all holy Obedience continually, fearless of a thousand Difficulties which may be in the Way. We shall be *more than Conquerors thro' HIM that hath loved us.*

You will want to know, my Brother, how it is with me.—I rejoice to tell you, That I live under *great Grace,* tho' a *great Sinner;* and find my Lord's Strength, daily made perfect in my Weakness. I see and feel more of my own Emptiness and Vileness; and rejoice greatly in the All-cleansing Blood, and All-sufficient Fulness, of my own dear *Lord Jesus.* CHRIST loves *me* infinitely! I love HIM, tho' alas! but weakly. He pities and pardons me continually. He renews my strength daily. And yet, Oh *yet,* He hath not *cast me off, for all that I have done!* In a Word, *my Beloved is mine, and I am His:* He dwells in and with *me* here; and shortly will make me perfectly like Him, and take me up to dwell with HIM for ever where He is. Oh pray, that I may love and serve Christ *more;* who am under such infinite Obligations! And praise Him on my Account.—*Great Grace be with you!*—I am,

Dear Sir,

Yours for ever in JESUS,

——— ———.

LETTER IX.

To Mr. B________r.

Reverend and very dear Brother,

Grace unto you, and Peace be multiplied,

YOUR very kind Letters, I joyfully receiv'd. I bless *God* for them both, and return *you* a thousand Thanks. The kind Expressions of your Love to unworthy *me,* affect my Soul. I wonder that the Lord should give such a vile Sinner, so much Room in your Heart, and in the Hearts of his dear Children with you. But all is of *Grace:* And let Free-Grace have *all the Glory!* I assure you, my honour'd Brother, I accept your Love, with sweet Surprize. The GOD of Love reward you a *Hundred-fold!* I am very unworthy of Love from you, dear Sir, and the dear Saints with you; and much more to be honour'd by you. But if Christ's Father, and my Father, will cast Honour upon so despicable a Worm, in my feeble Attempts to serve Him, as a rich Donation of infinite Grace; I cast my Crown down at his Feet, and say, *Salvation and Glory, and Honour and Blessing, be unto GOD, and to the LAMB for ever!*

And now, my dear Brother, you will think, if I lov'd you, why did I not answer your first Letter sooner? Allow me to say, dear Sir, my Soul loveth you, is knit to you in the Lord, and much I desir'd to send you a Line in Testimony hereof. But indeed Brother, I have been prevented from Time to Time, and could get no Leisure until now. When I receiv'd your first Letter, *&c.* there were sent me divers Letters from *L*___ _______*n,* which requir'd speedy Answers of some length. This, with other Work, which my dear Lord successively call'd me to, prevented my *writing* unto *you.* I believe you will excuse me. Yea, and be induc'd to praise the Lord with me, if I tell you, That by one of my poor Letters, wrote upon Request to a young Man in

L_n, who was in Darkness and Perplexity about the State of his Soul, the Lord brought him out into glorious Light, Liberty and Joy. So that he now tells me, "He feeds no more on *Husks,* but on heavenly *Manna,* and can't help declaring to all, what *great Things* God hath done for his Soul!" He tells me likewise, "That the Reading of my Works, (poor as they are) was a Means under God, of awakening him to *adore Free-Grace,* and the Mystery of *Electing Love.* Tho' at first (he says) he was much confus'd about it, while carnal Reason, Self-Righteousness, and the Favour of the World were in Opposition to it. But now, (says he) all those thick Clouds are dispersed." He enjoys sweet Freedom in the Lord, is join'd in Society at the Tabernacle, lives joyfully under the bright Shine of a Gospel Ministry, and is become a glorious Soul.—Brother

L_s, writing to me of him, says, "Oh I have brave News to tell you. Glory be to our dear *Emanuel* for your Writing! For they have been the Means of awakening dear Brother

C_ns. Indeed he is become a sweet Soul, a Champion for the LORD of Hosts; and walks sweetly with our SAVIOUR Day by Day."—

Oh this was brave News indeed to my poor Soul! And the Lord sent it at a seasonable Time. When but the Night before, Satan had rais'd up one of our Lord's Servants, to be his Instrument, to disswade me from Writing for Christ. This wounded me at Heart, till recollecting myself, I knew it was the Enemy's Voice, in that of my Friend's, to hinder me in my Lord's Service: Upon which I got fresh Strength.—And lo, the next Morning, my kind Lord, to comfort my poor Heart, sent me the above News!—Oh then, I had Reward enough, of all my weak Labour. I thought it well worth the while, to spend my whole Life in writing for Christ, were it to a *Methusalah*'s Age, *to win one Soul to JESUS to adore Free-Grace in Him!*

Another Instance of divine Kindness, I may add. Some Months ago, a dear young Woman told me, "That in Reading my Letter to the *Negroes,* the Lord overcome her Soul with the Love of Christ to poor Sinners, gave her to see her Misery without Him, to mourn for all her past Neglect of Him, and to seek Him most earnestly: (She has now found Him) Altho' before she was quite careless about attending upon the Worship of God, and without Concern for her poor Soul."

These Things are the LORD'S *Doings,* and are *marvelous in my Eyes!* Oh that you, and all the Saints with you, would praise the LORD with me, for this his wondrous Kindness to the Chief of Sinners!—I should not have took up your Time, my dear Brother in telling these Stories, but to get my Lord some Glory; as I am confident you will rejoice with the *Bridegroom,* to see Him have the *Bride*; and with the least of his *Friends,* (that deserves not the Name) who, in boundless Grace, He has made of any Use, to win some of his *Enemies.*

Once more, let me add, all the wondrous Grace, which the Lord hath shewn to his vile and worthless Worm, in making me of Use to *any,* (I would humbly say by Way of Wonder at his Love, to *many)* of his dear called Children, to help their Faith and Joy! And then let me say, *Oh praise the LORD with me, and let us exalt his Name together!*—Oh my dear Brother, I hint not these Things, as if I had done any thing for *Christ,* but to shew you what great Things he hath done for *me.* For my own Part, I lie down in my Shame, and Confusion covers me, at my Vileness and Unprofitableness, under such bright Displays of infinite Favour. And as enabled, cry, *Grace, Grace!*

I thank you, my dear Brother, that you, and the Saints with you, bless the Lord on my Account, and remember me in your Prayers. I thank you likewise, that you put me in Remembrance of the Lord's loving Kindness towards me. He blest it to raise my Wonder at infinite Grace, to excite my Praises, and to humble me for all my Insensibility and Unthankfulness. This Expression of your, broke my Heart: "Indeed, my dear Sister, I must tell you, that I think, you ought to love your Lord *much;* having not only much *forgiven,* but also much *given you.*" I could read no further, but fell down before the Lord, was melted into Tears of Love, Joy and Humiliation, ador'd his infinite Love to me, and bewail'd my little Love to *Him.* I told Him then, and oft since, what his dear Servant said to me. I acknowledg'd that I ought to love Him *much*, I lamented that I lov'd Him *little*, and pray'd Him to *baptize me with Fire.* Oh my Brother, if you knew what a vile, wretched, ungrateful Creature I am, and how little I love the *Lord,* for his great Love to *me,* you would be astonished! No *Love,* but that which has the Fulness, the Strength, the Unchangeableness and Eternity of the GODHEAD in it, could bear with my Ingratitude and Provocations! But oh! *our* JEHOVAH, *can* love whom He *will,* be gracious unto whom He *will,* and have Mercy upon whom He *will,* tho' the very Chief of Sinners! All his Dealings with vile, ungrateful me, convince me more and more, of the infinite Greatness and Freeness of his Love. *Herein is Love, not that I loved GOD, but that HE loved me!* Not that I love GOD, but that HE loves *me!*

I dare not say, That the Love of God, doth not engage me to love Him. For from blessed Experience, I must say, *I love Him, because He first loved me.* But my Love to God, is so little, to what it ought to be, and to what I earnestly desire it should be, that it seems as nothing in my own Sight. I see such Heart-Enmity against GOD, and such woful Fruits of it in my poor Soul, that pains my Heart exceedingly. Oh! my Love to *Christ* is so weak, so inconstant a Flame, or rather, so small a Spark, so oft wrapp'd up in Ashes, that I should utterly sink and faint, under the Weight of my Ingratitude, if his free, infinite Love to *me,* his strong Love, to change me into his own Image, did not support and revive me.

And sometimes I am tempted, "To do no more for Christ, unless I lov'd Him more That all the Labour of my Hands will be in vain, of no Account with the Lord Jesus, at the great Day, unless He had my Heart in it." Yea, "That all that I have done and said to excite others to love Christ, will rise up in Judgment against me, unless I lov'd Him more myself."

But then my poor Soul is help'd to say, "Well, my Lord forgives my little Love; and therefore I'll love Him as I can." "If my Labour should be in vain at last, if my Lord should take no Notice of any Thing I ever aim'd to do for Him, when He comes to give Rewards unto his Servants according to their Works, because He hath so little of my Heart in the Labour of my Hands; yet if Christ may be glorify'd in me, and his Children comforted and strengthened in the present State; I'll go on to serve Him and His to the utmost of my Power." And tho' all that I have ever said about Christ, should in some sort, rise up in Judgment against me, because I love Him no more; yet if thereby I may win other Souls to love Him, and bring Glory to Him, and Happiness to them, that Way; I'll submit to my own Shame, and endure all Things for Christ and His." Yea, I sometimes think, "If I was to go to Hell at last, as I know, thro' Grace, I shall not, I would do all I could, to serve Christ and his People now: Esteeming it my unspeakable Happiness, and Matter of my Joy and Thanksgiving, to glorify Christ, and serve his People."—Oh how do I love the Glory of Christ, at Times! And how doth my Heart rejoice, if by any Means, I may comfort and strengthen his dear Children! If my Lord by me, will send them any Refreshment in this weary Wilderness!

But dear Sir, I know why I thus write to you. In the greatest Part of this Letter, I have been carried quite beyond my first Intention. Oh help my by your Prayers! Certain it is, that I love my lovely, loving Lord but *little.* Pray that my Love to *Him,* may be a pure, keen. solid, lasting Flame. That He would make me like his *Seraphims,* in flaming Love to Him, Zeal for his Service, and quick Dispatch of his Work. But oh, what do I ask? Can a Worm of the Earth, a Sin-burden'd Worm, serve the Son of God like the heavenly Host, those pure, those winged Flames in the Love and Service of JESUS? No!—*Angels* fly: *Worms* creep. But oh that my Love was sublimated! That in my little Measure, I might be made a Creature, *akin* as it were to Angels! Oh methinks, if I had all the Love to Christ, that ever possess'd and *created Mind,* in my *little Soul;* I would pour it out upon GOD'S Beloved, upon *my* Beloved at JESUS' Feet, that ineffably *fair,* that *altogether lovely ONE!* But oh my narrow Soul, my little Love to so great an Object! Oh my great Ingratitude to so glorious a Lover, as the Son of GOD, my dear LORD JESUS!

Nevertheless, my Brother, such is the boundless Love of CHRIST to me, that He will call me *his Love, his Dove, his Undefiled!* He will say to me, *Thou hast Dove's Eyes. How fair is the Love, my Sister, my Spouse! How much better is thy Love than Wine! And the Smell of thine Ointments than all Spices!* My JESUS, will not lose my *weak Service,* because of my *little Love;* but wash away its Impurity in his own Blood, perfume it with his much Incense, and present it in his own Perfections, unto his and my Father, HOLINESS TO THE LORD: And will find it unto Praise, and Honour, and Glory at his Appearing. He will not *so* notice *my* Want of Love, as to forget my weak Attempts to draw *others* to love Him; but call even *that, My Kindness;* and pardon all that was *lacking* in myself. Yea, wrap me up for ever in the Arms of his infinite Love, and crown me with endless Glory!—Oh my Brother, who would not *love* such a Bridegroom! Who would not *serve* such a Master, whatever Temptations one may have to the contrary! And lo, He will give us the Victory over *these,* and then crown is as Overcomers. Yea, heighten our Glory so much the *more,* than if we had met with *no Opposition.* Our Lord will say to us, in our abiding with Him in the Service He calls us to now, amidst all the Temptations we meet with to the contrary, as of his Disciples of old, *Ye are they which have continued with Me in my Temptations: And I appoint unto you a Kingdom, as my Father hath appointed unto me.*—Oh this is *the LORD!* This is *our GOD! These are Parts of his Ways: But how little a Portion is heard of HIM!*—But to return.

The whole of your Letter was sweet and savoury to my Taste, refresh'd my Bowels in the Lord, and strengthened my Hands in his Work. And with you, and the dear Family, I rejoice and give Thanks, for the late wonderful Appearances of the Lord, for and with you. And the more, as the same is an Answer of my poor Prayers. Much I was concern'd when I heard, that dear Mr.

W________d was prevented coming to you at the Time he intended. Not but I rejoiced for his Stay in *England,* where he is much wanted. But I was griev'd for *you,* knowing how much you long'd to see Him, and fearing his further Absence from you would discourage your Hearts. And earnestly I pray'd, that the Lord would visit you *Himself,* and make you glad with his Presence. And when I receiv'd the News of it, much I rejoiced.

Your last Letter, my dear Brother, is a Means of renewing my Joy, and further exciting my Thanks and Praise, to your God and mine, who has dealt so graciously with us both. I thank you for putting me in Mind of the great Goodness of our own God, in granting unto you the great Blessings, which I was perswaded He had in Store for you, (that you as his escaped Remnant, should yet take Root downward, and bear Fruit upward) and in answering my Desires therein. Doubtless our God, loseth much of his Glory, as a God hearing Prayer, for want of our particular Notice of the Petitions we put up to Him, and the Answers we receive from Him. And we also, much of that Encouragement to seek Him, and Confidence which we should other wise have in Him.

Fear not, my dear Brother, your taking up too much of my Time, in reading, or answering your Letters from *Bethesda.* If the sovereign Lord of all, will please to indulge unworthy *me,* with such great Favours, and make any thing so poor a Worm may write, of Use to your dear Souls; I give *Him* the Glory, and rejoice over *you,* with exceeding great Joy. Oh how gladly would I be a Servant of you all, if the Lord would please so to honour me! *I live, if you stand fast in the Lord.* Sweet were your Words to me, and well might you say, "If our Redeemer has receiv'd this Gift, and bestow'd it on you freely for us, you are happy in using it for Him and us."—*Happy indeed,* my Brother. Oh *who am I, and what is my Father's House,* that the LORD should bring me *hitherto?* That he should make so unworthy a Worm, of any Use to his dear Family at *Bethesda! Is this after the Manner of Men, O LORD God! According to thine own Heart, and for thy Word's Sake, hast Thou done all these great Things, to make thy* Worm *know them!*—Indeed my Brother, I look upon every Part of my Work for Christ, as a Part of my Inheritance. I see with Joy, Wonder and Praise, my Border pass on from Letter, to Letter, from Answer to Answer, according to the Line of my great Inheritance, in my Time-State, which was cast for me, by infinite Wisdom and Grace, from Eternity.

Fear not *troubling me,* my dear Brother, with *your Complaints,* nor that any of the dear Children of God should do so. It is our Privilege, a Part of the Communion of Saints, to unbosom our Souls to each other, to bear each other's Burdens, to seek each other's Good, to rejoice with them that rejoice, and to mourn with them that mourn. The more *free* you are with me, the more *kindly* I take it, the more my Spirit runs into yours, and interests itself in your Concerns. God grant me a Bosom large enough, to embrace all his Children, and to receive all their Cases with the greatest Sympathy!

As for yourself, my dear Brother, JESUS has the Care both of you, and your Work. He bears you Name, your Person, and your Judgment, continually upon his Heart and Arm, before his and your Father. Doubt not of the Lord's having Work for you to do, of one Kind or other, in one Place or other, so long as He continues you in this World. Do the Work of the Day, and take no anxious Thought about what you shall do To-morrow. Your Master will shew you your Work, as your every Day's Employment comes up before Him. And lo, for all your Work, you have a Sufficiency of Strength, in the LORD, your great Magazine, your glorious Store-House, in whom *all Fulness dwells.* It is the Glory of the Gospel, that it is *The Ministration of the Spirit;* and of Gospel Ministers, That they are to *preach the Gospel with the Holy Ghost sent down from Heaven.* Wisdom and Strength, Boldness and Utterance, for every Thing you are to say or do for Christ, is provided for you, and shall be given you at the appointed Hour. When your Lord calls you to any Piece of Work for HIM; in his Strength, and cloth'd with his Majesty, go forth, fearless of the Faces of Men. He *will give you a Mouth and Wisdom, that your Adversaries shall not be able to gainsay, nor resist.* Oh, *no Mouth,* like that of *Christ's* giving! *No Wisdom,* like that of *his* bestowing! *No Strength,* like that immediately, and continually receiv'd from HIM! Oh 'tis *brave* saying and doing, walking and running for CHRIST, under *such Assistance.*—That we run not before the Lord sends us; we must wait till we see our Call clear, before we attempt any Thing our Minds incline to, or are exercis'd about.—And that we be not negligent in following Him; as soon as we know the Lord's Mind about any Piece of Service, we must attempt it immediately, without conferring with Flesh and Blood.

As to your leaving *Bethesda* for a while, I would very tender, dear Sir, of saying any Thing to disswade you from it, if your Mind inclines thereto. Not knowing, but the Lord has Work for you to do elsewhere. And I know the Lord can raise up another, to feed and watch over his dear Sheep and Lambs, of which you have now the Charge. But I confess, whether from my Weakness, or not, the Thing seems grievous to me. Clear was your Call to *Bethesda;* wonderful the Lord's Loving-kindness, in giving such a dear Shepherd to his little Flock; great is the Work the Lord has enabled you to do for Him there, great the Assistance and Success afforded; and great the Privileges precious Sould have enjoy'd under your Ministry. Yea, great is the Delight your Lord has taken in your Service there; and great shall be your Crown of Glory, when HE appears. Great then should your Satisfaction be, that it is the Lord's Mind you should depart; before you leave his dear Flock, and so important a Trust which He has put into your Hands.—And if you *must* go: *The Lord go with you!* And may *the GOD of the Spirits of all Flesh, set a Man,* fill'd with Wisdom and Grace, *over his Congregation* at *Bethesda.*

Dear Sir,

Ever Yours,

——— —————.

LETTER X.

To Mrs. B________r.

My dear and honour'd Sister in Christ,

I Kindly thank you for your Letter. The Account you give me of the Lord's gracious Dealings with your Soul, rejoiceth mine. I see you are CHRIST'S *own.* And believe it, He will *love you unto the End.* His Love towards *you,* was from of Old, from everlasting. His manifested Love, when you knew him not, nor the Way of his Dealings with those on whom his Heart is fix'd, was a Light-giving, a Life-breathing, a Soul-attracting Discovery, made at the appointed Time. And since that Day of Power, everlasting Love has follow'd you, has highly favour'd you, with the Holy Spirit's Witness with your Spirit, that you are a Child of God; has restor'd your Soul, after Backslidings, and made your renewed Life, a Means to quicken others.—*Great* and *distinguishing* Favours indeed! And yet *these,* my dear Sister, are but the Beginnings of Love's Displays towards you. To the End of Time, and to a never-ending Eternity, will the LORD your Lover, follow you, with bright and increasing Shines, of his infinite, free, everlasting Kindness.—Oh! If GOD *loves;* He will love like HIMSELF! If God loves as a SAVIOUR; He will *save* like GOD; — How full; how great, how glorious then, must your Salvation be; if therein the infinite Glory of JEHOVAH, as the God of Love, is for ever to shine! What Depths, will infinite Love save you from! What Heights, will it save you to! What Sins, will it not forgive! What Provocations, will it not pass by! What Iniquities, will it not subdue! What Enemies, will it not conquer! What Succours, will it not afford! What Supplies, will it not grant! What Victories will it not give! What Graces, will it *not* work! And what Glories, will it not bestow!—Oh my Sister, you are under *the Love of GOD!* Which as an infinite Sun, will cast upon you the resplendent Rays, of its immense and unchangeable Glory, thro' Time, and to Eternity!

And tho' in the present State you must meet with Vicissitudes, a thousand Variations of your Frames and Circumstances; yet all these are under *Love's Management.* When Clouds and Darkness cover you, they are but to commend, and set off *Love's Glory,* so much the more, in its Darkness-dissipating Shines. After dark Nights, you shall have bright

Days. After a cold, barren Winter, you shall have a reviving Spring, and a warm and fruitful Summer. *Love's Eye* will look you out of Darkness, Sorrow and Death, into Light, Life, Joy and Glory. And by every of its renewed Shines, will further display its unsearchable Riches, its bright and immense Glories!

And Lo, my dear Sister, *Love* has the Care of you, when Darkness covers you. Amidst darkest Dispensations, blackest Apprehensions, greatest Desertions, sorest Temptations, strongest Corruptions, and in all your most weak, cold, and contracted Frames, *Love* is at *work* for you; tho' then, in a great Measure imperceptibly to your Sight. By *these,* Love will humble, and empty you, in order to fill and exalt you. By *these* Love will shew you more of your exceeding Blackness, your Ill-deservings, and Hell-deservings; in order to ravish your Heart with its own infinite Brightness, as a Sin-pardoning, Grace-giving, All-conquering, and All-enriching, Flow, of Immensely Free and Sovereign, unchangeable and everlasting Favour! Thus Love *prepares you,* by Darkness, for Light; by Night, for Day; by Winter, for Summer.

And lest you should utterly lose *Sight* of *Love's Glory,* and your Spirit *fail* for want of its native Displays, and sensible Operations; your Night, your Winter-Seasons, shall not be *too long.* Swift-wing'd *Love,* will *haste,* to *look* your Darkness, into Day, your Winter, into Summer, by its radiant Beams, its quickening Influences; to fill you with the Joy of *Sense,* after it hath try'd your *Faith.*

This, my dear Sister, shall you be car'd for and comforted, humbled and rais'd, and every Way sav'd by *infinite Love,* thro' a Succession of Days and Nights; until Night and Darkness, are swallow'd up in eternal DAY. Until Winter is *past and gone,* and an everlasting Spring, an eternal Summer *comes on.* When you shall live for ever, under the bright, immediate, uninterrupted *Shine* of *infinite Love,* darting out all its immense Glories upon you, unto Bliss and Joy, *Endless* and *Unknown!* Then lo, *Your Sun shall no more go down; but the* LORD *shall be your everlasting* LIGHT, *and your* GOD *your* GLORY!

Mean Time, my dear Sister, *see* what a Refuge you have in God! what a Covert under the Shadow of JEHOVAH'S Wings; whereunto you may continually resort, in every Time of Trial and Distress! *Infinite Love,* will never wax weary, of keeping and defending you, of succouring and saving you. *Love* will pity and pardon, strengthen and comfort you; subdue your Iniquities, increase your Graces, prevent your Fears, and grant your Desires; and in a full and everlasting Salvation, will do for you *exceeding abundantly, above all that you can ask or think!* Oh come, rest your weary Soul in *Love's Bosom.* Cast yourself, with all your Heart-Griefs, Miseries, and Wants, into *Love's Arms.* They stand wide open to receive and embrace you, and are well prepar'd, to ease, comfort, and save you to the uttermost. Cast all the Care of your Salvation upon the GOD *of Love,* who careth for you. And only be careful in every Path of Duty, to *love HIM,* who *first loved you.* Love Him as you *can*, my Sister. I know you are griev'd at your little Love. But the GOD of Love, forgives you, calls for your Heart, and will not despise the least Breathing of your Soul towards Him; but delight in it thro' his dear Son, in whom He accepts, both your Person and Obedience. He sees with infinite Pleasure, your mystical Completeness in Christ *now;* and that personal Completeness thro' Him, which you shall have *ere long;* which Glory you shall grow up to, thro' the Influences of his own Grace. And as a *Father,* you have his *Heart.* Therefore walk before him in *Love,* as his *dear Child,* unspeakably *dear* to Him in the *Beloved of his Soul.* Oh *kiss* and *embrace* your Father, like a fond child. Infinite Love *permits it, allows you* a holy Familiarity with GOD in CHRIST. Oh stand not at a *Distance,* since you are made *so nigh!* You may have Access with *Boldness* thro' the Blood of JESUS, unto *His* and *your Father.* And when you can't vent the *Love* of your Heart in clasping about Him, in praising and adoring Him; Oh fall down at his Feet and mourn, that you can love Him *no more,* and pray Him to *enkindle you* with *His Fire.* One Way or other, or rather both Ways, let the *Love* of your Soul, your *Soul* in Love, be cast as a small Drop, into the unfathomable Ocean of the *Love* of God, into the God of Love! *Unto whom be Glory thro' Jesus Christ, World without End.* Amen.

Indeed, my dear Sister, The Lord's breaking in upon your Spirit, and enlarging your Heart to bless Him, when He took away your Child; notwithstanding the contracted Frame you was in, the Depth of your Dejection, and the Strength of your Affection towards a dying Comfort; was a wonderful Appearance of GOD for you. From whence you may learn: The Freeness of his Love; the Greatness of his Care; All-sufficiency of you *own* GOD, to give you in HIMSELF, a full and complete Happiness, tho' all Creatures and Things should be taken from you, and your own Heart and Flesh fail you. GOD, who was then *the Strength of your Heart,* is and will be *your Portion for ever;* your present and eternal ALL! Wherefore cleave unto Him, and live upon Him as *such.*—Into the sweet strong Arms of *everlasting Love,* I commit you: To be carried by *Grace,* into *Glory.* Where shortly I hope to meet you, and join with you, and the innumerable Multitude of Saints and Angels round the Throne, in singing *Hallelujahs* unto GOD and the LAMB for ever.—Pray and give Thanks for me, who am

Yours Affectionately in our Sweet
LORD JESUS,

——— ———

LETTER XI.

To Mr. H_______m.

My Dear and Honoured Brother in Christ,

WHAT shall I say to my dear Brother, whom JESUS loves, whom I love? I'll put you in Mind of your *Blessedness,* declar'd by our Lord's own Mouth, *Matt.* v. 3. *Blessed are the Poor in Spirit: for theirs is the Kingdom of Heaven.* Oh my Brother, little do you think, how great that *Grace is,* which has made you *poor in Spirit.* An Infinity of Grace, in the Forgiveness of all your Sins, was laid as the Foundation of that great Work of God upon your Soul, in shewing you your own Poverty. Upon which all the exceeding Riches of JEHOVAH's Grace were to be expended, (display'd, not exhausted) in raising up the rich and stately Structure, of your endless Glory. If *Grace,* an Immensity of Grace, had not been prepar'd for *you* in Christ, before the World began; you had never been prepar'd for *it,* in the present Time.—And *how* prepar'd? Not by your own Goodness, but by a Discovery of your own Wretchedness. Of your exceeding Sinfulness; of the overspreading Pollution of your whole Nature. Of your exceeding Weakness; of your utter Insufficiency to do any Good, to do any Thing towards your own Salvation to make yourself righteous before, or accepted with God; or to subdue Sin, and sanctify your Nature.—Are you so *poor,* that in yourself, you neither *have* any Thing, nor can *do* any Thing, that is truly good? Are you nothing in yourself, but an Heap of Miseries, Weaknesses, and Wants? Do you *see* this to be your Case, and *groan* under it?—Oh *happy, thrice happy Soul!* Your *Blessedness,* is beyond the Expression of an Angel's Tongue! *Yours is the Kingdom of Heaven!* The Kingdom of Grace here, and of Glory hereafter! Free, rich, reigning Grace, will do *all* for you, that can do *nothing* for yourself. *Grace* will forgive your innumerable Transgressions; will follow you, even in your Life's End, with fresh Applications, and renewed Manifestations of free, abundant Pardon. *Grade,* will subdue all your Iniquities, will bruise all your spiritual Enemies, under its mighty Feet, and cause you to set your Feet upon the Necks of them. *Grace* will break all your Bands and Fetters from off you, will deliver you from every Snare, restore your Soul, renew your Graces, increase your Comforts, supply your Wants, heal your Backslidings, and love you freely: Yea, love you into Light, Life, Liberty, Joy and Glory, perfect and eternal!—You have Happiness *enough,* my Brother, a boundless, endless Store, in that you are *under the Reign of Grace. Grace,* will never quit its Throne, nor cast off its Subjects, nor wax weary of displaying its Glories, and casting Abroad its Riches upon them, with an holy Profuseness, according to the Liberality of a GOD! Of the GOD of *all Grace!* And this from an Infinity, an Eternity of *Love towards them!* Come, my Brother, lie down and rest by *Faith,* in the Bosom of that *Grace, which reigns thro' Righteousness unto eternal Life, by Jesus Christ our Lord.* For Thousands, and ten Thousands of Sins, of Provocations, of Weaknesses in *you;* shall but make Room for the more abundant Displays of *reigning Grace,* in the Variety, and Immensity of its infinite Glories!—That you may daily live, as a Subject of the *Kingdom of Grace,* under its Soul-overcoming, its Heart-changing, and Life-transforming Shines; until you are blest with the *Kingdom of Glory* which awaits you; is the hearty Desire of, Dear Sir,

Your most Affectionate, tho' unworthy
Servant, in our fairest, dearest,
sweetest LORD JESUS,

LETTER XII.

To Mr. P________m.

My dear and honour'd Brother in Christ,

UNTO you at this Time, I thought not of writing. But not knowing but you might be in an unbelieving Frame, a distemper'd Child; and looking upon you as a beloved Child, unspeakably *dear to Christ;* you was *dear to me.* Mine Heart was turned within me, and write I *must.* And our Lord's Dealings with *Thomas,* encourag'd me hereto.

What then shall I say to you, my dear Brother? I tell you, JESUS *loves you.* Has lov'd you anciently, loves you infinitely, and will love you eternally. He lov'd, and liv'd, lov'd, and dy'd, lov'd, and rose, lov'd and ascended, loves, and sits in Heaven for you. To save you to the uttermost, to bring you up to sit with Him in Glory.

'Twas *this Love,* that laid hold on you, when dead in Sins, posting on to Destruction; and gave such a mighty Turn to your Mind, that set your Face *Sion-ward,* to seek, and follow hard after JESUS, a naked CHRIST, altho' in Nakedness, or thro' a thousand Difficulties that might be cast in your Way, to that Land where JESUS is.—Oh my Brother, if *Christ* had not first left all, *his* great *All,* for *you,* you had never been made willing to leave *your* little *All* for *him.* The *World,* would have held you, as it doth Thousands, to their eternal Ruin; if *Christ,* that left his Glory for you, had not drew your Heart off, from all the empty Shews of this World's Glories. *Sin* and *Satan,* would have held you fast, and forever have refus'd to let you go; if *He* who knew no Sin, had not been made Sin for *you,* if *He* who is the Prince of Life, by his own Death for you, had not destroy'd the Destroyer, and deliver'd *you* from the Power of Darkness, from the Soul-killing Reign of Sin and Satan. Oh the infinite Grace, the Almighty Power that *set you free!* You was drawn with the *Cords of the Man Christ,* with the *Bands of his Love,* when you first began to *love and seek* JESUS. *Many are call'd;* are left to make Excuses, go their Way, and Christ hears no more of them. But *you was drawn.* Christ would not, could not, be without *you.* And you, under the

All-attracting Influence of his Love and Loveliness, could not, would not, be without *Him*. CHRIST, CHRIST, none but CHRIST! A thousand Worlds, are nothing to *me*, without JESUS! Thus your Soul ran on crying, seeking *Him*, who was then seeking *you*. And oh! When CHRIST and you *met*, in the first Manifestations of *his Love*, and Expressions of *yours*, how *sweet* was that Meeting! You met, never to *part* more. Of *twain*, you become *one*, inseperably, and eternally *one*. CHRIST gave himself to *you*, in an everlasting Covenant; you gave yourself to *Him*, to be His forever. CHRIST took *you*, for better, for worse, to nourish and cherish you, to love you invariably, thro' ten thousand Variations in your Frames, and Behaviour towards *Him:* Yea, to love you into perfect and unchangeable Glory, and unto the endless Ages of Eternity! You took CHRIST, with his *Cross*, as well as his Crown; yea, esteem'd *that*, a Crown unto you; resolving thro' his Grace to follow him, thro' evil Report, and good Report, thro' Joys, and Sorrows; yea, tho' it should be, thro' *much Tribulation;* until you reach'd Glory with Him. A Fig for the World, then! CHRIST was All to *you!* And you all for *Him!* The Marriage was made between Christ and you. Your *beloved* was *yours*, and *you His*. And that was *enough:* You needed no more, to make your Joy full.

And tho', my Brother, since then, you may have Cause to lament the Loss of *your first Love;* your Maker, your Husband, has not lost *his first*, his great, his infinite *Love to you!* He *knew that you would deal very treacherously*. And yet, in the Kindness, in the Faithfulness of a GOD, of JEHOVAH, He *betrothed you unto himself for ever*. He *rests* in his Love towards you. His whole Soul is at Rest, in his Love-Delights in *you*. And He will never seek another Object of his Complacency, instead of *you*, for all your Unkindness to *Him*. No, He *rests undisturb'd*, in his deep, still, immeasurable *Love!* Saying, *Here will I dwell for ever*, (this Soul shall be the Object of my eternal Love) *for I have desired it*.—And lo, my Brother, He will be *silent*, because of his *Love*. He will not, in vindictive Wrath, make mention of your Sins, nor rebuke you for them; but bury them all in the infinite Depths of his Grace, and the Merits of his Blood. The LORD your Husband, *hateth putting away*. He will not *cast you off, for all that you have done*. But by the fresh Displays of his infinite Love to *you,* will draw you into the fresh Exercise of Love to *Him.* Yea, increase the same, until you are made *perfect in Love,* a glorious Soul, all-enlarg'd, and meet for the Marriage-Glory with your Royal Bridegroom, in the heavenly World. Where, as one well saith, "CHRIST shall enjoy his Bride, without any Reluctancy, or Unsuitableness in her; and she enjoy her Bridegroom, without any Vail upon his Face. Love shall have its full Vent, on both Sides. The mutual Yerning of Bowels, shall be satisfy'd; and the Voice of *Come,* from HIM above, and from her below, shall period itself, in one eternal, inseperable *Meeting."* Let me add, in Love-Enjoyment, in Glory-Communion of an endless Duration!

Mean Time, my Brother, CHRIST *remembers you,* (and oh, with what Delight!) *the Kindness of your Youth, the Love of your Espousals, when you went after* HIM *in the Wilderness, in a Land that was not sown.* When, forsaking the Pleasures of *Sense,* you followed a naked Christ by *Faith,* in such thorny Ways, as no natural Man will walk in. And you that have borne the *Cross,* shall shortly wear the *Crown.* You have your Lord's Word for it, That *you that have forsaken all, and followed Him; shall have an Hundred-fold in this World; and in the World to come, Life everlasting!*

What say you now? Do you *believe* CHRIST's *Love?* If you *doubt it;* reach out the Hand of your *Faith,* and thrust it into his *Side,* pierc'd by your Sin of *Unbelief.* And put your Finger into the *Print of the Nails,* the Wounds which your *Sins* did make in your crucified Lover, those indelible *Characters* of his *Love! And be not Faithless, but believing.* Let Faith and Love, clasp about your once dying, your now living SAVIOUR, and say with *Thomas, My Lord, and my God!—Wishing all Grace and Peace,* may abound towards you, like a *River;* and requesting your Prayers and Thanksgivings for me; I remain,

Dear Sir,

Yours, most Affectionately in JESUS,

LETTER XIII.

To Mrs. *P_______m.*

My dear and honour'd Sister in the Lord,

I Thank you for your kind Letter. I love you in the Bowels of Christ. Glad should I be to serve your Faith, and help your Joy in the Lord. Great is the Grace shewn to *me,* and much I rejoice over *you,* in that the Lord has been pleas'd to make any Thing of mine, of *Use* to your precious Soul. I sympathize with you in your Temptations, by which you have been hinder'd from Writing. Yet a little while, and our Communion will be free and full, uninterrupted and eternal. Shortly, we shall be with Christ; and no more troubled with Sin and Satan.—No more Discord, Disaffection, or Dis-esteem among Saints then. We shall be *made perfect in one.* In one Body, in one Love-Glory. We shall love and honour one another then, as Fellow-Members of Christ, our glorious Head. Yea, love and honour Christ, in each other. His Image being perfected in us, and his Glories cast upon us, we shall shine in each others Sight, to our mutual and eternal Endearment, like so many Suns in the Kingdom of our Father: And his infinite, all-surpassing Brightness, which casts our Lustre, be admir'd and ador'd, in and by all.—So perfect shall be the *Love-Unity* of all the Saints! So great the Glory of that *Oneness* among *themselves,* which our Lord has pray'd for! Yea, we shall be *one* in the *Son,* and in the *Father.* There will be such a Love-Union and Communion, between GOD and us in CHRIST, such displaying, and enjoying of infinite Glories, such a Delight in the infinite JEHOVAH, to make *us* blessed, and in *us,* to bless and adore *Him* for ever; that will raise our Glory high, far above all our present Thought!

And to this Glory, my dear Sister, you are growing up, as a Child, and Heir of God, and a Joint-Heir with CHRIST; notwithstanding all your present Weakness, and exceeding Sinfulness. JESUS has the Care of your Growth. And *increase* you shall, *with all the Increases of* GOD, even by those very Things and Times, wherein you seem to *decrease. The* LORD *is your Shepherd: You shall not want:* Feeding, healing, thriving. He has laid down his Life for *These;* and his Power, Grace and Faithfulness, is engag'd to bestow them. The Care of our Growth, in a Way of Duty, is *ours;* in the Way of Privilege, GOD's. We have such a Shepherd, that loves and cares for us infinitely; and that one Way or other, will increase us continually. And to his all-wise, and all-gracious Conduct, we may, we ought, to commit ourselves joyfully.

The Heart, my dear Sister, yours and mine, our *old* Heart, *is deceitful above all Things, and desperately wicked.* We don't know a thousandth Part of that Depth of Sin, of that Hell of Iniquity, which is in our corrupt Nature. None but the great JEHOVAH, hath search'd this vast Abyss! And unto HIM, its amazing Depths, are all naked and bare.—And yet from a Depth of *Love* in *his Heart,* infinitely greater, he hath took up a sovereign Resolve, to be *gracious* unto us, vile Sinners, merely because he *will* be gracious.—And how wonderful is it, that to be gracious unto *us,* to pardon all our Heart, Lip, and Life-Wickedness, to pity us under it, and save us from it; God the Father, should lay it upon his *own Son!* Should make HIM *Sin for us, that we might be made the Righteousness of God in Him!*

Oh my Sister, God the Father, looks upon us in his *Son,* thro' his infinite Satisfaction, and glorious Perfections, as *All-fair,* and without a *Spot;* notwithstanding all the Spots and Deformities which are in *us! He hath remov'd our Iniquities as far from us, as the East is from the West.* Those distant Poles, may sooner meet, than our Sins be judicially charg'd upon us. *When the Iniquity of* Israel *is sought for, there shall be none, and the Sins of* Judah, *they shall not be found:* Because the Lord hath *pardon'd them.* As God looks upon us in his crucify'd *Son, he hath not beheld Iniquity in* Jacob; *neither hath he seen Perverseness in* Israel. Our *Sins* are cover'd with an infinite Satisfaction, and remov'd by an infinite Discharge. God, with the Eye of his *Justice,* sees no Sin in *us,* as he beholds us in *Christ;* even while, with the Eye of his *Omniscience,* he sees us in *ourselves,* in all our amazing Vileness, as *chief Sinners.*—And having imputed our Sins unto *Christ,* and his Righteousness unto *us,* and freely pardon'd and justify'd us, thro' his active and passive Obedience; he will remove Sin out of our *Nature.* It shall be destroy'd in us personally, as it was destroy'd in Christ mystically. From the infinite Merit of Christ's Satisfaction, and the infinite Virtue of his Discharge; Sin shall be destroy'd by an infinite Power, from out of *us,* both Root and Branch. For,

As our Lord is made unto us *Righteousness;* so likewise, *Sanctification.* Christ has a pure Heart for *us,* to answer all the Impurity of *ours,* and make us such holy Creatures, representatively in *Himself,* as a Holy GOD can delight in. And as the inherent Purity of *Christ's Nature,* as the Man JESUS was personally, and immeasurably fill'd with the Holy Ghost, is made ours to represent us, so from his communicable Fulness of the Spirit of Grace, shall *our Natures* be made pure and clean. As we are perfectly holy *in Christ* representatively, we must be made so in our *own Persons* influentially. God the Father, hath predestinated us to be *conform'd unto the Image of his Son.* And the Lord the Holy Ghost, has begun, and will compleat this *good Work* in us, and bring us up shortly, in our *own Person,* to that Pattern-Glory, which we now have *in Christ.*

Mean Time, we must live by *Faith;* and *reckon ourselves to be dead indeed unto Sin, and alive unto God,* perfectly so, *in Christ Jesus our Lord,* mystically: that we may enter into the *Rest* of an assured Perswasion, that we shall be so personally. The *one* being the Foundation of the *other,* the Spring and Source of our desired Perfection.

Again, we may rest by *Faith,* in assured Hope of perfect personal Holiness thro' Christ, from that Omnipotence of *Power,* which has been already display'd, in the begun Work of Grace in our Souls, and which stands *engag'd* to perfect it. Alas! our *own Strength,* is much too weak, to mortify the least sin, or to add to the least Grace in our poor Souls. But the *Almightiness of* JEHOVAH, the Omnipotence of an *infinite Arm,* is engag'd for us in both.—Let us then, my dear Sister, in the Way of our Duty, wait for Divine Influence. *In well-doing,* let us continually, *commit the Keeping of our Souls* into the Hands of our own GOD, *as unto a faithful Creator.* Who having created us anew in Christ Jesus; will maintain and perfect our new Life, until all Sin and Death, is swallowed up in *Victory,* and *we appear with Christ in Glory.*

And from that compleat Salvation, my dear Sister, which you now have *in Christ,* and shall shortly have *thro' Him;* lay out yourself, your time and all, to love and serve your SAVIOUR. Who so inexpressibly *lov'd,* doth and will *love you!* Who tho' he was *Lord of all,* emptied himself of all his Glory, took upon him the *Form of a Servant,* and served on Earth for you; to set you with *Him,* on his *Throne* in Heaven! Oh, never was such a *Lover,* as our *dear* LORD JESUS! Never was such *Service,* as the *Lord of Glory,* perform'd for *us!* In Love *unknown,* he served for his *Bride,* spent his whole *Life,* yea, *dy'd* on the Cross, in *her Service!* Was made a *Curse,* to make *her blessed!* Endur'd *her Hell,* that *she might* have *his Heaven!* Took upon his Holy SELF, all *her Uncleanness;* that with his *own Blood,* he might wash her from all her Impurity, array her with his own Beauties, and marry a *vile Beggar* to himself, to inherit with HIM, the *Throne of immortal Glory!*—And shall we not *love him?* Shall we not say, in all holy Obedience, *Worthy is the* LAMB *that was slain, to receive Blessings, and Honour, and Glory, and Dominion; for ever and ever. Amen!—Great Grace be with you!*—With dear Love, I am,

Yours in CHRIST for ever,

——— ———

LETTER XIV.

To Mr. G_______t.

My very dear and honour'd Brother, in our sweet JESUS,

YOUR most acceptable Favours, I receiv'd. The Lord reward your Labour of Love an *hundred-fold!* I am most unworthy of the least Regard from any of the *King's Sons.* Free Grace, has put me among *the Children.* But surely I may, I must say, I am the *least* and *last,* the *vilest* and most *unworthy* of them all. If the *Grace* of the King our *Father*, was not infinite and unchangeable, immensely free and sovereign, he would not suffer vile *me,* to abide in his House, nor to be look'd at with an Eye of Favour, by any of the Princes of his Family. But oh, by Grace *unknown!* He washes away my Impurity, hides my Deformity, arrays me with his own Beauty, casts upon me some sparkling Rays of his own Brightness, and lets many of his *better Children* love me! And, oh surpassing Wonder! HIMSELF loves me; notwithstanding all that Unloveliness, and vile Ingratitude which his Holy Eye sees in me! Me, my Father *loves,* my elder Brother *loves,* my glorious Comforter *loves; me,* not my *Vileness;* but yet it's me, with a *nevertheless,* with a *notwithstanding* all my exceeding Sinfulness! Oh *Grace,* infinitely rich, free and superabounding! Oh *Love,* infinitely higher than the Heights of my Provocations! Broader than the Breadth of my overspreading Pollutions! Deeper than the Depths of my Vileness and Ingratitude! Longer than Time! Long as Eternity, past and to come! Oh Sin-pardoning, Sin-subduing, Grace-giving, Glory-bestowing *Love!* Oh *Love,* that will love me into its own Image! Into as great a Purity and Holiness, as if *Sin* had never entred! Yea, into a higher Life and Glory, than perfect *Adam* was possess'd of! "Oh free, infinite, eternal and unchangeable *Love,* in *thee* my little, vile, weak Soul *rest!* Work all thy Wonders for and upon me, until thou hast made me *perfect in Love,* a *glorious Piece* of thy *great Workmanship!* And then all my By-past *Blackness,* shall for ever commend, and set off thine infinite *Brightness,* serve to enhance thy *Glories,* and to exalt thy *Praises,* unto *Ages without End!* Then as a *Drop,* receiving all my bliss from *thee,* into *thee* I'll flow, with all the Praise, the unfathomable Ocean of my endless Glory."

Most kindly I thank you, my dear Brother, for the Account you gave me in your Letter, of the Lord's *gracious Dealings with you.* I read it with Tears of Joy. I adore the Grace that has sav'd your dear Soul, that has pluck'd you, as a *Brand out of the Burning,* and snatch'd you as a *Prey*, out of the *Jaws* of the Devourer. Oh *Grace, Grace!* Take the Praise from us, and all the Saints and Angels, *World without End. Amen.* Oh my Brother, you are *Love's Prey.* Infinite Love hath rescu'd you, from those infinite Depths of Woe, you was just upon the Brink of. And which *Way* did Love do it? It did it by Covenant-Engagements from *Everlasting,* and by Covenant-Performances in the *Fulness of Time.* It did it by *Price,* in order to do it by *Power.*

Think, Oh think, what *Love* it was in the *Father,* to lay all your Iniquity upon his *own Son!* To resolve from *Everlasting,* Not to impute your Trespasses unto *you,* but unto *HIM!*—What *Love* was it in the *Son,* to take *your Load,* (that would have sunk *you* into eternal Perdition) upon *his Back!* Your vast Debt upon Himself, and engage as your *Surety,* to pay it to the very last Mite!—And what *Love* was it in the *Holy Spirit,* to become the Unction, the Anointing, to qualify the Man JESUS, with all Gifts and Graces, for his Work of *Saving you!* And thus to *resolve*, To fit Him for it, and carry Him thro' it, for *you,* before the World began! Yea, and in Consequence hereof, to engage to become your Sanctifier, Indweller and Comforter: Notwithstanding He foresaw all your Vileness and Ingratitude, even after his begun Work upon you, and gracious Abode in you!—Oh don't you shrink to *Nothing* as it were, under a Sense of your own Littleness and Vileness, before the Majesty of *infinite Love:* While you see yourself thus taken up into the Thoughts of the Three-one GOD, before the Mountains had a Birth, or the World's Foundation was laid! Oh what was *you,* what was *I,* little, vile, despicable *Worms,* that *we* should be thought on in great Grace, by the Great JEHOVAH, before Time began! Aye, God-provoking, Hell-deserving *Wretches,* that *we* should be *so loved! We* that were Enemies, Rebels, Traitors. Surely we may say, with amazing delightful Wonder, *Herein is* Love, *not that we loved GOD, but that He loved* us!

Think again, What *Love* it was in the *Father,* actually to give his Son for *you,* in the *Fulness of Time!* To charge all your Sins upon *Him,* and wound the Darling of his Soul for *you!* Oh, when it came to the Trial, God the Father so loved *you,* that He withheld not his *only son,* but deliver'd Him up to Death for *you! It pleased the Lord to bruise Him,* to *put Him to Grief,* to lay the *Chastisement of your* Sin, that procur'd your *Peace, upon Him:* That *with his Stripes you might be healed!*—What *Love* was it in the *Son,* actually to take upon his Innocent, Holy SELF, all your Guilt and Uncleanness, to stand charg'd with all your Crimes, to drink the Cup of Wrath, that amazing Cup of Indignation, and give up his Life a *Sacrifice,* in *your Soul's stead!* That when it came to the Trial, that *He* must die, or *you* perish, when He began to *feel* that dreadful Shower of Divine Vengeance to be poured down upon Him, which made his Soul *exceeding Sorrowful, even unto Death;* that *then* He should not turn back, nor repent what He had engag'd to do, but with infinite Resolution, *endure the Cross, and despise the Shame* for *you!* When no less a Price than his *own Life,* who was an infinite Person, could be *your Redemption!*—And what *Love* was it in the *eternal Spirit,* to *strengthen* the Man JESUS, to offer up Himself a Sacrifice for *you!* To set the *Joy* of his Father's Glory in your Salvation, *before Him,* for which He endur'd the Cross, and obtain'd for *you* eternal Redemption! Oh what *Love* was it in the *Three-one GOD,* thus to redeem you by *Price,* in order to redeem you by *Power!*

And when that Day of Power came on, wherein you was to be rescu'd as a *Prey,* out of the *Teeth* of the devouring Lion; Oh what a miserable Case did Love find you in! What a willing Slave to Sin and Satan? What a Heart-Enemy to God? What a loathsome Creature was you *then,* in the Eyes of infinite Purity? And yet, with what an out-stretched Arm, did infinite Love *save you!* How were the Flood-gates of infinite Mercy *pull'd up,* the Sluices of infinite Grace *open'd,* thro' the Wounds of your dear Redeemer: And like an All-overflowing *Flood,* or rather a boundless *Ocean,* swallow'd up all your Mountainous *Sins* in its unfathomable *Depths!* And sav'd your *Soul* unto Joy and Bliss, in the Right and Title, First-Fruits and Earnest, of immeasurable *Heights!* Surely, my dear Brother, you may well say of your Redemption, both by Price and Power, "*I am Love's Prey.* Infinite Love hath *brought,* hath *rescu'd* me, from endless Misery and Death, unto eternal Life and Glory!"

And tho' your Redemption by *Power,* is at present but partial and initial; it shall shortly be compleat and total. Because that same infinite Love which began it, is engag'd to finish it. *Being confident* (says the Apostle) *of this very Thing, that He which hath begun a good Work in you, will perform it until the Day of Jesus Christ,* Phil. i. 2. From this Word, *perform it,* we may learn, That when Christ by his Spirit *apprehends us* in Grace, it is to *perfect us* in Glory. To make us as perfect as we shall be at the Day of Christ. When our Souls shall be perfectly conformed to his Image, to the Glories of his Soul, and our Bodies fashion'd like unto his glorious Body. *Grace,* and *Glory,* are but two different *Parts* of the same *good Work,* as comprehensively taken. Grace, is *Glory begun;* And Glory, is Grace made *perfect.* And therefore He that hath wrought the Work of Grace in us, is said to have *begun* the good Work; and in maintaining and raising it into Glory, to *perform it.* And that same Almighty HE, who began our new Life, will perform the begun Work of his Hands, and perfect the Design of his Heart concerning us; from that same Infinity of Love, Power and Faithfulness, in which it was begun. And for this we are call'd to live by *Faith.*

Hence then, my dear Brother, in the Way of your *Duty,* in all appointed Means for the Mortification of Sin, and Growth of Grace, wait you continually for *Divine Influence.* And especially live by Faith on Christ, for every *Day's Supply* of all Grace. Commit your weak Soul daily, into the hands of your Almighty SAVIOUR, to be kept from all Evil, and strengthened unto every good Work, to the Exercise of all Grace, and the Denial of all Ungodliness. And thus by Faith, lie down and *rest,* in the Bosom of infinite Love, Power and Faithfulness; and take an holy *Ease,* from all anxious Cares and perplexing Fears, about your Growth in

Sanctification. For the GOD *of Peace will sanctify you wholly, in Spirit, Soul and Body. Faithful is HE that hath called you; who also will do it.*

I should now, my dear Brother, attempt an Answer to your last kind Letter. But have left myself but little Room, and by the few last Hints above, have glanc'd at some Parts of it. I rejoice that the Manifestation of God's *free Love,* sets your Heart against *Sin,* and engageth you to *strive against it.* In which good Work, I pray you to continue unto the End. Our Lord will have us strive against Sin in a *Way of Duty:* And when we see our own *Weakness,* will therein make *his Strength perfect,* and crown our Endeavours in a *Way of Mercy.—Natural Violence,* is not *God's Way* of mortifying Sin. This is to be done, only thro' the *Spirit of Christ,* and *Faith* in the *Redeemer's Blood.* Yea, let me say, It is the Redeemer's *Arm alone,* that can and will do this Work for us *Efficiently;* tho' under his Influence, He calls us to attempt it *Instrumentally.* And, *He that believeth, shall not make haste:* To leave the Path of Duty appointed for him to walk in, nor to step out into By-paths of his own Invention; but shall quietly wait for God's Salvation. It glorifies our Lord, he accounts it a *Bowing,* a *Submiting* to Him, and *Exalting* of Him as the great SAVIOUR; to say in Faith, under the deepest Feeling of our own Weakness, unto assured Confidence and Soul-Rest, *In the LORD have I Strength:* And to *glory* in Him thereupon.—And tho' my dear Brother, you are sometimes *foiled*; Thro' Christ's Conquest for, and in you, you shall be *more than a Conqueror.* Tho' *a Troop should overcome you, you shall overcome at the last. In Patience* then *possess your Soul;* Give not out the Fight, but *endure Hardness as a good Soldier of Jesus Christ.*

And to encourage you hereto, consider, GOD, your own GOD, is always the *God of Peace,* unto you in CHRIST. He *forgives your Iniquities, and will remember your Sins no more.* His Heart is in an infinite Flame of Love towards *you,* when yours is the coldest towards *Him.* Yea, let me say, He looks upon you under all your Diseases, with an infinite *Pity;* and from his infinite Grace, will *heal all your Backslidings, and love you freely.* Wherefore return unto Him continually, confess your Iniquity, believe his Grace, and set about your Work, of *perfecting Holiness,* cheerfully. God the Father is well pleased with you *in Christ:* He views you *compleat* in his spotless *Son,* even *now,* lacking *nothing.* And with infinite Delight, *rests in his Love, rejoicing over you with Singing.* In Christ then, by *Faith,* view yourself a *spotless Beauty,* an Object of *God's Complacency.* There's no Deadness, Forgetfulness of God, or Indifferency towards Him, appears in *you,* as you stand *in Christ.* You are every Way such a One, as you stand in CHRIST, even in respect of *Sanctification,* as GOD can *delight in.* You are *dead to Sin, and alive unto GOD,* perfectly so, in CHRIST. And the more you view this by Faith, the greater Freedom of Access will you have to God, thro' his holy Son, the more Strength against Sin, and Encouragement to personal Holiness.—You ask me, my dear Brother,

"How a Soul, after sweet Manifestations of God's Love, can account for its, not only losing the *Sense* of them, but also its falling into a *light* and *forgetful Frame of Mind*, concerning God's manifesting Himself unto it?" I answer:

First. Our sweet *Sensation of divine Love,* that which is more immediate and efficacious, depends upon the immediate *Shine of it* on the Soul; and is lost by *intervening Clouds,* when glorious Love, is vailed from our Sight, and its bright, warming Beams, which had wont to be cast upon us, are *intercepted.* Just as our pleasant *Feeling* of the Heat of the *Sun,* depends upon its immediate *Shine;* and is lost when its warming Rays are *withdrawn.*

Secondly. Our falling into a light and forgetful Frame, concerning God's manifesting Himself unto us; proceeds from our Mind's being *diverted* unto other Objects, which engross our Attention, or snatch away our Thoughts from those divine Manifestations, on which they were once intensely fix'd.

Our losing our sweet Sensation of divine Love, thro' the Withdraw of its Shine; may be accounted for, either,

1. From the *sovereign Pleasure of Jehovah:* Who in infinite Wisdom, for his own Glory and our Good, oft sees it meet to hide his Face from his dearest Favourites. And, *If He hideth Himself, who can behold Him?* Or,

2. From our *provoking the Lord,* to withdraw from us: *Our Sins having hid his Face, and seperated between us and our God.* And,

Our falling into a light, and forgetful Frame, concerning the Lord's manifesting of Himself unto us, thro' our Mind's being diverted to other Objects, which engross our Attention; may be accounted for,

1. From our *exceeding Sinfulness,* our natural Bent to backslide from God, to forsake the LORD our Husband, and go after other Lovers. And,

2. From the many *Temptations and Snares* which are laid for our taking, by the Enemy of Souls, thro' the various Occurrences of this present Life: By which we, sinfully *yielding,* are drawn off from *God,* and lose the quick Remembrance of *Him,* e're we are aware; yea, are lost as in a Wood, among Creature-Vanities and Vexations.

And sad, my dear Brother, lamentable it is, when this is our Case. And yet too too often, is this the Case with God's *own People. Can a Maid forget her Ornaments,* (saith the Lord) *or a Bride her Attire? Yet my People have forgotten ME Days without Number,* Jer. Ii. 23. Oh horrid Ingratitude! What, *God's People,* whom He chose to be his peculiar Treasure, whom He redeem'd with an out-stretched Arm: *forget* HIM, their *Ornament,* their *Glory,* and his manifesting Himself to them as such in *infinite Love!* And that, *Days without Number! Oh foolish People and unwise, thus* evilly *to requite the* LORD for his great Goodness, his distinguishing, boundless Grace!—And will He *yet* say of them, They are *my People?* Oh Heart-melting, Soul-humbling, All-attracting *Love!* Oh inseperable Love! What, will not the Lord *cast off* his People, for all that they have *done?* Oh, *no,* He will not, for his *great Name's Sake:* Because it pleased the LORD to *make them his People.* And will He still *love* such an adulterous Bride? Oh, *yes,* He will: Because his Love is infinitely great, free and unchangeable! *The Love of the LORD!*—And by his All-overcoming Love, will He bring her again into conjugal Love and Duty to Himself. And tho' He should *chastise,* it shall be in *Mercy:* It shall *spring* from Love, and *end* in Love. *She went after her Lovers, and forgot ME, saith the LORD. Therefore behold I will allure her, and bring her into the Wilderness, and speak comfortably to her. And I will give her her Vineyards from thence, and the Valley of Achor for a Door of Hope, and she shall sing there, as in the Days of her Youth, and as in the Day when she came up out of the Land of Egypt. And it shall come to pass at that Day, saith the LORD, that thou shalt call me Ishi*:--(my Husband) *And I will betroth thee unto Me for ever,* Hos. ii. 13, *&c.* Oh infinite, eternal *Love!* How *mighty* is its Efficacy on the *Soul,* when shed abroad in the Heart by the *Holy Ghost!* This is *our* GOD! My Brother. This is *his Love!* Which will save *you,* will save *Me,* and all his *Chosen,* from the deepest Misery, to the highest Glory!---

In the Heart and Arms of your *own* GOD, the God of *Love,* I leave you. Wishing abundant Life and Liberty, from the Lord your Life, who was *bound,* to set you *free:* And a joyful taking up of *his sweet Cross,* who endur'd a *bitter Cross for you,* until you are *crown'd in Glory with Him:* I remain. Dear Sir, with great Affection,

Yours in CHRIST for ever,

______ _____.

LETTER XV.

To Mrs. R________r.

My dear and honour'd Sister in the Lord,

I Thank you for your Letter. I am glad you got the Victory over Self and Satan, to write to one of your Fellow-Members in the Body of Christ. Your thinking of *me* above what is meet, hindred that free Communion which ought to be between Members of the same Body. *We* are *nothing;* CHRIST is *All,* and *in* all. He is our Head, we are his Members; He is our Father, and we are his Children. Let us love, and converse familiarly with each other as such.

I rejoice in the Wonders of God's Love towards you, and praise Him on your Account. Oh my Sister, you and I, tho' far distant in Place, and born in divers Nations, are of that Number, who were gathered into *one in Christ,* by God's *electing Love.* That were chosen in Him and given to Him, as his Body, as his Bride and Spouse, before the Foundation of the World. We are of that *Church,* that Universal Church of God's Chosen, which Christ *loved,* and *gave Himself for: That He might sanctify and cleanse it, by the Washing of Water, by the Word, That He might Present it to Himself a glorious Church, not having Spot or Wrinkle, or any such Thing; but that it should be Holy, and without Blemish.*

Hence it was, my dear Sister, from our being gather'd into Christ by Election, from our being gather'd into one in Him, by Redemption; that we are gather'd into Christ by efficacious Grace, in special Vocation. That *we,* who were once *afar off,* are made *nigh by the Blood of Christ,* and are *no more Strangers and Foreigners, but Fellow-Citizens with the Saints, and of the Houshold of God.* Oh how high are our Privileges! How great were the Miseries we are saved *from!* How great are the Glories we are saved *to!* That we have at present in Grant, First-fruits and Earnest; and shall have ere-long, in full Possession! Oh the Glory of that *City,* which our God hath *prepared for us! There shall in no wise enter into it any Thing that defileth, nor that worketh Abomination.* Its Inhabitants shall be all Holy. *The City hath no need of the Sun, nor of the Moon to shine in it: for the Glory of GOD* shall *lighten it, and the LAMB* shall be *the Light thereof.* What do you think of it, my Sister? Little do you think, what great Glories, your own GOD has prepar'd for *you.* They are *so great,* that his own *Greatness,* and *Goodness* as GOD, and as *your* GOD, is for ever to shine forth therein! The Grace by which you are saved, is *great Grace.* And *great* is the *Glory,* which this Grace will bestow. *It doth not yet appear what you shall be. But when CHRIST who is your Life shall appear, you also shall appear with Him in Glory.* So great, that *Eye hath not seen, nor Ear heard, neither hath it entered into the Heart of Man* to conceive a Thousandth Part of its Brightness! GOD set his Heart upon *you* of Old, and for his *great Love* wherewith He loved you, even when *dead in Sins,* in his *rich Mercy,* forgave you all Trespasses; and *Quickened you together with CHRIST,* both mystically and influentially: *That in the Ages to come,* to the endless Ages of Eternity, *He might shew the exceeding Riches of his Grace, in Kindness towards you thro' Christ Jesus.* Think, oh you *Heir of GOD,* you *Joint-Heir with CHRIST,* of your *great,* your *glorious Inheritance!*—You rejoice in the *Earnest* of it. Well you may: It is GOD'S Earnest, a Part given you of the Whole. Remember likewise, that the whole of your Inheritance, is given you in the *Right* of it, by an absolute irreversible *Grant.* You have eternal Life in its Greatness, Fulness and Glory, in the Right of it, as a Believer in the Son of GOD. And you have the begun Possession of it, by the Holy Spirit as an Earnest. Free-Grace, has made you a *Child, an Heir of* GOD *thro'* CHRIST. You are brought into a Family, where *Grace reigns to eternal Life.* No more to *go out,* to *lose* your sonship, and become a *Servant,* a *Stranger,* a *Foreigner;* but to *abide in the House forever,* among the free Children by Grace, and Heirs of immortal Glory.

Good, my dear Sister, has it been for you, that you have been *afflicted.* Your Afflictions were to bring you to the *House of Mercy,* where *special Mercy* was to be shewn to your *precious Soul.* Oh it was free Mercy, rich, everlasting Mercy, that convinc'd you of your Misery by Sin, and Desert of eternal Vengeance. That shew'd you the Ransom of God's finding, and deliver'd your Soul from going down to the Pit. Glorious was the *Exchange* indeed, when you *lost your Husband,* a Creature, a dying Worm of the Earth; that the LORD of Hosts, your Maker, your Redeemer should *become your Husband.* That when you *lost your Son;* the Son of GOD should be *given you.* That when you *lost your earthly Inheritance;* the heavenly Inheritance should be *bestow'd.* Never, never will you be able to tell out the *Glories* of this Exchange! You must for ever delightfully enjoy, but can never fully express them. It's a Task too great for an *Angel's Tongue,* to count up those vast Treasures of Grace and Glory, which you have in GOD! His own *Immensity,* is known to none but HIMSELF. And all the immense Glories of JEHOVAH, in the Gift of himself unto you in Christ, as your GOD and Portion, are made over to *you,* for your Bliss and Enjoyment; to make you happy, to the utmost of your Creature-Capacity! Infinite Love, made *All* in GOD, *yours;* laid up all the Treasures of Grace and Glory, for you in CHRIST, according to the Infinity of JEHOVAH's Wisdom! And from thence they shall be handed down unto you continually, thro' Time, and to Eternity. Infinite Love, my dear Sister, the Streams of rich, free Grace, thro' a crucufy'd JESUS, will follow you all along thro' the Wilderness, until you reach *Canaan's Land;* when you shall be swallow'd up in Love's Ocean, and live amidst the *Pleasures,* the full Joys, which are GOD's *Right Hand for evermore.*

I rejoyce, my dear Sister, that you have had precious Experience of the streaming Love of GOD towards you; that it has follow'd you, even into those Depths of Distress, which you had brought upon yourself by Sin. That the LORD your Lover, who will *never, never leave, nor forsake you, forgave your Iniquity, heal'd your Backslidings, and lov'd you freely.* And that from hence, your Heart was directed into the *Love of* GOD, in its Sovereignty, Independency, Unchangeableness and Eternity. The *Faith hereof,* is a mighty Bulwark against *Fears,* a glorious Cordial against *Faintings* a sweet Allurement, and strengthning Encouragement to *follow the* LAMB, *even whither soever he goeth.*—And if the Lord calls you, my dear Sister, to follow hard after him in the Dark, and enables you then to *trust in him,* and to *stay yourself upon your own* GOD; much will this be for the Glory of his great Name, for your present Advantage, and for the Enhancement of your future Crown. Here we must live by *Faith:* Hereafter, we shall live by *Sight!*—I commit you as a tender Lamb of CHRIST's Fold, to the Love and Care of your great Shepherd; who loves you infinitely, and will save you fully and eternally. May *his Grace be with your Spirit!* And you *increase with all the Increases of* GOD!—So prays, my dear Sister,

Your most Affectionate Friend,
Who would gladly be your Servant,
For JESUS' Sake,

——— ———

LETTER XVI.

Feb. 28, 1743.

To the dear Family at *Bethesda;* assembled by the Father of Mercies, to be his Care, his Delight, his Habitation,

Grace and Peace be multiplied.

Honour'd Brethren,

I Thank you for your kind Acceptance of the feeble Lines I sent you, and for your kind Answer by that dear Servant of Christ, and your Minister, Mr. *B_______r.* I rejoyce and glory with you, for the great Goodness of *God,* towards *you,* the Beloved of his Soul, in the late glorious *Visitations* with which you have been favour'd.

You have seen, my dear Brethren, the Wonders of God's Love and Power, in your Deliverance from *cruel Enemies,* that sought your Lives.[1]

—Oh, why did he not give you up into the Hands of them that hated you? Who said in their Hearts as proud *Pharoah, I will pursue, I will overtake, I will divide the Spoil: My Lust shall be satisfy'd upon them, I will draw my Sword, my Hand shall destroy them.* Oh ye children of the living God, why did not your heavenly Father *give you up?* Was it because you were such *obedient Children,* that had not provok'd the Eyes of his Glory? Were there not Thousands of Provocations in the holiest of you all? I know you will say, "Not for our *Goodness,* did our GOD deliver us." No, my Brethren, he wrought for his *Name's Sake.* In the Infinity of his Love, he said concerning you, *How shall I give thee up,* Ephraim? *How shall I deliver thee,* (into the Enemy's Hands) Israel? *How shall I make thee as* Admah? *Shall I set* thee *as* Zeboim? (As the People of my Wrath) *Mine Heart is turned within me, my Repentings are kindled together. I will not execute the Fierceness of mine Anger, I will not return to destroy* Ephraim; *for I am* GOD, *and not Man, the Holy* One *in the midst of thee, and I will not enter into the City.* No, my Brethren, the LORD your own God, did not enter in amongst you, as a Destroyer, with his sore Judgments; but according to his promise, became *a Wall of Fire round about you,* to defend *you,* and destroy your Enemies: And HE has since appear'd, as *the Glory in the midst of you.* Oh my Brethren, *the Right Hand of the* LORD, *is become glorious in Power; the Right hand of the* LORD, *hath dashed in Pieces the Enemy.* And you to your *Bethesda,* the Father of Mercies brought in Safety, after your Flight for Fear of the Enemy. Where, secure and joyful, under the Shadow of his Wings, you have abode ever since.

And lo, my Brethren, not only did the Lord do you *Good,* but he *rejoyced* over you herein, with his whole Heart, and with his whole Soul.

---

[1] The *Spaniards* who invaded *Georgia,* in the Year 1742, and design'd to cut off the Family at *Bethesda,* Root and Branch. But God defeated the proud Enemy, who came in with 5000, by a *few* of the *English* Forces, who were in all, but 900. Of the *Spaniards,* there were 200 slain and taken; and but *five* of the *English.* The Particulars of the Invasion and Deliverance, were so wonderful, that it is said, "The like is hardly to be parallel'd in late History."

And as a Testimony hereof, he call'd *you* to rejoyce with *him*. The great Master of the Family, return'd *with you,* return'd *to you with Mercies.* He made a *Feast* for his dear Servants, his Children, his Bride and Spouse, that he and you might mutually *rejoyce together.*

And may I not say, That this was an *Emblem,* a faint Resemblance, of that glorious *Feast,* which the LORD of Hosts will make for his People, after all their Dangers, Difficulties, and Travels in the Wilderness are over; and he brings them home to his House, his Palace Royal in *Heaven?* Oh the ineffable Glories of *that Feast!* The Joys, the Triumphs of *that Day,* when all the *Enemies* of God's People, are wholly and for ever overcome! When the *Children* of his eternal Love, thro' a thousand Deaths and Dangers, are brought safe into their *Father's Arms!* When the *Bride, the Lamb's Wife,* the Purchase of his precious Blood, the Conquest of his Love-Power, array'd with her Bridegroom's *Glories,* and made the *Perfection of Beauty,* shall be brought by *him,* into his immediate Embraces, and presented to *himself,* and before the Presence of his *Father's Glory!* Oh, it will be with *exceeding Joy!* Exceeding far, all our present Conception, or Expression. The whole Court will ring for Joy. GOD, the Father, Son and Spirit, will rejoyce over *us,* and in our Salvation, with *singing.* And *we* the saved Ones, shall rejoyce in saving Love, and in the GOD of our Salvation, each one for ourselves distinctly, and jointly with, and for each other, shout forth *Hallelujahs.* While Myriads of wondring *Angels* on every Side, assist the Joy, and join the Praise with their loud *Amens.* Oh my Brethren, what a joyful, what a glorious Feast will the *Marriage-supper* of the LAMB be! How will the bright Sun of *eternal Love,* cast upon us its direct and immediate Rays! How will the *Glory of* GOD *and of the* LAMB, shine round about us, into us, and thro' us on every Side! What rich Dainties, what Delicates of Love's preparing, what mingled Wine, what Royal Wine in Abundance, reserv'd for *that Day,* shall then be brought out, and set before us: When our Lord makes us *sit down to Meat, to eat and drink with him at his Table in his Kingdom!* And, oh, astonishing *Love!* HIMSELF the King of Glory, will *serve us!* Will carve all our Portions with his *own Hand,* and put the Cup of Consolation into *ours;* that sweet, that exhilarating Cup of Joy and Life, procur'd and prepar'd for *us,* by *his* once drinking the bitter Cup in our Stead, the Cup of Sorrow and Death! Then we shall sit down to Meat, never to rise up from Table more! Oh my Friends, little do you think, how *welcome* the King of Glory will make you, when he sets you as so many Princes around his Royal Board! Oh then, he will open all his *Heart* to you, and tell such Stories of *Love,*as you never before heard! Then, he'll shew you all the *Way he led you thro' the Wilderness,* in all it's various Windings and Turnings, that it was all *right.* Then, in infinite Grace, he will recount all your *Services,* and say so *much* of all that you have thought, said or done for HIM, that you cannot *Think.* The Greatness of his Love herein, was much of it to be let out upon your Spirits here, is *such*, that it would dissolve your earthly Tabernacles, and make the Frame of Nature fly in Pieces. But when the King of Glory, sets you at his *Love-Board,* you shall be *strong* to bear *Love's Weight,* its fresh and constant *Flows,* without staggering, or reeling at its *infinite Greatness!* Never was such *Table-Conference,* as shall be between CHRIST and *you, then.* Oh my Brethren, you shall *all lean on* JESUS' *Breast at Supper-Time,* at this his *Love Feast,* of endless Duration! You shall see your Lord as HE *is,* without a Vail upon his Face, be made perfectly like him, and folded up in his sweet Embraces, to the *Days of Eternity!* GOD *shall wipe all Tears from your Eyes: And there shall be no more Death,* (in Soul, nor Body; no more Distance from GOD, no more Inactivity, or Dulness in his Service) *neither Sorrow, nor Crying, neither shall there be any more Pain: For* these, as *former Things, shall be wholly pass'd away.*

What then shall I say to you, oh you *Children,* you *Heirs of* GOD, that will shortly be the *Peers of Heaven?* Will you not *love the* LORD *the* LAMB; who *hath loved you, and washed you from your Sins in his own Blood, and made you Kings and Priests unto GOD and his Father?* Will you not *all,* jointly, and particularly, in the Service he calls you to, pour out your Souls in *Love,* into the Bosom of *your Beloved?* For the Honour of HIM, who endur'd the *Cross,* to *crown you?* Come my Brethren and Sisters, the LORD the LAMB, forgives all the Imperfection of your *Obedience,* buries your *Sins* in the Depths of the Sea, records all your *Services,* and will bring them forth before Men and Angels, *unto Praise, Honour, and Glory at his appearing. Wherefore gird up the Loyns of your*

Mind, be sober and hope to the End, for the Grace that is to be brought unto you at the Revelation of Jesus Christ. In every Thing give Thanks; Rejoyce evermore; Pray without ceasing. Be strong, and work; for the LORD is, and will be *with you.*—Excuse this long Digression. May the Lord make it of some Use!

Again, my dear Brethren, being return'd to *Bethesda, your* GOD, not only rejoyc'd *your Hearts* with his Love, who before were gather'd unto *Christ;* but also gather'd *other Souls* unto HIM, the Sent SAVIOUR; to your, and their Glory and Joy.—May the Lord still bless, and increase you, even into a *Multitude;* like as He did his People in *Egypt!*

And now my honour'd Brethren, since the LORD has appear'd so signally for and amongst you; I beseech you to *walk worthy of HIM,* as your *own GOD.* To trust in Him, if He should seem to slay you. To submit to his holy Will, if he should cover you with Clouds and Darkness, as a Family, or as particular Persons. To adore and bless Him, in and for all his Dealings with you. And to wait and pray for his promis'd Grace, when He will *again bring you forth to the Light, and you shall behold his Righteousness.* His Faithfulness to his Covenant-Engagements, to be, to appear to be, *your* GOD; and in owning you for *his People,* and dwelling with you as such, by the visible Tokens of his Presence.—You remember, my dear Friends, that before your late *bright Days,* it was a Time of *Darkness* with you. That then you waited for your GOD; and He did not disappoint your Expectations, but appeared among you in his Glory, to your great Joy, and sweet Surprize. And now He has given you such a Lump of *Sense,* to help your *Faith;* will you not believe in the *Dark,* if the Lord should *call you to it?* Let me say, The LORD *expects* you should trust Him *now.* Oh my Brethren, your GOD is not *gone,* when you lose the *Sight* and *Feeling* of his Presence. He dwells in the midst of you, as the LORD *your God,* as *mighty to save,* resting in his unchangeable Love towards you, and waiting for the fit Season to deliver you; even when He clothes Himself with such *thick Darkness,* that you cannot *see Him,* nor your Prayers pass *thro' it,* to your Perception. And if you *love the Lord,* if you would *honour Him* at such Seasons; Oh, *believe.* Believe Him to be your *own GOD,* that will work all Things together for his Glory, and your Good. Lie at *Anchor* in the Bosom of infinite Love and Faithfulness, when *roughest Tempests* beat upon you. *Cry unto the LORD in your Trouble, and He will bring you out of your Distresses. He will make the Storm a Calm; and bring you to your desired Haven.* And then you shall praise Him for *his great Goodness, and for his wonderful Works* towards you.

And are there any of you that *groan* under your Unbelief, Impatience, Unthankfulness, and unsuitable Returns to the Lord, for his great Goodness? Oh my Brethren, your Heavenly Father forgives you, is the GOD of Peace towards you, and from an Infinity of Love and Bowels, pities you under all your Weaknesses, Temptations and Distresses. *He will turn again, He will have Compassion upon you: He will subdue your Iniquities:* And HE *will cast all your Sins into the Depths of the Sea.*—And be not discourag'd my dear dear Brethren, at any of your *Trials:* All shall be *well.* All shall end in GOD'S Glory, and turn to your Salvation. And fear not, if the Lord should lead you, even you that have believ'd thro' Grace, *in Paths that you have not known.* For lo, HE is with you, and *will make Darkness Light before you, and crooked Things straight. These Things will He do unto you, and not forsake you.*

And now my *dear little Children,* you *tender Lambs* of Christ's Fold, that have lately been gather'd by your *great Shepherd's Arm;* what shall I say to *you?* I'll tell you of your *Father's Love. Little Children, your Sins are forgiven you for* Christ's *Name's Sake.* You are *passed from Death to Life, and shall not come into Condemnation.* God has made an everlasting Covenant with you in Christ, *That He will not turn away from doing you good.* He hath promised to be *unto you a Father, and that you shall be his Sons and Daughters.* Oh my little Children, you are *born,* new born, *To an Inheritance incorruptible, and undefiled, and that fadeth not away, reserved in Heaven for you.* And lo, *you are kept,* and shall be, *by the Power of God thro' Faith unto Salvation.* The Lord that hath call'd you by Grace, will bring you into Glory. None of your Soul-Enemies shall destroy you, shall ever pluck you out of JESUS' Hands. You are not, shall not be left alone, in your own Strength, which is but Weakness, to grapple with Corruption and Temptation, and to get to Heaven as you can. No, you *tender Lambs,* JESUS your *Shepherd* hath an *Arm* to gather you from all your Wanderings, to support and comfort you under all your Faintings, and to defend you from all your Enemies. *He will gather* you *with his Arm, and carry* you *in his Bosom;* will feed, guide and keep you all along thro' this Wilderness, until he has brought you to the Heavenly *Canaan,* that Land of Rest which your Souls desire.—And tho' you shou'd lose your *Comforts,* my dear Children, those Joys of God's Favour, which at first fill'd your Hearts; don't think you have, or shall lose your *God;* or your Interest in your Dear *Lord Jesus.* No, my little Children, Whom the *Lord loveth,* He loveth unto the *End,* for ever. He that at first manifested his Love to you, will always abide the *Same,* the very Same in his infinite Grace to you, as He *said unto you at the Beginning.* The LORD loves you *freely;* not for your Goodness, but because He *will* love you. He foresaw all your Sins, and Unkindnesses to Him; and if He had not had Love enough in his Heart, to pardon and pass by *all;* He would never have *told you of his Love:* He would not have begun to love you, if He had not design'd to love you unto the End. And God's Love will not only pardon all your Sins, but also subdue, and destroy them for you. *By little and little,* He will drive out all your spiritual Enemies from before you, until *you* be increased in Grace, and made perfect in Holiness. For which End the Holy Spirit of God, is given to *dwell in you, and abide with you for ever.* And remember, CHRIST is your *Righteousness* before GOD. He washes away all your Sins in his own Blood, and clothes your naked Souls with his Obedience. Which is a glorious Robe, without a Spot; and it covers you all over, from Head to Foot, and makes you appear exceeding beautiful in the Sight of God. God loves you *in Christ;* and delights to see you draw nigh to Him as a *Father,* thro' his *Dear Son.* You are *imperfect* in yourselves; but *complete* in Christ. You have a Thousand *Wants;* but Christ has *all Fulness,* treasur'd up in Him for you, to be given you in every Time of Need.—Wherefore, Oh you *new-born Babes,* who *have tasted that the Lord is gracious, desire the sincere Milk of the Work, that you may grow thereby.* Pray, read, hear, and meditate on the Word of God. Lay the Mouth of your Faith to the Free Promises, those Breasts of Consolation. For God has declar'd, You *shall milk out, and be delighted with the Abundance of* that *Glory,* which He has prepared for you. And so shall you, *little Children,* increase in Grace, until Grace is made perfect in

Glory. *Commit the Keeping of your Souls to* JESUS. And HE'll *preserve you safe unto his Heavenly Kingdom. His Grace be with your Spirits!* Amen.

And shall I not say a Word to *you* of the dear Family; who are yet *unconverted?* My Bowels yern towards *you.* Oh poor Souls! You must *perish,* if you are not *born again.* If you flee not by Faith to Christ; to Deluge of God's Wrath, will certainly destroy you. Oh you perishing Sinners, What think you of our JESUS? *He is able to save* you *to the uttermost.* Will you not *seek Him while He may be found?* Are you willing to *perish* out of *Bethesda,* where so many Souls find *Mercy?* Oh cry unto the Lord Day and Night, and give Him no Rest until *you* are among that happy Number. Our GOD, *keepeth Mercy for Thousands!* And who knows but it may be for *you?* God has call'd many of late among you, out of Darkness into his marvellous Light; has Ark'd them in CHRIST, before the Waters of his Indignation come down upon the ungodly World. And lo, in our JESUS, there is *yet Room* for Thousands! And *you* are call'd to *come in.* Oh may God's compelling Power reach your *Hearts!* And then you'll come *freely.* Who knows, perhaps some, or all of *you,* may be the *next* that Jesus Christ may save at *Bethesda.* Therefore pray, and wait for his Salvation. And the Lord *prevent* secure Souls, and *satisfy* longing Souls, *early with his Mercy!* That for *your Conversion, Bethesda* may be again a House of *Joy,* a House of *Glory.*

I return now, to take Leave of *you,* my dear Brethren and Sisters, who already *believe in* JESUS, and have *Life thro' his Name.* And unto *you* let me say, *Be perfect,* (Labour after a growing Conformity to Christ, in Heart, Lip and Life) *be of good Comfort, be of one Mind, live in Peace; and the* GOD *of Love and Peace shall be with you.*—The Lord hath done great Things in *England* and *Scotland* by your dear Mr. *W__________d.* And still he has much Work to do *here.* All Grace abounds towards him. "Tho' set in the Front of the Battle, he tells me. He is still more than a Conqueror thro' *Emanuel's* Love." When his Master gives him Leave, he'll come to you again. In Patience possess your Souls, and believe it will be in the best Time.—*Great Grace be with, and upon you all!*—Pray, and give Thanks for me, who am,

Yours most Affectionately

In our dear LORD the LAMB,

LETTER XVII.

To Mr. W_______d.

Reverend and very dear Sir,

MOST humbly I thank you for your kind Letter from *Biddiford.* It refresh'd my Spirit. The Lord reward all your great Kindness to little *me,* every Way like his Great SELF!—I rejoyce to hear, that the *Lord's Hand* was with you in your *Work,* even to the last of your Stay in *England.* From the Beginninng of your last Visit to these Lands, even to the End of your Stay with us, hath the Lord in a singular Manner own'd and blest you.—I rejoice and give Thanks, for that marvellous Deliverance which God wrought for you, when your Life was in such imminent Danger; and that the cruel Assault was over-rul'd for the Furtherance of the Gospel. Your *Life,* my dear Brother, is in the *Lord's Hand;* and none of your Enemies shall take it from you, before the *Lord's Time,* to love your Spirit Home into his own Bosom. You count not your *Life* dear unto *yourself,* that you may finish your Course with Joy, to testify to all, the Gospel of the Grace of God. But precious is your Life in the Sight of the LORD. And so will your *Death* be, if JESUS should call you to die a *Martyr,* and be sacrificed for his Truth and Cause; to serve the Faith of Saints, and in Love to poor Sinners.—Oh my honour'd Brother, faint not at your *Tribulations for us,* they are *your,* they are *our* Glory. But rejoyce to *be a Partaker of the Afflictions of the Gospel, according to the Power of God.* Of which you have had such abundant Experience, in seasonable Succours, Supports, and Assistances, in all your Times of Need hitherto. And still, oh still, *the Grace of* CHRIST *is sufficient for you, and his Power shall rest upon you. Afflictions,* and the *Gospel,* are *inseparable.* Not a Soul that knows, and bears Witness to the Gospel, in the Life and Spirit of it, but must endure Afflictions, in a Degree proportionable to his Appearance for Christ, and Labours in his Gospel. Opposition from the prophane World, from carnal Professors, aye, and from Believers themselves, under one Prejudice or other, cast into their Minds by the Prince of Darkness, must the Witnesses of CHRIST, his Gospel-

Labourers meet with.—But so great is the *Grace* of the Gospel, to support us, that the *Afflictions* of the Gospel will not sink us. So great is our *Reward* in the *Work* of the Gospel, in the happy *Fruit* thereof, to our Lord's Honour in the Salvation of precious Souls, and in that *Crown of Righteousness* which awaits the Labourers in Christ's Gospel, at his appearing; that we may well *reckon* with the Apostle, *that the Sufferings of this present Time, are not worthy to be compared with the Glory which shall be reveal'd in us.* Sweet was this Word to *me,* with respect to *you,* "With Persecutions." Your *Persecutions,* my Brother, are Part of your *Reward,* of that Reward which our Lord gives you, in forsaking *all,* to serve *him* and *his.* They are your Glory *now,* and resplendently will appear to be so, in the *Days of* CHRIST.—Labour, and suffer then, O dear man of GOD, for the dear LAMB, who has lov'd, and bought you with his Blood; and like him, your great Pattern, *for the Joy that is set before you, endure the Cross,* until you are *crown'd in Glory with him.*—That *all Grace* may abound *towards you,* and *by you* to Thousands of Souls in *America;* that you may ride in *Triumph* as it were, to your *dear Family,* and see their *Faces* as the Face of GOD, and mutually tell of the *Wonders* his Love hath wrought for you, to the *Glory of God by Christ,* and to your *exceeding Joy thro' him;* is the earnest Desire of the *least of Christ's,* who with a Heart brimful of Love to you for JESUS' Sake, subscribes,

Reverend Sir,

Your most Affectionate

Humble Servant,

______ _____.

A LETTER
ON THE
BEING and WORKING
OF
SIN,

In the Soul of a *justified Man,* as consistent with his *State* of Justification in CHRIST, and Sanctification through HIM:

WITH THE

NATURE of his OBEDIENCE, and of his COMFORT, consider'd: As the one is *from* GOD, and the other *to* HIM; notwithstanding his Corruptions may be *great,* and his Grace *small* in his own Sight.

EPISTLE to the READER.

Christian READER,

As our dear SAVIOUR has blessed the following LETTER to my Soul, *to whom it was first sent; and as the pious and useful Author (not doubting but it well be bless'd to others also) has been directed to publish it: I humbly beg Leave to recommend it: As it may be a Means of establishing them in our SAVIOUR's free, and unchangeable Love to Sinners.—And that it may be render'd* profitable, *may the* Lord Jesus *sprinkle it with his* own Blood, *and say to it,* Go and prosper exceedingly.

I also take Liberty to acquaint you, my Christian Friend, and Fellow-Sinner, (to the Glory of God our Saviour) that the Lord was pleas'd at first to open my Eyes, in reading the Writing of the Author. The only Thing that seem'd *to induce me to read them, was, their being wrote by a* Woman: *Which made me have them in some Esteem, tho' ignorant of what they contain'd. But at length, the LORD made them a great* Blessing *to me, and I gladly embrac'd every Opportunity of pursuing the same. And thro' them was convinc'd of these great Truths: "That I was saved freely by Grace, thro' Faith." And, "That the Righteousness of Christ, was imputed to all that believe in his Name: &c."—That they may have (through the eternal Spirit) a still* greater Blessing *attending them; and if they contain any Thing contrary to his Mind and Will, may he blot it out; and whatever is agreeable, may he* seal it *with his Blood upon the Reader's Heart!*

So pray the Vilest, but one of the LORD's Redeem'd, and your very happy Brother in the Knowledge of the LAMB's Death and Smart,

WILLIAM COLLINS.

THE
BEING and WORKING
OF
SIN,

In the Soul of a *justify'd Man,* consistent with his *State* of Justification in CHRIST, and Sanctification thro' HIM, *&c.*

Dear Sir,

THROUGH the Goodness of GOD, I had the Privilege and Pleasure of receiving from my dear Friend, Mr. *H__________t,* a Letter of yours wrote to him; wherein you gave some Account of your Experience, and desir'd his Thoughts about the *State of your Soul:* Which he desired me to *answer.* And gladly, dear Sir, I embrace the first Moment's Leisure for this Service. May our dear Lord, by me, the Chief of Sinners, send you an Answer of Peace!

Glad am I, dear Sir, that you have a painful "*Sense,* of your miserable Condition by Nature, and that you are fully *sensible,* that none but CHRIST, the great Physician of Souls, can bring you Health and Cure." A Sense of *these Things*, Sir, are peculiar to those that are *New-born.* It is the New Creature's *Sensation* of what is contrary to it, under which it groans, and of what is agreeable, for which it longs. You may read your own Experience in that of the Apostle *Paul's,* Rom. vii. From ver. 15. to the End; and take the Lord's own Word for it, as to your *State,* that you are a Man *in Christ,* and that there is *no Condemnation* to you, tho' there is so much *Sin* in you, seen, felt, and groan'd under by you. c*hap.* iii. 1.

In answering your Letter, Sir, I shall consider, 1. Your Complaints of the Being and Working of Sin. 2. Your Desire after filial Obedience. 3. Your Comfort in CHRIST. 4. Your Fear that it is not right. And 5. Conclude with a Word of Advice. I begin with,

I. Your *Complaints* of the Being and Working of *Sin.* And as to your being "Vile, Sir, full of Evil, dead to every good Word and Work, serving God with your Mouth, while your Heart is far from him, and in a Word, vile as the Devil himself:" All this is very consistent with the *Justification* of your Person, thro' the Blood and Righteousness of Christ, and with the *Sanctification* of your Nature, by his Holy Spirit, or your being a renew'd Man, in all the Powers and Faculties of your Soul, unto Influence extending to all the Members of your Body, and to the Whole of your Conversation.—If you ask, *how? I answer:*

The opening to you the Plague of your own Heart, is from a special Work of the Holy Spirit of God upon your Soul, in quickning you influentially through Christ, upon the Bottom of your being quickned in and with him mystically. It is from your being cut off from your old Stock, the first *Adam*, and graffed into *Christ*, the second *Adam*, that this Life, of Sensation of your own Death, springs into your Soul. It is from the New-Creation Work of God upon your Soul, from his *commanding the Light to shine into your Heart*, from his making you a new Creature in *Christ*, that you discover your own Darkness, as an old Creature in and from *Adam*.—And the Discovery of your own Misery and Wretchedness, from the overspreading of that unfathomable Depth of Sin, that Hell of Iniquity, which is in your vile Heart, is the LORD's killing you *sensibly*, in order to make you *sensibly* alive. It is God's bringing the *Commandment* home to your Soul, in its Spirituality, that you *thro' the Law, might die to the Law*, or die to all Hopes of Life by your own Obedience. In a Word, it is God's making you *sick, Heart-sick*, his giving you a deep, felt *Sense* of your Sickness, of your deadly Disease, that you might see your *Need* of the great *Physician*, and look to HIM for healing.—And by the same Grace that shews you your Misery, you have a Discovery of the Remedy. Such a Discovery of the Excellency and Suitableness of CHRIST, as an All-sufficient SAVIOUR, that strongly attracts your Heart after him, and sweetly allures you to put your Trust in a crucify'd JESUS, to look to, and depend upon his Obedience alone, for all your Righteousness before, and Acceptance with God.—And as a guilty Sinner's trusting in the crucify'd SAVIOUR, looking to, and depending upon the *Obedience* of that ONE, by whom all the *many* that shall be saved, are and shall be made *righteous*, for his own Justification and Life in particular; is *believing:* So God *imputes* the Righteousness of his Son, unto all the Ends of Grace, unto *that Soul*. For, *by him all that believe are justified from all Things, from which they could not be justified by the Law of Moses*, Acts xiii. 39.—And this Justification, is *Justification of*

Life. The justify'd Soul, is not only deliver'd from all the *Curses* of God's Law, from all Wrath and Death in the Law's Sentence; but hath also a Right given him to all the *Blessings,* both of the Law and Gospel; to all Blessings, of Nature, Grace and Glory. And *receiving Abundance of Grace,* thro' *the Gift of Righteousness, shall reign in Life by Christ Jesus:* notwithstanding all that Sin and Death which works in him, and is painfully felt by him.—And as God in justifying a Sinner thro' his dear Son, doth not consider him in himself as *righteous,* but as *ungodly;* and as the Soul that believes on Christ for Justification, in that Act of Faith, doth not look on his own *Righteousness,* but upon his *Ungodliness,* to be justify'd and sav'd from it; and as the whole of God's Salvation, in the *Right* of it by his free Promise, belongs to that Soul, notwithstanding its Ungodliness: So, dear Sir, the *Justification* of your Person, thro' the Blood and Righteousness of CHRIST, is and may be very consistent with that Abundance of *Sin,* with those Aboundings of *Iniquity,* which you see and feel in your corrupt Heart.

Again, dear Sir, the *sanctification* of your Nature, by the Holy Spirit, or your being a renewed Man, in all Powers and Faculties of your Soul, unto Influence extending to all the Members of your Body, and to the whole of your Conversation; is and may be very consistent with your most grievous *Complaints* of the Being and Working of *Sin,* in Heart, Lip and Life. Because, the sanctifying Work of the Spirit, tho' it is *perfect* with respect to *Parts,* as every Part and Power of the Soul is *sanctify'd;* is yet *imperfect* with respect to Degrees, there being no Part of Power of the Soul, that is sanctify'd *throughout.* And so, tho' all the Members of the Body of a sanctified Man, are yielded *as Instruments of Righteousness unto Holiness,* just so far, and so long as they are under the sanctifying *Influences* of the Holy Ghost; yet as the Being of *Sin,* remains in the Soul that acts those Members, so when *that* prevails, the Members of a holy Man's Body, may be sadly abus'd to be *Servants unto Iniquity.* And thus, tho' a sanctify'd Man, is *holy in all Manner of Conversation,* as Holiness is the general Scope of his Actions; yet thro' the Prevalency of indwelling *Sin,* he may at Times be hurried away, and carry'd Captive as it were, into some particular Actions that are *sinful.* And most certain it is, the best Actions of the holiest of Men, are woefully *mix'd* with Sin; so that all the Saints while in this mortal State, are very far from Perfection in Holiness. And yet, as all the Powers of their Souls are in Part *sanctify'd;* as all the Members of their Bodies, so far as under the Influence of Grace, are yielded unto *God;* and as the whole of their Conversation, in their general Course, is *Holiness to the* LORD: So they are, and may be properly said to be *Holy Men,* and so the Lord Himself styles them in his Word, notwithstanding all that Unholiness which remains in them, in Heart, Lip and Life.—Hence the Saints, who are said to be *the Temples of the living God,* in whom God *dwells* and *walks,* and to whom he is and will be a *Father* in Christ, are exhorted to *cleanse themselves from all Filthiness of the Flesh and Spirit,* and thus to go on, *perfecting Holiness in the Fear of God,* 2 Cor. vi. 16,--18. and vii. 1.—See then, dear Sir, how consistent all your grievous Complaints of *Sin* are, with the Safety and blessedness of your *State,* as justify'd, and sanctify'd in and thro' CHRIST.—Again, The Happiness of your *State,* Sir, doth further appear, from,

II. Your *Desire after filial Obedience:* "To serve the Lord, not out of *Fear*, thro' a Dread of Punishment; but out of *Love*, from his infinite Love and Grace to Hell-deserving Sinners." This, dear Sir, is an Evidence, that the Love of Christ strikes your Heart, and forms its own Image there. *The Desire of a Man is his Kindness,* Prov. xix. 22. And that same *Grace,* which has wrought this Desire in your Heart, and maintains it in all your Services, will call your Obedience, the Obedience of *Love:* However weak it be. The *Spirit of Adoption,* is at the Bottom of this *Desire;* and the Disposition of a *Child,* is manifested thereby. Which is proper to a Man that is *in Christ, a New Creature.* See how the Apostle describes such, by giving an Account of his own Experience, and that of all the Saints in this Regard, 2 Cor. v. 14, 15. *For the Love of Christ constraineth us, because we thus judge, that if one died for all, then were all dead: And that He died for all, that they which live,* (that are made spiritually alive, justify'd and sanctify'd thro' the Death and Resurrection of Christ) *should not henceforth live unto themselves, but unto Him which died for them, and rose again.* There is not a Person in the World, that is constrain'd by the Love of Christ, to serve him; but hath had the Love of God shed Abroad in his Heart by the Holy Ghost; but hath had a

Principle of Love to Christ, wrought in his Soul, by the transforming Influence of his first Love; but hath the Spirit of Sanctification dwelling in him, to prepare him as a Vessel of Mercy for future Glory. This is the grand Difference, between a *justify'd* and an *unjustify'd Man,* between a *regenerate,* and an *unregenerate Soul:* the *one*, doth all he doth in Religion, from a predominant Principle of *Self-Love,* under the Influence of *slavish Fear;* the *other,* doth all, from a predominant Principle of *Love to Christ,* under the Influence of *Child-like Freedom.*—Hence those that are spiritually alive, are said to be *dead to the Law,* (to their own Obedience for Life) *by the Body of Christ;* (who fulfill'd the Law's Precept, endur'd its Penalty, took up their full discharge, and was publickly justify'd in their Name and Room) *that they should be married unto Him, as raised from the Dead,* that they might *bring forth Fruit unto God,* Rom. vii. 4. And thus also, they are said to be, *no more Servants, but sons, and Heirs of God through Christ,* Gal. iv. 7. And to be *Free-Children,* not of the Covenant of Works, but of the Covenant of Grace, *Ver. 31.*

And tho' dear Sir, you complain of base *Selfishness* in your Observance of religious Duties; as "a Desire after the Praise of Men, and a Fondness to be thought religious by others:" Yet is not *Self,* the sole Motive, whence your religious Performances spring. This is inconsistent with your *Desire after Child-like Obedience,* of serving God out of *Love* to Him. And therefore you *err,* in saying, *Self,* is the sole Motive of your Obedience, and in calling contrary Thoughts, *Self-Flattery.* For, blessed be God, there is good Ground for that great *Unwillingness,* which you find in your Heart at Times, to think that *Self,* is the sole Motive of you acting according to your Duty.—For tho' there is much of the Pharisee in the *Christian,* yet is not the Christian a *Pharisee* in Religion; tho' there is much Hypocrisy in the truly *gracious Soul,* yet is not the gracious Soul a *Hypocrite;* tho' there is much of Selfishness, in a Man that *loves God above all,* yet is not *Self,* the predominant Principle of such a Man's Actions in Religion.—You say, Sir, "The Glory of God, hath the *least Room* in your Heart." And what if I should say, it hath the *greatest Room* there? And what if both should be *true,* at different Times, and in different Senses? The Glory of God, hath the least Room in your Heart, consider'd as *corrupt,* and when *Corruption* prevails. And yet, the Glory of God, hath the greatest Room in your Heart, consider'd as *sanctify'd*, and when the *New-Creature Life* in your Soul, hath Liberty to act according to its own Nature.

Be intreated then, to view yourself in a *complex* Consideration; as having *two Natures* in your Soul, *Sin* and *Grace;* which are directly contrary to, and alternately prevail against each other.—Consider likewise, that the Life of Grace in your Soul, hath Liberty to act *singly* and *purely;* by reason of that Body of Death, which you always bear about with you, by reason of indwelling Sin, which cleaves to, and blends itself with your most religious Actions: So that your best *Righteousnesses are as filthy Rags.*—And again, consider, That as a New Creature in Christ, the *New-Life* in your Soul, is the *reigning Principle,* from whence all your religious Performances *spring:* And that according to this *holy Principle,* your religious Actions are denominated *Holy;* notwithstanding all that Uncleanness, which continually adheres to them, from that Sea of Sin, that overflowing Fountain of Corruption, which still abides and works in your Soul.—So that, tho' base *Selfishness* cleaves to your holy Actions, in a greater or lesser Degree, more discernibly, or indiscernibly; yet are you not a *self-seeking Hypocrite,* nor is *Self,* but the *Glory of God,* the Principle of your religious Performances.

For I humbly think, that those selfish Thoughts, which croud in upon the Minds of God's Children, when they are about to do any Thing for God, do rather follow *after,* than go *before* a religious Person, in his religious Performances. According to *Rom.* vii. 21. *I find then a Law, that when I would do Good, Evil is present with me. When I would do Good:* There's *Grace* in the Soul, aiming at the Glory of God. *Evil is present with me:* There's *Sin,* aiming at Self-Gratifications; that follows hard upon the Heels of Grace, and as it were comes up with it, either to hinder a religious Action, or to spoil it, by endeavouring to direct it to a wrong End. *For I delight in the Law of God,* says the Apostle, *after the inward Man,* Ver. 22. There's the *New Nature* in the Soul, the *main Spring* of a New Creature's Actions. *But I see another Law in my Members, warring against the Law of my Mind, and bringing me into Captivity to the Law of Sin, which is in my Members,* Ver. 23. There's the old, *corrupt Nature,* that dwells in the same Soul; the Power of Sin, that working in the several Members of that Body of Death, makes *War* against the Power of Grace in the Heart: and too often prevails, to bring the Man, as a New Creature, into *Captivity to the Law of Sin,* which is in his old, corrupt Nature. And when this is the Case, either more inwardly or outwardly, if it is but for a Moment, the renewed Soul groans, and bewails its Misery, with an *O wretched Man that I am, who shall deliver me from the Body of this Death!* Ver. 24. Until, turning its Eye unto *God its Saviour,* it spies sufficient Help, and full Redemption prepar'd for it; and again proceeds in its Course of Obedience to God, from a native Love to, and Delight in his Law. And happy is that Man, who blest with spiritual Wisdom, can form a right Judgment of his own Experience in these Regards: And distinguishing *himself,* from *himself,* himself as *corrupt,* from himself as *sanctify'd,* draws up that just Conclusion concerning himself in both Respects, as the Apostle doth: *So then with the Mind* (the new Nature) *I myself serve the Law of God; but with the Flesh* (the old Nature) *the Law of Sin,* Ver. 25.

But whether vile, selfish Thoughts, press in upon the Mind of one that loves God supremely, *before* he engageth in any religious Duty, or *after* he is engag'd therein; they are equally *hateful* to a godly Man, to the new Nature in his Soul, which denies, and opposeth them as Parts of Ungodliness, and presseth forward in holy Obedience, with a Desire after the Glory of God in all. Whence it is evident, that the Principle of Grace in a regenerate Man, is the *leading Principle* of his religious Actions.

Now then, dear Sir, let me ask you, whenever base, selfish Thoughts present themselves to your Mind, tho' at first they may have some pleasing Influence upon the *corrupt Part* of the Will; yet as soon as you have the Liberty of Reflection, and the Will as an *entire Faculty,* hath Freedom to act: Do you *like,* or *dislike* them? Do you *allow,* or *disallow* them? Are they your *Desire,* or your *Grief?*—If the *Latter;* be assur'd, that there is a true Principle of *Love to God,* wrought in your Soul, that supremely aims at *his Glory* in your religious Performances. And that these vile Thoughts, are the *War* that Sin makes against Grace, which hath the *Throne* in your Heart, the *Opposition* that you meet with from your Lord's Enemies, while your labouring Spirit, with its Weights upon its Back, strives to get forward in the Service of HIM *whom your Soul loveth.*

And lo, as selfish Thoughts are you Weaknesses, your Diseases, your Heart-griefs; your heavenly Father will not look upon you under *These,* with a wrathful Eye. He will not lay these your Iniquities unto your Charge, but in infinite Love to your Soul, He will *cast all your Sins behind his Back.* And in boundless Compassion, will He pity your diseased Soul, *as a Father pitieth his Children,* and *spare you, as a Man spareth his Son that serveth him.* For, *Who is a God like unto him that pardoneth Iniquity, and passeth by the Transgression of the Remnant of his Heritage?* Wherefore go on to serve Him with Chearfulness; for *He will subdue your Iniquities, and cast all your Sins into the Depths of the Sea.* And such is the infinite Grace of our glorious Master, CHRIST, that He will call *that, Service,* which by Reason of its *Imperfection,* deserves not the *Name.* And our Love therein, *Fair,* notwithstanding all the Spots and Blemishes with which it is attended. Our Dear Lord, from the Infinity of his Love, well knows how to *cleanse* both our Persons and Services in his own Blood, to *array us* with his own Beauties, and then to call us *All-fair.* Yea, *Hephzi-bah,* the LORD's *Delight!*—I come now, Sir, to consider,

III. Your *"Comfort in* CHRIST: Which you have at Times, and want to know from what *Spirit* it proceeds." And I am bold to say, That your glorious Comfort, proceeds from the *Holy Ghost,* the glorious Comforter, who dwells in your Heaven-born Soul. It is HE, who undertook the Whole of your Salvation, in the Application-part of it, that has shewn you your own Misery by Sin, that shews you the Glory of CHRIST, the great SAVIOUR, and gives you gracious Hints, "That HE will have Compassion on you, and lead you out of the Vale of Sin, into the Light of glorious Grace." From whence the Language of your Soul is, *I know that my Redeemer liveth,* &c. No *Spirit,* dear Sir, but the Spirit of CHRIST, gives such Comfort to any *one Soul.* And you may know that this your Comfort is from the Divine Spirit, both from the Matter and Effect of it.

1. From the *Matter* of it, which is CHRIST, reveal'd in your Soul, as an All-sufficient SAVIOUR. This is the Work, the peculiar Work of the Holy Ghost the Comforter, as sent from the ascended SAVIOUR,

into the Hearts of the saved ones. For which see *Joh.* xvi. 14. HE shall *shall glorify* ME: (saith our Lord) *for He shall receive of mine, and shall shew it unto you.* That Spirit that *glorifies* CHRIST, that shews the SAVIOUR's Glories to a Sin-benighted Soul; is no other than the *Spirit of* CHRIST, the Holy Ghost, the promised Comforter. The Person of the *Comforter* is known, by the promis'd *Comfort* which He affords.—Again, dear Sir, this may be known,

2. From the *Effect* of it: Which is *Faith,* produc'd in your Heart: Whence you are enabled to say, *I know that my Redeemer liveth, &c.* Which includes in it, 1. A *Knowledge* of you own Captivity to Sin. 2. A *Conviction* of your own Inability to deliver yourself from your sore Bondage. 3. A *Discovery* of an All-sufficient Help, a Redeemer of God's providing, for lost Sinners. 4. A *Looking* unto Him alone, for your full Redemption, And 5. Some Degree of *Persuasion* of Interest in Him: That He is your *Goel,* your *near Kinsman,* who assuredly will perform the Kinsman's *Part,* in redeeming you from all Misery, unto all Glory.—And this is true, living *Faith, the Faith of God's Elect,* which is wrought in none but those, who *shall be saved in the* LORD, *with an everlasting Salvation.* Thus the Old Testament Saints, who *all died in Faith, not having received the Promises,* (in their Fulfilment by the Incarnation of our Saviour; as you now, have not receiv'd the Fulfilment of the Promises, of your complete Redemption thro' Him) *saw them afar off, and were persuaded of them, and embraced them,* Heb. xi. 13. *Faith* then, being the Effect of your Consolation; be assur'd, dear Sir, that your Comfort proceeds from the *Spirit of God.* That Spirit, that works Faith in CHRIST, by his comforting Operations on the Soul; is indeed the *Spirit of* CHRIST. Hence the Holy Spirit is stil'd, *The Spirit of Faith*, 2 Cor. iv. 13 *We having the same Spirit of Faith.* And He is so, 1. As He works a *Principle* of Faith. 2. As He presents the *Object* of Faith. And 3. As He enables the Soul to *act* Faith. And thus, Faith is said to be a *Fruit of the Spirit*, Gal. v. 22. A Principle of Faith, an Eye to see CHRIST, the Spirit of Faith hath wrought in your Soul: The Object of Faith, when He comforts you, He presents to the Eye of Faith: and by his own Strength, and in his own Light, while resting on, and shining into your Soul, He enables you to put forth Acts of Faith.—Thus, *Faith* being the Effect of your Comfort;

it is an undeniable Evidence, that the Holy Ghost, the Comforter, is the *Author* of it.

Well, dear Sir, may you style your Comfort, "*Glorious Comfort.*" For while you are favour'd with it, you *rejoice with Joy unspeakable, and full of Glory.* Heaven, as it were comes down to meet you, and you have a sweet Foretaste of the Fruits of that good Land. Which is an assuring Pledge, that you shall one Day enjoy the Glories of that *Kingdom,* which was *prepared for you from the Foundation of the World.* Hence the Holy Spirit, the Comforter, in his comforting Operations, (which transport the Soul, as it were, from Earth to Heaven, and set it a longing for immortal Glory) is said to be an *Earnest,* 2 Cor. v. 5. And the Saints in the Enjoyment thereof, are said to have the *First-Fruits* of the Spirit, *Rom.* viii. 23.

And wonder not, dear Sir, That this your transporting Comfort, is but "*Momentary, transitory, visionary;* that it no sooner almost *affects* you, than it *leaves* you." For *such* are the Comforts of the Holy Ghost, which the Saints enjoy, while in this World.—Visionary, indeed they are, that is, to *Faith:* Because Faith receives, those glorious Glances, which the Holy Spirit presents. Whence it is said to be *The Evidence of Things not seen,* by an Eye of Sense, *Heb.* xi. 1.—Momentary, and transitory likewise, the Comforts of the Holy Spirit are, which He affords his People in the present State. Else the Condition of the Saints while in the Body, could not so fitly be styl'd, a State of *Absence from the Lord,* and they said to *walk by Faith, not by Sight,* 2 Cor. v. 6, 7. When the Holy Ghost shines in upon our Souls with a Ray of glorious Comfort, and we are taken to the Mount of Vision, and blest with the transporting Glances of the Glory of CHRIST; it fares with us, as with the Disciples when in the Mount, while they were saying, *Lord, it is good for us to be here:--Let us make Tabernacles,--a Cloud overshadow'd them,* Mat. xvii. 4, 5. And as it was with the *Disciples,* even so it fares with *us:* When they were going to *Emmaus,* and *Jesus drew near, and made their Hearts burn within them, while He talked with them by the Way, and opened to them the Scriptures;* no sooner almost were *their Eyes opened, that they knew Him;* but *He vanished out of their Sight,* Luke xxiv. 31.—Indeed the Lord is a Sovereign, and acts as such in comforting his People. While his comforting Influences upon some Souls, are of a shorter, and upon others, of a longer Duration; and so likewise are experience'd by the same Soul, at different Times. But extraordinary Comforts, do not ordinarily last *long;* either as to the present Vision of the Glories presented to our View, or to that Degree of Influence, with which the glorious Prospects were attended. Though there ever after, remains a precious Remembrance of the infinite Glories we have seen, and at Times, a precious Savour of the ineffable Sweets we have tasted; unto an answerable Degree of Influence, which extends to the Whole of our Conversation.

But, however *short,* the comforting Influences of the Holy Ghost may be, if they last but for a *Moment,* as to their immediate Emanations on the Soul; the Comfort convey'd thereby, is *everlasting.* Not in the *Subject,* in us, whose Frames vary; but in the *Object,* in the God of all Consolation, who is unchangeably the same, and whose infinite Glories are then present to our View. The Holy Ghost, in those Moments of Discovery, shews us Things as they *are.* Where our Help lies, tho' we have destroy'd ourselves; and that Sufficiency of Help which is provided for us, and which will bring all Salvation to us. And thus, *our Lord Jesus Christ himself, and God even our Father, which hath loved us,* are said to have *given us everlasting Consolation, and good Hope thro' Grace.* Whence the Apostle pray'd for the *Thessalonians,* that their *Hearts might be comforted,* further comforted, under renewed Influences) and so they *stablished in every good Word and Work,* 2 Thes. ii. 16, 17.

And tho' the Moments of our Comfort may be but *short;* they are exceeding *sweet.* One *Moment's* Enjoyment of CHRIST, and of GOD in him, is far preferable, to an *Age* spent in Creature-Delights! Hence the Psalmist *David* cries out, speaking the Language of the Saints, and their different Experience from that of Sensualists, LORD, *lift thou up the Light of thy Countenance upon us.* THOU *hast put Gladness in my Heart, more than in the Time when their Corn, and their Wine increased,* Psal. iv. 6, 7. And *Whom* (says Asaph) *have I in Heaven but* THEE? *And there is none upon Earth that I desire besides* THEE, Psal. lxxiii. 25.

Again, though the comforting Influences of the Holy Ghost, are but as it were for a *Moment;* yet are those happy Moments frequently *repeated* to the dear Favourites of Heaven, in whom the Lord the Comforter dwells, and whose Consolation, he hath engaged to maintain. If our Lord withdraws from us, as to his comforting Presence by the blessed Spirit, he will not leave us always, nor long without Comfort. He *will see us again, and our Hearts shall rejoyce, and our Joy, no Man shall take from us,* John xvi. 16,-22. The Holy Ghost, in his comforting Operations, is that *River,* that full, free, flowing River of Life, *the Streams whereof, shall make glad the City of* GOD, and every Citizen of Mount *Sion,* Psal. xlvi. 4. *Whosoever drinketh of the Water that I shall give him,* saith our Lord, *shall never thirst; but the Water that I shall give him,* (the Holy Ghost, in his sanctifying and comforting Influences) *shall be in him a Well of Water, springing up into everlasting Life,* John iv. 14.—Oh dear Sir, your Consolation shall never fail; because the Comforter shall never be taken away from you. He that *dwells in you, shall abide with you for ever.* And renew and increase your Consolation here; until it rises hereafter, to be *a River to swim in:* Until you are blest with the full and immediate Vision of your own GOD in CHRIST, in whose *Presence is Fulness of Joy,* and at whose *Right Hand, there are Pleasures for evermore!*—In the next Place, Sir, I am to consider,

IV. Your *Fear* that your Comfort is not *right:* "Because it leaves you to a *Heart* corrupt and abominable; that there is no Amendment in your *Heart,* that *that* is the *same* as it always was, if any Difference, *worse;* tho' a formal Amendment be produced in you *Life."* From hence, Sir, you are at a *Loss,* whence your comfort proceeds, and fear it is not from the *Spirit of God,* but from *Satan,* transforming himself into an Angel of Light, to deceive your Soul. "Because your Comfort, doth not produce those *Graces* in your Heart, which are mentioned in the word of God, as *Fruits of the Spirit."*—Your Comfort, dear Sir, I am well satisfy'd, is from the *Spirit of God.* For no such Comfort can *Satan* give, that makes the Redeemer *precious,* tho' it were but for *one Moment,* to any *one Soul.* Your Comfort arises from gracious Hints, that the SAVIOUR will have Compassion on you, and save you from *Sin;* not only in its Guilt, but also in its Filth, Power and Being. Which is an Evidence, that a *holy Nature* is wrought in your Soul, which groans under your own Sinfulness, and thirsts after Holiness: And likewise, that your Comfort is from *God;*

because God's Salvation, in all its Parts, comforts you. Such Comfort, can no unregenerate Soul *receive,* nor Satan *give.* It comes down from God our Father, thro' Jesus Christ, by the Spirit of Grace into your Soul.—And no reason have you to fear, that it is not from *God,* because you don't find your Heart to be *amended* thereby, but that it is rather *worse.* For it is *Light,* that discovers *Darkness.* It is *God's Light,* shining into your Heart, that shews you the Blackness and Vileness of your *own Nature.* Hence you think your Heart to be *worse,* because you see *greater and greater Abominations,* in that All-Fulness of Sin, that unsearchable Depth of Iniquity which lurks there.—But to answer this Part of your Letter, more distinctly, and shew you in what Sense, your Heart *is* made better by your Comfort, and in what *not;* I must have Recourse to the Distinction which I have already made.

Know then, dear Sir, that you are to distinguish *yourself,* from *yourself,* yourself as *corrupt,* from yourself as *sanctify'd.* And so, you have in you, both a *new Heart,* and an *old:* Grace and Sin, both dwell together in the *same Soul,* yea, in the *same Faculties.* Your *old Heart,* the Corruption of Nature, is not to be *mended,* or made better by your Comforts, but to be *destroy'd.* According to *Rom.* vi. 6. *Knowing this, that our old Man is crucify'd with him, that the Body of Sin might be destroy'd, that henceforth we should not serve Sin.* And the Body of Sin is not destroy'd at *once,* but by *Degrees. By little and little* will the LORD our God, drive out these Enemies, our Corruptions, from before us; until we be increased, under the renew'd Comforts of the Holy Ghost, to inherit the promis'd Glory. And the *Discovery* of Sin, such a Discovery thereof, that makes it loathsome to the Soul, and puts it upon looking to Christ for Deliverance, and breathing after the same; is no small Part of the *Destruction* of Sin. It is the Destruction of its *Reign;* and an Evidence, that Grace hath the *Throne* in the Heart. And where the Reign of Sin is destroy'd in the *Heart,* it shall not reign in the *Life.* However turbulent and troublesome it may be at Times, either in Heart or Life; it is an Usurper upon the New-born Soul, and is not yielded to by it, as such, as its approved, rightful Sovereign. But *subdu'd* and *destroy'd* it shall be, by auxiliary Supplies of Grace and Strength, out of Christ's Fulness, as the King and Saviour of the New-born Soul.—And as for your *new Heart,* your Soul as renew'd, that shall be made *better,* by the glorious Consolation which is given you. The Exercise and Increase of every Grace, being the direct Tendency, and blessed Effect, of all the Comforts of the Holy Ghost.—To this you'll reply:

Aye, but this is that which stumbles me, and is the Cause of my Fear: I do not find that my *Graces* are increased by my *Comfort.*—To this, let me say,

If you would see the *Fruit* of your Comfort, in the *Increase* of your Graces; look for it just *when* you are comforted, and so *long* as your Consolation abides. To look for *Fruits* of Comfort, immediate inward Fruits, when comforting Influences are *withdrawn;* is just like looking for the bright Beams of the Sun, when it don't shine, but is vail'd with a Cloud: Or, like looking for Summer-Fruits, in the Winter Season.—How is it then with you, dear Sir, in those happy Moments, when glorious Comfort breaks in upon your Heart? Don't you *then* find, Faith and Love, Hope and Joy, Humility and Self-Denial, Zeal for God's Glory, and Gospel-Repentance, some or all of these Graces, at one Time or other, to be upon the *Flow,* just when the Consolations of God *flow in* to your Spirit, and while they *abide* with your Soul? Is not CHRIST precious to you at *such Seasons?* Is not *Sin* loathsome and grievous? Are you not *then* willing to take up your *Cross,* and *follow the Lamb' whithersoever he goeth?* And don't you *then* long to *glorify God* upon the Earth? If *so*, your *glorious Comfort*, hath *glorious Fruits.*—And from these immediate Fruits thereof in your *Heart*, there are more remote Fruits of it in your *Life,* in a Gospel-Conversation. Which you unfitly call, "*A formal Amendment of Life.*" Because you see the Corruptions of your Heart, to be as *great* as ever, and the Graces of your Soul, appear so *small* in your own Sight.—But be of good Cheer, Sir, your Comfort is from GOD, and is attended with those blessed *Fruits,* which in the Divine Word, are said to be *Fruits of the Spirit.* And under further and greater Consolations, you shall see further and greater Fruits unto Holiness. Your *old Heart,* your Iniquities, shall be *subdu'd,* and your *new Heart,* your Graces, shall be *strengthned.* Because CHRIST *lives, you shall live also,* Joh. xiv.19.—In the last Place, Sir, I shall,

V. Conclude with a Word of *Advice.* And briefly, let me say, *Make* CHRIST *your* ALL. *Look to* HIM *for all.* And *wait upon* HIM, till *all Salvation* is brought unto you.

1. *Make* CHRIST *your* ALL. That is, *esteem* Christ to *be,* all that God the Father has *made him unto you. Wisdom,* to direct you; *Righteousness,* to justify you; *Sanctification,* to make you holy; and *Redemption,* to deliver you from all Bondage, and to bring you into the full and glorious Liberty of the Sons of God.—You see, my dear Brother, how *imperfect* you are in *yourself.* But *your* JESUS, is *all Perfection* unto you. *You* are all Want; but CHRIST is all Fulness. And *you are complete in* HIM: *Lacking Nothing.* Even *now;* tho' *so incomplete* in yourself.—And therefore,

2. *Look to* CHRIST *for all.* For HE is your All to GOD, and your All to *you.* Your all to GOD. In that He continually presents your Person and Services, before the Father, without a Spot: *Holy, unblameable, and unreproveable in his Sight,* unto *all pleasing.* Or, renders you an Object of *God's Delight;* as wash'd in his Blood, cloth'd with his Righteousness, and adorn'd with his Perfections. And so *your Beauty is perfect, thro' his Comeliness which he hath put upon you.*—And the more you view your Compleatness in Christ *mystically,* the more will your *personal* Holiness increase. The more you look upon yourself to be dead indeed unto Sin, *mystically* in Christ, the more will you die to *Sin personally.* The more you reckon yourself to be alive unto God, *in Christ,* to be *presented so,* in the Fulness of *his Life;* the more spiritual Life will you feel *in your own Soul.* And the more you view the *Iniquity of your Holy Things,* continually borne away by your *great High Priest above,* and they presented in his shining Perfections, HOLINESS TO THE LORD, the more holy will your *Service be.* For a glorious *Influence,* from the Death of Christ, beheld by Faith, flows into the Soul, for the Mortification of Sin: From the Life of Christ, to increase Life in us: And from the Acceptance of our Services in Christ's Perfections, to make our religious Performances, more perfect.—Look then to CHRIST for *all,* for all your Compleatness, as HE is your All to GOD, *representatively.*

Again, Look to CHRIST for all, as HE is your All to *You, influentially.* For in *your* JESUS, there is *all Fulness;* not only for

Representation, but also for Communication. Oh dear Sir, CHRIST, that has *begun* to destroy Sin in your Soul, that has given it its Death's Wound, will never *leave,* till He has *quite* subdu'd it under your Feet, and destroy'd the very Being of it out of your Nature. JESUS, that has *begun* to make you *alive to God,* that has begun this good Work in you, will continually flow out upon your Soul, with *fresh* quickening Influences, until all that Death which now works in you, shall be swallowed up of *perfect Life,* and *immortal Glory.* The LAMB that hath bought you with his Blood, and conquer'd you by his Power, that hath given you a Heart, a Desire to serve Him; will enable you to serve Him more and better, until that which is in *Part* shall be done away, by the Coming of that which is *Perfect.* And then you shall *see his Face, his Name shall be in your Forehead,* and under the everlasting *Flows* of reigning Grace, you shall serve Him *perfectly* and *eternally,* among the Saints and Seraphs that are round his Throne.—And therefore,

3. *Wait upon* HIM, till *all Salvation* is brought unto you. All Salvation is laid up in CHRIST *for you,* and shall by Him, most assuredly be brought *unto you.* Wait upon Him, then, dear Sir, *Wait, I say, upon the* LORD: *And He shall strengthen your Heart, and save you to the uttermost.*—Wait upon him in the Use of all the *Means* of Grace; and so shall the *Grace* of the Means flow down upon your Soul. The more diligent you are in all Respects, in *seeking the* LORD; the more abundantly shall you *find Him,* as the God of all Salvation unto *you.* For, *He hath not said unto the Seed of* Jacob, *seek ye* ME *in vain.* The most *diligent Christians,* have the most *thriving Souls.* Because God's Free-Grace, which bringeth Salvation, *calls* for our Diligence, and delights to *crown it.*

Abide in CHRIST by Faith, and come unto Him daily, as an empty, helpless Creature in yourself, to receive Supplies of Grace, out of his Fulness. And upon every new Discovery of *Want,* sit not down in *wretched Self,* mourning and discourag'd; but instantly attempt your Duty, to go out of yourself to CHRIST, by a fresh Act of *Faith,* for all the *Supply* you need. When Water in the Stream, Grace in *you,* fails; the Fountain, CHRIST, is always full and free. One great Reason, why we have so *little Grace* in us, is, Because we abide so *much at Home,* in *ourselves,* seeking to live upon our own Stock; instead of going out to CHRIST, to live in, and receive from, *His* inexhaustible Fulness, continually. The greatest Strength of inherent Grace, is not sufficient to uphold the Soul one Moment, without renewed Influences from CHRIST. *The Youth,* young Men that are strong in Grace, that live upon their inherent Stock, *shall faint,* yea, shall *utterly fall. But they that wait on the* LORD, *shall renew their Strength:* Tho' the weakest Souls, *they shall mount up with Wings as Eagles, they shall run and not be weary, they shall walk and not faint.* Because *the everlasting God, the* LORD, *the Creator of the Ends of the Earth, who fainteth not, neither is weary, giveth Power to the Faint, and to them that have no Might,* HE *increaseth Strength,* Isa. xl. 29, *&c.*

And abiding in CHRIST by Faith, go on to serve Him in *Love,* having Respect unto all his Commandments.—*Keep your Heart with all Diligence.* Watch your *Thoughts,* that they run not out from GOD, to needless Things, and sinful Objects. And whenever they attempt it, in the Name and Strength of the LORD, call them back instantly, that at his Requirement, you may give him your *Heart.*—Maintain a due Care of your *Words, that no corrupt Communication proceed out of your Mouth, but such that is good to the Use of edifying.*—And in the whole of your *Conversation,* make it your Business continually, under the Teachings of Divine Grace, to *deny Ungodliness and worldly Lusts,* (to deny them in their first Rise in your Heart, in order to a Denial of them in your Life) *and to live soberly, righteously and godly in this present World.*—Delight in the precious *Word of God;* read, hear, and meditate thereon.—Be as frequent as may be in *Prayer,* if you can spend but a few Minutes at a Time; and labour to keep your Heart *always* in a praying Frame.—Let the *Saints, the Excellent of the Earth,* be your Companions.—*Redeem the Time,* it is very precious: And labour to improve it all, some Way or other, for the Glory of God, and your own, and others Advantage.—And whenever your Hands and Feet are *defiled,* (as Defilement will continually cleave to your Works and Walk) *wash by Faith,* in the *Fountain set open for Sin, and for Uncleanness,* in the *Blood of Christ, that cleanesth from all Sin.* That so, having *your Conscience purged from dead Works,* you may go on to *serve the living God, perfecting Holiness in his*

Fear.—Labour to *do* as much, as if you was to be *saved* by your *Doings.*—And when you have done *all,* say you are an *unprofitable Servant;* and expect all your *Salvation* to be, as indeed it is, of pure, free, infinite *Grace.* Lay all your Obedience joyfully *down,* at the Feet of CHRIST, who obey'd and dy'd for *you:* And desire to be found in HIM, and *his Righteousness* alone, for all your Acceptance with GOD, both here and hereafter. –Thus, *make* CHRIST *your* ALL; *look to* HIM, *for All;* and wait upon HIM continually, by *Faith* and *Love,* in *Hope of his Salvation:* And HE the great SAVIOUR, will bring *all Salvation* unto *you;* for Soul and Body, for Time and for Eternity.

You seem to be at a *Loss,* Sir, by what you add towards the Close of your Letter, "Whether your want of Amendment of Heart, is for want of a *right* Application of your Comfort." And to this, I would just give a Hint or two. In the Application of Christ, and the Joys of his Salvation to us, there is to be consider'd, both, the Work of the *Holy Spirit;* and *our Acts of Faith.*

1. *The Works of the Holy Spirit:* Or, his revealing Christ and his Salvation to our Souls, unto some Degree of Assurance of Interest, and a proportionable Measure of sanctifying Influence. And in *this,* there can be *nothing amiss.* The Holy Ghost, always applies *right.* But as the Work of Sanctification, in the Mortification of Sin, and quickning us to live unto God, is to be carry'd on by *Degrees;* we must not expect it at *once,* upon our first Comfort; but to advance continually with our renewed Consolations, under gracious Influences of the Holy Ghost the Comforter.—Again, In the Application of Christ, and the Joys of his Salvation to us, there is to be consider'd,

2. *Our Acts of Faith:* Or, our receiving by Faith, what the Holy Ghost reveals, and improving the same, unto the Mortification of Sin, and quickning us to Holiness. And in *this,* our Obedience of Faith, there is *much amiss.* Not that Faith, so far as it *applies,* doth not apply *right.* But there is much *lacking in our Faith.* We are *slow of Heart to believe,* to receive the Consolations, which the Holy Ghost gives, according to the Measure fo the Spirit's Revelation. We either put them away from us, and *refuse to be comforted;* or suffer our Comforts to be wrested out of our Hands by Satan and Unbelief, as if they did not belong to *us,* by Reason

of our great Sinfulness. And so our Love to God, and Zeal for his Glory, our Hatred of Evil, and Strength to oppose it, are *weakned.* For we *love God, because he first loved us;* and just so far as we *believe his Love. And this is the Victory that overcometh the World.* And all our spiritual Enemies, *even our Faith,* I John v. 4.

If then, dear Sir, you would apply Christ, and the Joys of his Salvation *aright;* come to the SAVIOUR daily, as a *poor Sinner,* with all your Miseries and Wants. Come upon the Gospel-Call, which is, to *whosoever will.* And being come, *take the Water of Life,* receive CHRIST and all his Grace, *freely.* As exhibited to your Faith, by the Word and Spirit of God: Without staying for a Sight of your own Goodness, before you *believe* the Grace of the Gospel is for *you.* And so will your Sanctification *increase* continually. For as the Salvation of GOD in CHRIST, is for *Sinners;* and in all its Parts, is of one pure Piece, of free, infinite, sovereign *Grace:* So the more we believe it as *such,* the more we receive the strong Consolation, which a GOD that cannot lie, hath given us, even to every poor Sinner that flees to CHRIST for Refuge; the more shall we increase in *Holiness,* the greater *Saints* shall we be.—

And now, dear Sir, that the Grace of CHRIST may be with your Spirit; that you may increase with all the Increases of GOD; that the Lord may direst your Heart into the Love of GOD, and into the patient Waiting for CHRIST: Until *all Salvation* is brought unto *you,* from all Misery, unto all Glory; is the hearty Prayer of,

Dear Sir,

Your Friend that loves you

In the Bowels of JESUS CHRIST,

——— ———

A
LETTER
ON THE
Duty and Privilege of a *Believer,* to live by Faith, And to improve his Faith, Unto Holiness.

To the Society at the Tabernacle, *in* London, *a Friend and Servant of theirs, wisheth* Grace and Peace, from God our Father, and from the Lord Jesus Christ.

My dear and honour'd Brethren,

I Rejoice to hear, that some of your dear Souls, begin to taste the ineffable Sweetness of a Life of Faith on the Son of God, even when you have not the Delights of spiritual Sense. That, my dear Brethren, is most properly a Life of *Faith,* which is not founded on spiritual *Sense.* That Persuasion of Interest in Christ and all his Fulness, which is not built upon gracious Frames and inward Feelings; but upon the Promises and Declarations of Grace made to Believers in the Book of God, upon the Word and Oath of a God that cannot lie; is Faith *indeed,* or that which by Way of Eminence, may be styl'd *Faith.* Permit me then, my dear Brethren, to give you a Hint,

I. That it is the Duty and Privilege of a Believer, to live by Faith. And,

II. To improve his Faith unto Holiness.

First, That it is the Duty and Privilege of a *Believer* to *live by Faith,* is evident; in that *this is God's Commandment, that we should believe on the Name of his Son Jesus Christ,* 1 Joh. iii. 23. That we should believe his infinite All-sufficiency, his Ability and Willingness to *save;* his being call'd of *God* to this Work, to save Sinners to the uttermost; and his infinite Faithfulness to God that appointed him, and to his own Promise, to give *Rest,* present and eternal Rest, eternal Life and

Salvation, to every weary, heavy-laden Soul, that believes on him, or comes unto him at his Call, *Matt.* xi. 28. It is our Duty, not only to *believe on the Son of God,* or to come to him as poor perishing Sinners in ourselves, *for* eternal Life; but also to be persuaded, that *believing,* we have *Life thro' his Name,* or eternal Life in him, according to *his*, and his *Father's Promise.* And to hold fast this our Confidence, notwithstanding all our Vileness and Unworthiness. We ought to believe, that we have eternal Life *in Christ,* in the Right of it, by the full, free and irreversible Grant of a GOD that cannot lie; amidst all the Variations of our own Frames: And that we shall have the complete Enjoyment of it *thro' Christ,* even when we see or feel but little of its glorious Beginnings in *ourselves.* That having believed on Christ *for it,* we *have it* in him, and shall *enjoy it* thro' him. And to doubt it, because of our own Sinfulness and Unworthiness; casts a very great Dishonour upon the infinite Grace and Faithfulness of GOD. For, *He that believeth not* God, *hath made him a* Liar, *because he believeth* not *the Record that God gave his Son. And this is the* Record, *that God hath given to* us eternal Life: *And this Life is in his* Son, 1 John v. 10, 11. Oh the horrid Nature of *Unbelief,* of this *easily besetting Sin!* How often doth *it,* and *we* thereby, give the *Lye* to a GOD of infinite *Faithfulness! He that hath the Son,* Saith the Apostle, *hath Life; and he that hath not the Son of God, hath not Life. These Things have I written unto you that believe on the Son of God; that ye may know ye have eternal Life, and that ye may believe on the Name of the Son of God,* Ver. 12, 13. The Apostle's Scope in these Verses is, 1. To shew that Difference of *State,* which is between a *Believer,* and an *Unbeliever.* A Believer hath the *Son;* an Unbeliever hath *not* the Son. A Believer hath *Life* in the Son; an Unbeliever, not having the Son, hath *not* Life. And 2. To excite Believers to their *Duty,* of believing their *Interest* in Christ, and their *Right* to eternal Life in him. *These Things have I written unto you that believe on the Son of God, that ye may* know (or have a full Assurance) *that ye have* eternal Life, *and that ye may* believe *on the Son of God.* Or hold fast this your Confidence, amidst a thousand Discouragements, from within and without.—Thus it appears to be the *Duty* of a Believer to live by *Faith,* or steadily to believe his Interest in Christ, his Right to eternal Life, and that he shall have the full Enjoyment of it thro' him; even when he hath not spiritual *Sense,* or a joyful Feeling of the Increase of spiritual Life in himself. And as it is his Duty; for his *Privilege.* For, while a Believer lives by *Faith,* and so far as he is in the Exercise thereof, his soul hath *Rest,* and is fill'd with *Peace and Joy.* Thus, *Heb.* iv. 3. *For we that have believed, do enter into Rest.* And 1 *Pet.* i. 8, 9. *Whom having not seen, ye love; in whom, tho' now ye see him not, yet believing, ye rejoyce with Joy unspeakable, and full of Glory. Receiving* (by a full Persuasion in yourselves, from the Witness of God in his Word) *the End of your Faith, the Salvation of your Souls.* Oh the Rest, the Peace and Joy, that fill the Soul in the Exercise of *Faith! Unbelief,* my dear Brethren, so far as we yield to it for want of *Sight;* not only dishonours GOD, but straightway brings *us* into Darkness, Weakness and Bondage. But *Faith,* pure Faith, on *Things not seen,* gives Light in Darkness, Strength in Weakness, and Liberty in Confinement.

To beget all spiritual *Faith,* there must be a spiritual *Evidence* given. The Object of Faith, must be presented to the Eye of Faith, in such a Manner as is suited to draw out the Act of Faith, to receive its Object: Either, 1. Singly and purely, according to its own Nature, which is to credit *Things not seen.* Or, 2. In a amix'd Way, as the same Things are clothed with sensible *Effects,* perceptible to *Sight.*

We have both *these* exemplify'd in the *Resurrection* of Christ, and in his *Appearance* to his Disciples. In the Word which our Lord gave to them before his Death, *that the Son of Man must be kill'd, and after three Days be raised again from the Dead,* Mat. xvi. 21. In the same Word which his *Angel* put the Women in Mind of that sought him at the *Sepulchre,* and at our Lord's Command bid them, *go tell his Disciples, that he was risen, went before them into* Galilee, *and that there they should see him as he said unto them,* Mar. xvi. 5, *&c.* And in the same Message, which *Jesus* himself sent the Women with to his *Brethren,* Matt. xxviii. 10.—Which was *Evidence* sufficient for them to have *believed* his Resurrection upon. Whence, as they did *not;* our Lord upbraided them with their *Unbelief and Hardness of Heart,* Mark xvi. 14. Luke xxiv. 25.—They wanted *Sense* to help their *Faith.* To *see* a risen Jesus, before they *believ'd* his Resurrection. Our Lord indulg'd them; He *appear'd* to them, and shew'd them his *Hands and his Side,* John xx. 19, 20. *But* Thomas *was not with* *them when Jesus came. And when the other Disciples told him they had seen the Lord;* he resolutely said in Unbelief, *Except I shall* see *in his Hands the Print of the Nails, and put my Finger into the Print of the Nails, and thrust my Hand into his Side, I will not* believe, Ver. 24, 25. *Jesus* therefore, when he appear'd again to his *Disciples,* Thomas being with them; as soon as he had saluted them all with *Peace be unto you:* He instantly, in boundless Compassion and infinite Condescension, thus address'd his unbelieving *Thomas: Reach hither thy Finger, and behold my Hands; and reach hither thy Hand, and thrust it into my Side; and be not* Faithless, *but* believing. Upon which, *Thomas* in the Language of Faith cry'd out, *My Lord, and my God.* A flood of joyful *Sense,* being let in upon his Soul; it set *Faith* upon the Flow: Out it went unto its *Object,* claim'd its *Interest: My Lord, and my God!* Then said *Jesus* to his believing *Thomas, Because thou hast* seen me, *thou hast* believ'd: *Blessed are they that have* not seen, *and yet have* believed, Ver. 26, &c.

Our Lord here, states the Difference, between believing *without,* and *upon* Sight, and pronounceth a peculiar Blessedness upon the *latter,* or declares those to be eminently *blessed,* who had *believed,* and had *not seen,*--By which perhaps our Lord might respect the Faith of those *Women,* who *believed* his Resurrection upon the Credit of his own *Word* given them before his Death, which they *remembred* when put in Mind of it by the Angels at the *Sepulchre,* who declar'd to them that *he was risen, as he said unto them,* Luke xxiv. 6, 7, 8. Upon which they return'd to *bring his Disciples Word.* And that they *believed* his Resurrection, is evident, in that *they departed quickly from the Sepulchre, with* Fear, (or Reverence) of this wondrous Work of God) *and* great Joy, *Matt.* xxviii. 8. Their *great Joy,* sprang from that *full Persuasion* which they had upon the Credit of the Lord's *Word,* that he was *risen.* They remembred his *Word,* when put in Mind of it by the Angels, and believ'd the *Fulfilment* thereof, which they acquainted them with. And hence with great Joy, they ran to *tell his Disciples;* even before they had *seen Jesus himself.* For, *As they went, Jesus met them, saying, All Hail. And they came and held him by the Feet, and worship'd him: Then said Jesus unto them, Be not afraid: Go tell my Brethren, that they go into* Galilee, *and there shall they see me,* Ver. 9, 10.—But when they *told his Disciples all these Things,* (what Jesus had said to them about his Resurrection before his Death; what the Angels had told them as to the Fulfilment thereof; and that Jesus himself had sent them to acquaint them herewith, and that they should shortly see him) *their Words seemed to them as idle Tales, and they believed them not,* Luk. xxiv. 11.—Thus the *Disciples* would *see* Jesus, before they *believed* his Resurrection. And when he appear'd unto them, said, *Peace be unto you: And shew'd them his Hands and his Side: Then were the Disciples glad when they saw the Lord,* John xx. 19, 20. When these Disciples *saw* their risen Lord, their *Faith* in his Resurrection according to his Word, sprang: As did the *Faith* of poor *Thomas,* when the Lord *appear'd* unto him.—But the *Women,* believed his Resurrection according to his Word, *before* they had seen the risen SAVIOUR. The one believ'd *without,* the other *upon* Sight.—And unto this our Lord might have Respect, when he said to Thomas, *Because thou hast seen me, thou hast believed: Blessed are they that have not seen, and yet have believed.* As well as to the Faith of the Old Testament Saints, who *saw the Promises afar off, were persuaded of them and embraced them;* and *died in the Faith* of them, altho' they had *not* receiv'd the Fulfilment of them, or *seen* the Truth of God's *Word,* clothed with visible *Effects.*

And there is, as hath been hinted, a peculiar *Blessedness* in believing without Sight. In that, 1. It gives more *Glory* unto *God,* for the Soul to credit his naked *Word,* before it sees it array'd in answerable *Effects.* To believe what God hath said, merely because HE hath spoken it, and thence to expect the Performance thereof, in the Face of a thousand Difficulties; brings much Glory to *God.* And 2. To believe without Sight, gives *Rest* and *Joy* to the *Soul,* in a stable Promise, an All-producing Word, before the blessed Effects of it, spring to the Joy of Sense; and frees the Soul from that *Perplexity,* which otherwise fills the Mind, between the giving and fulfilling of a Promise, when there are Deaths pass over it. Thus of *Abraham* it is said, *And being not weak in Faith, he consider'd not his own Body now dead, when he was about an hundred Years old, nor yet the Deadness of* Sarah's *Womb. He staggered not at the Promise of God thro' Unbelief; but was strong in Faith, giving Glory to God. And being fully persuaded, that what he had promised, he was able also to perform,* Rom. iv. 19, 20, 21. And, *We that have believ'd,* Saith the Apostle, *do enter into*

Rest, Heb. iv. 3. Into the present Rest of Faith, in Assurance of future Glory; before we enter into the Rest of Vision, in the Enjoyment thereof.

This then, my dear Brethren, shews us the *Excellency* of a Life of pure Faith, of believing without Sight, when we have not gracious Frames and inward Feelings, or the Prop of spiritual Sense to assist our Faith.—Unto every one who hath seen his Misery by Sin, and his Danger of God's eternal Wrath, if he abides in a State of *Unbelief;* who hath had a Discovery of Christ the great SAVIOUR, the only Refuge which God hath provided for poor Sinners, and has been enabled to flee unto Him by *Faith:* Unto that Soul, God hath given an everlasting Security, That he *shall not perish, but have everlasting Life.* The Soul that at the Gospel-Call, has run into Christ by Faith, as *an Hiding-place from the Wind, and a Covert from the Storm,* is eternally secur'd in Him, from endless Misery, unto endless Glory. Unto every and all of those, who have *fled to Christ for Refuge, to lay hold on this Hope set before them,* the LORD hath given his *Word and Oath,* that by these *two immutable Things, in which it was impossible for* GOD *to lie, these Heirs of Promise might have a strong Consolation,* Heb. vi. 17, 18. Oh my Brethren, when the SAVIOUR receiv'd you as perishing Sinners, to save you to the uttermost; God gave you his *Word of Promise,* his great unchanging *Word,* as it stands in his *Book,* for your Salvation. Yea, did he not apply some Promise or other to your *Hearts,* and persuade you thereby, of your everlasting Security in JESUS?—And tho' that Life and Power, that Savour and Sweetness, which attended the Moments of Application, may be worn off your Spirit; yet those Grants and Bequeathments made by the Promise, as it stands in God's *Book,* and when apply'd unto *you,* are invariably the same. The *Promise,* yea, *all the Promises of God* to you, *are Yea, and Amen in Christ,* 2 Cor. i. 20. A constant *Yea,* a fixed *Amen. The Gifts and Calling of God are without Repentance,* Rom. xi. 29. Remember, that *all the Promises of God* to you, are made in *Christ:* In Him who is your ALL. Whom God hath made unto you, *Wisdom and Righteousness, and Sanctification, and Redemption,* 1 Cor. i. 30. They are made in the unchangeable JESUS, who hath for you an unchangeable *Fullness:* By Virtue of which you are and shall be rendred for ever, the Objects of God's Delight. They are made by the LORD *Jehovah,* who *changeth not.* They are made for your *Security;* they are made for your *Consolation.* And that your Security might be *double,* and your Consolation *strong;* to God's unchanging Word, he hath added his inviolable *Oath.* And, because he could swear by no *greater,* he hath sworn by *himself: That in Blessing he will bless you.* In which is included, the Forgiveness of all your Sins; the Justification of your Persons; the wondrous Privilege of your becoming the Sons of God; your Right to Grace and Glory, and to all good Things; the Sanctification of your Natures, by the Word and Spirit, thro all the Changes which pass over you; and the complete Glory of your whole Persons, or your being rais'd up in Conformity to Christ, unto the Enjoyment of eternal Life with Him. What a wondrous ALL of Blessings then, is compris'd in the Word and Oath of GOD, which are given unto you in CHRIST! The *Promise* is the Expression of God's *Mind,* of *the Thoughts of his Heart* towards you in his dear Son; which *stand fast unto all Generations.* And the LORD having given you his great *Word;* the infinite Truth and Faithfulness of *Jehovah,* are engag'd to make it good. And as in infinite Condescension and amazing Goodness, the LORD hath added his solemn *Oath* to his great Word; how strongly hath He *bound himself to save you?* A Word so *great,* cannot be *broken.* An Oath so *solemn,* cannot be *violated.* And so great a BEING, so strongly engag'd, will not, *cannot lie.* It is *impossible* that he should, both with regard to his immutable Nature, and to his solemn Engagements. The *Promise,* the Word that is gone out of his Mouth, stands for ever fast upon the solid Basis of the great unchanging *Purpose* of his Heart. And the Oath of GOD, stands in *Himself,* as firm *as* Himself. For the LORD, in swearing by HIMSELF, by all that is in HIM, hath engag'd all his infinite Perfections to perform it, to save his People to the uttermost. And both the Word and Oath of GOD, being given us, not only for our Security, but also for our Consolation, and for this End in Particular, as is specify'd, That we who have fled for Refuge to lay hold on the Hope set before us, might have *a strong Consolation:* How great is our *Unbelief,* when we receive not so great a *Witness?* And how great is our *Folly,* when we refuse to be comforted with so great a *Consolation,* as the Great JEHOVAH hath given us?

The Word and Oath of GOD, given to *Believers in* CHRIST , being the solid everlasting *Ground of Faith;* Here Faith should *rest,* when it han't the Prop of spiritual *Sense* to lean on.—Most kindly our Lord at first, indulges his weak Children, applies his *Promises* with glorious Power in their Hearts, and clothes them with such great and sensible *Effects* upon the Soul, that bear down *Unbelief,* and draw out *Faith,* to claim its Interest in the Promise, in the promis'd SAVIOUR, and in his Salvation. And the New-born Babe in Christ, finding itself by the Promise, to be brought forth as it were into a new World; from Darkness and Death, Weakness and Bondage, Sin and Sorrow, into Light and Life, Liberty and Strength, Joy and Holiness; is apt to think, that these blessed and sensible Effects of the Promise, will always *abide* upon its Heart.—But the Lord designs to learn his Child to walk by *Faith,* when it han't the Supports of spiritual *Sense* to bear it up. And for this Reason among others, withdraws his Sun-like Face, and calls the Soul when it *walks in Darkness,* and hath *no Light* of Sense to go by, to *trust in the* LORD, *and to stay himself upon his God.*—But oh, the Soul being inured to a *Prop,* knows not how at first to go *alone.* Sense being *gone,* its Faith begins to *fail.* Because the Soul believ'd the *Promise,* as to its own Interest in it, rather upon those gracious *Effects* of it, which it once saw and felt in *itself,* than upon the infinite Grace, the Almighty Power, and unchangeable Truth and Faithfulness of GOD the Promiser. It is true, the Faith of a Believer, ultimately centers in *these,* and the Soul don't know at first, that it leans too much to *Sense,* and goes thro' *gracious Effects,* to take up the *Promise of Grace.* But it is manifest that it doth; in that when the Promise is as it were *stripp'd* of present sensible Effects on the Heart, the Soul finds it a hard Task, to believe a *naked Promise,* to trust in a *naked Word,* merely upon the Credit of the *Promiser.* Without are *Fightings, and within are Fears.* Satan, by his Temptations, with all his Power, opposes the Soul's believing without Sight. An unbelieving Heart, raises a thousand Objections; and the Soul stands trembling, and knows not how to set one Foot forward by Faith, when Sense is gone.—And utterly would it *cast away its Confidence,* if *everlasting Arms* were not *underneath,* to support the Soul, and strengthen it for Acts of Faith without Sight; to *trust in the* LORD, even when he seems to *slay it,* and to *hope in his Word,* even *against Hope,* or in the Face of a thousand Difficulties and Discouragements.—And then, the Soul having found a solid Basis to rest on, an Anchor-hold in Storms, and being enabled by Faith to honour GOD; God will honour *Faith,* and break forth again upon the Soul with further Shines of his infinite Kindness, tho' the fresh Application of the Promises, to comfort and strengthen the Soul after its Conflict.—And thus the LORD teacheth his Children to trust Him, when He hides Himself from the House of *Jacob,* and to stay upon their God, when they walk in the Dark; and also, to look and long for the Light of his Countenance, to turn Night into Day, and Winter into Summer. And thus to walk on with God in the Faith of his Promis'd Grace, thro' various Changes inward and outward, in the present Time, until the unchangeable State of their promis'd Glory, their eternal Glory comes.

Are there any of you then, my Brethren, that have not yet been taught a Life of *pure Faith,* of trusting in, and resting on the Promise of God's Grace, when you don't see the gracious Effects thereof in your own Heart? What shall I say to *you?* Oh dear Souls, you forget the glorious Person in whom the Promise was made, and thro whom it is to be fulfill'd unto you. Hath God promised you eternal Life, as *Believers in Christ?* Is this the Voice of his Promise, as it stands in his *Book?* Was this its Voice when apply'd by the Spirit unto your *Hearts?* Oh consider, it was made in CHRIST in him *who of God is made unto you, Wisdom, and Righteousness, and Sanctification, and Redemption.*—What, doubt the *Promise,* because you see your own *Folly?* Oh remember, CHRIST is *your Wisdom.* Made so of GOD, by Constitution, by Appointment. Your Wisdom, to *represent you wise,* without the least Spot of Folly before God. Your Wisdom, to be communicated, to make you *wise inherently,* unto increasing Degrees, until a Perfection of Wisdom be given you.—what, afraid the Promise don't belong to *you,* because of your *Unrighteousness?* Oh consider, CHRIST is *your Righteousness.* His complete Obedience is imputed to *you,* and you accounted by *God,* and *presented to Him,* completely righteous therein.—What, refuse to be comforted by the *Promise,* because of your *Unholiness,* because of your remaining Corruptions, and the Imperfection of your Graces? CHRIST is *your Sanctification.* In his perfect personal Holiness, as your Head, you as Members of his Body, as Branches in him your holy Root, are *presented completely holy unto God.* And in him your Treasury, your Store-House of all Grace and Glory, you have a Fulness to be *communicated,* in further Measures, unto higher Degrees, until you are fully wrought up into a complete Conformity to *Christ,* to God's *First-born,* your glorious Pattern and Exemplar.—What, think you are not the Lord's *Free-Men,* according to *Promise,* because you are still in some Degree, *bound* by Sin and Satan, overcome by these Enemies, and brought into *Captivity;* and thereby, into *Bondage-Frames?* Oh see, CHRIST is *your Redemption?* In him your Redemption is complete. As you stand before God in a arisen JESUS, *Sin* hath no more Dominion over you; *Satan's* Power is quite destroy'd; and the *Law* is perfectly fulfill'd. *In Christ,* you are *Free-Men indeed:* Completely redeem'd from all Slavery, into full and glorious Liberty. In him the Work is completely and for ever done. And by Virtue of that complete Redemption by *Price,* which you now have *in Christ;* you shall ere-long be completely redeem'd by *Power,* in all Respect, in your *own Persons,* from all Misery, unto all Glory.—Oh doubt not your Interest in the *Promises of* GOD, because of your own *Wants and Emptiness;* since they are made unto you in CHRIST, who is *All Fulness,* and *your* ALL. *And ye* (saith the Holy Ghost) *are compleat in Him,* Col. ii. 20. Not ye *shall be,* tho' that is a Truth contain'd in other Texts; but ye *are* complete in Him. Your Completeness in Christ, my Brethren, is so full, so unchangeably perfect, that nothing can be taken from it, nor added to it. It rises not with your holy Frames, nor sinks when they fall. God hath given you a complete Head, a full Completeness in him, and an everlasting Acceptance in the *Beloved.* In HIM, you are every Way such as GOD can delight in. And all the Promises being made unto you *in Christ,* in Him your perfect, your acceptable *Head;* there are none of your personal Imperfections, that can, or shall, hinder the Performance thereof unto you, *through Him.* And as the Promise is the Expression of God's *Heart,* of the sovereign Resolve of his *Will,* to be gracious unto you in and thro' his dear Son; It stands in the infinite, immutable Grace of JEHOVAH's *Nature,* quite independent on *your Goodness,* and can nave fail, so long as GOD endures. Oh my Brethren, you *little Things,* What, doubt the *Love of God,* and the *Promise* of his Grace, because you see no *Worthiness,* no *Loveliness* in yourselves? Little do you think, How *freely,* how *greatly* GOD loves you! He loves you like his *Great* SELF! Yea, the *Love* of God to you, is HIMSELF loving you! And can you *measure* the Heighth, the Depth, the Breadths, and Lengths of infinite *Love?* No; it *passeth Knowledge!* Is far beyond the *Search* of finite Understanding! None but GOD himself, perfectly *knows* the infinite Glories, the Freeness, the Sovereignty, the Strength, the Greatness, the vast Infinity and Eternity of his *Love* unto *you.* All the Fulness of GOD, is compris'd in his *Love.* The Promise Stands in infinite *Love,* as well as in an infinite *Person,* infinity *beloved;* and from thence, thro' *Christ,* shall have a glorious Fulfilment, to the most unlovely, unworthy, poor, and needy *Souls,* that hang upon the Promise of Grace held forth to Sinners, in the Word of the Gospel. Oh my Brethren, *The* LORD *your GOD* (thro' the once-bleeding, now risen, interceding, and reigning LAMB) *in the Midst of you is mighty; He will save, he will rejoice over you with Joy: He will rest in his Love, he will joy over you with Singing,* Zeph. iii. 17. Doth GOD *rest,* complacently and continually rest in his Love towards you in CHRIST: And will not *you rest in it?* Is it the infinite Resolve of GOD's *Heart,* to save you thro' CHRIST: And will you not *believe it?* Will GOD *rejoice over you,* to do you Good with his whole Heart, and with his whole Soul, and joy over you therein with *Singing:* And shall not *your* Hearts and Souls, *sing and rejoice,* in and with *Him?* Oh hearken to your Lord's Voice, even you who are the weakest Lambs of Christ's Fold: For unto you he saith, *Rejoice in the Lord always: And again I say, Rejoice,* Phil. iv. 4.—And hence, my Brethren, While you live and walk by Faith, I would give a Hint,

Secondly, That it is the Duty and Privilege of a *Believer,* to improve his Faith, unto *Holiness. Abide in me,* saith our Lord, *and I in you. As the Branch cannot bear Fruit of itself, except it abide in the Vine: No more can ye, except ye abide in me. I an the Vine, ye are the Branches: He that abideth in me, and I in Him, the same bringeth forth much Fruit: for without me, ye can do nothing,* John xv.4, 5. Believing our Interest in JESUS, it is our Duty to go out of our empty needy Selves, unto the Fulness of Christ by Faith, to derive Life and Strength from Him continually, to maintain and increase our Graces, and to enable us for all holy Duties. And the more we improve our Faith of Interest in Christ, to abide in Him as our Root of Influence; the more Sap and Nourishment shall we derive from Him, to enable us to bring forth Fruit unto God. The more will our dear Lord, and His, and our Father, be glorify'd in us, if we bear much Fruit. And the greater our Obedience of Faith and Love is; the greater will be our Lord's Joy in us, as obedient Children to Him, as fruitful Branches in Him; and the more abundant will be our own Joy. As, Ver. 8,-11. *Herein is my Father glorified, that ye bear much Fruit, so shall ye be my Disciples. These Things have I spoken unto you, that my Joy might remain in you, and that your Joy might be full.* Those are fruitful Christians, glorious Souls, who improve their Faith of Interest in Christ, unto abiding in Him, and deriving from Him continually; in Order to their walking with Him closely, in the white Garments of a Gospel-Conversation, or in *all Manner of holy Conversation and Godliness.* Faith and Holiness, are closely *connected* in the Gospel of Christ. *And having an High Priest over the House of God:* Says the Apostle, *Let us draw near with a true Heart, in full Assurance of Faith, having our Hearts sprinkled from an evil Conscience, and our Bodies washed with pure Water. Let us hold fast the Profession of our Faith without wavering, (for He is faithful that hath promised) And let us consider one another to provoke unto Love, and to good Works,* Heb. x. 21, 22, 23. And thus he addresses the Saints, 2 *Cor.* vii. 1. *Having therefore these Promises, (dearly beloved) let us cleanse ourselves from all Filthiness of the Flesh and Spirit, perfecting Holiness in the Fear of God.* The Lord that was the *Author,* will be the *Finisher of our Faith:* And yet we are exhorted to *hold fast our Confidence. The God of Peace will sanctify us wholly:* And yet we are exhorted to *Cleanse ourselves, and to perfect Holiness in his Fear.* Which shews us, That the same Work, which is God's *efficiently,* is ours *instrumentally:* Or, that *God* will do it for us, in the Use of those *Means* which He hath appointed. And as *holding fast the Profession of our Faith without Wavering,* we are exhorted to *provoke one another unto Love, and to good Works:* And as *having these Promises,* we are exhorted to *Cleanse ourselves,* &c. It shews us, that *Faith* and full *assurance* of Faith, hath a glorious *Influence* into *Holiness,* and is a strong *Motive* thereunto. And therefore the Apostle *John,* when he says, in the full Assurance of Faith,

Beloved, now are we the Sons of God, and it doth not yet appear what we shall be: but we know, that when He shall appear, we shall be like Him; for we shall see Him as He is, 1 John iii. 2. He adds, *And every Man that hath this Hope in him, purifieth himself, even as He is pure,* Ver. 3. And, *He that saith he abideth in Him, ought himself also so to walk, even as He also walked,* Chap. ii. 6.—Thus it appears to be the *Duty* of a Believer, to improve his Faith, unto *Holiness.* As we ought to take up our *Faith* of Interest in Christ and his Salvation, first and principally, upon the Credit of the free and faithful *Promise* of a GOD that cannot *lie,* made in his Book, and apply'd to the Heart of every one that believeth in JESUS; and to hold this fast in the Face of a thousand Discouragements from the Strength of remaining Corruptions, and the Weakness of our Graces: So likewise, for the *Glory of God,* we ought to improve Faith, unto *Holiness.* And as this is our Duty; so our *Privilege.* For our own *Comfort* too, ought we thus to put *Faith out to Use.* Inasmuch as when *Faith* at God's Command, goes out directly to its *Object; Sense* by his Appointment, come in, in an orderly Way, to corroborate and strengthen *Faith's Testimony.* And therefore saith this Apostle *John, And hereby we do* know *that we know him, if we keep his Commandments,* 1 John ii. 3. And thus the Apostle *Paul, and we desire that every one of you do shew the same Diligence, unto the full* Assurance *of Hope unto the End,* Heb. vi. 11. And as, my Brethren, our Growth in Grace, and in the Knowledge of Christ, will be proportionable to our Diligence in the Use of Means; as God's manifestative Glory and our present Comfort are greatly concern'd herein; So likewise is our future *Crown of Righteousness,* that Reward of good Works, which of the freest Grace, awaits Believers at Christ's Appearing. As 1*Cor.* iii. 13, 14. And thus the Apostle *Peter* exhorts the Saints, unto whom *are given exceeding great and precious Promises, that by these they might be Partakers of the Divine Nature, having escaped the Pollution which is in the World through Lust: Giving all Diligence, add to your Faith, Virtue; and to Virtue, Knowledge; and to Knowledge, Temperance; and to Temperance, Patience; and to Patience, Godliness; and to Godliness, brotherly Kindness; and to brotherly Kindness, Charity. For* (saith he) *if these Things be in you, and abound, they make you that ye shall neither be barren nor unfruitful in the Knowledge of our Lord Jesus Christ. But he* *that lacketh these Things, is blind, and cannot see far off, and hath forgotten that he was purged from his old Sins.* (The Believer, that don't give all Diligence, to add to his Faith, Holiness; weakens his confidence in the Forgiveness of Sins, and raises Mists of Darkness, to obscure the Glory thereof from his View) *Wherefore the rather, Brethren, give Diligence to make your Calling and Election* sure: (To make it stand forth to be seen in the Fruits of it, to the glory of God, as it were unshaken before all; that by contrary walking, your Interest in electing and calling Grace may not seem to totter, or fall, to the View of others, nor yet appear uncertain in your own Sight) *For if ye do these Things,* saith the Apostle, *ye shall never* fall. (From your own Steadfastness in Faith and Holiness, while another outruns you, and takes your Crown) *For so an Entrance shall be ministred unto you* abundantly (as rich Heirs of Glory, filled with the Fruits of Righteousness) *into the everlasting Kingdom of our Lord and Saviour Jesus Christ,* 2 Pet. i. 4, *&c.*—

Unto you then, my dear Brethren, who are enabled to *live by Faith,* when you have not spiritual *Sense,* gracious Frames, and joyful inward Feelings to rest on; unto *you* let me say, As you are blest with the Faith of your Completeness *in Christ; Follow on to know* HIM, *the Fellowship of his Sufferings, and the Power of his Resurrection* more and more in your *own Souls* daily. You are now complete *in Christ.* You are shortly to be so *thro' Him,* in your *own Persons.* Oh, Abiding in Christ by *Faith,* hasten on, in the Use of all the *Means of Grace,* unto that *Day's Glory!* I know that the Love of Christ, and of God in Him, will *constrain you;* that Assurance of Faith, hath a glorious *Influence* into all holy Practice. But yet, my Brethren, the Lord sees we need, and we ought to suffer, *The Word of Exhortation.* For as Satan tempts us to *Unbelief,* from our Incompleteness in *ourselves,* while we look for spiritual *Sense* to assist our *Faith,* for personal Holiness, to help us to believe the Promises, or first and primarily to take up our Faith of Interest in them from thence: So when we are blest with the Faith of our Completeness *in Christ,* when the glorious Influence which attends the Moments of Discovery, is worn oft our Spirits; Satan may tempt us to *carnal Security.* And our own slothful Hearts, may insensibly sink into *spiritual Laziness,* and a Neglect of that vigorous Pursuit after *personal Holiness,* which is call'd for of those who believe their *Completeness in* JESUS. As on the one Hand, being tempted, we adhere too much to *Sense,* before we will *believe:* So on the other Hand, it is possible that we may be tempted, when we begin to *go by Faith,* to have too great a *Disregard* of spiritual Sense.—I speak not thus, my honour'd Brethren, as if I knew, or thought, that this was the Case with any of *you.* But I only give a Hint, that in this Respect, as well as in others, we *all* ought to beware of *Satan's Devises;* who at all Times, and by all Ways, seeks to hinder our Faith and Holiness. And also to keep up an holy *Watch* over our own *wicked Hearts,* which are naturally bent to Backsliding from God. Let us *first* be concern'd about our Duty, and to enjoy our Privilege, of *Believing without Sight,* of Believing our Interest in Christ, had his Salvation, merely upon the Credit of the free Promise of the faithful and unchanging God, amidst a thousand Changes in ourselves: and *next,* let us most earnestly labour after *Sense,* or the sensible Enjoyment of God, and an entire Dedication to Him. If we duly regard the *former,* we can't be too much in earnest about the *latter.* Sense is an unspeakable Privilege, when it is *added* to Faith. When Sense is kept in a due Subordination of Faith, and follows it in its appointed Order; it is like adding another Sail to a Ship, to make its Motion more swift. Let Faith be the main *Top-sail;* and Sense as a *lower Sail,* will be of vast Advantage. When Faith and Sense are *join'd,* or Faith and all the other Graces are in *Exercise,* in the Duties and beauties of Holiness; when all Sails are *up,* when all Sails are *fill'd* with the glorious Gales of the *Holy Ghost;* That soul hath *full Assurance,* or in *full Sail of Faith,* runs sweetly and swiftly, as it were directly before the Heavenly wind, unto its desired Haven of *eternal Glory.* Those are glorious Christians, who in an unshaken Faith of their Interest in Christ, and in God thro' Him, are *Men:* And yet in their Desires after Communion with God in Love, or a frequent *tasting that the Lord is gracious,* to influence their Souls into all gracious Practice, are like *newborn Babes.* Oh my Brethren, our Lord, our God, is a *Lover:* And He takes an infinite Pleasure in his *People's Love.* In our loving of *Him,* who first loved *us.* Our loving Lord, delights to have us like *fond Children,* that want always to hang on the *Breast,* and be dandled on the *Knee,* and that can't endure their Parent's *Absence.* Highly our Lord commended the Church at *Ephesus* for her Obedience, *Rev.* ii.

2, 3. *Nevertheless,* saith he, *I have somewhat against thee, because thou hast left thy* first Love, Ver. 4. We should have more of our Lord's Presence, if we could not be contented without it, if we did not let Trifles and Creature-Vanities run away with our Hearts. *Therefore* (saith the Prophet) *Thou hast forsaken thy People, the House of* Jacob, *because they be replenished from the* East, *—and they please themselves in the* Children of Strangers, *Isa.* ii. 6. It was well said by a dear Servant of Christ, "*Faith* carries it above all the Graces, in Point of *Justification:* But *Love* above all, in Point of Christ's *Manifestation of Himself.* Christ knows what it is to *love;* and no Soul shall *die* for the *Love of Him." Fond Souls* that love the Enjoyment of Christ, and are earnest to shew their Love to Him in keeping his Commandments; shall be eminently blessed with *his,* and with his *Father's Presence.* According to his Promise, John xiv. 21, 23. *He that hath my Commandments, and keepeth them, He it is that loveth me: And he that* loveth me, *shall be* loved *of my* Father, *and I will* love him, *and will* manifest myself *unto him.—And* we *will* come *unto him, and make our* Abode *with him.*—Come then, my Brethren, you that are blest with the Views of your *Completeness in Christ,* and with the Faith of *Interest* in God's eternal and unchangeable *Love thro' him;* with this strong *Wine* of the Gospel, refresh'd as *Giants,* rejoice to run the *Race* that is set before you, in all holy Obedience. Oh, none have such Furniture of Holiness, and are under such high Obligations to this glorious Liberty, as those Christians, who are blest with the Faith of Assurance, with the View of their unchangeable Completeness in Christ, amidst all the Variations of their own Frames. Come, my Brethren, look to CHRIST, your glorious *Pattern:* See you not, how perfectly *dead you are to sin, and alive unto God in Christ?* Rom. vi. 11. See you not the complete Glory of the second *Adam,* and your Completeness in Him? Oh remember, that as is the *Head,* so must be the *Members.* As is the *Heavenly Man,* so must those be that are *Heavenly.* Such they *are* in a begun Measure; such they *shall be* in the highest Perfection, *1 Cor.* xv. 48. Are you *dead to Sin in Christ?* Oh, *Let not Sin live and reign in your mortal Body, that you should obey it in the Lusts thereof,* Rom. vi. 12. Are you *alive unto God in Christ?* Oh rest not in *dead lifeless Frames;* but seek renewed Quicknings, from Christ your living Head, from Him the second *Adam,* who is to you, *a quickning*

Spirit, 1 Cor. xv. 45. Is your *Fruit unto God,* found *in Christ,* your *green Fir-Tree?* Oh rest not in a *barren, fruitless Condition* in your *own Souls;* but in the Use of all appointed Means, seek for fresh divine Influences, that you may have your *Fruit unto Holiness;* the *End* whereof will be *Everlasting Life,* Rom. vi. 22. Are you made *nigh* unto God *in Christ,* admitted into the highest Favour and Fellowship? Oh endure not *Distance* from God in your *own Souls;* you are called into *Fellowship with the Father, and with his son Jesus Christ: Draw nigh to God, and He will draw nigh to you,* Jam. iv. 8—Oh my Brethren, May we not blame *ourselves* for our own Deadness, Unfruitfulness, and Distance from God? Hath HE ever *said to the Seed of* Jacob, *seek ye ME in vain?* Do we not rather *lie down* upon a Bed of Sloth, when our *Beloved* withdraws himself; then *arise* to seek Him in the Use of *Means,* till the *Grace* of the Means flows down upon us, and quickens us to a holy Earnestness, and Restlessness of Spirit, until we *find him whom our Souls love?* In a Word, my Brethren, Are we *complete in Christ?* Do we *believe it,* and so enter into *Rest by Faith?* Never let us *rest from Duty,* till in conformity to him, we are *compleat in ourselves.* Let us not think, *That we have already attained, or that we are already perfect:* but let us *follow after, if that we may apprehend that* (perfect Holiness and Glory) *for which also we are apprehended of Christ Jesus,* Phil. iii. 12.—And now, my dear Brethren, *That the God of Peace, may fill you all, with all Joy and Peace in Believing; sanctify you wholly in Spirit, Soul and Body: And preserve you blameless unto the Coming of our Lord Jesus Christ:* Is the hearty Desire of,

My Honour'd Brethren,
Your most Affectionate Friend
And humble Servant,
In our glorious LORD,
The once Slain, now
Reigning LAMB,

______ _____.

FINIS.

ERRATA.

[Errata corrected in text]

2

LETTERS
ON
Spiritual Subjects,
AND
DIVERS OCCASIONS;
SENT TO
RELATIONS and FRIENDS.

By One who has tasted that the LORD is Gracious.

LONDON:

Printed; and Sold by JOHN OSWALD, at the *Rose and Crown* in the *Poultry*, near the *Mansion-house;* and EBENEZER GARDNER, at *Milton's Head* in *Grace-church-street.* 1740.

[Price Bound One Shilling and Sixpence.]

THE

AUTHOR's EPISTLE

TO

The Persons to whom the following LETTERS were wrote.

My dear Friends,

As many of you have testify'd your kind Acceptance of these Tokens of my Love, when they were wrote to you, and that the Lord was pleas'd to make them of Use to your Souls; so I doubt not your Acceptance of them, now they are presented to you in Print. Especially since, together with those which were wrote to any One of you in particular, there are several more which were wrote to other Friends, which are here presented to your View, which otherwise you might not have seen.

And as to those of my Friends, to whom I have wrote Letters, which are not inserted in this little Tract; I intreat that they will not take it as a Mark of Disrespect, that their Letters were not plac'd among the rest. For, of many of the Letters which I have wrote, I kept no Copies; and those Copies which I did preserve, which are still in my Hands, were too many to be inserted in this Book, if it had been twice as large as it is: So that as to them, God only knows whether they'll ever see publick Light.

Perhaps some may think, that if any of my Letters were Printed, it wou'd have been more proper to have had them done after my Decease; and of this Mind I had us'd to be myself. But as others have thought, that if they were publish'd now, they might be of present Use, and have therefore desir'd the same, unto which I have consented; I hope none will be offended, that they are done while I am living; since, for that reason, I have entirely conceal'd my Name. And I well know, that all that is valuable in them, is from the Lord; and that all the Imperfection that is in them, is mine. But if God will ordain Strength to any of his Children, by the Lispings of so weak a Babe; as it will be my Joy, so He shall have all the Praise.

And therefore, as to these Letters which are now extant, if God hereby may be glorify'd, and his People reap any Advantage; I shall have my End in their Publication. And for this, I intreat you all, that are my Friends, to help, by your Prayers, your Friend that loves you in the Bowels of JESUS CHRIST.

LETTERS

ON

Spiritual Subjects, *&c.*

LETTER I.

To Mr. W. *and* E. C.

Dear Brother and Sister,

MAY the Peace of God that passeth all Understanding, keep your Heart and Mind thro' Christ Jesus!

I am exceeding glad that you are helpt to bear your Loss patiently; believing that the Lord will do you good by it. Our dear Father, never takes any good Thing from us, but in order to give something better. He has taken away your Pebbles, to give you Pearls; Empty'd you of Riches in Shew, to fill you with True Riches, and Never-failing Substance. Bless him therefore, for Taking as well as Giving. His Love cast the Lot this Way; Believe it, and you'll like it well. A little Grace is better than much Gold. You will be great Gainers by your Loss, if the Lord give you submission to his sovereign Dispose under it, Acquiescence with his good Pleasure in it, and a further Acquaintance with Himself, as your everlasting ALL by it. Mr. *Rutherford* calls the World, "The Clay-portion of Bastards; not the Inheritance of Children." 'Tis a great Thing for a Saint that is rich in this World, to be throughly sensible of its Nothingness; and to live beside his outward Enjoyments, upon that Infinite, Inexhaustible Fullness he has in God. The Creatures stand as a Blind between us and Him. And God loves his Children so, that he calls for our Hearts; and rather than want 'em, he'll strike the Creatures dead, that Himself, the Life of all our Joys, might be exceedingly endear'd to us. He'll dry up the Streams of Creature-comforts, that our thirsty Souls may learn to drink their Fill at the Fountain-Head. And so great is his Grace, that it pleaseth him well, to see his Children come to his Bosom for all they want, when starv'd out of Creature-Supplies! Oh what Fools are we to catch at Shadows, and let go the Substance, the Sum and Quintessence of all our Bliss! Oh how happy should we be, if infinite Sweetness did always ravish our Souls, and unheart us from all the Creatures! Oh, the Crystal Streams, which proceed out of the Throne of God, and of the Lamb, how sweet are they at the Well-Head! What a pure River of Water of Life should we swim in if we always liv'd in God! This will be our Life in Heaven, to the utmost Perfection; and happy they, who are aspiring after the rising Glory, and highest Degree of it here on Earth!

The Father of Mercies, and God of all Comfort, fill you with all Joy and Peace in Believing!

I am Yours in Christ for ever, &c.

LETTER II.

To Mr. W. *and* E. C.

Dear Brother and Sister,

AS to my Health, Blessed be God, I am not worse than I was when Brother was here. I dwell in a crasy Tabernacle, which I think, sometimes, is near its Dissolution. But I rejoice in that *House,* that *Building of God, Eternal in the Heavens,* which I know, thro' Grace, is prepar'd for me. I *in this Tabernacle groan, being burdened,* by reason of that Sinfulness, and Weakness which attends, and renders me incapable either to know or serve the Lord as I would, and as perfect Spirits do: and this makes me long for the Time when *Mortality shall be swallowed up of Life.* We have no reason to be afraid of a separate State; for *Blesses are the Dead which died in the Lord,* Rev. xiv. 13. Nor yet should the Saints be afraid to die; as if they should be forsaken, and left to go thro' the last Trial alone. No, our God will be with us when we come to the River Death; he will divide the Water before us, and so marvellously appear in carrying us thro' it, that we shall take thence a Memorial of his

Infinite Grace and Faithfulness; as the Children of *Israel* did when they passed thro' the literal *Jordan,* Josh. iv. 7. We should come up from the Wilderness, even to the last Step of it, leaning upon our Beloved; who hath said, *I will never leave thee, nor forsake thee,* Heb. xiii. 5. This Word *Never Leave thee,* reacheth thro' our whole Lives, even unto Death; yea, into Death, thro' Death, above and beyond Death, even to an endless Eternity. And unless everlasting Arms could wax weary, unchangeable Love alter, and Infinite Faithfulness fail, we have no reason to be afraid; No, not *in the Valley of the Shadow of Death,* Psa. xxiii. 4. Our God will be *our Refuge and Strength, a very present Help in* that *Time of Trouble,* Psa. xlvi. 1. And as he will be *the Strength of* our *Heart,* when *Heart and Flesh fail* us, so, our *Portion for ever,* or our eternal Lot. And oh, who can count up a thousandth part of those vast Treasures of Glory we have in his immense BEING, as he has made over his Great SELF to us in Christ! Why should we then, that are *the King's Sons,* be *lean from Day to Day?* The Lord grant us true Greatness of Mind, that with a *Princely* Spirit, we may behave as *Heirs* of Glory under our present Trials!

Wishing all Prosperity, and begging a Share of your Prayers, I commit you to *Israel's* Keeper, and rest,

With dear Love, Yours in the Lord, &c.

LETTER III.

To Mr. W. *and* E. C.

Dear Brother and Sister,

Grace and Peace from God our Father, and from Jesus Christ our Lord, be multiply'd unto you.

I am persuaded, that the Lord is doing you great Good by the great Exercises you meet with. *As many as* the Lord *loves,* he *rebukes and chastens.* The Lord help you to believe, that all your Trials are so many fresh Tokens of that boundless Love, which is in his Heart towards you: and to receive them from his Hand accordingly, with Submission, Patience, Cheerfulness and Thankfulness! Your *light Affliction,* which is *but for a Moment, worketh for you a far more exceeding and eternal Weight of*

Glory; while you *look not at the Things which are seen, which are temporal, but at the Things which are not seen, which are eternal.* Patience is a perfecting Grace: and we are exhorted to *let Patience have its perfect Work, that* we *may be perfect and entire, wanting nothing,* Jam. i. 4. When the Saints, (as one well says) have learn'd to bear a Cross, they shall wear a Crown. Our dear Lord Jesus, *tho' he were a Son,* (such a Son!) *yet he learned Obedience by the Things which he suffered.* And the Members must be conform'd to their Head, in Sufferings, as well as in Glory, to meeten 'em for their Inheritance, and prepare 'em for their Crown. Let us reckon then, that all our Time-Trials, (as they flow from God's Love, thro the Blood of Christ, and are under the sanctifying Influences of the Holy Ghost) to be *greater Riches than the Treasures of* Egypt, or this dark World.

And now, that you both may be *strengthned with all Might, according to God's glorious Power, unto all Patience, and Long-suffering with Joyfulness,* is the earnest Desire of

Yours, &c.

LETTER IV.

To Mr. H. T.

Dear Sir,

My beloved Brother in Christ,

IT is upon my Heart to write a few Lines to you, to beseech you, in the Bowels of Jesus Christ, and by all that Love and Grace which has been display'd in your Salvation, that you walk worthy of the Vocation wherewith you are called. Oh, *remember, That in Time past,* you was a *Gentile in the Flesh.* And at that Time, you was a *Stranger* to God, and an *Enemy in* your *Mind, by* reason of *wicked Works.* That then, being under the Government of *the Prince of Darkness,* you had your Conversation among *the Children of Disobedience,* walking according to *the Course of this World, fulfilling the Desires of the Flesh and of the Mind;* and was *by Nature a Child of Wrath, even as others.* And, oh, what did Free-Grace, and boundless Mercy do for you in that Day! When the Lord pass'd by you, and saw you *polluted in* your own *Blood, dead in Sins,* and said unto you, *Live!* Surely, your *Time,* That Time, was a *Time of* LOVE! What Sins did Free-Grace forgive! What Provocations did it pass by! How throughly did it Wash, Purify, and Beautify your Soul! What a glorious *Robe of Righteousness* did it cast over you! How richly did it anoint you with *the Oil of Gladness,* the Spirit of Grace, as a Sanctifier and Comforter! And in a Word, what a rich *Crown* of *Loving Kindness* did it set upon your Head! So that you was *exceeding beautiful,* and did *prosper into a Kingdom;* being made by Jesus Christ, a *King,* and a *priest* unto God and His father!

And now, what think you do you owe to Free-Grace! Is it not worthy to be glorify'd by your whole Spirit, Soul and Body? When you was first espoused to Christ, did you not give him your whole self? Did you not count him worthy of all Love, Duty, and Glory? Did you not Then like his *Kingly,* as well as his *Priestly* Office? And count Obedience to his Scepter your high Privilege, as well as Forgiveness of Sins thro' his Blood? And is your Mind alter'd now? Do you think Jesus Christ is less worthy of your Love, Duty, and Glory now, than he was Then? Is he less excellent in Himself? or in any of his Glorious Offices? Or is all his Excellency, Love and Grace to you, of little worth? of no Force to constrain you to live to Him? Oh, my dear Brother, what an abominable, hateful Thing is Sin! What a Dishonour doth it cast upon, and how contrary is it to God, Father, Son, and Spirit! How doth it slight and thwart the Design of the Father's Love, which was to make us perfectly holy! How doth it contemn the Grace of Christ, and contradict the End of his Death, which was to purify unto Himself a peculiar People, zealous of good Works! And how doth it slight and thwart the gracious Design of the Holy Spirit, who has taken Possession of our Souls, to work us up into a full Conformity to Christ, our holy Head! and how, by sin, do we grieve him! *Depart from us, we desire not the Knowledge of thy Ways,* is the Language of every Sin to each of the Three Persons in the glorious Godhead. By every Act of Sin, we do as it were, renounce our Allegiance to God in Christ, and to Him, as *Sion's* King; and, as far as in us lies, put ourselves afresh under the Dominion of *Satan;* preferring the

Prince of Darkness, and his hellish Dictates, before the Prince of Light, and the glorious Teachings of his Word and Spirit! Oh, horrid!

And as for ourselves, Oh, what a Soul-destroying thing is Sin! Every Sin is a Step taken back towards *Egypt's* Land; towards that Nature-Darkness, and Bondage, from which Free-Grace, boundless Mercy, and Almighty Power set us free. 'Tis making a *Captain* to return into *Egypt;* lothing the heavenly *Manna,* and longing after the *Flesh-pots,* the *Onions* and *Garlick,* the abominable Fare we once fed on, while in the Kingdom of *Satan,* when we *drank Iniquity like Water.* It brings Death upon our Comforts, Fruitfulness, and Usefulness in the World: for *if we live after the Flesh,* we *shall die.* By Sin, we lose our Opportunities of glorifying God upon the Earth; and so, that Praise, Honour, and Glory we should otherwise receive in the Day of Christ. Yea, as by Sin we dishonor God, and abide not in Christ; so we shall be ashamed before Him at his coming. If we should be sav'd at last; yet how sad will it be to lose all our Works? For that *fiery Day* will *try* all *the Works* of God's dear Children. *If any Man's Work abide, he shall receive a Reward: If any Man's Work be burnt, he shall suffer Loss: But he himself* (upon the bottom of Sovereign Grace) *shall be saved, yet so as by Fire;* or as a Person just escapes, with his Life, the Violence of the Flames, and has all his Goods consumed. 1 *Cor.* iii. 13, *&c.* This is our *Seeds-time,* and every Thought, Word and Action, may fitly be compar'd to *sowing of Seed.* And *he that soweth to* his *Flesh, shall of the Flesh reap Corruption; but he that soweth to the Spirit, shall of the Spirit reap Life Everlasting;* or that *incorruptible Crown of Glory,* for which the Apostle says, He, and the Saints *ran* their Christian-Race, *Gal.* vi. 8. 1 Cor. ix. 25.

Upon the whole, my dear Brother, have you been *joined to Idols?* Oh say, *What have I to do any more with* them? Have you turned away from the Lord? Oh return unto *Him* again! For he is *Merciful* and *Gracious,* and will not *cause his Anger to fall upon* you. He'll have Mercy upon you, and *abundantly pardon. If we confess our Sins,* (over the Head of the great Sacrifice, looking by Faith afresh upon Christ, who once *bare* them *in his own Body on the Tree) he is faithful and just to forgive us our Sins, and to cleanse us from all Unrighteousness.*

And as a Means to make you hate sin, and strengthen you against it, look upon it oft thro' the Glass of a crucify'd Jesus. Bring it, by Faith, to the Cross of Christ, and see if there is not Virtue enough in the Blood of your crucified Saviour, to *crucify the Flesh with the Affections and Lusts.* And whenever you find your Heart enclined to any Evil, think thus; What did my dear Lord once bear for my Sin? Can I love that, which was so hateful, and lothsom unto Him? Can I take Pleasure in That, which fill his bitter Cup? Can I take Sin by the Hand, and thereby take up a Sword as it were to wound and pierce my Lord afresh? Have I not pierc'd him enough already? Can I not be contented without plucking the Crown from his Head, who dy'd to crown me? I intreat you to think thus; yea, I charge you in the Name of the Lord, to put these Questions to your Soul, in an *Hour of Temptation.* And if they will not move you; you may be sure, that your Soul is in sad Case, and greatly *harden'd thro' the Deceitfulness of Sin.* And every fresh Act of Sin will harden your Heart more and more, and make you less capable to resist Temptations; until, perhaps, you provoke the Lord to give you up to the Power of Sin and Satan, in such a Manner, as at present you little think of; and also to bring a severe Rod upon you by his own Hand. Believe it, that sinning against God will be *Bitterness* in the End. And Sins against Light and Love are the most presumptuous, and of the deepest Dye. Again, as a Means to keep your Heart in a holy Bent against Sin, be frequent in secret Prayer, ejaculatory, at least; ask Help of God; try this Weapon of All-Prayer. And read and meditate on God's Word. If we were diligent in the Use of Means, to keep our Hearts in an holy Frame, we should not be so apt to fall in with Temptations as we are. If we were fill'd with the Spirit of Grace, the Life and *Sap* of our holy Root, we should be like green Wood, not apt to take Fire. But it is our Dryness, because we *abide not* in Christ by Faith, that ruins us. Once more, another Means I intreat you to make Use of, is, Watchfulness. Watch the first Motions of Sin, and kill 'em in the *Bud.* Beware likewise, that you go not to the *String's-End.* As it were; that you go not to the utmost of that Liberty you think you may have, and yet keep from the Act of Sin. Dallying with Temptations, is entering into them. Converse with Satan is the ready

Way to be overcome. If we wou'd not yield to any Act of Sin; let's beware that we yield not to a pleasing Thought about it.

And now, That the Grace of Christ may be sufficient for you, and his Strength made perfect in your Weakness, is the earnest Desire of,

Sir, Yours in the Lord, &c.

LETTER V.

To R. K.

Dear Sister in our Precious Jesus,

LEST you should question my Love, tho' in Haste, I wou'd write a few Lines. We have had many sweet Feasts with our Beloved in the Wilderness: But the richest Provisions, and the best Wine are reserved till the last; and the Marriage-Supper hastens. The Lord grant you may grow in Grace, and in the Knowledge of Christ! Oh, how little have we seen of his transcendent Beauty! We have beheld so much of his Glory, as to make him *the chiefest of Ten Thousand* in our Esteem: But there is enough in him to fill Men and Angels with new Wonder to all Eternity! Christ's Riches, are absolutely unsearchable; a Mine that we can never bottom to Eternity! We shall see more and more of his Glory, as we pass on towards Perfection; and Oh, the wonderful Grace that is to be brought unto us at our Lord's next Appearing, which, in a Way of Eminence, will be *The Revelation of Jesus Christ!* The Views of his Glory, which we have had here, tho' true and real, yet are so small, that if compar'd with what we shall have then, it will be as if we had never seen him; and as if he was but then reveal'd to us. We shall be so ravish'd with the Views of his Glory, that we shall never be able to look off his bright Face for ever.

I am Yours in Christ, &c.

LETTER VI.

To Mrs. E. B.

Much honour'd and beloved Sister,

Grace and Peace be multiply'd unto you, thro' the Knowledge of God, and of Jesus our Lord.

Yours I received, and return you abundant Thanks for your great Kindness shewn towards us, and unto me, who am the most unworthy, *and less than the least of all* Christ's. And none of your Kindness shewn towards my dear Lord, in the weakest of his Members, shall be unrewarded at his next Appearing.

If you smelt any Fragrancy on us, it was Christ's Sweetness cast upon us that delighted your spiritual Sense. And if *an Unction from the holy One,* a Drop of that holy Oil cast upon a Creature, be so fragrant; what must the immeasurable Fulness of the Lord's Anointed, the Christ of God, be! *For God giveth not the Spirit by Measure unto Him.* Oh the transcendent Fragrancy of our Beloved! *The Smell of His Garments* delight the Saints, both in the upper and lower Worlds. There are little Sparks of Beauty and Excellency scatter'd up and down in the Creatures; especially among *the Saints, the Excellent of the Earth,* as new Creatures: but all Beauties, in their flaming Glories, are summed up, and radiantly shine in the Person of Christ, as God-Man! There is in Christ, not only the Beauty of the whole Creation, but even uncreated Beauty itself. What's all the Beauty of the Creatures, of Men and Angels, in both Worlds, if compar'd to his; in whom *the Fulness of the Godhead dwelleth Bodily!* None in the Heavens can be compared unto the LORD, none among the Sons of the Mighty can be likened unto the LORD; the LORD, the Mediator. No, the Heavens praise him as God's WONDER! *Psal.* lxxxix. 5, 6. The glorious Hosts of Saints and Angels above, under the surprising and increasing Displays of his Glory, eternally adore that uncreated Beauty and Brightness which shines forth in our exalted Jesus! The crowned Saints *cast down their Crowns* before his Throne, and shrink to nothing, as it were, in themselves, before the Displays of his infinite Majesty, Love, and Grace! *Rev.* iv. 20. The whole Host of *Seraphims,* Angels, and Archangels, *vail* their *Faces,* and *cover their Feet,* as unworthy to stand in his Presence, or to look on the refulgent Brightness of his unsearchable Glory; as the *Train* of divine Perfections *fills* the *Temple* of his glorified human Nature! *Isa.* vi. 1, 2. And as for the Saints below, when favour'd with the least Glimpse of his Glory, he is the *chiefest of ten Thousand* in their Esteem, and *altogether lovely!* They have *none in Heaven* but him, nor upon *the* Earth that they desire besides him, or in comparison with him. *Song* v. 10, 16. *Psa.* lxxv. 25. Oh how happy, are those Souls who have an Interest in this great Lord Jesus! And are blest with the transforming Shine of his inconceivable Glory! Oh, what Folly are we guilty of, when we forsake this *Fountain of living Waters,* and *hew out to* ourselves *broken Cisterns that can hold no Water!* Jer. ii. 13. When we forsake the infinite Fulness of Christ, and seek Contentment in Creatures, and Creature-Excellencies! *The Way of Life is above to the Wise:* Prov. xv. 24. The Way of Faith, by which Life is possest and enjoy'd, is, to live out of ourselves, upon the Christ of God, in all his infinite Fulness and Fitness to save Sinners, from the Depths of Misery, to the Height of Glory.

Dear Sister, you say, "That I will not allow you to put Ifs, concerning your Interest in the Lord Jesus." But if I would not; it is not for Want of Bowels towards you, nor Sympathy with you in all your Soul-Distresses. No, I can say, thro' Grace, that, in the Bowels of my dear Lord Jesus, I have a compassionate Tenderness towards all his suffering Members; and, in an especial Manner, an inward Fellow-feeling with the Lambs of his Flock, under all their Harassings by the *roaring Lion:* and glad, exceeding glad should I be, if by any Means, I might be made helpful to 'em in the Combat. But having seen somewhat of that Dishonour Unbelief brings unto God, and found what Discomfort it has brought to my own Soul; I would exhort my dear Brethren and Sisters, to take God at his Word, as to their eternal Salvation, in looking unto Jesus; and to hold fast the Confidence of their eternal Security, in the Face of ten Thousand Difficulties, and seeming Contrarieties, merely upon the Word and Oath of a God that cannot lie: who has laid himself under such Engagements, on purpose that *the Heirs of Promise might have strong Consolation, who have fled for Refuge to lay hold upon the Hope set before 'em.* Heb. vi. 18. The Lord, would not only have us to be safe, but to know our Safety, in fleeing to his dear Son for

Life. And when the Saints exhort one another to *hold fast the Beginning of* their *Confidence stedfast unto the End;* their Design herein, is, that God might have the Glory, and they the Comfort of this great Salvation. Nor are such Exhortations in vain: The Lord often blesseth them, as a Means, to encourage his dear Children in the *good Fight of Faith.* And I am perswaded, that God's fearful-hearted Ones would not so often speak the Language of Unbelief, if they did consider, what great Dishonour it casts upon God, in each of the three glorious Persons, as they have been, and are jointly engag'd in the Work of our Salvation; and likewise, how much they weaken their own Hands thereby. A few Thoughts, and Words of Faith, in a Time of Darkness, brings more Honour unto God, and Comfort to the Soul, than we are aware of. A Believer, by every Act of Faith, doth as it were afresh *set to his Seal that God is true;* and likewise *enters into Rest.* John iii. 33. Heb. iv. 3. Every Act of Faith brings present Honours to God, and Rest to the Soul. And, as Acts strengthen Habits; so every Act of Faith strengthens the Habit of Faith, and tends to weaken and subdue the Power of Unbelief. Whereas, by yielding to Unbelief, we give God the Lie, and weaken our own Hand; We thereby render ourselves more uncapable to fight it out in Faith, against the Powers of Darkness. We are exhorted to *take* unto us *the whole Armour of God,* that so we may be *able to withstand in the evil Day, and having done all to stand.* Eph. vi. 13. "Tis always an evil Day with God's Children, when they are assaulted about their Interest in the Lord Jesus: And if we have not then this Piece of Armour, the Helmet, on our Heads, the Hope of Salvation, (the objective Hope of Salvation, or the Ground we have of Hope of Salvation) the Enemy will wound us exceedingly.

As to the various Temptations, Darkness, and the Power of Unbelief, you are exercis'd with; *the same Afflictions are accomplish'd in your Brethren that are in the World.* The Children of God are all try'd in these respects, more or less. And 'tis well for us, that we have a sympathizing high Priest, who can have Compassion according to the Measure of our Distress; who has been *tempted in all Points like unto us,* that from an experimental Feeling of the Power of Temptation, he might know how, in the tenderest Bowels, to succour us when tempted. Not a Sorrow pierceth our Hearts, but our dear compassionate Head feels it: And he lives in Heaven, on purpose to save us out of all our Distresses, by his Advocacy and Intercession with His and Our Father, in the Virtue of his Great Sacrifice, and in the Interest of his Great Person. So that we are exceeding safe, who have trusted our Souls in the Hands of this Jesus, with whom the Father is well pleased, and in whom his Soul delighteth; so that he can deny him nothing that he asks. Yea, it shall certainly be well with us; since the Father himself loveth us; and from thence called his own Son to this Office of High-Priest for us upon the Throne, on purpose that the glorious Fruits of his Love, in our complete Salvation, might be communicated to us, in a Way of Honour to all the divine Perfections. And as we are safe, and it is, and shall be well with us, so we have great reason to be *exceeding joyful in all our Tribulations;* while we *fill up that which is behind of the Afflictions of Christ in our Flesh.* Col. i. 24. For even now, while we are Combatants, we are *more than Conquerors, thro' him that hath loved us,* Rom. viii. 37. *And if we suffer with him, we shall also be glorified together.* Ver. xvii. Our glorious Captain will *cover* our Heads *in the Day of Battle;* and as he has overcome For us, so he will certainly overcome In, and By us: He'll give the Victory on our Side, either actively, or passively. For tho', like *God,* a *Troop* may *overcome* us, yet *we shall overcome at the last.* If Sin and Satan should give us a Foil, then our dear Lord Jesus will lead us afresh to his Death; and so we shall overcome, passively, by the Blood of the Lamb. And then, having renewed Peace, under the Sprinklings of the Blood of Jesus, our Faith shall be rais'd up again, to bear a fresh Testimony for God, against the Prince of Darkness, and all the Powers of Sin; and so we shall overcome Actively. *Rev.* xii. 11. All the Weakness and Sin that attend us in the Conflict, forgiving Love will bury in the Depths of the Sea; and every Act of our tried Graces, *shall be found unto Praise, Honour, and Glory at the Appearing of Jesus Christ.* And when once we get to *the City of Habitation,* the *Rest that remains* for us, we shall bless God for all his Dealings with us, and admire the Conduct of wise Love, in *all the Way it led us thro' the Wilderness;* while we see every weary Step wisely over-ruled to make our Rest so much the more glorious. We shall then see, that we could not have been without any, the least of all our Trials, whatsoever they be; but God would have had less Glory, and *we* less Happiness. If we *are in Heaviness thro' manifold Temptations,* there's an absolute *Need* of it; that God might have his manifestative Glory, in our Deliverance, in all those various Rays which infinite Wisdom ordain'd; and that *We* might have that full and comprehensive Salvation, unto which we were appointed. Our suffering State will be quickly over; our reigning State hastens. And mean while, *our light Affliction,* which is but *for a Moment, worketh for us a far more exceeding and eternal Weight of Glory.* Let us then be *Followers of them, who thro' Faith and Patience,* do now *inherit the Promises;* reckoning *the Sufferings of this present Time not worthy to be compared with the Glory that shall be revealed in us,* 2 Cor. iv. 17. Heb. vi. 12. Rom. viii. 18.

I am glad, my dear Sister, that at Times, you are favour'd with Soul-amazing Prospects of your near and high Relation unto God in Christ; which humbles you in the Dust, before the Majesty of that Grace which shines forth herein. This is no less than Heaven begun in your Soul, a Sweet Fore-taste of that inconceivable Glory, you shall e're long have the full Possession of. A Cluster of *Canaan's* Grapes is brought you in the Wilderness; that so you might know, by spiritual Sense, as well as by Faith, that the Land whither you are going, is an exceeding good Land. And what tho', at other Seasons, thro' the Power of Unbelief, you may be kept low in your Soul; yet this makes no Change in your High Relation to God in Christ, nor in those high Privileges you have in Him. *If we believe not,* and so want the Joy of God's Salvation; *yet He abideth faithful, and cannot deny Himself,* in the unalterable Word and Oath which is gone out of his Mouth concerning it; and so the Salvation itself is eternally secur'd to us. When Darkness covers us; *The Darkness and the Light are both alike to Him:* and at such Times, we are especially call'd to live by Faith; to trust in the LORD, and *stay ourselves* upon our God, *Isa.* l. 10. He is Our God still, even when we have *no Light* of inward Comfort to walk by; and are ready to be driven away with Temptations: and it is the Excellency of Faith, to trust in *Jehovah,* and stay itself upon him, as its own God, at such Seasons.

You can with Comfort remember the Time past, when you was enabled to crowd thro' all your own Unworthiness, and inward Corruptions, to *Touch the Hem* of Christ's *Garment;* which you found to be *Healing* to your Soul. And as you have *received Christ Jesus the Lord,* so *walk in him,* Col. ii. 6. As we came to Christ at first, as undone Sinners in ourselves, to receive that free and full Salvation of God, prepar'd for us in Him; even so let us come unto him all our Days under a deep, and increasing Sense of our Emptiness, to be continually supply'd out of his inexhaustible Fulness. Faith is a Grace ordain'd of God, to take possession of Christ, and of Eternal Life in him: And let us be assured of our Eternal Safety, having run into Christ, the City of Refuge. How much sin soever there may in such a Soul, there is no Condemnation to it. No, blessed be God, our State in Christ, alters not a jot, with our Frames. The Discoveries of God's Favour towards us in his Son, may vary; but his Love, in itself, is as unchangeable as his Being. 'Tis an everlasting Round, that gloriously encloseth us from Eternity to Eternity. We are enclos'd in Grace by Father, Son, and Spirit; set in Grace in our Enclosings, as the precious Stones in *Aaron's* Breast-plate were set in pure Gold, *Exod.* xxviii. 20. So we are set, and have an eternal Fixation, an unchangeable Standing in Grace, *Rom.* v. 2. God's Love, like the Sun in the Firmament, always keeps a steady Course, whether we behold it, or Clouds hide its Glory from our View. And so various are its Emanations, that our Sight is much too weak to take in the full Glory of its Rays. Love walks in such various Ways, such unthought-of Paths, that we are often at a loss to trace its wondrous Steps in the mighty Race it runs. It will take up Eternity to admire its mysterious Circuits, in all its rich Aboundings according to the manifold Wisdom of God.

Grace be with you. Amen.

I am Yours in Christ, &c.

LETTER. VII.

To Mrs. M.

Dear Sister, whom I love and honour in the Lord,

I Rejoice with you, for the exceeding Riches of boundless Grace extended towards you, not only in the Salvation of your Soul; but also in that Assurance of Faith you are favour'd with : and likewise, that your longing Soul, under the ripening Influences of *the Son of Righteousness,* hath a *Desire to depart, and to be with Christ, which is far better.*

But yet, my dear Sister, I beseech you, *suffer that Word of Exhortation,* Jam. i. 4. *Let Patience have her perfect Work, that ye may be perfect and entire, wanting nothing.* Be willing to stay the Lord's Time; and fear not your losing any thing thereby. Christ comes *into his Garden to gather Lilies,* as soon as ever they are fully ripe for his own Bosom. He will gather you in, as a *Shock of Corn in its Season;* and not let you stay in the Field too long, to your Damage. No, your stay in the World is to prepare you for Glory; that Glory, which is laid up for you, and shall shortly be put upon you.

But it may be, you will say, "If I saw that Work go on, I should be willing to stay; but instead of being more prepar'd for Glory, I think, I am more unmeet."

But as to this, God is the best Judge of our Meetness for Glory; as also, of the Ways, Means, and Time to meeten us. Perhaps, you may not feel such a vehement Flame of Love, Joy, and Zeal as you was wont; and yet your Faith, Humility, and Patience may be greater. There's a Variety of Graces, in the Souls of the Saints; and each must have its Exercise, and proper Time of Trial.

If you have not now such Manifestations of Divine Favour, to the inflaming of your Love; yet it may be you may glorify God more, by believing in the Dark, by trusting in him when he seems to slay you, by cleaving to him when he seems to cast you off; as counting him both able and faithful, that hath promis'd, even in the Face of ten thousand Deaths and Difficulties, with which you are surrounded.

If, thro' the Lord's withdrawing his sensible Presence, and an increasing Sight of your own Corruptions, you do not shoot upwards in Spiritual Joy, as you was wont; yet you may grow more downwards in Humility, and Self-abasement.

And tho' your Zeal, in a way of active Obedience, may want that vehement Flame it once had; yet your Patience in passive Obedience, or your Fitness to endure a Variety of Trials, may be greater. And so you are still upon the Increase, even when you seem to decline.

And as to those very Graces, which seem to wither; there may not be such a Decay in them as you think of. They may decay in some Respects, and yet increase in others. For tho' the Edge of your spiritual Affections, may not be so keen; yet your Love may be more solid, and keep a more steady Course in all the Paths of Obedience; even in the Want of those sweet Allurements, which first inticed you into the Wilderness. Your Joy may be more pure; more in the Lord, and in what you are in him; tho' less in Self, and spiritual Enjoyments from him. And your Zeal likewise may abound more and more in Knowledge, and in all Judgment, tho' the first Flashes of it may be over, which, ordinarily, are not so well regulated. And thus your personal Meetness or Preparation for Glory increaseth continually, even at those very Times, and by those very Means which seem to lessen it.

Therefore, *let Patience have its perfect Work, that ye may be perfect and entire, wanting nothing.* If you was to be taken to Glory, before you had pass'd thro' the whole Course of Trials appointed for you, there would be something wanting in your Preparation for it. The *Measure of* your *Stature in Christ,* as a Member of his Body, and of that proportionable Glory which shall be put upon you, is appointed by God the Father: And the Holy Ghost, keeping this Pattern in his Eye, is now working you up into that Conformity to Christ, to which you was predestined, by all the Changes and Trials which pass over you, both inward and outward, in order to bring you up to that full Glory reserved for you. Every Act of our tried Graces *shall be found unto Praise, Honour, and Glory at the Appearing of Jesus Christ,* 1 Pet. i. 7. And were they to have no Trial, how could they have an Opportunity of acting?

And as the Holy Ghost has taken Possession of us, to Work us up into a full Conformity to Christ, both in Holiness and Glory; so in carrying it on, he oft works, as it were, under-ground, out of our Sight: For in infinite Depths of Wisdom, we are curiously wrought in secret; so that our spiritual Growth, and increasing Meetness for Glory, are rather to be judg'd of in general, by Faith, taking in the Declaration of God in the Promise, *Psal.* xcii. 12, *&c.* than by Sense, or the present felt Exercise of this or that single Grace.

And since our Lord first suffer'd, and then entred into his Glory, let us be willing to *follow his Steps,* and *run with Patience the Race that is set before us;* looking unto that Eternal Weight of Glory, which our *light Affliction* now *worketh for us.* And in all our Sufferings according to the Will of God, let us *commit the keeping of our Souls to him in Well-doing, as unto a Faithful Creator,* who will perfect what concerns us, and not forsake the Work of his own Hands. Yea, let us value Life, with all its Trials, while it is continu'd, as a great Blessing; and labour to improve it, as a Opportunity put into our Hands to glorify God on the Earth: And when all the Work is done upon us, and by us, that was design'd, and we, in all respects, fully meetned for Glory, we shall not stay here a Moment longer, but be immediately loved home unto Christ's, to be glorified with him for ever.

And now, that you may be *strengthned with all Might, according to his glorious Power, unto all Patience, and Long-Suffering with Joyfulness,* until you are fully made meet for, and taken up into the Possession of your Inheritance with the Saints in Light, is the earnest Desire of

Yours in the Lord, &c.

LETTER VIII.

To a little handful of Christ's Lambs at C---n E---d.

Grace and Peace be multiplied unto you, from God our Father, and our Lord Jesus Christ, by the Blessed Comforter.

Dear Friends, I long after you all in the Bowels of Jesus Christ, that your Hearts might be comforted, your Hope increased, and your Faith establish'd upon Him, *the Rock of Ages.* And having but little Time to speak with you Face to Face, when I was last with you, I was desirous to have a little Converse with you by Writing. I find Sin is your great Burden, which fills you with Fears, lest you should one Day perish. But as to this, remember that Sin, all the Sins of all that shall be saved, were once laid by God the Father upon his own dear Son. *All we, like Sheep, have gone astray: we have turned every one to his own Way, and the LORD hath laid on him the Iniquity of us all,* Isa. liii. 6. And as God the Father made all our iniquities at once to meet upon Him, the spotless Lamb if his own providing, and wounded Him for our Transgressions; so Christ *bare our Sins in his own Body on the Tree;* and *gave* up *himself a Sacrifice* in our Room and Stead; by which he has *put away Sin,* and for ever *made an End of it,* 1 Pet. ii. 24. Heb. ix. 26. And as he has destroy'd Sin in himself, and given us a compleat Victory over it in Him; so he will e'er long destroy it in us perfectly, by the Power of his Holy Spirit, in the Virtue of his God-like Blood. Our *Old Man was crucified with Christ, that the Body of Sin might be destroy'd,* Rom. vi. 6. Sin is condemn'd to die, by the dying of the Lord Jesus, and therefore shall never condemn us. No; tho' Sin, Original and Actual, has abounded in such an amazing Manner, in its Guilt, Filth and Power; yet, blessed be God, where *Sin abounded, Grace* did *much more abound; That as Sin has reigned unto Death, even so Grace might reign thro' Righteousness unto Eternal Life, by Jesus Christ our Lord,* Rom. v. 20, 21.

How did Sin [abound,] even our Sin, in *Adam's* first Transgression? How has it abounded in that universal Corruption of Nature, which has overspread the Elect of God, as well as others, as Descendants from fallen *Adam?* And how has it abounded in all those filthy Streams which this filthy Fountain has been sending forth in all Ages, in Thought, Words, and Ways, even in the Chosen of God themselves? How far are the Aboundings of Sin, in these respects, beyond the Comprehension of any Creature!

And yet, *Where sin abounded, Grace* did [much more] *abound:* when the LORD, the Father, took our Sins, the Sins of the whole Elect, and bundled 'em up, as it were, into one Iniquity, which he laid upon his dear Son; who being an infinite Person, was well able to bear all that inconceivable Wrath, which a Sin-revenging God pour'd out upon him, as the due Desert thereof. By which he made a full Satisfaction to injur'd Justice, and an everlasting Peace between God and us; reconciling all the Divine Perfections, which gloriously harmonize in the Salvation of Sinners by the Blood of his Cross; and reconciling us too, in the Body of his Flesh thro' Death, when he gave himself a Sacrifice in our Stead. Whereupon God, as *the God of Peace,* did *bring* him *again from the Dead,* or raise him up from under all that Guilt, Curse, Wrath and Death he bore for us; and thereby, at once, did openly acquit and discharge him, as a publick Person in our room; and also freely, fully, and eternally forgive us all our Trespasses, and raise us up to endless Life and Glory in him, our great Representative. Thus Grace did much more abound. Grace was not only a Match for Sin, and so could not be overcome by it; but it was stronger, infinitely stronger than Sin, and so overcame it, even to a compleat and eternal Victory. Yea, Grace did much more abound, not only to an utter Destruction of Sin, in its Reign unto Death; but further also, in bestowing upon us such Life and Glory in Christ, as the Fruit of his Death, which is far superior unto that we had in *Adam*. Oh, the Super-aboundings of Grace! This [much more] who can search the Dimensions of it!

And Grace [did] *much more abound:* 'Tis put in the past Tense, to shew both the Earliness of it, and also the Foundation of its After-display in Christ, and glorious Reign thro' him. Oh the Earliness of this Grace! How did it super-abound in the everlasting Purposes, Counsels, and Covenant of the Three-One God, over all the Aboundings of Sin, fore-view'd even before Time commenc'd! And this was the Foundation of that bright Display which was made of it in the Death and Resurrection of Jesus Christ. And how did Grace, the Grace of all the Three Persons in God, super-abound, when Jesus died for our Sins, and was rais'd again for our Justification, and set down at God's right Hand, as our Representative and Forerunner! For Father, Son, and Spirit, had an equal Hand in these Wonders of super-abounding Grace. The Father laid Sin upon his own Son, and pour'd out upon him all his Wrath; the Son bare and endur'd the same; and the Holy Spirit, by his Almighty Influence, enabled Christ, as Man, to *endure the Cross,* and *despise the Shame, for the Joy he set before him.* And all the Three, in boundless Grace to us, were jointly concern'd in Christ's Resurrection, and Ascension to Glory, as our Head and Representative. And thus Grace [did] much more abound, [in] Christ, as the Foundation of its glorious Reign by him.

Grace did much more abound; that as Sin has reigned unto Death, even so Grace [might] *reign thro' Righteousness unto eternal Life, by Jesus Christ our Lord.* Sin has reigned in its Guilt, Filth and Power: It has reigned unto Death, unto bodily Death, unto Soul-Death, unto Time-Death, and Eternal Death, which, as *the Wages of Sin,* is the due Desert of every Sinner. But *Grace reigns unto* [Life], thro' [Righteousness]; the Righteousness of Christ, or his compleat Obedience, both active and passive; and so, according to the Righteousness of Jehovah's pure Nature, and his holy Law: and it reigns [by] Jesus Christ, the Anointed Saviour, as our Lord. Thus Grace reigns unto Life; Life of Justification, Sanctification, Consolation, and Glorification, and in all, unto Eternal Life; partial and initial in this World, and compleat and total in the World to come.

Well then, dear Souls, what become of Sin? Oh, look to Christ, once crucify'd, and there see Sin compleatly finish'd in him, with all its woful Effects, and for ever made an end of. Yea, see in a risen and glorified Jesus, what full, transcendent, unchangeable and eternal Life and Glory, God's super-abounding Grace has bestow'd upon you in him! Here's a Foundation laid, that is every way large enough to bear all that vast Superstructure of our personal Salvation, from all Misery, unto all Glory, which one Day shall be laid upon it, when the whole Elect, being compleatly fav'd, both mystically and personally, in, and thro' Christ, shall for ever, with Shoutings, cry, *Grace, Grace unto it!* Lift up your Heads therefore, and be not afraid of the Condemnation of Sin: It once reigned unto Death in Christ for you, when he died in your Stead; and even so, Grace shall reign, by him, unto Eternal Life, in your compleat Salvation. Sin, in its Guilt, shall not destroy you: *for there is no condemnation to them that are in Christ Jesus,* Rom. viii. 1. Sin, in its Filth, shall not make you loathsome in the Sight of God: *for the Blood of Jesus Christ his Son, cleanseth us from all Sin,* 1 John i. 7. *Sin,* in its Power, *shall not have Dominion over you; for you're not under the Law, but under Grace,* Rom. vi. 14. And Sin, in its Being, shall not always abide in you neither; your Heaven-born Souls shall not be always vext with the Being of this hateful Thing, Sin: For your *Spirits,* at the Moment of Death, shall be *made perfect* in Holiness, *Heb.* xii. 23. And there shall be no Defilement, no unclean Thing, either in your Bodies or Souls, when you enter into the *new Jerusalem,* Rev. xxi. 27. You shall then be unblameable *in*

Holiness, before God *in Love,* Eph. i. 4. Thus gloriously will Grace reign unto [Life], over all that Sin and Death that works in you. And be not cast down, because you have no Worthiness: For it is [Grace] that reigns, free Grace, that seeks none of the Creature's Goodness to be a Motive of its Reign. Be not discouraged by the Strength of your Soul-Enemies; for it is [reigning] Grace, all-conquering Grace, that is infinitely able to subdue all the Opposition it meets with. And let not your own Unrighteousness hinder your Faith and Joy in this Grace: For it reigns thro' the Righteousness of another; thro' Christ's [Righteousness], not your own. And tho' you have no Strength of yourselves to do any thing for your own Defence and Safety, or for god's Glory; yet this Grace will do all for you, as it reigns by Jesus Christ our Lord. By [Christ], not yourselves: The whole of your Salvation is committed into Christ's Hand, not your own. And Grace reigns by Christ, as [Jesus], a Saviour, that is infinitely able to save to the uttermost; and by him also, as [Christ], the Anointed of the Father, a Saviour in Office, that is authoriz'd and appointed of God to work out all that Salvation for his People, which Free-Grace bestows. And it reigns also by Jesus Christ, as [LORD] over all Creatures, and Things in Heaven, Earth and Hell; and by him also, as [Our] Lord, our Head, our Husband; one in the nearest Relation to us: Whose Love engageth his Power, as well as his Faithfulness; who exerciseth his Kingly Authority over all Things, in an especial manner for the Good of his Church; breaking his Enemies with his Rod of Iron; and defending, and governing his People by the sweet and powerful Scepter of his Grace, whereby he is *able to subdue even all Things unto himself.* What are all our Enemies? Men, Sin, Satan, Death and the Grave? Tho' like mighty Mountains, before our *Zerubbabel* they shall become a *Plain: And he shall bring forth the Head-Stone* of our Salvation, by the same Free-Grace that laid its Foundation, to the endless Wonder of Men and Angels, and the eternal Glory of the Three-one God; the exceeding Riches of whose Grace will shine forth herein, to the innumerable Ages of a glorious Eternity!

But after all, it may be, you will say, "These are glorious Privileges for those who are interested in 'em; but how shall we know that they belong to us?"

In answer to this, consider, that the Persons, over whom Sin shall not have Dominion, either in its Guilt, Filth, Power, or Being, are such, all such, and none but such, that are, not under the Law, but under Grace. All that ever shall be saved, have been, are, or shall be brought from under the Law, to submit to the Reign of Grace.

And those Persons are under the Law, (in the Sense I here intend it) who like and approve of the Old Covenant, as it makes Doing the Condition of Life; and accordingly, they cleave to the Works of their own Hands, and endeavor to establish their own Righteousness, as the Matter of their Justification before God. Tell such Souls of Jesus Christ, his Blood and Righteousness, and Free-Grace in him, as the alone Way of Salvation; and that Faith in him, is the Means appointed of God for a poor Sinner's Enjoyment of all that Life and Glory which is bestow'd by God's Free-Grace, without the least Work, Worth, or Worthiness in the Creature; and it is very unsavory to them. They don't like to hear of Christ's Righteousness, and God's Free-Grace in him, in the Point of Justification, to the utter Exclusion of their own Works. No, they seek Life, *as it were, by the Works of the Law:* They can't think, that what Christ has done and suffer'd, is sufficient to save them, without they do something themselves, to add unto it, or rather to be found in without it. For they like not the Obedience of the Son of God: They see no Beauty in this glorious Robe, and so reject it; and seek to dress themselves up in the *filthy Rags* of their own Righteousness. And as they see no Need of Christ's Righteousness, so, nor of his Strength neither; they think, that they have Power in themselves, to do what God requires, whenever they please to exert it; and so they like not, but reject Christ as a Root of Influence; and bring forth all their wild Fruit, from, in, and to themselves, under the Influence, and for the End of the Old Covenant. Thus, rejecting the Saviour of God's providing, they would fain, in the Pride of their Hearts, save themselves. And as for God's free Sovereign Grace in Christ, by which he saves a Sinner, without any of his own Works, their Hearts rise against it: They will not be beholding to Free-Grace for Salvation; but seek to earn it by the Works of their own Hands. And the Souls which thus cleave to the Law, (living and dying in such a State) shall be found under it at the awful Day of Judgment; and must then hear what it speaks unto them, in all the amazing Curses of it, and bear the Weight of that inconceivable Wrath, which is the due Defeat of every Transgressor while Sin, Death, and Hell have an eternal Dominion over them. This then is the Condition, and will be the End of all those who live and die under the Law. *For by the Deeds of the Law shall no Flesh be justified in* the *Sight* of God, *Rom.* iii. 20. *For as many as are of the Works of the Law, are under the Curse,* Gal. iii. 10. *And what things soever the Law saith, it saith to them who are under the Law,* Rom. iii. 19. But then, who are they that are under Grace?

The Persons *under Grace* (in the Sense I here intend) are such that are convinc'd of their own Insufficiency top save themselves, and of Christ's All-sufficiency to save even the very Chief of Sinners; which draws out their Souls into earnest Desires after Life and Salvation, by God's Free-Grace in him. These like and approve of the New Covenant, in which the Salvation of Sinners stands alone upon absolute Grace. These have had a Discovery of God's Holy Law, as it requires perfect and perpetual Obedience, in Heart, Lip, and Life; and upon every Failure, curseth the Transgressor: And in the Light the Holy Ghost sets up in such a Soul, it sees its Contrariety to God, and his Holy Law, in Heart as well as Life; it sees its own Inability to do any Duty in that perfect manner the Law of God requires; it sees, That when it *would do Good, Evil is present with it;* and that if God was to deal with it according to his righteous Law, it must perish for ever. And now the Soul begins to die unto the Law, or to all Hopes of Life by the Works of its own Hands. And further, to make the Soul *dead* indeed *to the Law,* (as a Covenant of Works) the Lord goes on to reveal his Son, in such a Soul, as having been made under the Law, to fulfil all its Requirements, and suffer all its Penalties for all that shall be saved; whereby he becomes *the End of the Law for Righteousness to every one that believeth,* Gal. iv. 4. Rom. vii. 4 and x. 4. And proportionable to the Revelation of Christ made to the Soul, it sees a Soul-attracting, Heart-ravishing Beauty and Excellency in him, and his Salvation; which draws it out into earnest Desires to have him for its Portion, to be wash'd in his Blood, to be supply'd from his Fulness, and found in his Righteousness before God. Now the Soul sees, that if ever it is saved, it must be by God's Free-

Grace in Christ; and prostrates itself at the Throne of Grace intreating Divine Mercy to be extended to it, as a miserable undone Sinner. And it is likewise convinc'd of the Necessity of Faith in Christ, that it must believe, or perish; and accordingly, it looks unto him alone for Salvation; it attempts to come to him, and rest its Soul upon him; and under a felt Sense of its own Weakness, it cries out, *Lord, I believe; help thou mine Unbelief,* Mar. ix. 24. Thus it sees a Need of Christ's Strength, as well as his Righteousness; and is glad that the Salvation of a Sinner, from first to last, is all of one pure Piece of Grace. And tho' the Soul mayn't have full Assurance of its own Salvation, by God's Free-Grace in Christ, and so not full Joy in it; yet it likes this Way of Salvation, and desires, above all things, to have an Interest in it. And a Glimpse of it now and then, which it gets in a Promise, or an Ordinance, begets in it a secret Hope, and glads its Heart more than if the whole World was given it. For, when once the Soul is remov'd from an Old Covenant-bottom, if its Hope was not fixt on New Covenant-Grace in Christ, it would utterly sink into Despair. And there is such an Agreeableness between the Principle of Grace in a new-born Soul, and the Doctrine of Grace reveal'd in the Gospel; that the Soul would not part with that little Hope it has of eternal Life in Christ, for all the Treasures of the Universe. And the Souls which thus cleave to Grace, are undoubtedly under it now, and shall be found so in the Day of Christ, to their unspeakable Joy and Glory.

Well then, dear Hearts, if you have not a full Assurance of your Interest in Christ, and his Salvation; yet, if you desire him above all things, and that Free-Grace would do all for you in the Matter of Salvation, you are certainly under the Dominion of Grace. For the Desires of your Souls, cleaving to Grace, are their submitting unto its Reign. And this Grace that has begun to reign over you, will reign on, notwithstanding all the Opposition it meets with in you, even unto eternal Life; or your complete Salvation from Sin and Death, to endless Life and Glory.

Grace be with you. Amen.

I am Yours in Christ, &c.

LETTER IX.

To Mrs. L.

Dear Friend,

I Am far from thinking it any Trouble to answer your Request, in giving you my Thoughts concerning those Scriptures which your Mind has been exercis'd about: For if I could be any way helpful to thy Soul, I should rejoice, and be exceeding glad. Take therefore the following Hints briefly.

John xii. 47. *And if any Man hear my Words, and believe not, I judge him not: for I came not to judge the World, but to save the World.* Our Lord in these Words declares, That *if any Man hear his Words,* i.e. the Doctrine which Christ, his Apostles and Ministers preach, with a natural or external Hearing only, and so believe not in a saving manner, that he judgeth him not; that is, it was not Christ's immediate Work in the Days of his Flesh, nor is yet, while the Gospel is preach'd, to judge and condemn Unbelievers. *For I came not to judge the World* (says he) *but to save the World.* Our Lord's first Coming was not Judgment, but to publish, and work out Salvation. And while the Gospel is preach'd, it is the Time of Christ's *Long-suffering,* wherein he *waits to be gracious* to poor Sinners: But when he shall appear the second Time, he'll come to Judgment; and then all those who shall be found to have liv'd and died in Unbelief, as Despisers and Rejecters of Christ, and his Salvation, shall be judged and condemned by him, with a *Depart ye Cursed, into everlasting Fire, prepared for the Devil and his Angels.*

And now, methinks, this Text should be matter of Encouragement to thee, in thy present Case. Dost thou see thyself to be a poor Sinner? And art thou afraid to draw nigh to God, or lift up thine Eyes to Heaven, because thou art so vile? Yea, dost thou fear that thou art yet in a State of Unbelief, that thou hast never yet put forth one Act of Faith upon Christ? Why, he did not come to condemn thee, to deal with thee according to thy Sins, and send thee to Hell presently. No, he came to save Sinners, even the very Chief of them: And he has wrought out a full and complete Salvation, that is every way sufficient for thee; that is large enough to deliver thee from all thy Fears, to supply all thy Wants, and to satisfy all thy Desires: And this Salvation is proclaime'd in the glorious

Gospel, as infinitely free for the most Undeserving. If thou hast no Worthiness, nothing to bring to God, thou mayst have Salvation freely, *Isa.* lv. 1. Yea, if thou hast a longing Desire after it, thou art the Soul that Christ invites to take thy Fill freely: *If any Man thirst,* (says he) *let him come unto me, and drink,* John vii. 37. *And let him that is a thirst, come: And whosoever will, let him take the Water of Life freely,* Rev. xxii.17. There is an infinite Fulness of Life and Salvation in the Lord Jesus Christ, for the worst off Sinners; and there is Salvation in no other: And therefore, if the Cry of thy Soul is, *What must I do to be saved?* Thou art commanded, even Thou in particular, to *believe on the Lord Jesus Christ;* and in so doing, thou hast the faithful Promise of a God that cannot lie, that *thou shalt be saved,* Acts xvi. 31. And Believing is looking unto Christ alone for Salvation, *Isa.* xlv. 22. Asking it of him, *John* iv. 10. Coming to him for it, *Mat.* xi. 18. Trusting in his Name, *Mat.* xii. 21. and committing thy Soul into his Hands, *2 Tim.* i. 12. And wouldst thou Believe? Why, venture, in the face of ten thousand Sins, Fears, and Discouragements, to cast thyself down at Jesus Feet, and say, with the poor Lepers, *Lord, if thou wilt, thou canst make me clean,* Luke v. 12. *a*nd with the *Publican, God be merciful to me a Sinner,* Luke xviii. 13. And thou shalt find Grace in his Sight; his Mercy will bid thee live; thou shalt *pass from Death to Life, and never come into Condemnation,* John v. 24.

Philemon xv. *For perhaps he therefore departed for a Season, that thou shouldst receive him for ever.* The Apostle *Paul*, in these Words, puts *Philemon* in mind of the wonderful Grace and Providence of God, in over-ruling the Departure of *Onesimus, for a Season* from him his Master, as a Means of his Conversion to Christ, that so he might *receive him for ever:* Not merely now as a Servant, but as a Brother in Christ, which is a Relation that can never be dissolved. *Onesimus* was Servant to *Philemon,* he wrong'd his Master, ran away, and was brought by some means or other) into the Prison where St. *Paul* was: Upon which the Apostle preaches Christ, and the Word of his Grace to this poor Sinner; and the Power of God accompanying the Word of the Gospel, gave it Entrance into his Soul, form'd the New Creature there, and enabled him to believe in Jesus: Upon which the Apostle rejoiceth, and acquaints *Philemon* with this wonderful Grace, exhorting him to receive *Onesimus, not now as a*

Servant, but as a Brother beloved in the Lord, with the same Kindness and Joy he had us'd to shew unto the Apostle himself, who lov'd him as his own Soul.

And was there such Grace in the Heart of God towards *Onesimus?* What Encouragement may this be to thee? The Lord is as full of Love and Bowels now as ever, and extends the same Free-Grace, and boundless Compassion to Sinners now, as then. And did mighty Grace lay hold upon *Onesimus,* when he was in the Height of his Rebellion; when he had just added Theft to all his other Sins, and ran away from God, as well as from his Master? Then sure, nothing is too hard for reigning Grace; it can conquer the most rebellious Creature, and pardon the greatest Sins. None of all thy Sins, tho' great as Mountains, and numberless as the Stars, can hinder thy Salvation, if the Lord resolve to be gracious unto thee: No, *where Sin abounds, Grace much more abounds.* None of thy Sins are too great for reigning Grace to pardon, for omnipotent Grace to subdue. Grace will reign gloriously, displaying its Riches upon a Vessel of Mercy, in its complete Salvation, notwithstanding all its Unworthiness, and Provocations, its Ill Deservings, and Hell-deservings; no Opposition shall stand before it: If God say, I will be gracious to this or that Soul, neither Sin within, nor Men and Devils without, shall hinder its Salvation. Hope therefore in this Grace: For the *Lord takes Pleasure in them that fear him,* (that call upon his Name) *in them that hope in his Mercy,* Psa. cxlvii. 11. And never was any Soul ashamed of its Hope and Confidence in God: No, *Blesses is the Man whose Hope the LORD is,* Jer. xvii. 7. Put thy Trust therefore in the Shadow of his Wings, in the Mercy of God in Christ, and thou shalt never be ashamed nor confounded, World without End, *Psa.* xxxvi. 7. *Isa.* xlv. 17. Again, did God, in his all-wise Providence, who *works all Things after the Counsel of his own Will,* over-rule the Departure of *Onesimus,* to bring him under the Apostle's Preaching, which was the Means of his Conversion? Then 'tis plain, that there is an appointed Time to bring Souls home to Christ; *a Day of Power,* in which they shall be *made willing,* Psa. cx. 3. And what if I should say, I hope this Time of Love is come unto thee, and this Work of Power begun upon thee. Once more, did God over-rule the Departure of *Onesimus* from his Master *for a*

Season, that so he might *receive him for ever,* and that with Advantage? Even so, let me say, did God over-rule his Peoples Departure from him in the Fall, and in this Time-State, to commend his Love the more in bringing them again to himself, to receive then for ever, in an higher Relation, and Glory, than they had when they were with him in their first Father, *Adam.* And what if the Lord, in his Thoughts of Love towards thee, did suffer thee to depart from him for a Season, that so he might bring thee again to himself, and receive thee for ever! He tells thee in his Word, that thou hast *departed from him by Sin,* Ezek. vi. 9. he bids thee return again, and says, thou *shalt find Mercy,* Isa. lv. 7. And has promis'd to receive thee, 2 Cor. vi. 17. And those whom Christ receives, he receives for ever. His Arms stand wide open to embrace thee; and if thou art helpt to return to him, he says, he *will in no wise cast* thee *out,* John vi. 37. He will *receive* thee *to the Glory of God,* Rom. xv. 7. He will *keep* thee *by his thro' Faith unto Salvation,* 1 Peter i. 5. And suffer neither Sin, Men, nor Devils to *pluck* thee *out of his Hands,* John x. 28.

2 Cor. iv. 3. *But if our Gospel be hid, it is hid unto them that are lost.* The Apostle *Paul,* in these Words, speaking in his own Name, and in the Name of the other Apostles, calls the Gospel of Christ, *Our Gospel;* because it was the Ministry which they had received of the Lord Jesus, the Message they were sent to publish, and the glad Tidings which they preach'd. And as they preach'd the Gospel of Christ with the greatest Evidence, and clearest Demonstration; so the Holy Spirit attended their Ministry, and made it *the Power of God,* unto the Salvation of Multitudes; who receiv'd the Truth in the Love of it, upon the fullest Conviction, and with the highest Assurance. Upon which the Apostle utters these Words; *but if our Gospel be hid, it is hid unto them that are lost.* As if he should say, "We have preached the Gospel of a Crucified, Risen, and Ascended Saviour, so plainly, convincingly, and powerfully; that if it be hid unto any Souls, they are certainly in a lost Condition." That is, they are at present *Dead in Sins,* they are not *New Creatures;* and so have no Spiritual Eye to see the Glory of Christ which brightly shines in his blessed Gospel; they are under the Government of Satan, who *blindeth* their *Minds;* they are still in the State wherein they were born, going astray from God, and not yet *returned to the Shepherd and Bishop of Souls.*

Again, if the Gospel be always hid unto any Souls, they are such which are irrecoverably lost; if after all the preaching of Salvation by Jesus Christ, there be any that live and die ignorant of, and in enmity to the glorious Gospel, they are certainly such who perish for ever.

And now, if thou shouldst be afraid, that thou art at present in a lost Condition; yet, were it so, thou art not in a hopeless Condition. For all the Chosen of God, who are now found by the great Shepherd, and called to be Saints, were once in a lost State by Nature, as well as thee. All Christ's Sheep, which his Father gave him, went astray by Sin; and turning every one to his own Way, they lost and destroy'd themselves' or brought themselves into such a miserable Condition, that they were utterly undone: And had neither Will, Skill, nor Power to deliver themselves from that perishing State in which they were involved. But such was the infinite Grace of God the Father, that he laid their Sins upon his own Son; and such the boundless Grace of Christ, that he died for them, in their stead, to bring them again to God; and such is the astonishing Grace of the Holy Spirit, that he quickens 'em when dead in Sins, gives them to see their own Misery, and Christ's Excellency, and brings them home to him, their great Shepherd. Art thou *lost?* it was Such Christ *came to seek and save.* Luke xix. 10. And he *goeth after that which is lost until he findeth it, and when he hath found it, he layeth it on his Shoulders, and bringeth it home rejoicing; saying to his Friends and Neighbours,* the Saints and Angels, *rejoice with me, for I have found my Sheep which was lost.* Luke xv. 4, 5, 6. Christ took such Pleasure in saving lost Sinners, that he died for them, that so he might accomplish it; yea, he now lives in Heaven to intercede for them; and when, as a Fruit thereof, they are brought home to his Fold, he rejoiceth over 'em to save them *to the uttermost.* Therefore be not discourag'd, for if thou art lost, Christ can find thee, and if thou hast no Power to return, he can lay thee on his Shoulders, and bring thee Home; yea, if thy Case was so miserable, that thou hadst no Will to return, Christ can make thee willing in a Moment; for he is in all respects, *mighty to save.* But if he has given thee a Will, a Desire to return unto God in Christ, he has already found thee out, and laid hold on thy Heart by his Almighty Power, and he'll bring thee home to God, both here in Grace, and hereafter in

Glory, presenting thee with exceeding Joy. If he has given thee a Sight of thy own Misery, and a Glimpse of his Beauty, so as to beget a Desire in thy Soul after him, the Gospel of Christ has already begun to shine into thy Heart, and it shall shine more and more until *the perfect Day;* and it shall never be hid unto thee, as it is unto them that are lost.

1 Cor. xv. 2. *By which also yea are saved, if ye keep in memory what I preached unto you, unless you have believed in vain.* The Apostle *Paul,* having preach'd the Gospel of Christ unto the *Corinthians,* and particularly the great and comfortable Doctrine of the Resurrection; he here exhorts them to a constant Remembrance thereof, it being of so great Importance. There were, at that Time, some in the Church at *Corinth,* who were so far fallen away from the Doctrine of the Gospel, as to deny the Resurrection of the Dead; for which Reason the Apostle insists largely upon that Article in this Chapter. In the *first Verse,* he professeth to declare afresh the Gospel that he had formerly preach'd to them, which they had receiv'd, and wherein they, professedly, did stand. *By which,* says he, in this *second Verse, ye are saved, if ye keep in Memory what I preached unto you, unless ye have believed in vain.* It seems to me, that the Time-Salvation of the Saints, from Errors, Heresies, and Soul-Distresses, is what the Apostle here intends; which is closely connected with a believing Remembrance of the Doctrines of the Gospel, and particularly this of the Resurrection. In like manner as he says, *We are saved by Hope.* Rom. viii. 24. Which is evidently intended of our Time-Salvation: for in no other Sense can we be said to be saved by Hope; for when once we come to the Enjoyment of that Salvation hoped for, the Exercise of that Grace ceaseth; as her there argues, *for Hope that is seen, is not Hope.* And then in the last Clause, *unless ye have believed in vain,* he sweetly puts them in mind how they did at first receive the Gospel, and this Doctrine of the Resurrection; how they once saw a Glory in the Resurrection of Christ from the Dead, to discharge them from Sin, and raise their Souls to Life here, and their Bodies unto Life eternal, at the Morning of the Resurrection. And, as if he should further say, can you now easily part with what you once liv'd in the Faith of? Have you believed in vain? Is the Faith you once had of these great Things, become a light Matter, an empty Thing? Or can you let your doctrinal Faith of

the Gospel lie by in your Judgments as a useless Thing? Have you not a continual Need of exercising Faith therein, when without it you can neither live safely from Heresies, fruitfully unto God, nor joyfully to your own Souls? This your Time-Salvation, as your Privilege, being closely connected with your Duty, in a believing Remembrance of the Doctrines of the Gospel, which you did receive: This, in brief, I take to be the Meaning of the Words. For there are none that believe in Jesus for eternal Life, that can believe in vain, in this respect; No, they *are passed from Death unto Life, and shall never come into Condemnation.* Their eternal Salvation is not uncertain, but absolute: It stands immoveably fixt upon *Christ,* the unchangeable *Rock of Ages,* by the immutable *Word* and *Oath* of a *God that cannot lie.* John v. 24. Mat. vii. 24, 25. Heb. vi. 18. Tit. i. 2.

Well then, if as a perishing Sinner, thou fleest *for Refuge* to *lay hold* on *Christ, the Hope set before* thee, thou shalt be eternally saved: Upon thy first Act of Faith, as soon as ever thou art got into the City of Refuge, thou wilt be eternally safe, for ever out of all Danger of everlasting Misery; and as an *Inhabitant of the Rock,* thou mayst *sing,* beginning the Work of Praise here, which will be thy eternal Employment in Heaven. And if it is the Duty of Believers to keep up a quick and constant Remembrance of the glorious Gospel which they have receiv'd, in order to their Time-Safety, Fruitfulness and Comfort; then do thou also labour to think and meditate upon every Truth of the Gospel, every Beam of Light that springs into thy Mind, under the preaching or reading of the Words of this Life: For this will be an effectual Means to preserve thee from Soul-Distress in an Hour of Temptation, to strengthen thy weak Hope, and encrease thy Joy.

1 Cor. xiv. 38. *But if any Man be ignorant, let him be ignorant.* It seems, by the Coherence of these Words, that there were some in this Church of *Corinth*, who were greatly puff'd up with Pride, and a vain Conceit of their being spiritual, even to a slighting or despising the Dictates of the Apostle, under the immediate Inspiration of the Holy Spirit: And there having been such abundant Evidence of his Apostleship, and that it was the Truth of *Christ* which he preach'd and wrote; if after all, there were any who would willfully shut their Eyes

against the Light, and pretend Ignorance; he, in these Words, resolves to leave them, and take no further Pains for their Conviction. *If any Man be ignorant, let him be ignorant.* 'Tis as if he should say, "If after all the Signs of an Apostle, which have been shewn in me, and that abundant Demonstration of the Spirit with which I preach and writ the Gospel of Christ; any Man who thinks himself spiritual, will not behold my Mission from *Christ,* nor acknowledge my infallible Guidance into all Truth by the Divine Spirit; let him remain just were he is, *let him be ignorant* still."

But there is no Reason for thee to be discourag'd from this Text: If thou seest thyself to be an ignorant Creature, and groans under it, this is no Threatning to thee, that thou shalt abide in thy Ignorance still. No, the Lord *Jesus Christ* is *made* of God *Wisdom,* unto such that have none at all. 1 Cor. i. 30. His Father has call'd him to the Office of Prophet, on purpose to teach the ignorant, to *open their blind Eyes: Isa.* xlii. 7. And he has promis'd to *bring the Blind by a Way that they knew not, to lead them in Paths which they have not known, to make Darkness Light before them, and crooked Things straight. These things,* says he, *will I do unto 'em, and not forsake them,* Isa. xlvi. 16. *He can have Compassion on the Ignorant, and them that are out of the Way,* Heb. v. 2. If the High-Priest under the Law could have Compassion, much more can *Christ,* whose Bowels are infinite. Wast thou the most ignorant Creature in the World, Christ can teach thee efficaciously, or teach thee to profit; that is, he can remove thy Ignorance, and give thee the Knowledge of himself, and of the Father in him; *whom to know is Life eternal,* John xvii. 3. If Christ *teach thee to profit,* he will do it as the LORD thy God by a creating Power, *Isa.* xlviii. 17. If Christ will shine into thy Heart, *to give thee the Light of the Knowledge of the Glory of God,* as the God of all Grace in him, thy Darkness shall flee before it. If he say but the Word, *Let there be Light,* as he did in the first Creation, immediately the Light appears, and the darkest Soul is *made Light in the Lord.* Be encourag'd therefore, to come unto him under all thy apprehended Darkness, and cast thyself down at his Feet, and say, *What I know not, teach thou me,* Job xxxiv. 32. For he is infinitely *able to save* thee, in this respect, *to the uttermost.* In him *are hid all the Treasures of Wisdom and Knowledge:* His Wisdom is infinite, his

Power Almighty, and his Compassions boundless. And this mighty Saviour, is a Saviour in Office, it is his Office to teach poor Sinners that are ignorant; and he is *good and upright,* and he will do it, *Psal.* xxv. 8. He will *teach Sinners,* because of the infinite Goodness of his Nature, and because he is *upright* also, or *faithful to him that appointed him,* and to his own Engagements also, by Covenant and Promise: And never did any Soul perish for want of Knowledge, that waited upon him for teaching; no, he'll make the Way of Life so plain, that *a way-faring Man, tho' a Fool, shall not err therein,* Isa. xxxv. 8.

The Grace of Christ be with thy Spirit.

I am Thine in Him, &c.

LETTER X.

To Mrs. S.

Dear Friend,

Having heard how the Tempter made use of that Word, *Hab.* ii. 4. to distress thy Soul, it was on my Heart to write a few Lines to acquaint thee with what I take to be the Meaning thereof. *Behold, his Soul which is lifted up, is not upright in him.* The Intent of the Holy Ghost in these Words, is, to set forth the perishing State of an Unbeliever: And here is, 1. A Description given of him, that he is such an one *whose Soul is lifted up.* And, 2. Here is a Declaration made concerning him, that his Soul *is not upright in him.*

The Person that is here said to be lifted up, is such as one that is lifted up in Pride, or a vain Conceit of the Sufficiency of his own Righteousness to stand in before God, and to screen him from his vindictive Wrath. It is such an one that , *Pharisee* like, exalteth himself, commends his own Righteousness, and dares to plead it before God, as the Cause why his Wrath should turn away from him. Thus there were some among God's Professing People of old, who, being lifted up in a Conceit of their own Righteousness, pleaded their Innocence, as the Cause why his Anger should turn from them. But this their Confidence in their own Righteousness, and of their Deliverance upon that Bottom, the Lord tells them that he *rejected*, and that he would *plead with* them, *because they said they had not sinned*, Jer. ii. 35, 37. Thus an Unbeliever is here describ'd, as one who, in this Sense, is lifted up. And then we have

The Declaration that is made concerning him; *Behold*, says the Lord, look upon the Man that is thus lifted up, *his Soul is not upright in him*. It is a legal Uprightness that is here intended: And it is as if the Lord should say, "In vain doth that Soul plead his own Righteousness for Deliverance from my avenging Justice, who cleaves to the Works of the Law, as the Matter of his Justification before me: For such is the Purity of my holy Law; that it will find innumerable Faults with his pretended Obedience; the Crookedness thereof will abundantly appear, when compar'd with the Straightness of that perfect Rule. And such is the Strictness of my Justice, that to vindicate my own Honour, I must pour out my Wrath, according to all the Curses of my righteous Law, upon that Soul who dares to trust in his own imperfect Obedience, in the *filthy Rags* of his own Righteousness: his Soul is not upright in him; and therefore his external Obedience can't be so. My Law requires Soul-Uprightness, or perfect Conformity in Heart, Lip, and Life, in that Person who will be justified thereby: And since his Soul is not upright, it will condemn him, and he must die the Death, who will dare to stand at the Bar of my Justice, to be try'd by my holy Law." And that this is the Declaration the Lord here makes concerning an Unbeliever, or the Soul that is lifted up, is plain from the opposite, or what stands oppos'd to this, in the latter Part of the Verse; *But the Just shall live by his Faith:* Especially, if we look upon this Text, as quoted by the Apostle, to prove, that the Justification of a Sinner before God, stands alone in his Free-Grace, thro' the imputed Righteousness of Christ, to the utter Exclusion of the Works of the Law in that Point, *Gal.* iii. 11. *But that no Man is justified by the Law in the Sight of God, it is evident:* For, *the Just shall live by his Faith.*

The Just]. There is no Way for a Sinner to be just with God, but by the Blood and Righteousness of Christ. And in this Way, God can be *Just, and yet the Justifier of him which believes in Jesus,* that desires to be found in him, and looks for Salvation from him alone, *Rom.* iii. 26.

Shall live]. The eternal Life, or Salvation of a Sinner, stands alone in God's Free-Grace, thro' the Blood and Righteousness of Christ, *Eph.* i. 7. *In whom we have Redemption thro' his Blood, the Forgiveness of Sins, according to the Riches of his Grace.* Rom. v. 19, 20, 21. For *as by one Man's Disobedience, many were made Sinners; so by the Obedience of one shall many be made righteous. Moreover, the Law enter'd, that the Offence might abound: But where Sin abounded, Grace did much more abound: that as Sin hath reigned unto Death, even so Grace might reign thro' Righteousness, unto eternal Life, by Jesus Christ our Lord.*

By his Faith]. Or that which his Faith lays hold of. For when the Lord is about to make any Soul a Partaker of this Salvation, he shews it its own Sinfulness and Misery, and that it is utterly impossible for it to be saved by the Works of the Law, or by its own Obedience to the Law; because it can do nothing in that perfect Manner which the Law of God requires; and therefore inevitably comes under the Curse for every Failure: upon which the Soul dies unto all Hope of Life by the Works of the Law: And then he opens to it a Way of Life, that in all respects suits an undone Sinner, by his Free-Grace, thro' a crucified and risen Jesus; and begets Faith in the Soul, or a secret Persuasion that there is enough in Christ, and what he has done, to save it. Whereupon, the Soul ventures into Christ, tho' it sees itself overspread with Sin, as with a Leprosy, and says, *Lord, if thou wilt, thou canst make me clean.* And the Lord, to shew his infinite Grace, as will as his Ability to save, immediately says, *I will, be thou clean,* Luke v. 12, 13. By which he conveys a full and everlasting Salvation to that Soul. And thus *the Just shall live by his Faith. For unto him that worketh not,* that brings none of his own Works to justify him before God; *but believeth on him that justifieth the Ungodly;* that draws nigh to God upon his Throne of Grace, and pleads the Extension of his Mercy and Grace thro' his own Son; *his Faith is counted for Righteousness,* or that which his Faith lays hold on, the Blood and Righteousness of Christ, God the Father imputes or reckons unto him, as the Matter of his Justification, and declares his Acceptance of him, and Well-pleasedness with him in his dear Son, *Rom.* iv. 5. Thus *the Just shall live by Faith,* in respect of Justification: For that Soul that looks for all its Acceptance with God, by his Free-Grace, thro' his dear

Son, shall never die; but is *passed from Death unto Life,* John v. 24. And the justified Soul, having an indefeasible Right to all that immeasurable Fulness of Life in Christ, it is its Duty and Privilege to live by Faith in respect of Expectation; looking for a continual Communication of Life out of Christ's Fulness, for the full Supply of all his Wants, thro' Time, and to Eternity: And in this respect, it is to live by Faith, until Faith is swallow'd up in Vision. In these Words then, we have two Sorts of Persons spoken of, Believers, and Unbelievers; the one lifted up in a Conceit of their own Righteousness; the other just, or justified in Christ's; and the End of the One, which is Death, imply'd, in that he is not upright, and so under the Law's Curse; and of the other, which is Life, declar'd, *Behold, his Soul which is lifted up, is not upright in him; But the Just shall live by his Faith.*

And now, dear Soul, it is evident, that it was the Father of Lies who apply'd these Words unto thee, to afflict and distress thy Heart: He apply'd 'em to the wrong Person; since thou wast mot lifted up in a Conceit of thy Righteousness, but in the Hope of God's free Mercy, thro' the Blood and Righteousness of his Son. And in this thou needest not fear being lifted up too high. No, poor Soul, hast thou been humbled in the Dust, under a Sense of thy own Vileness? Thou art then that *Valley* which the Lord has promis'd to *exalt.* xl. 4. Hast thou no Righteousness of thy own, and so art low in thy own Eyes? Thou shalt be exalted in Christ's *Psal.* lxxxix. 16. And as thy Person is exalted in this, far out of the Reach of all thy Soul-Enemies; so, in the Lord's time, thy Faith also shall be exalted, and thou shalt rejoice in his Name all the Day-long. *Go* on therefore *in the Strength of the Lord, making mention of his Righteousness, even of his only:* And fear none of thy Enemies, Sin, Men, nor Devils: For none of them shall be able to condemn thy Soul, to *pluck* thee out of Christ's *Hands,* or separate thee from his Love; which is *better than Life* natural, and in which there is Life for thee, both spiritual and eternal. And whoever, or whatever would discourage thee, Christ bids thee to *rejoice in* him, and that *always* Phil. iv. 4. Christ got the Victory over all thy Soul-Enemies, by the Strength of his mighty Arm; and he gives it unto thee, *Col.* ii. 14, 15. *Psal.* xcviii. 1. *1 Cor.* xv. 57. Rejoice therefore in his mighty Conquest; for thou dividest the Spoil.

And fear none of those Things which thou may'st suffer from the Malice of Satan in any of his wicked Instruments: For if thou shouldst have Tribulation *ten Days,* during the Time appointed of the Lord; as he bounds their Rage, so he'll over-rule thy Sufferings for his own Glory, and any Good; while thy *light Affliction which is but for a Moment, worketh for thee a far more exceeding and eternal Weight of Glory,* 2 Cor. iv. 17. *Reckon* therefore, *that the Sufferings of this present Time, are not worthy to be compar'd with the Glory which shall be revealed in thee.* Rom. viii. 18. *Rejoice* that thou art *counted worthy to suffer Shame for his Name: For if we suffer with him, we shall also be glorified together. Be faithful therefore unto Death;* and Christ will *give thee a Crown of Life,* Rev. ii. 10.

Into Christ's Arms I commit thee, to support, defend, and embrace thee, while passing thro' a World of Trials, until he bring thee home unto himself, to be *forever with* him *to behold* his *Glory;* and rest, with dear Love,

Thine in Him, &c.

LETTER XI.

To Mrs. G.

Dear Friend,

Having heard of thy Soul-Distress, and thy Fear lest the Promises of God do not belong to thee, I was willing to write a few Lines unto thee. And if thou hast seen thy lost Condition by Sin, that thou art forever undone without an Interest in Christ, and hast a Desire to be saved by him alone; there is a full and everlasting Salvation in Christ prepar'd for thee, which thou art call'd to receive freely. *This is a faithful Saying, and worthy of all Acceptation, that Jesus Christ came into the World to save Sinners,* (says the Apostle) *of whom I am chief,* 1 Tim. i. 15. If thou seest thy self to be a chief Sinner, it was such Christ came to save. If thou *labour* under, and art *heavy laden* with Sin; it is thee, in particular, that Christ calls to *come unto* him, and has promis'd to *give* thee *Rest, Mat.* xi. 28. "Aye, sayst thou, if I had an interest in the Promises, I should think myself happy." Why, poor Soul, all that Life and Salvation for Sinners, which is declar'd in the Promises, is summed up in Christ. Lay hold therefore upon him by Faith, who is *the Hope set before* thee in the Gospel, as infinitely free for the worst of Sinners; and thou mayst lay claim to all the Promises. For *all the Promises of God are in him; yea, and in him, Amen.* 2 Cor. i. 20.

They are all of them [in] him. And that Soul that looks unto Christ alone for Salvation, believeth in him, is entred into him as its City of Refuge, its Place of Defence, and Soul-Rest. And there it is well provided for, exceeding safe, and eternally secure: For,

[All] the Promises of God are in him, yea. Perhaps thou seest a Glory in a particular Promise, and think'st, Oh how glad should I be if this Promise was mine! Why, if thou hast a Desire to be found in Christ, thou art in him; and so all the Promises are thine: not one, two, or three only, but all the Promises of God: Not a Promise in the Bible, but belongs to that Soul, who commits itself into the Hands of Christ to be saved by him. Hast thou done so? thou art rich enough: Thou hast all that thou canst desire; yea, and infinitely more. For *Eye hath not seen, nor Ear heard,* The glorious things which God hath *prepared* for that Soul, who runs, as a perishing Sinner, into the Name of Christ as the mighty Saviour, to shelter itself in him, who is an Hiding-place from the Wind, and a Covert from the Storm of divine Vengeance. If thou hast ever put forth one Act of Faith upon Jesus, or cast one Look unto him for Life; thou hast Christ, and eternal Life in him; all the Promises of God are thine; and thy Riches, in that one great Promise of the new Covenant, *2 Cor.* vi. 16. *I will be their God,* are infinitely greater than Man or Angels can reckon up.

And as all the Promises of God meet in Christ, so they are in him [yea]: They all agree, as with one united Voice, to grant that full and comprehensive Salvation, which is in Christ, to every believing Soul, with one *Yea.* They are not *Yea* and *Nay;* some of them *Yea,* and others *Nay;* But *in him they are all Yea.* And as they are *all Yea* in Christ, so in him they are *always Yea;* not *Yea* at one time, and *Nay* at another; but a fixed, eternal *Yea.*

And as all the Promises of God are in Christ, Yea, as they are all, and always of one Mind in the Grant of Salvation unto every one that believeth in Jesus; so likewise they are all of them in him, *Amen.* They all stand in him confirmed, with God's *So let it be,* or So it shall be; which efficaciously produceth all the Salvation granted. And since all the Promises of God, are in Christ, *Amen;* there is an absolute, infallible Certainty of the Performance of all the good Things which the Lord hath spoken. Then surely *the Heirs of Promise* may have *strong Consolation.*

But it may be, thou wilt say, "I fear I am not one of the Heirs of Promise." Well, dost thou see thyself to be a perishing Sinner? Dost thou know that there is Salvation in Christ? And hast thou a Desire after it? Why, then ask him for it; and he will in no wise send thee away empty. *If thou knewest the Gift of God,* (said our Lord to the *Samaritan* Woman) *and who it is that saith unto thee, Give me to Drink, thou wouldst have asked, and he would have given thee living Water,* John iv. 10. Then *open thy Mouth wide;* for he has promis'd to *fill* it, Psal. lxxxiv. 10. Thou needest not be afraid of asking more Grace than Christ has to bestow, or is willing to give to the most Unworthy, the very Chief of Sinners. And never did any Soul ask Christ for *the Water of Life,* Grace here, and Glory hereafter, but he gave it its Fill *freely. Ask* therefore, and thou shalt *receive; seek,* and thou shalt *find; knock, and it shall be open'd unto thee,* Mat. vii. 7. For Christ lives in Heaven on purpose *to save* them *to the uttermost,* who come unto God by him, *Heb.* vii. 25.

And now, that you may be enabled to flee for *Refuge to lay hold on* Christ, *the Hope set before* you, and as an *Heir of Promise* have *strong Consolation* in him, in whom *all the Promises of God are Yea and Amen, to the Glory of God by us,* is the earnest Desire of

Your loving Friend in the Lord, &c.

LETTER. XII.

To Mr. L.

Dear Sir,

Grace, Mercy and Peace be multiplied unto you, from God the Father, and from Jesus Christ, by the blessed Spirit.

You told me, to the Joy of my Heart, that you hop'd Christ was precious to your Soul. And if thou hast seen thy own Misery by Sin, that thou art for ever undone without him; and hast also had a Glimpse of his Glory, Excellency, and Suitableness as the alone Saviour, he is precious indeed unto thee, *the Chiefest of ten thousand in* thy Esteem. Whatever others think of Christ, thou hast high and honourable Thoughts of him, and of what he has done and suffer'd for the Salvation of Sinners, and of what he is now doing for them in Heaven, to save them to the uttermost who come unto God by him. Yea, has not thy Soul fell down, and ador'd him, in those happy Moments wherein thou hast beheld his Glory? And has not a Sight of his Beauty wrought in thee Soul-endearing Thoughts of this lovely Jesus? And tho'; perhaps, thou couldst not say, *this is my Beloved, and this is my Friend;* with a a full Persuasion that he was thy Saviour; yet, has not a Glimpse of his Excellency attracted and drawn out thy Soul into earnest Longings, Pantings, and Breathings after him, and an Interest in him, as the Sum of all that Happiness thy Soul could crave, both in this World and in that which is to come? I know, it is so with those Souls that see Jesus, just in those Moments in which his Glory is presented to their Eye. And has it been thus with thee? Hast thou ever had such a Glimpse of Christ, that drew thy Soul after him, and made thee cry, "Lord, give me Christ, whatever thou deniest me of: Let me have him for my Portion; and as to other things, deal with me as thou pleaseth: A World, without Christ, will not satisfy me: Give me Christ, and I have enough!" If these are the Breathings of thy Heart, thou art a Believer, whether thou know'st it, or not. And Christ is thine, everlastingly thine; and neither Sin, Death, nor Hell shall separate thee from his Love. Thou art exceeding safe. And mayst be very joyful: For in having Christ, thou hast Life; Life of Grace, and Life of Glory. All Things are thine: Thou shalt have all that Happiness, both for Soul and Body, which God sees best for thee in this World, and a boundless Ocean of Joy and Glory beyond it, to a never-ending Eternity. Hast thou committed thy Soul into Christ's Hands? Thou art his Care: Thou art Christ's, not thy own: He has taken the Charge of thee; and as such, he'll keep thee safe, defend thee from all Dangers, strengthen thy Grace, and meeten thee for Glory. He will preserve thee *from falling,* and *present* thee *faultless before the Presence of his Father's Glory with exceeding Joy.*

Then *cleave* to the Lord *with full Purpose of Heart:* Go on venturing thy Soul in the Hands of Jesus, trusting in him when he seems to slay thee, and waiting for him when he hides his Face from thee: And thus follow the Lamb whithersoever he goeth, in all the Ordinances of his own Appointment here, and thou shalt certainly be found among the Lamb's Company, who shall sit down with him on his Throne, and be crown'd as Overcomers, at his next Appearing. Make haste, and don't delay to keep his Commandments: Do not let Satan and Unbelief hinder thee any longer from giving up thyself to the Lord, and his Service: For thy Working time for God will be soon over. Oh! hast thou not been thy own long enough already? Wilt thou not from this Time give up thyself to the Lord? *Wilt thou not,* says he, *from this Time cry unto me, My Father, thou art the Guide of my Youth?* Jer. iii. 4. "How long will it be, as if the Lord should say, e're thou own me for thy Father, and follow me as a Child; trusting in me for Strength and Guidance to conduct thee safe thro' a World of Trials, into my own Bosom? Wilt thou not from this time cleave to me?" So would I say unto thee: Wilt thou not from this time be the Lord's? Remember, *the Day is far spent;* and what thou dost for God, thou must do quickly: *Boast not of tomorrow; for thou knowest not what a Day may bring forth,* Pro. xxvii. 1. Therefore *whatsoever thy Hand findeth to do, do it with thy Might,* Eccles. ix. 10. Wast thou to live to the Age of *Methuselah,* thy God is worthy to have all thy Love, and all thy Obedience, to have all thy Time spent in his Service: But alas! thou hast but an Inch of Time left, a short Space; Death and Eternity hasten upon thee; and then thuo'lt not repent that thou gavest up thyself to the Lord so soon, or begans't to serve him so early; but rather, that thou didst not begin sooner, and hast done so little for God. It will be to the Honour of those Souls, in the Day of Christ, who have trusted in the Lord, and follow'd him in the Face of ten thousand difficulties from within, and from without. Their Faith and Obedience shall then be own'd and crown'd, by Free-Grace, in the Sight of Men and Angels: Whereas those of the Saints, who, thro' Satan and Unbelief, have been hindred from following Christ in this World, according to his Appointments, will be asham'd before him at his Coming. Their *Works shall be burnt up;* and they'll *suffer loss,* tho' they themselves *shall be saved, yet so, as by Fire.* Therefore let us that have believ'd in Jesus, prize our present Moments, and labour to improve 'em, as an Opportunity put into our Hands to glorify him that hath lov'd us, by shewing our Love to him in keeping his Commandments. His Servants shall eat when others are hungry; they shall drink, when others are thirsty; they shall rejoice, when others are ashamed; they shall sing for Joy of Heart, when others shall howl for Vexation of Spirit, *Isa.* lxv. 13, 14. *If any Man serve me,* says our Lord, *let him follow me; and where I am, there shall my Servant be: if any Man serve me, him will my Father honour,* John xii. 26. And what canst thou desire more? Oh happy, thrice happy Souls, who are in such a Case! Who is like unto 'em, *a People saved of the LORD!*

The Grace of Christ be with thy Spirit. Amen.

I am, with all due Respect,

Yours in him, &c.

LETTER XIII.

To the Lady H.

My dear Christian Lady,

I Beg you'll please to pardon my Boldness, in giving you the Trouble of this; which I should not have presum'd to do, if I was not comfortably persuaded that you are an elect Lady, that love the Lord Jesus, his Cause, and People, even the very meanest of them; and therefore will patiently attend to the Chatterings of a Child that cannot speak.

The Apostle *James* exhorts the Saints he wrote to, to rejoice in the Lord, in those various Stations in which the divine Providence had plac'd 'em in this Life, *Jam.* i. 9, 10. *Let the Brother of low Degree rejoice in that he is exalted; But the rich, in that he is made low.* Oh what distinguishing Grace is it to you, my dear Lady, that has made you low in your own Eyes! Since not *many wise, not many mighty, not many noble are called,* as *1 Cor.* i. 26. What Grace is it, that you should be one of those few! an

Object of electing Love, and a Subject of calling Grace, when thousands of your Rank and Quality are passed by! Oh, how many of the great Men of this World have *their good Things, their Portion in this Life?* While the LORD is your *Portion,* your Time-Lot, and your eternal All! He did not think these things good enough for you; no, he set his great Love upon you from everlasting, and gave you a Portion that is every way answerable to the infinite Love of his Heart, which is no less than his Great SELF! And having blest you with this Portion before Time, in his everlasting Covenant with his Son; so, when the appointed Moment of Calling-Love came on, he sent his Holy Spirit down into your Heart, to shew you the Vanity and Emptiness of all worldly Glory, and to ravish your heart with infinite Sweetness, uncreated Excellency, that so you might seek for, and find a Soul-satisfying Rest in GOD : possessing your vast INHERITANCE in him, by Faith which is in Christ Jesus. The Riches, Honours and Pleasures of this vain World, (which Mr. *Rutherford* calls, "The Clay-Portion of Bastards") had never lost their Beauty in your Eye, if the Spirit of the LORD had not blown upon the Glory of his lower Creation, and made it wither like the mown Grass in your Sight, *Isa.* xl. 7.

What innumerable Multitudes are there of the World's great, wise, mighty and noble Men, who continually dote upon its gilded Toys, and empty Nothings; as if there was a Happiness in 'em agreeable to the nature of an immortal Soul? And You had never found them to be unsatisfying *Husks,* if you had not been one of God's Children, for whom the *Bread* of Life is prepared in your *Father's House.*

Again, what Multitudes are there, that dote upon their own Excellencies, their natural Endowments, and moral Performances; as if they were some of the most beautiful Creatures in the World? And even dare to about *to establish their own Righteousness,* as their justifying Dress before God? And you likewise had been of this miserable Number, if the Spirit of the LORD had not blown upon created Glory, in this respect also. Your natural Excellencies and Performances had never lost their Brightness in your Eye, if the Spirit of the LORD had not given you a Sight of the transcendent Glory, and infinite Excellency of the Person and Righteousness of Jesus Christ; to attract your Soul after him, as the chiefest of ten thousand, the fairest in both Worlds, the Sum of all your Happiness, and Center of your Desires! 'Tis the Soul-ravishing Beauty, the adorable Excellency of Christ, the Glory-Sun, darted by the Spirit upon the Eye of your Faith, which has put out the Light of Creature-Beauties, and extinguish'd them out of your Sight; so as to make you say, with the *Psalmist,* Psa. lxxiii. 25. *Whom have I in Heaven but thee? and there is none upon the Earth that I desire besides thee.* And with the Apostle *Paul,* Phil. iii. 7, 8, 9. *But what Things were Gain to me, those I counted Loss for Christ. Yea, doubtless, and I count all Things but Loss, for the Excellency of the Knowledge of Christ Jesus my Lord: for whom I have suffer'd the Loss of all Things, and do count them but Dung, that I may win Christ, and be found in him; not having my own Righteousness, which is of the Law, but that which is thro' the Faith of Christ, the Righteousness which is of God by Faith.* Oh what a special Privilege is this, to be made so low, as to be beholding to Christ for all! For all Happiness, Life and Glory, in this World, and that to come! Well may *the Brother,* or Sister, *of high Degree rejoice, in that* they are *made* thus *low:* Forasmuch, as the Lord, by this Work of his Grace, is preparing that Person for a Life and Glory that is far superior to all earthly Enjoyments; yea, no less than the high and eternal Exaltation of the heavenly State!

Has it been thus with you, my dear Lady? Has the Lord stript you naked of created Excellencies? 'Tis in order to fill, satisfy, and clothe you with his own immense Glories! What reason then have you to rejoice in the Lord, both now, and for evermore? And believe it, that your high Station in the World (what Thorns and Briars soever attend it) was appointed for you, by the same infinite Love that ordain'd your eternal Salvation: Like it therefore, as the Choice of infinite Wisdom, the Way laid out for you to a City of Habitation; and labour to improve it to the Honour of that Grace which has sav'd you. The Lord may have intended three Things, principally, hereby; 1. To commend or set off the Glory of distinguishing Grace the more in your eternal Salvation. 2. To give you an Opportunity to glorify God the more on the Earth. And, 3. By this, as a Means, to enhance your future Crown.

How will distinguishing Grace shine in your Salvation, when you shall be plac'd at *Christ's* Right Hand, openly acquitted, discharg'd and blest; and as such, call'd to *inherit the Kingdom,* that Kingdom of Glory, *prepar'd for you from the Foundation of the World;* while Thousands of illustrious Souls, the Great, Rich, Mighty, and Noble of the World, shall tremble at the *Lamb's Wrath,* and *call to the Rocks and Mountains to fall on them, and hide them from the Face of him that sits on the Throne, and from the Wrath of the Lamb, when that great Day of his Wrath is come,* wherein none of them *shall be able to stand!* Matth. xxv. 34. Rev. vi. 15, 16, 17. And how will it raise your Notes of Praise high, when, with the redeemed Company, you join to sing *the Lamb's new Song,* saying, *Worthy is the Lamb who was slain, and has redeemed us unto God with his own Blood, out of ever Kindred, Tongue, People, and Nation, and has made us Kings and Priests unto our God!* Rev. v. 9. Oh! to see yourself redeem'd by the Lamb's Blood, from all Misery, unto all Glory, out of the great and mighty People of the Earth; while they are left to perish in their Sins, and sent away from *Christ* into eternal Torments! How will this raise your Wonder at distinguishing Grace, and advance your *Hallelujahs!*

Again, What if God, by your high Station in the World, puts an Opportunity into your Hands to glorify him the more on the Earth? The LORD rais'd *Moses* to that high Pitch of Honour in *Pharoah's* Court, that so he might have an Opportunity to glorify God, and to exercise his Graces in denying himself, taking up his Cross, and following Christ: For which his Faith is so commended, *Heb.* xi. 24, 25, 26. *By Faith Moses, when he was come to years, refused to be called the Son of Pharoah's Daughter; chusing rather to suffer Affliction with the People of God, than to enjoy the Pleasures of Sin for a Season; esteeming the Reproach of Christ greater Riches than the Treasures in* Egypt: *For he had respect unto the Recompense of the Reward:* If *Moses* had not had so much to lose, how could his Faith and Love, in his Self-Denial, forsake all for God, have shone so conspicuously? Of what an excellent Kind did his Faith appear to be, when, at once, he left the Pleasures, Honours, and Treasures of the Court, and the Crown of *Egypt* too, which in all Likelihood he might have enjoy'd; refusing to be call'd the Son of *Pharoah's* Daughter; and chusing rather to suffer Affliction with the People of God? He stepp'd down at once from all his Court-royalty, not for any of the Gratifications of Sense, but to suffer Affliction: Instead of being a Prince, he becomes a

Servant, a mean Shepherd, and earns his Bread by keeping of Sheep; and this he did of mere Choice; he was not constrain'd thereto, and so submitted to it, but he chose it. Oh, strange Choice, in a Worldling's Eye! None but them that have the same Faith which *Moses* had, will make such a Choice. But however strange this Choice might seem to *Pharoah's* Courtiers then, or to Unbelievers now, it was not an irrational one: No, *Moses* had the highest Reason for what he did; he acted herein very confidently with spiritual Reason, or the Principles of Reason sanctify'd. And therefore the Holy Ghost gives us the Cause of this wonderful Effect: *For he had Respect unto the Recompense of the Reward.* The Eye of his Faith look'd beyond the Things of Time and Sense, to that transcendent and eternal Glory, which is to be reveal'd in the Saints. He had Soul-ravishing Views of the Infinite Glory of that GOD, who had said to *Abraham,* and in him to all his Seed, *Fear not, for I am thy Shield, and thy exceeding great REWARD,* Gen. xv. 1. And he look'd to the Glory of that happy Day, when a *Crown of Righteousness* shall be set upon the Head of every Overcomer; which drew on his Soul to run in that Way which let to so glorious an End. So that he did not choose to suffer Affliction merely for its own sake, but as it was the Way appointed of God for his People to pass thro' unto the Heavenly Kingdom. He chose to suffer Affliction with the People of God, to cast in his Lot among them, to fare as they did, for present and future, for Time and for Eternity. And this because they had JEHOVAH for their God; such a GOD, that made them the only HAPPY People, in all Conditions, in all Times, and unto all Eternity. And this glorify'd God exceedingly, in that he preferr'd him above all; above all those high Enjoyments he had in *Pharoah's* Court: Yea, he saw such a transcendent Glory in this GOD, as he is to be enjoy'd in and thro' *Christ,* that made him esteem even the very Reproaches he should suffer for his Sake, to be greater Riches than the Treasures in *Egypt.* And thus it was apparent that he made God his chief End, in that he forsook all, and follow'd him, thro' thick and thin, better and worse; that so he might have the present and eternal Enjoyment of him, as his chief Good, and Soul-satisfying ALL! And tho' the poorest Believer in the World has *obtain'd like precious Faith* with *Moses,* which prodeceth answerable Effects in his proper Sphere, yet

Moses had a greater Opportunity to glorify God, in this Respect, in forsaking Abundance for him, because of his high Station in the World. And tho' your Ladyship is not call'd, as *Moses* was, to a personal forsaking of your high Station, yet you are call'd to a cleaving unto *Christ* in it; which can't be done without leaving the Pleasures, Riches, and Honours of it in Heart; chusing rather to suffer Affliction with the People of God, than to enjoy the Pleasures of Sin for a Season; esteeming the Reproach of *Christ,* greater Riches than the Treasures of the Universe. And if your Ladyship's Station was not so high, you could not have such an Opportunity to glorify God, by forsaking so much for him, which his Omnipotent Grace enables you to do, under the Soul-attracting Displays of his infinite Sweetness, and transcendent Glory. And therefore,

Once more the Design of God, in your high Station, is, to prepare you hereby for your future Crown. It is indeed a thorny Place, where you, as one of Christ's Lilies, grow; and no wonder if they often scratch and tear you. If you was *of the World, the World would love its own; but because Christ has chosen you out of the World, therefore the World hateth you.* But *remember, it hated Christ before it hated you.* And I doubt not your Willingness to fare in the World, as Christ did, to stay for your Glory, till the whole Course of your Sufferings are fulfill'd; as knowing that *if* you *suffer with him,* you shall *also be glorify'd together:* The Way to the Kingdom lies *thro' much Tribulation:* But your dear Lord Jesus will be a Companion with you in it. Not a Sorrow pierceth your Heart, but Christ feels it; yea, takes it as done to himself: He is privy to all your Distresses, and in dear, sympathizing Love, will support you under 'em, sanctify you by 'em, and deliver you from them. When you have no Christian Friend or Brother by, to tell your Case to, Christ is with you then, who is *a Friend that sticketh closer than a Brother; a Friend that loves at all times, a Brother born for Adversity;* on Purpose to know Adversity, that he might sympathize with you in it, and save you from it; unto whom you may freely open all your Heart, in the Faith of his infinite Bowels to pity you, and Power to help you. For he'll not only compassionate you in all your Griefs, but in infinite Grace and Faithfulness, he'll richly supply all your Wants. And when you ha'n't Opportunity to converse with Christian

Friends, labour to improve that Season, by acquainting yourself more intimately with the Lord Jesus: Drink at the Well-head, the Fountain is infinitely sweeter than the Streams; and you shall never come to his Bosom, and be sent away empty. Go on therefore, right noble Lady, to cleave unto Christ, by Faith, and every Grace, taking up his Cross daily, and following the Lamb withersoever he goeth; reckoning, *that the Sufferings of this present Time are not worthy to be compared with the Glory which shall be revealed in you.* Take Pleasure in denying yourself, in all Respects, for Christ: Be glad that you have any thing to part with for him that has lov'd you. Christ took Pleasure in denying himself, his Great SELF, for you. And Oh! what did ye deny himself of, when, in infinite Love, he left his Glory in Heaven, became a *Man of Sorrows,* and dy'd on the Cross for you, to redeem you from Sin and Death, to endless Life and Glory! And what can be too dear to part with for your dear Lord Jesus? I'm sure, nothing that he calls for, while your Eye is fixt upon his boundless Love, and your Soul chang'd *into the same Image.* Rejoice therefore that you are *counted worthy to suffer Shame for his Name;* and esteem *the Reproaches of Christ,* your great and substantial *Riches.* For all the Flouts and Frowns you meet with for cleaving to Christ, his Cause, People, Word and Ordinances in this World, will be as so many Jewels to enrich your Crown in the World to come. Oh, what a rich, massy, embelish'd Crown, will Christ set upon the Heads of those Saints, who have left all, and follow'd him amidst ten thousand Reproaches! *Ye,* (saith our Lord) *which have follow'd me, in the Regeneration, when the Son of Man shall sit on the Throne of his Glory, ye also shall sit upon twelve Thrones, judging the twelve Tribes of* Israel. *And every one that hath forsaken Houses, or Brethren, or Sisters, or Father, or Mother, or Wife, or Children, or Lands for my Name's sake, shall receive an Hundred-fold,* (even in this present Time) *and shall inherit everlasting Life,* Mat. xix. 28, 29. Christ has *Thrones* for his suffering Saints, which are far superior to all those petty Glories, of which the Princes and Potentates of this World boast. And as for Crowns, Christ has *a Crown of Life, a Crown of Righteousness, a Crown of Glory,* which he'll give to every Overcomer, at his glorious Appearing and Kingdom, *Rev.* ii. 10. *2 Tim.* iv. 8. *1 Peter* v. 4. When, of the freest Grace, he'll *give Rewards unto his Servants, and to his Saints, and to all that fear his Name both small and great,* Rev. xi. 18. And then the raised Saints, those starry Glories of the first Resurrection, being marshall'd into Order, shall shine forth in their different Orbs, with an heavenly Lustre, and a World-confounding Splendor: And those shall shine the brightest in that Day, who have been enabled to do and suffer most for Christ in this. For every of their Services, even the meanest, shall then receive a full and proportionable Reward. *1 Cor.* xv. 41, 42. *Matt.* v. 11, 12. And chap. x. 41, 42. *Blessed then is the Man that endureth Temptation; for when he is tried, he shall receive the Crown of Life, which the Lord hath promis'd to them that love him,* Jam. i. 12.

I am, with the greatest Respect, Your Ladyships, at all Obedience in the Lord, &c.

LETTER XIV.

To Mrs. S.

Dear Friend,

Grace unto you, and Peace be multiply'd.

OUR Lord, *John,* iii. 3. Affects the Necessity of the New-Birth, and *ver.* 5. Declares what kind of Birth he intends, *viz. Of Water and of the Spirit; i.e.* of the Word and Spirit of God; without which no Man *can see,* that is, enjoy, or *enter into the Kingdom of God.* The reason of it is this; because, in order to all kind of Enjoyment, there must be an Agreeableness in the Person or Thing enjoying, with the Person or Thing enjoyed. This the Apostle declares, *1 Cor.* ii. 14. *But the natural Man receiveth not the Things of the Spirit of God: because they are Foolishness unto him; neither can he know them, because they are spiritually discerned.* He receives them not, because they are Foolishness unto him; and they are so, because he cannot know them; and the Reason of this, is, because they are spiritually discerned; and he being but a natural Man, has no spiritual Eye, no Organ suited to behold a Glory in spiritual Things, which can only be spiritually discerned.

Thus, in the Works of Nature, the All-wise Creator form'd all his Creatures with a Capacity suited to live, act, or be in that proper Element, Sphere, or Place which he had design'd for them; as Birds in the Air, Fishes in the Water, *&c.* And as for Man, the Top-piece of the Creation, in whom the whole was, as it were, epitomiz'd, or summed up; how curiously was he wrought, when he came out of his Maker's Hand? How excellently was he fitted to enjoy all that great Happiness which was prepared for him! His Soul, as it came out of his Creator's Hand, was excellently fitted to enjoy Communion with God, as the God of Nature, displaying his Glory in the Creatures; and his Body, how wonderfully was that fram'd to enjoy the Creatures in this World? How excellently were all his Senses fitted to their proper Objects? His Eye to behold the Glory of the Sun, the Variety of Creatures, and the Beauty of Colours? His Ear to converse with Sound? His Palate to taste Meats? His Smell to take in Scents? And his Feeling to judge of solid Bodies, perceptible by that Sense? And as it was in the Formation of Man, so, in some measure, it is in his Generation: For, when a Child is born into the World, it is, in these respects, suited to, and has a Desire after the Persons and Things which are therein; and without this, it could have no Enjoyment of the good Things of Life.

And as it is in the Works of Nature, so in the Works of Grace: For, as this World is prepar'd for the Child's Enjoyment, and then that is generated, and born in order to enjoy it; so there's a Kingdom prepar'd for the Children of God; and the Soul must be regenerated, new-born, or born again, before it can see it. There being the same Necessity that the Soul be born into the World of Grace, before it can enjoy that; as there is that a Man should be born into the World of Nature, before he can enjoy this.

And now, methinks, I hear thee say, "All this I am convinc'd of; but I greatly want to know whether I am one of those who are new-born." If this be thy Case, then as the Lord to tell thee, and he'll give thee an Answer of Peace in his own Time. There are two Ways whereby a Soul comes to know that it is new-born: The first is, by the Revelation of the Spirit, bearing witness to the Soul, in some Word or other, where this Truth is declar'd. the second is, by his enabling the Soul to discern its own Acts in divine Light; and to draw Conclusions from its discerned Acts of Grace, that it has the Principle. And in both these Ways, the Lord can give thee Satisfaction in an instant, if it pleaseth him. But generally speaking, it is some Time ere a Child of God can draw steady Conclusions of its being new-born, from its own Acts of the new Life. And therefore thou mayst be new-born, tho' thou dost not know it!

A living Infant, you know, when first born into the World, hath Life; but it doth not know it. It had a secret Life from its first quickning in the Womb; and from thence a secret Motion: but as soon as it is born, it begins to live visibly to others: but yet the Child itself knows nothing of the Matter. It crys, desires the Breast, tastes the Milk, and is satisfy'd; sees the Light, and feels the Heat with Pleasure; all which are visible Demonstrations of its Life to By-standers; but the Child knows nothing of it, because it is not capable of Self-reflection. And thus it is with a new-born Soul: There's a secret Work of God upon the Heart, a Principle of Life given; and from thence some secret Motions and faint Stirrings now and then, under begun Convictions, before it is brought forth into the visible Life of Grace; which discovers itself, as soon as ever the Soul is born again, in the Breath or Cry of the new Creature, its Desires, its Discernings, and its Enjoyments: Which, when communicated to grown Christians, they know such a Soul is one of Christ's new-born Babes; altho' this Child itself is not yet capable so to reflect upon its own Acts, as to conclude its Life from thence.

And if this be thy Case, that thou canst not pass a Judgment from what thou hast experienced, that thou hast the Life of Grace, or art new-born; then tell me, as a rational Creature, how it is with thee? For as such, thou canst tell what the Acts of thy Soul have been; altho', as a new Creature, thou mayst not yet be come to such an Exercise of thy spiritual Senses, as to know those Acts to be Acts of Grace, and a certain Demonstration of thy being born again.

Well, a living Child sees: What hast thou seen? Hast thou seen thyself to be a Sinner by Nature, as well as by Practice? In Heart, as well as Life? And that thou art utterly undone, and must perish for ever, without an Interest Jesus Christ; as being utterly unable to do any thing to deliver thyself from the Wrath to come? Hast thou seen thy own

Righteousness to be but *Filthy Rags?* And thy own Strength, to do any good, but Weakness? Again, hast thou seen an Excellency in Christ, as a complete Saviour, that is exceeding suitable to thy Case as a lost Sinner? And hast thou any Discernings of the Glory of God's Free-Grace and Mercy in Christ? Thou hast then the new Creature's Eye, discerning Faith, even the Faith of God's Elect.

And, from these Discernings, hast thou been made to cry unto the Lord. To lament thy Sinfulness before him, and to supplicate his Throne for Mercy, praying him to give thee Christ, whatever he denies thee of? Thou hast then the new Creature's Breath, which flows from none but those that have the new Creature's Life.

Again, what are thy Desires? Are the Longings of thy Soul after the Free-Grace and Mercy of God in Christ, as held forth in the Promises, those *Breasts of Consolation?* Thou hast then the new Creature's Appetite, and art certainly born of the Word and Spirit of God.

Once more, what are thy Enjoyments? What satisfies and pleaseth thy Soul best? Has the Free-Grace of God, and of the Lord Jesus Christ, been sweet and savoury to thee in a Promise, or in an Ordinance to the refreshing and satisfying of thy Soul for some Moments; just so long as thou hast the *Breast* in thy Mouth, the Grace of the Promise *milk'd* out to thee? Then thou hast *tasted that the Lord is gracious,* and art one of Christ's new-born Babes. And hast thou ever felt any refreshing Warmth and Comfort in the Love of God, which, like Fire, has warm'd and heated thy cold Soul? Thou hast then that Satisfaction which is proper to a new Creature: and it is evident, in all these respects, that thou art certainly born again. And as such, thou shalt see, that is, enjoy *the Kingdom of God,* as a kingdom of Grace here, which is a Kingdom of Power, *Righteousness, Peace, and Joy in the Holy Ghost;* and thou shalt enter into the Kingdom of Glory hereafter, as being made *meet* to be a Partaker of the *Inheritance of the Saints in Light.* For he that is thy God *hath prepar'd for* thee *a City,* and *wrought* thy Soul *for this self same thing.* There being never a Soul in the World that is thus wrought upon, but is *a Vessel of Mercy prepared unto Glory,* by a saving Work of the Holy Ghost upon it, as well as in the Purpose of God concerning it.

Go on therefore, as a *new-born Babe*, to *desire the sincere Milk of the Word*, the unmixed Grace of the Gospel; and fear not to receive it, that thou mayst *grow thereby*. For it is on purpose for thee, to maintain and increase they begun Life of Grace in thy Soul, until it is perfected in the Life of Glory. Rejoice then, thou Lamb of Christ, for thou art exceeding safe under thy kind Shepherd's Care: he'll *gather* thee *with his Arm*, and *carry thee in his Bosom;* he'll *lead* thee *into green Pastures, beside the still Waters*, and make thee to *lye down safely*.

I am, with dear Love,

Yours in him, &c.

LETTER XV.

To Mrs. C.

Dear Sister,

I Greet you in the Lord, wishing *Peace*, from *the God of Peace*, to be extended towards you *like a River*.

I should have wrote to you before now, but I have been hindred, partly thro' the Affliction that has attended my Yoke-fellow, and my own personal Weakness, under which I often groan, because I can do so little for my dear Lord Jesus. Oh, how am I prevented from serving Christ as I would, by reason of the Body of Sin that dwelleth in me, and the Weakness of my natural Frame! But yet, in Faith, I look forward to *the Day of* my *Redemption, and rejoice in Hope of the Glory of God*, when I shall have done with all natural and sinful Weakness too, and be for ever fill'd with Strength to know, love, and glorify God perfectly. Here we have Weakness attending our Souls, as well as bodily Weakness, to conflict with. What qualms, sick, and fainting Fits come over our Spirits now, at times, while the Body of Sin and Death works in us? But in Heaven, *Mortality shall be swallowed up of Life. The Inhabitant* of that City *shall say no more, I am sick;* for Sin, with all its Effects, shall be for ever destroy'd. God will root the Being of Sin out of our Nature, at Death; and perfect Conformity to Christ shall take the Place that Sin once had in our Souls: And he'll deliver our Bodies too from the Domination of Death, at the

Resurrection-morn, fashioning them *like unto* the *glorious Body* of Christ. And then Sin and Death will, apparently, be swallow'd up in the Victory of everlasting Life. Oh the Glory of that State, when we shall never have a vain Thought more! An unbelieving Thought more! A heartless, listless Thought for God more! But shall have our whole Souls intensely fixt upon him, beholding his bright Face, fir'd with love to him, and fill'd with Zeal for his Glory, ascending like a perpetual Flame, in eternal *Hallelujahs!* Then we shall be fitted for Glory indeed, both in its Enjoyment and Employment. We shall see the Lamb's Face, and the Face of God in him, and *cast* down our *Crowns before the Throne,* while we ascribe Salvation, Glory and Honour unto God and the Lamb for ever. We shall then be able to bear that *Weight of Glory,* which is now prepared for us; which, was it to be let out upon us here, would crush our weak Nature, and break down our feeble Frame, under the majestick Greatness thereof. This *new Wine* of Glory would *burst* our *old Bottles,* the old Frame of our Nature. And therefore the *Vessels of Mercy* must be *prepar'd* for, before they are fill'd with Glory; and when we are prepar'd for it, we shall everlastingly be fill'd with it. God the Father *prepar'd* us *for Glory,* in his Eternal Choice of us in his Son, fore-appointing us to that great End. God the Son prepar'd us for Glory, when, in Love to the Church, he *gave himself for it, that he might sanctify and cleanse it with the Washing of Water by the Word,* that he might *present it unto himself a glorious Church, not having Spot or Wrinkle or any such thing.* And God the Holy Ghost prepares us for Glory, by that *good Work* of Conformity to Christ, which he hath *begun in us,* and will *perfect* upon us, both in Soul and Body. And when, from the Love of God, in his three glorious Persons, we are fully made *meet for* our *Inheritance,* we shall enjoy it: As soon as ever we are come to Age, we shall enter upon the full Possession of that inconceivable Glory, and endless Life we have in the LORD, as our *Portion!*

Lift up thy Head therefore, my dear Sister, under all the Trials thou meetst with in this present Time; for the Lord, by these, is preparing thee for endless Glory. The *everlasting Arms* are *underneath,* to support thee; they are round about, to embrace and defend thee; and they are always at Work upon thee, to polish and prepare thee for Glory, by every

Stroke that toucheth thee. And tho' Trials may be grieving to thy frail Flesh; yet thy God will exercise thy Faith, and every Grace by 'em, and make them to *yield* thee *the peaceable Fruit of Righteousness,* in that *Crown of Life,* which the Lord has *promis'd to them that love him,* when they are fully try'd. Therefore endure Temptation, looking to the Glory which shall be reveal'd; for there is a peculiar Blessedness attending it. When a new Trial comes, think thus with thyself; "Now my God is about to make me more like Christ; 'tis the boundless Love of my Father's Heart, that gives me this Cross to bear; that so I might be conformable unto Christ in Sufferings: Looking therefore unto my Lord, who *endur'd* his *Cross for the Joy set before him,* and leaning upon his Strength, I'll take up mine, and bear it after him, until I reach Glory with him." Gold must be refin'd from its Dross, before it can shine forth in its native Glory. So must the Saints, in the Furnace of Affliction, before they shine forth in that Glory which shall follow. Therefore prize your Trials, and be thankful for 'em; for they all *work together for* your *Good,* under the efficacious Influence of eternal Love, infinite Wisdom, and almighty Power. And since our *light Affliction* which is *but for a Moment, worketh for us a far more exceeding and eternal Weight of Glory;* what Cause have we to rejoice in Christ now? and *to comfort one another with these Words,* that *we shall,* ere long, *be for ever with* him?

Fare ye well in the Lord. In him, with dear Love, I am yours for ever, &c.

LETTER XVI.

To Mr. C.

Honour'd Brother,

Grace and Peace from God our Father, and from Jesus Christ our Lord.

Your God is *the God of Peace;* and your Jesus, the Lord of Peace, the King of Peace; that made Peace for all his Subjects, and gives it to 'em by the blessed Spirit, as the Comforter. Having therefore *your Feet shod with the Preparation of the Gospel of Peace,* go on cheerfully thro' a World of

Trials, and fear none of the rugged Way you meet with. For having *Peace with God, thro' Jesus Christ,* and your Faith cloth'd herewith, you may safely tread your roughest Way, as being well fenc'd and secur'd for all harm. Remember, if your Trials are great, and your Way thorny, your *Shoes* shall be *iron and Brass,* and *as* your *Days,* your *Strength:* You shall have Strength proportionable unto every Day of Trial. What tho' you have no Strength of your own, to endure the least Affliction, to the Glory of God; yet you have Strength enough in your Head: Say therefore, in Faith, as it was long ago foretold, *In the LORD have I Strength,* Isa. xlv. 24. For unless the everlasting Strength of JEHOVAH could fail, you shall not want fresh Supplies when you are just ready to faint. No, *he giveth Power to the Faint, and to them that have no Might he increaseth Strength. And they that wait upon the LORD, shall renew their Strength, they shall run and not be weary, and walk and not faint:* And if they meet with Trials, which are like mighty Mountains in their Way, they shall *mount up with Wings as Eagles,* and fly over them, *Isa.* xl. 29, 31. Therefore fear none of your Trials: For infinite Wisdom ordain'd 'em, infinite Love bestows 'em, and almighty Power over-rules them for the Glory of God, and your Advantage. Grieve you they may; but destroy you they cannot. And learn, my dear Brother, to look for your Peace where it is, even in the Bosom of Christ: *In me,* says he, *ye shall have Peace.* He has told you, that *in the World ye shall have Tribulation:* therefore think it no *strange Thing.* For all God's Children have their Trials, those very Trials which were appointed for them. Therefore say, with *Job, He performeth the Thing that is appointed for me,* Chap. xxiii. 14. Those very Trials you meet with were fore-appointed for you, as a Means to try and exercise your Graces. Your kind Father designs to make you a *Partaker of his Holiness,* by every Chastisement that passeth over you. He designs your *Profit* herein, to brighten and increase your Grace, and thereby to prepare you for your future Crown.

And if you find your Afflictions to be a Means of sending you often to the Throne, and exercising your Graces; if you learn Obedience by the Things you suffer; you have great Reason to bless God for them, and for a sanctify'd Use of 'em. And don't let Satan rob God of the Glory, nor you of the Comfort, of his Kindness to you herein. For Afflictions could work no Good in thy Heart or Life, if God did not work by 'em. And that God that works by 'em, could as well work without 'em, was it his Pleasure. He could fill our Hearts brimful of Grace, without Trials as a Means, was it his Will. But since infinite Wisdom saw it meet, that *thro' much Tribulation* we should *enter the Kingdom,* let us submit with Thankfulness, and like the Way that leads to so glorious an End. God did not appoint Affliction merely for its own sake, but as a Means to purify his Children. *By this,* says the Lord, *shall the Iniquity of Jacob be purged, and this is all the Fruit to take away his Sin,* Isa. xxvii. 9. Fiery Trials are to brighten our Graces, and consume our Dross. Rejoice therefore, as *knowing that Tribulation worketh Patience,* (It works it, because God having appointed it as a Means, works by it unto this End) *and Patience, Experience; and Experience, Hope,* Rom. v. 3, 4. And as our God designs to increase our Graces by Affliction; so to prevent us from Sin thereby. And 'tis wondrous Grace to be either prevented or restor'd from Sin, by any Trial we meet with. The Lord knoweth that our Hearts are *bent to Backsliding* from him; and therefore, in infinite Grace, he says, *I will hedge up thy Way with Thorns, and make a Wall, that she shall not find her Paths. And she shall follow after her Lovers, but she shall not overtake them; and she shall seek them, but shall not find 'em,* Hos. Ii. 6, 7.

Here's preventing Mercy stopping up our Way of sinful Delight in the Creatures. But what would all this do upon our Spirits, if God was not to work upon our Hearts in these thorny Dispensations? Why, just nothing at all that is good: We should not get a jot nearer the Bosom of God thereby, but rather, like the Wicked, fret under his Hand, and blaspheme his Name. But behold, that same Grace that hedgeth up our Way with Thorns, and thereby prevents us from taking up our Rest in the Creatures, doth absolutely engage to work efficaciously upon our Souls, in turning them to God by these thorny Providences; as it follows,

Then shall she say, I will go and return to my first Husband, for then it was better with me than now, [Then] shall she say: When? why, when her Way is hedg'd up, when all the Creatures she seeks to delight herself in, scratch and wound her. Aye, and then *she* [shall] *say,* (it is not said, she *will* say; but she *shall* say) Efficacious Grace will make her say: And what shall she say? Why; *I will go and return unto my first Husband; for then was it better with me than now.* Here's God's *shall,* before her, *I will:* Efficacious Grace secures her Will, and sweetly allures her into the Bosom of God, under fresh Discoveries of his Relation to her, as her Husband; giving her a quick Remembrance of that infinite Sweetness she once tasted in him, and a delightful Prospect of those transcendent Privileges, which are only to be enjoy'd in Communion with him. *I will go and return to my first Husband; for then was it better with me than now.* 'Tis as if she should say, "The Creatures grieve me, and I do but wound my self, in seeking Delight in 'em: *I'll go* therefore unto Christ, *my first Husband,* who is all Love, as well as Loveliness, and will therefore readily receive me again; *for it was better with me* when I lived in his Bosom, *than it is now* I have forsaken him: I'll therefore return again unto him, as my complacent Rest, my Soul-satisfying All."

And, Oh, happy Souls, who are thus wrought upon under Trials, and brought to the Bosom of God by Afflictions! Has this been thy Case, my dear Brother? *It is the Lord's doing,* and let it be *marvellous in* thy *Eyes.* If he brings thee to himself, what matter how? And be assur'd, that none of thy Afflictions, whether from within or from without, could, of themselves, bring thee to the Bosom of God under any Trial. No, 'tis he himself that brings thee, whenever thou art brought. Praise his Name therefore, in that he deals with thee as a Child, blessing his Rod, to make thee holy. The Ungodly never have one sanctify'd Affliction in their whole Course: But unto us that believe in Jesus, Afflictions are Fining-Pots, to make us bright and glorious. They are all mercies to us: They flow from Mercy, they are manag'd by Mercy, and they end in Mercy: For God cannot be disappointed of his Design therein; to wit, his own Glory, and our special Advantage. There is something to be done upon us in all the Changes which pass over us: One Providence has one Thing to do upon us; another, another; and God, in and by all, is working us up into Conformity to Christ in Holiness, in order to our being conformed unto him in Glory. And whatever he does with us, he is still carrying on our Salvation, in that Way which infinite Wisdom sees best for us. Therefore *cast* thy *Care upon him that careth for* thee; and follow thy Lord in all his Ordinances, and in all his Providences: For thy dear Lord Jesus will be thy Guide and sweet Companion thro' the Wilderness, until he bring thee home to Glory, and set thee before his Father's Face, in whose *Presence is Fulness of Joy,* and *Rivers of Pleasure for evermore.* Say with *David,* 2 Sam. xxiii. 5. *Altho' my House be not so with God; yet he hath made with me as everlasting Covenant, order'd in all things and sure: For this is all my Salvation, and all my Desire, altho' he make it not to grow.* I am,

with dear Love, yours in the Lord, &c.

LETTER XVII.

To Mrs. B.

Dear and Honour'd Sister,

Grace unto you, and Peace be multiply'd from God our Father, and from Jesus Christ our Lord.

Having heard of thy Distress, by reason of the Loss of near Relatives, it was on my Heart to write a few Lines unto thee. And I would say unto you, as our dear Lord to his Disciples, *let not your Heart be troubled, neither let it be afraid,* John xiv. 27. Be not troubled for the Loss of your dear Relations: For it is the Lord's Hand that took them away; and he has done all things well; well, for his own Glory, and well, for your Soul's Advantage: He has done all so well, that nothing could be better than it is. You know he has a sovereign Right to give Mercies to his Creatures, or take them away as he pleases; but he exerciseth this Sovereignty towards his Children, in a way of special Love and Grace. And if you cou'd believe stedfastly the Love of your Father's Heart, in these smart Strokes of his hand; you would see no Cause to be angry, like *Jonah,* for the Loss of his *Gourd,* Chap. iv. 9. But rather, to say, with *Eli, It is the LORD: let him do what seemeth him good,* 1 Sam. iii. 18. And with *Job, the LORD gave, and the LORD hath taken away; blessed be the Name of the LORD,* chap. i. 21. But, my dear Sister, I trust you are not angry at what the Lord has done, but only troubled for your Loss.

But as to this consider, you have not lost your God; you have Him still; and in having Him you have all, even in the Want of all; and therefore need not be much troubled. Let them be at their Wits End, and break their Hearts for the Loss of Creatures, who have no Interest in God: But as for us, that have the LORD for our Portion, we are so rich, that we can never be made poor; and so happy, that we have always Cause of rejoicing; and it well becomes us, when we have nothing of the Creature to rejoice in, to possess all Things in GOD, and glory in Him as our ALL! May not Christ say to thee, my dear Sister, as *Elkanah* to *Hannah, Why weepest thou? and why eatest thou not? and why is thy Heart grieving? Am not I better to thee than ten Sons?* 1 Sam. i. 8. Is not Christ better than ten Sons? Infinitely better than all the Creatures, both in the upper and lower Worlds? And hast thou him, and yet troubled! Oh wipe thy Eyes, and weep no more for the Loss of the Creature, when thou hast the Creator! for the Shadow, when thou hast the Substance! for a Beam, when thou hast the Body of the Sun! for the Stream, when thou hast fhe Fountain! and for a Drop, when thou hast the Ocean! If there is not enough in Christ to fill thy Heart with Gladness, then go on to mourn; but if there is, pass off from the Creatures, run to his Bosom, and solace thyself with his infinite Sweetness, his boundless Excellencies, and his incomprehensible Glory! Are the Creatures gone? Thou hast not lost much; nay, nothing of that full and comprehensive Happiness, which God has prepar'd for thee in his Son. Hadst thou once some Sweetness in the Creatures, and dost thou now want it? Care not much for it; since Christ stands in all Relations to thee, and will fill them up with his own infinite Sweetness, thro' Time, and to Eternity. There are no Comforts in the Creatures, but what God puts into 'em; and none to be enjoy'd in them, but what are mixt with Crosses. But in Christ, there's Joy without Sorrow, Light without Darkness, Sweet without Bitter, and Life without an End! Thy Husband, Christ, ever lives, and ever loves; and *because* he *lives,* thou *thou shalt live also;* thy Life is secur'd in his. Think but, in Faith, which Christ is to thee, has done, and will do for thee; and I dare say thou'lt want none but him, to make thy Happiness complete. He has infinite Bowels to compassionate and succour thee in all thy Distresses; infinite Wisdom, to order all Things for the best for thee; infinite Patience, to pass by all thy Provocations; infinite Mercy, to forgive all thy innumerable Transgressions; infinite Fulness, to supply all thy Wants; infinite Power, to defend thee from all Harms, and save thee from all

Misery unto all Glory; and in infinite Faithfulness, he *will never leave, nor forsake thee!* Others may leave thee, but *Christ* will never fail thee. Friends may *stand aloof from thy Sore;* but *Christ* will *know* thy *Soul in Adversity.* Yea, saith he, *the Mountains shall depart, and the Hills be removed; but my Kindness shall not depart from thee, nor the Covenant of my Peace be removed, saith the LORD, that hath Mercy on thee,* Isa. liv. 10. And what canst thou want more? Oh, nothing but the Enjoyment of *Christ,* to make thee perfectly happy! Labour therefore, to live upon him, as thy Time-Portion, as well as thy eternal ALL: For this will be for his Glory, and thy Comfort. It will be for the Glory of thy Lord, if thou put him for a Well, a never-failing Well of Consolation, while thou art passing thro' the *Valley of Baca,* this World of Trials; and in acquainting thyself with him, thou shalt have Peace; such *Peace* that the *World* can neither *give,* nor take, such *Joy* that a *Stranger intermeddleth not with.*

"Aye, sayst thou, but this is my Misery, I am so chain'd down to Sense and sensible Enjoyments, that my Soul is oft *in Prison,* and I *cannot come forth* into the Liberty and Sweetness of my Lord's Bosom." Well, if this be thy Case, *Christ* can come to thee, when thou canst not come to him: He can come *leaping on the Mountains, skipping on the Hills;* those Hills of Difficulty, which are too great for thee to climb over to get to him; and such his Grace, that he will come. *I will not leave you comfortless,* says he, *I will come unto you,* John xiv. 18. And if *Christ* comes unto us, he brings all Salvation with him: He brings Life, Light, Liberty, Joy, Glory, all that our Souls can want. He can, with a Word of his Mouth, break our Bands asunder, knock off our Fetters, strengthen our weak Faith, and give us Access, in an Instant, into the glorious Liberty of the Sons of God. So mighty is our Beloved, that he *can* do it; so gracious, and so faithful, that he *will* do it. Thy Maker, thy Husband, will have compassion upon thee in all thy Soul-Distresses, as well as in all thy outward Troubles; and he'll comfort thee in all thy Tribulation. Thy dear Lord Jesus will be thy Companion all the Way thro' the Wilderness: Do not think that thou art left to go thro' the World alone: No, thou hast thy Beloved with thee, to conduct, support, comfort, and protect thee in thy Passage home to Glory. And when thou dost not see his Face, believe it, his Heart is the same towards thee as ever; and thou art then call'd to live by Faith, rejoicing in Hope of the Glory of God: For tho', *for a small Moment he may forsake thee,* as to his sensible Presence, yet, (as he'll never forsake thee as to his real, gracious Presence, so) *with everlasting Kindness he will have Mercy upon thee:* And he'll quickly take thee up to Glory, where thou shalt see his Face, without the least Cloud to interpose for ever. And then he'll *wipe all Tears from thy Eyes,* and open the Mystery of his Providences, which here thou hast been try'd with, as having been all consistent with his everlasting Kindness towards thee, and subservient to thy eternal Salvation. Therefore lift up thy Head; for what *thou knowest not now, thou shalt know hereafter.*

The Grace of our Lord Jesus Christ be with thy Spirit. *Amen. I am, with dear Love, yours in him,* &c.

LETTER XVIII.

To Mrs. L.

Dear Friend,

NOT having Ability of Body to give you a Visit, I was willing to write a Line to you under your present Concern. And I would say unto thee, as *Paul* and *Silas* to the Jaylor, *Acts* xvi. 31. *Believe on the Lord Jesus Christ, and thou shalt be saved.* God the Father, from his great Love to poor Sinners, even when they were *dead in Sins,* did give his own Son to be their Saviour; he call'd him to this work, and anointed him for it; and when he sent him forth into the World, he gave *this Commandment* to lost Sinners, that they *should believe on the Name of his Son Jesus Christ,* 1 John iii. 23. *And this is the Will of him that sent me,* saith our Lord, *that every one that seeth the Son, and believeth on him, may have everlasting Life,* John vi. 40. And this Lord Jesus is infinitely *able to save* them *to the uttermost, who came unto God by him,* Heb. vii. 25. And to shew that he is as willing as he is able, he says, *Come unto me, all ye that labour, and are heavy laden, and I will give you Rest,* Matt. xi. 28. And he has given the highest Assurance of Happiness unto that Soul which believes in him: *John* iv. 46. *Verily, verily, I say unto you, he that believeth on me, hath everlasting Life.* And believing on *Christ* is, *looking* unto him for

Salvation: *Isa.* xlv. 22. *Committing* the Soul into his Hands, to be kept from eternal Misery, and brought unto eternal Glory, *1 Tim.* i. 12. 'Tis *trusting* in his Name, *Matt.* xii. 21. and *resting* upon him, as *the Foundation* God has *laid in Sion;* or 'tis the Soul's laying the whole Weight and Stress of its Salvation, building all its Hope of Life upon *Christ* alone, from a discerning of his Preciousness, as that *Rock against* which *the Gates of Hell shall not prevail, &c. 1 Cor.* iii. 11. *1 Peter* ii. 7. *Matt.* xvi. 18.

Well then, dost thou see thyself to be utterly undone by reason of Sin? Here's a Saviour provided, and a great One: Look unto him, and thou shalt live for ever. However great thy Sins are in themselves, or appear to be in thy View, they are not too great to be pardon'd; *Christ* is infinitely greater, as a Saviour, than thou canst be as a Sinner. He is mighty to save; yea almighty. He says, *Look unto me, and be ye saved, all the Ends of the Earth,* Isa. xlv. 22. He commands Sinners at the greatest Distance, to look upon him the great Saviour; and unto every Soul that looks, he says, *Be ye saved:* he is so mighty to save, that he saves with a Word of his Mouth. And that because he is God; as it follows there; *for I am God, and there is none else.* So that his Almightiness, as God, is engag'd to save every Soul that looks unto him for Life. Yea, all the Perfections of his Nature are engag'd for the Salvation of that Soul; his infinite Love, Mercy, Wisdom, Truth, Faithfulness, *&c.* And is not here enough to save thee? Look to him therefore, and thou shalt be saved. Thou shalt be saved, whoever says nay: If Satan says nay, or if thy unbelieving Heart says nay, it matters not; Christ's Word shall stand, and bring all Salvation to thee, notwithstanding all the Opposition that can be made against it. He would have thee look to him as God; and that will answer all thy Objections. What are all thy *Crimson* and *Scarlet*-dy'd Sins, before the infinite Merit of his Blood, that *cleanseth from all Sin!* Isa. i. 18. 1 John i. 7. What's all the Power of thy spiritual Enemies, before the omnipotent Strength of the LORD thy Saviour! Who *travels in the Greatness of his Strength* to save Sinners, and *tread* down their Enemies! *Isa.* lxii. 1. What is all thy Unworthiness and Sinfulness, before free, reigning Grace, and boundless Mercy, in its glorious Superaboundings! *Rom.* v. 21. *1 Tim.* i. 14. If the Lord will be gracious to thee, and will shew Mercy on thee; who, or what shall hinder it? Remember, he will be gracious to thee as GOD; and if thou wantest all the Mercy and Grace that is in him to save thee, thou shalt have it, if thou lookest, as a perishing Sinner, unto *Christ* alone for Salvation. When *Christ* saves a Sinner, he does it *with* his *whole Heart, and* his *whole Soul,* Jer. xxxii. 40, 41. Every one he saves is as much interested in all the Grace of the Saviour for his Salvation, as if *Christ* had never another in the World to save, besides him. And what thinkest thou now? Is all the Grace that is in *Christ,* enough to save thee? Believest thou that he is able to do this? Aye, sayst thou, if I was one of his; but that I am afraid of.

Well, if thou canst not come to him as a Child; come, as the Woman of *Canaan,* who thought herself to be unworthy as a *Dog,* and plead for the *Crumbs* which fall from the Childrens Table; and *Christ* will say unto thee, as he did unto her, *O Woman, great is thy Faith, be it unto thee even as thou wilt,* Matt. xv. 27, 28. Come therefore, come as thou canst, with all thy Misery, and cast thyself down at Jesus Feet, and thou shalt find Mercy. For *he that believeth on him, shall never be confounded* 1 Peter ii. 6. *Seek the LORD* therefore, *while he may be found, and call upon him while he is near.* For he hath said, *Let the Wicked forsake his Way, and the unrighteous Man his Thoughts; and let him return unto the LORD, and he will have Mercy upon him, and to our God, for he will abundantly pardon,* Isa. lv. 6, 7. Come therefore, come, and try what infinite Mercy will do for thee: For there never was any poor, needy Soul that came to the *Throne of Grace* to *find Mercy,* however great his Sins and his Wants were, that was sent away empty, nor shall be, unto the World's End; since Christ *ever liveth to save* them *to the uttermost,* who *come unto God by him,* Heb. vii. 25.

Wishing Grace, Mercy, and Peace may be multiply'd unto thee, in the Manifestation of free Pardon, to the filling of thy Heart with Joy unspeakable, and full of Glory, *I am,*

with dear Love, thine in the Lord, &c.

LETTER XIX.

To Mr. W. G.

Dear Brother, whom I love, and honour in the Lord,

YOUR Labour of Love, which you have shewed towards his Name, Gospel, and Cause in B—s, shall be abundantly own'd, and crown'd in the Day of *Christ;* when you shall find, to your unspeakable Joy and Glory, that none of your Labour has been in vain in the Lord. Wherefore be stedfast, unmoveable, always abounding therein. I rejoice that the Lord has given you a large Heart, and an open Hand for him, who gave himself, his great Self for you. Surely I can say, with *Deborah, My heart is toward Governors of* Israel, *that offer'd themselves willingly to the Help of the Lord,* Judg. v. 9, 23. I am glad that the Love of Christ constrains you to give up yourself and your all unto him. And, believe it, my dear Brother, you shall lose nothing by it. Our Lord has told us, that *a Cup of cold Water* given *to a Disciple, in the name of a Disciple,* or because he belongs to Christ, *shall in no wise lose* its *Reward.* And when he appears the *second Time, without sin, unto Salvation,* he comes to *give Rewards unto his Servants, and to all that fear him, both small and great,* according to their Works. And oh, how brightly shall the Saints then *shine in the Kingdom of their Father,* with a proportionable Glory, unto al their various Services which they have been enabled to do for God in this present State!

'Tis true we owe ourselves, and our all, had we ten thousand times more than we have, to our dear LORD; whom we can never, no not to Eternity, sufficiently love, serve, and honour, for what he is in himself, unto us, and has done for us: So that our utmost Service is our Duty; and could we do all that is commanded, we should still be but *unprofitable Servants: For who hath given him,* (in a Way of Desert or Merit) *and it shall be recompensed to him again?* No, *all Flesh* here must *be silent before* the LORD of GLORY! And the Saints have such a Sight of the Lamb's Worthiness, and of their own Unworthiness, that their Mouths, of all other, are stopped; they'll never open their Mouth before him, and say, we have done many mighty Works in thy Name, which deserve thy Notice: No, the Remembrance of their own Shame, together with the Soul-ravishing prospects of his Glory, will make them shrink to nothing before his infinite Majesty, Love and Grace, in the Review of their best

Services; saying, *Lord, when saw we thee an hungred, and fed thee?* &c. *Ezek.* xvi. 63. *Matt.* xxv. 37.

But yet, such is the boundless Grace of our Lord and Master, our Friend and Brother, our Head and Husband, that none of our Services, no not the least that we are enabled to do for Him, shall go unrewarded. He'll call the Performance of our Duty, Kindness; the Acts of our Service, Friendship; *Jer.* ii. 2. *Jam.* ii. 21, 23. And infinite Love will reward 'em, according to the Estimate it puts upon them. *Ye are they,* saith the Lord, *which have continued with me in my Temptations. And I appoint unto you a Kingdom, as my Father hath appointed unto me: That you may eat and drink at my Table in my Kingdom, and sit on Thrones, judging the twelve Tribes of* Israel, *Luke* xxii. 28, 29, 30. Oh, infinite Grace! How will our Lord honour his Servants! He calls us *Friends;* and then advanceth us as such. He *works all our Works in us* and by us, and then calls 'em ours. He enables us to overcome, and then crowns us as Overcomers; granting us to *sit with* him *in his Throne,* as he overcame, and is *set down with* his *Father in his Throne.* And herein he acts like himself, as the God of all Grace! while every Saint shall *receive his own Reward,* according to his own Labour, *Rev.* iii. 21. *1 Cor.* iii. 8. Blessed then are those Servants, which can do most for Christ in this Day; since, in that Day of his Kingdom, he'll *gird himself, make* them *sit down to Meat,* and *come forth and serve* them, *Luke* xii. 37. A Phrase that has more Grace in it, than we can take in! Wherefore, my beloved Brother, *Stand fast in the LORD,* abounding in his Work; as having *respect unto the Recompense* of the REWARD!

Wishing you may have the Joy, as a Friend of the Bridegroom, to see him have the Bride, (in the Success of the Gospel, in the Conversion of many in B---s)

I am, with dear Love, and due Respect,

Yours in the Lord, &c.

LETTER XX.

To Mrs. S.

Dear and honour'd Sister,

Grace unto you, and Peace be multiplied.

It is the Pleasure of the Lord, your Father, to lay his chastening hand upon your Body; but since this very Chastisement flows from the boundless Love of his Heart, and was determin'd by his infinite Wisdom, for his own Glory, and your Advantage, receive it with Thankfulness. You'll bless God for it, when you come to Heaven; and see how needful it was for you to pass this Way, thro' this Affliction, to Glory: Therefore begin the Work of Praise now. the Lord's Design herein, is not to destroy, but to refine you; to make you more conformable unto Christ, your glorious Head, in Suffering: And as Christ first suffered, and then entred into his Glory, so must you. There's a Glory to follow the Sufferings of Christ mystical, as there was of Christ personal. The Members must have Fellowship with their Head, first in Sufferings, and then in Glory: *For if we suffer with him, we shall also be glorify'd together,* Rom. viii. 17. We should look upon the Sufferings of Christ with a double View.

First, As he suffered in our stead, to satisfy Justice, and bring us to God, *1 Peter* iii. 18. And so, we don't suffer with him. No, blessed be God, *of the People there was none with* him, in this respect, *Isa.* lxiii. 3. Our mighty Mediator, on whom the Father *laid Help,* stood alone, in the Greatness of his Strength, as God-Man, under the inexpressible Weight of our Sins, and his Father's Wrath, pour'd out upon him thro' the Curses of a broken Law; issuing in that overflowing Deluge of Afflictions which he endur'd, when for us he became the *Man of Sorrows;* when *he was wounded for our Transgressions, and bruised for our Iniquities.* And hereby he has for ever satisfy'd Law and Justice, and fully taken away the Curse out of all our Afflictions: For having drank up the Wrath-Cup, he left not one Drop for us. So that in this respect, we don't suffer with him: No, such was the boundless Grace of God towards us, that he suffer'd, and we go free! But then,

Secondly. Christ also suffer'd for us, leaving us an Example, that we *should follow his Steps,* 1 Peter ii. 21. *It became him of whom are all things, and by whom are all things, in the bringing many Sons unto Glory, to make the Captain of their Salvation perfect thro' Sufferings,* Heb. ii. 10. It was a Design becoming the infinite Wisdom of *Jehovah,* to make his own Son, as the *Captain* of their Salvation, the great Leader of his People, *perfect thro' Sufferings.* God ordain'd his own Son, in his assumed Man-Nature, first to *suffer,* and then to *enter into his Glory;* first to pass thro' all Sufferings, and therein to exercise all Graces, and at the End of his Race to be crown'd with all Glory; that so he might become the great Pattern of Obedience unto all his junior Brethren, and the Exemplar of that Glory, which they shall arrive unto when their suffering State is ended, as *1 Peter* ii. 11, 12, 13. with *Heb.* xii. 2. And as Christ's Sufferings are propos'd as an Example of our Obedience, and we enabled to tread in his Steps; so the Head and Members have a Community in Sufferings. Or, we may be said to suffer with him, as I humbly conceive, in these four Respects: 1. In that the Origin, Source, Spring-head, or first Rise of Sufferings, both to Christ and us, is the Father's Love. 2. In that we bear Afflictions, under the Infleunces of the same Spirit in our Measure, as Christ did. 3. In that we have the same End in View, in our patient enduring Affliction, to wit, the Glory of God, as Christ had. And, 4. In that our Sufferings serve as a Foil to set off the Glory which shall succeed 'em, as Christ's did. Suffering, both to Christ and us, while by the same Spirit we learn Obedience under it, is but a Preparation for Glory: As the dark Ground, the Limner says, is in order to commend and set off the fair and beautiful Colours which he designs to draw upon it. And Oh, how glorious will Christ, whole Christ, Head and Members be, when all that Glory is laid upon 'em, which was ordain'd to follow their Sufferings! *Oh thou Afflicted, tossed with Tempest, and not comforted, Behold,* saith the Lord, *I will lay thy Stones with fair Colours,* &c. *Isa.* lxiv. 11, 12. And Oh, how glorious will the Church appear, in the *New Jerusalem* State, when this Promise shall have its full Accomplishment, when the *fair Colours* of Glory are laid upon her *Stones,* which before were carv'd, and prepar'd by Affliction to receive it! Affliction, to God's People, under the Management of infinite Wisdom and Grace, is like the Carving of Letters in Stone, in order to overlay 'em with Gold.

Well, my dear Sister, since you suffer with Christ, you need not be very sorrowful under it; you have a sweet Companion in all your Tribulation. Your dear Lord Jesus interests himself in all your Sorrows; *I was sick,* &c. says he, *Matt.* xxv. 36. And, says *Paul, I fill up that which is behind of the Afflictions of Christ in my Flesh,* Col. i. 24. Since this Affliction in your Flesh is Christ's, fear not a glorious Issue. You are one of those Sons that are to be brought to Glory; and in Conformity to the First-born of the Family, you are to be lov'd home, thro' Affliction. *Christ* has gone before us, thro' Affliction and Death, up to Glory; and taken the Curse and Bitterness out of our Pains, and the Sting out of our Death; and now 'tis sweet following our Fore-runner, who is for us entred into the Presence of his and our Father. I say, following of him; because our Faith is to eye *Christ* as gone before us into Glory. But let us not think that he is so gone, as to leave us alone in a World of Trials. No, no; we have our Beloved with us, his Arm to lean on, and his Bosom to rest in, all the Way we come up from the Wilderness. He has said, *I will never leave thee, nor forsake thee,* Heb. xiii. 5. And the Grace and Faithfulness of this Promise secure his Presence with us, thro' Life, thro' Death, and to Eternity. And if the Lord is with us, who, or what need we fear? So that we *may boldly say, The Lord is my Helper, I will not fear what any Creature,* or thing *can do unto me.* For *neither Death, nor Life, nor Angels, nor Principalities, nor Powers, nor Things present, nor Things to come, nor Height, nor Depth, nor any other Creature, shall be able to separate us from the Love of God which is in Christ Jesus our Lord,* Rom. viii. 38, 39.

And now, that you may be *Strengthned with all Might, unto all Patience, and Long-suffering, with Joyfulness,* is the earnest Desire of,

Your humble Servant in the Lord, &c.

LETTER XXI.

To Mrs. K.

Dear friend, and honour'd Sister,

I Beg leave to return humble and hearty Thanks to you and Mr. K. for all that great kindness you have shewn to the Cause of Christ here, in its low Estate; and unto us the least in our Father's House. And be assur'd, that none of your Labour of Love shall in any wise lose its Reward. The Lord abundantly inrich your Souls with his Grace, and cause you to inherit Substance, the *true Riches,* where neither *Moth nor Rust can corrupt, nor Thieves break thro'* to *steal.* All things here are Shadows, that have nothing in them suited to the Nature of an immortal Soul: The best of worldly Enjoyments are empty, and passing away; but the Riches of Christ, are both durable and unsearchable! And oh that the Lord, the Spirit, may give unto you a Sight of your Interest in those immense Treasures! If we have Christ, we have all; all for Time, and all for Eternity! Oh the exceeding Preciousness of Christ! and the Happiness of that Soul who is interested in him! Neither Men nor Angels can tell it out. The whole World, with all the Variety of Creatures and Things in it, can't fill the Heart of one Man. But One Christ can fill the largest Soul, yea, Millions of them, both in the upper and lower Worlds, at once: Because his Fulness is infinite! Oh, what a *goodly Heritage* have they, that have Christ for their *Portion!* And how happy are they who love him most, and serve him best! Oh, what a glorious Master is Jesus Christ! who makes all his Servants *Kings!* who has *Thrones* and *Crowns* for every one of them; who pardons all their Sins, accepts all their weak Services, and in infinite Grace rewards them! Yea, that gives them no less than his great SELF! And the eternal Enjoyment of him, as their exceeding Great REWARD! What a Thraldom is the Service of Sin, and how doth it debase and ruin the Soul! But the Service of Christ is perfect Freedom, and the highest Honour! The whole Hosts of Angels and Arch-angels, with the *Spirit of just Men,* now *made perfect* in Heaven, think it both their Honour and Happiness to serve and glorify Jesus Christ. What an Honour then is it for a a mortal, sinful Worm, to be admitted into the Service of this Great LORD! And a kind of Fellowship with the glorious Family above! Oh, little doth the World think, what an honour and Happiness it is to serve Christ Here! Nor yet what Glory he hath in reserve for his Servants hereafter! Christ's Servants wear Royal Apparel, and are feasted as so many Princes, even here; but the World don't see their Glory, not know their Enjoyments, because they are of an heavenly Nature; and so too bright and high to be discern'd by the natural Eye, or for the natural Man to conceive of! Oh the amazing Difference Christ puts between his Servants, and the Servants of Sin and Satan, even in this World! *Behold*, says he, *my Servants shall eat, but ye shall be hungry; behold, my Servants shall drink, but ye shall be thirsty; behold, my Servants shall rejoice, but ye shall be ashamed: Behold, my Servants shall sing for Joy of Heart, but ye shall cry for Sorrow of Heart, and shall howl for Vexation of Spirit,* Isa. lxv. 13, 14. Christ's Servants have heavenly *Manna* to eat, a *pure River of Water of Life* to drink of, the *Streams* whereof till them with Joy and Gladness, and make then break forth into singing, even in this World; while the Servants of Sin have just the Reverse. But oh, when Christ comes again, *in his Father's Glory, in his own Glory, and in the Glory of his holy Angels,* what a Difference will he put between 'em then! When they that fear the LORD shall shine forth with an heavenly Splendor, as Jewels made up; and have such an astonishing Glory put upon them, that the Ungodly, to their utmost Shame, and everlasting Confusion, shall *discern between the Righteous and the Wicked, between him that serveth God, and him that serveth him not!* Mal.iii. 17, 18.

Wishing Grace and Peace from God our Father, and the Lord Jesus Christ, by the blessed Comforter; *I am,*

with dear Love and Service to your whole Self, yours in the Lord for ever, &c.

LETTER XXII.

To Mrs. D.

Dear Sister,

Grace unto you, and Peace be multiplied.

Having heard, that you are much cast down in your Soul, under a Sense of your own Unworthiness, and afraid, on that account, that you are none of the Lord's; I was willing, according to your Desire, to write a few Lines unto you. And this I would say to thee, that among all the innumerable Multitudes of God's People, there never was, nor will be one that was saved, because they were worthy of God's Love, or of any its glorious Fruits. No; Salvation, from Foundation to Top-Stone, is all of one pure Piece of Grace. Free-Grace is the Chariot that conveys all God's Chosen home to Glory. If Salvation was of Works, and to be bestow'd upon condition of the Creature's Obedience and inherent Goodness, then you might be discouraged, if you saw the want of these things in yourself; and conclude that there was no Salvation for you. But since Salvation is of Grace, free, absolute, unchangeable and infinite Grace, why mayn't it be for thee? Thy Unworthiness can't hinder: Because Free-Grace delights to glorify its Riches, in saving to the uttermost, those that are most unworthy. God has *concluded* his Chosen, all *in Unbelief, that he might have mercy upon all. And where Sin has abounded, Grace doth much more abound,* Rom. xii. 31, and v. 20. How unreasonable then is it for thee to conclude that thou art not the Lord's, because thou art unworthy; when all his are such? Yea, let me say, there are none but his, that see themselves to be such.

As God's Design, from everlasting, was to glorify his Grace to the utmost, in saving a Remnant of poor Sinners, whom he had set his Heart upon, and chosen to Life Eternal; so, *in the Fulness of Time,* he sent his Son to die for 'em; and at the appointed Moment, when their personal Salvation is to begin, he sends forth his Spirit into their Hearts, to convince them their great Unworthiness of any Favour, in order to make them willing to be beholding to his rich Mercy and Free-Grace for the whole of their Salvation.

For by nature, all *Adam's* Posterity are under the Covenant of Works, and seek Life by the Deeds of the Law. And so blind is proud Man, and so deceived by Satan, that he thinks there is some Goodness in his Heart or Life, which renders him worthy of divine Mercy and Favour; which he dares to plead before God, as the *Pharisee, God, I thank thee, I am not as other Men;* or if this is not the Language of his Mouth, how often doth he *bless himself in his Heart,* in his supposed Goodness? And so long as the Soul rests upon this Bottom, it is impossible for it to enjoy Salvation; God's Way of saving Sinners, and the Way such a Soul would be saved in, being so diametrically opposite. "I have done this and that, and the other, saith such a Soul, Lord, save me." There's no Salvation, saith the Lord, by the Deeds of the Law; I save none but miserable Sinners, that can do nothing to help themselves, but are utterly undone; my Design is to glorify my Grace in saving such; and no Soul shall perish, that is willing to be saved this Way? But alas, an unregenerate Man don't like this Way of Salvation: No, he chuses to cleave to the Works of the Law; and living and dying in that State, being under the Curse, he must perish for ever.

But when God is about to apply Salvation to an elect Vessel, he empties such a Soul of all its conceited Goodness, and gives it to see its own Ill-deservings, and Hell-deservings; he shews it its Misery, and reveals the Remedy; in order to make it willing to be saved in his own Way, and to fill it with Mercy, Grace, and Glory in this World, and that which is to come. *God be merciful to me a Sinner,* is the Plea of such a Soul. *I will be merciful to thy Unrighteousness, and thy Sins and thy Iniquities I will remember no more,* is the glorious Answer that it receives from the Lord. Salvation by Grace, the Soul pleads for: This is according to God's Heart, and the eternal Designs of his Kindness; and Salvation by Grace, he bestows upon that Soul.

And is it thus with thee, my dear Sister? Dost thou see thy own Vileness and Unworthiness, and desire to be saved alone by Grace: Be of good Comfort, for thou art a Vessel of Mercy; prepared unto Glory. God's free, full, and everlasting Salvation was prepar'd for thee; and thy Heart, by the Work of the Spirit, is prepar'd to receive it: And what then shall hinder thy Enjoyment of it? Thou art certainly one of the Lord's; or else thou hadst never been made willing to be saved in God's Way. Art thou *willing* to be saved by Jesus Christ? 'Twas *in the Day of his Power,* that thy stubborn Will was subdu'd, and sweetly drawn into Subjection to himself, as the alone Saviour. Thy Salvation is already begun; and fear not the full Accomplishment of it. Christ has saved thee, to Willingness; and will give thee all that Salvation thy willing Soul desires. And what tho' thou art vile, and wretched in thyself; there's Grace enough for thee in the Heart of God, and Salvation enough in the Person of Christ, which thou art call'd to receive freely. *Come* therefore, *boldly to the throne of Grace;* for thou shalt *find Mercy, and Grace to help in Time of Need,* Heb. iv. 16. *Open thy Mouth wide,* saith the Lord, the Desires of thy Soul, for all the Grace and Salvation thou needest, *and I will fill it,* Psal. lxxxi. 10.

Thy Sins, tho' an huge Mass, yet, were they ten thousand times more and greater than they are, are no more, when cast into the infinite Grace of God, and the infinite Merit of Christ's Blood, than a small Stone to the immense Ocean; which is no sooner cast therein, but it is cover'd, and swallow'd up of its unfathomable Depths! Honour therefore the God of all Grace, by believing his Grace sufficient to save thee, by casting thyself into the Arms of his Mercy, and by crediting his infinite Faithfulness, as a God that cannot lie; who has said, *they that trust in the LORD, shall be as Mount Zion, that shall never be removed: They shall never be ashamed nor confounded, World without End,* Psal. cxxv. 1. Isa. xlv. 17.

And now, that the *God of Peace* may *fill* thee *with* all *Joy and Peace thro' Believing,* is the earnest Desire of

Thy Loving Friend in the Lord, &c.

LETTER XXIII.

To Mrs. B.

My very dear Sister,

MY Soul is troubled at the present Distress you are under. *If one Member suffer,* all the rest sympathize. But oh, the infinite Tenderness of your Head in Heaven! Not a Sorrow pierceth your Heart, but he has an inward Feeling of it. And his Bowels yern towards you, even now there is such a Cloud upon his Face, and he seems to speak against you: He yet *earnestly remembers* you *still.* Aye still, notwithstanding all the Contrarieties you see and feel in yourself. What tho' you have an Hell of Iniquity in your Nature, as much, in your Apprehension, as there can be even in the Devil's themselves; yet this alters not Christ's Heart towards you one jot. God has resolv'd that Sin shall never out-do his Grace; but that *where Sin has abounded, Grace* shall *much more abound.* What tho' the Sin of your Nature appears, in your Sight, like a mighty Ocean, that would swallow you up; yet 'tis no more than a Drop, if compar'd with the infinite Ocean of Christ's Love, and the Merit of his Blood, which has swallow'd up all your Sin. Your Heart can't be worse than what the Lord speaks of the Hearts of Men in general, *Gen.* vi. 5. *And God saw that the*

Wickedness of Man was great in the Earth, and that every Imagination of the Thoughts of his Heart was only evil, and that continually. And yet this did not alter God's Heart to a *Remnant* in his Son, that were as bad as the *rest.* Your being as bad as them that perish, don't put you into a perishing State with them. And when God would set off the Greatness of his Love to his own People, he does it by putting them in mind of their being as bad *by Nature* as the rest, *Mal.* i. 2, 3. *Was not* Esau Jacob's *Brother? Saith the Lord: Yet I loved* Jacob. So that there is no reason for you to conclude, that you are not the Lord's, because you see yourself to be as bad as others.

But it may be, you'll say, "tho' God's People are as bad as others *by Nature,* yet *Grace* makes a Difference."

'Tis true, there is a new Nature given; but yet the old Nature in all its Parts and Branches. And if you had not a new Nature, you could not see that Mass of Iniquity in your old.

The Apostle, in the *seventh* of the *Romans,* cries out as a *wretched Man,* by reason of that *Body of Sin and Death* that dwelt in him. He complains not of this or that Member only, but of a *Body of Death,* in all its Parts and Members; a complete Body of Sin dwelling in him. And yet, in the Triumph of Faith, could bless God for a complete Victory in Christ, over Sin and Death at the same Time.

But it may be, you will say, "that the Carriage of your Soul towards God has been so froward and rebellious, that it can't agree with the Nature of a Child."

With the new nature of a Child, blessed be God, it cannot: For there is a Principle of Love in your Soul, that will make you *lothe yourself in your own Sight, for all your Abominations;* when God breaks out upon your Spirit again, with shining Discoveries of abundant Pardon, and gives you to see that he is *pacify'd towards you for all that you have done.*

But that Frowardness and Rebellion may and doth agree with the old Nature that dwells in God's Children; see, *Isa.* xlviii. 4. *Because I knew that thou art obstinate, and that thy Neck is an Iron Sinew, and thy Brow Brass.* And *ver. 8. yea, thou heardest not, yea, thou knewest not, yea, from that time that thine Ear was not open'd: For I knew that thou wouldst deal very treacherously, and wast call'd a Transgressor from the Womb.* And yet notwithstanding all this see the Grace that breaks forth in the next *three Verses: For my Name's sake will I aefer mine Anger, and for my Praise will I refrain for thee, that I cut thee not off. Behold I have refined thee, but not with Silver; I have chosen thee in the Furnace of Affliction. For mine own sake, even for mine own sake will I do it; for how should my name be polluted? And I will not give my Glory unto another.* Who could have thought, that ever such an obstinate, stiff-necked, treacherous dealing one, that was a *Transgressor from the Womb,* should be called God's *Chosen?* And that he should resolve to *refine* such an one in the *Furnace of Affliction,* for his *own Name's sake;* taking all his Motives from within himself, from his own Heart, when he could find none but the contrary in the Creature's Nature and Carriage?

See also another Instance of God's Kindness to a Froward Child, *Isa.* lvii. 17. *For the Iniquity of his Covetousness was I wroth, and smote him: I hid me, and was wroth, and he went on frowardly in the Way of his Heart.* What could one now think that the Lord should say concerning such an one, but I'll destroy him? But oh! Behold the Grace that straightway breaks forth towards this rebellious Creature; *I have seen his Ways, and will heal him: I will lead him also, and restore Comforts unto him, and to his Mourners!* Ver. 18. *I have seen his Ways:* (what Ways?) "Not his holy Ways; for as if the Lord should say, he has provoked me by his Iniquity to smite him. Not his believing, submissive Ways; for instead of learning Obedience by the things he suffers, he's worse and worse, more froward and rebellious under my chastning Hand. Nor yet his repenting Ways; for instead of bemoaning himself under his Peevishness, and turning to me with all his Heart, he goes on frowardly, as in a Course of Fretfulness and Rebellion; in the Ways of his own Heart, not in the Ways of my Precepts. And yet for all this, *I will heal him:* Tho' I might destroy him, if I was to deal with him after his Carriage towards me. I might say, go on in thy own Ways, to thy own Destruction; and bring upon thyself deserved Ruin. But, in the Super-aboundings of my Grace, *I will heal him.* He has wounded himself, and is ready to die of his Wounds; but I'll bind up his wounded Spirit. Darkness covers him, so that he can't see the Way of Faith, nor has he Strength to set one Foot forward therein; but *I will lead him also.* I'll take him by the Arms, and support him under his present Weakness; and also teach him to go again in my Ways, notwithstanding his present Ignorance. And tho' he has lost the Joys of my Favour, which had wont to be the Strength of his Spirit; and thinks I am become his Enemy, because he finds so much enmity in his carnal Mind against me: Yet my everlasting Kindness shall break forth upon him again, like the Sun from under an Eclipse, and fill his Heart brim-full of Joy, even to running over: For I will not only *restore Comforts to him,* but *to his Mourners,* who shall rejoice for his Consolation."

What think you, my dear Sister, of this Grace? It is sufficient to save you; yea, let me say, it is more than enough. Had you ten thousand times more Sins than you have, you could never spend the exceeding Riches of Grace; the Treasures of which, laid up in Christ for you, are inexhaustible. Grace is a Spring that can never be drawn dry! 'Twill rise higher than your Sins, let them be ever so much exalted; 'twill *spring up,* even *into everlasting Life.* Grace has *Depths,* infinitely deeper than the greatest Depths of your Sins and Miseries! *Heights* infinitely higher than the Heights of your Provocations! *Breadths,* infinitely more extensive than the Aboundings of your Iniquities! And *Lengths,* infinitely longer than your Sins, either in Commencement, or Duration! Grace laid the Foundation of your Glory in Christ, before Time or Sin entred; is now managing the Superstructure, by all the Changes which pass over you; and will lay the Top-Stone, when Sin and Time shall be no more, out-living them to an endless Eternity! I might multiply Instances of Grace; but the Time would fail me. The whole Gospel, both in the old and new Testament, is one entire Declaration of the Wonders of Grace, and the Depths of Mercy to unworthy Creatures, and miserable Sinners!

But it may be, in the Depth of your Distress, you'll *refuse to be comforted,* and say, "All this is not for me."

But remember God's own dear Children have said so in times of Darkness, as you, who yet have been made to say the quite contrary, when the Light has broke out upon them again. When *Heman* was brought forth into the Light, and could call God, the God of his Salvation, read what an Account he gave of the Darkness he had been in, and what he said while it lasted. That he was *counted with them that go down to the Pit, free among the Dead,* &c. Psal. lxxxviii. And the Church,

Lam. iii. 18. did say, in Unbelief, *My Strength and my Hope is perished from the LORD.* And yet, *when God* broke out upon her Spirit afresh, she could say, *the LORD is my Portion: therefore will I hope in him.* And from her own Experience, encourage others to *hope, and quietly wait for the Salvation of the LORD;* telling them, that *the LORD is Good to the Soul that seeketh him;* that he *will not cast off for ever; but tho' he cause Grief, he will have Compassion according to the Multitude of his Mercies;* as Ver. 24, *&c. Sion* said, *the LORD had forsaken* her, *and forgotten* her; when yet she was *graven upon the Palms of his hands, and her Walls were continually before* him, *Isa.* xlix. 14, 16. *David, the Man after God's own Heart,* when in sore Trials, and all things seem'd to go contrary to what had been told him, in the Name of the Lord, said, in his unbelieving *Haste, All Men are Liars,* Psa. cxvi. 11. He was so far from believing God's Kindness and Faithfulness towards him in his Troubles, that he said, he should perish; and that they that spoke otherwise, told him Lies. And yet, after all this, he was made to sing gloriously of God's Mercy and Faithfulness in his *well order'd Covenant;* and to die in the Faith of its being *all* his *Salvation,* 2 Sam. xxiii. 5. And tho' you can't at present *believe, yet he abideth faithful, he cannot deny himself,* 2 Tim. ii. 13. Nor can your *Unbelief make the Faithfulness of God of none Effect,* Rom. iii. 3. Your Unbelief can't rob you of your Interest, tho' it does of your Comfort.

And if you not only cannot believe, thro' Weakness, but will not believe, thro' Obstinancy; yet Christ has had such among his dear Children. *Thomas* said, *I will not believe,* John xx. 25. And yet the Grace of Christ conquer'd his stout Heart, and sweetly drew him again, in the Exercise of Faith, to say, *My Lord, and my God,* Ver. 28. And thus, thro' Grace, it shall be with you.

Christ cannot part with you, if you could with him. He has resolv'd that *none shall pluck* you *out of* his *Hands,* John x. 28. None of all the numerous Sins of your Nature, let them be ever so strong; no nor all the Legions of Devils in Hell, or wicked Men on Earth, should they be all combined together against you, shall be able to move you one Hair's-breadth from that Security you have in Christ's Hands. The Father gave you to him; and the Love of his Heart engageth his Power to hold you fast. Yea, tho' in Unbelief you would throw yourself out of his Arms; yet he will never let go his Love-hold of you. For this the Lord, the God of *Israel* saith, *He hateth putting away,* Mal. ii. 16.

And tho' the Lions roar upon you in this dark Night, yet they shall not devour you; because the *Lion of the Tribe of* Judah is stronger than they. He has them in Chains, and sets Bounds to their Rage. And he will ere long arise for your Help; the *Morning Light* will ere long break out upon your Soul; and then these fierce *Beasts of Prey* will haste to their *Dens,* Psal. civ. 22. And the new glory of the Light, breaking forth out of thick Darkness, will be amazingly glorious, and exceeding pleasant to behold. This is one Reason why the Lord suffers Darkness to seize the Spirits of his Children; that so, when the Light of his Face shines upon them again, it may be exceeding precious in their Esteem.

And while the Darkness lasts, I would beg of you to beware of making hasty Conclusions, either of yourself, or of God's Thoughts and Ways towards you. Because you can't make a right Judgment of these Things now. And hereby you'll dishonor God's Grace, and *grieve the Spirit,* by which you have been *seal'd* in times past, as well as *pierce* yourself *thro' with many Sorrows.*

Again, I would intreat you, *not to forsake assembling* yourself with the Saints. *There the Lord has commanded the Blessing, even Life for evermore.* Where can you go? Christ has *the Words of eternal Life,* John vi. 68.

But it may be you will say, "I shall perish; and to what End should I wait upon God?"

But oh, that you could resolve with yourself, That if you do, it shall be at Jesus' Feet; following him, tho' he should go from you; and *trusting* in him, tho' he should *slay* you. This would glorify God exceedingly, as well as confound the Enemy. And remember how the Woman of *Canaan* sped, when she would take no Denial, *Matth.* xv. 28.

I commit you to *the God of Peace,* who shall *bruise Satan under your Feet shortly;* and *after* you have *suffered a while, stablish, strengthen, and settle you,* 2 Peter v. 10. Longing for the Day-break of your Deliverance,

I rest, with sympathizing Love,

Yours in the Lord, &c.

LETTER XXIV.

To Mrs. E. D.

Dear Sister,

Grace and Peace be multiplied unto you, thro' the Knowledge of God, and of Jesus our Lord.

You told me, at parting, that you should be glad to hear from me, if I had any Word from the Throne concerning you. And having desired of the Lord, that he would give me one, if it was his Pleasure; in the Night, when I was thinking of you and your Trials, that Word was brought to my Mind to write unto you, *Isa.* liv. 5. *For thy Maker is thy Husband, the LORD of Hosts is his Name:* And oh, that the Lord the Spirit, would please to lead you into that near, sweet, inseparable Relation, Christ and you stand in to each other; while, with this Text, as with a Finger, he points the Eye to your Faith to look upon the bright Glories thereof!

Fear not, (saith the Lord, in the preceding Verse) *for thou shalt not be ashamed: neither be thou confounded, for thou shalt not be put to Shame: for thou shalt forget the Shame of thy Youth, and shalt not remember the Reproach of thy Widowhood any more.* And the Reason of these Privileges promised, both here, and in the Day of Christ, is given in the following Verse: *For thy Maker is thy Husband, the LORD of Hosts is his Name,* &c. Oh, think upon this wonderful Declaration of Grace made in these Words!

Think a while upon the Person here spoken of; *thy [Maker]* whose *Name* is *the Lord of Hosts!* This is no less than *Immanuel,* God with us, God in our Nature, the eternal Son of the eternal Father, who did assume our Nature into personal Union with himself. He is a divine Person, that has all the essential Glory of the Godhead in him; and therefore said to be the [LORD], JEHOVAH, which is a Name proper to God, and incommunicable to any Creature: And this LORD, as Mediator, is likewise to be considered as Man; for his human Nature is necessarily included in these Characters which are given of his Person; to wit, a Husband, and a Redeemer.

Well, this is the Person spoken of: But look upon him now in his divine Nature, as *thy Maker the LORD of Hosts;* who has an infinite Fulness of Life and Being, in and of himself; and has given Life and Being to all Creatures and Things. 'Tis HE that is adored and worshiped by the angelick Host above; Angels and Archangels *vail* their *Faces* before him, as unworthy to look upon his infinite Glory, and *cover* their *Feet,* as unworthy to stand in his Presence! It is HE that is adored and praised by *the general Assembly and Church of the First-born,* the Saints now in Heaven. And 'tis HE, that is greatly *feared,* i.e. worshiped and obey'd, in the *Assemblies of the Saints* on Earth; while he's *had in Reverence* of all that are round about him in the Church below! Yea, 'tis HE that has all Creatures and Things at his Command: Before him the Devils tremble, and under his Feet the Wicked of the Earth shall be trodden down! But Oh! who can set forth a thousandth Part of his infinite Glory! 'Tis far beyond the Capacity of Men or Angels, in the upper or lower Worlds, fully to take it in, or tell it out. Oh how far is the Line of created Understanding, in its greatest Perfection, from fathoming this infinite, unsearchable Depth! What the can a Babe say? Only this. Look upon his fair Face, who is *the Chiefest of ten thousand!* and oh, that the Lord the Spirit would give thee an amazing Prospect of the Glory of thy Beloved!

Well, this glorious Person, who is the Wonder of Saints and Angels, the Terror of wicked Men and Devils; who can make Worlds at his Pleasure, and dash his Enemies into eternal Perdition with a Word of his Mouth; this is HE, that in infinite condescending Grace, has stooped down to take thy [Husband.] Oh amazing! *Thy Maker,* who has a far greater Right to dispose of his Creatures as he pleases, than the *Potter* has *to made one Vessel unto Honour, and another unto Dishonour,* he has set his Heart upon thee, and given himself to thee as thy Husband! Oh, astonishing! What, God love Creatures! JEHOVAH set his Heart upon the Work of his Hands! And that he should do it in such a distinguishing Way, take one, and leave another, choose one, and refuse another: How rich and sovereign is this Grace! And how sweet is this Word [Thy]! that he should give himself to thee, to be thy Husband, and betroth thee unto himself for ever, while thousands are passed by! He has indeed given himself to thee in all Relations; as Father, Brother, Friend, *&c.* in all which his Love shines gloriously: But oh, this sweet Relation of an Husband! What, has he given himself, his great Self, to be one with thee for ever! Oh, the Height, Depth, Breadth, and Length of this Grace!

Again, consider, this Relation is no empty Name, no unfruitful Thing: Wondrous are the Effects of that Love which entred into this Relation, and flow thro' it. And this shineth forth in the Word [For], *For thy Maker is thy Husband,* &c. as it stands connected with the glorious Privileges promis'd in the precedent *Verse.* All thy present and future Happiness is secured in this Relation, as the Effect in its Cause. But this is a Field too large for me to enter far into. All that I can do is only to point thine Eye to it, and leave thy Faith to trace its wondrous Paths, by the Leadings of the Word and Spirit of God.

Look therefore upon the Love of thy Husband: And all the glorious Fruits of it, which flow thro' this Relation he stands in to thee. Other Husbands may enter into this Relation, and what the Love of it, or their burning-hot Love may soon grow cold. But as Christ's Heart was in a Flame of Love towards thee, when he gave himself to thee to be thy Husband; so it abides *yesterday, to day, and for ever* the same. He *rests in his Love,* and will never cast thee off, or seek another Object instead of thee. No, he has said concerning thee, that thou art his *Rest,* the Rest of his Heart *for ever;* and he is *the LORD that changeth not;* as not in his Nature, so nor in his Love: Therefore this Relation is no empty Name. Nor yet will it appear to be an unfruitful Thing, if thou consider what the Love of thy Husband has done, and will do for thee.

For as he gave himself to thee, to be thy Husband; so he has gloriously, transcendently, above and beyond all the Creatures, acted in all his Riches: *Thy glory,* says he, *which thou gavest me, I have given them,* John xvii. 22. So that what Christ has is thine, as thou art one with him. Yea the Love of this thy Husband, engaged him to become thy Saviour, thy Surety, to redeem thee from all Misery, unto all Glory; when thy Fall in the first *Adam* was fore-view'd in all its woful Effects. Thus his Love work'd before Time. Look upon it also in its glorious Fruits in Time: 'Twas a mighty Stoop of his Love, to take thy Nature, to stand in thy Room, to obey the Law for thee, to bear thy Sins, to pay thy Debts, by giving up himself a Sacrifice in thy Stead, when thou wast a Transgressor, and hadst treacherously departed from him. And as his

Love went thro' Death for thee, so in Love he rose for thee, entred into glory for thee, and ever sits at the right Hand of the Father, making Intercession for thee, until thou art saved *to the uttermost*. And as a Fruit of this thy Husband's Love, the Holy Spirit was sent down into thy Heart, to quicken thee when dead in Sin, to shew thee thy own Misery, and his Excellency, to enable thee to flee unto him for Refuge, whose Heart and Arms stand open wide to embrace thee, and to cause thee to fall in Love with him, who long since had set his Heart upon thee. Look also on the Fruits of thy Husband's Love, in clothing thee with his Righteousness, in supplying thee out of his Fulness, in giving thee his Flesh and Blood to eat and drink, that thou mayst live for ever; and in all that glorious Care which he exerciseth towards thee in all the Way he leads thee thro' a World of Trials. Once more, think what his Love will yet do for thee in time to come. He'll never leave thee in the Wilderness, he'll over-rule all things for thy good, he'll defend thee from all Enemies, he'll perfect thy Grace in Glory, he'll take thy Soul into his Bosom at Death, and thy whole Person at the Resurrection-Morn: And then, for ever folded up in his sweet Embraces, thou, with the rest of his redeemed Ones, shalt admire, adore, and enjoy his Love, and sing the new Song; *Unto him that loved us, and washed us from our Sins in his own Blood, and hath made us Kings and Priests unto God and his Father; to him be Glory and Dominion for ever and ever.* Amen.

I am Yours in Christ, &c.

LETTER XXV.

To Mrs. S. C.

Dear Sister,

Grace and Peace be multiplied unto you, from God our Father, and Jesus Christ our Lord.

When I had concluded to write unto Sister *D.* my Heart began to yearn towards you, and I desir'd the Lord, if he had any thing to send unto you by me, that he would give me a Word; and presently, *Matt.* xxviii. 20. was brought to my Mind. *And lo, I am with you always, even unto the End of the World.* Amen. This Promise was given to the Apostles, and in them to all Christ's Ministers, to encourage them in their Lord's Work, thro' all the successive Ages of Time; and it likewise contains in it, a gracious Declaration of Christ's Presence with all his Children, according to their several Stations and Employments, even unto the World's End; and so it is matter of Encouragement to every Believer, to follow Christ in all his Appointments, and to give up themselves to him, in all manner of Obedience.

This Promise is ushered in with a Note of Attention, [Lo] and calls upon you, my dear Sister, to behold, to look upon the Grace of your Beloved, which shines forth herein. Cast your Eye therefore upon the Person promising, [I]; *I am with you,* &c. And *see* his personal Perfections, and Bridegroom-Compassions, as your Head and Saviour; view him in his Love, Grace, Mercy, Power, Faithfulness, *&c.* for it is no less than himself, his great Self, in all his immense Perfections, who has engaged to be with you!

Listen also unto the Voice of your Beloved, or unto what he declares unto you herein. *I am with you, &c.* [With] you; oh amazing! This is a Promise of his special gracious Presence with you in the Church, and in the World; in the House of God, and in your own House. With [You], in distinction from the World. He'll *manifest* himself *unto* you, but *not unto the World:* No, they *see him not,* but you shall *see* him: For having set his Heart upon you, he'll dwell with you, and display his Grace, and all his glorious Perfections, every way answerable to the Greatness of his Person, and the Nearness of that Relation you stand in to him. And tho' you mayn't always have his sensible Presence, yet even then, you have his real Presence with you. *I* [Am] *with you,* says he, really, for your Advantage, even when you want the Sense of it, for your Comfort. And how long will Christ be with you? why, not now and then for a Fit, and be gone, but [Alway], In all Times, Places, and Cases whatsoever; *even unto the* [End] of *the World;* that is, as it respects thee in particular, unto the End of thy Being in the World; and as it respects his People in general, unto the very End of the World itself. And this our Lord confirms, with, [Amen]. This is Christ's *Amen,* or *so be it,* who with a Word could make Worlds, and with a Word can speak into Being all that vast Happiness which he has prepar'd for his People. In this Word therefore, by this *Amen,* he at once grants, and irreversibly confirms this wonderful Promise of his Presence with his People, even unto the End of the World.

Well then, my dear Sister, since Christ is, and will be with you; what canst thou desire more? He has all Power in his Hand to help thee, and he has all Grace in his Heart to do it; and he is the Lord that is faithful, who will be as good as his Word. Thou hast Christ, and thou hast all! Thou hast him in all Relations, thou hast him in all Conditions, thou hast him unto all that Salvation and Glory thy longing Soul can desire! Live upon him therefore as thy all! Creatures may fail thee, Relations and Friends may desert thee; but Christ will *never leave, nor forsake thee.* Thou hast his *Arm* to lean on, and his *Bosom* to rest in, all the Way thou comest up from the Wilderness. Is Christ with thee? thou canst want nothing, either for Soul or Body: Since he has infinite Fulness to supply thee, and infinite Love to *nourish* and *cherish* thee, even *as his own Flesh.* He that has all, can no more let thee want any thing which he sees good for thee, than he can *deny himself:* Because he loves thee as himself. Submit to his Wisdom therefore, *in all the Way* he leads thee *thro' the Wilderness:* For he'll bring thee by *a right Way to the City of Habitation.* And what tho' he should lead thee thro' much Tribulation; since Christ is thy Companion, thou needst fear nothing. If he suffer thee to be cast into a burning fiery Furnace, himself will be with thee there, and thou shalt walk at Liberty amidst fiery Trials, and shalt not be consumed. He'll go before thee to lead thee in the Way thou shouldst go, and be with thee every Step of it to keep thee Company, and he'll be behind thee too, as thy *Rere-ward,* to defend thee. He'll be a *Wall of Fire round about* thee. *And the Glory in the midst of* thee. Then surely thou mayst sing in Sorrow, since Christ is with thee in all thy Distresses; to defend thee from all Dangers, to sympathize with thee in all thy Griefs, to bear the heaviest End of thy Burdens, to support thee under 'em, to sanctify thee by 'em, to pardon all thy Weakness in bearing 'em, and compleatly to deliver thee from them, in his own Way and Time, which will be most glorious! Thy dear Lord Jesus will be with thee even until Death; unto death, in death, and thro' Death; and then he'll *wipe all*

Tears from thine *Eyes,* and take thee up to be with himself forever, to enjoy a blest Eternity in the Vision of his, and his Father's Face, in that Life and Glory which is yet unknown!

That *the Peace of God which passeth all Understanding,* may *keep* thy *Heart and Mind thro' Christ Jesus,* is the earnest Desire of

Yours in Him, &c.

LETTER XXVI.

To Mr. B. M.

Dear Brother,

Grace and Peace be multiplied.

WHEN I had a Word from the Lord for Sister *C.* I was loth to leave you out; and therefore desired that he would send something unto you also. And that Word was brought, *Gal.* v. 1. *Stand fast therefore in the Liberty wherewith Christ has made you free.*

We were by Nature, under the Law, and as Transgressors, under the Curse, under the Dominion of Sin, and the Government of Satan, and (as in ourselves considered) obnoxious to divine Vengeance, both here and hereafter: from all which, Christ hath made us free. And this Freedom is a complete and everlasting Liberty, in which it is both our Duty and Privilege to stand fast.

We were indeed under the Law; but [Christ], God-Man, the Anointed of the Father, our God, our Kinsman-Redeemer, was *made under the Law, to redeem* us *from under* it, as a Covenant of Works, by fulfilling all its righteous Commands in our stead; and to redeem us from its Curse likewise, by *being made a Curse for us.*

We, in all respects, were under the Dominion of Sin; but Christ *was made sin for us,* to redeem us from it, and for ever make an end of it.

We, by Sin, had put ourselves under the Dominion of Satan, that Prince of Darkness; but Christ, by being *made Sin for us,* and dying a Sacrifice in our stead, has *destroyed him that had the Power of Death,* and delivered us from that dreadful Bondage in which we were held.

We, *by Nature, were children of Wrath even as others;* but Christ has bore all that divine Vengeance that was the due Desert of our Transgressions; by which he has for ever delivered us from vindictive Wrath, both in this World, and that to come.

And as he has delivered us from the worst of Slavery, so he has likewise brought us into the most glorious Liberty: He has made us *Free Indeed!* For in giving himself a *Ransom* for us, he redeemed us, not only from all Misery, but unto all Glory. He has given us a Right unto all the Privileges of the Sons of God, both here in Grace, and hereafter in Glory. Thus the Son has made us [Free]. And this Freedom is complete, and everlasting, in himself, for his whole mystical Body. And as we are now made free in him, so we shall ere long enjoy a complete and everlasting Freedom in our own Persons, by and thro' him. Mean while we should live by Faith, or [Stand] fast in that complete Freedom, that eternal Perfection we have in him.

Well then, my dear Brother, has the Holy Spirit of God been sent down into thy Heart, to quicken thee when *dead in Sin,* to shew thee the Misery of thy natural State, and to enable thee to *flee* unto Christ *for Refuge?* And has he at times, *bore witness with thy Spirit,* that thou art a Child of God, and enabled thee to cry unto him, *Abba,* Father? Why, thou art one of them that Christ hath made free. He hath made thee free perfectly, and eternally in himself, as I hinted before; and he has also, in some Sense, made thee free in thy own Person too. He has delivered thee from the Law, from the Dominion of Sin and Satan, and from the Wrath to come; and he has given thee, as a Believer in him, a visible right unto all the Privileges of the Sons of God, both here, and hereafter: And he'll complete thy personal Freedom by the same Grace that begun it. Therefore *stand fast in* that [Liberty] *wherewith Christ hath made* thee *free.*

Stand fast: This Word implies Opposition. Satan, and Unbelief will oppose thy standing where free Grace hath set thee; and that legal Spirit that remains, even in God's free Children themselves, will oppose their standing fast in this Liberty. Satan seeks to draw God's free Children into Bondage-Frames; because he knows how much Dishonour it casts upon their Redeemer, and that glorious Liberty wherewith he has made them free; and also because he knows how much it will entangle, and perplex their Souls, and hinder their Peace, Joy, and Usefulness. Oh! he hates to see us stand [Fast] in this glorious Liberty; he envies Christ the Honour, and us the Comfort of this great Salvation. Watch therefore against all the Assaults of the Enemy, from what Quarter soever they come; and endeavour to keep thy Ground, and to stand it out bravely in Faith; having on *the Breast-plate of Righteousness,* (Christ's Righteousness) thy *Loins girt about with Truth,* (the Truth of God in the Promise, and the Truth of Christ's Salvation) thy *Feet shod with the Preparation of the Gospel of Peace,* for *an Helmet, the Hope of Salvation,* and *praying always with all Prayer and Supplication in the Spirit, watching thereunto with all Perseverance:* For this will tend to thy Redeemer's Honour, and to thy Comfort. And remember, that whatever Enemy attacks thy Faith hates thy Lord, and his Glory; and hates thee too, thy present Joy, and future Crown. Therefore be strong, and play the Man; and know, that if the Enemies should prevail at times, to bring thee into Bondage-Frames, yet they shall never bring thee into a Bondage-State. No, for thou art redeemed out of the House of Servants; Thou art *no more a Servant, but a Son; and if a Son, then an Heir of God thro' Christ.* Wherefore, my Beloved Brother, *So stand fast in the LORD!*

In him I am Yours, &c.

LETTER XXVII.

To Mr. P. N.

Dear Friend,

Grace be with you, Mercy, and Peace from God the Father, and the Lord Jesus Christ.

When I was determined to write to our dear Brother, and Sisters, you being, I trust, a longing Soul, I found a Desire to have somewhat to send unto you. And that Word was brought to my Mind, *Rev.* xxii. 17. *And the Spirit and the Bride say, Come. And let him that heareth say, come. And let him that is a thirst come. And whosoever will, let him take the Water of Life freely.* This Scripture will doubtless have its full Accomplishment in the *New Jerusalem* State of the Church; but yet there is a Voice in it now, a Sound of Abundance of Grace unto every poor Soul that is set a longing for Christ, and his Salvation.

These are the Words of the Lord Jesus Christ, who *sent* his *Angel* unto his Servant *John, to testify these Things in the Churches,* as *Ver.* 16. In this 17 *Verse* he continues his Speech, and tells us who they are which proclaim the Grace of the Gospel to poor Sinners, and invite them to partake of it. And,

First, Here is the [Spirit], the Holy Ghost, who was given upon Christ's ascension, to glorify him in the Churches, and in the Hearts of all God's Chosen. *The Spirit saith, Come.* He that *searcheth the Depths* of God, the Depth of his Counsels, Covenant and Promises, that knows what vast Provisions of Grace are made for poor Sinners, and what infinite Love towards 'em, and Readiness to receive 'em, there is in the Heart of God the Father, and in the Heart of Jesus Christ, he says, *Come.* This Word [Come], notes out that Fulness of Grace and Glory, which is provided for the Supply of poor Sinners in the Lord Jesus Christ, that Readiness there is to receive 'em, and gracious Invitation which he gives unto them. "*Come,* as if he should say, *For all things are now ready;* all Grace and Glory your needy Souls can want, for Time or Eternity. *Come,* Christ's and his Father's Heart and Arms stand open wide to embrace you. *Come,* the Lord invites you to come, and partake of all freely; you are welcome to all his Grace; it is his Will that you should come, it is his Desire that you should come; therefore come away speedily." Thus *the Spirit saith, Come.* And he saith so, as a Comforter in Office, as sent from the Father and the Son to draw poor Sinners unto Jesus Christ; which Work of his, he gloriously and efficaciously performs, when he speaks unto the Heart; and thereby, at once, sweetly allures and constrains the Soul to come. Oh the efficacious Drawing of the Holy Ghost! Never had any Soul seen Christ's Beauty, been sick of Love for him, or have come unto him for Life, if the Holy Ghost had not allured it by infinite Sweetness, and drawn it by Almighty Power! *The Spirit saith, Come;* and thereby he draws poor Souls into conjugal Affections to the Lord Jesus Christ, a visible conjugal Relation to him, and

Communion with him. And upon this, Christ hath a Bride, a visible Church on Earth. And therefore,

Secondly, The Bride saith, Come. The [Bride]; Believers congregated in Gospel-Order, gather'd into a Church-relation, by solemn Covenant, giving up themselves unto Christ as their Head and Husband, and professing Subjection to him. And this Church, the Bride, is stiled *the City of God,* Psal. xlvi. 4. Where the Crystal *Streams of the River of Water of Life* run. And she, having had such rich Experience of that Fulness of Life and Grace that dwells in, and flows thro' her Beloved, to the satiating of her longing Appetite; and also such rich Discoveries, that there is in him, not only infinitely enough for her, but also for all the Chosen of God, even unto the World's End; she, from her own Experience, and at the Command of her Lord and Husband, proclaims, by her Ministers, these glad Tidings; and invites poor Sinners unto Christ, the Fountain of Life, to drink, yea, drink abundantly. "*Come,* says the Bride, (unto poor awakened Souls) I was once as miserable as you, as poor and thirsty as you; but when the Spirit said, *Come,* I ventur'd in to my Lord and Husband, as God's Salvation for the Chief of Sinners; when I was almost famished with Thirst, and ready to faint away with Longings after Jesus Christ, and Fears that I should not find him; when I was just ready to perish, under the apprehended Wrath of God, the Temptations of Satan, and the Corruptions of my own Heart and Ways; and I found in him, my Saviour, a *pure River of Water of Life,* which is infinitely enough to satisfy and solace me thro' Time, and to Eternity; yea, I found in Christ, not only an infinite Fulness of Life, but also an infinite Freeness to communicate the same, notwithstanding all my Unworthiness. And as I found enough in Christ for me, so in him I see an inexhaustible Fulness for you, an infinite Store, that can never be drawn dry! And this my Lord and Head bids me to proclaim unto you, and invite you to come. *Cone* therefore, you, my *Companions,* that *hearken to* my *Voice,* you longing Souls, that are set *athirst* for *the Water of Life;* venture in to Christ, and take your Fill of all his Grace: For it is a River of Life, that is full, free, and everlasting! Thus *the Bride saith, Come.* But in the next place."

Thirdly, Christ commands him that heareth to say, Come. *And let him that* [heareth] *say, Come.* This may denote particular Believers, who have *Ears to hear what the Spirit saith to the Churches,* and likewise what the Bride says to poor Sinners in her Beloved's Name: And these, tho' not join'd to Christ's visible Church, (and so distinguished from the Bride) from their own Experience of his Grace, and from those Discernings they have had of what the Spirit the Bride says, are commanded to say, *Come.* "'Tis as if Christ should say, you my Children, that are afraid to follow me in the Ordinances of my House, who have not yet arrived to that Strength of Faith, and visible Love-Communion with me as my Bride hath, don't you be silent; do you say, *Come:* Tell poor Sinners what you have seen and heard of me, and invite 'em to come; concern yourselves in that glorious Work in which the Spirit and the Bride are employ'd, and in which my Heart is so deeply engaged." And Christ, by this Command, not only binds them to this Duty, but likewise gives them Strength for the Performance of it; he hereby speaks into Being what he calls for; as he did, when he said, *Let there be Light, and there was Light.* And so it carries in it a prophetic Description of what such Souls do, and shall say: But it is put in the Form of a Command, to excite their Obedience; because of the Backwardness of such Souls to proclaim Christ and his Grace to others, who are under prevailing Fears themselves, or at least not so openly favoured with Communion with Jesus Christ as his Bride is. *Let him that heareth say, Come.* And then,

Fourthly, The Lord Jesus Christ himself comes in and says, *And let him that is athirst Come: And whosoever will, let him take the Water of Life freely.* These are the Words of Christ, who once died, and now lives to save Sinners; in which he declares his infinite All-Sufficiency *to save* them *to the uttermost,* his Readiness to receive 'em, and the kind Invitation he gives 'em to partake of all his Grace; and to answer all the Objections which are apt to rise in the Hearts of such that are *athirst* for *the Water of Life,* he makes this royal Proclamation from his Throne: *And whosoever will, let him take the Water of Life freely.*

And now, my dear Friend, how is it with thee? Hast thou seen thy Sin and Misery by Nature, that thou art utterly undone without Christ?

Hast thou had any Discernings of his Beauty, and All-Sufficiency to save, even the Chief of Sinners? And hast thou been set a longing, a thirsting after an Interest in him, and his Salvation? Why, thou art the Person thus invited to come. *The Spirit, the Bride,* and *he that heareth say, Come.* And lest, after all, thou shouldst be afraid that Christ's Heart is not towards thee, He says *Come;* and what wouldst thou have more? Oh! *grieve not the Holy Spirit,* by slighting his Call, do not slight the Bride's Voice in her Ministers, nor yet the Voice of him that heareth, nor shut thine Ear to the Call of Christ himself! Thou art call'd, and call'd again. Art thou *athirst?* Thou art the Man that Christ calls to come unto him and *drink.* But it may be thou wilt say, "I am athirst for Life and Salvation by Jesus Christ; but I am afraid I am not one of them that it is designed for; and I am so unworthy, I am afraid it will never be bestowed upon me." These thy Fears Christ foresaw, and provided a Cordial for thee beforehand. Listen therefore, and receive in Faith, the Life-giving Words of his Mouth, in this royal Proclamation from his Throne: *And whosoever will, let him take the Water of Life freely.* He says, *Whosoever* [Will]: Hast thou a Will? Thou art the Man he speaks to, as much as if there was never another in the World in thy Case. Aye, sayst thou, 'I have a Will, but I have no Worthiness; my Heart hangs back, I am afraid to venture.' Hark then, what he says unto this. *Let him take the Water of Life freely.* [Let] him, &c. This is Christ's Grant of Life and Salvation unto thee. Oh! Open the Mouth of Faith, and take thy Fill. Christ bids thee *take the Water of Life freely.* [Freely]! This will reach thy Case, if thou wast the most unworthy Creature under Heaven: For here's no Condition, nothing to be done by thee to procure or earn this *Water of Life.* No, it is set abroach *freely,* for thy thirsty Soul to take its Fill both here and hereafter. Again [Freely]! 'Tis as if Christ should say, *Drink, yea, drink abundantly:* Thou needst not fear drinking the River of Life dry: There's such an infinite Abundance of Grace and Life in me, that thou mayst take thy Fill, however large thy Desires are; and when thou hast it, there will be never the less in me. There's an infinite Fulness of Grace and Life in Christ, for every thirsty Soul. And this shines forth in the World [The], *Let him take* the *Water of Life;* not[Of] the Water of Life; as if one was call'd to take a Part, and another another, just as much as they needed. No, Christ calls every thirsty Soul that has a Will, a Desire to be saved by him, to take up and possess by Faith, all that infinite Fulness of endless Life and Glory that is in him. To take it all up at once, and live upon it as its own, in the Right of it, as well as to derive thence a present and successive Supply of all its Wants thro' Time, and to Eternity. So that here is Grace enough for thee; 'tis as full as it is free; and in both respects it is infinite! Come therefore, at Christ's Call, and venture thro' ten thousand Difficulties, to take the Water of Life freely. Come as thou canst, take in as much as thou canst; attempt thy Duty; Christ will strengthen thy Faith ere thou art aware. And if thou canst take but now and then a Sip of the Water of Life, know, for thy Comfort, that the whole River of it is thine.

One more, does *Christ* say, *Come, Let him take, &c.* These Words have in 'em, not only the sweetest Invitation, but also, an efficacious Voice of thy Saviour, as thy King; which, in his own Time, will ripen thy Faith into that Motion he now calls for; and command off thine Enemies, which now hinder thy coming, and taking *the Water of Life freely.*

Grace be with thy Spirit.

I am Yours in Christ, &c.

LETTER XXVIII.

To Mr. E. S.

Dear Brother,

Grace and Peace be multiplied unto you, from God our Father, and our Lord Jesus Christ, by God the Comforter.

When I had concluded to write to the rest of our dear Friends, I was desirous to send a Line unto you, as a Token of my Love; and that Word dropt on my Heart for you, *Psal.* xlv. 2. *Thou art fairer than the Children of Men.*

I know that you have seen much of *Christ's* Beauty, Excellency, and Glory already, to the attracting your Soul after him, to the transforming you into his Likeness, and to the filling of you with Joy unspeakable, and glorious: But there is yet more, infinitely more to be beheld in your Beloved, who is the *Chiefest of ten thousand,* and *altogether lovely!*

You have seen much of the Beauty of the Saints, which has drawn out your Love, and knit your Soul to 'em, as your own Company, as *the Excellent of the Earth, in whom is all* your *Delight.* They are indeed *Jewels* in *Christ's* Esteem, and have a sparkling Glory on them; but remember, 'tis his Sun-like Face that casts their Lustre; they shine forth in the Glory of his Rays. Theirs is but a derived Beauty from his incomparable Fairness! And is no more, if compar'd with his, than the smallest Atome to the whole Mass of Earth, a Drop to the Ocean, or a Beam to the Sun! No, nor so much neither: For *Christ* is *Fairer,* infinitely fairer than these, who are the fairest of the Sons of Men. Some of the Saints shine forth more eminently in one Grace, and some in another; and a Difference will be seen among the starry Glories of the first Resurrection: But all Excellencies meet in *Christ,* as the Circumference-Lines in their Center, as the scatter'd Beams in the Body of the Sun. So that look upon the fairest of the Children of Men, in their fairest Condition, in this World or that to come, and *Christ* far exceeds them all. But oh, my weak Eye! How little can I take in of the Glory of this bright Object! Oh, how little have I seen! And how little can I say of his Soul-ravishing Beauty! Of his adorable Excellency! I would only point you to him, my Brother, and say, as *John* the *Baptist, Behold the Lamb of God!*

Behold the Christ of God! Look upon him in his transcendent Fairness; he's *fairer than the Children of Men:* Fairer, in his Relations, as Head, Husband, Brother, Friend, &c. fairer in his Love, Mercy, Grace, Wisdom, Power, Faithfulness, &c. Fairer, in his Covenant-Engagements; fairer, in his Conception and Birth; fairer, in the Performance of his Life; fairer, in the wonderful Atchievements of his Death; fairer, in his great Resurrection; fairer, in his glorious Ascension; fairer, in his Exaltation now in Heaven: And as he now is, (by Covenant-Settlement) so he will ere long appear; fairer than the Children of Men, in his Glory-Reign; and fairer also in his last great Judgment of Men and Devils, at the End of Time: And then among the innumerable Company of glorified Saints and Angels, he'll shine forth for ever, as infinitely fairer than the Children of Men! While himself, their eternal Sun, darts forth upon them all their bright and endless Glory! But oh, the unsearchable Riches of *Christ's* Fairness! Neither Men nor Angels can fully know, or set it forth!

That *the God of our Lord Jesus Christ, the Father of Glory, may grant unto you the Spirit of Wisdom and Revelation in the Knowledge of him,* who is infinitely *fairer than the Children of Men;* to the changing you *into the same Image from Glory to Glory;* to the preparing you for abundant Usefulness in this present Time, and a weighty Crown at *Christ's* Appearing, is the earnest Desire of

Yours, in our own Lord Jesus, &c.

LETTER XXIX.

To Mrs. E. G.

Dear Friend in the Lord,

Grace unto you, and Peace from God our Father, and from Jesus Christ our Lord.

Having heard of your present Distress, by reason of *atheistical* Thoughts, I was willing to write somewhat unto you. And I would advise, as the Lord shall enable you, to *three Things.* As,

1. Be not over-much cast down by reason of your present Exercise. For *the same Afflictions are accomplish'd in your Brethren which are in the World.* Think not you Case singular: For many of God's Children have been engag'd with the *Powers of Darkness,* in the same Combat that you now are; and thro' the *Captain* of their *Salvation,* have got a triumphant Victory over them.

2. When these vile Thoughts press in upon your Mind, endeavour to cast them out with as much Lothing, and as little Distress as you can. This was Mr. *Janeway's* Advice to a Friend of his, troubled with blasphemous Thoughts, "They are, says he, the Morsels which Satan would have you swallow down," And therefore cast them out with Lothing; but be not distressed: For they are not your Sins, any further than consented to. "They are, say he, Satan's Strivings to ravish the Spouse of Jesus; for which he shall pay dear one Day." And so far as they

are a Burden, an Affliction to the Soul, so far as it crys out against them, so far they are a Force put upon it. And the Case is the same with that of the *betrothed Damsel,* under the Law, who was not to die, if a Man met her in the Field, and forc'd her; because she cried out, and there was none to deliver her, *Deut.* xxii. 25, 26, 27. But suppose the worst that can be, that thy Heart joins with Satan herein, and so thou becomes guilty, and filthy hereby: (And how far our wicked Hearts join Issue with Satan in his vile Suggestions, God only knows; I am apt to think, we seldom, if ever, come off without some Measure of Guilt and Defilement). Yet thou hast no Reason to be distressed with a desponding Fear, as if there was no Help for thee in God. For were thy Sins ten thousand times more and greater than they are, the Multitude of God's great Mercies infinitely exceed them. And if he resolve to be gracious to thee, and to shew Mercy on thee, down they must fall before pardoning Grace, and overflowing Mercy, as the *Egyptians* did, in the Red-Sea, and rise no more to condemn thee. Were thy Sins as *Scarlet,* red like *Crimson,* the Blood of *Christ* can make thee *white as Snow.* And therefore,

3. Whenever Sin and Satan assault you, labour, upon the first Onset, *to flee for Refuge to the Hope set before* you; to haste away to *Christ,* that *Man who is an Hiding-Place from the Wind, a Covert from the Tempest, as Rivers of Water in a dry Place, and the Shadow of a great Rock in a weary Land,* Isa. xxxii. 2.

Doth the Wind of Temptation blow hard upon thee? *Christ* is *an Hiding-Place from the Wind.* Not only from the Wind, the great Whirlwind of God's Wrath, which shall drive away all that are found out of *Christ,* like *Chaff,* into *everlasting Burnings;* but he is also an Hiding-Place from the Wind of Satan's Temptations, where thou mayst be exceeding safe from all Harm, in the most evil Day that can befall thee. *The Name of the Lord,* the Lord Jesus the great Saviour, *is a strong Tower* for a poor Sinner; *Oh! run* into it; and thou shalt be *safe*, Prov. xviii. 10. Do, as the *Psalmist* said he would, *Psal.* lvii. 1. *Under the Shadow of thy Wings will I make my Refuge, until these Calamities are overpast.* Dost thou see thy Sinfulness and Misery by Nature, doth the Enemy pursue thy Soul? Hath he smitten thy Life down to the Ground, dost thou feel the Pain of his *fiery Darts,* and canst thou not do any thing to save or deliver thyself *from the Wrath to come,* from that inexpressible and eternal Misery which is the due Desert of every Transgression? Why, *Christ* calls thee to look unto him, as once *made Sin and a Curse* for poor Sinners, *by* whose *Stripes we are healed.* He says, *Look unto me, and be ye saved, all the Ends of the Earth,* Isa. xlv. 22. Oh, cast up thine Eye therefore unto a once crucified Jesus; see him, bearing Sin, and the Wrath of God, and making a full Satisfaction to divine Justice for such poor Souls that see they have not a Mite to pay; see him, conflicting with the Powers of Darkness, and gaining a complete Victory over them, that we might be deliver'd from Satan, who had the Power of Death. Yea, cast up thine Eye to a risen Jesus; see him, discharg'd from Sin, having for ever made an End of it; see him, justify'd in the Name and Room of poor Sinners, who have no Righteousness of their own, to stand in before God; see him, ascending up on high, leading *Captivity captive,* that we might be set free; see him, enthron'd at God's right Hand, *exalted as a Prince and a Saviour, to give Repentance unto* Israel *and Remission of Sins;* and as a compassionate High-Priest, that knows how to succour the Tempted, having once suffer'd himself, being tempted in all Points like as we are, that he might sympathize with us under Temptations, shield and support us in them, and deliver us from them: View him as he ever liveth to make Intercession, and as such, *able to save to the uttermost,* all them *that come unto God by him.* Thus look unto *Christ* the great Saviour, as an undone Sinner in thyself, for thy own Salvation; cast thy Soul into his Arms, at the Feet of his Mercy, and rest upon his faithful Promise: He says, *Thou shalt be saved.* He bids thy weary, *heavy laden* Soul, to *come unto* him; and he has promis'd to *give* thee *Rest,* Matt. xi. 28. His Arms stand wide open to embrace thee; and he's infinitely more willing to receive thee, than thou canst be to commit thy Soul into his Hands. Then venture, with innumerable Sins, innumerable Fears, and thro' innumerable Oppositions, to cast thyself upon *Christ,* the mighty Saviour, and thou shalt be saved *to the uttermost.* Thou must believe, or die; rest upon *Christ,* and run into him, or perish: Therefore stand not to hesitate whether he will save thee, or not; but venture in unto him, and say, with *Esther, I will go in unto the King, and if I perish, I perish;* and the royal Scepter of his Grace shall be holden out, for thee to touch, and live.

Doth Satan assault thee with the Wind of Temptation, to drive thee away from *Christ?* Oh, run the faster to him, and he'll hide thee from all Evil, and screen thee from all Danger: For never did any Soul perish, or want Succour, that *fled* unto *Christ for Refuge.* He will *cover* thy *Head in the Day of Battle,* and send thee suitable Grace and Strength, according to thy Day of Trial. *Christ* has all the *Legions* of Devils in his Power, and *gathers* the *Wind* of Temptation in his *Fist,* as well as he doth the natural Wind. *And in Measure when it shooteth forth, he will debate with it.* He'll not *suffer you to be tempted above that you are able, but will with the Temptation make a Way to escape, that you may be able to bear it,* Isa. xxvii. 8. 1 Cor. x. 13. He'll not let it blow too hard upon thee while it lasts; nor will he let it blow upon thee always neither. For his is *full of Compassion,* and will not *always chide.* He *knoweth our Frame; and remembreth that we are Dust,* Psal. ciii. 14. He knows the Power of Temptations, the Pain of Satan's *fiery Darts;* having once felt them in the Days of his Flesh: And therefore from his own Experience, he'll not only sympathize with thee in them, but graciously deliver thee from them. He'll *rebuke* the Tempter, and cause the Wind of Temptation to cease, and create a *Calm* in thy tossed, troubled Soul, by a Word of his Power, when the appointed Moment of thy Deliverance is come; as he rebuk'd the natural Wind, and it obey'd him, *Mar.* iv. 39. Therefore run to *Christ* for Shelter; and *resist the Devil, and he'll flee from you,* Jam. iv. 7. When he sees that those very Temptations, by which he design'd to drive you away from *Christ,* are a Means of your fleeing the faster to him.

Again, do the Waves of inward Corruption, agitated by Satan, beat vehemently against thy Soul, like a mighty Tempest, which threatens to swallow thee up? *Christ* is a *Covert from this Tempest:* Run unto him therefore, as once *made Sin,* and now exalted to save Sinners, and thou shalt be secure from all Harm. Sin shall never condemn that Soul, that flees unto *Christ* for Salvation. No, *Christ's* Death will be the Death of Sin, and the Life of that Soul, that flees unto him for Safety. Christ crucify'd, is such a Covert from the Tempest, to the Soul that runs into him, that not a Drop of divine Wrath shall ever light upon it. Christ has so born Sin, Curse, and the Wrath of God, that he hath for ever born it away from that Soul: And God as the God of Peace, freely, fully, and eternally forgives all its Iniquities, even all manner of Sin and Blasphemy whatever, whereby it has transgressed against him. And as Christ is a Covert from the Tempest of Sin, in its condemning Power; so also from its tyranizing Power, unto every Soul that flees unto Him for Relief. He *will subdue our Iniquities* for us, as well as *cast all our Sins into the Depths of the Sea,* Mic. vii. 18. Christ can keep thee from fainting in the Combate, and enable thee to hold out in the Storm; unto *the set Time to favour* thee, in a peaceful Calm, come. And then, with one Word of his Mouth, he'll silence the Billows of Corruption; as, in the Days of his Flesh, he *commanded the Sea,* and it *obey'd* him; as well as *the Wind,* and it *ceased.* For he *ruleth the raging of the Sea* of Corruption, when *the Waves thereof arise, he stilleth* them; as he doth the Raging of the Waters in the natural Sea, when it is most tempestuous; saying, *Hitherto shalt thou come, and no further;* and *Here shall thy proud Waves be stayed,* Psal. lxxxix. 9. Job. xxxvii. 11. How blessed then are those Souls who take Sanctuary under the Shadow of his Wings! That harbor in him, who is a Covert from the Tempest!

Further, is thy thirsty Soul almost parch'd up with the Heat of Temptations? Is the World a dry Place to thee, that cannot afford thee one Drop of spiritual Refreshment, or Soul-Consolation? In this Case, Christ is *as Rivers of Water in a dry Place.* As *cold Waters to a thirsty* Traveller, that's ready to famish for Thirst, under the parching Beams of the Sun; so, and much more is Christ, unto the Soul that *panteth* after him. Oh, the reviving Efficacy, the transcendent Sweetness, the abundant Fulness of *Christ,* as the Fountain of Grace, unto that Soul that is *ready to perish* for Want of it; when once it is led by the Spirit, to lay the Mouth of its Faith to this *Fountain of living Water!* Here it may Drink its Fill, and bathe itself in Pleasures, with Joy unspeakable and full of Glory! Nor is he only as Waters in a dry Place, when *Christ* and the Soul first meet, for its present Refreshment; but he is also, as Rivers of Water, for its constant Supply. *Christ* is not like a *failing Brook,* which in the Summer's Drought deceives the thirsty Traveller; which, perhaps, was once full for his Refreshment, but now empty, and can afford him none: But *Christ* is as a River, *a broad River with Streams.* For so this *Glorious LORD will* be unto us, Isa. xxxiii. 21. While passing thro' this

Land of Drought, this Wilderness-World, unto the Heavenly *Canaan.* He'll be a River of Life, for Fulness, to supply our Wants, however great our Necessities be; a River, for Freeness, however unworthy we are; and a River, for Duration, to supply us continually; yea, as Rivers of Water in a dry Place: There is in *Christ,* not only a full, free, and perpetual Supply of Grace; but of all kinds of Grace; There is in him a glorious Variety, that is every way sufficient to answer all our Wants, to satisfy all our Desires, and to fill us with all kinds of heavenly Pleasures and new Delights, thro' Time, and to Eternity! He'll be as Rivers of Water of Life unto us here in Grace, and hereafter in Glory! Then haste away to this living Supply!

Once more, Is thy Soul weary, and almost tired out, by reason of the continual Persecution of the Enemy, which, like the Sun upon Travellers in hot Countries, beats upon thy Head, and makes thee ready to faint and die for want of a little refreshing Shade? Why, *Christ* is also *as the Shadow of a great Rock in a weary Land,* in this weary Wilderness. Come, *sit down under his Shadow,* and thou shalt find *great Delight.* His cooling Shade will refresh and comfort thy weary Soul. He is as the Shadow of a Rock, which none of the penetrating Beams of the Sun can pierce thro', to molest or annoy thee; of a great Rock, that is large enough to cover thee all over. Here thou mayst sit, and take an holy Ease: For this Rock will defend thee from all Harm and Danger: Aye, and which is more, this Rock will supply thee with all heavenly Necessaries. For herein, *Christ* transcends all natural Rocks.

A weary Traveller may be glad to *embrace the Rock for a Shelter,* and sit down under its Shade for a while, to refresh him from the scorching Sun: But if he sit there long, he may starve and die for want of Sustenance: For nothing of that Nature can the flinty Rock afford him. But 'tis not so with that Soul who sits down under the Rock, *Christ.* No, wherever *Christ* is a Rock for Defence, he is also a Fountain, a Store-house for Supply. To that Soul that has *the Munition of Rocks* for its *Defence, Bread,* the Bread of Life, shall be given, and its *Waters,* of Consolation, shall be *sure,* Isa. xxxii. 16. Thus the Spouse, speaking of *Christ* under the Metaphor of an *Apple-Tree, I sat down,* says she, *under his Shade with great Delight, and his Fruit was sweet unto my Taste,* Cant. ii. 3. There is in *Christ,* all kinds of refreshing Shade, and all kinds of nourishing Supply. And, in a Word, there's enough for thee in him, to save thee from all Misery, unto all Glory, thro' all Times, and unto all Eternity! But what shall I say? There's more in *Christ* than Words can express, than the Tongue of Men and Angels can tell out, or their Hearts conceive, to an endless Eternity! Oh, *Come and see!* Come, and taste, that *the Lord is Good!* And *blessed are all those who put their trust in him.* Psal. xxiv. 8.

And now that you may be *drawn by the Cords of Love* into the swiftest Motion after Christ, and the nearest Communion with him, to your full Joy, and complete Deliverance, is the earnest Desire of,

Your Affectionate Friend, and humble

Servant in the Lord, &c.

LETTER XXX.

To Mrs. E. B.

Dear and honour'd Sister,

Grace unto you, and Peace be multiplied, from God our Father, and our Lord Jesus Christ, by the blessed Comforter.

I am given to understand by Sister *J---n,* that you are exercis'd, both with Affliction of Body, and Darkness of Soul; and I sympathize with you herein. But *think it not strange,* my dear Sister, *concerning the fiery Trials* you meet with, *as if some strange Thing had happen'd unto you.* Remember, the *LORD hath his Fire in* Zion *and his Furnace in* Jerusalem. *Isa.* xxxi. 9. To refine, not to destroy his People. God sends Afflictions upon his children for their good: Sin and Satan, indeed aim at our Destruction herein; but God bounds their Rage, and over-rules their Malice, to issue in his Glory, and our Salvation. The Design of Sin and Satan, is, the Destruction of our Graces, as well as of our Persons; and therefore they blow up the Fire of Affliction to the utmost, and would continue it until we are consumed. But, "Hold, says the Lord, my Children are my Gold, precious in my Esteem; and thy must pass thro' the Fire to be refined, but not lie there till they suffer Loss." And therefore when we are in the Furnace, our God sits by, to see that the

Fire be not too hot, nor continu'd too long upon us; as *the Refiner* watcheth his Gold, manages it while in the Furnace, and takes it out thence, when it is fully purify'd, *Mal.* iii. 3.

Well then, my dear Sister, since you are one of them who are precious in the Sight of the Lord, you must pass thro' the Fire of Affliction: But since it is the LORD's Fire, which he has appointed, which he manageth, and which he'll restrain at his Pleasure, trust thyself in the Hands of thy infinitely wise and gracious Refiner, and thou shalt come out of it, both with present and eternal Advantage. This Affliction, as an Instrument in the Hand of God, the Almighty Agent, is at Work upon thee, and for thee, to exercise and increase thy Graces here, and to prepare thee for thy future Crown. Therefore endure the Trial: *For blessed is the Man that endureth Temptation: For when he is tried, he shall receive the Crown of Life, which the Lord has promis'd to them that love him,* Jam. i. 12.

But it may be, you say, Aye, if I was sure that I was one that lov'd God, I should patiently wait for, and expect an happy Issue: But I am afraid lest I should deceive myself, deceive others, and at last come short of that Rest which remains for the People of God.

As to these thy Fears, and ten Thousand more of a like Nature, which may arise in the Heart in a Time of Darkness, they are altogether groundless; and tho' they may rob thee of thy Comfort, they cannot rob thee of thy Safety in Christ, nor of that Inheritance which is reserved for thee in Heaven. No, blessed be God, you are still just where Free-Grace set you: God has fixt you in his Son, and laid you, by Faith, upon Him *the Rock of Ages;* and now, your Salvation stands as immoveable as the Rock on which it is founded. The *Rain* may *descend,* the *Floods come,* and the *Winds blow,* all kinds of Afflictions and Temptations together, may beat vehemently against your Faith of Safety in Christ, but your Security in him shall never fall; because *founded upon a Rock,* that is able to bear the greatest Weights which are laid upon it, and to secure the Building from all Dangers, in the greatest Stress of Weather which can possible befal it. The Rock of Immutability is still beneath you; and unless Christ could sink, your Soul, the Salvation of it, I mean, that leans upon him, can never fall. You may fall as to your Frames, but can never sustain one

Shake as to your State. No; *The Foundation* God has laid *in Sion,* is a *Stone,* a *try'd Stone, a precious Corner-stone, a sure Foundation; and he that believeth on him, shall not be confounded,* Isa. xxviii. 16. 1 Peter ii. 6. And now, let all the Objections be brought out, that all the Legions of Devils, and Armies of Corruptions combin'd, can raise against the Salvation of that Sinner that looks unto Christ for Life, and down they must fall before the Grace of this Promise: God's Word shall stand, to the eternal Salvation of that Soul, and the Confusion of all its Enemies.

The Lord well knew, what mighty Assaults would be made upon the Faith and Comfort of his Children, and therefore added his Oath to his Great Word; That by *two immutable Things, in which it was impossible for God to lie, we might have a strong Consolation, who have fled for Refuge to lay hold upon the Hope that is set before us,* Heb. vi. 18. And have not you, my dear Sister, in Times past, *fled* unto Christ *for Refuge?* Yea, don't you even now? Dare you flee unto any other than the Name of the LORD, the great Saviour, as your *strong Tower,* for Safety? And if you dare not, why should you question your Safety; since God's Word assures you of it? God says, The Soul that *runneth* into *the Name of the LORD,* is *SAFE,* Prov. xviii. 10. Satan and Unbelief say, Nay; and produce ten thousand Evidences against such a Soul, in its own Heart and Life. And thus there is a Strife: Well, God adds his Oath; he comes in on the Side of his Child, whose Life seems to hang in Suspense; *and because he can swear by no greater, he swears by* HIMSELF: That is, he engages all the Perfections of his Great BEING, for the Salvation of that poor Sinner, who flees to Jesus, the sent Saviour: and accordingly, as the infinitely Wise, True, and Faithful God, gives Testimony of the same; which, with Reverence be it spoken, is the highest ASSURANCE the GODHEAD is capable of giving! And if the Witness of faithful Men is to be receiv'd, *the Witness of God is greater,* 1 John v. 9. And if *an Oath among Men is to them an End of all Strife;* what a *Confirmation* must the *Oath* of JEHOVAH be!

Well then, my dear Sister, since the faithful God stands for thy Salvation, on the one Side, and the Powers of Darkness stand against it, on the other: I would say unto thee, as the Apostles, in another Case, *Whether it be right in the Sight of God, to hearken unto you* (for thee to hearken unto Sin and Satan) *more than unto God, judge ye.* Attempt thy Duty then, oh thou fearful-hearted one, by a fresh Act of Faith, as one of God's Witnesses, to *set to* thy *Seal that He is* TRUE: To stand thy Ground, *in the Liberty wherewith Christ has made* thee *free;* even in the very Face of the Enemy: (and well thou mayst, since the LORD stands with thee) and thy Soul shall *tread down Strength,* and *put to Flight the Armies of the Aliens,* Armies of unbelieving Thoughts, muster'd up by Satan the Prince of Darkness. And if thou canst not say, with *Thomas, My Lord, and my God;* yet indulge not that Monster Unbelief, that dares, in the Face of so much Assurance, to give the faithful God the Lie! But whenever the Enemy bears hard upon thee, that thou shalt perish; endeavour to flee to Christ, as a helpless, perishing Sinner, in thyself, and commit thy Soul afresh into his Hands, to be kept till *the Day of Redemption.* And in so doing, thou wilt honour God, thy Soul will find Rest, and Satan will be forc'd to flee. For when he sees that those *fiery Darts* he shoots at thee, to drive thee off from Christ, are a Means to hasten thy Flight to him, he'll retire. Therefore learn the Art of War, and stand to thy Arms, as a valiant Soldier of Jesus Christ; opposing the Enemy with *the Sword of the Spirit, which is the Word of God;* holding up Christ by Faith, on every Side, to resist the *fiery Darts* he shoots at thee, from what Quarter soever they come. And if at any time he gives thee a Foil, then run to thy *Rock,* and hide thee, into the *Name of the LORD,* thy *strong Tower,* where thou shalt be *safe,* and set aloft out of the Reach of thy Enemies.

But it may be, thou wilt say, "Alas, I am so confused and dark, so weak and wounded, that I can neither stand my Ground for Christ, nor run to him."

If this be thy Case, then know for thy Comfort, that the *Captain of* thy *Salvation* stands for thee, and will come to thee, when thou canst not come to him. Thy Compassionate High Priest has Bowels for thee, every way proportionable to the Measure of thy Distress. He's a Man of Bowels, Yea, the God of Bowels: The Compassions of our Gospel High Priest are infinite! And having himself *suffer'd, being tempted in all Points like unto us,* he is *able* also, from an inward, experimental Feeling of the Power of Temptations, to *succour* us when *tempted.* And as he has an

Ability of Bowels to pity us, and an Ability of Strength to help us; so he has also Authority from his Father, the broad Seal of Heaven, to be our Physician to heal us; and he's *faithful to him that appointed him.* So that our Jesus is just such a Saviour as we need. *The Spirit of the Lord GOD,* says he, *is upon me, because he hath anointed me to preach good Tidings to the Meek; he hath sent me to bind up the Broken-hearted, to proclaim Liberty to the Captives, and the Opening of the Prison to them that are bound; To proclaim the acceptable Year of the LORD, and the Day of Vengeance of our God, to comfort all that mourn: To appoint unto them that mourn in* Zion, *to give them Beauty for Ashes, the Oil of Joy for Mourning, the Garment of Praise for the Spirit of Heaviness, that they might be called Trees of Righteousness, the Planting of the LORD, that he might be glorify'd,* Isa. lxi. 1, 2, 3. This was the Work the God of all Grace sent him about; and oh, with what amazing Tenderness doth he perform it! *He healeth the Broken in Heart, and bindeth up their Wounds,* Psal. cxlvii. 3. *He says to the Prisoners, Go forth; to them that are in Darkness, Shew yourselves;* and then again *they feed in the Ways, and their Pastures are in all high Places, They shall not hunger nor thirst, neither shall the Heat nor Sun smite them: For he that hath Mercy on them shall lead them; even by the Springs of Water shall he guide them,* Isa. xlix. 9, 10. And thus the Lord Jesus will deal with you, my dear Sister; therefore *be strong, fear not: Behold your God shall come with Vengeance,* (to destroy all thy Enemies, who shall be found Liars unto thee) *even God with a Recompense,* (for all thy waiting for him) *he shall come and save you,* Isa. xxxv. 3.

Into his Arms I commit you; earnestly desiring that happy *Morning* of divine Favour, which shall arise upon your Soul, when the short *Night* of your present Weeping is over: Christ will *see you again, and your Heart shall rejoice, and your Joy shall no Man take from you.* And, mean while, tho' Clouds and Darkness cover thee, Commotions and Tempests shake thy Mind; yet all is clear, as to thy State, in the upper Region of Christ's Love!

In Him, with dear Love,
I rest Yours, &c.

LETTER XXXI.

To Mr. W. *and* E. C.

Dear Brother and Sister,

I Beg leave to return you hearty Thanks for all your Favours. I am very sorry to hear of your Troubles; and should rejoice to hear of the Kindness of the Lord, in granting you a sanctify'd Use of 'em, and an happy Deliverance from them. Let us not think it strange, that *in the World we have Tribulation;* but rather rejoice, that in Christ we *have Peace,* amidst all the shaking Storms and surging Waves that pass over us. Vanity and Vexation are wrote upon all the Creatures: No Satisfaction or Rest for our Souls, but in the Bosom of God. *Riches make themselves Wings, and flee away;* but they that have Christ for their Portion *inherit* a *Substance,* that can never be lost or lessen'd. God in Christ is Substance; all Things else are Shadows. If we seek Happiness in Creatures; they'll all say, eventually, 'Tis not in me. But so far as God hath our Hearts, so far we are at rest. Because the infinite Fulness of his perfect and immense Being is a satisfying Good, to the most enlarged Desires of the Heaven-born Soul. All Things below God are subject to change, are passing from us, and we from them; but *Jehovah,* our Portion, changeth not; nothing can separate him from us, nor us from him. Oh, blessed is the Man whose God is JEHOVAH! When the Lord empties us of Creatures, the Language of his Grace and Providence is, *Come, my People, enter into your Chambers, and hide yourselves:* Come into my Bosom, take up your Delights in me; I will be all unto you, when every thing else is gone: *Hide* yourselves under the Shadow of my Wings, until these Calamities are *overpast.* And oh, happy Soul, that is fill'd with God, when empty'd of the Creature! Oh blessed Exchange! Yea, may we not say, oh happy Trial, oh blessed Affliction, that has drawn me off from the Circumference-Lines of Creature-Perfections, to rest in GOD, the Center of all my Blessedness!

The God of Peace sanctify wholly and meeten you daily for *the Inheritance of the Saints in Light,* which is *incorruptible, undefiled, and fadeth not away!* Begging your Prayers, I rest,

Yours in Christ for ever, &c.

LETTER XXXII.

To Mr. H.

Dear Sir, my honoured and beloved Brethren in Christ,

IT was with Concern that I heard Mr.O—read a Letter of yours, wherein you gave some Account of your inward and outward Trials: And therefore I was desirous to write a Line, in hopes it might be convey'd to you. And, be of good Comfort, my Brother, you have one Friend, that you may have Communion with at all times, and it is not in the Power of any Creature to intercept it. Jesus Christ can send from Heaven unto you by his Holy Spirit, and give you to know his Mind; and you, by the Assistance of the same Spirit, may fully open your Heart unto him: And no Creature can hinder it. Oh, prize your Friend in Heaven, and labour after a more intimate Communion, and greater Familiarity with him, now your Converse with Friends on Earth is in a great measure cut off. This, indeed, is hard Treatment from the Creature: But remember 'tis a kind of Persecution that you suffer for Jesus' Sake; and, like your Lord, learn Obedience by the Things you suffer, and endure the Cross for the Joy set before you. For this shall turn to your Salvation, and Glory in the Day of Christ. It may be, the Lord may have design'd, (for look unto him in it, thro' and above the Creature) by cutting off the Streams, to bring you to drink more immediately at the Fountain-Head. And that is infinitely better. Certain it is, that the Voice of your Beloved's Grace, in this Providence is, *O, my Dove, that art in the Clefts of the Rock, in the secret Places of the Stairs, let me hear thy Voice let me see thy Countenance; for sweet is thy Voice and thy Countenance is comely.* Your dear Lord Jesus hath desired a more free and intimate Communion with you. Indeed, he loves you: He loves you dearly, he loves you strongly, he loves you unchangeably, and he loves you eternally. Oh, Come and see. Come, and prove his Grace! Come, and see how good the LORD is! How much better he will be to you than ten Sons, than all the Creatures! Acquaint now thyself with him, and be at Peace: thereby Good shall come unto thee. Perhaps, by this Providence, well improv'd, you may have a greater Experience of the Sweetness, Fitness, Fulness, Excellency and Glory of Christ's Friendship than ever. And from hence, with the greatest Solace and Admiration, commend him unto others, with a *This is my Beloved! and This is my Friend!*

And have you sinn'd against your Friend? Have you griev'd your Friend? Oh, grieve with him! But do not think that he will forsake you: For thus the LORD the God of *Israel* saith, *he hateth Putting away*. If the LORD your Friend, had not had Love enough in his Heart to pardon all your innumerable Transgressions, and to pass by all your great Provocations, he would never have begun to love you; he would not have set his Heart upon you in Christ, in the Beginning of his Way, before his Works of old; nor yet would he have begun to manifest his Love, by calling you out of Darkness, into his marvellous Light. For God's Love begun, must run on to all the happy Objects thereof in one eternal Round, unto Ages without End. And that it might do so, infinite Wisdom divided a Water-course, thro' a crucify'd Jesus, for Love's overflowing Waters, that so reigning Grace might superabound over all our abounding Sinfulness, to the Honour of all the divine Perfections. Your God, my Brother, foreview'd all your Iniquities, in all their Aggravations, and yet, in the Greatness of his Love, he resolved to be gracious unto you, and to have Mercy upon you, in the free, and full Forgiveness of them all. He knew that your Neck was an Iron-Sinew, and your Brow, Brass; and that you would deal very treacherously; and yet he resolved, that nothing, none of all your Unkindness and Ingratitude should ever separate you from his Love. Oh, Behold this Love, and adore it! Behold it, and let your Heart melt into Gospel-Repentance before it! Behold it, until you feel an attracting Efficacy in it, and are changed into its Likeness! What, will not the Lord cast you off for all that you have done! Will he not deal with you after your Sins, nor reward you according to your Iniquities! Altho' they are more highly aggravated, and in some Sense greater, as you are one of his Favourites, for whom he has done such great things, than theirs can be, who are the People of his Wrath, against whom he hath Indignation for ever! Will he not turn you into Hell, with the Nations that forget God! Oh, Let this set your Heart against Sin! Let this Love engage you to give a Bill of Devorce to it! and to say, with *Ephraim, What have I to any more with Idols?* Oh, my Brother, The Lord expects you should return unto him again. Shall he turn away, says he, and not return? And, go, says he, proclaim these Words towards the North, (to my Children, who by Sin have lost the sweet Beams of my sensible Favours, that like the South-Wind, had us'd to blow upon their Souls with its refreshing Gales; and are got into the cold Point, having lost their first Love, and their Hearts almost frozen against me, and are apt to think that my Love towards them, is as cold as theirs towards me) and say unto them, *Return thou backsliding* Israel, *saith the LORD, and I will not cause mine Anger to fall upon you: for I am merciful, saith the LORD, and I will not keep Anger for ever. Only acknowledge thine Iniquity, that thou hast transgressed against the LORD thy God, and hast scatter'd thy Ways to the Strangers under every green Tree, and ye have not obeyed my Voice, saith the LORD. Turn, O Backsliding Children, saith the LORD, for I am married unto you, &c.* You see, my dear Brother, how the LORD calls upon you to return. Turn not therefore away from him; for the LORD will not forsake his People for his great Name's sake, because it hath pleased the LORD to make them his People. I am glad that you have been helpt to plead his Promise with him; that he will never leave you, nor forsake you: It is a Token of his never-failing Kindness, and of the fresh Visits thereof towards you. Go on to put the Promise in Suit: For the God of all Grace, will not, cannot deny himself. Consider likewise, what Encouragement you have to approach the Throne of Grace, to find Mercy, and Grace to help in Time of Need; since you have a Jesus, that is entred into Heaven for you with his own Blood, and there lives for you, as your advocate and Intercessor, to save you to the uttermost. And cast not away your Confidence, which hath great Recompense of Reward. It is, as Dr. *Goodwin* observes, one great End of Satan, in tempting us to Sin, to weaken our Faith. Let us therefore beware of this Device. And when we have fallen, let us not yield to unbelieving Fears about our Interest in God, or our being in a State of Grace; but rather, in the Faith of our Relation to him, let us return, and say with the Prodigal, *Father, I have sinned against Heaven, and in thy Sight, and am no more worthy to be call'd thy Son.* For *if we confess our Sins, he is faithful and just to forgive us our Sins, and to cleanse us from all Unrighteousness.*

With a Word or two of Caution and Exhortation, I'll conclude. And beware, my dear Brother, of yielding to any Sin. For hereby you will greatly dishonor God, grieve the Comforter, weaken your own Graces, strengthen your Corruptions, and unfit yourself for the Lord's Service. And in order to avoid sinful Acts, watch against sinful Thoughts, keep your Heart with all Diligence. Oh, let it not steal out from God, the Sum of all Perfection and Bliss, to seek Delight in the Creature, or any base Lust. Abide in Christ by Faith, and he will abide in you by his Spirit: and so you shall mortify the Deeds of the Body. Live in a constant Dependence on Christ, and Independence on yourself. For Inherent Grace, as you well observe, is not able to keep us in a Time of Temptation, without fresh Influence from above. Be diligent in the Use of Means: Read God's Word, and meditate therein Day and Night. Be frequent in secret Prayer: and neglect not public Ordinances. Let the Saints be your own Company: Delight in them who are the Excellent of the Earth. Flee youthful Lusts. Your Age, and the Place you live in, calls for great Watchfulness. Your Temptations are strong: Oh, be you strong, to resist them, in the Grace that is in Christ Jesus! Remember, he has Crowns and Thrones for every Overcomer. If you seek the Lord early, and follow him fully in your present youthful Day, as it will be greatly to his Honour, so to your own exceeding Joy, and unspeakable Glory. You are call'd to wrestle with the Powers of Darkness, both within and without: and had therefore need to have on the whole Armour of God, that you may be able to withstand in the evil Day, and having done all, to stand. You are call'd to run your Christian Race, for an incorruptible Crown: Keep it in sight, to animate you in your Course: That you may so run, as to obtain the invaluable Prize of eternal Glory!

Grace be with you, *Amen.*

I am, Sir, yours in the Lord, &c.

LETTER XXXIII.

To J. M.

Dear Sister,

Grace and Peace be multiplied unto you thro' the Knowledge of God, and of Jesus our Lord.

Having heard that you are yet on this side Glory, travelling thro' the Wilderness, it is on my Heart to have a little Talk with you by the Way. But by reason of Distance, Paper-converse is all that can be attain'd. 'Tis the Pleasure of our dear Father, to exercise thee in a very particular Manner, and to continue it long upon thee: But be not cast down hereat, as if some strange Thing had happened: For as many as the Lord loves, he rebukes and chastens. But it may be you'll say, "My Affliction is very uncommon, has lasted a great while, and it is like to endure so long as I'm in this World."

Well, be it so: Yet remember that God's special Love to you ordain'd this particular Trial; and his everlasting Kindness keeps it still upon you. This was the Means infinite Wisdom pitch'd on, for the Display of boundless Love to you. By this, you are to be made conformable to Christ in Sufferings, and meetned for a Conformity to him in Glory. Since Free-Grace has saved you, give it leave to carry on your Salvation in its own Way. What tho' you pass thro' much Tribulation, the Kingdom's at the End. I doubt not, but the Lord, at times, has opened much of his Love to your Soul in the present Afflictions: But the brightest Discoveries are behind. The great Opening of God's Heart, in the Gift of every Trial, is reserved for us till we get over *Jordan*, on the other side Death, into the Land of Promise. Then we shall remember all the Way the Lord led us thro' the Wilderness, and see it was a right Way to a City of Habitation. Then the Mysteries of Divine Providence shall be unfolded, the Cloud taken from off every dark Dispensation, and the Vail from our Understandings. There, the secret Springs of boundless Love, Infinite Wisdom, and Almighty Power, which ordain'd, managed, and over-ruled every Scene of Providence, for the Glory of God, and our Advantage, shall at once be laid open: For we shall see as we are seen. We shall bless God, when we come to Heaven, for every, even the bitterest, sharpest, longest Affliction, that attended our mortal Life; because we shall see how the Lord uninterruptedly carried on the Designs of his own glory and our Salvation, by every Change that pass'd over us. Mean while, we must live by Faith, and labour after an encreasing Submission to the Divine Will, under the sorest Rebukes, and a Blessing of God for every Stroke, till Grace is swallowed up in glory: When our Wills, with the highest Complacence, shall everlastingly flow into the Will of God. And even now, we have reason, not only to be patient, but also to rejoice, and glory in Tribulation. And was the Eye of our Faith strong enough to pierce the Cloud of afflictive Providence, and discern the Love of our Father's Heart, which, as an infinite Deep, coucheth beneath, and is the Spring of every Dispensation, we should sing in Sorrow, take Pleasure in Distresses, and glorify God in the Fires. *Our light Affliction,* saith he Apostle, *which is but for a Moment, worketh for us a far more exceeding and eternal Weight of Glory,* 2 Cor. iv. 17. There are three Things comprised in these Words, which I desire you may be enabled, frequently, to meditate upon. *First,* the Lightness of the Saints Affliction. *Secondly,* The Shortness of it. And *Thirdly,* The Advantage of all their present Trials.

First, The Lightness of the Saints Affliction: Our Light Affliction. It's not said, the Afflictions of the world are light: But our Affliction is light. And it is so, if compared with what we have deserv'd, and the Damned in Hell endure. Light, if compared with what Christ once bore, when for us he was, the Man of Sorrows, and acquainted with Grief. Light, because by virtue of Christ's Suffering for us in our room and stead, the Curse is taken out of all our Afflictions. Again, they're light, because omnipotent Strength is engaged to support us under 'em: Underneath are the everlasting Arms. We have not, are not, shall not be left to go thro' any Trial alone. The God of *Jacob* in our Refuge and Strength, a very present Help in Trouble. The Lord Jesus is our sweet Companion in Tribulation. He is with us, to sympathize with us in our Sorrows, to sustain us under our Burdens, to pardon all our Unbelief and Impatience, when in the Furnace; and at last compleatly and gloriously to deliver us, and bring us forth as Gold seven times refined. No Affliction, indeed, for the present is joyous, but grievous to our frail Flesh. It is so in itself, but much more so to us; because we live so much by Sense, and so little by Faith. Every Trial that passeth over us, hath a light as well as a dark Side: And we should look upon every Affliction with a double View: As 'tis oppressing and grieving to weak Nature, it is, in itself, Evil; and calls for Submission to the Divine Will. But then, as the same Affliction is view'd, as flowing from God's Love, and effectually managed for his Glory, and our Advantage; so 'tis good: and ought to be matter of our Joy and Thanksgiving.

Let's leave it then to them that have no Interest in the God of all Grace, to think Afflictions heave: For wo to them that are alone. But for us, that are interested in God, in all his Persons, and in all his Perfections, as engaged in Covenant for our good let's go on rejoicing in Tribulation; esteeming all our Afflictions, as indeed they are, light.

Secondly, The Shortness of the saints Affliction, is matter of great Consolation: 'tis but for a Moment. A Moment is but a short space, the smallest Division of Time. And unto this of a Moment, are our longest Afflictions compared. Suppose they should last as long as we are in this World: Yet, even our whole Life, if compared with a vast Eternity, is but like a Moment. And, as Mr. *Dod* well says, "What can be great to him that counts the World nothing? Or long, to him that counts his Life but a Span?" Oh! were we more frequent in our Converse with Eternity, it would make the Afflictions of this present Time appear short. Did we live more in the Views of approaching Glory, we should remember our Afflictions as Waters that pass away; that are here one Moment, and gone the next. But alas! such is our Folly, that we are taking Thought for a great while to come: And so make our apprehended, future Trials, present Distresses. Whereas, were we under the most pressing Weights, and did take Thought for no more than the Day; (and *sufficient to it, is the Evil thereof*) living by Faith on the Borders of Glory, as just entering into the Mansions of Rest; it would alleviate our Sorrows, and make the longest Trial appear short. Could we thus reason with ourselves every Day, "Well, I'm got one Day nearer home; the Afflictions of the past Day I shall never go thro' any more: And perhaps, before I see another Day in this World, I may see Glory's Day; a Morning that will have no Clouds nor Evening to succeed it: No Sorrow, Sin, nor Death to darken its lustre." Oh, what a Means would this be to increase our Patience, and make us of an enduring Spirit! And what matter of Comfort is it, that while our short-lived Afflictions last, Christ will be with us in 'em? He's with us when we pass thro' the Waters, that the Rivers don't overflow us; that the swelling Waves of Affliction don't overwhelm us: And when we walk thro' the Fires, that the Flames kindle not upon us, that fiery Trials don't consume us. The Priests Feet were to stand in *Jordan*, till all *Israel* was clean passed over. So our dear Lord Jesus will stand amidst our Distresses, dividing the Waters before us, till all his Children are clean passed thro' 'em. His Presence with us in Affliction, will make it light; and his delivering Kindness out of it, will make it short. But,

Thirdly, the Advantage of the Saints Affliction, is also an Encouragement to Faith and Patience: It worketh for us. But what doth it work? Why, no less than Glory! And it works Glory for us, as it prepares us for it. Glory was prepared for us, and settled upon us, in God's everlasting Covenant with his Son, before the World was. And Affliction is a Means, infinite Wisdom, Power, and Grace makes use of, to prepare us for Glory: That Glory which was got ready for us before Time, and will last to an eternal Space beyond it. And who would think much to endure Affliction, that sees it is but for the Trial, and perfecting of his Graces; and that the Exercise of each might be found unto Praise, Honour, and Glory at Christ's Appearing?

Now then, let's bring things to the Ballance of the Sanctuary, and learn to judge of 'em aright. Let's amass together all the Afflictions of a Believer's Life, and put 'em in one Scale, and Glory in the other; and see if that don't infinitely outweigh them! especially, if we cast in the additional Weights that are on Glory's Side: Here's Affliction on the one Side; but Glory on the other: Light Affliction, for a Moment; but a Weight of Glory; yea, an exceeding, a *far more exceeding and eternal Weight of Glory!* Well might the Apostle say, *For I reckon, that the Sufferings of this present Time, are not worthy to be compared with the Glory which shall be revealed in us,* Rom. viii. 17.

Dear Sister, you are straitned in me, a poor, contracted, narrow-mouth'd Vessel, that can take in, or let out but little: But you're not straitned in Christ. The Lord enlarge your Capacity, to take in

Abundance of himself in the glorious Promises! And open unto you such Views of the Inheritance of the Saints in Light; which may cause you to go comfortably thro' your present Trials: and at last give you a triumphant Passage thro' the Valley of the Shadow of Death, under the bright Shines of his Face, beheld by Faith; until Faith is swallowed up in Vision!

So prays, yours in the Lord, &c.

LETTER XXXIV.

To E. H.

My dear Sister in Christ,

I Greet you: wishing Grace and Peace may be multiply'd unto you, thro' our Knowledge of God, and of Jesus our Lord.

Yours I receiv'd, and rejoice to hear how our gracious God is carrying on his Work in your Soul. It is our unspeakable Privilege, that our Lord's Fulness cannot decay. 'Tis hence we have receiv'd all our Supplies hitherto. And tho' we are still as needy Creatures as ever, yet the Fulness of Christ abides unchangeably the same. As it is an overflowing, so an ever-flowing Fountain; which fills the Saints in both Worlds. 'Tis hence the Saints have, do, and shall receive thro' all the Ages of Time: and this will fill us to an endless Eternity, without the least Waste. Let all the Saints in Heaven and Earth drink, yea, drink abundantly, drink their Fill out of the Fulness of Christ; yet can they not sink this Fountain one Hair's Breadth. Because our Maker is our Husband: The LORD of Hosts is his Name. The grace of Christ, as the Church's Beloved, is not the Grace of a mere Creature: then it would be soon dry'd up and gone: But it is the boundless, infinite, inexhaustible Grace of JEHOVAH, the Rock of Ages, who changeth not! Oh the transcendent Fairness of our Beloved, as he is our GOD, as well as our Goel, or Kinsman-Redeemer! What sweet Fellowship may we have with the infinite Grace of the boundless Deity dwelling in our own Nature! Here, divine Terror shall not make us afraid; because infinite Majesty is cloth'd with our Flesh. We may well hold fast our Confidence, since we have such a great High-

Priest, Jesus the Son of God, passed into Heaven for us. Jesus, born of the Virgin, to be a Saviour; and yet the Son of God in our Nature! The Bowels of Christ, our Gospel High-Priest, are truly human, and yet infinite: Because of the Union of the Divine and Human Nature in the wonderful Person of our Beloved. What Encouragement is this to our Faith? We may come daily with our empty Souls to our full Jesus. Our Wants are innumerable; but there's enough in Christ to fill us: Yea, there's a Redundancy, more than enough. The Vessels of Mercy are and shall be cast into this Ocean of Glory, contained in it, and fill'd with it; but they can never contain that, which contains them; because the most enlarged Capacities, even of glorify'd Saints, are still but finite: and the Glory of God, into which they are cast, is infinite; an immense Sea, without either Shore, or Bottom!

The Lord help you, my dear Sister, to abide in Christ by Faith, and to come to him daily with all your Wants: His Power, Grace, and Faithfulness are all engag'd to grant you a rich Supply. To live by Faith on the Son of God, in the every Day Work of a Believer. And when you can't come to Christ, in the Views of your Marriage-relation to his Person, and Interest in his Fulness, you may come as a poor perishing Sinner in yourself, unto him the exalted Saviour, who is mighty to save, whose Office it is to save the chief of Sinners; even all them that come unto God by him. And such is his Grace, that in no wise he will cast out any poor Soul that comes to him. No, tho' it be ever so unworthy, vile, wretched and miserable; there's Strength enough in his Arm, and Grace enough in his Heart, to save to the uttermost. It matters not how great our Wants be, when we come to an infinite Fountain. It is no more for Christ, to fill the vastest Desires of the most needy Creature that ever came to him, than for the Sea to fill a Cockle-shell. Nay, 'tis not so much: For tho' there is a sort of Immensity in that vast Confluence of Waters; yet they may be lessened. But the Fulness of Christ is properly infinite, and therefore not subject to the least Diminution.

But I must conclude, desiring that the God of our Lord Jesus Christ, the Father of Glory, may grant unto you a more abundant Measure of the Spirit of Wisdom and Revelation in the Knowledge of

Him, whom to know, is Life eternal. With dear Love to yourself and all Friends,

I rest Yours in Christ for ever, &c.

LETTER XXXV.

To P. W.

My dear Sister,

I Rejoice to hear of your Health, and with your Soul may prosper exceedingly. Dear Child, work while it is Day. Improve all the Time the Lord gives you for his Glory: For this will be for his Honour, and your own Joy, both now and in the Day of Christ, Oh, be diligent, that you may be found in him in Peace, without Spot, and blameless! Christ will never leave thee, nor forsake thee: His Grace will be sufficient for thee: Therefore lay out thyself for him, all manner of Ways, at all Times, and in all Places. Keep the Crown in View, to quicken and encourage you to *run with Patience the Race that is set before you.* Who would not work for Christ, that glorious Lover! That glorious Master! Who HIMSELF will be our exceeding great REWARD! But ah, Wretched me! How ungrateful, disingenuous, rebellious, and slothful have I been! 'Tis well for me that Free-Grace reigns, reigns thro' Righteousness, a better Righteousness than mine, unto eternal Life; and that where Sin *has abounded, Grace doth much more abound.* Was it not so, I should never be saved. But, blessed be God, I see, to my unspeakable Joy, the whole of my Salvation, founded in, and secur'd by free, reigning Grace! But then, what a Debt of Love, in all holy Obedience, doth a saved Soul owe unto its Saviour! Oh here, I fall short, vastly short of what is my Duty; and so of that Glory I ought to give him. Oh Wretch that I am, doth Christ delight to glorify me: and shall I dare, by my Negligence in his Service, to slight his Honour! And yet thus evilly have I done innumerable Times. Oh, "I must go into Heaven, (as Mr. *Rutherford* says) Free-Grace's Divour." And, "Surely I shall die, minting and aiming to be a Christian." But then, oh, then, I shall be a Christian indeed! As full of Christ, as like him, and as able to serve him, as now my Soul longs to be!

Oh, pray for me, that while I abide on this side *Jordan,* I may be blest with a growing Communion with Christ, an increasing Conformity to him, and a more abundant Service of him! And the Lord grant you these three Blessings!

I rest Yours, &c.

LETTER XXXVI.

To T. W.

Dear Brother,

I Bless God for Christ: And because he lives, I live also. Oh, my Brother, what Grace is it to us, that our Union to Christ, our Life, cannot be broken! And, oh that our Faith of Interest in him, in his Person and Fulness, may daily engage us to live to him, who died for us, and rose again! Oh that we might not be contented to live at the poor, low, carnal Rate at which the most of Professors and Church-Members live at this Day! Our Lord *has his Fan in his Hand; and he will thoroughly purge his Floor.* Oh, when the Lord shall search *Jerusalem* with Candles, who may abide the Day of his Coming? Let us therefore watch, and keep our Garments. And whatever others do, let us labour to improve all our present Moments, some way or other to glorify God, that so when our Lord appears, we may be found of him in Peace: And have his *well done,* as *good and faithful Servants.* Oh, how blessed a Thing it is, to say with the Apostle, *for me to live is Christ!* 'Tis sweet to live for Christ here, as well as to live with him hereafter. Oh what a glorious Master is Jesus Christ! How glorious is his Service! And what a glorious Reward will he bestow upon his Servants, when he bids them *enter into the Joy of their Lord!*

Wishing a rich Increase of all Grace, unto all Glory; and desiring your Prayers for us,

I rest, Yours, &c.

ERRATA.

[Errata corrected in text]

3

LETTERS

ON

Spiritual Subjects,

AND

DIVERS OCCASIONS;

SENT TO

Relations and Friends.

By One who has tasted that the LORD *is* GRACIOUS.

VOL. IV.

Wherefore comfort yourselves together, and edify one another, even as also ye do, 1 Thess. v. 11.

LONDON:

Printed by J. HART, in *Poppings-Court, Fleet-street:* And sold by J. LEWIS, in *Bartholomew Close* near *West Smithfield;* and E. GARDNER, at *Milton's-Head,* near *Aldgate,* 1746. [Price stitch'd Nine-pence.]

LETTERS
ON
Spiritual Subjects, &c.

LETTER I.

To Mr. and Mrs. *W-----s.*

My Dear and Honour'd Parents,

I Rejoyce to hear of your Welfare. It must needs be well with *us,* in every State, that are so nearly related to, and so well secur'd in CHRIST. Infinite Love, chose us in Him, before Time began; united us to Him, unto our Life from Him, when the LORD passed by us, saw us in our *Blood,* and said unto us, *Live.* Infinite Love, acquainted us with our Misery, reveal'd the Remedy, shew'd us our Danger, presented our Refuge, enabled us to flee unto, into CHRIST: And then the LORD *shut us in.* By his great *Word,* his irreversible *Oath,* given for our Salvation: That thenceforth, we might have *strong Consolation.*—We are *Heirs of Promise,* My dear Parents: And therefore our Inheritance is secure. Oh were we to *earn an* Inheritance in GOD, by the Works of our own Hands, by our own Obedience to the *Law;* we must go without it for ever. But an Inheritance by *Promise,* suits us. This great Inheritance of the LORD, for our Portion, given us by *free Promise,* and confirm'd to us in the LAMB'S *Blood;* displays the *Glory* of Sovereign Grace, and well *agrees* with our Poverty. An Inheritance given us by free, unchanging *Promise,* with the *Yea,* and *Amen.* of GOD upon it in CHRIST: must needs be *ours,* and for ever *sure* to us, notwithstanding all our Unworthiness.—But oh, what reason have we to lament, that we have behav'd no more, like *Heirs of Promise!* For myself, I mourn, I lament over all my unsuitable Behaviour, to that infinite Favour, which is cast upon me by the GOD of all Grace, in making me an *Heir of Promise!* Oh my *Sins,* since the Lord acquainted me herewith, deserve the hottest *Hell!* And yet, to the Glory of boundless Grace, my Inheritance is *secure!* The Mercies of God's everlasting Covenant, to me in Christ, are *sure Mercies!* Because they are *free* Mercies, *unconditional* Mercies: That don't stand upon my little, fickle Obedience; but upon the immutable Grace, the unchanging Truth and Faithfulness of the great JEHOVAH! And the Greatness and Eternity of the REDEEMER'S Merit!—This comforts me greatly, humbles me deeply, and attracts me strongly, to *love* HIM, that GOD of Love, *who first loved,* who will always love *me.*—But oh, what can I do for *Him,* who has done so much for *me!* Ah *little, very little,* if compar'd with the *great Obligations* I am under! Yea, *nothing* can I do for GOD, but what his *free Love* enables me to do. And then of his *own,* I give him. And in infinite Grace, he *accepts* my little Mite! But surely, if of his Stock, I had an Angel's Store; I would lay it out, to a *Methusalah's* Age, to endless Days, to glorify the GOD of Grace, of all Grace, who has made me an *Heir of Promise!* In Heaven, I shall love and serve him perfectly and eternally. And I long to do both increasingly, while on this Earth. Help me by your Prayers.—*The Grace of Christ be with your Spirit.*—I am, my honour'd Parents,

Your most dutiful Child.

LETTER II.

To Mr. *P--------ll.*

My dear Brother in Christ,

I Thank you for your Letter. I rejoice in what God hath done for your Soul. Truly, if the LORD had been minded to *destroy you,* he would not have shewed you *these Things:* Viz. The Plague of your own Heart; The Insufficiency of your own Righteousness; And the Excellency and Glory of *Christ,* as the only SAVIOUR: Whence you desire to be found in *him,* wash'd in his Blood, cloth'd with his Righteousness, and saved in him with an everlasting Salvation; to the endless *Glory* of rich, free, sovereign *Grace.* These are such Things, that God reveals to none but those who are *Vessels of Mercy: Whom he had afore prepared unto Glory.* CHRIST is *yours,* and you are *his,* and neither Sin, Death nor Hell, shall ever *separate you from his Love.* He has begun your Salvation; and he will finish it. He hath given you precious Faith; and he will perfect it. And your very *Desire* to be found in Christ; is an *Evidence* of your Faith in him, and Love to him. It was foretold concerning Unbelievers, That when they *see Christ,* in the outward Revelation of him, there would be to them, *no Beauty in him that they should desire him,* Isa. liii. 2. And on the contrary, it is said of Believers, *unto you that believe he is precious,* or desireable, *1 Pet.* ii. 7. Not one Soul, that *desires Christ,* shall ever *die* for Want of him. Not one Soul, that sees Christ to be *Altogether Lovely,* but stands in a *Marriage-relation* to him, in an indissoluble Union to the Lord of Life and Love. Not one Soul, that is made *willing* to be saved in God's Way, by his Free Grace, thro' the Lamb's Love and Blood, Righteousness and Power; but shall be *saved by him to the uttermost,* from all Misery, unto all Glory. The *Desire* of the Soul going out after Christ, is its *coming* to him. *And him that cometh unto me,* saith our Lord, *I will in no wise cast out,* John vi. 37. No; CHRIST receives that Soul, unto the Glory of GOD: To save him from endless Misery, to everlasting Glory. And there is such an infinite Fulness of all Salvation-Blessings in *Christ,* for the most poor and miserable, wretched and naked *Sinner,* that comes to him, that he need fear *no Want.* There is Salvation-Help enough in *Christ,* to answer our extensive Destruction, in and of *ourselves.* To make us as free from Sin, in its Guilt, Filth and Power, as holy to God, and as happy in him, as *Adam* was, before his Fall: Yea, to raise us to an higher Life and Glory. Our Lord is come, that we might have *Life,* and have it *more abundantly.* And all the Fulness of CHRIST, is made over, by the Word and Oath of a GOD that cannot *lie,* unto the most miserable, needy *Sinner* that comes unto him.—Come then, come again and again, with your every Day's Wants and Miseries, unto the Fulness, the Mercies fo the great SAVIOUR. And thence you shall receive, and *Grace for Grace.* The Arms of Christ, stand open to receive you. You will honour the Redeemer's Love, Blood and Fulness, his Power and Faithfulness, if you come to him daily, and cast yourself upon him, as a most miserable Sinner, for a full Supply of all your Wants. And I can tell you from his

Word, and from my own Experience, that he will not send you *empty away*.

I am glad that you have such a Sense of *Sin*, that you can *justify God*, if he was to send you to *Hell*, and acknowledge his Righteousness therein; that you would love him, and his Righteousness therein; that you would love him, and speak well of his Goodness to others. Yea, that the very Thoughts of God's being *glorify'd*, if you was to be *damned*, afford you some *Pleasure*. These Things are an Evidence, of true Love to God in the Heart. Of *that Love*, which whoever hath it, shall *never* go down to Hell. Of *that Love*, which is a *Preparation* for Heaven, and the very *Beginning* of it in the Soul.

And as a Thought, that God would be *more* glorify'd in your Salvation, than in your Damnation, is *more* pleasant to you; Let this move you to come with Alacrity, unto *Christ for Life*. For in the Salvation of Sinners by *Jesus Christ*, all the Perfections and Glories of *Jehovah*, radiantly shine, and are harmoniously display'd. Here, in the Salvation of chief Sinners, thro' the crucify'd SAVIOUR; *Justice and Mercy are met together, Righteousness and Peace, do kiss each other*. This is the Way that infinite Wisdom has devised, that infinite Grace has provided, that the LORD himself hath chosen, for the most refulgent Display of his infinite Glory.

Like then, what GOD likes. Embrace his SON held out freely unto you in the Gospel. It will please the Father *well*, if you lay hold by Faith on the great SAVIOUR, for yourself as a *chief Sinner*. *This is a faithful Saying, and worthy of all Acceptation, that Jesus Christ came into the World, to save Sinners, Chief Sinners*. Oh, accept of *him*. Take him for *yourself*. CHRIST is a *free Gift*. You may have him *without Money*, and *without Price*. The Father bids you, the Son bids you, the Spirit bids you *receive him*. And unto *you*, the Lord will give *Power*, Privilege, a Royal Grant, with efficacious Influence, *to become a Son of God*. An *Heir of* GOD, *and a Joint-Heir with* CHRIST! Come again and again to the Lord Jesus. Let this be your Life continually. "Unto whom *coming* (says the Apostle) as "unto a living Stone, &c." Oh stand not gazing upon your Sins and Miseries, till you lose yourself in a Maze: But haste away to CHRIST, upon the first Sight of them. His Name is called JESUS: *For he shall save his People from their Sins.* Honour him then, in this his Office as a SAVIOUR, by coming to him for all Salvation, for all Grace and Mercy, as being in yourself a miserable Sinner. And Christ will make you a glorious Saint, or *sanctify you wholly, in Spirit, Soul and Body, and present you Faultless, before the Presence of his* Father's *Glory, with exceeding Joy.*

Be not surprised at the Being and Working of *Sin* in you. The *Canaanites* dwelt in the Land, to learn *Israel* War. And by *little and little,* the LORD will drive them out from before us, until we be increased in Grace, to inherit the Glory prepared for us.—As to your *Unbelief;* distinguish between a *State* of Unbelief, and the Workings of Unbelief, between *total,* and *partial* Unbelief. You are not in a *State* of Unbelief. But you, and every Believer, have *Unbelief,* remaining and working in the Soul where *Faith dwells.* And as Unbelief opposes, more or less, our Acts of Faith continually; we are call'd to *fight the good Fight of Faith.* And the more *frequent* our Acts of Faith on Christ are, the *weaker* will the Power of Unbelief grow in our Souls. It is no *proud Presumption,* but *humble Faith,* for a poor *Sinner,* to come repeatedly to the merciful SAVIOUR, and rest his weary Head in Christ's Bosom; believing, according to his Promise, *that he will give him Rest,* from all his Sins and Fears, and to the utmost of all his Desires, both of Grace and Glory.

It was not *Satan,* to deceive you, but the *Spirit of God,* to comfort you, that apply'd those Scriptures to your Heart, which were pleasant to your Soul. And *those,* and *all* the Promises of God, are yours in *Christ.* They are all *yea,* and *Amen,* unto you in *him.* And in looking for the *Effects* of the Promise, to know if it was from the *Lord;* seek the *immediate* Effects of it in your *Heart;* just *when* and *while,* the Word abides with Power on your Mind; And the *remote* Effects of it in your Life, just *so far* as the Promise influenceth your Heart. To look for immediate, inward Effects of the Word, when the Power of it is gone *off* the Mind; is like looking what o'Clock it is by the Dial, when the Sun don't shine on it.—Don't wonder, that you have a *Heart,* and a *Heart;* a Heart for *God;* and a Heart that *departs from him.* Since in your Soul, there are *Two Natures:* The new Man, and the old. Since in your corrupt Nature, there dwelleth *no good Thing;* and in your new Nature, tho' all Good dwells, yet is it *weak,* and *imperfect.* Grace is in its Infancy, and therefore at Times, overcome by the old Man, by the Power of Corruption in your Soul. But your *little Grace,* being *Christ's Life in you;* shall be maintain'd and increas'd from his Fulness, until all Sin and Death, is *swallow'd up* of perfect Holiness, Life and Joy for evermore.—*Head-Knowledge* of Gospel-Truths, is a *Privilege.* Pray for the Holy Ghost's *Fire,* to enkindle them in your *Heart,* and change your *Soul* into the Image of Christ by them.—I am glad that my printed Account of the Lord's Gracious Dealings with *me,* has been blest to *you,* to encourage you to hope in, and seek for, his rich, free, abundant Grace, to be display'd towards you. *Your Heart shall live, that seeks* GOD. I hope to think on you before the Lord; and shall be glad to correspond with you, if his Glory and your Joy may be promoted thereby. Committing you to the Care of CHRIST the great Shepherd; I am, Sir,

Yours affectionately in Him,

——— ———

LETTER III.

To Mrs. *A.* and Mrs. *M. W-----s.*

Dear Children,

I Rejoyc'd to hear, that you were under any Concern about your precious Souls, and inclin'd to seek JESUS. An Interest in CHRIST, is the *One Thing needful.* If we have *this,* we shall be eternally happy; if we have it *not;* eternally miserable. *The Wages of Sin is Death: But the Gift of God is eternal Life, through Jesus Christ our Lord.* God hath given, and will give, to poor Sinners, *eternal Life:* And this Life is in his *Son.* He that findeth *Christ,* findeth *Life,* and shall obtain *Favour of the* LORD. O my dear Children, we are all of us, born into this World, most miserable *Sinners.* We are quite undone; we have *destroy'd* ourselves by Sin. But for ever adored be God's Free Grace! In Christ the *Saviour,* is our *Help.* It hath pleased the Lord, to lay *Help,* the Help of Sinners, upon one that is *mighty.* Upon the mighty SAVIOUR, who is able and willing, to save to the Uttermost, even all that come unto God by him. There is all Fulness in Christ, to answer your every Want. All the infinite Treasures, the inexhaustible Stores of Grace and Life, are laid up in Christ; on purpose for the most poor and miserable, blind and naked, and Law condemned Sinners that come unto him. Do you *see* your Misery? Do you *want* Mercy? Is God's free Mercy in Christ, *desirable* to you? Then are *you*, you as it were by Name, call'd by JESUS, to *come* unto him, and *drink:* To take your Fill freely, of all lthe Grace you want, to save you from all Misery, unto all Glory. He will not send you *empty away.* His Love, his Mercy, his Power, his Faithfulness, are all engag'd to save you. He will not, he cannot deny himself. He will in no wise cast out, any poor Soul that comes unto him for Life. And do you begin to *see* any Beauty in Christ? Any Precociousness in his Blood? Any Glory in his Righteousness? Any Excellency in his Fullness? Then remember what he says for your Encouragement: *I love them that love Me, and those that seek Me early shall find Me,* Prov. viii. 17. Christ first loved *you;* or you had not been drawn by a Sight of his Beauty, to love *him.* He first desir'd to save *you;* or you had not been desirous to be saved by *him.* Christ was first willing to be married unto *you;* or you had not been made willing to have *him,* the LORD of Hosts, your Maker, your Redeemer, for your Husband. And if *Christ* is willing to embrace you as his own, in the Arms of his infinite Love; and *you* are willing to be folded up for ever in his sweet Embraces: *What can hinder?* Oh give up yourselves to JESUS, to be entirely *his;* and HE will be entirely *yours.* And the Day of your *Espousal* unto him, will be the Day of the *Gladness of his Heart.* Oh did you see but a thousandth Part of his infinite Worth, did you taste but a thousandth Part of his infinite Sweetness, your Souls would be *sick of Love* for *him, the Chiefest among ten Thousand!* For HIM, that fair, that incomparably fair, and *altogether lovely* ONE! Oh dear Children, CHRIST is a Well of Life, a Sea of Bliss, a Mass of Treasure, that is Bottomless, Boundless, Endless! In HIM, all Beauties, and Glories, all Delights, and Perfections, both created and uncreated; do jointly and for ever *meet!* Neither the Tongues of Men, nor of Angels, were they employ'd to an eternal Space, could tell you the one *Half,* no nor the ten *Thousandth Part* of his infinite Glory! Oh seek an intimate Acquaintance with JESUS! Nothing like *this,* to tell you what JESUS is. CHRIST is best *known,* by a real Enjoyment, a feeling Possession, and humble Adoration, of his great, his glorious, his blissful

SELF! Hereby your Souls will be filled with all the Fulness of GOD; changed into the same Image, from Glory to Glory, in this World; until you see CHRIST as he is, are made perfectly like him, and appear with him in the Glory of the World to come.—*Grace be with you!* I remain

Yours most affectionately,

——— ———

LETTER IV.

To Mr. and Mrs. W------s.

My very Dear and much Honour'd Parents,

WITH Gladness I received your kind Letter. As it is your Desire, my dear and honour'd Father, *That Christ may be magnified in your Body, whether it be by Life, or by Death:* So I know it will be your Joy, if the Lord Jesus, will please in his infinite Grace, to say of any of *your Offspring, I am glorify'd in them.* The Hope of *This,* yea, the Joy of it, when my dear Lord is graciously pleas'd to hint it to my Spirit, concerning my unworthy *Self,* fills me with Heart-melting Wonder, Love and Thankfulness. And how greatly hath the Lord blest you, in *others* of your Offspring! What a Joy will it be to you at the last Day, to see us *all* rais'd up unto *Life eternal,* to inherit Glory with *you!* To say, like your Lord, concerning all your dear Children, for whom you have pour'd out so many Prayers and Tears, and whom so often you have kindly instructed and exhorted; *Lord, here am I, and the Children which Thou hast given me!* How will it rejoice your dear Soul, to see that none of us are lost; but all brought safe by God's Free-Grace, to his eternal Glory! To see us *all,* each one in our own Place, as so many bright Jewels, clad with an amazing Splendor, and fixt by the King of Glory, to his Crown Royal, for ever and ever! Oh when *We,* by our Lord, are presented *Faultless,* before the Presence of the Father's *Glory,* together with *you;* it will be with *exceeding Joy!* We shall each one rejoice in our *own* Salvation, with a Joy that far exceeds all present Thought; and have an additional Joy in the Salvation of *each other.*—And this Glory, my honour'd Parents, hastens upon us, and all the Chosen of God. *This Mortal must put on*

Immortality. This *earthly Tabernacle*, must be *dissolved*. That so we may be *clothed* with that *House*, that *Building of God*, that ineffable Glory, prepar'd for us, *Eternal in the Heavens*. Oh my dear Parents, your dear Lord Jesus will be with you, in all your Pains and Afflictions, thro' the Infirmities of an advanced Age. The Lord will make all your *Bed* for you, when *sick*. And when *Death comes*, and no Creature can help you: Then, then will the LORD be your Helper. He will *never leave you, nor forsake you:* No, not in Death's Water. *Jesus* your High Priest will go before you, make a Way for you, and bring you safe over *Jordan*, into the promis'd *Land. The Eternal* GOD *is your Refuge: And underneath* you, in your last Trial, will be *the everlasting Arms*. These Almighty Arms, will keep your Spirits from sinking, when your Bodies must fall by the Stroke of Death. The soft Embraces of those sweet Arms, will refresh your Souls, and ease the bitterest Pains that your outward Man may feel. And not the least Pain, not he least Sickness you may endure, to bring down your mortal Frame; but will serve as a *Foil*, to set off that immortal Glory you shall enter upon: In EMANUEL'S Land, where the Inhabitant shall not say, *I am sick. There* I shall shortly *meet you.*—And let us remember, that Death comes to us as a *Blessing*. *Death* to us, will be an Entrance into *Life*. We shall never be free from Sin, perfectly holy, nor fully happy, we shall never be as we would, nor should be; till we see JESUS as He is.—I remember you before the Lord; and beg your Prayers for me: Who with a Heart brimful of Love and Duty, subscribe, my honour'd Parents,

Your most obedient Child,

——— ———

LETTER V.

To Mr. F-----o.

Dear Sir,

I Hope that your dear Soul grows in Grace, and in the Knowledge of CHRIST. That you see more of your own Miseries and Wants, as a poor *Sinner;* and rejoice in the Mercies, Merits and Fulness of the glorious SAVIOUR. Oh blessed be God, our dear Lord Jesus, is just such a Saviour as we *need!* His precious *Blood,* cleanseth us from *all Sin:* His glorious *Righteousness,* clothes our *naked Souls:* And his inexhaustible *Fulness* of Grace and Glory, will maintain and perfect our *Graces,* and give us the full Enjoyment of *Glory,* in and with him, unto Ages without End! Oh let us come daily to our dear Lord Jesus, and commit our Souls into his Hands, to be saved to the uttermost. He *can,* and *will* save us. He is in *Office* to save us, as our Prophet, Priest and King. And has given us his great Word of Promise, That the Soul that *cometh unto him, he will in no wise cast out.* Our Lord saveth *Sinners.* He delights to save. He will not upbraid us with the Number, the Greatness, the Aggravation of our Sins. For, *tho' we have done as evil Things as we could;* yet he saith, *Return again unto me.* Oh dear Sir, This is the Voice of GOD our SAVIOUR, of the LORD, the LORD GOD, *Merciful and Gracious: Forgiving Iniquity, Transgression and Sin!* And oh how *abundant* is he, in his *Goodness and Truth,* towards poor Sinners! Our dear Lord, is *a Friend of Publicans and Sinners.* A loving, tender *Friend,* an omnipotent, faithful *Friend,* the only, and everlasting *Friend* of Sinners. *This* MAN, CHRIST, *receiveth Sinners, and eateth with them.* The SAVIOUR *receives Sinners,* to save them from all their *Sins.* He receives them freely, fully, and perpetually, into his own All-gracious and Almighty Hands. To heal their Wounds, to bind up their Sorrows, to beautify their Souls, to keep them from Falling, and to present them Faultless before the Presence of *His,* and of his *Father's* Glory, with exceeding Joy! And oh how *familiar* doth the dear SAVIOUR, delight to be with the Chief of Sinners, that see their Misery, and prostrate their Souls at his Feet, to find Mercy! He not only receives them to the Glory of God, to save them from endless Misery, unto eternal Glory, with all the infinite Grace, with the boundless Compassions of a GOD: But he rejoiceth over them, thus to do them Good, with his whole Heart, and with his whole Soul: He *eateth* with them; He makes a Feast for them, and feasts with them, saying, *Eat, O Friends, drink, yea, drink abundantly, O Beloved.* Thus kindly doth the great SAVIOUR, invite the Chief of *Sinners,* to feed upon himself, as the sacrificed LAMB, to drink deep Draughts of his bottomless, boundless, endless Love, which is infinitely better than Wine: To receive all Salvation-Blessings in and with him, unto eternal *Life* by him, altho' to procure the same for us, he poured out his Soul unto *Death!* And oh the hearty *Welcome,* the kind Appellations that he gives us: *Eat, O Friends, drink, yea, drink abundantly, O Beloved!* As if he should say, "You are heartily *welcome* to all Grace and Life, thro' my Love and Death: Come, take your Fill freely: You have all Salvation in me, with me, with all my Heart, with all my Soul. Joy and rejoice in and with *me:* I joy and rejoice with *you,* for all *your Bliss.'*—And lo, he doth not say, 'Come, you *Enemies,* that have pierced me to the Soul with your Sins; come take the Blessings of Life, procur'd for you by my Death: But, Eat, O *Friends!* I forgive all your Heart-Enmity against me, and all the woful Fruits of it in your Lives, wherein you have behav'd like Enemies to me. I am *your Friend* indeed: I dy'd for you when *Enemies.* I have reconcil'd you *in*, and will reconcile you *to* myself, by my Death, perfectly. And now, I call *you* no more *Enemies,* but *Friends.* I esteem you so really, I call you so cordially. An everlasting Friendship is begun, shall be perfected and maintained, between you and me. Little do you think, what a *Friend's Heart,* I have towards you: Nor how greatly as *my Friends,* I rejoice over you! Eat, O *Friends!*—Drink, yea, drink abundantly, O *Beloved!* I don't call you, *The People of my Wrath,* even you that are the Chief of *Sinners,* who come in at my Call, to feast upon my Flesh and Blood; but the *Children of my Love.* Come, drink *abundantly:* You have all *freely.* You can never drink my Love, my Life, the Well of your Salvation *dry:* Nor think, what an infinite Spring of Bliss, I, in my infinite Love, will be unto you, who are by me, so infinitely *beloved!*"—Thus heartily doth the SAVIOUR *welcome Sinners*, Thus freely doth he *receive them*, and thus kindly *address them!*—And since our Lord, the Friend of Sinners, delights to be thus gracious to them, and familiar with them; let us then, encouraged by his Love, Blood and Fulness, approach his Presence freely, with all our Wants continually: *To receive Mercy, and find Grace to help in every Time of Need.*—Wishing a Life of joyful Communion with God; a growing Conformity to Christ; a fruitful Life on Earth, to his Honour; and a weighty Crown of Glory with him in Heaven: I remain, Dear Sir,

Your very affectionate Friend and Servant
In our Glorious LORD,

LETTER VI.

To Mrs. W-------r.

My Dear Sister in Christ,

I Hear, that you have been *afflicted.* I doubt not, you can say, That this Affliction has been *good* for you. It was sent, my dear Sister, as the Lord's Messenger, to bring you a Token of your Father's Love. It was sent to be manag'd by the Lord's Hand, for the Trial of your Graces, and to meeten you for Glory. I hope you receiv'd it with Humility, Submission and Thankfulness. That you neither *despis'd the Chastening of the Lord, nor fainted when rebuked of him.* Because of his infinite *Love, shed abroad in you Heart by the Holy Ghost:* Which, like strong Wine, supported your Spirit. It is good for us to endure Chastening. *Behold,* saith the Apostle *James, we count them happy which endure.* And, *Blessed is the Man that endureth Temptation; for when he is tried, he shall receive the Crown of Life, which the Lord hath promised to them that love him.* Oh my dear Sister, let us love and adore our GOD in *every Thing.* He loveth and blesseth *us* in *all Things.* In Bitters, in Sweets, in Comforts, in Crosses. All Things, wisely *mixed,* and graciously *over-ruled,* together work for God's Glory, and our Advantage; both present and eternal. Oh *happy,* thrice *happy, are the People whose God is the* LORD! Happy are they in all Cases, happy at all Times. Because GOD their Happiness, is present with them, hath the Care of them, and will never leave them, nor forsake them. The LORD being *our Shepherd, we shall not want:* Feeding, Leading, Healing. Our Souls, our Bodies are his Care. *As the Heaven is high above the Earth: So great is his Mercy towards them that fear him. As far as the East is from the West: So far hath he removed our Transgressions from us. Like as a Father pitieth his Children: So the* LORD *pitieth them that fear him.* His Bowels yern towards us, whenever he useth his Rod upon us. But when he sees that we *need it;* his Love will not let *us want it.* So *great* is his Grace! Nor will he let us be *always* under Chastisement. *His Anger endureth for a Moment: But in his Favour there is Life.* The Life of all our

Joys, abides in his Love, as the Water of the Stream, abides in the Fountain, is derived from it, and maintained by it. Little Interruptions of his manifestative Favour, we must expect here; tho' there is not the least, in the infinite Love of his Heart. But *Goodness and Mercy* in their native Displays, in various, plenteous, lasting Streams, *shall follow us all the Days of our Life,* through Time; and waft us into the Ocean of Love, Life and Glory, where we shall have full Joys, to a long Eternity.—I commit you to the tender Love and Care, of your dear Lord Jesus; and in him, my dear Sister, I am,

Yours very affectionately,

——— ———

LETTER VII.

To Mr. H-------d.

My very dear Brother, in our sweet LORD JESUS,

Gladly I embrace the first Moment's Leisure to write to you.—Kindly I thank you for yours. I am glad the Lord puts it into your Heart to long to hear from me. I hope he designs to send some Refreshment to your dear Soul, by so weak, so vile a Worm. Oh my Brother, if our dear Lord would carve you a Portion from his own Table, and put it into my poor, empty, tottering Hand; how gladly, in his Strength would I run to bring it you! I feel that I *love you* in the Bowels of JESUS CHRIST; but it is HE only can *fill you.* And fill you he *will,* brimful of Grace and Glory, in his own Time. *If the* LORD *had been pleased to destroy you,* my Brother, *he would not have shewed you these Things.* He would not have shewed you the Depth of your Misery by Sin, the Insufficiency of your own Righteousness, and the Excellency of CHRIST, in his glorious Person, and all-sufficient Fulness, as a compleat SAVIOUR: To raise your Estimation of HIM, as the *Chiefest among ten Thousand,* and to put you upon the Search after him, as *your Beloved.* CHRIST was prepar'd on purpose for *you,* my Brother; and you are prepar'd for the Knowledge of *Him.* And what they shall *hinder* your Enjoyment of him, thro' Time and to Eternity? I am sure it is not the Greatness of your *Sin,* by Nature or

Practice, that can do it, tho' of all Sinners, *you* was the very *Chief.* It is a *faithful Saying,* (you may venture your Soul, and eternal All upon it) *That Jesus Christ came into the World to save Sinners, chief Sinners!* And how *worthy is this if all Acceptation!* Will you *accept it,* my Brother? Will you as a most miserable Sinner, cast yourself down at the SAVIOUR'S Feet, and say, "Lord I take *thee,* as the Father's Gift to the Chief of Sinners: I lay hold on *Thee,* as held out to the Hand of my Faith, in the free Promise of the glorious Gospel, for the very *vilest* of all." If you *will have* CHRIST, my Brother, you *may,* you *shall.* Oh never stand hesitating, whether the SAVIOUR is for *you!* and whether your *Sins* will not shut you out from the SAVIOUR'S Arms! But stretch out the Hand of Faith, and take him as a *free Gift* to the Chief of Sinners. You can but be the *Chief.* As such then *receive him,* only *receive him,* and he is *Yours* for ever. Flee into the SAVIOUR'S open Arms, and say, "Lord, I am such a miserable Sinner, that I shall sink into the lowest Hell, if thou dost not save *me,* if thou dost not open wide thy merciful Arms, and let me into thy Self, and all thy Grace. And I have heard what *Wonders* thy Love and Blood have wrought, in saving M*anasseh, Paul* and *Magdalen.* I have heard likewise, That thou art *able to save to the uttermost,* even *all them that come unto* GOD by *Thee.* LORD JESUS, save *me!* Glorify the Infinity of thy Grace, in my Unworthiness! The Immensity of thy Mercy, in forgiving my great, numberless, and aggravated Transgressions! And the Omnipotence of thy Power, in my utmost Weakness! Lord, shew what a Wonder thou canst work in saving such a great Sinner, from all Misery, unto all Glory! And Heaven shall for ever ring with thy Praises."—Oh cast yourself down at JESUS Feet, all over-spread with the Leprosy of Sin, from Head to Foot, no Part clean, and say, "Lord if thou wilt, thou canst make me clean." And the compassionate SAVIOUR, will stretch out his Hand of Power and Grace, give you a saving Touch, and will say, with an all-efficacious Voice, 'I Will: Be thou clean.'"

I make no doubt, my Brother, that you have already *believ'd* on the Lord Jesus, and that the Actings of your Faith towards him, have frequently been after this Manner. And *as you have received Christ Jesus the Lord, so walk in Him.* Your Comfort-Life depends on it. We pinch and starve our Souls, by staying at Home in Self-wretchedness; instead of going out daily, upon every Conviction of Want to the CHRIST of GOD, to possess that full and everlasting Salvation, provided and exhibited in him, for the Chief of Sinners. Oh my Brother, whenever you are afraid, whenever your Heart trembles because of your *Sins,* venture in to CHRIST instantly. Stand not to hold Parley with Sin and Satan, whether you shall *believe* or *not?* But say as *Esther, I will go in unto the King;--and if I perish, I perish.* And CHRIST will hold out the *Scepter* of his Grace, for you to *touch* and *live.* Let your Acts of Faith on JESUS, be like Wave upon Wave, rowling apace after one another. *Haste, haste* you into the Bosom of CHRIST. *Flee apace* unto HIM, your strong, your glorious City of Refuge, the only Hope set before you in the glorious Gospel. It is *ill* abiding without, to hear the Threats of Pursuers that seek your Life, and will have the Blood of all, that get not into CHRIST by Faith. And tho' you have already believ'd in JESUS, and so your *State* is *safe;* yet if you forsake your Resting-place, and wander into the forbidden Grounds of doubting and Despair; the Pursuers will be after you, a dreadful *Sound* will be in your Ears, and your *Life,* to you; will seem to hang in *Suspense.* Wherefore get by Faith into CHRIST, your quiet, full, and glorious Habitation.

And whenever you come to CHRIST for Life, or look to JESUS for Salvation; believe that he will *give you of the Fountain of the Water of Life freely;* and that you *shall be saved,* merely because HE *has said it,* who is GOD, and cannot lie, deceive, change, or repent? So shall your Joy be full, and your Holiness great. So shall your Soul be marvellously strengthned in your Conflict with the Powers of Darkness, if you thus march boldly on against them, under the Banner of the SAVIOUR'S LOVE.

Glad am I, to see you so sensible that you are a *Sinner,* a *great* Sinner. That you know a *little* of CHRIST, and pray for further Teachings. And that you esteem it a Favour above all Things, to have this Petition put up for you, 'God be merciful to such a Sinner!' Oh my dear Brother, be not dismayed because you are such a *great Sinner.* For your JESUS is a *Great* SAVIOUR! HE is *mighty to save!* It's well you know a *little* of CHRIST: For that Knowledge is *saving.* In that you have *eternal Life!* And tho' you know *but* a little of CHRIST, you are Interested in his

Great SELF, and all his infinite Fulness! CHRIST, and all his Grace are *yours!*—What are your *Sins* then, tho' *red, like Scarlet and Crimson?* In the Virtue of his GOD-like Blood, they shall be *white as Snow and Wooll!* What is the *Guilt* of Sin, before the SAVIOUR'S *All-attoning Blood!* What is its amazing *Filth,* before this *cleansing Fountain!* What is its mighty, turbulent Strength, before the SAVIOUR'S *Sin-subduing Arm!* Aye, and what is the *Being of Sin,* its rooted Fixation in our Nature, before the *All-destroying Power,* and *All-perfecting Grace* of CHRIST! That will sanctify us wholly, Soul, Body and Spirit, and set us blameless and faultless, without Spot or Wrinkle, or any such Thing, perfect in Holiness, to its Height and Glory, before *His,* and his *Father's* Face for ever! Oh my Brother, *Sin* shall never be too hard for the *Grace* of CHRIST! Grace shall *reign* over Sin, until it is utterly destroy'd! Until all *Mortality,* Sin and all the Effects of it, respecting both our Souls and Bodies, shall be *swallowed up of Life!*—But my Brother, such is the infinite fullness of the LORD our SAVIOUR, that the greatest of mortal Saints, know but *little* of his Glory! The one *Half,* the ten *thousandth Part,* has never yet been *told us!* Yea, the SAVIOUR'S Fulness and Riches, are absolutely *Unsearchable!* A Mine of immense Treasure, a vast SEA of GLORY, that can never be *emptied,* nor *bottom'd,* by Saints and Angels to the Days of ETERNITY!—And lo, the *Mercy* of GOD in CHRIST, is *infinite!* It is JEHOVAH'S Mercy! It is HIMSELF resolving to be *merciful!* And can you *spend it,* my Brother? Can you *draw it dry,* with your Thousands and Ten Thousands of Wants? No, no; the innumerable Multitude of saved Sinners, that have been, or shall be saved even to the World's End, can never *sink* the GODHEAD *one Hair's Breadth!* They may *draw Water* continually, *drink,* and drink their *Fill,* out of this *Well of Salvation,* and still it will be as *Full,* as *Deep,* as *All-overflowing* as ever! Oh my Brother, put your *Trust* under the Shadow of JEHOVAH'S Wings: And you shall *see* that his *Mercy* is upon you from *Everlasting to Everlasting!—the Love of God our Father, the Grace of Christ, and the Comforts of the Holy Ghost be with you.* Amen. As enabled, I shall make mention of you before the LORD: And remember, dear Sir,

Yours most Affectionately in JESUS,

——— ———

LETTER VIII.

TO MR. L--------S.

My dear Brother in CHRIST,

I Rejoice that GOD *who commanded the Light to shine out of Darkness, hath shined in your Heart, to give you the Light of the Knowledge of the Glory of* GOD *in the Face of* JESUS CHRIST. Out of CHRIST, GOD is a *Consuming Fire;* and we, *Sinners,* can no more *stand* before him than dry Stubble, before a devouring Flame. But in CHRIST, all the Glories of the GODHEAD shine, in the bright Form of LOVE! GOD is the GOD of *Peace,* to every poor Sinner that draws nigh to him thro' the LAMB'S *Blood. Fury is not in* HIM, unto such Souls. All the essential Perfections of JEHOVAH, are on their Side, engag'd by his infinite LOVE, to fulfill its glorious Design, in their compleat Salvation: The *Glory* of GOD therefore, may well be said to be in the *Face,* in the Person of CHRIST; for there it is fully, resplendently, and will be eternally display'd. And the *Knowledge* of the Glory of GOD, the GOD of all Grace, which casts its refulgent Rays thro' the sent SAVIOUR, on the Chief of Sinners, when GOD shineth to give it in their Hearts, must needs be a Life-giving, an All-surpassing, a glorious, marvelous LIGHT!—Oh my Brother, What Grace, is it, that ever the least Beam of this Glory, should dart into *our Souls!* Should shine into *our Hearts,* out of that thick, that total Darkness, which Sin had cover'd us with ! 'Tis *Light of Life:* Life out of Death, Life that will swallow up Death, and spread its Glories over all, unto the fair bright DAY, of Light and Life, perfect and eternal! Oh how rich, free, and distinguishing is JEHOVAH'S Grace unto *us,* that the LORD should thus arise upon *us,* unto Light of Life; while *Thousands* round about us, *sit in Darkness and the Shadow of Death!* We, as our Lord, must say, *Even so Father, for so it seemed good in thy Sight.*—I am glad you feel the sweet Influence of GOD'S Heart-enlarging Love. Oh may we feel it more and more, until we are deliver'd from all Straitness, and brought into the full and glorious Liberty , reserved for the Sons of GOD!—Indeed my Brother, it is a very great Blessing, to see the Plague of our own Hearts;

to have a quick and painful *Sensation* of the Being and Working of *indwelling Sin,* and earnest *Longings,* and inexpressible *Groanings* wrought in our Souls, after a full and eternal *Freedom* from it. For not a Soul that doth experience these Things, but hath received the blessed Comforter, and felt his blessed Operations, is prepared for strong Consolation, and shall be a Partaker of present, and everlasting Salvation thro' JESUS CHRIST.

Little Crosses we must meet with, my Brother, from our Father's dear Children, our Shepherd's dear Sheep and Lambs. But what are these to that *great Cross,* which our Lord once bore for us! And what are the *little Trials* we meet with now and then from our *Brethren,* to those *great Ones* which our Lord meets with from *us,* and from all his *own,* scatter'd over the whole Earth, every Day, Hour and Moment! And what are our *little Trials* to our *Great* LORD, for whose Sake we are call'd to bear them! Once more, What are our *little Crosses,* our light, momentary Afflictions, to that *great Crown,* that *far more exceeding and eternal Weight of Glory,* for which by them we shall be prepared! All our *Sufferings,* as well as our Faith and Joy, are *Gifts* of our Father's Love. *It is given us on the Behalf of Christ, mot only to believe, but also to suffer for his Sake.*—Then let us receive all our Grieving Things from the Hand of GOD thankfully; and ask for Grace to endure them meekly and patiently, and to improve them wisely and faithfully. For not the least *Evil* we thus receive from God, endure from men, and improve to the Glory of Christ, but shall be to our present and eternal *Advantage.*—Oh my Brother, if Christ bears with so *much* Unkindness from us daily, shan't we bear with the *little* we now and then meet with from our Brethren? If our Lord forgives us *ten thousand Talents,* shall not we forgive our Brother an *hundred Pence?*—We have need to say, *Lord, increase our Faith!* If we had more *Faith,* we should have more *Love* to Christ and His; *bear* all Things for his sake and theirs; *shew forth* his Meekness and Gentleness, Goodness and Kindness to all; *Glorify Him* in all, and receive *Good* by all, unto a rich Increase of Grace in this World, and great Glory in that which is to come.—*The Grace of our Lord Jesus Christ be with your Spirit.* In HIM I am,

Ever Yours,

LETTER IX.

To Mr. and Mrs. W------s.

Ever dear and honour'd Parents,

OH what an unspeakable Privilege is it, that our JESUS never forgets *us!* His Eye is upon us, his Care is over us, and his Love is always in an infinite Flame towards us. Well he *sees* all our Griefs, and *knows* our Sorrows. Not with a regardless Eye, and unaffecting Notice. But seeing, he *sees,* and knowing, he *feels,* unto an inexpressible Sympathy, and an infinite Resolve of Mercy, to bring us full and glorious Deliverance, by his Wonder-working Arm. Our dear compassionate Lord, makes every trying Case of *ours,* as it were his *own* by Sympathy; and thence to us as his, he shews the richest Mercy. And never shall we want Mercy in the *Stream,* while Mercy in the *Fountain* endures. So long as *Christ* abides, a *merciful High Priest over the House of God,* while the Name of *Jesus,* our everlasting Father, is *Jehovah merciful,* and the Mercy of his *Heart* endures, who is the eternal I AM; the House of GOD, the Children of JESUS, can never want the Mercies of his *Hand,* in that Manner, Measure and Time, which infinite Wisdom sees best.—No, my dear Parents, let us *fear the* LORD *and his Goodness;* for there is *no Want to them that fear Him.* Let us go on to *hope* and *trust* in him, and to *wait* for him; and we shall not be *ashamed.* Early will the Lord *satisfy* us with his *Mercy,* and supply all our *Need* according to his own Riches in *Glory.*— Unto the LORD, the LORD *God, merciful and gracious,*--I commit you, and requesting your Prayers, I subscribe, my honoured Parents,

Your most Dutiful Child,

——— ———

LETTER X.

To Mr. P--------ll.

My beloved Brother,

I Han't Time to write as I would. But a Hint I wou'd fain give you, as to what you wrote in your last to Mr. *T----y.* You desir'd him 'To thunder out the *Law* to you, if he knew how.'—Oh dear Sir, What, so great a *Sinner,* as you see yourself to be; and want to lie at *Sinai's* Mount? Can you bear its fiery Flashes? Can you endure its roaring thunder? Don't you remember the Terror which attended the giving of the Law? How the People, when they saw the *Thundrings and Lightnings, the Noise of the Trumpet, and the Mountain smoaking; removed, and stood afar off?* And that so *terrible was the Sight,* that even *Moses* said, *I exceedingly fear and quake?* Oh, a *Sinner,* cannot meet God at *Sinai,* but must meet *Death. Our God,* is there a *consuming Fire,* and we as dry *Stubble,* that cannot stand before him. Oh my dear Friend, would you run into the *Fire?* Know you not, that the Flashes of God's fiery Indignation thro' the Curses of a broken Law, would *consume you?* That the Thunder-bolts of his flaming Wrath, would strike you *dead?*

"Aye, you will say, I know, that my Heart cannot *endure,* nor my Hands be *strong,* if God was to deal with me, a miserable *Sinner,* according to his righteous *Law.* I don't want to abide for *ever* under the Terrors of the Law: But only to lie at the Foot of *Sinai,* to hear its Thunders, till I throughly know my Misery as a Sinner, and my Heart is turn'd against every Sin."

Oh dear Sir, The Terrors of the *Law,* will sooner make you run away from GOD, that turn your Heart from *Sin;* tho' they are useful to *convince* of Sin. Nothing but the Grace of the *Gospel,* can set the Heart against *Sin,* and win the Soul to GOD.

You say, Sir, 'You have never been under the *Law?*

It is a *Mistake.* You have heard what *Things the Law saith,* till your Mouth is *stopped,* you are become *guilty* before God; and acknowledge his *Justice,* if he was to send you down to *Hell.* Thus you have heard the Law in its *Curses;* and say, they are *righteous.* You have likewise heard it in its *Requirements;* and dare not meet it with your own imperfect *Obedience,* as your justifying *Righteousness;* but desire to be clothed with

Christ's Obedience. Thus, by the *Law,* in the Hand of the *Spirit,* have you been *prepared* for the *Gospel.* And unto you that see and groan under your own Misery as a *Sinner,* unto *you,* I say, the SAVIOUR is given, unto *you,* all the *Grace* of the *Gospel* belongs.—Come, dear Soul, come into the *Wounds* of the *once-bleeding* LAMB! Hear the *Grace,* the *Peace,* which they proclaim to you. These will give you the *deepest Conviction* of Sin's *exceeding Sinfulness;* will make it most *hateful* in your Sight; will *strengthen* your Soul to wage Wars against it; and in the End will give you a complete *Victory* over it.—*Great Grace be with you!* I am, dear Sir,

Yours most Tenderly in JESUS,

——— ———

LETTER XI.

To Mr. C------ns.

My dear Brother in Christ,

YOURS I receiv'd; I thank you for it. It brought glad Tidings to my poor Soul. Much I rejoice in *your Salvation.* And most humbly and thankfully, I adore that infinite *Grace,* which made my poor Labours, a *Means* of your Awakening, and Enlightning in the Knowledge of CHRIST; and of bringing you out of Darkness and Bondage, into the glorious Light, and joyful Liberty of the Sons of GOD. *This is the* LORD'S *Doing; and it is marvellous in my Eyes.* Oh how *richly* hath my Lord rewarded my *poor Labours! Your* being brought to *adore* Free-Grace, and the Mystery of Electing Love *hereby,* to a comfortable *Knowledge* of your Interest in CHRIST, and to the *Enjoyment* of sweet Freedom in HIM; is such a *Reward* of my Work, that is and will be the Matter of my Joy in God, and Thanksgivings to him, unto *Ages without End!* Oh *Grace, Grace!* My *Labour* has not been *in vain in the Lord!* Oh that I may *always abound in his Work!* May *this,* with every other of his Love-cords, *bind me!* The Lord knows, I have *aim'd* singly at his Glory, and the Good of Souls, in all my Attempts to lisp out the Grace of GOD in CHRIST. And therefore my Joy is *full,* when I hear of any Honour brought to his great Name, and any Advantage to precious Souls thereby. I think it well worth the while, to labour for my Lord, in his delightful Work, were it to a *Methusalah's* Age, to win *one Soul* to JESUS; to refresh and comfort *any* of his dear Sheep and Lambs. But oh, with how many *rich,* and *royal* Rewards, doth the Prince of Grace, crown the *weak,* and *short* Labours of his most vile, and unworthy Worms, whom he delights to favour! Oh had I a thousand Hands, and a thousand Lives; CHRIST and *His* should have them all. The LAMB that has bought me with his Blood, is infinitely *worthy,* of ten thousand, thousand Times more Service, and Glory than *I can give!* And yet, in infinite condescending Grace, he accepts my *little Mite!*

Oh my *dear Child,* you have a *Father,* that loves you *infinitely!* That lov'd you *eternally,* before Time, or Sin enter'd! That lov'd, that loves you *unchangeably!* That gave *Himself* for you, in Love unknown, *freely,* when in his Fore-View, an Enemy; That has given you his *Holy Spirit,* that has forgiven *all our Sins,* that has lov'd you into Communion with him in the *Life of Grace;* and will love you as his *own,* thro' all Deaths and Dangers, to be for ever with him in the *Life of Glory!*—God the Father, Christ's Father, and your Father, lov'd and chose you of *old,* from the free, sovereign good Pleasure of his own Will. He gave you to Christ, to be redeemed by him, and saved to the uttermost.—God the Son, lov'd and bought you with his *Blood,* from Sin and Misery, to Grace and Glory. He has given you a Right of full Deliverance from the former, and of full Possession of the latter.—And God the Holy Ghost, has lov'd and *quickned* you, when dead in Sins, to a new Life, in and with Christ; and will maintain and increase it, until all *Sin and Death,* is swallow'd up in the Victory of *Life eternal.* The Three-One GOD, *loveth you.* Embraceth you in the Arms of *Everlasting Love;* hath done, doth and will do, thro' Time, and to Eternity! None of all your Enemies, either within or without, shall ever pluck you out of your SAVIOUR'S *Hands. Neither Death, nor Life, nor Angels, nor Principalities, nor Powers, nor Things present, nor Things to come, nor Height, nor Depth, nor any other Creature, shall be able to separate* you *from the Love of God which is in Christ Jesus our Lord.*—What have you then to *do,* my dear Child, but to *commit* the Keeping of your Soul, continually, in Well-doing, unto HIM on whom you have believed? And to *love* the God of Love; in all holy Obedience, until, *holy and without Blame, before God in Love, you appear with* CHRIST *in Glory!*

I rejoice that you are join'd in Society with the *Saints,* got to your *own Company,* and live joyfully, under the bright Shine of a Gospel-Ministry. Great Grace be with you! Great Glory awaits you! Live and walk as the *Redeemed of the* LORD. As one that is called into *Fellowship* with Saints, with Angels, with GOD himself, Father, Son, and Holy Ghost! Oh may the great Delights of your *present Feast* on heavenly *Manna,* continue and increase, until the superior Glories, and ineffable Sweets of your *everlasting Feast* come on! When you shall sit down at the *Marriage-Supper of the Lamb,* never to rise up from Table more! Of which your present Feast, is a sweet *Foretaste,* a most sure *Earnest!*—Into the Arms of CHRIST I commit you, my *little Child;* to be kept from the Evil of the World, sanctify'd thro' the Truth, and nourish'd up in Faith, unto *eternal Life.* Oh may you be nonour'd to know, to love and serve CHRIST, much in *this present World!* And may you shine forth in his Glory, as a bright Star for ever and ever, in the World to come! So prays, my dear Brother,

Yours most affectionately, in our
Glorious LORD *the* LAMB,

——— ———

LETTER XII.

To Mr. W-------s.

My dear Brother,

I Should rejoice to hear from you. I hope your Soul prospers, that you *grow in Grace, and in the Knowledge of* CHRIST. *Whose you are, and whom* I trust, you desire to *serve,* more and better daily. As for *me,* I have been, I am, a Favourite of Heaven, tho' the *least* of Saints, and the *Chief* of Sinners. Bless and adore the Lord, for all his Grace, to vile, unworthy *me.* And pray for me, that I may love *Him* who first loved, who will always love *me.* Oh the infinite *Freeness of* GOD'S *Love!* Had he look'd for Qualifications, for *my Goodness;* it had never been fix'd on me. I have been *rebellious* against the LORD, ever since I had a Being. Aye, and ever since he brought me out of *Egypt's* Land. And well he *forknew* how rebellious and ungrateful I should prove, and how *treacherously* I should deal with *him.* And yet he resolv'd to *love me freely!* Thus he has lov'd me hitherto; and thus he will love me even unto the End. And when he has lov'dd me into perfect *Likeness* to him, into the Image of his own Love; then I will love him *perfectly* and *for ever.* Now I *groan,* I lament, it is the greatest Burden my Soul feels, that I love my God *so little!* That I *have* lov'd, that I *do,* that I *can* love him so little! *Oh wretched me! Who shall deliver me from the Body of this Death!* From this Heart-Enmity against God, which sadly works in my corrupt Nature! *Thanks be to God thro' Jesus Christ! There* my Victory is compleat, my Deliverance is wrought out; and thence to *me,* a full, a free, an everlasting Salvation shall come. Help me by your Prayers, for much of the Holy Spirit, that I may glorify my own GOD, the GOD of *Love,* in doing and suffering his whole Will, as becomes a dear Child of his, in this little Inch of Time which may remain to me.

For yourself, my dear Brother, abide in CHRIST by Faith daily; cleave unto him in Love continually; walk in every Path of Duty cheerfully; watch against Sin earnestly; and with All-prayer, pray without ceasing perpetually. That you lose not your Opportunities of glorifying GOD upon the Earth, and fall not into Temptations to his Dishonour. Both which will grieve you exceedingly, when your Time is almost gone, and blest Eternity is coming on. Oh how happy should we be, if we liv'd every Day, as if it was our last Day! And was as careful to improve all our Time for GOD, as we shall wish we had done, when Time with us shall be no more!—Wishing all Grace, unto all Glory: I remain, my dear Brother,

Yours most Affectionately,

——— ———

LETTER XIII.

To Mr. W------rd.

My dear Brother in Christ,

Grace unto you, and Peace be multiplied, from God our Father, and from the Lord Jesus Christ.

YOURS I receiv'd; I thank you for sending a Line to poor me. If the Lord will please to send you any Thing by *me,* I shall rejoice. There is not a Drop of Refreshment in any Creature, unless the LORD fills it. And if a Creature is ever so full in itself, and labours ever so much to communicate to others; not one Drop of Comfort can we receive thereby, unless the LORD gives it. Which should teach us, an entire Dependance upon GOD, for all the Supplies we want; and Ascription of Glory to him, when he extends his Grace unto us, which Way soever it flows.

I rejoice, That you have a painful *Feeling* of that Body of Sin which dwelleth in you, of your old, corrupt Nature, receiv'd from the old *Adam.* This is a *Sensation,* that none have, but those who are *new Creatures in Christ.*—And as all your Hope of eternal Salvation, is fix'd alone, upon the rich, free, sovereign Grace of God in CHRIST; it is *good Hope.* A Hope that will not fail, of which you shall not be ashamed. That same *Free-Grace,* which wrought the Grace of *Hope* in your Soul, and which is the *Object* of your Hope, will maintain your Hope, and give you all hoped-for Blessings, freely, fully and eternally.

I am glad that you have a Desire to die for Christ, (if he calls you to it) and with his People, rather than to enjoy the Pleasures of Sin for a Season. This *Desire* of your Heart, your Lord will call your *Kindness* to him. And however weak it be, he will not *break the bruised Reed, nor quench the smoaking Flax:* But bind up and strengthen your weak Grace, and nourish and increase it into a pure Flame.

And as to that Fear of *Falling,* of denying your Lord with Oaths and Curses, rather than *die* for him; that fruitless Fear which torments your Heart: It flows from the Workings of remaining Unbelief, from an Aptness to live upon your own Stock, upon that little Grace which is in *you,* rather than upon those vast Stores, that immense Fulness of Grace which is in CHRIST.—Oh my dear Brother, What, *afraid,* that you shall not hold out, because you feel so little Strength in *yourself?* You have forgotten where your *great Strength lieth.* Not in *yourself;* but in the LORD! In the LORD JEHOVAH, in whom there is *everlasting Strength.* Even in HIM, who as the *Creator of the Ends of the Earth, fainteth not, neither is weary.* JEHOVAH-JESUS, is your *Strength.* And can you spend those vast Treasures that are in HIM? Can you draw the Well of Salvation dry? With your thousands, and ten thousands of Wants? Millions of needy Souls, with innumerable Wants, have been supply'd from thence; and still the Well of Life is as full as ever! CHRIST is as full for *you,* my Brother, as he was for the first needy Soul that ever came unto him. Oh come, poor, weak Thing, and lie down by Faith in the Bosom of your own Lord Jesus, in the Bosom of that infinite Fulness, that everlasting Strength which is in HIM; and take an holy Ease, from all anxious Thought and perplexing Fear, because of the little Strength which is in *you!* "Can you by taking Thought, add one Cubit to your Stature?" Why will you thus depart from the LORD your Rest, to launch forth into a Sea of Trouble? What, *fear,* because you have so *little Strength?* Alas! If you had as much Strength of inherent Grace, as *Peter* had, when he said, "Tho' I die with thee, I will not deny thee:" If you trusted to it, as he did; you would *fail.* If you had as much Strength as perfect *Adam;* it would not be sufficient to keep you. His Will was perfect; he might have stood, if he would; but being mutable, and standing upon his own Legs; *down he fell.* If you had as much Strength as the *Angels* had in Heaven, before they sinned and became black Devils; if you trusted to it, as they did, and would none of CHRIST; *down you wou'd fall.* Why then will you stand mourning over *your little Strength,* since there is Strength enough in CHRIST, to make you stand? And all the Strength of the omnipotent JEHOVAH, in HIM, is held forth in the free Promise, as a Bosom for your weak Soul to rest in? Come, *Bow to the* SAVIOUR: He accounts it an Honour done to him, when a poor Sinner, in his utmost Weakness, says by Faith, "In the LORD have I Strength." When he says so, by Way of Dependance upon his Fulness, and by Way of Persuasion, that he shall be supply'd from thence. Oh come, cast your Care upon CHRIST! In well-doing, commit the Keeping of your Soul unto him, as unto a faithful Creator; who will not forsake the Work of his own Hands, nor suffer the weakest Soul, that rests on *him* to *fail.* No. *The Youth shall faint, and young Men* in Grace, that depend upon their inherent Strength, *shall utterly fall.* But weak Souls, even such that have *no Might, that wait upon the* LORD, *shall renew their Strength. They shall mount up with Wings as Eagles, they shall run and not be weary, they shall walk and not faint,* Isa. xl. 30, 31. Yield not then to perplexing Fear of Want, because you have a few single Pocket-pence, but a little Grace, a little Strength in *you;* since all the Treasures of Grace and Strength, in our everlasting GOD, are yours in CHRIST, and to be communicated for your full Supply, in your every Time of Need. Oh my Brother, trust in the LORD, and be not afraid. For while CHRIST endures, the Soul that trusts in *Him* shall not *fail.* "Because CHRIST lives, you shall live also."

As to the Times, I think they look *troublous.* But our Lord has said, "See that you be not troubled." It appears to me, to be the *Midnight-State* of the Churches; and that by the late Out-pouring of the Spirit upon that dear Servant of *Christ,* Mr. *Whitefield,* and his Brethren, the *Midnight-Cry* is begun. Surely, *The Bridegroom cometh.* It is Time for the Virgins to *arise* from their carnal Security, to *trim their Lamps,* and go forth to *meet Him.* Some of us begin to *awake,* and look about us. Others are still fast *asleep.* But as the Cry grows louder, in the Ministry, and in tremendous Providences, all the *Virgins* shall be roused up, and *go forth,* with Zeal and Expectation, in all the Ways of his Appointment, to *meet the Bridegroom.* And to awaken the sleeping Saints, to some Purpose, I expect a sore Stroke upon the Churches. To be blest by the Holy Spirit, to the *Living in Jerusalem,* for their further Purity, and to prepare them for their future Glory. I think the Powers of *Antichrist,* making War with the *Lamb,* will prevail, *to scatter the Power of the holy People, for a little Season.* And that the LORD will *hide* the most of *his* in his *secret Chambers, until the Indignation be over-past.* That he will be *with those,* that may be call'd to witness for him and his Truth, even unto *Death.* And that then, the *Lion of the Tribe of Juda,* will arise, and deliver his People, and tear his Enemies in Pieces. That *Sion* shall rise and shine, and be *the Praise of the whole Earth;* and that *Babel* shall fall, never to *rise more.* The Church will be in the greatest Trouble, just before her brightest Glory. And if the Spirit of Persecution which appears in this

Nation, should be the Beginning of an approaching Shower; let none of us that believe in Jesus, be distrest for fear of the Storm. Since our Lord will be with us in it, and be unto us, *An Hiding-place from the Wind, a Covert from the Tempest, as Rivers of Water in a dry Place, and as the Shadow of a great Rock in a weary Land.* And, "When these Things begin to come to pass, saith our Lord, lift up your Heads; for the Day of your Redemption draweth nigh."—Salute, in my Name, all the Saints with you. May *Great Grace* be upon them all! And every one of us, be *Followers of them who thro' Faith and Patience inherit the Promises!* Pray for *me.* The LORD be with *you!* In HIM, Sir, I am

Your affectionate Friend and Servant,

——— ———

LETTER XIV.

To Mr. P------fs.

Dear Joseph,

I Thank you for yours, I han't had Time to send you a Line till now, and am oblig'd to be short. Oh dear Child, you are straitned in *me;* but have an Infinity of Love and Grace, of Care and Tenderness, in the Heart of *Christ* towards you. The great Shepherd, loves all his Sheep and Lambs, even to the least and last, with an *infinite Love.* He watcheth over them with an *infinite Care,* and rejoiceth to do them Good, with an *infinite Joy.* Neither the Tongues of Men, nor of Angels, are able to set forth a Thousandth Part of that *Dearness,* which the *least* of Christ's, stands in to *Him.* He loves the least of his Sheep, of his Brethren, of his Members, as *Himself.*—By Love *unknown,* he enclos'd them, in his Covenant Engagements with the Father, before Time had its Being, or the Mountains their Birth.—Love *unchangeable,* brought the Son of God out of the Bosom of the Father, to die for his Sheep in the Fulness of Time. Ah! What were *we?* Were we *worth* any thing? No, no; we were worthless, loveless, loathsome and abominable. Poor and miserable, wretched, blind and naked. Not Friends, but Enemies, posting on in a Course of Ungodliness, to eternal Ruin. Sin had entred, Wrath was denounced, and endless Death, just ready to swallow us up. But, oh *stupendous* Love! *Knowledge-passing* Love! The son of God would *die* in our Room! Die we must, if JESUS had not given his Life, his Soul, in our Souls stead. The *good Shepherd,* saw the *Wolf coming,* just ready to devour us; and he did not *fly,* but *laid down his Life for the Sheep.* He endur'd that Death, which *we* must have suffer'd, had not *He* dy'd, that *we* might live. And this because we were his *own,* given him of the Father before the World was, and lov'd by him, with an infinite, unchangeable Love.—And from his *Love,* that was *strong as Death,* to die in our Stead, and conquer Death for us; he resolv'd to bring us to *Himself;* unto Faith in him, and Obedience to him here; and unto Glory with him hereafter. *And other Sheep I have,* saith he to the *Jews, which are not of this Fold; them also I must bring.* His infinite Love and Faithfulness, laid him under this *Necessity.* And describing his *Sheep,* his *called* Sheep, and their Privilege, he says, *My Sheep hear my Voice, and I know them, and they follow me. And I give unto them eternal Life, and they shall never perish, neither shall any pluck them out of my Hand,* John x. 27, 28.

And han't you *heard Christ's Voice?* Hath he not gone after you, when running away from him, and caus'd you to hear a Voice behind you, saying, *This is the Way, walk in it?* Han't the language of Christ to you, been after this Manner, 'Turn, O poor Sinner, I dy'd for such as *thee.* I am the *Way* to the Father; come unto *me,* and I will give thee *Rest;* walk in *me,* and I will give thee *Life?'* Yea, hath he not said unto *you* in particular, *I have loved thee with an everlasting Love?* And have you not felt an Almighty Power in the Voice of Christ, that sweetly drew your Soul *to Him,* and engag'd you to follow *after Him?* If *so,* you are one of *Christ's Sheep;* and he *will give unto you eternal Life, and you shall never perish, neither shall any pluck you out of his Hand.* Neither Men, Sin, nor Satan.—There's an infinite Fulness of Life in Christ, who is your Life, to swallow up all that Deadness, under which you groan. Your good Shepherd, is *come that you might have Life, and that* you *might have it more abundantly.* Wherefore, seek him for it most earnestly.

And the Ordinances of Christ are his appointed Means, for the Conveyance of Life into the Souls of his dear Sheep and Lambs. There he *leads them into green Pastures, and makes them lie down beside the still*

Waters, of Grace and Peace, to their Refreshment, Strength and Joy. And therefore, to be without the Life-giving Presence of Christ, in his publick Worship; ought to be esteem'd by us, as one of his Rebukes. *As many as he loves, he rebukes and chastens;* and sometimes chastens them in this Way; which calls them to the fresh Exercise of Humiliation and Repentance.—Wherefore rest not without the quickning Presence of Christ, in the Ministry of his glorious Gospel. But humble your Soul before him, and give him no Rest in private, until he is found of you in his publick Worship. Invite your Beloved to go with you. Tell him, you cannot *live without him,* that Ordinances, will be *Wells without Water, Clouds without Rain,* if HE doth not *fill them.* Plead his Promises, and his wonted Grace to his Own; and pray him to *remember you with the Favour that he beareth unto his People,* and to *visit you with his Salvation: That you may see the Good of his Chosen, rejoice in the Gladness of his Nation, and glory with his Inheritance.* JESUS is a *Lover;* and in infinite Condescension to such Worms as *we,* the Objects of his Love, he delights in *our Love,* and to have us *fond* of his Presence. Oh could we not be *contented* without our Beloved; we *should not* be without him.—That *the Grace of Christ may be with your Spirit,* to set your Soul a longing for him, and seeking after him, until you find the quickning Presence of the Lord your Life, unto your exceeding Joy; is the sincere Desire of

Your Friend that loves you in the Bowels of Christ,

LETTER XV.

To Mr. and Mrs. G------n.

My dear Brother and Sister.

YOU dear Children of our Father's Love, you who are dear to me in the Lamb's Love and Blood, why should *we* fall out in our Way to Heaven? If I had offended *you* in anything, I would freely ask you to forgive me; and as you have been angry with *me,* without Cause, I most freely forgive *you,* for *Jesus* Sake, who hath forgiven *us.* Oh dear Children, why should we be *Twain,* since Jesus dy'd to make us *one* in himself? Why should we rob our Lord of the Joy of his Heart, in *not loving one another, as he hath loved us?* Christ loves *us,* notwithstanding all our Peevishness and Frowardness towards *him;* and *so* ought we to love one another. Methinks, dear Children, I could gladly *wash your Feet.* I feel a sweet, springing Love to you as the *Lord's,* and as nearly related unto *me* in him. And oh, what a *Joy* would it be to me, to *ease* and *comfort* your burden'd Minds! To *pour Oil and Wine into your wounded Spirit!* To *bind and strengthen your Arm!* Oh dear Children, our gracious Father, will not *cast us off, for all that we have done!* Let us *return* unto him, whenever we have *departed* from him; for he is always the *God of Peace* to us, thro' the *Lamb's Blood.* And as such, he *will bruise Satan under our Feet shortly, and sanctify us throughout, in Spirit, Soul and Body.* We are under the Forgiveness of Sins. We are justify'd by Blood, and our Iniquities shall be subdu'd. God our Father, hath nothing against *us,* as we stand in *Christ. He hath not beheld Iniquity in Jacob, neither hath he seen Perverseness in Israel,* And shall we have any Thing against each *other?* See you not the Design of the Enemy, to separate *us,* for whom *Jesus* bled, and pray'd, that we might be one? Oh let our Heaven-born Souls, unite in one, *more than ever!* Let Satan get nothing by this his Attempt to bruise our *Heel,* but a greater Bruise of his own *Head.* Let him know, by our fresh *Endearments* to each other, that we are too closely *knit* by the Lamb's Blood, ever to be *separated.*—So shall we walk before God our Father as his dear Children, unto *all pleasing:* So will our Lord have *Joy in us:* And so shall our own, and other Souls, reap *great Advantage.—Great Grace be with you!* I am

Yours affectionately in the once Bleeding LAMB,

——— ———

LETTER XVI.

To L------s.

My dear Brother in Christ,

I Long to hear how your Soul prospers. The Lord is good to *me,* infinitely, incessantly, and will be eternally good to poor, wretched, *sinful me.* The LORD is good to *all,* in the Bounties of his Providence; his common Goodness extends itself to all the Works of his Hands. But oh, *The great Goodness,* the special, the distinguishing Goodness of God, *towards the House of Israel! We* that have found Grace in the Sight of the LORD, *we* that believe in JESUS, are interested in all Goodness of JEHOVAH'S Nature, in all the Goodness of his everlasting Covenant, his new Covenant of Free-Grace, thro' the Son of his Love. And conform'd it is, even an Immensity of Goodness, or rather, the LORD himself, the immense Ocean of Goodness, to us, for our Portion, by the Blood of the sacrificed LAMB. Oh, our GOD has *made,* has *cut* a *Covenant,* and passed between the Pieces; the divided Parts of our Lord's human Nature, when the Soul of our crucify'd Jesus, was separated from his sacred Body. All the Grace that was given to us by Grant, in God's everlasting Covenant with his Son, before the World was, is confirm'd unto us as Sinners by the LAMB'S Blood. It pleased the LORD to lay on HIM, the Iniquity of *us all,* of all his Chosen; and to bruise him for our Sins, to wound him for our Transgressions, to pierce him to the Soul, by the Sword of his Justice, until it was fully satisfied, compleat Payment made, and eternal Redemption obtain'd for us.—and then, lo, our Covenant-God, thro' the Peace-making Sacrifice of his Son, became the *God of Peace* unto *us.* And as such, *brought again from the Dead, our Lord Jesus, that great Shepherd of the Sheep, thro' the Blood of the everlasting Covenant.* And exalted him to his own Right Hand, to save us *influentially* in our own Persons, as he had done *mystically* in himself; to save us by *Power,* in the Application of Salvation, as he had done it by *Price,* in the Impetration, or working out of Redemption.—And this, of God's being our *own God,* the *God of Peace* unto us in Christ, is as the *Waters of Noah unto him. For as he hath sworn that the Waters of Noah should no more go over the Earth; even so hath he sworn* thro' a bleeding JESUS, *that he will no more be wroth with us, nor rebuke us.*—No, *we* that were chosen in Christ before the World began, *we* that were in him by Representation, when he dy'd a Sacrifice for us on the accursed Tree, and *we* that are now in him by Faith, that have run into the SAVIOUR'S Name, as our strong Tower; *we* are for ever *safe* from God's vindictive *Wrath.* There was Peace made between all the divine Perfections on our Account, for our Salvation, and Peace made for us, by the Blood of Christ's Cross. And the LAMB that made it by his Death, maintains it by his Life, while *he ever liveth,* by his Advocacy and Intercession, to *save us to the uttermost.*

Who then shall break *Friendship* between God and us? Who, or what shall *separate us* from the *Love of God* which is in *Christ Jesus our Lord?* Who shall *rob us* of our Portion in JEHOVAH? Who, or what shall *infringe,* or *lessen* that Ocean of Goodness, which we have in his great BEING, in his inviolable Covenant, in his sure Promises, which all have the *Yea,* the eternal *Yea,* and the fixed *Amen* of GOD upon them in CHRIST? Can *Satan* rob us of our Portion in GOD? *No,* the LAMB has destroy'd the Power of that roaring *Lion.* Can the *World* with all its Snares rob us of our Inheritance? *No,* JESUS has *overcome it.* Can *Sin,* that worst of Enemies, rob us of our GOD, our CHRIST, our Portion in Grace and Glory? *No;* it is *finish'd,* Transgression is made an *End of,* in our dear dying *Lord;* and by the Almighty Efficacy of his Death, it shall be subdu'd, and utterly destroy'd in *us.* JESUS, that was once *dead,* is now *alive,* and *lives for Evermore.* And *because* HE *lives, we shall live also. We* that are *dead* with him, in a begun Measure, to the Pleasures of Sin, and the sensitive Delights of this World, *we* whose Souls pant after heavenly Enjoyments; *we* are well provided for, well secur'd, *our Life is hid with* CHRIST *in* GOD. While CHRIST abides, *we* are secure; while GOD endures, *our Life* cannot be lost. This Ocean-Fulness, will flow out upon us, in various, fresh, perpetual Streams of infinite Goodness, thro' Time; until we are wafted into GOD in CHRIST, our Sea of Goodness, to live amidst the Pleasures which are at his Right Hand, to a blest Eternity.—Oh my dear Brother, let us receive the strong Consolation by Faith, and improve it by Love, in all holy Obedience, to the Glory and Joy of our dear Lord, and to ours with him, when he appears.—*The Grace of Christ be with your Spirit.* Pray for

Yours most affectionately in JESUS,

——— ———

LETTER XVII.

To Mr. S-------s.

Dear Sir,

I Greatly rejoice in the Wonders which God's Free-Grace hath wrought for poor *Plymouth*. The dear Mr. *Whitefield*, a little before his Departure from us, acquainted me in a Letter, that he had lik'd to have been *murder'd* in his Bed, at your Town. But oh how I rejoic'd to hear, afterward, that God over-rul'd this Providence, to bring many Souls under the *Sound*, and under the *Power* too, of his blessed *Gospel*, by that his dear Servant, who was so basely treated! Who is a God like unto our GOD! How wonderful are his Ways, his Ways of Providence, his Ways of Grace, towards his own chosen People! Many of whom lay in a perishing Condition at poor *Plymouth*, cast *out into the open Field* of this World, among dying Souls, *polluted in their own Blood*, most miserable, loathsome Objects; helpless of themselves, unpity'd, and without Help from others. But lo, the God of all Grace, *passed by*, and being *rich in Mercy, for his great Love wherewith he loved them, even when dead in Sins*, he said unto them, *Live!* Yea, when he saw them in their *Blood*, in all their Nature-Defilement, by original and actual Sin, he said unto them, *Live!* And their Time was the Time of *Love!* Of Love's Manifestation, of Love's Application, of Love's Triumph over all their Enmity, to the endless Praise of its own Glory! Of its Heights, its Depths, its Lengths and Breadths, which are immeasurable and infinite! Every Way worthy of GOD! Oh then it was, that the God of all Grace, *washed* these his beloved Ones with *Water*, yea, he throughly washed away their *Blood* (their Guilt of Sin) from them. He *justify'd them freely by his Grace*, thro' the Sin-cleansing *Blood* of the Slain LAMB. He anointed them with *Oil*, pour'd upon them his *Holy Spirit*. He deck'd them with *Ornaments*, beautify'd their Souls with every *Grace*. Yea, he *sware* unto them, and entred into a *Covenant* with them, and they became *his*.—Oh glorious *Grace*, of a Sin-pardoning GOD! Oh glorious *Power*, of a Sin-subduing *Arm!* Of an *Almighty*, All-conquering, Soul-wooing, Soul-winning, Soul-saving *Lover! Plymouth* would *none* of Christ. But CHRIST would have *some Souls* in *Plymouth*. And oh *happy they*, who were made *willing in the Day of his Power!*—And are *you*, my dear Brother, among that happy

Number! Oh do all you can, to love and serve your SAVIOUR! His *Grace be with your Spirit.* In JESUS our sweet Lord, I am, dear Sir,

Your affectionate Friend and Servant,

—— ——

LETTER XVIII.

To Mrs. M------t.

My very dear Sister in Christ,

I Hope you experience, that the Lord's Goodness and Mercy, follow you hitherto. And after you still, the glorious Flows thereof shall run, even all along thro' the Wilderness, until you reach *Canaan's* Land. That Land of Love, Life, Joy and Glory, into which your *Forerunner, is for you entred.* JESUS is gone up to his *Father's House, to prepare a Place for you.* And soon will he come by Death, to receive your Spirit into his own Embrace; and again at Judgment, to redeem your Body from the Grave, and to receive your whole Person to himself; to see him as he is, to be perfectly like him, and to serve him incessantly, among the Saints and Seraphs which are round his Throne.—Oh my dear Sister, the Glory of that Day hastens, when we shall all be gather'd together unto Christ, and unto one another, in and with him. *And so shall we be for ever with the Lord.* Surely our dear Lord Jesus, *comes quickly.* He is on his Way: He is gathering in his Chosen, in many of the dark Places, of this, and other Lands. *There is an Handful of Corn in the Earth, upon the Top of the Mountains;* (where there is not much Likelihood that Corn should grow) a few despised Instruments, who are almost every where spoken against, whom God hath raised up, to preach the Gospel of his Son Jesus, with glorious Seccess. *The Fruit thereof, shakes like Lebanon,* And by and by, *They of the City, shall flourish like the Grass of the Earth.* The Churches, which now generally languish, under the Withdraw of the divine Presence, Power and Glory from amongst them; shall again be revived. *Unto us* among them, *who fear the* LORD'S *Name,* shall *He* the *Sun of Righteousness arise, with Healing in his Wings. And we shall grow up, and go forth as Calves of the Stall.* Well-fed, and fat, as living Sacrifices, *Holiness unto the* LORD.—*Pray,* my dear Sister, *for the Peace of Jerusalem:* For the Comiong of our Lord's Kingdom, for the bringing on of Latter-Day Glory. For the Prosperity of the Lord's Work, which he is now about in the World; and for the Support and Success, of the poor, hunted, persecuted Labourers, which the Lord is pleas'd to make use of therein. And so will our Lord, the *Bridegroom* of the Church, call you one of his *Friends;* and the Church's Glory shall come on, as an Answer to your Prayers.—That our dear Lord Jesus, may support you and your dear Yoke-fellow, under all the Afflictions which you may be called to endure; that your Strength may be equal to your Day; that you may be enabled to glorify GOD in the Fires, and be prepared for endless Glory, by all your present Trials; is the earnest Desire of, my dear Sister,

Yours for ever, most Affectionately,
In your LORD *and mine,*

——— ———

LETTER XIX.

To Mr. F-------o.

Dear Sir,

IT is indeed a Miracle of Mercy, that we, *Sinners,* are out of *Hell;* who are in ourselves, such fit Fuel for *everlasting Burnings!* But oh, *Jesus,* our Sacrifice, has endur'd the Fire of divine Wrath, that we who look to him for Salvation, might be deliver'd from the Wrath to come.—I trust, my dear Friend, that you have seen such a Need of Christ, that you must perish for ever without him. And such an Excellency in him, that he is unto you, *The Chiefest among ten Thousand!* Don't you see such a Loveliness in *Jesus,* at Times, when you get a Glimpse of his Glory, that you can say with the *Psalmist, Whom have I in Heaven, but* Thee! *And there is none upon the Earth that I desire besides* (or in Comparison with) Thee! If so; you are a *Believer in Jesus.* For, *unto you therefore which* believe, *He is* precious. And as a Believer in the Son of God, you have *Christ* for your Portion, and all *Life* in and with him. *Your Beloved is* yours *and you are* his. He loves you as his own, he loves you as himself. He loves you freely, infinitely, unchangeably, and will love you eternally.

Be *free* then, *very free,* with your *own Lord Jesus.* Oh come to him daily, and tell him all your Griefs. Shew before him all your Trouble, and open every Sore, that pains and afflicts you. Your *Jesus,* is a *Physician,* that well knows how to heal all your Wounds, and bind up your Sorrows. For *Skill,* there is none like him; his Understanding is *infinite!* For *Tenderness,* he is all-surpassing; his Compassions are *bottomless, boundless, endless!* And for *Power,* he can do *all Things;* he is the LORD *Almighty!* And you cannot please him better, than to commit yourself daily into his Hands, with all your Diseases, your Soul-sicknesses, for *Him* to heal and cure you. Oh dear Sir, he will *rejoice,* to take you into his *Care,* and to *save you to the uttermost.* He will rejoice over you, thus to do you *Good,* with his *whole Heart,* and with his *whole Soul.* Yea, he accounts it his *Honour,* that you honour him as the great *Saviour,* when you come to him as a miserable *Sinner,* for all the Grace and Salvation you want, for Time, and for Eternity. You can't want *more,* than he has to bestow, and will rejoice to give. Oh come to *Jesus,* with all the *Wants* you are made sensible of; and when you want a *Sense* of your Misery, bring *that* Want with you also. The Fountain, *Christ,* is *full* and *free.* He will not send you *empty away.* Oh be *frequent* in your Acts of Faith upon Christ. *Unto whom* coming, □ saith the Apostle. It is the great Work of a Believer, to come unto Christ *continually,* to *receive of his Fulness, and Grace for Grace.* Oh how *blest,* are they, that abide in Christ by *Faith!* And how blest are they, that abide in Christ by Faith! And how *sad* is our Case, when we depart from him, by an evil Heart of *Unbelief!* Oh it is *sad* walking in the World, *without Christ!* Without *Nearness* to him, and *Fellowship* with him! *They that are far from him, shall perish; but it is good for us to draw near unto God.* Let us watch and pray, that we may *abide* in Christ by Faith, and *walk* with him by Love.—And whenever we backslide from him, thro' our wicked, deceitful Hearts, the Snares of the World, and the Temptations of Satan; let us confess our Iniquity before the Lord, and instantly cry unto him, with the *Psalmist, I have gone astray like a lost Sheep; seek thy Servant.* And say unto our Souls, as he did, *Return unto thy Rest, O my Soul; for the* LORD *hath dealt bountifully with thee.*—Wishing

Grace and Peace may be multiply'd unto you, thro' the Knowledge of God, and of Jesus our Lord: Unto his tender Love and Care, I commit you: And in Him, dear Sir, I am,

Your affectionate Friend and Servant,

——— ———

LETTER XX.

To Mr. H------s.

My very Dear and much Honour'd Brother,

Grace unto you, and Peace be multiplied.

I Humbly thank you for your dear Letters: They refresh'd my Bowels in the Lord. Your inward Affection to me, that Fellowship you have with me in the Truth, and that Willingness which is in your dear Heart, to suffer a Child to cry *Hosanna to the Son of David!* And especially, the Hints you gave of the coming of our Lord's Kingdom, did much comfort my Soul.—May the Lord reward all your Kindness to *me,* an *hundred-fold* into your *own Bosom!*

As to myself, my Brother, I am a *poor Sinner,* sav'd by God's *Free-Grace,* according to its own Riches! Oh what Wonders has God's Free-Grace wrought for *me!* How has he delighted to love me! But oh, my *Unkindness* to my kind Father, breaks my Heart! I am *pained* at my very Soul, to feel the Workings of Sin in my corrupt Nature. And even *surprized* to see such a Depth of Iniquity in my vile Heart, after so long an Acquaintance with JESUS, and such abundant Displays of Grace that I have been favour'd with. And under this, I am frequently *tempted to think,* "That God will *cast me off* as to Usefulness, and use such a vile Sinner no more unto any of his dear Children." And I am sure, that if he was not God, the LORD *that changeth not;* he *would* do it. And under the Views of my own Vileness, I also find an *Aptness* to sink into Dejection of Spirit. I find it exceeding difficult to take in, and keep up a due Sight and Sense of Sin, without sinking into an unbelieving Heaviness, at such Times when I am not sensibly under those full and overflowing Tides of Love and Grace, which bear down all before them. Oh this Sin of Sins,

Unbelief! It is the *Source* from whence all Sin *springs,* and the *Gulph* into which all Sin *flows!* Satan stirs up the Corruptions of the Heart, all seated as it were in Unbelief, and tempts God's People to *Sin:* And by the Motions of other Sins, stirring, or yielded to, either more inwardly or outwardly, he tempts them to *Unbelief.* And this is the worst Sin of all. In as much as the Soul hereby, so far as it prevails, casts the highest *Dishonour* upon the Grace of God, and the Fulness of Christ: as if there was not *Enough* in the infinite Grace of JEHOVAH, in the infinite Merit of CHRIST'S Blood and Righteousness, and in the infinite All-sufficiency of his Fulness, to *answer* the Souls Wants, and even infinitely to *exceed* them! Oh this Sin of *Unbelief,* this staying at Home in Self-wretchedness, instead of going out to Christ, and to God in him, so far as it prevails, is a tacit *Rejecting* of the SAVIOUR, and of all the Grace exhibited in him, by the glorious Gospel, for the chief of Sinners! Happy should we be, if upon every Conviction of our own Emptiness and Vileness, we pass'd the next Moment out of *ourselves,* into CHRIST, and there clos'd with the glorious Remedy provided for our miserable, helpless Souls! Oh what a God-honouring, Soul-nourishing, and comforting *Life* is a Life of *Faith on the Son of God!* All Glory be to God's Free Grace, this, in the main, is *the Life which I now live in the Flesh!* But, yet to my Grief, I feel the secret *Workings of Unbelief* in my Soul, and that I am *tempted to it,* upon the new Discoveries of my own Vileness. And under the Views hereof, I am further *tempted,* to cast off the Service of God, so far as it respects my making Mention of him unto others; after this Manner: "You see how vile you are; say no more for God, appear no further, keep Silence, unless you was better."

But oh, my dear Lord, doth not leave me to the Power of these Temptations. In infinite Grace, he forgives all my sins, and yet employs me in his Work! He appears again and again, to find me something to *do* for him, and frequently gives me to hear, that *He does* something by *Me, vile Me!* even when I have said, Time after Time, *I am cast out of his Sight!* Oh *Free Love!* He shews me the horrid Nature of Unbelief, and strengthens my Soul to believe on him, for his Honour and my Joy, in the Face of a thousand Difficulties and Discouragements. And by the sweet alluring Language of his Love, He draws on my Soul to serve him in the Liberty of his dear Children, and causes me to appear for him in the Work he calls me to, with an holy Boldness, in his own Strength and Worthiness; notwithstanding all that Vileness and Unworthiness which I see in myself, and that Satan objects against me.

Oh my Brother, I see, that the *Whole* of my Salvation, in all and every of its *Parts,* stands alone upon God's rich, free, sovereign *Grace,* reigning in glorious Triumph through a crucify'd JESUS! This *Grace* began my Salvation in Quickning me when dead in Sin! This *Grace* has maintained and increas'd my new Life hitherto, through a Thousand Deaths and Dangers! And this *same Grace,* will carry me safe through a World of Sin and Sorrow, into the World of Glory, in its own Everlasting Arms! Oh help me to bless and praise my God, for his *great Grace* unto *Me!*

I Rejoice much in our Lord's Kindness to *You;* in that he increaseth you with all the Increases of God. In that he strengthens you with all Might by his Spirit in your inward Man, makes you valiant for his Truth upon the Earth, laborious in his Service, and abundantly successful in your Labours. Go on, my dear Brother, in the Lord's Strength to serve him. Your Service is *acceptable* to your great Master, *profitable* to his dear Children, and *delightful* to your own Soul. Your *Work* is honourable and sweet, and your *Reward* will be Great and Glorious. Oh labour hard for CHRSIT, according to his Working, in your little Inch of Time; an Eternity of Rest awaits you in his, and in his Father's Bosom! *The Grace of our Lord Jesus Christ be with your Spirit.* I forget you not before the Lord. Pray for, Dear Sir,

Yours Affectionately in our Glorious Head,

——— ———

LETTER XXI.

To Mr. H------d.

My beloved Brother in Christ,

GLAD was I of the Line you sent me, which signify'd your Desire to hear from me.—My Time now allow'd me to write, is very short, and

I am unacquainted with your present Frame. But in the general, I find you want *Good.* Let me therefore say unto you, as *Eliphaz* to *Jeb, Acquaint now thyself with him* (with God in Christ) *and be at Peace: thereby* Good *shall come unto thee.* Oh you *tender Lamb* of Christ's Fold, your *Shepherd's Heart* is concern'd for you, his *Bowels yern* towards you; and in boundless Compassion, with everlasting Kindness, will he *gather you* by the Strength of his Arm, and *carry you* safe in his Bosom, through a Land of Pits and Snares, and fiery flying Serpents, unto the Land of Rest; where *Sorrow and Sighing shall flee away, and everlasting Joy shall be upon your Head!* Your Weakness, Sickness and Diseases, shall never turn away the Heart of your Tender Shepherd from you! But having loved you with a free, infinite *Love;* his Love towards you, will draw out the *Compassions* of his Soul, so much the more, to help, relieve, and save you to the uttermost! *The whole* (says He) *need not a Physician, but they that are Sick.* Oh, JESUS CHRIST, has a special Regard to his *sick Children,* and takes a peculiar Delight in healing their Souls, and binding up their Wounds! If Christ *lose one of his Sheep,* if one of them be driven from his Fold and expos'd to imminent Danger; such are his infinite Bowels towards it, that he doth as it were *Leave the Ninety and Nine, and goeth after that which is lost until he find it. And when he hath found it, he layeth it on his Shoulder, and bringeth it Home rejoicing.* Oh my Brother, if such was your Case, that there was no Pity for you in any of the *Creatures;* you have Tenderness enough in CHRIST'S Heart, a boundless endless Store, of Love-Grace, and Mercy, to relieve and solace you in all your Miseries! Come, *try* the Compassions of JESUS! The GODHEAD is in Him! His Bowels are *Infinite.* His Mercies are *Tender Mercies,* that are easily *touch'd* with the *Feeling* of your Miseries! *Tender,* to sympathize with you in them, to relieve you under them, and to deliver you from them. Oh, CHRIST hath a *tender Heart,* and a *tender Hand* to bind up *wounded Spirits!* Your Miseries can be but *Finite;* but the Compassions of CHRIST are *Infinite!* They know neither Bound, Change, nor End! But spread themselves in glorious Triumph over all! Oh come, cast your Soul, put your Trust under the Shadow of his Wings, until your Calamities are overpast! He will not *Frown you away:* but, *open his Arms,* his Bosom, and let you into *all his Grace!* And lo, *The* FATHER *himself loveth you!* It will please the *Father well,* to see you come unto him by *Jesus Christ.* HE *delighteth* in Mercy, in exercising Loving Kindness to the most miserable and unworthy. The FATHER'S Love is great, free, unchangeable and eternal! And through the crucify'd, risen, and ascended SAVIOUR, he will display his Mercy, Love, and Grace, in its exceeding Riches, unto Ages without End! God's *Design* in saving Sinners by Jesus Christ, is to *magnify* his Mercy, to *glorify* his Grace, to *commend* his Love, and set if *off* in all its native Glories, before all intelligent Beings. And therefore, *Where Sin has abounded, Grace doth much more abound.* Oh the infinite Fulness of *Grace!* The Glory of this *much more!* GRACE triumphs over *Sins,* over *Miseries,* over *Wants* innumerable, in the *Salvation of Sinners* unto Life eternal! It *fills* Valleys, *covers* Mountains, and like a mighty Deluge, *prevails* in its infinite Strength, and *spreads* its immense Glories over all!

"It rises, see, it drowns the Hills,
'T has neither Shore nor Bound;
Now if we search to find our Sins,
Our Sins can ne're be found!"

Oh the infinite *All-prevailings* of GOD'S free, rich, reigning GRACE! Eternity will be little enough to *adore* its Wonders, and *sing* its Praises! Oh *submit* to this GRACE, *rejoice* in this GRACE, *adore* and *praise* this GRACE, in Heart, Lip and Life, until *Time's Praises* are swallow'd up in blest *Eternity's* louder HALLELUJAHS!

Unto the Love and Care of our *Great Shepherd,* I commit you. Pray for, my dear Brother,

Yours most Tenderly in JESUS,

———— ————

LETTER XXII.

To Mr. L------s.

My dear Brother in Christ,

I Thank you for your kind Letter. I rejoice in the Lord's Goodness to *you* and *others,* in applying his own Truths with Power to your Hearts, so weakly stammer'd out by a *Babe.* I rejoice in the Lord's Kindness to *me,* in making my weak Attempts to serve him and his People, acceptable to *you. Not unto us, not unto us,* O LORD, *but unto thy Name be all the Glory!*

Glad am I to hear, what Haste our Lord makes, that his glorious Kingdom comes, that he has begun to *shake* the Nations. Oh may the Shake be *general,* and the *Desire of all Nations come!* My dear Brother, we had need be *ready.* There is no time for us to *sleep now. The Bridegroom cometh!* Oh let us *arise, and trim our Lamps,* lest he find us unprepared! Surely that great and wonderful Work which Christ is doing in the World at this Time, calls aloud upon us, *Christians,* to arise from our carnal Security, to put off the Deeds of Darkness, to put on the Armour of Light, and as Children of Light, to stand prepar'd for the Glory of the approaching Day. Even of that bright DAY, *when the Knowledge of the* LORD, *shall cover the Earth, as the Waters do the Sea!* When *Jew* and *Gentile* shall be brought into *one Fold,* and *one Lord shall be Shepherd over them!* When *the* LORD *shall be King over all the Earth, shall reign in Mount Zion, and before his Ancients, gloriously!* Surely our Lord, in his Word, and by his Works says, *I come quickly.* Let us in Transports of Love and Joy say, *Amen! Even so, come Lord Jesus!*

I am glad my dear Brother, that you have *Boldness* thro' the *Goodness* that is in JESUS, even in the Views of your *Self-emptiness.* It is Christian-like, Believer-like, to be *nothing* in ourselves, and *All* in CHRIST, who is our ALL! Oh it requires much of the Wisdom and Strength of Faith, to look well into our own Vileness and Emptiness, without *unbelieving Dejection;* and to feel and see ourselves full and glorious, by our Lord's Beams and Streams, without *Self-exaltation!* Oh how apt are we to look upon ourselves in a *seperate View* from Christ! To look on our Wants, in a *seperate View* from his Fulness, and to look on our Supplies, in a *seperate View* from the glorious Fountain from whence they proceed! And so on the one Hand, to sink into *Discouragement;* and on the other, to make Idols of our Lord's *fair Jewels!* On we have *unbelieving, Self-exalting,* and in both, CHRIST-*Excluding Hearts.* The Voice of proud Unbelief, in all its various Workings is, *None of Christ! None of Christ!* And yet the Grace of our Lord Jesus Christ is *sufficient* for us: To forgive our Sins, to subdue our Iniquities, and to give us humble Faith, the Voice whereof, with a louder Cry, is, *None but* CHRIST! *None but* CHRIST! He is ALL, and in ALL! The LORD, and our LORD! And unto him be all the GLORY! and happy are the Souls whose Language is *this!* and happy they, when *this* is their Voice! CHRIST will say of them, in the Infinity of his Grace, from his own Beauties imputed and imparted, *Thou art All-Fair, my Love, there is no Spot in Thee!* And they again will reply, *Thou art Fair my Beloved; Fairer than the Children of Men,* Fairer than Angelic Glories, immensely Fair, and *Altogether Lovely!* How Blessed then are the Souls that believe in JESUS, and that have Communion with him by Faith! That have an Interest in CHRIST'S Love and Fellowship with him therein! And that this, my dear Brother, may be your daily Privilege, is the hearty Desire of your

Friend and Servant in the Lord.

LETTER XXIII.

To Mr. L------s.

My very dear Brother,

THE Account you gave me in your last, of the Lord's Dealings with your Soul, did much endear you to me, through his Working. Oh my dear Brother, you and I, and all God's Chosen, are loved with the *same Love.* With the infinite, free, unchangeable, and eternal Love of GOD! This Love was fix'd upon us of old, before time was, or Sin entered: Has found us out when afar off from GOD, and made us nigh by the Blood of CHRIST. It was because the LORD had *loved us with an everlasting Love,* that he *drew us with Loving-kindness,* unto Faith in JESUS. Oh the Sovereignty of *Grace,* that took *you,* and took *me,* while *others* were left, who in many Respects, were not so *bad* as we! Whoever is angry at *distinguishing Grace,* let *us* admire it, adore it, and shout its Praises, thro' Time and to Eternity. Let *us* cry, *Grace, Grace,* to the Whole of our Salvation by *Jesus Christ!* Love, infinitly *Free,* took us up in our perishing Condition, and gave us the Life of *Grace.* And in its sweet, strong, everlasting Arms, it will carry us into the Life of *Glory.* And there, with uninterrupted Shine, it will cast upon us its bright Beams, unto Bliss and Joy, full and immense, to the Days of Eternity!—*Rejoyce* then, my dear Brother, *in Hope of the Glory of* God. And, *Come up from the Wilderness, leaning upon your Beloved.* Who is *Yesterday, To-day, and for ever the* SAME, in his boundless Love to *you!* In HIM, I am Sir,

Your most affectionate Friend and Servant,

——— ———

LETTER XXIV.

To Mr. H--------d.

My dear and honour'd Brother,

Grace unto you and Peace be multipli'd, from God our Father, and the Lord Jesus Christ.

THUS we that believe in JESUS, may well greet one another. Since Peace is made for us by the Blood of Christ's Cross, and shall be extended to us like a River. God our Father, is the *God of Peace* unto us in Christ. Oh my Brother, you and I, have done as *evil Things as we could.* And yet, all is *Peace,* between God and us *still.* Our Original Guilt in our first Father *Adam,* that horrid Mass of Enmity against God, which was thence derived into our wretched Nature, that entire and continual Rebellion against our Maker, which we were guilty of before he call'd us by his Grace, and those many great and aggravated Sins, which we have been guilty of since we were under forgiving Love; rise to such a Mass of *Guilt,* that it is an astonishing *Wonder,* that we are not made Vessels of *Wrath* for ever! We have deserv'd nothing less, than God's fiery Indignation, to be persecuted with his Storm, and cast into the tempestuous Sea of eternal Vengeance.—But oh, did JESUS step into *our Place!* Did HE *bear* our Sin, *endure* our Hell, and *drink* up all that Wrath which was due to *us,* even to the last Drop, until he cry'd out, *It is finisht!*—What *Love* was this in the Son of God! What *Love* was this in the Father, To give his Son to be thus abas'd and crush'd, wounded and bruised to Death, even the Death of the Cross for *us!* For us *Rebels!* For us *Enemies!* For us that deserv'd to be Companions with *Devils,* in the *Lake of Fire* for ever! Oh, it is like GOD! A Love worthy of GOD! In which the infinite Glories of the GODHEAD shine, and will be radiantly display'd, to the endless Wonder and Praise of Men and Angels! It was *you,* my Brother, it was *me,* that JEHOVAH *so loved!* Can we *sound* the Depths of Love's Ocean? Can we *take* the Breadths of this boundless Sea? We may dive into it, but can never *Bottom* it. We may *swim* in it, but can never pass *over* it. Infinite *Love,* is beneath us, above us, behind us, before us, in the Depths and Heights, the Breadths and Lengths of its own *Infinity!* And this Love, my Brother, dy'd in *Blood,* thro' the Death of JESUS, is a Sea of *Life* unto us! Here we have the free, the full, the eternal Forgiveness of all our Sins. A Robe of justifying Righteousness, more glorious far, than Angels wear. A Fulness of all Grace, to supply us, to enrich is, to delight us, a boundless, endless Store. And a Fulness of all Glory, of inconceivable Bliss, in the Right of it now, and shall have the Enjoyment of it e'er long, in the immediate Vision of GOD and the LAMB for ever.

Sweet to me, dear Sir, this Morning, were the first and second Verses of the twenty third Psalm. My Heart was inclin'd to acquaint you with it. Ancient was the *Father's Love,* free, rich, distinguishing was *his Grace,* in giving us to *Christ,* as *his Sheep;* and in commanding him to lay down his *Life,* and take it *again* for us, to save us to the uttermost. And the boundless Love of *Christ,* his free, rich, sovereign *Grace,* in accepting us at the Father's Hand, as his *Sheep,* in taking the Charge of us as *such,* although himself was to *die* in our Stead, to redeem us from all Misery, unto all glory; doth far surpass *Knowledge.* All the World are not Christ's Sheep. Why was *you?* Why was *I?* How is it that *we* should find such Grace in the Sight of the LORD? It can be resolv'd into nothing less, than the sovereign *good Pleasure* of his *own Will.* It can only be answer'd by this great Resolve of his Heart: "I will be gracious to whom I will be gracious, and will shew Mercy on whom I will shew Mercy." Let us admire, let us adore it. Strange! That it shou'd be *us,* that the LORD resolv'd to be gracious to, and to shew Mercy upon! But so it is: The LORD is *our Shepherd!*—We shall not *want.* No, his own Life has been paid, to procure for us a full *Supply.* He leads us into *green Pastures:* that deserv'd to dwell in a barren Land, where no Salvation-Blessings spring. He maketh us to lie down beside the still *Waters:* that deserv'd not a Drop of Comfort, nothing but the Damned's Fare; to be tormented in the *Flames of Hell,* without a Drop of Water to cool our Tongue. He makes us to lie down and rest by the *still* Waters; that have deserv'd to be all expos'd to the Waters of *Trouble.* Strange! That the glorious LORD, Father, Son, and Spirit, should be unto *us*, that have done so wickedly, that have so much Wickedness in us, a *River* of Grace and Peace, of Love and Life, a *glorious broad River with Streams;* where no Enemy can come to destroy us: When from our God, there is *no Peace to the Wicked!* Oh my Brother, the GOD *of Peace* is our Portion, thro' the LAMB'S *Blood!* Thus to us, the *Legatees,* the *New Testament,* with all its glorious Gifts and Bequeathments, stand *confirmed.*

Go then, you Son of Peace, you Heir of Peace, *preach Peace by Jesus Christ, to them that are afar off, and to them that are nigh.* Tell Saints of their peaceful State. Tell Sinners, there is Peace in Christ for the very Chief, that come in to him, the LORD our Peace. Preach the reconciling Word: And the God of Peace will slay the Enmity in the Hearts of his People thereby.—That *the Peace of God which passeth all Understanding, may keep your Heart and Mind thro' Christ Jesus;* is the sincere Desire of, dear Sir,

Your Affectionate Friend and Servant,
In the Glorious LAMB.

LETTER XXV.

To Mr. C------ns.

My dearr Brother in Christ,

I Kindly thank you for your Letters. The first of which brought me Tidings of great Joy, with Respect to the Coming of our Lord's Kingdom, and especially in the Army. Oh may it rise and shine, till the whole Earth is filled with its Glory! In vain the Powers of Darkness, oppose the Lord of Light, the LORD our Light, the glorious Sun of

Righteousness, who is rising upon his People, with Healing in his Wings. All opposite Power must stoop to the supreme Dominion of the glorious LAMB; when HE takes unto himself his great Power, and reigneth: by the Sceptre of his Grace, to save his People, and by his Iron Rod, to dash in Pieces his Enemies. The Powers of *Antichrist,* will make *War with the Lamb;* but the LAMB shall *overcome them.* And however grieving the Approaches of Christ's Kingdom may be to the Men of the World; "Let the Children of Zion be joyful in their King:" and say with united Voice, *Come Lord Jesus, come quickly!*

As to yourself, my dear Brother, I mourn, I rejoice with you, for your different Experiences of the Power of Sin, and the Power of Grace. Well it is for you and me, that tho' *Sin* works in us, and too often prevails as an *Usurper;* yet it hath not the *Throne* in our Hearts. *Christ* reigns there; and *Sin* shall not have Dominion over us. Because we are *not under the Law,* as a Covenant of Works; which condemns for Sin, which gives no Strength against it: But *under Grace;* which forgives our Sins, and subdues our Iniquities.—Howbeit, tho' a Christian is, and ought to be *passive* to the Reign of Grace; he is call'd thereby, to be *active* in a Way of Duty; to maintain a strict Guard over his Thoughts, Words and Actions, to watch and pray always, lest he enter into Temptation.—And thus the Promise, "Sin shall not have Dominion over you; for you are not under the Law, but under Grace:" And the Exhortation, "Let not Sin therefore reign in your mortal Body, that you should abbey it is the Lusts thereof:" do well agree. The Grace of God, doth not set *aside* Duty; but *calls* for it. Carnal Security, is the Bane of Christianity. "Be sober, be vigilant, saith the Apostle *Peter,* for your Adversary the Devil, goeth about like a roring Lion, seeking whom he may devour." He will either put Souls upon *working* for Life; or having Life, to *cease* from working. To *fear* that their Sins will never be forgiven; or being pardon'd, to be *fearless* of Sin. He will put Believers, either upon *doubting* of the Truth of Grace in their Hearts; or having a Persuasion thereof, to be *proud* of it. He will either *dissuade* us from Duty, because of our *Weakness;* or put us upon *attempting it,* in our *own Strength, &c.* And our vile *Hearts,* always join with *Satan.* And both agree to draw us into *Sin.* We walk as it were, in the midst of *Snares,* And therefore we had need walk *watchfully.* We are never so *weak,* as when we think ourselves *strong.* So near to *nothing,* as when we think ourselves to be *something.* Nor in so much Danger of *falling,* as when we think we *stand.* For, "Pride goeth before Destruction; and a haughty Spirit before a Fall." *Self,* even gracious Self, *admir'd,* is made an *Idol* of; and *trusted in,* will *deceive us.* Every Idol must be *abolish'd,* that the LORD alone may be *exalted.*

But oh, what a Mercy is it to us, that when *we fall,* we are not *alone!* That there is One to help us *up,* our strong *Lord Jesus,* whose almighty Arm, *upholdeth all that fall!* Who limits our Falls, that tho' we fall partially, we fall not utterly! Who forgives our Sins, heals our Backslidings, and over-rules our Falls, to make us more watchful of our Steps! Oh it is well for us, that we are *Christ's Care;* that He hath a constant *Hold of us;* else we should fall into *Perdition,* we should fall, and *rise no more.* But *everlasting Arms* being *underneath us,* we are for ever secur'd from *that* Danger; and being round about us, they'll *raise us* when we slip: "When we fall, we shall arise; when we sit in Darkness, the LORD will be a Light unto us."—We never walk *safely,* but when we walk *believingly;* but when we *walk in Christ by Faith,* as we have *receiv'd him.* Oh when, thro' Unbelief, we begin to walk in *ourselves,* in the Strength of our *received Grace;* we soon get a *Fall.* When we begin to act, as if we thought we could do *without* Christ; our kind Lord, in Love to our Souls, will soon convince us of the *Need* we have of Him. When we foolishly think, we have receiv'd Grace enough to enable us to walk as *Saints;* we shall soon find that we are poor *Sinners.* And good it is for us to be thus *humbled;* that we may learn practically, our own Misery and Poverty, and to go out of ourselves, and all Self-Dependence continually, to live in, and depend upon the All-Sufficiency of CHRIST. In whom alone, all our fresh Springs, for every Grace and Duty are; and from whom they must be continually derived unto us, or the Exercise of our Graces, and the Performance of our Duties will instantly fail.

I rejoice with you, my dear Brother, that tho' you have had a humbling Proof of your own Vileness; you have a sweet Sense of forgiving Grace. That tho' you have felt the Weight of Sin more than ever, you are sweetly supported under it, by glorious Views of your Compleatness in *Christ,* tho' so incompleat in *yourself.* Oh, nothing gives the Soul, such sweet, solid Soul-Rest, as a View of our being dead to Sin in *Christ,* when we sadly feel it is alive in *us.* Nothing kills Sin more, nor strengthens the Soul more against it. When we see a complete Victory over our spiritual Enemies, obtain'd for us, and secur'd to us by our conquering Lord; we shall fight valiantly under the Banner of his Love, against all the Powers of Darkness.—Wherefore, "Be strong, my Brother, in the Lord, and in the Power of his Might." For HE that has done all *for* you, will do all *in* you; and prepare you by all your Trials, for that Service He has design'd you for in this World, and for the Glory which is prepar'd for you in the World to come.—Unto the tender Care of CHRIST, the great Shepherd, I commit you: And am, dear Sir,

Yours most affectionately in HIM,

——— ———

LETTER XXVI.

To Mr. L------s.

My very dear Brother in Christ,

I Thank you for yours received. I compassionate you in your inward and outward Trials. Be of good Cheer: All Things go *well.* All Things are *yours,* whether prosperous or afflictive. All Things work together for your *Good;* to ripen your Graces, and prepare you for your Crown.—"Aye, you will say, how can that be, when I don't see that I grow in Grace thereby?—Know you not, my Brother, that our Lord works by *Contraries?* that he often works under-ground, out of our Sight? That a Child of God may *grow* sweetly in Grace, when he don't *know* it? That he may grow *downward* in Humility and Self-abasement, when he don't grow *upward* in Love and Joy? That when he don't *feel* the Power of Christ resting upon him, to his growing up into Him, by the Exercise of Summer-Graces; he may grow *more* in a deep Sense of his own Weakness and utter Insufficiency to do any good Things, take *deeper* Root by Faith into the All-sufficiency of CHRIST, and by a humble and entire Dependance, cleave *closer* to Him than ever? And that Winter-Dispensations, *prepare* for Summer-Fruits? *Blessed* (says our Lord) *are the*

Poor in Spirit; for theirs is the Kingdom of Heaven. God's free, sovereign Grace, reigning thro' the Redeemer's Righteousness, will do *all* for them, that see themselves worthy of *Nothing;* will *enrich* those, that see they *want* every Thing. It is good for us to be emptied of Self, and Self-Dependance; to see ourselves to be nothing but a Mass of Weakness and Vileness. And the Means by which this is effected, thro' the over-ruling Power of Grace of God, are Times of Trial. Of the sensible Withdraw of divine Influences, of Temptations from Satan, of the Working of Corruptions, and of contrary Dispensations.—when by Reason of *These,* we cry out, *Wo is me, I am undone!* Then we shall be *made.* When thus *oppressed* and *distressed;* the LORD *will undertake for us.* There is Work for the SAVIOUR, when thus we see ourselves to be *poor Sinners.* There is Room for Free-Grace to display its *Glories,* when within and without, we are surrounded with *Miseries.* And when in all Respects, we see ourselves to be *Helpless;* the LORD, the Almighty GOD, will be our *Helper.* We can't have too many Miseries, for a GOD of boundless Compassions to be touch'd with. Nor too many Wants, for a GOD of infinite Fulness to supply. And *this* GOD, in infinite Faithfulness, *is our* GOD, *for ever and ever.* For Ever, thro' Time; and for ever, to Eternity. And what can we want more? Is God in CHRIST *ours?* Let us be *content* with our Portion. We have *enough* in HIM: We have *All.* We cannot, we shall not want *any good Thing.* Whatever infinite Wisdom sees best for us; infinite Goodness will bestow upon us; and infinite Faithfulness secures to us.—Sweet my Brother, was this Expression of yours to me: "A God keeping Covenant, is a SAVIOUR to some Purpose." Let me add, Unto all Intents and Purposes, relating to our present and eternal Salvation, from all sin and Misery, unto all Grace and Glory. Oh my Brother, your Covenant-God, will give you *Faith* to trust in him. He that was the *Author,* will be the *Finisher* of your Faith. His Faithfulness stands engag'd, to maintain, increase, and perfect the Work of Faith with Power. Your Soul, your Body are the LORD'S: The Redeemer's *Right,* and precious to him. And both, and all Things needful for both, are *His Care.*

Come then, lie down and rest in the Bosom of infinite Love, in the Bosom of God, your own God in CHRIST; who is and will be to you, *The* God *of Love!* Here all Things are provided for you, that you can possibly want. Pardon for your Guilt, Strength for your Weakness, Wisdom for your Folly, in a Word, *all Fulness* to supply your *every Need.* Commit your Soul, your Body, your Circumstance, into the Lord your Redeemer's Hands; and take an holy Ease, from all anxious Care about either. *Can you by taking* such *Thought, add to your Stature one Cubit?* Will you rob your Lord of his Glory as your *Leader,* by drawing out *Ways* for him to lead you in? Oh commit yourself wholly unto *his Conduct.* Lose your own Wisdom as Folly, in his infinite Understanding. *Believe now,* that he leads you by a Right Way to a City of Habitation; you shall *see it* to be so *e'er long.* If now you are call'd to follow him in the *Dark;* He will shortly bring you forth to the *Light,* and you shall behold his Righteousness. *In the Dispensation of the Fulness of Times, God will gather together in one all Things in Christ.* All his Dealings, with all his People, into one bright Form, one great Design of boundless Love, in a glorious Order of infinite Wisdom: And as such present them unto their View; to their endless Joy, and to his eternal Praise.—And mean Time, let us *believe,* when we can't *see, adore,* what we can't *comprehend;* and *in Patience possess our Souls,* thro' all that Distress and Perplexity, which attends Nations, Churches, Families and Persons, in these evil Times, which precede our Lord's Coming. He has told us before-hand, that *these Things must come to pass;* and bidden us *lift up our Heads,* at the Beginning of Sorrows: Because *the Day of our Redemption draweth nigh.*

As to the Persecution that our Brethren meet with, the LORD will be with them in it, and over-rule it for the Furtherance of his Gospel, the Good of Souls, and for their present and eternal Joy. The more God's People are *afflicted,* the more they *grow.* The Enemies shall never get them rooted out of the *Earth.* So long as CHRIST sits enthron'd for them in *Heaven.* Howbeit, the Powers of *Antichrist,* will make War with the LAMB; and they shall accomplish to *scatter the Power of the holy People,* for a *little Season.* That the Judgments of our Lord the King of Saints, may appear to be true and righteous, when he ariseth to save all the Meek of the Earth, and to break in Pieces the Oppressor. *The* LORD *of Hosts is with us, the* GOD *of Jacob is our Refuge.* Selah. *There is a River, the Streams whereof shall make glad the City of God.* GOD *is in the Midst of her, she shall not be moved:* GOD *shall help her, and that right early. Therefore we will not fear, tho' the Earth be removed, and tho' the Mountains be carried into the Midst of the Sea. Tho' the Waters thereof roar and be troubled, tho' the Mountains shake with the Swelling thereof.* Selah.—Into the Heart and Arms of CHRIST, I commit you. Who loves you infinitely, cares for you continually, and will save you completely. His Grace be with your Spirit! Pray for me. I am, dear Sir,

Yours affectionately in the Slain LAMB,

——— ———

LETTER XXVII.

To Mr. H------d.

Dear and Honour'd Brother,

YOURS I receiv'd, and return you Thanks for it. I rejoyce in the Lord's Loving-kindness to your Soul, and that his hand is with you in your Work.—May the Lord continue these great Favours, and increase you with all the Increases of God! Indeed my dear Brother, it is our Happiness and Glory to *feel* much of GOD in our Hearts. It is CHRIST *within,* inwardly enjoy'd, unto a growing Conformity to him, that makes the Soul *Happy.* I am entirely of your Mind, that "Religion don't consist in Disputes, but in inward Sensation and Experience." And lamentable it is, that in the Age wherein we live, there is so much resting in *Head-Knowledge,* without *Heart-Experience.* And where the Truth of Grace is in the Heart, that there is so much resting in *past Experiences,* without an earnest Concern after *Growth in Grace,* and an *Increase in the Knowledge of* CHRIST, or a daily Fellowship with CHRIST in his Death and Resurrection, unto full Joy and increasing Holiness. Oh what holy, happy Christians should we be, if we were earnestly concern'd about a daily *Knowing* of the Truth as it is in JESUS, in its Power and Efficacy on our Hearts, and reducing the same to an answerable *Practice* in our Lives! That Religion which consists only in *Head-Knowledge,* without *Heart-Influence,* is little worth.—Nor is that Religion which exalts *inward Sensation,* to a Neglect of *outward Revelation,* much better.—For without *Knowledge,* (the Knowledge of Gospel-Truths) the *Heart* cannot be *good.*

We must first *know,* to *feel,* and *feel,* to *do,* if what we do in Religion is *right,* either as to the inward Actings of our Minds, or the outward Actions of our Lives.—This is the Sum, my dear Brother: The Lord Jesus Christ and his blessed Truths, reveal'd in the Gospel *without us,* must first be reveal'd by the Holy Spirit *within us,* before we can feel the happy Influence of God's Salvation in our Hearts: And *so far* as Christ and his Truths are reveal'd in us, *so far* we are oblig'd to abide therein by Faith, to cleave thereto in Love, and to bear Witness for the same, both in Word and Deed, in our Lives.—Has Christ and his Truths been reveal'd to *your Mind,* my dear Brother, by the Word and Spirit of God? Have you *seen* the Glory, and *felt* the Power hereof? Then are you call'd to *hold fast that which you have received; that no Man take your Crown.*—Disputes in Religion, for *Dispute's Sake,* for *Humour's Sake,* are no better than *vain Jangling,* idle Contention, a wretched Mispence of Time, a Neglect of the Power of Godliness, and a means to promote Ungodliness and Irreligion. Disputes in Religion, to advance Error, and destroy the Truth, are *abominable.* But Disputes in Religion, for *Truth's Sake,* to advance the Truth against rising Error, are *commendable* and *profitable.* Such *Kind* of Disputes, maintain'd by the inspir'd Penmen, we have Instances of both in the Old and New Testament. To such *Kind* of Disputes, the Saints are exhorted, even to *contend earnestly for the Faith which was once delivered unto the Saints,* Jude 3. And the happy *Fruit* of such Disputes, is the *Advancement* of the Redeemer's Kingdom, and the *Downfal* of Satan's, the *Establishment* of Saints in the Doctrines of Christ, the *Deliverance* of their Souls from the Falshoods advanc'd by the Father of Lies, and the *Overthrow* of Men of corrupt Minds.—Such is the infinite Wisdom and Grace of our dear Lord Jesus, as the Head and King of his Church, that he would not suffer Errors to appear, if he did not design to over-rule them for his own Glory and his People's Good. When the Prince of Darkness with his Train, make War with the Lamb by advancing *Error,* darkning, shaking *Error;* our Lord thereby, will more abundantly manifest and confirm his *Truth,* and the *Faith* of his People therein: While *then,* in an especial Manner, he calls and spirits his Servants, his Witnesses, to lift up the *Standard* of Truth, against Error, and *fight* valiantly under HIM their great Leader, who for this End came into the World, *To bear Witness to the Truth.* And lo, our Lord will honour those who are his Witnesses, his Warriors for Truth in the Earth, and crown them as Victors, with heavenly Glory.—An absolute *Opposition* to all Disputes in Religion, is an apparent *Artifice* of Satan. And the manifest Design of the Enemy herein is, to darken the Redeemer's Glory, by a Cloud of Error, and have none to stand on Christ's Side, on the Side of Truth, to fan the Air, and drive away the Smoke of the bottomless Pit.

Perhaps my dear Brother, you may wonder I speak thus; but I would guard your Mind from that Snare into which others have fallen. Brother *R-----s,* and Brother *O------y* were drawn *off* from appearing on the *Side of Truth,* by *No Dispute in Religion,* until they *lost* the Truth.—And a sad Account I have in a Letter lately receiv'd from a Friend at *Ph------ia,* "That the *M-----n* Tenets spread very fast in that Place, that many Proselytes are made, and that hereupon Persons most sadly give up the Truth of Christ, and say, 'They will have nothing to do with Doctrines, or Principles in Religion.'"—May *the God of Peace bruise Satan under your Feet, and after all your Sufferings by his Temptations, stablish, strengthen, settle you!* May HE *deliver you from every evil Work, and preserve you safe unto his Heavenly Kingdom! The Grace of* CHRIST *be with your Spirit!* Into his Arms I commit you. Pray for,

Dear Sir,

Yours most affectionately in JESUS,

——— ———

LETTER XXVIII.

To Mr. L------s.

My dear Brother L------s,

I Kindly thank you for your last. It much rejoic'd my Heart, to hear that your Hope in God and Expectation from Him was strengthen'd. And that the sovereign Lord of All, was pleas'd to make my last a Means to comfort your dear Soul. The Account you gave me, of the Lord's making my poor Letters of such Use to you, melted me into Tears of Joy and Thankfulness. The Lord thereby enlarg'd my Heart to praise Him, and fill'd me with vast Desires to serve Him.

It is Christ's Voice unto you, "Rejoice in the Lord always, and again I say, Rejoice." GOD hath given you his *Son,* that unspeakable GIFT! See that for this, to the glorious Giver, your whole Life be *Thanks!* Oh my Brother, a heavy unthankful Frame, ill becomes those happy Souls, that have CHRIST for their Portion. God the Father lov'd you so, that He did not think the *World,* good enough to be *your Lot.* And therefore gave his *Son;* in whom all Fulness, even the Fulness of the GODHEAD dwells. Oh take up your *wondrous Lot!* And go thro' a World of Trials rejoicing. CHRIST is given you, and all Things with him freely. All Grace, all Glory, and all good Things. Life and Death, Comforts nd Crosses, Things present and Things to come: "All are yours, and you are Christ's, and Christ is God's." Wherefore behave with a true Greatness of Spirit, as an Heir of *All Things,* an *Heir of GOD, and a Joint-Heir with CHRIST!* Are your most grieving Things given you by infinite Love? And will you not accept of them humbly and thankfully? Your Troubles are all under the supreme Dispose of your all-wise and all-gracious GOD. And after you have been fully exercis'd thereby, they will yield unto you, the peaceable Fruit of Righteousness. Oh be in Love with every Thing that comes from the GOD of Love, to bring the Fruits of his Love to you here in Grace, and to prepare you for endless Glory.—Happy are you, that you *seek* JESUS: You shall *find Him.* "Your Heart shall live, that seeks GOD."—Be *earnestly* concern'd. For all Anxiety and Perplexity spring from *Unbelief. Faith,* lays the Soul to Rest in the Bosom of GOD, in the Midst of Trouble. "The Righteous shall flourish like the Palm-Tree:" under pressing Weights. And when Pressures will not conduce to your Fruitfulness; the Lord your Lover, will take them off your Shoulders. All Things are in *Love to you;* in all *give Thanks: And the Peace of GOD which passeth all Understanding, keep your Heart and Mind thro' Christ Jesus.* In HIM, dear Sir, I am

Yours most affectionately,

——— ———

LETTER XXIX.

To Mr. C------ns.

My dear Brother in Christ,

Grace unto you, and Peace be multiplied.—I thank you for your last Letter. I have just now been reading it, and was melted into Tears of Joy, for the Grace that saved *you;* and made *me,* in my poor Writings, a Means of your Acquaintance with the *Doctrines of Grace;* and I am persuaded, with the *Grace* of those Doctrines.—Oh *why* did not the Lord let you go down in the *broad Way of Destruction,* when posting on in *that* high Road? Because He had *lov'd and chosen you of Old!* Because He *had not appointed you unto Wrath, but to obtain Salvation by Jesus Christ.*—And when turn'd from a vicious Course, to a *strict Life,* and become a proud *Pharisee,* a Reasoner, a Disputer against that sovereign *Grace,* by which the Lord saves his Own; *Why,* oh *why,* did not he Lord let you go down to the Pit of Hell, with this *Lie* of your own Righteousness *in your Right Hand? Why* did He not resolve to punish you with everlasting Destruction, for your Enmity against, and Disobedience to the *Gospel?* Oh, not because you did not *deserve it;* but because He *would* be gracious! Because He *would* have Mercy upon you, merely from the sovereign good Pleasure of his own Will! Oh Sir, you was *without* GOD in the World, *afar off* from Him; an *Enemy in your Mind by wicked Works;* even by this wicked Work, of *going about to establish your own Righteousness;* and thereby refusing *Submission to the Righteousness of God.* You was a *Stranger* to CHRIST: Of *you,* a *Builder,* upon your own Doings for Life, was *Jesus Christ,* the *chief Corner-stone,* the *Foundation* which God has laid in *Sion, disallow'd.* Your Soul was brimful of Enmity against your SAVIOUR. You said unto Him, *Depart from me; I desire not the Knowledge of thy Ways.* And would He not take you at your *Word,* and say, *I'll leave thee; thou shall never have eternal Life by the Knowledge of* ME? Would He not let *you* go, with a *Thousand* that fall at your *Side,* and *Ten Thousand* at your right-Hand? Oh, *No!* But *why,* oh *why?* Was it because you was *better than they? No, in no wise.* But such was the Sovereignty, the Freeness, the Immensity of Christ's *Love to you,* that He *would not, could not,* let you *perish. You* he had known, and lov'd of *Old.* He had liv'd and dy'd, serv'd and sweat, groan'd and bled for *you,* to bring you into his own

Embraces. You was *his* by Right of Gift; the Father gave you to him before Time began. You was *his* by Right of Purchase; he bought you with his Blood, and gave his own Soul, in your Soul's Stead. And out of the Devil's Kingdom, out of the Jaws and Paws of the Devourer, he would have you. He resolv'd you should be *his* by Right of Conquest: to assail and overcome you, to allure and secure you to himself for ever. Oh my Brother, all the Passes and Avenues of your *Heart,* were barr'd and bolted against CHRIST. *Satan,* that strong One, arm'd with your *Sins,* and the *Curse* of the Law, kept the *House,* the Possession of your *Heart;* until a *stranger than he* came upon him, bound him, and spoil'd him of his Goods. Until the LORD your mighty Lover, in the omnipotent Strength of his own Grace, made his Royal Entrance into your Soul; brake the Gates of Brass, and cut the Bars of Iron in sunder, destroy'd your strong Enemy, and deliver'd you out of his cruel Hands. *The Son hath made you free:* And now you are *free indeed!* Free from the Guilt of Sin, and free from its reigning Power. Free from the Government of Satan, and the World's Jurisdiction. Free from the Law's Curse, the Hurt of natural, and the Danger of eternal Death. But what shall I say? A *compleat Freedom* from all your Enemies, and *glorious Triumph* over them, hath JESUS given you *in himself,* and will shortly give you *thro' him.* Your *mystical* Freedom from all Bondage and Slavery, and Right to all Glory, is complete in CHRIST. Himself hath made you free, perfectly free, in himself. And *personal* Freedom, every Way complete, in the free, the irreversible *Grant* of all Salvation, is given you by *Faith* in the SAVIOUR'S Name. And the joyful *Beginnings* of all this Bliss, you have in your *own Soul.* Which from its happy Dawn, thro' Almighty Love, shall advance apace to the perfect Day, to the Meridian-Brightness of that glory-Day, which awaits you.—*Stand fast therefore in the Liberty wherewith* CHRIST *hath made you free; and be not entangled again with the Yoke of Bondage.* CHRIST hath lov'd and bought, lov'd and rescu'd, lov'd and woo'd, and won you to *himself.*—And will you not now be *his?* Oh, from henceforth, *being deliver'd out of the Hands of all your Enemies, serve him in Holiness and Righteousness all the Days of your Life!* CHRIST will never let go his Love-Hold of *you.* Oh cleave you unto *him,* with full *Purpose of Heart:* And *follow the* LAMB, even *whithersoever he goeth.* Bear the *Cross;* you shall shortly wear the *Crown.* Most *sweet* is the Cross of blessed JESUS; and ineffably *great* that Crown of Glory, which he will shortly set upon your Head, as an Overcomer. Labour to keep it in View by Faith, to hearten you on, to *run with Patience the Race which is set before you,* until you *inherit the Promises.* And what that Glory will be, in its Perfection, Extension and Greatness; is beyond the Description of an *Angel's Tongue!* Oh, what will it be, to see CHRIST as he *is!* To be forever *with him!* To live under the direct Line of his *Love!* The all-enlightning, all - enkindling Rays of Love's flaming Glory, to the innumerable Ages of a bless'd Eternity!—

"Millions of Years, my wondring Eyes,
Shall o'er thy Beauties rove:
And endless Ages, I'll adore
The Glories of thy Love!"

That you as a *tender Lamb* of CHRIST'S Fold, may be guided and guarded by him the *great Shepherd,* and made to lie down in the fat, green Pastures of Gospel-Grace, beside the still, deep Waters of eternal Love, for your Refreshment and Growth in this weary Wilderness; until he brings you to the City which our God has prepar'd for you, and *presents you faultless before the Presence of his* Father's *Glory, with exceeding Joy:* Is the sincere Desire of, my dear Brother,

Your most affectionate Friend and Servant,
In our sweet JESUS,

——— ———

LETTER XXX.

To Mr. L------s.

My very dear Brother,

I Am glad the Lord made my last Letter of Use to you. As you said it was *close:* I suppose you might misunderstand some Expression therein. Perhaps *this:* "All Anxiety and Perplexity, spring from *Unbelief.*" By this, my dear Brother, I did not intend *total,* but *partial* Unbelief. Nor to signify thereby, that the Anxiety which was in your Mind, was an Indication of your being in a *State* of Unbelief. There is much *unbelief* remains in *Believers,* even in the *strongest* of them all. The Workings whereof, ought to be reduc'd to their proper Principle, from whence they flow. And to *watch,* and *oppose* the same, is an excellent Piece of the *Wisdom* of Faith. We should not *doubt* our being Believers, because Unbelief *works* in us; but rise up as such, in a holy Indignation against this great Sin. This easily-besetting Sin, that robs God of his Glory, as our great SAVIOUR; and as of our Comfort in his great Salvation. Though, Thanks to the God of all Grace! it cannot rob us of our Interest in *him,* and his infinite Love and Care; nor seperate us one Moment from his tender Regard: However frequently it may suggest to *Sion's Children,* that *Sion's* GOD hath *forgotten* and *forsaken* them.--Be of good Cheer, my Brother; *Christ* lives for you and in you; and *you* shall live in and with *him,* both in Grace and Glory.—*Peace be unto you.*—In the Bowels of Jesus Christ, I am, dear Sir,

Your most tenderly,

———— ————

LETTER XXXI.

To Mrs. C------pe.

My very dear Sister in the Lord,

I Sympathize with you in your long Affliction; be of good Cheer: It is the Fruit of your Father's Love. It springs from Love, it shall be managed by Love, and it shall end in Love to your dear Soul. Your sweet Lord Jesus will be with you, now you are passing through the *Waters* of

Affliction; and the *Rivers* shall not overflow you. Surely in the *Floods of great Waters,* your *Sins* shall not come *nigh* you, In the Imputation of their Guilt, nor in their deserved Punishment. Upon Christ, your Surety, God the Father laid all your Iniquity; and your dying Lord, by giving himself a Sacrifice in your Stead, hath forever make an End of your *Sin.* Even *yours,* who have fled for *Refuge* as a perishing *Sinner.* To the once-bleeding *Saviour,* to lay hold on *him,* that glorious *Hope* set before you in the Gospel. *Christ,* your *Passover,* was sacrificed for *you.* And *God,* even your Father, beheld the *bleeding Lamb,* was satisfy'd for your Sins, and hath removed them as far from you, as the *East* is from the *West;* and is and will be unto you, *the God of Peace.* All is *Peace,* my dear Sister, between *God* and *you* in Christ. There is no *Wrath* in your present Cup of Affliction; nor shall the *Wrath to come* ever touch you. *Christ* is an *Hiding-place* to you, from that *Wind,* a secure *Covert* from that *Tempest.* And as *Rivers of Water,* will your *Jesus* be unto you in a *dry Place;* in your Passage thro' this Wilderness, this Vale of Tears.—Go fearless then, with your *own Lord Jesus,* through all the Afflictions of *Life;* yea, thro' *Death* itself, when he calls you to pass thro' that dark Valley, to the Mount of eternal Life and Glory. For lo, *the eternal* GOD *is your Refuge; and underneath are the everlasting Arms!* Since God the Saviour is your Refuge, my Sister, you shall be well defended. Since his everlasting Arms are underneath you, they'll support you well. They'll bear you up under pressing Griefs, and raise you to Joys and Glories, where Sorrows and Miseries cannot come.—I rejoice to hear, that you are resolved to *rest on Christ.* And well you may, my dear Sister, rest all you *Weight* as a poor *Sinner,* upon Christ the great *Saviour,* as the Building rests upon the Foundation: For the *Rock of Ages,* can never sink beneath you. It is safe venturing into *Eternity,* upon *Christ,* that *sure Foundation* which God hath laid in *Sion.* It is an impossible, that any one Soul should *perish,* that rests on *Jesus,* as that *God* himself should be *unfaithful;* who hath said, that *he that believeth on* Christ, *shall not be ashamed.*—Glad should I be, my dear Sister, if the Lord would please to rebuke your Illness, and to restore you to us again. But if the Time is come, for you to be taken up to the blest Assembly above, your Happiness will be ineffably greater. To be *with Christ,* bless'd with the immediate Vision of his Face, and a full

Conformity to his Image, is *far, far better! Glory, Glory* dwelleth in *Emanuel's Land!* We that are left behind, shall soon follow you, and with all the Lord's Redeemed, shall join in Hallelujahs unto God and the Lamb forever and ever.—Into the Arms of *Jesus* I commit you; who will *never, never, leave* you, *nor forsake* you: Who will not *fail* you, when Friends, and earthly Comforts cannot *help* you. No, Cisterns of Creature-Comforts are *dry,* and can't afford you one *Drop* in your greatest *Need;* then will the LORD be unto you, a *Fountain* of Life and Joy; the *Strength* of your *Heart,* and your *Portion forever!*—In *him,* my dear Sister, I am

Yours most Affectionately,

——— ———

LETTER XXXII.

To Mr. W------rd.

My very dear Brother in Christ,

I Thank you for your Letter, the Lord made it a Blessing to me, a Means to excite my Joy in him and Thanksgiving to him, to humble me before him, and to strengthen my Hand in his Work. Indeed the Lord hath done, and doth great Things for *me,* to shew his great Grace to the *Chief* of *Sinners:* And unto *him* be great and eternal Glory!

I sympathize with you, my dear Brother, in your present Temptations; altho', I have not been try'd in those Particulars. Having felt the Power and Pain of Temptations in other Respects, I can compassionate you, under your particular Exercises. The *same Afflictions* which every Child of God meets with, as to his particular Temptations, are accomplish'd in some or other of his *Brethren which are in the World.* And though every particular *Temptation* is not felt by every particular *Saint;* yet Temptations of all *Kinds* are cast among the Members of Christ as a collective *Body:* Whence all the Members from their own particular Experience, have a kindly Sympathy with each other in their particular Trials: And a *Collection,* an *All* of Temptations, was painfully felt by *Christ,* the dear *Head* of the Church; to fit him for a most intense

Sympathy with every of his *particular Members,* in every of their *particular Temptations;* himself having felt the *same:* Whence, from a Sea of flowing Compassions, an Infinity of yerning Bowels in his Heart, he affords them suitable Succour in every Time of Need. *He was tempted in all Points like as we are,* And *in that he himself hath* thus, *suffered, being tempted, he is able* thus *to succour them that are tempted.*—Be of good Cheer, my dear Brother, your compassionate Jesus, feels your Sorrows, and makes them his own by Sympathy; will support you under, do you good by, and deliver you from your present Distresses.—Flee to *Christ,* your Hiding-place from the Wind of Temptation; tell him how hard it blows upon you: And in infinite Grace, he will open his Bosom for your Relief, covert you in himself from the Storm, and cause you to take deeper Root through these Shakings, by which Satan wou'd tear you up from your Standing in Christ, and in the Truth as it is in Jesus. Venture to fight with Satan in your *own* Strength, nor with your *own* Weapons: But flee to the LORD your *Strength,* your *very present Help in Trouble,* and ask for Weapons out of his Armoury. And thus, *commit the Keeping of your Soul to Jesus;* and your Temptations shall *end well;* for the Glory of your Lord, the Captain of your Salvation, and for the special Advantage of your saved Soul. Flee as a feeble Creature in yourself, to the LORD the Rock of Ages, in whom is *everlasting Strength:* And as an *Inhabitant of the Rock,* you shall, yea, you may even now, *sing* a Triumph over all your Enemies, and say, *O my Soul, thou hast trodden down Strength: I am more than a Conqueror thro' him that hath loved me.*—Have you heard Christ's *Voice,* my Brother, and been drawn by his Grace and Power to follow him, to cleave to him, to commit yourself to him as a perishing Sinner, to be saved by him with a free, a full, an everlasting Salvation? Be well persuaded, from the Assurance given you by his sacred Word, that he gives unto you *eternal Life,* that you shall never *perish,* and that none shall *pluck you out of his Hand,* John x. 28. Strive they may, strive they will, even all the Powers of Darkness within and without you. But *alas!* for *them*, all *Hail* to *you!* They come too *late* to destroy you. The precious hands of Jesus, the strong Hands of his omnipotent Grace and Covenant-Faithfulness, in which you are inclos'd, do well secure you from the most cruel Efforts of your strongest Enemies.

Think it not strange, my Brother, that such Winds of *false Doctrine* are suffer'd to blow upon the People of God at this Time, and such fierce Winds of *Temptation* to assail them thereby. For whenever our Lord hath done, or is about to do great things for his Church, or for particular Souls, by the Holy Ghost, the Spirit of *Truth;* the Enemy Satan, the Spirit of *Error,* hath always done, and will do his utmost, to reproach and oppose the Work of the Lord, the Friend of Sinners. But not a Soul shall be shaken *off* from the Foundation *Christ,* that was ever built upon him; nor a Man *fall* from the *Doctrines* of Jesus, that independent on his own Wisdom and Strength, commits himself to the great Prophet and Head of the Church, and humbly waits upon the Lord for his Teachings to be given him, and his Power to rest upon him.

It is no new Thing, dear Sir, that those Persons you hint at, strive to draw us off from the *Truth* that we have heard and learned as it is in *Jesus;* by suggesting, "That it is but *Notion,* that we have received it by *Education,* from *Men, &c.* And are too full of our *own Wisdom,* as they call it."—For this has all along been the Way of those who would advance Errors, thus to endeavour to loosen Persons from the Truth, from the Doctrines of Christ, which they have been taught and receiv'd, and to make them become plain, simple Souls, like a blank Piece of Paper; that so they might be the more fit for them to write, or impress what Errors they please upon them. This is a great part of the *Subtilty* of the *old Serpent,* and one of the cunning *Sleights* of erroneous Persons, whereby they lie in *wait to deceive* unwary, simple Souls.—A Privilege very great it is when the Children of God are filled with all *Knowledge,* and spiritual *Understanding,* when the *Word of Christ dwells in* them *richly,* and they are enabled to hold fast the *Things,* the Doctrines of *Faith,* which they have been *taught.* For such blessed Souls, not being *Children,* but *Men* in Understanding, are not easily *tossed to and fro, with every Wind of Doctrine,* rais'd by Satan, and cast thro' Men of corrupt Minds. They are not *Reeds* shaken with the *Wind;* but in the Strength of *Christ,* fix'd upon *him* the immoveable *Rock,* held in his Hand, girt about with his Omnipotence, they stand like so many *Pillars,* with his precious *Truths* inscrib'd upon them, to bear a publick Testimony for the same before all. And from *these,* the Enemies flee, upon *these* they despair getting Advantage. It is the *simple Souls,* that *believer every Word,* that become an easy Prey to *Seducers:* It is those they seek for; it is such they labour to bring all to be, whenever they come.—But blessed be God, he hath had a Remnant, and will have in every Age of the Church, who fill'd with the Spirit of Truth, shall successfully oppose the Spirit of Error, and all the Instruments of advancing the same, under all the various Forms, of its Appearance. And blessed are those happy Souls, who are honour'd of God to be the Lamb's Witnesses, to hold forth his glorious Truths, against the black Falshoods of the roaring Lion. Who seeks thereby to eclipse the Light of *Emmanuel's* Kingdom, and make it a Throne of Darkness, like his own. To rob *Sion's* King of the Glory of his Crown; and his happy Subjects of their Obedience of Faith here, and so of their Crown of Glory with him hereafter. Altho, the unhappy Instruments made use of by the Prince of Darkness, may be *ignorant* of the *Depths of Satan,* of his Designs therein.

And tho', my dear Brother, some of the *Lamb's Witnesses,* may as it were for a Moment, endure the Torture of some *shaking Thoughts,* some Hellish Suggestions, shot into their Minds with an impelling Force; yet using that Piece of their Armour, *All-Prayer,* and holding up *Christ,* the *Shield of Faith,* on every Side, they shall therewith be able to *quench the fiery Darts of the Wicked.* And their *tried Faith,* which stands it *out* against the most furious Assaults; shall be found unto *Praise, and Honourn and Glory at the Appearing of Jesus Christ.* And over-rul'd their Trials shall be, to fit them more for their *Work,* of Witness-bearing for Jesus, in the present State. *Out of Weakness,* they shall be *made strong, wax valiant in Fight, turn to Flight the Armies of the Aliens,* and be crown'd at last *Overcomers.*

Whatever, my dear Brother, the poor blind *Heathens* might advance, in their Study of natural *Philosophy,* "That the greatest Attainment of Mortals was, To contemplate on *Things,* and leave them in *Suspense,* as being certain of *Nothing:*"—It is far otherwise with discerning *Christians,* in their Knowledge of *Christ,* and Study of *Divinity:* The *Book of God,* teacheth those who are bless'd with the glorious *Light* of it, quite another Lesson.—Here, in God's blessed Book, we have a most certain Account of the Things of *Nature:* Of their Original, Use, and End. That they deriv'd their Being from the great Creator's Word; that they are for his Glory, and as upheld by his Hand, subserve his Designs; and that they shall be dissolved at the Time appointed.—And in the Book of God, the Things of *Religion,* both natural and reveal'd, are display'd with the greatest Certainty and the brightest Glory.—Here the Being and Perfections of *God,* with the Worship due to him by his rational *Creatures,* as Things of the greatest Certainty, do shine most conspicuously.—And here also, the Revelation of *God in Christ,* and the Obedience due to him by *Christians,* are display'd with infallible Certainty, and shine with a peculiar and all-transcendent Glory. The Things of God, as the greatest Realities, dart upon us thro' his written Word, with an all-convincing and infinite Brightness. Here, in the blessed Gospel, the *Glory of God in the Face of Jesus Christ,* shines radiantly. The Glory of his Essence, of his Attributes, of his Persons, of his Counsels, of his Acts and Works of Grace, of his Means and Ends, in the Salvation of his People from all Sin and Misery, unto all Holiness and Glory: With the great and ineffable Things which God hath prepar'd for those that wait for him, both in the present and future World; and also, the sweet and strong Obligations to Duty and Gratitude which saved Souls are laid under, by the Love, Grace and Mercy of God their Saviour: As their present Privilege, and in order to their future Crown: All these, my Brother, as the greatest Realities, as infallible Certainties, from divine Authority, with an infinite Glory and Soul-transforming Energy, are presented unto us in the *Glass* of the *Gospel.*

And to suit a divine and supernatural *Revelation,* a special and divine *Faith,* or a *Faith of the Operation of God,* is given. Which is every Way fitted as a spiritual Eye, to converse with spiritual Objects, and is the Soul'd supernatural Capacity, to take in supernatural *Glories,* as infallible *Certainties,* in all the bright Forms of their Appearance, as they stand forth to be beheld in the divine *Revelation,* while a divine *Light,* by the Spirit of the Lord irradiates it.

Hence, *Faith* is said to be *The Substance of Things hoped for, the Evidence of Things not seen,* Heb. xi. 1. The *Things hoped for,* the *Things not seen,* are the *Things,* the invisible *Glories,* the infallible *Certainties* of a divine and supernatural *Revelation.* And these a supernatural and divine *Faith,* beholds and receives, according to their Presentation in the Gospel, as most *substantial:* Or, Faith gives a *Substance* to those Things in the Mind, which are declar'd in the Gospel to be greatest *Realities.* It doth as it were give *Being* to the Things hoped for, in the Soul, which are declar'd by the Word of God, to have the most solid and permanent *Being* in themselves. Faith makes them *Substance,* not *Shadow,* a mere *Phantasm,* or Appearance. And Faith is the *Evidence of Things not seen:* Of Things declar'd by the Word of God, which are not otherwise to be known; of Things hidden from the *Heathen* World, and from natural Men, in the nominal *Christian* World too; of Things past, present, or to come, that have not a present Appearance in themselves, or to the Views of *Sense;* but had, or shall have a real *Existence,* according to the Declarations made concerning them in the *Book of God.* Faith sees Things as they are there presented, and saith as God saith. Such and such Things have been, are, or shall be, saith *God:* Such and such Things have been, are, or shall be, says *Faith:* I see the Things which God hath spoken, they stand forth to my View, in their own Self-evident Light. Thus *Faith* is the *Evidence* of Things to the Mind, which are not at present *seen,* either by natural or spiritual *Sense.*—And as *great* an Evidence Faith is to the *Mind,* not to say a *greater,* of Things not *seen,* as the Eye is to the *Body,* of things *perceptible* to it, when *present* before it. When a Man by the Eye of his Body, *sees* the Sun in its own Light; he hath thereby the most demonstrative *Evidence* that there is a *Sun,* and that it *shines,* and needs not another to acquaint him therewith. So when a Man by the Eye of Faith, *sees* Christ the Sun of Righteousness in his own Light, in the *Light* of his *Word* and *Spirit;* he hath the greatest *Demonstration* in himself, that there is such a Person as the *Christ of God, the only begotten of the Father, full of Grace and Truth,* when he thus *beholds his Glory;* and needs not, under this Consideration, that another inform him thereof, but can join with the Apostles and primitive Saints, and say, *We see,* (I *see*) *Jesus.* And thus the *Things* of Christ, the Truths, the Doctrines, of Jesus, are beheld in the same *Light.* In the Light of *Christ* by his Holy *Spirit,* cast upon the Soul thro' the written *Word,* they are view'd, receiv'd, and evidenc'd to by *Faith;* as Things of the greatest *Reality,* of infallible *Certainty*, and of infinite *Glory.*

Now then, my dear Brother, to close up all briefly: Hath not the *Gospel* of Christ come unto *you,* not in *Word* only, but in *Power,* and in the *Holy Ghost,* and in much *Assurance?* Hath not the *Person of Christ,* in all his Glory and Fulness, as the only and all-sufficient Saviour, been reveal'd in, and made exceeding precious to you, as a perishing Sinner? And han't you felt an Heart-alluring, a Soul-overcoming Power attend the Moment of Discovery, by which you was sweetly and strongly drawn, to give up *yourself* entirely unto Christ, and to take *him,* and *God* in him, for your present and eternal ALL? And han't the *Truths,* the Doctrines of *Jesus,* been known, felt and tasted by you, in their Glory, Power, and Sweetness? Han't the *Things of Christ,* declar'd in the written *Word*, been reveal'd in you by the *Spirit*, and receiv'd and enjoy'd by *Faith,* with ineffable Delight, as Things of the greatest *Reality?* And have not the *Things not seen,* the *Things hoped for,* the Glories reserved for you in Heaven, been *realiz'd* and *evidenc'd* unto you? Han't they been made to you, *Substance,* and not *Shadow, Entity,* and not *Fancy?* Yea, han't you had a sweet *Foretaste* of that everlasting *Feast* which awaits you; by which its *Reality,* and Part of its ineffable *Glory,* have been initially *known* by you? And have you not receiv'd a most sure *Earnest* of your *Inheritance in Light;* a Part of the Whole, whereby the Whole hath been initially *possest* by you, and forever *ascertained* unto you? I am persuaded, my Brother, that you can give a positive Answer to these Queries; and that the *Torture* your Soul feels by the Rack of Temptations, upon which you are at present stretch'd, proceeds from your *Interest* in the *Things* of Christ, and your *Union* to *Him,* as your *Life,* your *Bliss,* your *All in All.* You wou'd easily *part* with what was not *dear* to you, and give up *that* you cou'd *live* without. But in these plundering, racking temptations, the Enemy would rob you of your *Substance,* and rend away your *Life,* which puts your Soul to *Pain.* But be of good Cheer; he is come too *Late* to gain his Ends. You have said, can, and shall say, with *Peter,* when ask'd if he and the rest of the twelve Disciples would go away from Christ? *Lord unto whom shall we* (shall I) *go? Thou hast the Words of eternal Life.* And tho' for a while, the Tempter may be suffer'd to stretch you as it were to the *Utmost:* Yet he shall not be able to *seperate* you from *Christ,* from the *Love of God,* nor from any of its glorious *Fruits,* prepar'd for, and secur'd unto you in *him.* The Bands, the Ties, the Ligaments by which *you* are fastned to you *Head* and *Saviour,* can never be *broken.* And, *After you have suffer'd awhile the God of all Grace, the God of Peace, will bruise Satan under your Feet, and perfect, stablish, strengthen and settle you.*—That this *Thorn in the Flesh,* this *Messenger of Satan sent to buffet* you, may be speedily remov'd and call'd off from you; and till then, that the *Grace of Christ may be sufficient for* you, and his *Strength* made perfect in your *Weakness:* So prays, my dear Brother,

Yours most tenderly in the LAMB'S *Bowels,*

______ _____

LETTER XXXIII.

To Mr. *P------ll.*

My Dear Brother in Christ,

SINCE as a poor *Sinner.* You would always be looking to, and loving of the *Savior:* will you not love him as your *King*, as well as your Priest and Prophet? Will not my dear Brother love the *Law* of Christ? You well know that our loving Lord hath said, *If ye love* ME, *keep my Commandments.* And the *Words* which he *spake,* he tells us, were not *His* (that is, not Originally, or only) *but the Father's which sent* him. The *Law of Moses,* the moral Law, as a Covenant of Works, did indeed bring into *Bondage.* But since Christ was made under it, and fulfill'd it for us, and has given it to us as the *Rule* of our Obedience; it is become *The perfect Law of Liberty:* And is of great, and perpetual Use to Believers: To shew us what is Duty, and what is Sin, to oblige us to the one, and to deter us from the other. The *moral Law* in the Hand of *Christ,* as given from the King of Saints to be a *Rule of Life,* to square our Actions by; is so far from bringing Believers into *Bondage;* that the more our Hearts and Lives are conform'd thereto, the more abundant, the more glorious is our *Liberty,* as the *Sons of God.* The *Law* to its Perfection, was in Christ's *Heart:* The *Law* to its Perfection, was in his *Obedience.* And the more we are conformed unto *Christ,* the more conformable shall we be in Heart and Life to the *Law of God.* And when made perfect in *Holiness,* we shall be perfectly conformed unto God's *holy Law.* And to a blest Eternity, shall *love the Lord our God with all our Heart, Soul and Strength, and our Neighbour as ourselves:* which is the *Sum* and *Substance* of the Law's Requirement. So long as the *Relation subsists* between the *Creator* and his *Creatures* of the Relational Kind, between the *Lord* and his *People,* between the *Saviour* and the *saved Ones;* I am persuaded, that the *moral Law* will *abide,* and be delightfully *obey'd,* by perfect Saints and Angels, in Bliss unknown, unto Ages without End.

The *Bible,* my dear Brother, that blessed Book, is indeed the *Book* of Books, and ought to be our chief Study. But let us not reject *other* Books, or neglect the reading of those wrote by Men, taught of God, and *mighty in the Scriptures.* We can't do this, without doing that which is forbidden in *God's Book:* viz. Without *quenching of the Spirit,* and *despising Prophecyings.* We can't neglect the reading of *such* Books of human Composure, which the Lord affords his People in this Day of glorious Light; without slighting of those *Gifts,* which the ascended Saviour gives unto his Church, for the Edification of his body, and neglecting the *Means* which the Lord affords us, of understanding his Mind in his own unerring Book. I look upon it to be one of *Satan's Devices,* to draw Men off from reading of Human Writings, by the specious Pretence of preferring the sacred Writings above all: That thereby, the Truths reveal'd, and the Errors discover'd in the Holy Scripture, might not be so fully *known,* as they are when the Scriptures are *expanded,* and consistently *open'd,* by Men that are gifted of the Lord to be Teachers of his People. And therefore, as it concerns Christ's Honour, and our own Edification, it is the Wisdom of Saints, not to be *ignorant* of this Device, nor *caught* in this Snare which is laid for their Taking.—That the *Holy Ghost the Comforter, may guide you into all Truth,* and give you Fellowship with the same, unto your present Joy, and future Glory: is the sincere Desire of, dear Sir,

Your affectionate Friend and
Servant in the LORD,

———— ————

LETTER XXXIV.

To Mr. L------s.

My dear Brother in our precious Lord,

YOURS I receiv'd, in which I perceive the kind Dealings of the Prince of Grace with you. In that having lov'd and bought you with his Blood, he resolves to have *all your Heart.* And therefore takes, and tears away your *Idols* from you.—Oh, my dear Brother, What Matter of Lamentation is it, that ever our wretched Hearts should slip away from CHRIST, that incomparably *fair,* that *altogether lovely* ONE! Whose *Love,* as well as Loveliness, is immensely *great,* and far surpasseth *Knowledge!* So *great a Lover,* as the LORD our Maker! And so *great a Love,* as to give his Life for Creatures, for Sinners, for Enemies, for such Wretches, who were brimful of Enmity against him: To espouse them to himself, and make them happy in, and glorious with him for ever! Oh *what Love, what Duty,* should such a *Lover,* and such a *Love* command from us, *the Beloved of the* LORD! How *great* is that Debt of Love and Loyalty, which the LORD'S *Redeemed,* owe to the LORD-*Redeemer!*—And yet, *Hear O Heavens, and be astonished O Earth!* We, even we who are married unto the LORD, and have been ineffably happy in the Enjoyment of his Love; are *bent to backslide from him, and to go after other Lovers!—Melt,* Oh our hard *Hearts!* Be *asham'd* and *confounded,* Oh our ungrateful *Souls!* And turn ye to the LORD with *Weeping,* and with *Supplication;* for still he will be *gracious!* Oh my dear Brother, our Lord *knew* that we would deal *very treacherously;* he knew *beforehand,* how rebellious and ungrateful we should prove: And yet he resolv'd to *die for us;* tho' he *foresaw,* that we should *little regard* his dying Love!—"Oh unheard-of *Lover!* Oh *Love* unknown! Woo us, win us to thyself! And change us into thy Love-Image! Lord, we can't *bear* to be thus ungrateful! And yet, alas! we *can!* Help *ourselves,* we cannot: Our Help is in THEE! Love us into *Love,* and *Thine* we will be for Ever!"

Oh my Brother, The Love of CHRIST *suits us.* It is the Love of the LORD! Which is Free without Motives! Great, without Measure!

Constant, without Change! Lasting without End! A Sin-pardoning, a Sin-subduing, an All-conquering, a Grace-giving, a Glory-bestowing LOVE! That will live and triumph in all its immense Glories, in our full Salvation and perfect Bliss, unto Ages without End!—Our Dear Lord, did not set *his Love* upon us, to leave us in *our Unloveliness.* No; CHRIST *loved the Church, and gave himself for it: That he might sanctify and cleanse it with the Washing of Water by the Word, That he might present it to himself a glorious Church, not having Spot or Wrinkle, or any such Thing; but that it should be Holy and without Blemish,* Eph. v. 25, 26, 27. The LORD our Lover, did not set his Love upon us and chuse us, because in his Foreview, we *were,* or *would be holy,* of and from *ourselves;* but that we *should be so,* in and from HIM. And well able is the Love of CHRIST, to go on with this glorious Design of his Heart, to *sanctify us throughout,* or to make us *glorious in Holiness;* because it is *strong Love!* Strong, infinitely strong, to pass by innumerable Provocations! And to overcome all Opposition! Oh my Brother, the whole *Weight* of our Sanctification, *rests* upon CHRIST'S *Love,* his Covenant-engaged Love! This solid Basis, bears the Building. And this glorious Power, will bring forth the Top-Stone.—Well, as you said, may we take Courage, that trust in JESUS; since HE has done all *for us,* and will do all *in us.*—Let us stand to our Arms, and in the Name of the LORD, set up our Banners against the Powers of Darkness. Our Captain will beat down our Foes before us; and crush all his and our Enemies, under his and our Feet. That mighty Love, which has made Sin a *Burden* to us; will free us from the Burden of *Sin.*—And let us tell other Souls, for their Encouragement, That the SAVIOUR can *love Sinners,* and that there is not a Soul in the World, that casts itself upon the SAVIOUR'S *Love,* for all Salvation; but shall, in *boundless, Love,* be saved by HIM to the uttermost! From the deepest Misery to the highest Glory, from the utmost of its Fears, and to the utmost of its Desires! Yea, unto such Heights of Glory, which Eye hath not seen, nor Heart conceiv'd!—Be strong, my Brother, be strong and fear not. JESUS *loves you:* And *that's enough.* The whole of our Salvation and Happiness is in it. You need not go out of the Love of CHRIST, from the Bosom of your Beloved, for one Moment's Deliverance from Misery, nor for one Moment's Enjoyment of Felicity. You have *All* in

HIM who is *your* ALL! Wherefore see that you live upon him as *such. Delight yourself in the* LORD: *And* HE *shall give you the Desires of your Heart.* And let every Soul, espoused to CHRIST, say,

"Why should my foolish Passions *rove!*
Where can such *Sweetness* be,
As I have tasted in *thy Love?*
As I have found in THEE!"

Great Grace be with you!—Pray for me.—That you more and more, *May be able to comprehend with all Saints what is the Breadth and length, and Depth and Height: And to know the Love of* CHRIST, *which passeth Knowledge, that you may be filled with all the Fulness of* God! is the earnest Desire of, dear Sir,

Your most affectionate Friend and Servant,
In our Fairest, Dearest, Sweetest LORD JESUS,

——— ———

LETTER XXXV.

To Mr. C------ns.

My dear Brother,

THE *Work* of God upon your Soul, appears to me very clear and full. But perhaps you mayn't have such clear Apprehensions, about the *Time* when the Power of God first wrought on your Heart. Several of God's dear Children begin to date their Conversion *later,* than the real Date of it is. This proceeds from an Apprehension, that the Soul's Conversion to God, begins at the Time when divine Consolations first overflow the Heart, and give the Soul Assurance of its Interest in the Lord Jesus. This being so sensibly sweet to the Soul, is remarked by it, for the *Day of God's Power.* And so indeed it may and ought, in regard of its being the more *full* and *sensible* Display of it; and the Time when the Soul is more *fully* and *sensibly* brought out of *Darkness, into God's marvellous Light.* But when *this* is so *fix'd,* for the Day of God's Power upon the Soul, as to *overlook* all the Operations thereof that went *before,* as *preparatory* to this; we have not so *full* an Apprehension of the Lord's

Work upon us, nor give him the *full Glory* of his saving Operations, as we should.

You say, my dear Brother, "That some Time after you was convinc'd of the Doctrines of the Gospel, you did not know God, experimentally." And yet tell me, a little lower, "That in the whole Course of this Exercise (wherein you was convinc'd of, and disputed for the Doctrines of Grace) you plainly saw your *Fall from God by Nature;*" or were convinc'd of your miserable State. This, my Brother, was a glorious *Effect* of God's saving Power, working upon your Heart.—In your former Letter, you told me, "That God had awakened you to *adore* Free-Grace, and the Mystery of electing Love; &c."

Now be pleas'd to consider, there is a vast Difference, between a *Conviction* of the Doctrine of Grace in the *Head,* and an *adoring* the Grace of that Doctrine in the *Heart.* The first usually goes before, and there seems to be a Necessity that it should, in order to the other. For the Understanding must first *know* the Truth, before the Will can *embrace* it.—A *speculative* Knowledge of the Truth, that goes no further than a mere outward *Notion* of it; may be found in a *natural Man.* This *Knowledge* of the Truth, is a *cold, unaffecting,* and *unattracting* Knowledge; that leaves the Will and Affections just where it found them. A natural Man, indeed, may have some *natural Pleasure,* in getting some *new Notions* of Truth; but no *Soul-Attraction* to the *Things* known, doth he experience thereby.—And however natural Notions of Gospel-Truths, may be *subservient* to a spiritual Knowledge of them; yet is a spiritual Discernment of the Things contain'd in those Notions, very *different* from a bare speculative Knowledge of them. In that, in the *one,* a mere empty Notion of the Truth, floats in the *Head;* which effects only an outward *Adherence* to it. But in the *other,* the Glory of Truth shines into the *Mind;* which produces a sweet and strict Adherence thereto, by all the inward *Powers* of the Soul. The Understanding *discerns* the Truth, in its Beauty, Glory and Excellency; the Judgment *approves* it; and the Will and Affections, *embrace,* and *clasp* about it. In a Word, the whole Soul, *unites* with the Truth, and is *chang'd* into the Image of it. And this you may see from two Texts. That the Truth shines into the *Mind,* in order to a spiritual *Understanding* thereof, see,

2 Cor. iv. 6. *For God who commanded the Light to shine out of Darkness, hath shined in our Hearts, to give the Light of the Knowledge of the Glory of God, in the Face of Jesus Christ.* Oh, when the least Beam of Light, the least Ray of any Gospel-Truth in particular, or of the Truth of the Gospel, the Way of Salvation by Jesus Christ, in general, shines in upon the *Mind,* with such a ravishing Beauty, and majestick Glory, that draws the Heart to *love it,* and makes the Soul *bow down before it:* This is a *saving Illumination,* a new Creation Light, set up in the Soul of a Vessel of Mercy, which is the very *Beginning* of its future Glory. It is God's *commanding the Light,* the Light of Life, spiritual and eternal, to shine out of spiritual *Darkness;* as in the first Creation, he *commanded the Light* natural, to shine out of natural *Darkness:* Or, it is God's *shining into our Hearts,* by a new creating Efficacy, to *give the Light,* not only of the *Knowledge* of God, but of the *Glory* of God, in the Face of Jesus Christ. Which Word imports, The ravishing *Beauty,* and All-attracting *Efficacy* of Gospel-Grace, darting in upon the Mind by a supernatural Revelation, which *unite* the Soul to the *Things* beheld, to the *Objects* revealed. This internal Revelation of Gospel-Truth, unites the Soul to the Things, the Objects reveal'd, in regard of *Approbation;* and sets it all in Motion, in regard of *Desire,* after the full Enjoyment of them, the nearest Coalition with, and most complacent Rest in them. And therefore, upon this *Hearing,* and *Learning* of the Father, the Soul *cometh* unto Christ. As,

John vi. 45. *It is written in the Prophets, and they shall be all taught of God. Every Man therefore that hath heard and learned of the Father, cometh unto me.* This *Hearing, and Learning of the Father,* is the same with his *shining into our Hearts, to give the Light of the Knowledge of the Glory of God, in the Face of Jesus Christ.* And from this saving *Illumination,* the Soul feels a sweet and strong *Attraction;* by which, being *drawn* with Cords of Love, it *cometh unto Christ.* First, in its *Desires* after him, as beheld, *altogether lovely!* Before it comes to him in the *Assurance of Faith,* to take up its Rest in him, and say, *My Lord, and my God!* The *first* of these, is true, saving *Faith,* as well as the *latter.* They are but different *Degrees* of the same *precious Faith,* which cleaves to, and clasps about the *precious* SAVIOUR. The first may *be,* where the latter is *not,* or is in a great

Measure *wanting*.—And the latter being more *sweet* and *joyous,* a more *sensible* Experience of divine Power on the Heart, and a more *full* Exercise of Faith on Christ; God's dear Children, do frequently date their Conversion from the *latter,* and too much overlook the *former.*—But wherever the Truths of the Gospel are *known,* and those in particular, which more immediately concern the Salvation of the Soul; and *so* known, in their Beauty and Excellency, as to *knit* and *unite* the Heart to them; or to draw out the Soul into *Desires* after, and *Adoration* of the Glories beheld, God in Christ, as the God of Grace and Peace, thro' a bleeding Jesus: That Man, *is a regenerate Man,* a *converted Man;* altho' he han't arriv'd to such a Degree of *Faith on the Son of God,* as to say, *Who loved me, and gave himself for me.* For the *Desires* of the Soul, *cleaving* to God in Christ, as the God of all Grace: are an Evidence, that the Soul is *turned* from Sin and Satan, from Self and the Law; or brought out of the State of *Nature's Darkness,* into the *marvellous Light of Gospel Grace:* In which *alone,* Salvation by Jesus Christ, is *discern'd, approv'd,* and *adher'd* to.

Now then, my dear Brother, consider, when you was *convinc'd* of the Doctrine of Original *Sin,* and Man's *Insufficiency;* did your *Convictions* thereof, reach no further than a bare empty *Notion* of these Truths, which floated in your *Head,* with respect to Men in *general?* Or did they reach *yourself,* and shew you that this was your *own Case* in *particular?* However the Beginning of your Convictions might reach your *Head* only; I believe they reach'd your *Heart* in the latter End of them. Else you could not say, 'That in the whole Course of this Exercise, you plainly saw your *Fall,* (your *own* Fall) from God by Nature.'—And when you was convinc'd of your own Misery by *Sin,* and Insufficiency to *help* yourself; you may observe, That you was remov'd from *Nature's Bottom,* from Self-dependance, and doing for Life. And when this is the Case with any Soul, if another *Foundation* was not laid for it to *rest on,* it would utterly *sink.*

Again, consider, when you was convinc'd of imputed *Righteousness;* was your Conviction hereof a mere empty *Notion* in your *Head,* that there was such a *Thing,* such a Provision of Grace made for the Salvation of *some?* Or did it reach *yourself* in particular, and shew you, that *you* must be sav'd in *this Way,* if ever you was sav'd at *all?* How did your Heart *behave* toward the Righteousness of Christ, when you was doctrinally convinc'd of it? Did you ever *see* any Beauty, Excellency and Glory in it? Did your Heart ever *fall down* before the Majesty of it; and *desire* for yourself, that you might be *found in Christ, and in his Righteousness alone, not having on your own Righteousness!* If *so,* the Conviction which you then had of imputed Righteousness, was *saving:* Or, a glorious *Effect* of the almighty Power of divine Grace, working upon your *Soul,* for your *everlasting Salvation:* Altho' you might not have a comfortable *Knowledge,* that the Righteousness of Christ *was yours,* until some Time afterward. Until the Time you date your Conversion from, when you could willingly have *departed to be with Christ:* Which must proceed from a comfortable *Persuasion* of your *Interest* in him.

But whether your Apprehensions about the *Time* of the Lord's first working upon your Heart, may be *clear* and *distinct,* or not: This may be Matter of Joy to you, that you can say, with the Man whose Eyes Christ had opened, *One Thing I know, that whereas I was blind, now I see,* John ix. 25.—And that your dear Soul continually may grow in Grace, and in the Knowledge of CHRIST, until that which is in *Part* is done away, and that which is *perfect* shall come: When you shall *know,* even as you are *known;* is the earnest Desire of, dear Sir,

Your tender Friend, in the Bowels of JESUS CHRIST,

——— ———

LETTER XXXVI.

To Mr. L------s.

Dear Brother,

I Thank you for your last kind Letter. I embrace the first Opportunity to answer it. I sympathize with you in the Bowels of JESUS CHRIST. Be of good Cheer, my Brother. For tho' you are under a *Cloud;* the *Sun* will break out upon you *again.* And mean Time, *your* JESUS is still the *same,* in his Person, Love and Fulness; the same for *you* as ever. The Changes which pass over *you,* make no Alteration in HIM. HE is in *one Mind,* to love you for ever, and save you to the uttermost; and none can *turn him:* None of all your Enemies within, nor without you. *Your* JESUS, in all his Dispensations towards you, is always *loving* and *saving you.* HE is always doing you *Good,* even by the greatest *Evils* that pass over you. Wherefore, *rest* by Faith in his Love, Wisdom, Power and Faithfulness. *Commit yourself,* and all your *Concerns* to your dear LORD JESUS, that cares for you as his *own:* And all Things shall end *well.* CHRIST is *All* for you to GOD, the *Whole* of your Acceptance with the Father, when your inherent Grace and Holiness are at the greatest *Height.* And when these are at the lowest *Ebb;* CHRIST'S Acceptableness to GOD, and *yours* in HIM, abates not a *Whit.* The Acceptance of your *Person,* in the great Person and Obedience of God's *Beloved,* is an *Unchangeable, everlasting* Acceptance: That neither *rises,* nor *falls,* with the *Variation* of *your* Frames. You are *compleat in* CHRIST: Nothing is wanting *there,* to make you a *perfect Beauty* in the Eye of GOD; even *now,* tho' you are so *imperfect in yourself.* And CHRIST is about the Work of *perfecting you,* in your own Soul. From *his* perfect Beauty *imputed,* a Perfection of Beauty shall be *imparted. Your* JESUS, is made of GOD unto *you,* not only *Righteousness,* but *Sanctification:* The communicative Fountain of it: That will *fill* all the Cavities of your Heart, all the Powers and Faculties of your Soul, your whole Nature, *brimful, running-over full,* for evermore!—And when our dear LORD is about to *fill us,* to add new Measures, and bless us with greater Increases of Holiness, HE always *empties us;* shews our great Emptiness and Want. And then, with his own infinite Fulness, HE flows out upon us, in rich Supplies, unto Joy and Bliss, that Strangers intermeddle not with!—And so wonderfully doth our LORD Work, that he makes us *holy,* even by that *Withdraw* of the sensible Influence of his Holy Spirit, which is the greatest *Burden* that our Souls feel. That is, HE *over-rules* every Kind and Degree of Withdraw of Influence, with whatever of Weakness and Evil we see and feel in ourselves at such Seasons, to make us *more holy,* and *stronger in Grace,* when He returns again with the quickning, strengthening, sanctifying Influences of his blessed Spirit! HE that hath *begun* the good *Work* in us, will *perform it:* And in infinite Wisdom, carries it on by *Contraries.* By a Variety of Frames, a Variety of Experience is given us;

and a Variety of Grace, or the various Displays of Grace, according to the manifold Wisdom of GOD, shall be usher'd in upon us. All Things are under a Blessing to us. Let us therefore love and bless GOD in all. Let us *watch* against *Sin,* and especially that *great,* that *Flood-gate* Sin, that lets in all other upon us, *Unbelief.* Let us *follow* after Holiness, *dread* Distance from GOD, and a selfish, careless, lifeless Spirit in Religion. Let us be *diligent* and *Conscientious* in Duty, and in the Path Way thereof, believing on CHRIST daily, for fresh Supplies of Grace, let us *follow on to know the* LORD: *And we shall know* HIM.—*Great Grace be with you!* Pray for,

Yours affectionately in CHRIST,

______ ______

LETTER XXXVII.

To Mr. C------ns.

My very dear Brother in Christ,

YOURS, I gladly receiv'd, and thankfully acknowledge. Your Letter, thro' the Lord's Working, gave me much Satisfaction and Pleasure. I rejoice that my last was made sweet to your Soul, and convincing to your Mind, with respect to the Lord's saving Operations on your Heart, being somewhat *earlier* than you thought of. For which we both, will join in Thanksgiving, now and for evermore.

I don't wonder, my dear Brother, considering your Circumstances especially, that you did not so particularly *notice* the Manner and Time of those *first* gracious Operations which you happily *felt.* The LORD the Holy Ghost, in his saving Work of Grace on the Heart, in producing, maintaining and increasing the new Life, often works, as it were under Ground, out of our Sight. It is one Thing to *feel* special, gracious Operations; and another, to *know* that they are saving, and what Part of the Spirit's Work to refer them to. Thousands of his blessed Operations, we soon let *slip,* and *forget* what he hath wrought for us. And those we remember *best,* Alas! By reason of Weakness, we see not a Thousandth Part of their *Glory!* We view the Holy Ghost's Work on our Hearts now, as it were in *scatter'd Parcels,* here one Piece, and there another, and see but *little* of the Order, Beauty, Variety and Glory of his harmonious Operations. But when the Whole of his Work upon us in Grace, in order to our Meetness for Glory, is finish'd, and we brought into the Land of Rest; we shall with inconceivable Joy *remember, all the Way which the Lord led us thro' the Wilderness.* We shall see, as it were with *one View,* the *Whole* of his great Work upon us and for us, in the State and Majesty of a GOD! In which he all along wrought, thro' ten Thousand Difficulties and Contrarieties in his Way: And then shall give him the full Glory of all his Grace. According to the utmost Measure of our Creature Capacity; tho' infinite Love, in its deserved Glory, adequate to the Displays thereof, will for ever remain in its own exalted Sphere, *for above all our Blessing and Praise!*

When God had reveal'd CHRIST in you, my dear Brother, He brought you a *Cross* to bear. And much I rejoice, that he enabled you to *take it up.* Tho' to follow your Lord, was to be slighted, set at nought, and deserted by all; even by the strict, *Pharisaical* Part of Mankind, as well as by the profane World. Oh my Brother, the *Cross,* the Cross of CHRIST, few will bear it. How many are there, that are under good Impressions at Times, and have some mind to *Christ,* at least, to *eternal Life,* that lose their *Souls,* because they will not, cannot take up the *Cross!* To follow Christ fully, is to lose the Favour of the World wholly. To part with every Thing that is desirable to a carnal Heart: As, Riches, Honours, sinful Pleasures, Self-Righteousness, fleshly Wisdom, worldly Worship, Friends, Relations, yea, even one's own Life, (if call'd to it) to hate and despise even *that,* in Comparison of CHRIST. And *who,* oh *who* will do *this!* What, part with *all!* Be stript quite *naked,* and naked follow a *naked* Christ, in the Face of Scoffs and Scorns, Cruelty and Rage, from Men and Devils! Oh, who *can,* who *will* do this! *None* but those happy Souls, who are blest with an internal Revelation of the SAVIOUR'S Glory, and a Heart-Attraction unto him thereby. Oh none but *they,* that see the *Pearl of great Price,* to be of inestimable *Worth,* will part with *all,* to secure *that Pearl.* None but *they,* who see the Person, Love, and Glory of CHRIST, to be infinitely more Worth than *Thousands of Worlds!* Will part with this *one* silly World for HIM. And *they,* were there *Millions of*

Worlds, more glorious far, would part with *all,* for *one* JESUS, and run on crying, (as that dear Martyr in the Flames) '*None but* CHRIST! *None but* CHRIST!' Oh, none but CHRIST, can satisfy a Soul that is born from *Above.* And with the blessed Enjoyment of HIM, in whom all the Fulness of the GODHEAD dwells, shall every such Soul, be fully and eternally *satisfied.*

See you not then, my Brother, the rich, free, distinguishing Grace of God, in *revealing his Son in you,* and in attracting your Heart after him by the Cords of his Love, in the *Day of his Power.* So that you forsook *all,* for *one* CHRIST! Oh happy, happy, thrice happy Soul! *All hail!* CHRIST is *yours,* and you are *his!* You have Happiness, Joy and Security enough. A Bundle of Bliss, a Mass of Treasure, a Sea of Delights, enough to fill every Corner of your Soul, was it ten thousand thousand Times more capacious than it is, brimful, running-over full, of Joy and Glory, thro' Time and to Eternity, in your *one* LORD JESUS! Oh *possess* your Portion. *Live* upon your Heritage. It is wondrous *Great!* Behave as an *Heir of* GOD! And let this little, dirty World, which Mr. *Rutherford* calls, "The Clay-Portion of Bastards," be under your Feet.—And still, my dear Brother, delight to *deny yourself* in all Respects for CHRIST; and taking up your Lord's *Cross,* follow hard after him daily. His infinite Love and Power, will make it *sweet* and *easy.* And oh the *Crown,* the immortal Crown of Glory, that awaits Cross-bearers! *If any Man serves me,* says our Lord, *let him follow me;* (let him deny himself, and take up his Cross and come after me) *and where I am, there shall also my Servant be: If any Man serve me, him will my Father honour.* By and by, you shall *see* CHRIST *as he is,* and be *for ever with the Lord:* Where Crosses shall be no more, but Joy and Glory in endless Store! And oh, my dear Brother, the *Smart* of all you ever endur'd for Christ, will not only then be *over;* but the Remembrance of every Cross you endur'd well, will yield you an eternal *Pleasure,* in as much as thereby, you glorify'd your *Lord* on the Earth: Which will enhance your Joy, when glorify'd *with him* in Heaven. And oh, the beauteous, the fair Colours of Glory, which our Lord will lay upon his Followers *there,* the Stones of his holy Temple, who have been carv'd and meetned by the Cross of it *here,* Those, my Brother, are the most holy, happy Christians, the most God-honouring Souls, and the richest Heirs of endless Glory, that do and suffer *most* for CHRIST in the present State. And especially the *Sufferers:* For, *Blessed is the Man that endureth Temptation: for when he is tried, he shall receive the Crown of Life, which the Lord hath promis'd to them that love him.* Wherefore, be in *Love* with the Cross of Christ; and ask for Wisdom and Grace, to bear it after him continually, in the same *Spirit,* shewing forth all those *Graces,* which so gloriously shone, in the *meek* and *lowly* Son of God! And unto *you,* who thus *continue with him in his Temptations,* will he *appoint a Kingdom.* Unto *you,* as an *Overcomer,* will he *grant to sit with him in his Throne; even as he also overcame, and is set down with his Father in his Throne.*

A glorious Privilege, indeed it is, my Brother, that tho' you have so much *Sin* in you, it doth not *reign* over you. The Reign of Grace has destroy'd the Dominion of Sin, will still subdue its Power, and utterly extirpate its Being, in the Lord's Way and Time. Wherefore, go on to look to JESUS, as once made Sin for you. Who has overcome Sin in himself, and will overcome it in you. And *reckon yourself* continually, *to be dead indeed unto Sin, and alive unto God in Christ Jesus.* For a glorious Influence you will derive from thence, to mortify Sin, and quicken Grace in you.—I forgot you not before the Lord. Continue to remember me. I esteem it a Privilege. The Lord will hear you. I and others will fare the better for it: And you in no wise shall lose your Reward.—My dear Love to the Brethren, May a Spirit of Love, Humility and Meekness reign amongst them: And those that minister unto them of the Word of Life, be esteem'd very highly by them in Love, for their Work Sake!—I commit the keeping of your Soul to the great Shepherd. May he deliver you from every evil Work, and preserve you safe unto his heavenly Kingdom! The Lord make you a burning and a shining Light in this dark World! And grant you an exalted Sphere, among the starry Glories of the first Resurrection!—Most heartily I bid you *farewel* in the Lord! And am, dear Sir,

Yours most affectionately,

In our dear JESUS,

——— ———

LETTER XXXVIII.

To Mr. W------rd.

My dear Brother in Christ,

YOUR last kind Letter I receiv'd, and return you hearty Thanks.—I rejoice for the great Things which the LORD hath done for your Soul. In revealing his dear Son in you, and in giving you Freedom of *Access* to the Father, thro' him, by the Holy Spirit; of *Entrance* into the *holiest,* by the *Blood of Jesus.* Christ, indeed, a crucified Jesus, is the only *Way* to the Father. On this *new,* this *living Way, thro' the Vail of his Flesh!* It is thro' this *rent* Vail of his human Nature, thro' his Soul and Body being *rent* asunder for us on the Cross, that we have *Access to God.* Unto God as the God of Peace, as the God of all Grace, as the God and Father of Christ, and our God and Father in and thro' him. On this Way of Access, thro' a dying SAVIOUR, suits a *Sinner well.* It is a Way of Life to *us.* And blessed for ever be the Lord our God, it is a *consecrated Way.* A Way that is consecrated for *us,* sanctify'd, or set apart for *us,* to walk in. It is an *High-way,* an *holy Way,* yea, *the Way of Holiness;* that is holy to *God,* that is holy for *us,* that makes all *holy,* tho' the vilest of Sinners in themselves, that walk in it by Faith. It makes us holy *representatively;* it makes us holy *influentially.*—Go on, my dear Brother, to *walk* in this Way. God the Father, likes a Sinner *well,* that comes unto him, thro' the active and passive Obedience of his Law-fulfilling, and once-bleeding *Son.* He sees no *Spot* in that Man; but beholds him *all-fair;* wash'd from all Sin in the Redeemer's Blood, and richly array'd with the glorious Robe of his perfect Righteousness. And in infinite condescending Grace, he says unto him, *Come near now, and kiss me, my Son.* God the Father permits a *Sinner,* yea, calls him, to be *familiar* with him thro' the SAVIOUR. He owns him for his Son, smells the Smell of his Raiment, drest in the Garments of his elder Brother, blesseth him, and saith, *See, the Smell of my Son, is as the Smell of a Field which the* LORD *hath blessed.*—Thus the Chief of Sinners, that come unto God by Christ, are *welcom'd* into his Presence, *pleasing* to him, and *blessed* by him, with all spiritual and temporal Blessings, in Measure, Manner and Time, (as to their Communication *thro' Christ,* upon the Bottom of their eternal Preparation for us, and Bestowment upon us *in him)* according to the

Infinity of *Jehovah's Grace: Wherein he hath abounded towards us in all Wisdom and Prudence.*

And tho', my dear Brother, you and others are cast out of Mr. *W-------y's* Society, for saying, "That Christ loves you, and will love you to the End." And, "That all your Perfection is in Christ, and in him alone." Be not grieved at it; since Christ admits you into more intimate Fellowship with *Him,* than many of your Brethren are favour'd with. Yea, so far as you suffer for the *Truth* herein, for your Witness-bearing for Christ; *Rejoyce, and be exceeding glad: For great is your Reward in Heaven.*—And as thro' remaining Darkness, there are now unhappy Differences among the Saints; Rejoyce in Hope of that happy Day, when we shall all *see Eye to Eye.* When we shall *all come in the Unity of the Faith, and of the Knowledge of the Son of God, unto a perfect Man, unto the Measure of the Stature of the Fulness of Christ.* And *Know, as we are Known.*

A glorious Truth, and an unspeakable Privilege it is, That Christ *loves his Own,* and will love them unto the *End.* And blessed, O blessed is that Man, who is favour'd with the Witness of the Holy Spirit, as to his own *Interest* in the SAVIOUR'S *Love!* In his free, unchangeable and everlasting Love! Oh what a comfortless Doctrine is that, Of *Falling from grace!* Of *Losing our Interest in the Love of* JESUS! Oh was there a Possibility of this; what solid Peace, what strong Consolation could any Soul have, that sees his own Vileness and Weakness? His Iniquity, and Inability to keep *Himself* from falling?

Indeed we are bid to *keep ourselves in the Love of God,* Jude 21. But the *Love* of God here, respects his *manifestative* Favour, and not the Love of his *Heart.* Which stands immutably the *same* in Himself, upon the sovereign good Pleasure of his own Will, to love us, and is quite *independent* upon our Goodness.—And in this Love we are bid to keep *ourselves.* Not *efficiently;* That is *God's* Work. And so *we are kept by the Power of God, thro' Faith unto Salvation.* But *instrumentally;* As our Duty is hereby enjoin'd, of being diligent in the Use of all those appointed *Means,* thro' which the Lord is pleas'd to bless us with the fresh *Displays* of his everlasting Kindness.—And if we are negligent in the Use of Means, *if we walk not in his Statutes, and keep not his Commandments;* our Father will rebuke us with the *Hidings* of his Face, with the *Eclipses* of his infinite Favour. *Nevertheless his Loving-kindness, he will not take away:* His Heart-Love, his Covenant-Love, He will not infringe. No, the Love of his Heart, fixt on us in Christ, the Resolve of his Will, to be gracious to us thro' him, and his Covenant with us in him, *stand fast unto all Generations.* And blessed is the Soul, that *stands fast* in the *Faith* of that *Love,* which stands *firmer* than the *solid* Mountains, and the *lasting* Hills. That was *from* Everlasting in Commencement, and is *to* Everlasting, in Duration, without the least Change, or Shadow of Turning.

And as to *absolute Perfection,* it is a most certain Truth, That there is none in *ourselves.* All our Perfection, in this Regard, is in *Christ,* and in *him alone.* And a most comfortable, glorious Thing it is, to view our Perfection in our perfect Head, in him, in whom we *are complete,* absolutely so, *lacking Nothing.* And a glorious Influence hath such believing Views of our Completeness in Christ, to make us personally, inherently, and increasingly Holy.

There is no Danger of asserting our absolute Perfection in Christ, and in him *alone;* so long as a *real,* tho' *partial Perfection* in *us,* is asserted together with it. That is, so long as the *new Man,* or *new Nature* in the Soul, is acknowledg'd, which is perfect as to *Parts,* tho' yet imperfect as to *Degrees;* and the Necessity of the *Truth* and *Increase* of inherent and personal Holiness, in Heart, Lip and Life, is asserted.

Our absolute Perfection in Christ, our complete Holiness in him is *God's Foundation,* upon which he builds our inherent and personal Holiness; upon which he begins, increaseth, and will perfect Holiness in *us.* And it ought to be *our Foundation,* upon which our Faith rests, and upon which it works, in all its Labour after an Advance of personal Holiness in *Heart and Life.*

In believing Views then, of our Completeness in Christ, of that Perfection which we now have *in Him,* and shall shortly have *thro' him;* let us labour to be *like him,* to grow up more and more into Conformity in him, as Members of such a holy Head, as Branches of such a holy Root.—So shall our Faith be strong, our Joy full, and our Holiness genuine and increasing. Or, rise apace, towards the Glory of that perfect Day, when *Holy and without Blame before* God *in Love,* we as his chosen, his redeemed, his sanctified Ones, shall be, *To the Praise of the Glory of his*

Grace, in Christ, thro' the endless Ages of a blest Eternity!—Wishing *all Joy and Peace in Believing;* and that *The God of Peace* may *sanctify you wholly, in Spirit, Soul and Body, working in you that which is well pleasing in his Sight thro' Christ Jesus:* In him, I am, dear Sir,

Your Affectionate Friend and
Humble Servant,

———— ————

LETTER XXXIX.

To Mrs. L------n.

My dear Friend,

YOU yold me your Concern, lest you should *perish,* by reason of your *Ignorance.* Glad am I, that the Lord hath *shewn you* your Malady, your Disease, your Soul-Sickness, which threatens your eternal Death. Now you are *sick,* you have *need of the Physician.* Now you see your Sickness as a Sinner, the SAVIOUR will be desired by you. It is the *Depth* of Soul-Misery, to be *insensible* of it. The *Strength* of our Spiritual Disease, to think that we are *Whole,* and that nothing *ails* us.—Oh the dreadful Misery of Thousands round about us, who are at *Ease,* and think all will be well with them at *last,* tho' they are just ready to *die in their Sins,* and to *perish for ever!* They are as it were, at the Edge of a Whirlpool, just ready to be swallow'd up in *endless Perdition;* and yet, alas, they *know it not!* They are *unconcern'd*; and wonder to see *others* so much concern'd about their Souls; and think their earnest Concern for Salvation, is but Folly and Madness. On *these* are they that are *Whole* in their Conceit, and have no sensible *Need* of the *Physicial.* These are they, that see no Beauty in the CHRIST of GOD, in the SAVIOUR of Sinners, that they should desire him. They hope to be sav'd from *Hell* at last; but as for Salvation from *Sin,* and all the woful *Effects* of it in their Souls, they are altogether unconcerned. And thus being insensible of their Misery by *Sin,* they neglect the Remedy, CHRIST, and his great Salvation. And abiding in *this State,* they must *perish eternally.* But when

God Designs Mercy for miserable Sinners, he quickens them to a *Sense* of their Misery, and thereby *prepares* them to receive Mercy.

Harken then, my dear Friend, are you *sensible* of your Misery? Are you *sick, Sin*-sick? The *Physician* is provided on Purpose for *you.* The SAVIOUR has Mercy in Store for *you.* You shall not *die. There is Balm in Gilead, there is a Physician there.* There is *Healing* for you in the Blood of CHRIST, there is an *Healer* in God's Covenant, a SAVIOUR provided, and a *great One,* that every Way suits your Case.—And since you need him, come to him. Oh *come,* and you shall be *welcome.* Come, tell the *Lord Jesus,* that you are an *Ignorant Creature.* He can have *Compassion on the* Ignorant, *and on them that are out of the Way.* He will not upbraid you with your Ignorance, but pity and compassionate your Soul under it. He has *Wisdom* enough in himself to *teach you,* to make you *wise unto Salvation. All the Treasures of Wisdom and Knowledge are in him.* And he is made of God unto us *Wisdom.* As all the Perfections of Wisdom and Knowledge meet in *him;* so they are treasur'd up in him for *us;* to be communicated to such foolish Sinners as *we.* He is a Saviour in *Office;* it is his Office to *teach the Ignorant.* God the Father has appointed him to save Sinners, from their Soul-destroying Ignorance. And, *Good and upright is the* LORD: *Therefore will he teach Sinners in the Way,* Psal. xxv.8.

Oh, the LORD the SAVIOUR is *good,* infinitely *good!* Good, to compassionate Sinners in their utmost Folly, according to the Measure of their Distress. As he is infinite in Wisdom, and fully knows the Case of every miserable Sinner that comes unto him; so he is a most *merciful High-Priest,* that is inwardly *touched* with a *Feeling* of all our Griefs. By an inexpressible Sympathy with us, he doth as it were, make them his *own.* His Heart is made of *Tenderness.* A boundless Sea of Compassions meet in it; into which, he takes the *Case* of every miserable Sinner that comes unto him.—And can he then send them *away empty?* No; he cannot thus *deny himself,* in his infinite *Goodness.* And therefore, because he is *good,* because he delighteth in Goodness, in free, unmerited Goodness, in boundless, unlimited Goodness, in exercising Loving-kindness; he will relieve us, notwithstanding our Poverty, and to the utmost of our Wants, according to his own unsearchable Riches, and immense Fulness,

And as the LORD the SAVIOUR is infinitely good; so he is infinitely *faithful* to him that appointed him, to God the Father, who call'd him to be our SAVIOUR, and to his own Engagements to save us, even every poor Soul, that comes unto God by him.—Come then, my dear Friend, come to *Jesus Christ,* and *shew before him all your Trouble.* Put your *Case,* commit your *Soul* into his Hands; and he will undertake for you. He *will not,* from his infinite Goodness, from his infinite Faithfulness, yea, let me say with Reverence, he *cannot* deny your Request: He will *save you to the Uttermost.* The SAVIOUR is GOD, and cannot *lie,* nor *repent.* The Word is gone out of his Mouth, in infinite Goodness, in infinite Faithfulness: That *he will in no wise cast out,* any poor, miserable Soul, *that commeth unto him,* John vi. 37. It is not possible that you should *perish,* it you *come to* JESUS. He will *receive you to the Glory of* GOD: To save you from endless Misery, to eternal Glory. Question not his infinite Goodness, doubt not his infinite Faithfulness: They are like the *great Mountains,* yea, *firmer* than the lasting Hills. *For the Mountains shall* depart, *and the Hills be* removed: But the *Kindness* of CHRIST'S Heart to Sinners, shall never *be removed.* His Grace, cannot *change.* His Compassions, never *fail.* Heaven and Earth pass away: But the Faithfulness of CHRIST to his Engagements, to his Word of Promise given to save Sinners, and every one that comes unto him, can never fail. Not a Jot, nor a Tittle of his Word, concerning their Salvation, shall pass away, until all be fulfilled.

And because the LORD the SAVIOUR is thus *good* and *upright,* merciful and true; therefore will he *teach* Sinners *in the Way.* Oh, they are *Sinners,* chief Sinners, unworthy, God-provoking, Hell-deserving Sinners, that the LORD the SAVIOUR delights to *save,* and is in *Office* to save to the *Uttermost!* He will teach these in the *Way,* in *The Way of Life, which is above to the Wise, to depart from Hell beneath.* He will teach Sinners, even the most ignorant, and make the Way of Life so plain for them, That a *way-faring Man,* a poor Soul that desires to go from Earth to Heaven, tho' a *Fool,* shall not *err* therein. And this because, He is given to be a *Light* to them that sit in *Darkness;* to guide our *Feet* into the *Way of Peace.* And has promis'd, to bring the *Blind by a Way which they knew not, to lead them in Paths which they have not known: To make*

Darkness Light before them, and crooked Things straight. And to *do these Things with them, and not forsake them,* Isa. xlii. 16.

See then, my dear Friend, what Encouragement you have to *come to* CHRIST. Oh stay not a Moment longer, doubting whether he will *receive you,* but come and *see.* Oh venture in to CHRIST: Say, as Queen *Esther, I will go in unto the King!—And if I perish, I perish:* And see if you find not *Grace* in the Eyes of the LORD. The SAVIOUR will hold out the *Sceptre* of his princely Grace, his promis'd Mercy, for you to *touch and live.* Cast yourself down at his Feet in all your Uncleanness, and say as that poor *Leper, Lord, if thou wilt, thou canst make me clean.* And JESUS, *Moved with Compassion,* will say unto you, as he did unto him, *I will; be thou clean.* CHRIST can save you with a *Word.* He can speak all Salvation to you, by Way of *Grant,* in an *Instant.* Even all that you want for Soul and Body, for Time and for Eternity. And his great Word, of free unchanging Promise, will bring all Salvation to you, thro' Thousands of Improbabilities, over Mountains of Opposition, thro' Seas of Difficulty, with glorious Triumph, to his endless Praise. And tho' he should seem to *hide* himself from you, and be *silent* for a while; you go not from him, follow him with your earnest Cries, until he gives you an *Answer of Peace.* When he *designs* Mercy for Souls, he often *tries* their Faith and Patience. Because he loves to display his Almighty Power in supporting us, under greatest Pressures; to see us follow hard after him, when he seems to go from us; to commend his infinite Grace, in bringing Salvation to us in the fittest Season; and thereby to endure himself, and his saving Love exceedingly to our Souls. Oh, *in the Mount,* the LORD will be *seen!* Our Extremity, is his Opportunity. Remember our Lord's Carriage to the Woman of *Canaan.* And if he should so try *you;* let seeming *Denial* of your Request, put you upon pleading with him more earnestly. 'Till he say unto you, as unto her, *O Woman, great is they Faith: Be it unto thee, even as thou wilt.—The Grace of Christ be with your Spirit!* So prays,

Your affectionate Friend,

——— ———

LETTER XL

To Mrs. M--------s.

My very dear Sister in Christ,

IT pleaseth the Lord to exercise me with much bodily Weakness. But blessed be his Name, he gives me sweet Submission to his Will, and Acquiescence with his good Pleasure. I long for nothing so much, as to believe in, love and adore my God in every Thing. Verily, *he hath done,* he doth and will do, *all Things well.* As is most conducive to his own Glory, our present Happiness, and eternal Bliss.—We are very apt to make *Mistakes:* Which is the Cause of much of our *Heaviness* under trying Providences.

We are apt to think, that this and the other *Thing,* would be for *God's Glory,* which we desire for that End. But our *great* LORD, who is *great* in Might, whose Understanding is *infinite,* doth perfectly see, that that *Thing* which he denies us of, or at that *Time,* in which he is not pleas'd to bestow it; would *not* be most for his Honour.—Oh my dear Sister, if we love above all Things, God's Honour; let us lay out in our projecting Minds, *this* and *that,* which he hath promis'd, according to the Rule of his Word; and let us bring the *Things,* we wish for, in earnest Prayer before him: Let us seek, yea, wrestle with him for the Performance of all his promis'd Goodness, of the good Word which he hath spoken, concerning his Church in general or particular, relating to our selves or others, about which our Desires are engag'd. And let us leave the *Manner* and *Time* of the Lord's bestowing the Things we request, entirely to *him:* Who is *wonderful in Council, and excellent in Working.* For there shall not *fail ought of all the good Things which the* LORD *hath spoken.* Nor will he fail to *satisfy us* with his infinite *Goodness,* as shall be most for the *Glory* of his great Name, And let us give him Leave to be Judge of that *himself;* and humbly bow unto his good Pleasure, and joyfully flow into his all-wise Dispose. Again, we are apt to think, that this and that *Thing* would be most for *our Happiness;* and to desire it for that End. But the LORD, who loves us infinitely, who is infinitely wise, doth well know, that those *Things* we seek, which he denies, or at those *Times* we wish, in which he gives them not, would *not*, augment our Bliss, but lessen it. Well our heavenly Father *knows* what we have *need of;* and that which is *good* he will *give;* and that which would do us *Hurt,* or at that Time, in which it would not be *best* for us, he will *deny* us of, however hardly we may take it.—Yet will he in no wise deny us any of the *Petitions* we ask of him in the Name of Jesus, according to his revealed *Will* in his *Word,* for his Glory and our Happiness; but grant them *all,* as a God *hearing Prayer,* either in the *Things* we ask, or in those that are *better;* at the *Times* we request them in, or at Seasons that are more *fit,* in which they shall appear most serviceable, beautiful and glorious.

Let us beware then, that we yield not to unbelieving *Heaviness* in trying Seasons; and cheerfully let us wait in *Faith,* for most gracious *Answers* to all our Prayers, from *Jacob's* GOD, who hath not said to the Seed of *Jacob, Seek ye* Me *in vain.* Let us go on to seek him, that we may glorify him; and *our Hearts shall live, that seek* GOD. Great shall be *his Glory,* in our Salvation; and *our Happiness,* in his Honour. *The* LORD *hath made all Things for himself;* and is *glorify'd* in all his Dispensations, both of Grace and Providence; and *most* glorify'd in those Ways and Times, in which he is pleas'd to work; and let *us* glorify him in *all.* We are happy in GOD, and in his *good Pleasure;* in his all-wise, all-gracious, and sovereign Dispose of all Things concerning us. And for his Glory, and our Happiness it is, to esteem Things as they *are;* and *in every Thing* to *give Thanks: For this is the Will of God in Christ Jesus concerning us.*—Wishing all Supports, under all Pressures, all Consolations, under all Dejections, all gracious Supplies, under all Trials, and all Assistance, for all active Service; *that the Name of our Lord may be glorify'd in you, and you in him, according to the Grace of God, and of our Lord Jesus Christ:* In him, my dear Sister, I am

Yours very affectionately,

——— ———

LETTER XLI.

To Mr. P-------ll.

Dear Sir,

I Should have been glad of a Line from you before this Time, and hope to hear from you soon. I trust, JESUS hears from you often, and that there is sweet Communion maintain'd between him and you. Oh dear Sir, he loves you infinitely! His whole Heart, is fix'd upon you in Love. *He is in one Mind,* to love you freely, fully, unchangeably and eternally; *and who can turn him?* None of all your Enemies, within or without, shall ever *seperate you from the Love of Christ.* He did not set his Love upon you, nor chuse you, because you was *better* than others by Nature; nor yet for your *forseen Goodness,* after your Conversion by Grace. Ah *no.* He *knew that we were obstinate, that our Neck was an Iron Sinew, and our Brow, Brass; and that we were call'd Transgressors from the Womb.* both in Nature and Grace. And yet, he *could,* he *would* love us; merely from the infinite Grace of his own *Heart,* and the sovereign good Pleasure of his *Will.* Oh how sad would be our Case, if the Love of *Christ's Heart,* in the least depended upon *our Goodness!* Alas, the Goodness of *our Frames,* is too oft like the *Morning-Dew, that quickly passeth away.* And we, wretched we, behave towards our kind Lord, as if we were not his special Favourites. *We forget God our Saviour, and lightly esteem the Rock of our Salvation.* Oh Soul-humbling, Heart-breaking Consideration! And especially, if we consider, that the LORD our Lover, will not *forget us,* nor *cast* us *out* of his Esteem, nor *off* from his kind Regard, for *all that we have done!* Oh, *who is like unto our God!* A GOD *that pardoneth Iniquity, that passeth by the Transgression of the Remnant of his Heritage, that retaineth not his Anger for ever: Because he delighteth in Mercy!*—And how should the bright Shine of *God's* all-overcoming Love, melt down our hard Hearts, into a swift Flow of Love and Gratitude to *him!* And how *doth it,* when the Energy of infinite Grace, of free, rich, distinguishing and eternal Grace, reacheth the Heart of a vile Sinner, of a backsliding Believer, in the great Power of GOD! Oh it is well for us that we are under *Grace.* Grace, *that forgives our Iniquities, that heals our Diseases! That redeems our Life from Destruction, and crowns us with Loving-kindness and tender Mercies! That satisfies our Mouth with good Things, so that our*

Youth is renewed like the Eagles! That maintains and increaseth our Life spiritual, unto Life eternal!—Unto this *Grace* I commit you, and am, my dear Brother,

Your very affectionate Friend and Servant,
In our altogether Lovely and Everlasting JESUS,

——— ———

LETTER XLII.

To Mr. L-------s.

My dear Brother in our sweet Lord Jesus,

MOST kindly I thank you for your Letter. Want of *Time,* not of *Love,* is the Cause why you hear no oftner from *me.* I have pray'd our *Dear Lord* to speak to you, when *I could not.* Oh *none* can speak like HIM! CHRIST has *the Tongue of the Learned,* and well knows how to *speak a Word in Season to him that is weary.* Oh, *None* can speak so seasonably, so suitably to *every* weary Soul, in *every* Kind and Degree of their Weariness, as the *anointed* SAVIOUR! Our All-Wise, and All-Gracious LORD! *Grace is pour'd into his Lips.* And from *his Mouth* such *gracious Words proceed,* that all *bear him Witness,* with Wonder, Love and Joy, that *hear* his glorious Voice! Oh, *never Man spake like this Man! His Lips are like Lillies, dropping sweet-smelling Myrrh!* Oh the *ineffable* Sweetness, the *refreshing* Fragrancy, the *Soul-quickning* Energy of our Lord's *Voice!* With a *Word of his Mouth,* HE ushers in Light, Life, Liberty, and Glory upon us at once! Such a *Fulness* of BLISS, that none can *conceive,* but the Souls that *enjoy it!* And by *Them* it is *inexpressible!* Unspeakably *blessed* then, must be those happy Souls, that hear, that know, *our Beloved's Voice!* For unto all the many *Thousands* espoused to him, scatter'd over the Face of the whole Earth, he speaks particularly and individually, in the Love, Grace, and Power of a GOD! In the Majesty of JEHOVAH! And as the LORD *their* GOD! And thus HE *commands Deliverances for Jacob,* Supports, Joys, Salvations, with an *All-endearing,* and *All-efficacious* Voice. As in the old Creation, HE said, *Let there be Light:* and there *was Light.*—Evident then it is, that *never Man spake like the Man* CHRIST!—

No Man can speak to the *Case* of any weary Soul, unless CHRIST puts a *Word* into his Mouth for *that Person*. And when Men have spoken to the Case, they cannot speak to the *Heart,* unless CHRIST takes the Words from *their Mouth,* and conveys them into the *inmost Soul,* by his *own* Almighty Breath. By the *Word of the* LORD, the Heavens of old were made and garnished: And by the *Word of the* LORD, are New-born Souls form'd and polish'd, until Grace is brightned into Glory. *Heart-work,* doth *all* belong to the SAVIOUR-GOD, whatever *Instruments* he is pleas'd to work by. Not a *Beam* of Light, Love and Glory, can penetrate our *Souls,* under the most bright and powerful *Discourse,* unless CHRIST the true LIGHT, shineth into our Hearts *therein*, and speaks unto us *thereby*. All our *Times of Refreshing,* come from the *Presence of the* LORD. It is CHRIST that *declares* his Father's Name unto us, either more *mediately,* or *immediately,* whenever the Love of GOD is shed abroad in our *Hearts,* and our *Souls* are changed into the same *Image,* from Glory to Glory.—What *Thanks* then should we give unto GOD for CHRIST! for this his *Unspeakable* GIFT! and for that spiritual Life, Joy and Glory, which our LORD is pleas'd to communicate to us, by his most Gracious and Efficacious *Voice,* which Way soever he gives us to *hear it!*—I rejoyce with *You,* and the rest of the Brethren, for that *Feast* you had at the *Tabernacle,* on your *Letter-Day*. It was the Love and Glory of our LORD, in himself and Works, which breaking out upon you, enlightned, and enkindled your dear Souls; and made them like an ascending Flame, in Prayer and Praise; which was most joyful unto *you,* and acceptable to GOD, thro' JESUS CHRIST.—Indeed my Brother, you then enjoy'd a *Taste* of Heaven's BLISS, the *First-fruits* of that GLORY which awaits you! And if a Taste be so *sweet,* what will the rich, the eternal *Feast be!* If the *News* of your LORD'S being on his *Way,* and of his *gathering* of the People unto HIM, was so *delightful* to your Souls; Oh what *ineffable Joy,* will fill your Hearts, when you shall *see him Face to Face!* When he comes in the *Clouds*, with ten Thousands of his *Saints,* in his *own,* and in his *Father's Glory,* and in the *Glory of his holy Angels!* When all the LAMB'S *Redeemed,* shall be gather'd together unto HIM, caught up to meet him in the *Air,* to enter into his *Joy and Glory,* and to *sing his Praises:* And so shall be for *ever with the Lord! Even so come Lord Jesus! Come quickly!*—In HIM, my dear Brother, I am

Yours Affectionately,

——— ———

LETTER XLIII.

To Mr. B--------m.

Dear Sir,

I Hope you experience that *Christ lives in you.* That your Life as a Branch in him your living Root, as in Union to him, as having Communion with him; is secretly maintain'd in the darkest and sharpest Winter-Seasons. And that it is richly increas'd unto a visible Branch-Glory, in those pleasant Sprint-Times of his manifestative Favour, which he is graciously pleas'd to afford you. If the Life of Grace in *us,* was not secur'd in Union to that Fulness of Grace, of Grace-Life, which is in *Christ;* it wou'd soon be destroy'd, by that Body of Sin and Death which works in us, and by the deadly Temptations of Satan and the World without us. But *our Life* of Grace, being *hid with Christ in God;* it shall never be totally extinguish'd in *us* by the greatest Damps that may be cast upon it. But maintain'd and increas'd it shall be, in Principle and Activity, under strongest Opposition, and after woful Decays, until it is perfected in the Life of Glory.

How *safe* then are we in *Christ!* What Cause have we to *Rejoyce in the Lord alway!* And to wait upon him continually for renewed Quicknings, whenever, with the Psalmist, we have the sad Experience, that *our Souls cleave unto the Dust!* Oh, our Dear Lord Jesus, our tender, compassionate Saviour, will *Remember us in our low Estate; because his Mercy endureth for ever!* The Love of his Heart towards us, is immense and unchangeable; His Care of us, perpetual; his Wisdom to restore us, is infinite; and his Power to save us to the uttermost, is Almighty. And into his All-wise, All-gracious, and Almighty Hands, let us *Commit the Keeping of our Souls,* thro' Time, the Meetning of them for Eternity, and the Raising of our Bodies unto endless Glory. For, *Of all that the Father hath given him, he will lose nothing but raise it up at the last Day.* And, *Present us Faultless before the Presence of his,* and his Father's *Glory, with exceeding Joy. And so shall we be forever with the Lord!*—With kind Service to Self and Spouse, I remain, dear Sir,

Your affectionate and obliged Friend and Servant,
In JESUS *our Lord, our Life, our* ALL,

——— ———

LETTER XLIV.

To Mr. M------s.

My dear Brother in Christ,

I Trust, you and your dear Yokefellow, have abundant Experience of the Lord's Goodness, since I saw you. Our dear Lord hath brought us far on our Way thro' the Wilderness, towards *Canaan's* Land. Yet a little while, and we shall *see* JESUS. *See him as he is,* be made perfectly *like him,* and *live* in his immediate Presence, under the bright, enkindling Beams of his Love and Glory, to an endless Eternity. My *dear Children,* you are the *Lord's;* his Heart is fix'd on you, his Care is over you, and all his Perfections are engag'd for you. All the *Fulness of* GOD, is *yours in Love.* Then, be sure, you can *want* nothing. God, your own God in Christ, will see to it, that you shall not want *any good Thing. Live* by Faith, upon your Portion in God, upon GOD your Portion. You can never *spend it. Draw Water with Joy out of this Well of Salvation:* You can never draw it *dry,* nor *sink it* an *Hair's Breadth.* Make GOD your ALL. He *is* so: *Believe* him to be so. And, put HIM for a *Well,* while passing thro' the Valley of *Baca,* this Vale of Tears. And *blessed, blessed* shall you be. For lo, this *Well of living Water,* in a thousand various Streams, will *spring up,* and run over, for your full and continual Supply, while you, rejoycing, *sing unto it.*

I am weak in Body; but my kind Lord, *stayeth his rough Wind in the Day of his East-Wind:* Sets Bounds to my Affliction, and says, *Hitherto shalt thou come, and no further.* Oh I find the GOD of *Jacob,* to be unto *me,* a *very present Help in Trouble.* He empties me from Vessel to Vessel, to refine me the more. He drives me by Afflictions, he draws me by

Mercies, from every Thing below *himself,* to live upon HIM, as my present and eternal ALL! And a glorious, Soul-satisfying ALL, is my GOD to *me.* Praise him on my Account; and lift up a Cry for your Friend that loves you.—Now, *The* GOD *of Peace, fill you with all Joy and Peace in Believing!* So prays, my dear Brother and Sister,

Yours in the LORD, our Love, our Life, Our All in All,

———— ————

LETTER XLV.

To Mr. W------s.

My very dear Brother,

WE live in a World of Snares: The Lord, who hath sav'd our Souls from Death, kept our Feet from falling! It is well that we are Christ's Care: Else we should fall, and rise no more. But, all Glory to the God of all Grace, we that have believed in Jesus, are forever secur'd from final *Apostacy!*—Yet much lies upon us, in Point of *Duty,* to watch daily, that we backslide not from GOD. That we are not content with Distance from him, and want of Communion with him; That we live not to his Dishonour, but actually in all Things to his Glory: Yea, that we increase in Faith and Love, and go on, 'perfecting Holiness in the Fear of God."—And blessed be his great Name, that whenever we fail, there is the Fountain of Christ's most precious Blood, to wash in; and an inexhaustible Fulness of Grace in him, to supply all our Wants, until Grace is ripened into Glory.—*The God of Love and Peace be with you!* I am, my dear Brother,

Yours most affectionately,

———— ————

ERRATA.

[Errata corrected in text]

4

LETTERS ON Spiritual SUBJECTS, AND Divers OCCASIONS; SENT TO RELATIONS and FRIENDS.

By One who has tasted that the LORD *is* GRACIOUS.

Wherefore comfort yourselves together, and edify one another, even as also ye do, 1 Thes. v. 11.

VOL. VIII.

LONDON:
Printed by J. HART, in *Popping's Court, Fleet-Street:* And sold by J. LEWIS, in *Pater-noster Row;* and G. KEITH, at *Mercers-Chapel, Cheapside.* 1750.
[Price stitch'd One Shilling and Three-Pence.]

LETTERS
ON
Spiritual Subjects, &c.

LETTER I. *To Mr.* W.

Ever Dear and Honour'd Father,

WITH abundant Thanks for all your Kindness, I send a Line to tell you, That the LORD is infinitely *Good* to *me,* even *still,* a SEA of *Goodness,* that flows out upon me in rich Streams of Loving Kindness continually! Oh how full is *my* JESUS! and how free in the Distribution of all his Grace to *me!*—And this JESUS, is *your* JESUS, my dear Father! This LORD, is *your Lot, your Part, your* GOD, *your Guide even unto Death, the Strength of your Heart, and your Portion for Ever!*—What then can you want? Oh live continually *upon,* and *to,* your own LORD JESUS! Labour after a *growing* Acquaintance with, and Conformity to Him, until that which is *Perfect* shall come. Oh how *rich* are you in CHRIST! In HIM, in whom all the unsearchable Riches, and Glories of the GODHEAD dwell! You have never yet seen a *Thousandth Part* of the Excellency of *your Beloved!* There is an unsearchable Depth, an infinite Height, a boundless Breadth, and an eternal Length, of *Glory* in *Him!*—But what shall I say? Words *fail;* there is such an Immensity of Glory *behind!* Neither the Tongues of Men, nor of Angels, can fully *Tell,* no, little can they *Tell,* were they employ'd to an eternal Space, *What your Beloved is!* HE IS WHAT HE IS! His Name is, I AM THAT I AM! No *Knowledge,* but that of *His Infinite Understanding,* is a Line long enough, to found this immense OCEAN of Glory! Or to *Tell what your Beloved is!*—But what HE *is,* He is for *You!* All his immense Glories, are a SEA of Bliss, for *You* to swim in, to live in, and to delight yourself with, thro' Time, and to Eternity!—Wherefore, Follow on to *Know Him,* and let not Trifles divert you from Him, or disturb your Rest in his Bosom. Possess CHRIST daily by Faith;

and in HIM you will be so *full*, that you can want *Nothing*, altho' you were surrounded with a *Thousand* Wants! And so *happy*, that you will fret at *Nothing*, altho' you were encompass'd with a *Thousand* Provocations! We can never want Happiness, not be pinch'd thro' with Miseries, unless we go out of our GOD! When we forsake our *Rest*, all is *Trouble*. When we return again to the Bosom of GOD, and so long as we abide there, *all is Peace*. Oh Happy is that Man, that delights himself in the LORD: For HE shall give him the Desires of his Heart!—Wishing all Peace and Prosperity; I request your Prayers: and am,

Ever Yours, at all Obedience,

LETTER II. *To Mr.* W.

Ever Dear and Honour'd Father,

YOUR kind Letter I receiv'd, and return abundant Thanks.—May the LORD bless you abundantly, in Soul, Body, and Circumstance! May you live *from Him*, and *to Him*, and rejoice in *Hope* of that happy Day when you shall live *with Him!* Yet a *little while*, and we shall *see* JESUS, be perfectly like him, and for ever with Him! The great Thing *now*, is to *serve Him*. This little Inch of Time, is all the Opportunity we shall ever have to Glorify Him before Men. Oh who would not work for such a Dear, Glorious MASTER, as CHRIST is! He will make all his Servants that work for Him *now*, sit down to Meat *erelong*, and HE Himself will come forth and *serve them!* Joy and Rest, Crowns and Thrones, of an eternal Duration, await the *Servants* of the *Prince of Peace!* Our Lives are just drawing to a Close. Oh let us labour to do something for CHRIST, before we enter into our eternal Rest! And when we can't honour Him in *Doing*, let us labour to glorify Him in *Suffering:* in patient, humble, thankful Submission, to all the Strokes of his kind Hand: That CHRIST *may be magnify'd in our Bodies, whether it be by Life, or by Death.*—Wishing all Prosperity, and requesting your Prayers; I remain, with the greatest Love and Duty,

Your obedient Child,

LETTER III. *To Mr.* I.

Dear and Honour'd Brother,

YOURS I receiv'd, and return hearty Thanks for it. Oh dear Sir, how blest are *you,* that you can say, "I know I am a poor vile *Sinner!*" That you have any Degree of *Feeling* of your lapsed degenerate State; *such* a Feeling of it, that makes you sensible of your *Need* of the SAVIOUR! This is a blessed Effect of the *Grace* of the *new Covenant;* and an Evidence that you are under it. We are all of us, even the whole Race of Mankind, while in a State of Nature, *Children of Wrath.* We are under the Declaration of Wrath in the Sentence of the Law, and filled with Wrath and Enmity against God. We are Enemies in our Minds by wicked Works. And being thus estranged from God, we have neither Will, Skill nor Power, to return unto him by Jesus Christ; and are cover'd over with a deep *Insensibility* of our extreme *Misery;* or in a Word, *Dead in Sin.*—But when the Time of Calling Love comes on, wherein the Chosen of God are to find Mercy, and to be brought under the Dominion of Grace; the LORD passeth by, sees them polluted in their own Blood, and in the Infinity of his Love, saith unto them, *Live.* And by that Life-producing Voice, takes away the *stony Heart out of their Flesh,* and gives them an *Heart of Flesh.* A new Heart, capable of a quick *Sensation* of their deep and extensive Misery; that hereby they may be *prepar'd* to receive that glorious Remedy, which was prepar'd for *them*, in GOD'S Counsels and Covenant about the *slain Lamb,* before the World's Foundations were laid. Oh this eternal *Love!* This free, this preventing *Love!* This Life-giving, saving *Love;* which *began* our Salvation in an infinite Depth of *Mercy;* and will *finish* it, unto unknown Heights of endless *Glory!*—Rejoice and be thankful then, my dear Brother, for that Knowledge which is given you, of your being a poor vile *Sinner.* And be assur'd, that you shall still *increase* in it, under the Teachings of the *Holy Spirit,* who is given to dwell in you for this blessed End, To *convince* you *of Sin.*

Again, How happy are *you,* in that you "know that *God so loved the World,* that He gave his *only-begotten Son,* to *die* for poor, vile, unworthy

Sinners!" Oh, *This* keeps you from *sinking* in deep Waters! From *perishing* in the miry Pit, the amazing Gulph of your own Vileness and Unworthiness; *Here's* the *Rock,* the strong, the eternal Rock, *the Rock of Ages* beneath you! And can you *sink,* think you, when so mightily *Under-propp'd!*—I compassionate you, my dear Brother, in that you can seldom say, "That the Son of God was given for *You* in particular."—Why do you *doubt it?* Is it because of your great *Unworthiness?* The SAVIOUR was given for the *most Unworthy. No Money, no Price,* is requir'd, to partake of CHRIST, and all the *Salvation* that is in *Him,* Do you *doubt* his being given for you in particular, because of that horrid Mass of *Iniquity* which is in your vile *Nature,* which too often works and prevails, in Thought, Word and Deed? The SAVIOUR was given for the *Chief of Sinners.* And who is a *God like* unto *our* GOD, *that pardoneth Iniquity,* that *passeth by the Transgression of the Remnant of his Heritage?* That multiplies to pardon, our multiply'd Provocations, according to the Immensity, and Eternity of his own Grace!—But if you *doubt* whether the Son of God was given for *you* in particular, consider, That He was given to be *believed in: That whosoever* believeth in Him, *should not perish, but have everlasting Life,* John 3. 16. This Word, *whosoever,* as it stands connected with what follows, is a glorious Call to *you,* to *me,* to every poor *Sinner,* and especially to such that see their Need of the SAVIOUR, to *believe on the Son of God:* And a glorious Description of the Person, and Persons that shall be *saved,* in Consequence of the SAVIOUR'S being given for every of them in particular, even for every of them that *believe in his Name.*—And if you doubt the *Truth* of your Faith in the given SAVIOUR; consider what *Faith* is. It is an hearty *Approbation* of CHRIST, as the *Project* of infinite *Wisdom,* and the *Provision* of infinite *Grace,* for the *Salvation* of *lost Sinners,* It is *such* an Approbation of the given SAVIOUR, that attracts the Soul after Him as *Altogether lovely;* and enables it to look *to,* and rest upon CHRIST *alone,* for its *own Salvation,* as held forth to poor Sinners, in the indefinite Promises of the glorious Gospel. In a Word, It is the Soul's *Persuasion* that CHRIST is the alone SAVIOUR; and its *Embracing* of Him as such.

Now then, my dear Brother, How is it with *you,* in those happy Moments when you are blest with some Prospects of the *Glory of*

CHRIST? Do you *like Him?* Is He *amiable* in your Eyes? Is He *All Desires* to you? Doth your Heart *cleave to,* and *clasp about Him,* as precious in *Himself,* and as precious unto *you?*—If so, you are one of them that *truly believe* on the *Son of God.* And for *You,* for *You* in particular, the great SAVIOUR was *given.* And as He was given *for* you, He is given *to* you; and in and with *Him,* all *Salvation,* is and shall be given you *freely.* You *shall not perish, but have everlasting Life.* God has given unto you *eternal Life,* in and with his *Son;* by the free, irreversible *Grant,* the free, unchanging *Promise* of the blessed *Gospel.* The *Word* is gone out of his Mouth in *Faithfulness;* He will not, *cannot lie,* nor ever *repent* of what He hath said.—Oh *set to your Seal, That* GOD *is true;* and *doubt* your Interest in Christ, his being given for you, and to you, *no more!* Your *Beloved* is *yours,* and you are *His.* You are *married* unto the LORD. And your Marriage Union, and his Relation-Love to *you,* which secures yours to *Him,* shall never, never be *broken.* But your Communion with Him, in Grace and Glory, shall from henceforth *increase,* thro' *Time* and to *Eternity!*

I am glad you think *meanly* of yourself. The meaner we think of *ourselves,* the more will our *Lord* be *glorify'd* in *us.* We are not saved, to be *something* in *ourselves;* but to be *All* in CHRIST. Oh how doth our accursed Pride, rob our Lord of his Crown!—What you *know* of the *Things of God,* is all of *Grace;* and more and more will the *Spirit of Grace* teach you.—Doubt not your *Call* to the *Ministry,* because you han't such *full assurance of Faith.* as some *others* have. Four our Lord saith, Let him that *Heareth* (that hath some good Measure of Knowledge in the Doctrines of Grace, and spiritual Gifts for the Ministry) *say Come,* Rev. 22. 17. It is as if our Lord should say, "Let such Souls, that have *heard* of my *Glories,* under the *Teachings* of my *Spirit,* invite poor *Sinners,* to come to ME the sent SAVIOUR; let 'em tell them of my Fitness, Fulness and Freeness to save to the uttermost. Altho' they han't such a full *Persuasion* of their *Interest* in me, as my *Bride* hath; as such Souls that have been more indulg'd with my Bosom-Embraces; who out of the Exuberance of their Joy and Love, most freely and naturally, say, *Come,*"—And tho' you mayn't yet have arriv'd at such a Degree of Knowledge in the *Mysteries of Grace,* as some *other* of your Brethren in the Ministry: Yet observe what our Lord saith in this Word, *Let him that* heareth *say Come.* "Not only him that *hath* heard, but him that *heareth,* that is still *learning* my Mind; let *Him* preach ME, so far as He knows me. And be a *Witness* of the Things which he hath *seen,* and also of those Things in which I will yet *appear unto him."*—And as the Lord favours you with his *Presence in Preaching,* and has given you some *Seals* of your *Ministry;* He has in these Respects, indulg'd you with *Lumps of Sense,* to encourage your *Obedience of Faith* therein.—Your compassionate MASTER, sees, yea, feels the *Pressures* you labour under; and will suitably *support you.* What tho' you are like a *bruised Reed;* He will not *break you.* Tho' like *smoking Flax;* He will not *quench you:* But *bind up,* and *strengthen* your Faith and Love, and bring forth for you, *Judgment unto Victory.*—That *all Grace may abound towards you,* is the hearty Desire of, Sir,

Your Affectionate Friend in JESUS,

and Servant for his Sake,

LETTER IV. *To Mr.* T.

My very Dear and Honour'd Brother,

YOURS I receiv'd, □ And who knows, my dear Brother, but *You* may be the *Man* whom the Lord hath made *Choice of,* by whose *Mouth* some of these poor *Souls* shall *hear the Word of the Gospel* and *believe?* Oh! come and see, if our Dear, our Great *Shepherd* hath not some of his lost *Sheep* to bring Home by *You.* Who knows but you may have some given you *here,* that shall be your *Joy,* and *Crown of Rejoicing* in the *Day of the Lord Jesus?* Oh my dear Brother, It is precious Work to Preach JESUS, that *Altogether Lovely* ONE! And Oh what a Privilege is it to be made a *Fisher of Men!* If the SAVIOUR hath Work for *you* to do *here,* my Brother, you *must* do it; as our Lord *must needs go thro' Samaria.* Come, my Brother, it's worth while to take a little Pains, to weary yourself to *serve* JESUS, your *Beloved,* the *Lord* that hath bought you with his *Blood,* and will crown you with his *Glory!* Come, come a *Wooing* for CHRIST. Come *Tell* of all his *Glory,* how highly his *Father* hath advanced him, and how willing he is to receive *Sinners* into his own Embraces. And *see* if there be any here, that are willing to be *Married* to the *Son of God,* to the *Heir of all!* And tho' you should be *weary* and fatigu'd in your Journey; remember, CHRIST was so, and sat thus on *Samaria's* Well. And yet He came with infinite Delight to do the *Will of his Father,* when *there* He was to bring Home that poor *Woman,* loved and chosen of Old, and other *Vessels of Mercy,* to HIMSELF, the *Well of Life,* to fill them with *Glory for Ever.* Come, my dear Brother, tho' you come thro' *Storms;* CHRIST will *Recount* all the weary *Steps,* you ever took in his *Service;* and richly will He reward your present *Labour,* with eternal *Rest,* with a *Crown of Glory that fadeth not away!*—Praying that the *Good Will of* HIM *that Dwelt in the Bush* may be with you, and that you may be brought amongst us, in the *Fulness of the Blessing of the Gospel of* CHRIST; I remain,

Dear Sir,

Yours most Affectionately in the LORD,

——— ———

LETTER V. *To Mrs.* M.

My Dear Sister in Christ,

I Hope you are still help'd to rejoice in the Lord, your own God, who will *never, never leave, nor forsake you.* All our Way thro' the Wilderness, was laid out for us by infinite Wisdom and Grace. All our Crosses and Comforts, were of old appointed, are wisely mixed, and shall be graciously and powerfully Over ruled, for the Glory of God, and our present and eternal Advantage. Oh my dear Sister, all Things are *well ordered* for us, in God's *everlasting Covenant.* Wherein he hath said, *I will be unto them a God, and they shall be unto me a People: and their Sins and their Iniquities will I remember no more.* And where Remission of these is, all Things must needs go well. For, *Blessed is the Man unto whom the Lord imputeth not sin.* Blessed is *he* in all Conditions: Every Thing comes to *him* as a *Blessing.*—And shall we be *afraid* of our Blessings? We have *God,* our *own God* in all, in every Cross, and in every Comfort, And is not HE enough to make the one *full,* and the other *sweet?* We need not *fear, tho' the Earth were removed, and tho' the Mountains were carried into the Midst of the Sea: Tho' the Waters thereof rore and be troubled, tho' the Mountains shake with the Swelling thereof:* (Tho' all be in Confusion round about us) since GOD *is our Refuge and Strength, a very present Help in Trouble:* And since, *There is a River, the Streams whereof shall make us glad,* in the most sorrowful Circumstances. Oh was it not for *Unbelief,* we should never be disquieted with any Thing that passeth over us. We may lye at Anchor, by Faith and Hope, in the roughest Sea. The Bosom of God, is a quiet Harbour, where we may delightfully rest, when all is tempestuous round about us. Had we more Faith in God, and Love to Him, we should never stir out of his Bosom, into Disquietude, to his Dishonour, and our own Grief, in the most trying Circumstances. Oh what Fools are we for so doing! If GOD cares for us; what need we be anxiously careful about *ourselves?* If HE has ordered all Things *well* for us, *so* well that nothing could be *better* than it is; what *Room* is there for Disquietude? *Surely every Man disquieteth himself in vain.* If we were *one in Will* with GOD, in every Thing, how *happy* should we be? What, for ourselves could *hurt us,* what could *grieve us,* if we had *no peremptory Will* to any Thing, but what is the *Will of God* concerning us? And in the Will of God, towards us in Christ, we have such a *Fulness* of *Bliss,* such an ALL of *Blessings,* that we need not go out of *it,* to desire any Thing *more.* Oh had we more *Faith,* we should *lie down* and *rest,* and solace ourselves continually with *infinite Fulness. Thou wilt keep him in perfect Peace,* saith the Psalmist, *whose Mind is staid on Thee.* Whenever therefore we are tempted to go out from the Bosom of God, and drawn off from Him, let us instantly say, with *David, Return unto thy Rest, O my Soul: for the* LORD *hath dealt bountifully with thee,* Ps. 116. 7. May *the Peace of God which passeth all Understanding, keep your Heart and Mind thro' Christ Jesus!* Requesting your Prayers; I remain, my dear Sister,

Ever Yours in CHRIST,

——— ———

LETTER VI. *To Mrs.* T.

My Dear and Honour'd Sister in Christ,

MOST heartily I thank you for your kind Letter. The Lord made it sweet and savoury to my Soul. I rejoice in the great Things which the Lord hath done for *You;* and adore his free, infinite, condescending Grace, in blessing my poor Labours for your Encouragement and Comfort. Never was any poor Sinner, so unworthy of so high a Favour, as *vile me!* But the LORD *will be gracious, unto whom He will be gracious.* And therefore it is, that unworthy *I,* have found *Grace* in his *Sight.* The Lord hath *chosen me, and not cast me away.* Not for my Fore-seen *Goodness,* did He chuse me; for I had *none.* Nor yet for my Foreview'd *Badness,* did He cast me *away,* tho' He *saw* what a vile, ungrateful, God-provoking Creature I *should be.* But from the sovereign good Pleasure of his *own Will,* He chose me in Christ unto eternal Life, and unto some Degree of Service to his better Children. That He might thereby commend his infinite *Love,* and the exceeding Riches of his *Grace* to the *Chief of Sinners,* to the eternal *Glory* of his *great Name.*—Help me then, my dear Sister, to praise this Grace, which casts on me its resplendent Rays, with such an amazing Brightness!

Oh, I must join with you, and say, "I am ashamed that I have made so little Progress, since my first setting out in the Ways of God." Oh that *I,* that have been so *greatly beloved,* should *love so little!*

You say, my dear Sister, "That it is no small Joy to you, tho' you do so little for your Dear Lord, that He enables me to do much." This is an Evidence that you *love* JESUS. Indeed I am asham'd of my little *Doings;* and more of my little *Love.* If our kind Lord, enables *me* to do more for Him, *one Way,* He may enable *you* to do more *another.* And if you think you can't *do* so much for Him as He enables me to do, you may *love* Him more. And that takes *Christ's Heart* exceedingly. Our JESUS is a *Lover;* and in infinite Condescension, He delights in *our Love. You* may bring more Glory to Him, in *loving Him,* and more delight his Heart, than poor, ungrateful *I,* with all my *little Doings.*—But why do I talk of *my Doings?* What *I* have done for CHRIST, is *his Word,* rather than *mine.* 'Tis *He* that works in me, both to will and to do, or *I* could do *nothing.* And when I look upon all the Work that CHRIST hath done by me, it appears *great,* a wondrous *Flow* of infinite Love to *me!* For which I owe Him *myself,* and Ten Thousand Times more *Praises,* than I *can give.* But when I look on what *I have done,* thro' his Assistance, it appears *little, very little,* when compar'd with what my Lord is *worthy of,* and with what my poor Soul wou'd gladly *do* for Him, if I *could.* And oh the *Imperfection* of my poor, little Doings! If my Lord's *Grace* was not *Infinite!* He would never cast a favourable Eye, upon any Thing I ever did for Him.—Oh, I must even drop *my* Doings. CHRIST'S Doings for *me,* doth as it were *swallow them up.* His *enabling* me to do any Thing, and every Thing I do for Him, His *pardoning* the Sin of my Doings; His *washing* my defiled Services in his own Blood; His *accepting* and *presenting* them in his own Perfections; And his boundless Grace, in *blessing* my poor Labours to the Souls of his Children; are such *Wonders* of infinite *Love,* such *Works* of my glorious *Lover,* that seem to swallow up all my little Doings, as a Drop I swallowed up of a vast *Ocean!*—And yet I know, the Prince of Grace, in the unsearchable Depth of his Love, will lose Nothing *He* has wrought by me, but call it *My Service;* and say, *I was hungry, and ye fed me, &c.*—Oh who would not *love* such a SAVIOUR! Who would not *serve* such a MASTER!

Come then, my dear Sister, the Grace of CHRIST is all *yours!* Your *Beloved* is *yours,* and *you* are *His!* Go chearfully on with the *Work* He *calls* you to. It is the *Generation-Work,* which his infinite Wisdom and Grace allotted for *you;* and that whereby He will account Himself *glorify'd* in you. If *I* am call'd to *one Service,* and *you* to *another;* we are both employ'd in the Service of the *same Lord.* As enabled then, let us give Him our *Hearts,* in what He calls us to; and so shall we walk before Him, as his dear Servants, as his dear Children, as his dear Bride, unto *all Pleasing.*

Be diligent, my dear Sister, in the Use of all appointed *Means,* for your Growth in Grace: Because GOD works by Means. And thus, in the Way of your Duty, cast all the Care of your Soul's Prosperity upon HIM, who is the *Author* and *Finisher* of your *Faith.* It was the LORD alone, that began the good Work in your Soul, and HE will finish it. CHRIST has the *Pattern* of all your *Glory,* given Him of the *Father;* and He will go on to polish and brighten you, until He has brought you up to your *designed Perfection.* Until he hath made you a *perfect Beauty,* brimful of Grace,

Glorious in *Holiness,* without a *Spot,* or *Wrinkle,* or any such *Thing:* And as such presents you to *Himself,* and to his *Father,* an Object of GOD'S Delight! A meet Subject of his Communion-Love, unto Joy and Glory, endless and unknown!

Yield not, my dear Sister, to such Fears, "That you han't believ'd *aright;* because you see such Vileness in your Heart." For none but those that have *true Faith,* have a *painful Knowledge,* of the *Plague* of their own *Hearts.* Such a Knowledge thereof, that makes them cry out, *Wo is me, for I am undone,* because of my *Uncleanness!* That makes them Heart sick of their *Disease,* and sick of Love-Desires after CHRIST, the glorious *Physician.*

But, my dear Sister, shall *you* fear your Interest in CHRIST, that have had such *assuring Testimonies* of his Love and Grace? What if you have lost the *Comfort* of those sealing Times; you han't lost the *Salvation* that was then seal'd to you. GOD'S *Yea* and *Amen,* are upon all the *Promises* of his *Grace* towards *You* in CHRIST. And HE cannot *change.* HE *is not a Man, that he should lie, nor the Son of Man, that He should repent.* Once hath HE sworn by HIMSELF: And He will not *alter* the *Thing* that is gone out of his *Mouth.* He hath given his unchangeable *Word,* his inviolable *Oath* for your *Salvation,* in *fleeing* to his *Dear Son* for *Refuge;* that your *Consolation* might be *strong.* Oh receive it, and hold it fast, let neither Sin nor Satan wrest it out of your Hands. If you *believe not;* HE *abideth faithful:* HE *cannot deny* HIMSELF. Your Dear *Lord Jesus,* and *God,* even your *Father,* in Him, pities you when weak in Faith, pardons all the Workings of your Unbelief, and calls you to take Him at his Word, to count Him both *able* and *faithful* that hath *promised,* to do what He hath spoken to you of. And thus to give Him *Glory,* in the Face of a Thousand Improbabilities, which may appear in your own Heart. GOD has given his Word, his Oath, That believing on his Son, *you shall not perish, but have everlasting Life:* That you shall be saved from all Sin and Misery, unto all Grace and Glory. And *that's enough.* Thousands of Oppositions shall *flee* before it, as the *Darkness,* before his All-creating *Word,* when He saith *Let there be Light; and there was Light.* GOD'S Love toward *You,* is free, and independent on any of your *Goodness;* infinite, and All-surmounting, over all your *Badness;* and his Truth and

Faithfulness, are as *permanent* as his BEING, who is, The Everlasting I AM! CHRIST is your *Light,* your *Life,* your ALL: And in HIM you are *complete,* who is *Yesterday, To-Day,* and *for Ever* the *Same.* And as sure as you are now complete in *Christ,* you shall be so *thro' Him.* Because HE *lives, you shall live also.*—Wherefore be *strong,* and *stand fast in the Lord,* my dear Sister. I am,

Yours most Affectionately in our Dear Lord,

——— ———

LETTER VII. *To Mr.* L.

My very Dear Brother,

I Kindly thank you for your last letter. I rejoyce to see the *Lord's Work* carried on in your *Soul;* and that you are help'd to commit the whole Management thereof unto *Him,* whose *Hands have laid the Foundation,* and will bring forth the *Head-stone,* the finishing Part, the Coronis of all, with Shoutings of *Grace, Grace unto it!* It was *Free Grace,* that *chose us in Christ,* before the *World began.* It was *Free Grace,* that *redeem'd us* by the *Lamb's Blood.* If was *Free Grace,* that *call'd us* out of *Darkness* into God's marvellous *Light.* It was *Free Grace,* that hath held our *Souls in Life* hitherto, amidst a Thousand *Deaths* and *Dangers.* And *Free Grace,* in its own everlasting Arms, will still bear and carry us, thro' various *Deaths,* unto further Increases of *Life,* until we are ripened for, and brought into *Glory.* Free Grace, laid the *Foundation* of our Salvation, doth effectually *manage it,* and will gloriously *finish it.*—Alas, we can't live one Moment, without fresh Supplies from *Christ;* nor do the least Thing in his Service, spiritually, without renewed Strength from *Him* continually.—And yet, oh wretched Creatures that we are! when our *Lord* fills us, how prone are we, thro' that accursed Pride which remains in us, to rob Him of his Glory, as if *we* were *something?* And when we have thus provok'd our Lord, our Life, our ALL, to withdraw from us, as it were for a Moment, and leave us to ourselves, to shew us we are *Nothing;* then, oh then, thro' wretched Unbelief, how prone are we to think, we shall never *see,* or *do* Good more?—But well our Dear Lord knows how to pardon, and pity us, to humble, and exalt us, to empty, and fill us; and by all, to bring us further out of ourselves, into Himself, and cause us to *grow up into Him in all Things, as our Head.*—And, oh, what an unspeakable Privilege is it, that we have *such a Head!* Such a Head of *Government!* Such a Head of *Influence!* The Father *gave Him to be Head over all Things to the Church, which is his Body, the Fulness of Him who filleth all in all!* Oh, were we *single Creatures,* were we not in *Union to Christ,* we could not *Stand,* were we ever so *perfect.*—The *Angels,* those Stars of Light, that were not secur'd by *Electing Grace,* and gather'd under *Christ,* as an *Head;* fell from their shining Orbs, and became *black Devils.—Adam,* that happy, that perfect *Man,* who came out of his Maker's Hand in a Fulness of Creation-Purity and Nature Bliss, standing upon his *own Bottom,* soon *lost it,* and became a miserable, guilty, filthy, *abominable Creature.*—How then should *we stand,* who have so little *Grace,* and so much *Sin* in us? And so many *Temptations* round about us? Whose Grace, is but as it were a *Spark,* amidst an *Ocean* of Corruption, agitated by fierce *Winds* of Temptation, which *threatens* its Destruction every Moment!—Oh here lies the Mystery, the Glory, the Security of a *Believer,* his Life is hid with CHRIST *in* GOD! A *Believer's Life,* is in Union to CHRIST, in an indissoluble Union, to an inexhaustible Fulness of endless Life, in the *Son of* GOD! A *Believer's Life,* is the Life of *Christ* in him. *He* lives; yet not *he,* separate from Christ, but CHRIST lives in *him.* And *because* CHRIST *lives,* and so *long* as CHRIST lives, a *Believer shall live also.* The weakest *Member* of the Body of Christ, is in Union to such a mighty *Head,* that he can never *fall.* That is, from his *new Life,* into the *Death of Unregeneracy.* No; CHRIST, in whom *all the Fullness of the* GODHEAD *dwells,* continually *holdeth his Soul in Life.*—And not only is his Life *maintain'd;* but it shall also be *increas'd.* The Life of CHRIST, in the Soul of a *Believer,* is an increasing, a Sin-killing, an All-conquering *Life.* CHRIST, his living Head, will live and reign in him, until all *Death,* of every Kind and Degree, is swallow'd up in *Victory:* Until all the Powers of his Soul, and all the Members of his Body, are filled brimful, of perfect *Life,* and endless *Glory!*

Then, my dear Brother, let us *bless* GOD for JESUS CHRIST, for this *his unspeakable* GIFT! Let us rejoyce in the *Lord* our *Life* always, notwithstanding all that *Sin* and *Death* which works in *us.* For *we are,* and shall be *more than Conquerors thro'* HIM *that hath loved us.* And in the Way of our Duty, let us leave our *Lord's Work,* in his own Almighty *Hands,* and follow on to *know* HIM, *the Fellowship of his Sufferings, and the Power of his Resurrection, that we may apprehend that, for which also we are apprehended of* CHRIST JESUS.—The dear LORD JESUS be with you! I am, my dear Brother,

Most Affectionately Yours in HIM,

———— ————

LETTER VIII. *To Mrs.* M.

My Dear Sister in Christ,

I Rejoyce to hear of the Lord's Goodness towards you, in upholding, and providing for you. I trust you feel the sweet Supports of the *everlasting Arms,* under all the Pressures you daily meet with. Every Child, my dear Sister, hath its Lot and Portion of *Trials,* each of us have our *own* Trials, which were appointed for *us,* by our Father's wise Love. And with our appointed Trials, a Sufficiency of *Grace* is provided for us, in God's *everlasting Covenant,* to carry us safely, profitable, and joyfully thro' them. Nothing comes to us by Hap or Chance. But every Thing we meet with, is the Fruit of *God's Counsel, the Counsel of his Will, the good Pleasure of his Goodness towards us in Christ. The* LORD *reigns for ever, even our* GOD. And therefore *the Children of* Zion, may *be joyful in their King.* For all Things must needs go *well,* for his Glory, and our Advantage, since all are in *his Hand,* are under the supreme Dispose of infinite Wisdom, Power and Grace. *Say to the righteous, It shall go* well *with him.* It goes *well* with the righteous, in *evil Times.* The LORD *hides them from Evil,* and under his Feathers are they secur'd from all Harm. Let Tempests rise, Winds blow, and Billows rore; those that are *Ark'd* in CHRIST, are *safe,* and may have *Rest* and *Joy* in troublous Times. Oh what can *hurt* that Soul, that dwells in CHRIST by *Faith!* If we abode in HIM, *Nothing* could hurt us. It is our going *out* of CHRIST, our departing from Him our Resting-place, by *Unbelief,* that wounds and grieves us.

Alas! when we go out of the Bosom of CHRIST, we go from *all Peace,* into *all Trouble.* Oh *Fools* that we are, and *slow of Heart to believe!* The least *Burden,* is much too heavy for *our Shoulders.* Why then, don't we cast all our Burdens upon the LORD, whose *mighty Shoulder* is well able to bear us, and all our Weights? Why don't we *cast all our Care upon Him that careth for us? Can we by taking Thought, add one Cubit to our Stature?* Why then are we so *foolish,* to go out one Moment from the Bosom of CHRIST? When shall we understand the *Wisdom of Faith,* to make CHRIST our ALL, to look to HIM for *all,* and quietly and thankfully, to leave *all Things,* in his All-wise, All-gracious, and Almighty *Hands?* Oh could we do so, all Things would be *well.* Our Lord would be *All* to us, supply all our *Wants,* and order all Things *for us;* every Way like his great, his glorious SELF! Oh, *a Life of Faith on the Son of God,* ought to be the constant Life of a *Christian.* It is a God-honouring, a Heart-cheering, a Soul enriching Life. Happy are they, who make the *Glory of God,* under every Trial, their greatest *Concern,* that have *no Will* but *His,* and that as having *Nothing,* possess *all Things* in HIM, who is their ALL! If CHRIST *is* ALL, and *our* ALL, if He has All in *Himself,* and will be All to *us,* what can we want *more?* What need we go out of our *Dear Lord,* one Moment, for any Advantage or Delight? What Good can we find *out* of Him, that is not to be enjoy'd *in Him,* transcendently, infinitely and eternally? Are Shadows *better* than Substance? Are Beams *better* than the Body of the Sun? Are Streams *better* than that broad River, that Ocean of Delights, which we have in the *Son of* GOD? What mean we, to catch at *Shadows?* To prefer *Trifles?* to *set our Eyes upon Things which are not?* Oh our Folly and base Ingratitude! Oh the infinite Grace of our forgiving God! Oh the All-conquering, the All-supplying Love, of our unchangeable Lord! Great Need have we to say, with the Disciples, *Lord, increase our Faith!* That so *the Name of our Lord may be glorify'd in us, and we in Him, according to the Grace of our God, and the Lord Jesus Christ.*—Wishing all Supplies out of Christ's Fulness, and requesting your Prayers for me; I remain, my dear Sister,

Ever Yours in our own LORD JESUS,

——— ———

LETTER IX. *To Mr.* H.

My very Dear and much Honour'd Brother,

I Long to hear from you. I forget you not in my Prayers. I hope the Lord will recover your Health, and spare you as a Blessing to his Church. I know you judge it far *better* to be *dissolved,* and to be *with* CHRIST. But surely we have Need of your Abode in the *Flesh* a while longer. Sometimes I think, 'You ripen so fast, that our Lord will gather you soon.' Glad am I, that under the rich Influences of Free Grace, you have been so mightily spirited for GOD, and borne upon the Wing in his Service. A rich, a weighty Crown of Glory, awaits you at Christ's Appearing. Oh dear Sir, go on still, to love and serve JESUS, to do and suffer for him, till Time is done, and blest Eternity comes on. And then you shall serve Him perfectly and for Ever, without Interruption, or Ceasation, among the flaming *Glories* of the *upper World!*—And oh, my dear Brother, remember *me,* a mourning Sinner, that longs to *love* JESUS. Oh pray that our Lord will *baptize me with Fire!* I am ashamed and confounded at my *little Love to Christ.* I am humbled, my Heart breaks, when I think how *much* there has been forgiven me, how *much* Favour bestow'd on me, how *long* I have been acquainted with the Prince of Grace, and yet that I love Him *so little!* Oh *wretched Sinner* that *I am!* I am no more *worthy* to be put among the *Children.* And yet Free Grace, has given me the *Relation* of a Child, tho' I deserve not a *Name* among the least and last of my *Father's House.* I am glad my Heavenly Father, my Elder Brother, my Sanctifier and Comforter, from an Infinity of Grace, know how to bear with, and cure me; to heal all my Diseases, and to beautify me with all those Graces, which I see upon others of the Family. Oh, if *Jehovah's Grace* was not *Free,* infinitely, unchangeably and eternally, *Free,* the lease Ray of it, had never shone upon vile, wretched *me!* But if the Lord *will be gracious* to the *Chief of Sinners;* who or what shall hinder Him? I am fully persuaded, that the *Grace of God,* is infinitely *sufficient* for me. And I rejoyce, I exceedingly rejoyce in this *Grace.* I cast my *Soul,* my *needy* Soul, upon this *Grace.* I know it will work *Wonders;* and I wait for its glorious Influences, to change me more and more, into the *Love-Image* of JESUS, the glorious *First-born* of Family. But oh! I am *pained* with my present *Unlikeness;* my base Heart, my ungrateful Carriage grieves me.—Oh my Brother, if you love me, pray for me, that my Lord will haste, to make me *like Him*, to make me *love Him*. That I mayn't always have such a contracted Soul, and so little in me, to delight and honour, my glorious Lord! my glorious Lover!—*Great Grace be with*, and *upon you* continually! I remain, Dear Sir,

Yours most Affectionately, in our own
Dear LORD JESUS,

———— ————

LETTER X. *To Mr*. S.

My Dear and Honour'd Brother,

YOURS I receiv'd, and return you hearty Thanks for it. I rejoice to hear, what God hath done for your Soul, in *shewing* you your lost, miserable State by *Nature*, in *revealing* his *Dear Son in you*, and his own infinite, free, everlasting *Love* towards you. Calling Grace, my Brother, is a Time-Fruit of God's Eternal Love. If you had not had an everlasting Standing in God's *old Love*, in the Grace of eternal *Election*, you had not been thus *drawn* with *Loving-kindness* in Time. And what was it, think you, that *mov'd* the Love of God towards you, that mov'd Him to Chuse *You*, and to resolve to be Gracious unto *You*, when he pass'd by *Thousands?* Was it your *forseen Goodness?* Was *you better* than those that *perish? No*, you'll say, *in no wise*. No, my Brother, we that are *Vessels of Mercy*, on whom God will made known the *Riches of his Glory*, of his glorious *Grace*, were of the *same Lump* with those who are *Vessels of Wrath, fitted to Destruction*. 'Twas nothing made *us* to differ from *others*, but the free, sovereign *Pleasure* of the great *Lord* of *Heaven* and *Earth*. We were no better by Nature, than those who are now in Hell. And tho' *Grace* has made a *Change* in us, had form'd Christ's Image in our Souls, and blest us with a begun Conformity to God's First-born; yet is *Nature*, *corrupt Nature*, even in us that are call'd by *Grace*, no better yet. In us, *that is in our Flesh, dwelleth no good Thing*. Nothing that is good, nothing but what is bad, even as *Hell of Iniquity*, abides still in our *vile Hearts*.

What then shall comfort us in our Conflicts with the Powers of Darkness? Oh it is GOD'S *Free Love!* His Sovereign *Love,* his Unchangeable, Everlasting *Love,* his Covenant-engaged *Love!* It is *This,* this *alone,* can give us *strong Consolation.* It was the good Pleasure of our Father's Will, to love us in Christ, with a Love that was and is, altogether *independent* on our Goodness. This free Love of God towards us, sought none of our Goodness, as a Motive of its Fixation upon us, nor doth it seek it as a motive of its Continuation to us. No, the LORD *loved us,* not because we were *better* than others; but because it *pleased the* LORD *to love us.* So Free, so infinitely Free was the Love of God, that He resolv'd to love us *without* our foreseen Goodness, *notwithstanding* all our fore-view'd Badness, to *bestow* all Goodness upon us, to *maintain* all Goodness in us, and in the End to *fill us* with all Goodness, with every Kind and Degree of *Goodness,* to the utter *Exclusion* of all our *Badness:* Or, in a Word, to make us *Holy, and without Blame before Him in Love,* and to keep us so, to the Days of Eternity!

And when Free Love has brought us up to our designed Perfection in *Grace,* we shall give it all the *Glory;* and wonder out *Eternity,* at distinguishing *Love,* while we each one for ourselves, warble out its Praises, with a Why *me, Lord!* Why *me!* Why should *I* be thus rais'd by Grace to eternal Glory, while a *Thousand* Sinners, no worse than I, fell at my *Side,* and *Ten Thousand* at my *Right Hand!* And all the innumerable Multitude of the saved Ones, shall jointly and together cry, *Not unto us, not unto us, O* LORD, *but unto thy Name,* unto thy Free Grace, in the whole of our *Salvation,* be the whole and eternal *Glory!*

And oh what Grace is it, my dear Brother, that mean Time, Heaven should come down to *meet us,* in this low Land! That now and then, under bright Displays of infinite Favour, we should be fill'd with heavenly Wonder and Joy, and thus begin the Work of Praise and Adoration, even while on this Earth! They are all *Heirs of* GOD, and have the *Earnest of the Spirit* given them, that are blest with these sweet Foretastes of *Glory,* of the *Enjoyment* and *Employment* of the *upper World.*

And having this Hope, thro' God's Free Love, of seeing JESUS as HE is, of being made like Him, and of being for ever with Him; what remains for us to *do* in the present State? Verily, it is only this, To *purify ourselves, even as* HE *is pure.* The Gospel of God's Free Grace in Christ, brings *all Salvation* to us: And, *only,* says the Apostle, *let your Conversation be as becometh the Gospel.* Oh what great, what high Obligations, doth God's Free, Eternal Love, lay us under to live to its Praise in the present Time! And the more the Love of God is shed abroad in our Hearts, the more holy, happy Christians, should we, shall we be. None are so Free, so gloriously Free, as those whom God's Free Love, binds most strongly unto all holy Obedience. *Bind us,* O LORD, for *ever,* bind us with Free Love! Then shall we be *Free indeed!*

Glad am I, my dear Brother, that you are helpt to *settle* upon GOD'S *everlasting Covenant,* his Covenant of Free Grace in CHRIST, which *is order'd in all Things, and sure.* This is a solid Foundation for our Faith and Hope, an immoveable Resting-place, amidst a thousand Shakings, from within and without. Our Frames continually *vary,* and *various* are the Dispensations which pass over us: But the *Covenant* of our God, doth not *Alter;* because the GOD of it don't *change;* and the *Head* of it, in whom all the Blessings of it are secur'd, is *Yesterday, To-Day, and for Ever the same.* Well then may this be our Support, both in Life and in Death. For *tho' our Flesh and our Heart fail us,* GOD, our New-Covenant GOD, *is the Strength of our Hearts, and our Portion for Ever. Tho' the Mountains and Hills shall depart,* the most lasting Parts of this lower Creation be dissolved, and Time itself put to a Period; GOD'S *Kindness* towards us in CHRIST, shall *not,* depart, but run on in its own everlasting *Round,* thro' *his Covenant of Peace,* which *shall not be removed,* unto our Joy and Glory, *Full* and *Eternal.*—Wishing a rich *Increase of all Grace,* unto a *weighty Crown of Glory;* and requesting your Prayers for me: I remain, Dear Sir,

Your Affectionate humble Servant,

In the LORD *the* LAMB,

——— ———

LETTER XI. *To Mrs.* T.

My very Dear Sister in Christ,

YOURS I receiv'd, I return you hearty Thanks. I rejoyce that you can say, concerning your late Trial, and your yet not ended Affliction, *Good is the Word of the* LORD, *which He hath spoken.* And that there was a *Need-be,* for your Exercise in these Regards.—Go on, my dear Sister, to believe the Love, and adore the Wisdom of your Heavenly Father herein. And to wait for the blessed Fruit of this his kind Chastisement. *Be in Subjection unto the Father of Spirits:* And *Life,* in the Increase of your Graces, in this World, and of your Crown of Glory in that to come, shall be the Effect of it.—And lo, God will be *glorify'd* in you, by this Trial, if you behave under it, like your *Lord,* and *learn Obedience by the Things which you suffer.* The State of God's *People,* and especially of his *Favourites,* in this World, is a *State of Suffering.* Whoever is at *Ease,* God's *dear Children,* his *beloved Ones,* shall not. They shall be *empty'd* from *Vessel to Vessel,* remov'd from *Trial to Trial,* to *refine* them the more. God will set the *Bush* He *loves,* on *Fire,* all on a *Flame.* But for the *Good Will of* HIM *that dwells in the Bush,* it shall not be *consumed* by the *fiery Trial;* but preserved *green* and *flourishing* under it: To the Glory of infinite *Power,* and boundless *Grace,* and to the Wonder and Praise of *Men* and *Angels,* thro' *Time* and to *Eternity.* Oh it's worth while, to *turn aside, to see this great Sight:* A *Bush on Fire and not consumed!* A *weak Child of God,* amidst *fiery Trials, uninkindled* by the Flame! Yea, full of *Sap* and *Moisture,* growing, and increasing thereby! In such a Case, we are made a *Spectacle* unto *God,* unto *Angels,* and to *Men.* GOD looks on us with infinite *Pleasure,* sees his own Glories display'd, and our Graces exercis'd, and says concerning us, as of his Servant *Job, Still he holdeth fast his Integrity.* And, *I have chosen Thee in the Furnace of Affliction. Good Angels rejoice,* to see the Favourites of Heaven behave under fiery Trials, as becomes their high Relation to GOD, and the Greatness of that Love and Duty which they owe to Him. And with Joy they *wing the Way,* to carry the Tidings up to the Throne and Court above. *Evil Angels,* are *confounded* at such a Sight. *Good Men* behold with *Wonder, Joy* and *Praise,* this glorious Sight, A flourishing Saint, amidst fiery Trials. The *World* of unconverted Men, stand *Agast.* The Conscience of some are struck with

Fear. The Souls of others *allur'd* to love and serve that GOD, who is so *good* to his suffering Servants, and works such *wonders* for them.—How *joyful* then, my dear Sister, would *we be* in *Tribulation?* And how *careful* of our *Behaviour* under it. to answer the great *Ends* of it, while we are thus made a *Spectacle unto all!*—And lo, the LORD that is with us *in* Trouble, will deliver is *out* of it; to his great Glory, and our great Advantage—Let us then, my dear Sister, take the *Prophets* and Saints of old, and our *Brethren* the Saints now, who behave under Trials as they ought, for *an Example of suffering Affliction, and of Patience.* Since we *have heard of the Patience of* Job, *and have seen the* End *of the* Lord: *That the Lord is very* pitiful, *and of* tender Mercy. And that *the* LORD *blessed the latter End of* Job *more than his Beginning.* And let *us,* with the Primitive Saints, *count them* happy *which* endure.—And see you not, my dear Sister, that he Lord has rather shaken his Rod at you, than laid it upon you? And that He has begun to deliver you? Wait a while, and Weeping will be over. The *Night is far spent,* a joyous *Morning* hastens. And the Lord grant You, and your dear Yokefellow, with the Saints he may minister to, a brighter Day of *Gospel-Glory,* than ever!—*The Grace of our Lord Jesus Christ, be with your Spirit!*—In HIM, my dear Sister, I am,

Yours most Affectionately,

______ _____

LETTER XII. *To* __ ____

My very Dear and much Honour'd Brother,

I Wish your Increase in *Grace* and *Gifts.* The Lord make you a bright *Star,* in the *Church-Heaven!* Clothe you with his *Glory,* and hold you in his *Hand,* unto abundant *Usefulness* in the present *State!* And grant you a luminous *Sphere,* among the starry *Glories* of the *first Resurrection!* Believe on Christ, Brother, for your every Day's *Fitness* for the great *Work* of the *Ministry.* Bring your empty *Sacks,* your repeated *Wants,* unto JESUS your *Brother:* Of *his Fulness* you shall *receive,* and *Grace for Grace.* The *Residue of the Spirit* is with *Him.* HE can fill you with the *Holy Ghost:* And let *that* be the Top of your Ambition. Had you all the *Learning* in the *Universe,* without the *Holy Ghost,* you wou'd be a sapless, favourless *Minister* of the *glorious Gospel.* But *fill'd with the Spirit;* your Learning shall be *sanctify'd.* and made *subservient* to your Lord's *Grace,* unto *his* and *your Glory.* HE can give you a *learned Tongue,* spiritually so, to *speak a Word in Season unto him that is weary;* make you *wise* to *win Souls;* and *successful* to *turn many to Righteousness:* Who shall be your *Joy and Crown* in the *Day of Christ.—His Grace be with your Spirit!* In Him, with the most affectionate Esteem, I am, Dear Sir,

Your sincere Friend and humble Servant,

LETTER XIII. *To Mr.* D.

My Dear Love,

WE have aim'd at the *Glory of* GOD; and may quietly leave *ourselves,* and *All,* in *his Hand. If he say, He has no Delight in us;* I trust our Souls, humbled in the Dust at his Feet, shall reply, *Here we are, let the Lord do with us, as seemeth good unto Him.* It has been some Refreshment to me, that whatever the Lord doth with *me,* He will get *Himself* Glory. If He cast me to the *Dunghil,* if there I may but have Grace to love and adore, to bless and magnify Him, and to sound forth his *Praises;* methinks I can humbly *submit* to his *Holy Will,* and sweetly *acquiesce* with his *good Pleasure.* I had a pleasant Thought, "That if I was to lose all my hop'd-for *Usefulness,* as God would be *glorify'd* thereby; I would rejoice in *his Glory* as *my Gain,* and take *that* for *my Heritage."* No Reason have we to be distrest, when Things seem to make most against us. Because, as we are brought to God by the Lamb's Blood, we are brought into a *Communion of Interests.* And if we had more Faith and Love, we should delight in God's Glory, as our Gain, whatever He doth with us. If we were not sinfully *selfish,* our own Advantage, would not give us a higher Joy, than God's Glory; but be in a due Subordination to it, and afford us the greatest Joy from it. We should rejoice in the Glory of God, for its *own Sake;* and in our Advantage, first and principally, as *God is glorify'd* thereby, and in a secondary Way, as *we are happy,* under the bright

Display of God's Glory; And in Thanks and Praise, return the Glory of all to Him, which is Bliss and Joy, we receive from Him. If we sink into *Dejection of Spirit,* as if we had nothing to *rejoice in,* tho' all Things are always for the *Glory of God;* it is an Evidence of inordinate *Self Love.* As on the other Hand, if we rejoice in the *Lord* and *his Honour,* when ourselves are *abased;* it is an Evidence, so far as we are enabled to do it, of *true Love* to God in the *Heart.*—But surely we talk like *Children,* when we say, Things make *against us;* we speak the Language of *Sense,* and not of *Faith.* For lo, all Things make *for us,* they together work for *our Good.* If they make against us in the *Particulars* which we desire, they make for us in the *Generals* that we wish, and serve to bring about every Jot and Tittle of that general and particular *Good,* which our All-wise, and All-gracious GOD hath allotted for *us.* It is not good for us always to be *exalted;* 'tis very profitable for us in the present State, to be sometimes in the *Valley of Humiliation.* Christ's *Lillies* in the *Valley,* with their *Heads bow'd,* in Faith and Love, to his *holy Will,* ripen apace for *Glory,* look very *beautiful,* and cast forth a *fragrant Smell.* "In the Valley of Humiliation, as Mr. *Bunyan* observes, the *Lord* of the *Pilgrims,* delighted much to *be.*" And shall *we* be unwilling to follow our *Master,* if He *call us* into it; since thro' his chearing Presence, and gracious Influence, we shall *sing there,* and be brought *thence* with Advantage? If *Winds* of Prosperity bear us *aloft,* lest we should be *exalted above Measure,* our Wise and Gracious GOD, will make Adversity a *Weight* for them. And left we should be too much deprest, *He weigheth the Waters* of Affliction *by Measure.*

Have we not then the highest Reason, humbly, cheerfully and thankfully, to commit ourselves to Divine Conduct? The LORD will never leave his *own,* in the most *distressing* Circumstances; nor suffer any Distress to *light* upon them, but what shall *issue* in their eternal *Joy* and *Glory.* What Faith and Love, what Joy and Thanks, do we then owe to the God of Truth and Grace? Our *Happiness* lies in *sanctifying the* LORD *God in* our *Hearts,* in every of his *Dispensations* towards us. In keeping close to God, in dwelling in Him, in walking with Him, and in casting all our Care continually, upon Him that careth for us. Our Life here, is one perpetual *Scene* of various *Changes:* All which, as wisely and graciously Over-ruled, by the Sovereign Lord of all, shall effectually prepare us for our *unchangeable* and *endless Glory* hereafter. The manifestative *Glory of God,* in every Thing that passeth over us, and our present and eternal *Advantage,* are inseperably *connected* with each other. Infinite Love, join'd them both together; infinite Faithfulness, secures the Links from breaking; and infinite Power, draws the unbroken Chain, thro' a continued Series of divers Events in Time, to the Glory of God, and ours with Him, to Eternity. And when the Whole of his Providential Dispensations towards us are *finish'd,* and all that Glory brought to his great Name by every Thing that was *design'd;* and all that Good brought to us, by all Things, which was *purpos'd: The* LORD *shall rejoice in his Works:* And pronounce concerning them, to the eternal Rest of his Soul, *They are all very good.* And when the Vail is taken off, and we see with one View, all the Works of God towards us, in their Variety, Harmony and Unity, exactly answering all the glorious Ends design'd; *we* shall *rejoice* with Him: And to the eternal Glory of his Name, and Rest of our Hearts, shall say, *He hath done all Things well!*—And the more we see, and say thus now, the more of *Heaven's Bliss,* we enjoy on *Earth.* Shall not *we* that are reconcil'd to *God* by the *Lamb's Blood,* be *one in Will,* be *one in Interest* with Him. If we *are not,* it makes *us* that are the *Friends of God,* look like *Enemies* to Him. Oh let not *God* and *us,* be *twain,* since *Jesus dy'd,* to make us *one* in *Himself; To whom be Glory and Dominion, for ever and ever. Amen.*—The Dear *Lord Jesus* be with thee! I remain,

Thy most Affectionate Spouse,

——— ———

LETTER XIV. *To Mr.* L.

Dear Sir,

Having heard, that you are under much Concern about your Soul, and distressed with Fear that you shall be *Lost:* I was willing to write a Line to you. To tell you that *Jesus Christ came into the World to save lost Sinners.* For this you have his own Word: *For the Son of Man is come to seek and to save that which was Lost,* Luke 19. 10.

We are all by Nature *Sinners:* guilty and filthy we were in our first Father *Adam,* by *his first Sin;* and have receiv'd a guilty, filthy *Nature* from him. And thus were *born* Sinners, and have gone *astray* from God, even from the *Womb.* And by every Sin, while we abide in a natural State, we go farther and farther off from God; and have neither Will, Skill, nor Power to return to him. And having forsaken our GOD, we have lost all true *Happiness* for our poor Souls which is only to be enjoy'd in *Him.* Having departed from our true and proper *Rest.*—And for our Sins, the righteous *Law of God,* pursues us with its Curse, and thunders out Wrath and Death against *every Soul of Man that doth Evil,* And thus, having *lost our* GOD, we have *lost ourselves;* lost all true Happiness, and brought upon us all Miseries in the Desert of them, and in the Beginnings of them too, in our Souls and Bodies, and are in apparent Danger of eternal Perdition. And by our Sin against God, *Satan* has got the Dominion over us, blindeth our Minds, hardens our Hearts, and leads us on in the Ways of *Sin,* down toward the Chambers of endless *Death.*—Thus all Mankind *lost by Sin;* and might justly have been *lost for ever,* in the Abyss of *Eternal Misery.*

But lo, *The Son of Man is come to seek to save that which was lost! God sent forth his Son made of a Woman, made under the Law, To redeem them that were under the Law.* The boundless Grace of God, provided a Redeemer for lost sinners. And this was no other than his own Son, *who thought it not Robbery to be Equal with* GOD. GOD *so loved* lost Sinners, *that He gave his only begotten* SON: To take our *Nature* into Union with his Divine *Person,* to become the *Son of Man.* That so *He,* who was the Son of God, and the Son of Man, that had both the Divine and Human Natures, in his one Person, might become *our* JESUS. That he in the same Nature that sinned, might destroy the Devil and all his Works, and save his People from their Sins, from that miserable lost State, which they had plung'd themselves into. And this He did by sustaining our Persons, taking our Law-place, bearing our sin, and Obeying, and Dying in our Stead.—By which in his own Person, He has wrought out a compleat Righteousness to cover naked Sinners; satisfy'd Divine Justice to the Full for our Sins; destroy'd all our Enemies, and *obtain'd Eternal Redemption for us.*—And having finisht the Work, God as *the God of*

Peace, brought him *again from the Dead thro' the Blood of the everlasting Covenant,* rais'd him from the Grave, as a triumphant Conqueror over Sin, Death and Hell; and exalted him to his own Right Hand, to save Sinners to the uttermost. That same JESUS, which sav'd Sinners compleatly by the *Price of his Blood,* when He dy'd for them upon the Cross; now lives for ever upon the Throne, to save them by the *Power of his Arm.* This *good Shepherd, that gave his Life for the Sheep,* will not suffer any one of them to be eternally *Lost.* But He will go *after that which is lost, until He find it; and when He hath found it,* He will *lay it upon his Shoulder, and bring it home* to the Fold, to his Church below, and to his Church above, both in Grace, and in Glory, *rejoycing.*

Then Sir, Are you *lost?* Jesus Christ can *seek and save you to the uttermost.* He came on *purpose* to save lost Souls; and in his Work He exceedingly *delights.* He shed his precious Blood for lost Sinners, that in the Virtue thereof, He might employ his infinite Power to save them. Are *you* wounded by Sin? CHRIST'S Blood can heal you. *With his Stripes we are healed.* Have *you* no Righteousness to appear in before GOD, that will bear the Test of his holy Law, and strict Justice? CHRIST has wrought out a Robe of Righteousness, to array naked Sinners, and make them appear Glorious in the Eyes of flaming Purity: His Name is THE LORD OUR RIGHTEOUSNESS. Have *you* no Strength to get the Victory over Sin, Satan and the World? Or to get out of the present Distress which you are in? CHRIST has an *Arm like* GOD, the *Arm of* GOD: In this LORD the SAVIOUR, there is Strength for the weakest Sinner: He can subdue your Iniquities, and bind all your spiritual Enemies: Bring you out of Darkness and the Shadow of Death, and break your Bands in sunder. Are *you* shut up as in Prison, under the Guilt and Power of Sin, and terrible Fears of Divine Vengeance? That JESUS who dy'd for Sinners, and bore the Wrath of GOD, to deliver us from the Wrath which is to come, is Authoriz'd by the Father, and Anointed with the Holy Ghost, to *proclaim Liberty to the Captives, and the opening of the Prison to them that are bound: To say to the Prisoners, Go forth, to them that are in Darkness, Shew yourselves.* Do *you* find that you have no Power to believe and repent? *Faith* and *Repentance* are the SAVIOUR'S *Gifts: He is exalted at God's Right Hand* to bestow them upon poor unbelieving, impenitent Sinners: *To give Repentance and Remission of Sins, thro' Faith in his Blood.* And he has promis'd to *pour the Spirit of Grace and of Supplications,* upon Souls that want Grace, and can't pray; that they may *Look upon Him whom they have pierced, and mourn, and be in Bitterness for Him.* Oh, Sir, CHRIST can give you a believing Heart, as broken Heart, a praying Heart, in an Instant. For He is *Mighty to save!* a GOD *working Wonders!* Yea, Wonders of Life for the Dead! In a Word then, Are *you* in a miry Pit, a Pit of Noise, where there is no Standing, where your Soul is terrify'd exceedingly, and from whence you can in no wise deliver yourself? JESUS can *bring you up from the miry Clay, out of this horrible Pit, and set your Feet upon Himself the Rock of Ages; and put a new Song into you Mouth, even Praise unto our* GOD, for a full and everlasting Salvation, which of his boundless Grace, He always bestows freely. You are not sunk too low, for *Everlasting Arms* to *reach you.* Therefore wait patiently upon the LORD.

And now, Sir, as I have hinted *Something,* tho' I han't told you a *Thousandth Part,* of the Excellency of CHRIST as a SAVIOUR: What do you *Think of Him?* Do you see any Suitableness in this mighty SAVIOUR, to your Case as a *perishing Sinner?* Do you see any Beauty in Him, whereby you desire Him? Are the Breathings of your Soul after CHRIST, as the Desires of *David* after the Water, when ready to die for Thirst, he said, *Oh that one would give me of the Water of the Well of* Beth-lehem *to drink!* Are these the Longings of your Heart, "Oh that CHRIST would give me Himself, and all that Life and Salvation that is in Him; that my thirsty, perishing Soul might drink its Fill, and live for ever!"—If so, then hear what he says to you: *I will give unto him that is athirst, of the Fountain of the Water of Life freely,* Rev. xxi. 6. *See:* Not a Soul that is *athirst* for CHRIST, shall perish and die for *Want* of Him! CHRIST, and all his Grace, is prepared on *purpose* for such Souls; and shall be bestowed upon them freely: Without Money, and without Price, without any Worth or Worthiness in them. They shall drink, and drink abundantly, thro' Time and to Eternity, of that *pure River of Water of Life, the Streams whereof make glad the City of God.*—Oh, Sir, if you apprehend yourself at *present* to be in a perishing Condition, you shall not be *eternally lost,* if you *look unto* JESUS. Cast your Eye therefore unto *Him,* as GOD'S

Salvation to the *Ends of the Earth.* He bids you *Look unto Him for Life;* and has said to every Looker, *Be ye saved.* He has granted Salvation to the worst, the chiefest of Sinners, that *look* to Him for it. And he will never, never *repent* what He has said, or be *worse* than his Word. He has said, *They shall come that were ready to perish.* Come then, dear Sir, cast your perishing *Soul* at the SAVIOUR'S *Feet,* and you shall *live for ever.* There is *Salvation in Him;* and there is *none* in any *other.* They must all *perish,* that do not look, that do not come to CHRIST: But not a Soul shall be *lost,* that comes at his Call, and casts itself in all its Misery, at the Feet of his Mercy. If you are afraid that you shall *perish,* come to JESUS. And if you fear that he will not *receive you,* come and *try.* You can *but* perish: Oh cast yourself at the SAVIOUR'S *Feet,* and resolve, That if you *do* perish, you will perish *There.* But Oh, be assur'd, tht *This is no perishing Ground.* For CHRIST Himself says to you, *Him that cometh unto Me, I will in no wise cast out,* Joh. vi. 37.—And it is no Sign that you shall be eternally *lost,* because you now *see* your perishing State. For when CHRIST seeks and saves *lost Souls,* He always shews them their *lost Condition;* that so they may be willing to be *found of Him,* and *sav'd by Him* from all Misery, unto all Glory. Wishing this Salvation, I am, Sir,

Your Affectionate Friend and Servant in the Lord,

——— ———

LETTER XV. *To Mr.* C.

Reverend and very dear Brother,

I Sympathize with you in your great Affliction, by the Withdraw of the Divine Presence, as to the warming, comforting, enlarging Influences of God's free Favour. Oh how sad is our Case, when our *Beloved* is thus withdrawn from us! When CHRIST our Light, our Life, our Joy, steps aside for a While, then Darkness, Death and Sorrow cover us. The Beasts of Prey roar against us, with a 'Where is now your God? He'll be favourable no more; your Strength and your Hope, your Life, your Joy, your Usefulness in the present State, are perished from the LORD. You looked for Light; but behold, Darkness. In vain you cry for Help; for the

LORD shutteth out your Prayers,' &c.—And happy is that Soul, who at such Seasons, is establish'd in the *Faith* of his *Interest* in God's everlasting *Favour.* An unspeakable Support in *This,* under greatest Pressures. Such a Man is arm'd against the Powers of Darkness. They can't pierce him to the Heart, as they do others of God's Children, with the Terror of an everlasting Separation from Him. Such a Soul, when stript of the Joys of spiritual Sense, can say in Faith, with the Church, *Rejoice not against me, O mine Enemy, when I fall, I shall arise; when I sit in Darkness, the* LORD, *shall be a Light unto me. I will bear the Indignation of the* LORD, *because I have sinned against Him, until He plead my Cause, and execute Judgment for me: He will bring me forth to the Light, and I shall behold his Righteousness,* Mic. vii. 8, 9.—And glad am I, my dear Brother, that this is *your* happy *Lot.* By Believing in the Dark, you will give Glory unto God, in his infinite Grace, Power, and Faithfulness; and hereby you will enjoy sweet Peace, in the Midst of Trouble.—I hope, my Brother, that our dear Lord is return'd unto you again with Mercies, before this Time. But if *not;* go on to trust in Him, tho' He should seem to slay you, to hope in his Mercy, tho' He should follow you with Rebuke, and to seek his Return, tho' He should seem to go further from you. And be of good Chear; for all Things shall issue well, shall together *work* for you *Good,* and *turn* to your *Salvation.*—Do you *groan* under Deadness, Darkness, Bondage: Oh *happy Soul!* 'Tis an *Evidence* of your *new Life,* that you are a *Child of Light,* and have formerly walk'd in the *glorious Liberty* of the *Sons of God.* Else you would not know what the *Want* of these Things is. Do you *groan,* because your *Beloved* has *withdrawn* Himself? 'Tis an Evidence, that *Christ* and *you,* have heretofore had sweet *Fellowship* with each other.—And lo, Those whom Christ *loves,* He loves unto the *End.* He will not, cannot hide Himself *long* from such Souls. His Withdraw, is but for a *Moment,* to set off the Glory of his *Return,* and further to display the Immensity, and Eternity of his *Kindness.* Those whom Christ *quickens,* shall never *die;* shall never lose their new Life, nor suffer any *Decays* thereof, but in order to their further *Increases* therein. Those whom Christ enlightens with the *Light of Life,* shall not *walk in Darkness;* in *total,* in abiding Darkness, nor in any *partial* Darkness, that shall not *end* in *Light,* and serve as a *Foil* to illustrate its *Glory.* And those whom the *Son makes free,* shall no more return to *Bondage;* to a *State* of Bondage, *nor shall* any *Bondage Frame* seise them, but shall be over-rul'd for their further *Freedom, their more glorious Liberty.—In Patience* then, my dear Brother, *possess your Soul,* and *wait* for your own *God;* and you shall not be *ashamed.* His Love, as it was free in its Fixation upon you, so it is and will be free, immensely free, in its Continuation to you, and in all its Emanations upon you. GOD'S *Love* is like HIMSELF, Great, Sovereign, Unchangeable and Eternal. And it is secur'd to *you,* in Itself, and in all its glorious Fruits, unto your full and eternal *Salvation,* by the infinite Faithfulness of the strong, the immutable JEHOVAH, in his everlasting, his well-order'd *Covenant.* Infinite Wisdom, for the further Display of infinite Love, sees it meet, my Brother, that *now for a Season, you should be in Heaviness thro' manifold Temptations, That the Trial of your Faith being much more precious than of Gold that perisheth, tho' it be try'd with Fire, might be found unto Praise, and Honour, and Glory at the Appearing of Jesus Christ.* By the Darkness that now covers you, the Lord is preparing you for Light. By Deadness for Life; by Bondage for Freedom; and by Shame for Glory: Both present and eternal. *For your Shame, you shall have double,* double Glory; *and for Confusion, you shall rejoice in your Portion. The Evening and the Morning,* you know, *were the first Day: &c.* Your present Darkness, is but the Forerunner of Light. Another *Day,* of further *Glory,* awaits you. The Lord hasten its happy *Dawn,* and make its *Meridian-Brightness great,* in your dear Soul, in your Family, and in the Church of God! So prays,

Dear Sir,

Yours most Affectionately in CHRIST,

——— ———

LETTER XVI. *To Mr.* L.

My Dear Brother in Christ,

I Heartily thank you for your last. By the Contents of it, I am made to admire the Riches of sovereign Grace, in *your,* in *my Salvation.* CHRIST, as the only Way of Salvation, is a *Path,* that the *Vulture's Eye,* that no unregenerate Man, tho' of the most piercing natural Wisdom, hath *seen.* 'Twas the same free, rich, infinite Grace, which provided CHRIST *for us,* that reveal'd Him *in us.* Ah, when *Nature* has done its utmost, to judge of *Salvation by Grace* it will still be an impenetrable *Mystery* to the *natural Man. The Things of the Spirit of God,* of the Father's, and of the Son's *Love,* in the Provision and Exhibition of the SAVIOUR, and in the Application of *Salvation* to the saved *Ones,* which the Holy Ghost reveals, are *not receiv'd* by the natural Man; *because they are Foolishness unto Him; neither can he know them, because they are spiritually discerned.* So great is the Power of Darkness, of the Soul-killing Influence of Sin and Satan, that it fills the Mind, and blinds the Understanding of the *natural Man;* and will hold him fast, as in a deep Dungeon, under the Bondage of the Law, without the least Beam of Gospel-Light; unless the omnipotent Power of Divine Grace, of the *God* and *Father* of our Lord Jesus Christ, *deliver him* from the *Power of Darkness,* and *translate him* into the *Kingdom of his dear Son.* Unless the Holy Ghost, sent from the Father and the Son, makes him a *spiritual Man,* creates a *Principle* of spiritual *Light* and *Life,* in his dead, dark *Heart;* and thereby makes him *meet* to be a *Partaker* of the *Inheritance* of the *Saints in Light.* Without the *Light of Grace,* without an inward gracious *Principle* of spiritual Light, which discerns and cleaves to the Light of Grace, to the *Doctrine* of Grace, in the outward Revelation; no Man shall ever see the *Light of Glory.* And nothing less than the omnipotent *Power* of the LORD alone, can create, or produce this Light in any one Soul.—What Reason then, have *we* to admire that Grace, that *saves* us thro' Faith, and gives us *Faith,* to receive Salvation alone by *Grace!* Oh, *Not of ourselves,* indeed, is Gospel-Faith; *it is the Gift of God.* A free Gift of his sovereign Grace, to those who were *ordained to eternal Life.* The LORD the Father, hath done more for us, in giving us *Faith,* to see the Glory of the LORD the Mediator, and the Excellency of GOD the SAVIOUR, in his Person and Work; than if He had given us *Millions of Worlds!* Oh what were they all worth, without, or in Comparison with his *Son! Without* the Knowledge of CHRIST, and of GOD in Him, whom to *know,* is *Life eternal!* Or in *Comparison* with that Knowledge!—Oh how evident is it, that the wise and learned World, with all their Learning and

Wisdom, are awful Strangers to *God,* to the *Lord Jesus Christ,* and to the blessed Operations of the *Holy Ghost!* Alas! the *World's \wise* and *prudent* Ones, know not the *Mystery of Faith,* nor the *Power of Godliness!* The *Kingdom of God,* of his Grace, is not *within them.* Hence they oppose and reproach, the Things which they understand not. Unto us, *Babes, it is given to know the Mysteries of the Kingdom, but unto them that are without,* even to the *Masters in* Israel, *all these Things are in Parables. Even so, Father, for so it seemed good in thy Sight!*—Let us adore the *Grace,* my Brother, that opened *our Eyes;* and pray that *the Eyes of the Blind,* of God's Chosen that are yet in Blindness, may *see out of Obscurity;* and that our Lord's Kingdom may come, over all the Opposition that stands in its Way; and rise and shine thro' all the Mists and Fogs, which are rais'd to obscure its *Glory. Grace be with you!* I am,

Yours most affectionately in the slain LAMB,

——— ———

LETTER XVII. *To Mr.* B.

Dear Sir,

THE *Sanctification* of a *Sinner,* by *Faith* in the SAVIOUR, is indeed a glorious *Gospel Mystery.* A Mystery, hid from the *natural Man;* and that, even by *spiritual Men,* is not well known, that is, practically understood. And yet a Mystery it is, of the greatest Concernment, both with respect to the Glory of God, and the Good of his People. Without some Degree of real-Acquaintance with it, a Man cannot be a *Christian.* And the more fully and sensibly he is acquainted therewith, the more *holy,* the more *happy* Christian is he. And the more is the God of all Grace in Christ, *glorify'd* thereby. Oh, a *Life of Faith* on the *Son of God,* is the every *Day's Work* of a Believer. Without it, we shall soon be *Backsliders* in Heart and Ways.—And oh the infinite Love, the boundless Grace of God, that tho' we are *bent* to Backsliding from Him, and are every Day guilty of it more or less; He will still call us, *His People,* and according to his Promise, will *Heal our Backslidings, and love us freely.* Aye, *freely* indeed! or He had never loved *us.* Us, that by Nature, were a

Sea of Vileness! A Hell of Iniquity! A Mass of black and horrid Contrariety to his infinite Purity! Us, that by Practice, were Transgressors form the Womb! And which is most amazing! Us, that since the Display of his infinite, all-attracting Grace, in the Forgiveness of our Sins, in the Sanctification of our Nature, and in the Admission of our Persons, into all the Royalties and Privileges of the Sons of God; have nevertheless, slighted his Love, despis'd his Commandments, forsaken the Lord, and gone after other Lovers! And yet, oh yet, GOD *loveth us!* Us, who are guilty of such Ingratitude, that is not to be found among the Damned! And this notwithstanding He *knew* beforehand, how *treacherously* we should deal with Him, how rebellious, how abominable we should be! Oh this was *Free Love* indeed! Free in its Fixation; and free in its Continuation, or it would not have *held* towards us till *now!* We have *try'd it,* by innumerable Provocations, by most aggravated Transgressions: Every of our Sins, who are so greatly beloved, so highly favour'd, being of a deep Dye, an extensive Guilt, a bloody Colour, And yet, all Glory to infinite, unchanging *Love,* thro' infinite, all-atoning *Blood!* our JEHOVAH, *consumes not the Sons of* Jacob, but *loves them freely still!*—And tho' the Lord, to bring his backsliding Children to a Sense of their Backslidings, puts them in Mind of their Folly and Ingratitude; yet such is his infinite Grace, that He calls upon them to return unto Him. *For pass over the Isles of* Chittim, *and see;* (saith the Lord) *and send unto Kedar, and consider diligently, and see if there be such a Thing.* (Look, as if the Lord should say, O my People, whether there be such an *Influence* of Folly and Ingratitude, to be found in the *ungodly World,* as is to be seen in *you!*) *Hath a Nation changed their Gods, which yet are no Gods? But my People have changed their Glory* (their God who is their Glory) *for that which doth not profit.—For of old Time I have broken thy Yoke, and burst thy Bands, and thou saidst, I will not transgress: When upon every high Hill, and under every green Tree thou wandrest, playing the Harlot,* Jer. ii. 10, 11, 20. And yet, saith the Lord, Chap. iii. 1. *They say, If a Man put away his Wife, and she go from him, and become another Man's, shall he return unto her again? Shall not that Land be greatly polluted? But thou hast played the Harlot with many Lovers; yet return again unto Me, saith the* LORD.—"Oh Free, Invincible, Everlasting Love! Overcome us, melt us, draw us! Then returning, under thy healing Influence, we will say repeatedly, after all our Heart, Lip, and Life-Backslidings, *Behold, we come unto Thee, for Thou art the* LORD *our God."*—Oh my dear Brother, what an unspeakable Privilege is it, that such poor backsliding Children as we, have such a merciful Father, that will not cause his Anger to fall upon us, tho' we have done as evil Things as we could! And how should this influence our Souls, into Childlike Ingenuity to our Heavenly Father? and Spouselike Loyalty to our Royal Bridegroom?—Surely it is our Wisdom as *Believers,* to come to the SAVIOUR daily, as being in ourselves, poor *Sinners;* and to abide in Him continually by Faith, to receive of his *Fulness,* and *Grace for Grace.* Even all Supplies of Grace, for multiply'd Pardon, abundant Peace, full Joy, renewed Strength, and increasing Holiness. So shall we be *filled with all the Fruits of Righteousness* here, *which are by Jesus Christ, unto the Glory and Praise of God.* And shall have an *abundant Entrance* hereafter, *ministred unto us into the everlasting Kingdom of our Lord and Saviour, Jesus Christ. To whom be Glory and Dominion for ever and ever.* Amen. Wishing all Prosperity: I remain, dear Sir,

Your obliged Friend and Servant,
in our Glorious Lord,

——— ———

LETTER XVIII. *To* -- --

Honoured Sir,

HOW glorious will be that State, when all the Saints shall *see Eye to Eye!* When we shall know, and love, and serve the Lord perfectly! When all our Death and Darkness, shall be swallowed up of Light and Life, full and eternal! That ineffable Bliss, hastens: Our *Lord comes quickly!* Let us by the Desires of our Souls, and in the Use of all appointed Means for our Growth in Grace, and Fruitfulness in good Works, press forward unto *that Day's Glory!* Yet a little while, and we shall *see* JESUS as HE *is,* be completely *like Him,* and *for ever with him!* And who can *tell* what Joys, what Glories, the Sight of our *Beloved's Face,* will cast upon *us,* to an *endless Space!* O my dear and honoured Brother, is CHRIST *yours,* and is HE *mine?* Let us rejoice in our wondrous LOT! Our present and eternal ALL! And may the *Love of Christ,* constrain us to *live to Him,* who *died for us and rose again!*

My dear Lord hath been with me in my Affliction; hath rebuk'd the Disease as an Answer of Prayer, and is raising me up to do a little Work for Him, I trust, which I long'd to finish, before I go hence, and be no more. O pray for a *double Portion of the Holy Spirit* to be poured upon me, that my redeemed Life, may be *doubly the Lord's!*—Sweet has a Thought of *living to the Will of God,* been to *me* of late, and particularly in *Sufferings:* by an humble, patient, sweet Submission to, and a joyful Acquiescence with, the *Will of God,* to give him the *Glory due to his great Name.* When we yield to any unmeet Heaviness under Trials, methinks we rather *die,* than *live,* to the *Will of God* therein—This, this of *Living to the Will of God,* is the daily *Work* of a *Christian.* To live to the Will of his *Promise* by *Faith,* to the Will of his □ Precepts in *Love,* and thro' both to live to the Will of his Providence, whether joyous or grievous, by a complacent *Flow* into *God's good Pleasure,* and an humble, thankful *Adoration* of HIM, in all the various Dispensations, of his invariable Love towards us.—Delightfully *sweet* is this our Work in *itself,* and thus to our abundant Joy is *experienced,* when the Power of Christ rests upon us for its *Performance:* And ineffably *great* will be our *Reward,* when, of the freest *Grace,* we are called to enter into the *Rest,* the *Joy,* the *Glory* of our *great Lord!* It becomes us, Sir, to *mourn* that we can live *no more* to HIM, who liv'd and dy'd, who rose and lives for ever for *us!* That we who are *bought with a Price,* can glorify God *no more,* in our Body, and in our Spirit, which are GOD'S! *This,* as the Case stands with *us,* (who being *sold under Sin,* oft experience, that when to *will is present* with us, *how to perform* we *find not,* this) is part of our *Work* and Labour of Love. Which our loving Lord, in the Infinity of his Grace, will call *our Kindness,* and in Love unknown, will accept and account as *our Service,* as if we had *done,* in some Sort, all that Work for HIM, which we fain *would* have done: And reward us he will, according to his *own Heart,* and every Way like his *Great* SELF! O what a glorious *Master* is *Jesus Christ!* None is *like Him* in *Grace!* May we *always abound in his Work,* to his present and endless

Praise!—That *the Love of God our Father, the Grace of our Lord Jesus Christ, and the Communion of the Holy Ghost* may *be with you:* is the hearty Desire of, Honoured sir,

Your most obliged Humble Servant,

——— ———

LETTER XIX. *To Mrs.* H.

My very Dear Sister in Christ,

AS the Lord hath fixed the *Bounds of our Habitation,* and the *Times before appointed;* we may be well assured, that for us his dear Children, He hath done all Things in relation thereto, so *Well,* that nothing could have been *better* than it *is.* His *Will,* in this Regard, being founded upon his *Counsel,* and his abounding *Wisdom and Prudence,* towards us, being according to the *exceeding Riches of his Grace.* Whence we should be induced to give *Glory,* to our all-wise, and all-gracious GOD. And as the Places and Times of our Abode were appointed; so likewise, our *Work* therein ordained. Our Work for *God* and his *People,* in relation to the Building, Beauty and Glory of the *Church,* the *City of the great King.* Thus God's People of old, *repaired the Wall of* Jerusalem, *every one over-against his House,* Neh. iii. 28. And thus we in particular, are especially call'd in Love to the *House of our God,* and for our *Brethren,* our *Companions Sakes,* to seek the *Good* of *Jerusalem,* the *Prosperity of Sion,* by Faith and Prayer, in the Places where *we live,* or *over against* the *Houses* where *our Lot* is cast. And as the *Lord* has chosen our Work for us, and the Places of our Residence in order to it; *we* should chuse the *latter,* as subservient to the *former.*—Glad should I have been, my dear Sister, if your Lot had been cast *here;* but as Providence at present fixes your *Abode* in the Place where you *reside;* believe that *this* is most for *God's Glory* and *your Advantage.* Such is the infinite Condescension of your Lord's Grace, that he will say, He hath *Need of you,* and of your Faith and Prayer, for the Advancement of his Cause and Interest, the Success of his Gospel, and the Good of his People in *N------n.* And you shall receive your *own Reward,* according to your *own Labour,* both in the present and future

World. You serve a *Master,* that is an *infinite Lover!* Whose *Grace* is boundless, changeless, endless! And who delights to shew its *exceeding Riches,* in the Fulness of your Time-Joy, and in the Greatness of your eternal Glory! Wherefore, go on the serve him to the utmost; and with the Enjoyment of HIM, you shall be richly blest. For His *Servants shall eat,* when others are *hungry;* His *Servants shall drink,* when others are *thirsty;* His *Servants shall sing for Joy of Heart,* when others *howl for Vexation of Spirit.*

I beg the Help of your Prayers, for the Advancement of our Redeemer's Interest in this Place. I hope the Lord will visit us with his Salvation, to revive his Work in the Midst of the Years of Trial; that this little *Tribe* be not cut off in *Israel.* It is now a Time of Distress, with most of the Churches of Christ, by the sad, felt Withdraw of Divine Influence. But at *Evening Time, it shall be light.* when our Hope is *cut off,* as it were, and Death and Darkness *feared:* Then is the *Lord's time* to *work Salvation,* and to arise upon us with the *Light of Life,* to our joyful Surprize, and his endless Praise. How good is it then, to *wait* for HIM, who *waiteth to be gracious?* For *the Needy shan't be always forgotten, nor the Expectation of the Poor, perish for ever.* And since the LORD is a *Refuge* for the *Oppressed,* a Refuge in *Times of Trouble:* Let us that *know his Name,* put our *Trust in Him.* Let us do it for his Honour and Pleasure, and for our Salvation and Glory. For, *The* LORD *taketh Pleasure in them that fear him, in them that hope in his Mercy.* And they that *know his Name,* by Way of *Trust,* as being honour'd by them, He will *deliver and honour,* with *long Life will He satisfy* them, *and shew* them *his Salvation.—Great Grace be with you!* With affectionate Esteem, I am, my dear Sister,

Yours in the Lord for ever,

——— ———

LETTER XX. *To ---- ----*

Reverend and dear Sir,

OUR glorious *Lord,* is a glorious *Lover!* A matchless *Lover!* And while for ourselves we *know,* his Knowledge-passing *Love;* O how sweetly, how strongly doth it *constrain us,* to *love Him,* in *keeping his Commandments!* And this Command of his in particular, "That we love one another, (in our little Measure) as HE in his (immeasurable Grace) hath loved us!" Gospel Obedience, the Obedience of Faith and Love, to the excellent and endearing Laws, of the Lord our Saviour-King, has its *Reward* in *Itself.* Our very Work, is our Wages: Or, our Employment, Enjoyment. And yet, in the Exuberance of our *Lord's Grace,* there is a *Reward of Glory* to come, which in Greatness doth far *surpass,* all our present *Thought!* How *blessed* then, are those happy Souls, who, *stedfast, unmoveable,* are *always abounding in the Work of the Lord: Forasmuch as their Labour is not in vain in the Lord!* This, Sir, is a Bliss common to all the *Saints,* in the Work allotted them in common as *such.*

But O what superior *Work,* or rather, what a superior *Kind* of the Lord's Work, is the *Ministry of the Gospel!* And what peculiar *Rewards,* are *Gospel Ministers* blest with, in the present and future *State!* How great is the Reward of their present *Work!* How great the Grace, that cast it on them as a *Service of Gift!* How great is the Reward of its present *Fruit,* in the Conversion of Sinners, and Edification of Saints: To the Glory of God by Christ, the Salvation of Souls, and their own unspeakable Joy! And how great will be the Reward of those that *turn many to Righteousness,* in the *Day of Christ!* They *shall shine* (in Glory) *as the Stars for ever and ever!*—And is this, Honour'd Sir, *your* delightful Work, *your* happy Lot: How *greatly* hath the *Lord loved you!* Of the *Grace of Christ,* towards a *Minister of his,* well may Men and Angels say, *Behold how* HE *loved him!*—I wish you abundant *Joy,* Sir, in feeding, and guiding the *Flock of* GOD, which He hath *purchased with his own Blood;* and a weighty *Crown of Glory,* when the *chief Shepherd shall appear:* And humbly request your Prayers for,

Reverend Sir,

Your most obliged humble Servant,

——— ———

LETTER XXI. *To Mr.* F.

Dear Sir,

I AM glad that the rich, free, distinguishing Grace of GOD to his Own, and towards yourself, as you hope you are one of that happy Number, affects your Heart, humbles you in the Dust before the Lord, and raiseth your Wonder and Praise. *Free Grace, reigning thro' Righteousness, unto eternal Life, by Jesus Christ our Lord;* is a glorious *Theme,* the Song of Saints and Angels, in the upper and lower *Worlds,* and will sweetly strike our Strings, unto increasing Melody, thro' the endless Ages of a blest *Eternity.* O for an increasing Display of its immense Glory in the present *Time!* That under the sweet Constraints of distinguishing, unchangeable, eternal Grace, we may be dedicated unto GOD, our Three-One GOD, in *all Manner of holy Conversation!*

It is indeed, Sir, the *last Time,* the Signs of our *Lord's Coming* are upon us. Happy will it be for those Servants of his, who shalt be found *watching.* Awful Warnings of impending Judgments, have been given to this God-provoking Nation, and the Two late Shocks of *Earthquakes* felt in *London,* are eminently such. By them Lord's Voice is to the City, "Repent, or I will come unto thee quickly: And ease me of mine Adversaries, and avenge me of mine Enemies." But O, who hears it! How few tremble at it! How many, what Multitudes, are secure, and go on still in their Iniquity! Tho' the *Lord's Hand is lifted up,* the *Wicked* will not see. But he *shall see:* (saith the Prophet) and see shortly, to his everlasting Destruction; if he will not see speedily, to a thorough Reformation, to a saving Turn unto God by Christ. Who as the great Saviour, is the only hiding Place for a poor Sinner, where he may be safe, from both natural, and moral Storms: When God ariseth out of his Place, to shake terribly the Earth, and to shake the Impenitent and Unbelieving down to Hell.

As to yourself, Sir, having fled unto Christ for Refuge from the Wrath to come, be not afraid with a dismaying Fear, of God's awful Judgments in the present Time. But, *Seek Righteousness, seek Meekness; it may be you may be hid in the Day of the Lord's Anger.* His Voice to his Own is, *Come, my People, enter thou into thy Chambers, and shut the Doors about thee: Hide thyself as it were for a little Moment, until the Indignation is overpast.* And happy, thrice happy are they, that hide themselves in *Christ,* and under the Shadow of *Jehovah's Wings;* they shall be safely preserved by *Grace* from all penal Storms, amidst the greatest Shakings, and Overturnings in *Nature.* God hath remarkable Deliverances in Store for them, that *sigh and mourn,* for all the *Abominations* in the midst of them, and that are committed by the Ungodly where they dwell: When *the Earth* (as was foretold) *shall reel to and fro like a Drunkard, and be moved exceedingly, the Transgression thereof* (of those that dwell therein) being *heavy upon it.* And if any of the Lord's People should fall in a common Calamity; that sore Judgment which will sink the Wicked into Damnation, shall raise a Saint to complete Salvation, and be to him, the very *Inlet* unto Joy and Bliss, ineffable and eternal! Therefore come what will, to those that are in Christ, *Say ye to the Righteous, that it shall be well with him.*

You desire my Thoughts, Sir, "Whether the Day of Grace may be past, with some poor Souls, before their Life is at an End." Please to take them thus: *The Day of Grace,* I humbly think, may be considered in a Three-fold Respect. As 1. The *Day* of the *Gospel.* 2. The *Day* of more than ordinary *Strivings* of the *Holy Spirit* with *Men,* in common *Convictions.* And 3. The *Day* of Christ's *Power,* the Power of his special *Grace,* on the Hearts of his *People.*

First. The *Day* of the *Gospel* may be stiled *The Day of Grace.* In that it is in itself glad Tidings, the Promulgation of the Grace of God, thro' Jesus Christ, to Sinners indefinitely: Or, to the very Chief of Sinners, without Exception of this or that Man; while its general Call is to all, *Come, for all Things are now ready; viz.* God has provided a full and free Salvation for perishing Sinners, thro' the crucify'd Saviour, and calls the very Chief of them to *Faith in Christ,* and *Repentance toward God,* to come in and partake of Gospel-Provisions, to their everlasting Salvation.

The Day of Grace, in this Respect may be *over* with some Souls, before their Life is at an End. As is evident by the Lord's Dealing with the unbelieving *Jews:* The Gospel was taken from them, and sent to the *Gentiles,* Act. xiii. 46. And whoever among the *Gentiles,* obey the Gospel, but make Excuses, like the *Jews,* have just Cause to fear, lest the Master of the House, the Lord of his Church, being *angry,* should resolve concerning them, That they *shall not taste of his Supper,* Luk. xiv. 24. That the Gospel shall be taken from *them,* or they from *it.* And this is sometimes done, by God's removing the Gospel from the *Place* where such Persons live, or by his removing *them* to another Place, where the Light of the Gospel doth not shine. And if the Gospel is not taken from the Place where such Persons live, nor they from it, God in Judgment, may justly give up those that *despise the Gospel,* that chuse *present,* before *eternal Things,* to an awful *Neglect* of this *great Salvation.* So that they may have no Mind to *attend* the Gospel, but while the *Light* shines upon *others,* be content *themselves,* to *sit in Darkness,* and in the *Shadow of Death.*

Secondly. The *Day of Grace,* may be taken for the *Day* of more than ordinary *Strivings* of the *Holy Spirit* with *Men,* in common *Convictions.* As, doubtless, the Spirit of Christ, in the Ministry of *Noah,* strove with the *old World.* And these Strivings of the Spirit, proceed from the Goodness of God, and natively tend to lead Men to Repentance, that they fall into Perdition.

But when these are rejected, God is provoked, and says of irreclaimable Sinners now, as he said of those before the Flood, *My Spirit shall not always strive with Man,* Gen. vi. 3. There are Times when Sinners under the Gospel, have more than ordinary Convictions of Sin, and Impressions upon their Hearts to seek God: And when these are not attended to, but slighted and despised; God may give up such poor Souls to the Hardness of their Hearts, and the Blindness of their Mind, and utterly withdraw from them those Influences of the Holy Spirit, with which before they were favoured. thus we are told of some, who being *past Feeling, have given themselves over to Lasciviousness, to work all Uncleanness with Greediness,* Eph. iv. 19. It doubtless becomes not us to say, who *hath,* or who hath *not,* provoked God so far, as utterly to withdraw the Influence of his Holy Spirit from them. Because we don't know, how far some Souls may be left to sin away Convictions, and yet afterwards be recovered. But if strong Convictions and Impressions, that are but of a common Kind, (and such are all those, that don't shew the Soul the Plague of its own Heart, unbottom it from Self-Righteousness, and allure it unto Jesus, as a complete Saviour, for its own Salvation); if these are sinned away, and a Person can work Wickedness without Remorse; doubtless such a Man, is in a very dangerous Case.—And perhaps the Day of Grace, in both these Respects, may be included in what our Lord said to *Jerusalem, If thou hadst known, even thou, at lease in this thy Day the Things which belong to thy Peace! but now they are hid from thine Eyes,* Luk. xix. 42.—But the Day of Grace may respect,

Thirdly. The *Day* of Christ's *Power,* the Power of his special *Grace,* on the Hearts of his *People.*

And this *Can't* be over, but shall certainly be experienced by every one of the Lord's People, *before* their Life is ended. This being the Covenant Promise of the Father, unto Christ his Son, *Thy People shall be willing in the Day of thy Power,* Ps. cx. 3. This is a Day of Grace *indeed!* The Day of Grace in other Respects, may be *resisted,* may be *over;* but this Day of Grace, is a Day of *Power,* of efficacious, irresistible *Love-Power,* that effectually *takes the Heart* and brings all adverse Power into *Captivity, unto the Obedience of Jesus Christ. Thy People,*--saith the Father, to the Son, *i. e.* those whom *I* have lov'd and chosen of old unto *eternal Life,* and given to *Thee,* to be *redeemed* from all Misery, unto all Glory; they *shall be willing.*—Almighty Love, Almighty Power engages for it. They shall be *willing.*—Not saved against their *Will;* but made *willing* to be saved in *God's Way.* By his Free Grace, without the Deeds of the Law, thro' the Blood and Righteousness of Jesus Christ; and to be saved unto Holiness here, as well as unto Happiness hereafter. And made willing they are, not by any *Force* put upon their Will, contrary to its *Inclination;* but by a most strong, and sweet *Allurement,* whereby the Will moves *freely,* in chusing that *supremely,* which the Understanding, from a supernatural Light shining upon it, sees *clearly,* to be the *greatest, chiefest Good.* And when thus made willing, so far as their Will is *renewed,* they are willing in the highest Degree; *Willingness,* in the Abstract, *Willingness,* in the Plural. And for their being thus willing, there is a *Day,* a set Time prefixed, that was Foreappointed in God's eternal Purpose. And that Day *shall* come, and *when* come, *Power* comes along with it; Satan-binding, Sin-killing, Soul-quickning, Soul-saving *Power.* The Lord, its infinite Lover, passeth by, sees it polluted in its *own Blood,* cast out into the *open Field,* a miserable, wretched, helpless Creature, and by his All-gracious, and All-efficacious Voice, says unto it, *Live.* Yea, when it is in its *Blood,* He saith unto it, *Live.* By which He communicates, and declares, *Life spiritual,* that shall by the same Almighty Power and Grace, be maintain'd and increased, unto *Life eternal.* And to shew the Source of this wondrous Change, He adds, And *thy Time,* this Day of Grace to thee, was the *Time of Love.* Of free, infinite, all-conquering, unchangeable and eternal *Love!* Ezek. xvi. 6, 8.

Thus, Sir, in this three-fold Respect, I humbly think, the Day of Grace may be taken. And you will easily see, that tho' the Day of Grace, in the two Former Senses, is sufficient to leave those who perish from under it, *without Excuse;* yet it is the Day of Grace in the latter Sense only, that is or can be, the Day of *Salvation-Power,* unto any *one Soul;* and that this Day of Grace, shall certainly be so unto *every Soul,* that was ordained unto *eternal Life,* wherein he shall be effectually called by *special Grace,* unto that *immortal Glory.*—From the two first, we may learn,

1. That it is the great Duty of all Men under the Gospel, to *comply* with the *Calls of it.* And that if they *neglect* and *reject* that great Salvation which the Gospel proclaims, even while it is called *To-day,* God may take the Gospel from them, or they from it, before they are *aware,* and deprive them of those Opportunities which they have slighted, which had a native Tendency to their Salvation, and which, despised, will aggravate their Damnation, when our *Lord shall be revealed from Heaven with his mighty Angels, in flaming fire, taking Vengeance on them that know not God, and that obey not the Gospel of Jesus Christ: Who shall be punished with everlasting Destruction, from the Presence of the Lord, and from the Glory of his Power,* 2 Thes. i. 7, 8, 9.

2. That every Soul ought to *beware* of striving against those Convictions and Impressions, which *tend* to their Reformation and Salvation. Inasmuch as they are the *Voice of* GOD, which ought to be *obey'd,* and which to rebel *against,* is a very great *Sin;* and will greatly increase their *Torment,* if God should withdraw from them the Influence of his Spirit, account them such that have *judged themselves unworthy of everlasting Life,* and leave them to perish in eternal Death, *Act.* xiii. 46.— From the Day of Grace in the last Sense we may learn,

1. That those who feel *Convictions,* should rejoice in Hope, that they may end in a saving *Conversion.* And let them know, that the Day of Grace is not *past* with *any one,* that feels the gracious *Power of God* working upon his *Heart.* And tho' the Soul may have sinned away Convictions Time after Time, and increas'd its Hardness of Heart and Blindness of Mind; yet *now, now,* if it has a *Desire* to return unto God by Christ, the Door of Mercy is *open;* and *To-day,* after *so long a Time,* the Lord calls it as a perishing *Sinner,* to flee to JESUS, the great Saviour, as the only Refuge and Hope set before it in the Gospel. And not a Soul that *comes in* at the Gospel Call, will our Lord *cast out,* but *receive him to the Glory of God,* to save him from endless Death, unto eternal Life, *Joh.* vi. 37.

2. That as there is such a Day of Grace, that is and shall be a Day of *Salvation-Power,* unto all the Lord's People; This may encourage all those, who have a painful Feeling within themselves, of *much Opposition* to their *own Salvation.* Not a Soul that is willing to be sav'd alone by God's Free Grace, thro' Jesus Christ, from all sin and Misery, unto all Holiness and Glory; but is one of the *Lord's People;* but hath felt the *Day* of his *Power* already upon its *Heart.* And that same omnipotent Grace, which hath *begun* in its new Life, will *maintain* and *increase* it unto Life eternal; will *vanquish* all Opposition, and *compleat* its Salvation. The Lord its *Saviour,* will be its *King,* to save it from *Destruction,* and with an *everlasting Salvation.* Mountains of Opposition, before our *Zerubbabel,* shall become a *Plain:* His Hands which have laid the *Foundation,* even his Hands shall *finish it,* and HE shall bring forth the *Head-Stone* thereof with Shoutings, crying, *Grace, Grace* unto it! *Zech.* iv. 7. And hence,

3. Let those who have been made willing in the Day of Christ's Power, learn to *admire* and *praise,* the rich, free, distinguishing *Grace of God* unto *them.* O how often have *we,* the *saved of the Lord,* slighted the Calls of the Gospel, made Excuses, and went our Way! Strove against Convictions, and repeated our Transgressions! And how justly might the Lord have said concerning us, as he hath done, and will do concerning others, *Because I have called, and ye refused, I have stretched out my Hand, and no Man regarded: but ye have set at Nought all my Counsel, and would none of my Reproof: I also will laugh at your Calamity, and mock when your*

Fear cometh, Prov. i. 24, &c. And yet, O yet, would not the Lord take us at our *Word,* and appoint us unto *Wrath,* which our *Sins* had deserved; but *compel* us to *come in,* that *his House* might be *filled! Compel* us to come in to *Christ,* unto our eternal Life by JESUS! What shall we say *of,* what shall we render *to,* this discriminating Grace, this infinite Patience, this All overflowing Mercy, and All-overcoming Kindness! In *all Manner of holy Conversation and Godliness,* let us, as the Lord's peculiar People, saved by Grace, in the Day of his Power, *shew forth the Praises of Him who hath called us out of Darkness, into his marvellous Light!* 1. Pet. ii. 9.—*The Grace of our Lord Jesus Christ be with your Spirit!* In HIM, I am, dear Sir,

Your sincere Friend and Servant,

——— ———

LETTER XXII. *To* ---- ----

My very dear Brother,

IF this is a false Report; beware of every Thing that may give any Occasion of Suspicion or Reflection. But if it be true; O *where are you!* What are you doing! Have you forgotten that vast Obligation which the Love of Christ, that passeth Knowledge, lays you under, to *live* unto HIM, who *died for you,* and *rose again?* Have you forgot the great Work of your Calling, which is, to be an *Holy Man* unto the LORD, or *dedicate* unto HIM, in *all Manner of holy Conversation and Godliness?* Are you not dearly bought with the *Redeemer's Blood?* Bought unto HIM? And will you deny the LORD of his *Right?* Of your little *Self,* who gave his great SELF for you! Be ashamed of such Injustice, of such Ingratitude. Let 'em not be seen in, be heard of *you,* the *Redeemed* of the LORD! O why do you thus forget HIM, who sav'd your *Soul* from the *lowest Hell!—Forger him,* did I say? That's not all, you *wound,* you *pierce him.* Was it not enough, that the Heart and Soul of Christ, were pierced once for you, when his *own Self* bare your *Sins,* in his *own Body on the Tree;* but will you pierce him *still!* Will you do that repeatedly and delightfully, under the Sorrows of which He groaned inexpressibly! O think, when you take an intoxicating Cup into your Hands with Pleasure, "*This, this* was *it,* that fill'd my *Lord's bitter Cup,* that Cup of *Wrath,* which made his *Soul exceeding sorrowful even unto Death!* Shall *I* drink that with Pleasure, which was to HIM so exceeding bitter! Shall *I* seek any Life of Delight in *Sin,* in *that* Sin, which caus'd *his* agonizing *Grief,* and accursed *Death!* Shall *I* this, *open all his Wounds!* And yield to that abominable *Sin,* even in the *Sight* of my *Lord,* (whose Eye is ever upon me) which actually caus'd, and instantly brings to his Mind, *His* exquisite *Sufferings!* Is any *Pleasure* I can now take in *Sin,* worth that *Grief* and *Displeasure,* which I shall hereby give to my *Lord afresh!*" Yea, think, "How shall I do that *abominable Thing* which *my Lord hateth,* and thus lay his *Honour* in the *Dust!* Dethrone HIM, who dy'd to crown *me!* How shall I thus *stumble* and *grieve the Saints,* and *harden Sinners* in their Wickedness! And how shall I thus, by *Sinning against* CHRIST, *wrong my own Soul!* Rob it of that Life of Joy, which is to be had in Communion with GOD, and Conformity to Him *here,* and of those additional Glories, which of the freest Grace, shall be the Reward of good Works *hereafter!*"—Thus, my dear Brother, thus think and reason with yourself, whenever tempted to sin against the Lord.

And examine how it is with you, after you have fallen into Sin. Do you look upon it as a *little, light Thing,* and make *Excuses* for it? Are you but little *concerned,* but little *pained* about it? And consequently, but little *humbled* before GOD for it?—If it's thus with you, your *Soul* is in a *pitiable Case.* God is withdrawn from your Spirit, you have left your first Love, and your spiritual Life is under an awful Decay. And *alarmed* you had need be, and stirred up to Duty *instantly,* lest you be *hardned* thro' the Deceitfulness of Sin *suddenly.* For tho' Sin hardens insensibly, by increasing Degrees, yet every Degree of Sin, hardens suddenly, and prepares the Heart for greater Sin, and greater Hardness.—And *dreadful* will the Consequents be, of *bold Sinning,* with *faint Concern,* unto every one who has *tasted* that the *Lord is gracious.* Such Backsliders are in Danger of provoking the Lord to give them up to the Power of Sin and Satan, to the Hiding of his Face, and the Rebukes of his Providence, to Soul-Darkness in this World, and to the Loss of that Praise, and Honour, and Glory, which otherwise they would have had in the World to come: And thus to cast them among the Number of those who *shall be saved,* so as by *Fire:* That lose all their Works, the Reward of an holy Life, which others shall receive in the Day of Christ.

But if the former is not your Case: If after any Fall into Sin, your Conscience being yet *tender,* you are *deeply pierced* with a Sense of *God's Dishonour* thereby, and of your great *Provocation,* and vile *Ingratitude* therein: If on Account thereof you are *deeply humbled* before the *Lord,* and *He,* in the Infinity of his Grace, speaks *Peace* to your troubled Heart, and thereby melts you into *Gospel-Mourning* for Sin, and raiseth in you holy *Resolutions* against it; if this is your Case: There is *Hope of Deliverance,* that God will *break your Bands,* and give you the *Victory* over that *Sin,* which now usurps with *Tyranny.* And for this Salvation, seek most earnestly.—And beware, that *after* Peace spoken, you *turn not again unto Folly.* For Sins of this Kind, are of the *deepest Dye.* of exceeding *great Guilt:* they dishonor *God greatly,* and wound the *Soul deeply.*—Wherefore *be sober, be vigilant,* watch against Temptations to Sin, and lift up your Heart to God for Strength to stand in the evil Day; *for your Adversary the Devil goeth about like a roaring Lion, seeking whom he may devour.*—That the *God of Peace* may *bruise Satan under your Feet shortly, sanctify you wholly, preserve you blameless, and present you faultless, before the Presence of his Glory with exceeding Joy:* is the hearty Desire and Prayer of, my dear Brother,

Yours most affectionately,

______ _____

LETTER XXIII. *To* ----- -----

My dear Brother,

HEALTH of Soul, is the greatest Blessing, Soul-Prosperity, the richest Mercy. *Near* to *God,* and beneath his Smiles, we *live;* but *far* from *him,* and frown'd away from his manifestative Favour, we *die.* Decay in the vigorous Exercises of our Graces, in our Fruitfulness and Usefulness, to God's Dishonour, and our own and others Grief. How is it with *you,* my dear Brother, are you blest with Fellowship with God, and thence enabled to walk in the Light, as He is in the Light, to purify yourself, even as Christ is pure? Or are you left to the Power of Sin, and under the awful Rebuke of Distance from God? *God* and *Sin, Light* and *Darkness, Christ,* and *Belial,* can have *no Fellowship* with each other. If Sin is indulged, God is displeased, his Holy Spirit is grieved, the Soul is wounded, and forsaken in Part and for a Time of its best Friend, and given up into the Hand of its Enemies. O, when *Israel* chose *new Gods,* then *War* was in the *Gates.* And to aggravate the Sin and Folly of God's People in their own Sight, the Lord saith, *Pass over the Isles of* Chittim, *and see; and send unto* Kedar, *and consider diligently, and see if there be such a Thing. Hath a Nation changed their Gods, which yet are no Gods? But my People have changed their Glory, for that which doth not profit,* Jer. ii. 10, 11. GOD is the *Glory* of his People; and yet so *foolish* are his backsliding Children, that they *change* their Glory, for that which doth not *profit.* "Do ye get any Thing, as if the Lord should say, by departing from Me?" O no; so far are we from gaining by Sin, that by every Act of it, we sustain the greatest Loss. We change our *Glory* for that which is *inglorious,* yea, for that which is most *vile* and *abominable,* and is and ought to be the Matter of our *Shame.* And hereby we become guilty of these two Evils, of *forsaking the* LORD, *the Fountain of living Waters,* and of *hewing to ourselves Cisterns, broken Cisterns, that can hold no Water.* Upon which the Lord saith, *Be astonished, O ye Heavens, at this,* Ver. 12, 13. And thus, from the Insensibility of his backsliding People, He addresseth the inanimate Creatures, *Hear, O Heavens, and give Ear, O Earth: for the* LORD *hath spoken, I have nourished and bro't up Children, and they have rebelled against me,* Isa. i. 2. And to shew their prodigious Stupidity, He adds, *The Ox knoweth his Owner, and the Ass his Master's Crib: but* Israel *doth not know, my People doth not consider,* Ver. 3. And to argue his People out of their base Ingratitude, He saith, *Have I been a Wilderness to* Israel? *a Land of Darkness? Wherefore say my People, We are Lords, we will come no more unto thee? Can a Maid forget her Ornaments, or a Bride her Attire? Yet my People have forgotten* ME *Days without Number,* Jer. ii. 31, 32. There is certainly no such Thing as *Stupidity* in the *sensitive Creatures,* when compar'd with that which is to be found in *Believers,* when departing from the *Lord,* we set up for *ourselves:* Our *own*

Will, instead of *God's,* for our *Law,* and the Gratification of our sinful Inclinations, instead of *walking worthy of God,* in all holy Conformity and filial Duty, *unto all Pleasing.* And as to *Ingratitude,* there is no such Thing to be found among the *rational Creatures,* towards their *Fellow-Creatures,* as appears in the *Children of God,* when *Jeshuran,* waxen *fat, kicketh!* When *nourished* by infinite Kindness, and indulg'd as the *Favourites of Heaven,* we despise the *Commandments of the Lord,* and rise up in Rebellion against *Him,* as if we were his *Enemies!* Nor can there be any such Ingratitude in the rational Creatures, towards *God their Creator,* who are Partakers of his *tender Mercies* in a Way of *common Bounty,* and yet are *regardless of Duty;* as is to be seen in *Believers,* when tho' the Objects of God's *special Favour,* we cast it behind our *Backs,* and by Sin trample it under our *Feet,* as if it was not worth a *Thought!* As if the *Mercies of God,* his special, Soul-saving *Mercy,* was not Motive sufficient to filial *Duty,* to engage us to offer up ourselves as a *living Sacrifice to his Glory, holy and acceptable* by *Jesus Christ!* O my dear Brother, *our Sins* are of a crimson, and scarlet *Dye. We* can't *sin* at a *cheap Rate.* Every of *our Sins,* that *believe in Jesus,* that are under *Forgiving-Love,* are of a more aggravated *Guilt* by *far,* than the Sins of those, who *do not know the Lord.* And deeper *far,* they pierc'd our dear, dying JESUS, than those we were guilty of, before we were *called out of Darkness, into God's marvellous Light.*—It is well for us, who are the chief of Sinners, that there is an Infinity of Merit in the *Blood of the Son of God!* Else, it could not *cleanse us from all Sin!* But, Glory be to God, Salvation by Grace, thro' the Blood of Christ, is infinitely *full* and *free!*—But, let us not *sin,* because *Grace abounds.* If there is any Spark of Ingenuity in our Souls, let us that *love the Lord, hate* this *Evil,* and with the utmost Abhorrence of it say, *God forbid!* Let the *Grace of God which bringeth Salvation, teach us, that denying Ungodliness and worldly Lusts, we should live soberly, righteously, and godly in this present World.*—I commit you as one of Christ's *Sheep,* loved, and bought with his *Blood,* to his tender *Care,* and saving *Power,* as the LORD our great, and good *Shepherd:* And am,

Yours very affectionately,

——— ———

LETTER XXIV. *To* ----- -----

My very dear Brother,

I AM distressed to hear of the lamentable State of your dear Soul.—Is the *Grief* you cause to your dear *Brethren,* and especially to your dear and honoured *Pastor,* whose tender Heart is ready to break with your Backslidings; *Nothing* unto *you?* Is the *Reproach* you bring to the *Name, Ways* and *People of God;* a *light Thing* with *you?* Is the *Displeasure* and *Grief* you give to the *Lord* that loveth you; unworthy of your *Notice?* What, *redeemed;* and not account yourself the *Redeemer's Right! Bought with a Price;* and not *glorify God with your Body and with your Spirit, which are* GOD'S! Have you forgotten the *Obligations* which boundless Love, reigning Grace, and pardoning Mercy lay you *under?* Have you forgotten your own *Engagements* to be the *Lord's?* What hath *Christ done to you,* my Brother, that you dislike your *Master,* and forsake his *Service?* Is *Satan* the best Master, and *Sin* the best Work, in your Esteem? What, *make a Captain* to *return to Egypt! What Fruit had you in those Things, whereof you* was once *ashamed?* In those *Evils,* whereof you ought now to be *ashamed?* Is not the *End* of those Things, *Death?* Yes, my Brother, as truly as the *Lord liveth,* the Word is gone out of his Mouth in Faithfulness, it shall not return void: *If ye live after the Flesh, ye shall die.* The Life of your Graces, the Life of your Glory, must and will *go,* by the Satisfaction of your Lust. Not the least *Sin* you commit, but will affect your *spiritual Life,* and detract from your *Crown of Life.* Will you let *another* take *your Crown?* No, rather, *So run, that you may obtain. The Lord is at Hand. The Judge standeth before the Door.* Know you not, that if any Servant of Christ, becomes so *evil,* as to say in his Heart, *My Lord delayeth his Coming, and to eat and drink with the Drunken: The Lord of that Servant will come at an Hour when he looketh not for him, and will appoint him his Portion with the Unbelievers?* Your *Time* is just gone; a vast *Eternity* hastens! Would you wish to enter the dark *Valley of the Shadow of Death,* with all that Darkness of *Guilt,* which such open Transgressions must bring upon your Conscience, if you are not awfully *hardned* thro' the *Deceitfulness of Sin?* If you don't see Sin in its Vileness and Blackness *now,* you will see it in its horrid Colours, in its Guilt and Aggravations, when you come to lie upon a *dying Bed.*

"Death puts on Things another Face,
Than we in Life do see:
Sin, Satan, Hell, Heaven, Life and Grace,
Then great and weighty be."

My dear Brother, if you go on in Sin, you may justly be left under the Hidings of God's Face, the Terrors of Conscience, and the fierce Assaults of the Enemy of Souls, so that you may endure a Kind of *Hell* in your *Spirit;* and not know but your *Portion* may be with *Unbelievers,* in the *eternal World,* when you are just entering upon an *endless State.*—For the Lord's Sake then, for his People's Sake, and for your Soul's Sake, *awake out of Sleep,* and venture not a *Step further,* in the *Paths of the Destroyer.* Let me intreat you without Delay, or Hindrance by any Business whatsoever, to set apart a Day of solemn Fasting and Prayer, to humble yourself before God for your Transgressions, and to intreat his forgiving Mercy and renewing Grace, for your speedy Restoration. Lest the Lord should say of you, as of his People of old, *Israel* would *none* of ME: *So I gave then up to their own Heart's Lust and they walked in their own Counsels.* Which brings present Misery, inexpressible. And the Loss of that Praise, Honour and Glory, which otherwise you should receive in Life eternal.—O that the Father of Mercies, the God of Compassions, would *pluck you* as a *Brand out of the Burning!* I commit you to his *tender Mercy:* and am, with *great Concern,*

Yours most affectionately,

——— ———

LETTER XXV. *To* ----- -----

My very dear Brother,

I Received your last kind Letter with great Joy, to hear of the Lord's Loving-kindness in *restoring* your dear Soul. *Who is a God like unto* HIM, *that pardoneth Iniquity, and passeth by the Transgression of the Remnant of his Heritage! He retaineth not his Anger for ever, because he delighteth in Mercy. He will turn again, he will have Compassion, he will subdue our Iniquities, and cast all our Sins into the Depths of the Sea.* O who would not *love* and *fear him!* How sad it is, that *we* the Redeemed, the Saved, the Restored of the LORD, should *sin* against him! And yet thus, wretched *we,* the Lord's People, are *bent to Backsliding from him!* Are you *redeemed,* Brother, *bought with a Price? Glorify* GOD *in your Body, and in your Spirit, which are his.* Are you *saved?* Let the *Love* of your Saviour, constrain you to *live unto* HIM *who died for you, and rose again.* Are you *restored?* Dread *returning again unto Folly.* Hath God the LORD shewed you *Light?* Bind the *Sacrifice* (your whole Spirit, Soul, and Body) with *Cords* (of his infinite Kindness) to the *Horns* of the *Altar:* To the efficacious *Power* of *Christ's Mediation;* who presents us, and all our Services, acceptable to God, to his and our Father. Commit the Keeping of your Soul daily into Christ's Hands. He would have his Children trust him with their Time-Preservation, as well as with their eternal Salvation. We little think what we *lose* for want of abiding by *Faith* in our dear *Lord Jesus,* in his immense Fulness, which only can be a sufficient Supply, for our extensive Emptiness. We, alas, too often go into a World of Snares, with a Sort of *Self-Dependence,* as if our inherent Grace, was sufficient to keep us; and so our Feet are caught in an evil Net, before we are aware. Whereas, if distrusting our own Ability to keep ourselves, we went out trusting in the LORD our *Strength;* we should be *safe,* by him directed, and upheld.—We have now, my dear Brother, but a little, a very little *Time* left, to glorify God in upon the Earth. O let us watch and pray, that it may be *all* devoted to his Honour. What can be too much, what enough, to do or suffer, for the Praise of that Grace which hath saved us! *The Love of God our Father, the Grace of our Lord Jesus Christ, and the Communion of the Holy Ghost;* call for our *whole Selves* continually, as a holy, living *Sacrifice,* to be offered up to the LORD'S *Glory.* But O how little *do* we, *can* we *pay,* of the Debt of Love we *owe!* Let us cast up our Accounts daily, reflect upon our every Day's Conduct; confess and bewail our Deficiencies, and fleeing for Pardon to infinite Grace, thro' all-atoning Blood, let us intreat restoring, strengthening, Soul-enriching Mercies. That taught by efficacious *Grace,* we may *deny Ungodliness* and *Worldly Lusts,* and live *soberly, righteously and godly, in this present World:* Hasting apace by abounding Thanksgiving, in practical Time-Praises, to the perfect Praises, and loudest Hallelujahs, of a blest Eternity.—To the tender

Compassion, and gracious *Protection,* of the LORD our *Shepherd,* I commit you: *His Grace be with your Spirit!* In him, with the dearest Love, I am,

Yours for ever,

——— ———

LETTER XXVI. *To Mr.* W.

Dear Sir,

YOU see what a *Trial,* my dear Yokefellow's *Death* would be to me at *this Time;* and will easily think, that I must be under some *Pressure of Spirit,* upon the least *Suspicion* of it.—But I feel *Everlasting Arms* underneath me. Cares, like a wild Deluge, wou'd break in upon me: But I wou'd *cast all my Care, upon* HIM *that careth for me.* I think it a most unreasonable Thing, for a Creature, and especially for a Believer, to take the *Government of the World,* upon his *own Shoulders,* by anxious *Thought for the Morrow: Which of us, by taking Thought, can add one Cubit to our Stature?* The Government of all Things, relating to the World, the Church, to Families, and particular Persons, even to the most minute Circumstance belonging to each; is devolved by the *Father,* upon the mighty *Shoulder* of our dear *Lord Jesus.* And *there* let it *rest.* I like it *well.* JESUS is my *King:* I know he will *save me;* and bring S*alvation* to my poor Soul, even by such Providences, which seem to carry *Destruction* in the very Face of them. All Things in Providence, are wrought according to the Counsel of *Jehovah's Will;* for the Glory of God, and the Good of his dear Children. HE *is wonderful in Counsel, and excellent in Working!* I see Him by Faith; I adore Him by Love; I wait for Him by Patience of Hope; even when his Footsteps are in such deep Waters, that Sense, neither natural, nor spiritual, can trace them. When I suppose the Worst, Sir, I think thus: 'What if this Trial should be attended with a Complication of Griefs? Who made it for me? It was *my* GOD! It was appointed for me, laid out for me of Old, by an infinity of Wisdom and Grace, for the Glory of God, and my Advantage. And what if God is to be *glorify'd* in me by this Trial?'—And then my Heart flows complacently into the Will of God, and says, "Lord, give me but Grace to glorify thee:

And Father, work thy Will."—Oh, dear Sir, GOD is my ALL! GOD in CHRIST is *my Portion!* I would live upon Him as *such;* and in Comforts and Crosses, in Life and Death, be wholly dedicated to *his Glory.* I would have no *Will,* but GOD'S; no *Interest,* but *His;* no *Care,* but to *glorify Him.* I think it a great Shame, for a Soul blest with Fellowship with GOD, to have a *contrary* Will, a *contrary* Interest to *His.*—And yet, alas, I am a feeble Worm, *crushed before the Moth!* Oh that the *Power of* CHRIST *may rest upon me,* and *his Strength be made perfect in my Weakness:* That in this Trial, I may walk *worthy of* GOD, *unto all Pleasing!*—For this, help me, dear Sir, by your Prayers. –And your Lord and mine, will richly reward your Kindness, like his Great SELF! I am persuaded, dear Sir, it wou'd rejoice your Heart, to serve CHRIST, in serving the least of His. And never was such a MASTER, as our JESUS! Himself will *serve* his *Servants! He will make them sit down to Meat, gird Himself, and come forth and serve them.* Oh wondrous Grace! What, the Lord of Glory, *serve* his creature-Worms! The Worms He *lov'd and wash'd in his own Blood,* to make them *Kings and Priests, unto God and his Father!*—"Oh our *Beloved,* draw us with the Cords of thy Love, bind us to be free in thy Service, to cast ourselves, our Time, and All, in all the little Love our Souls are capable of, as a Drop of Duty, into thy boundless Love, that Ocean of Glory!"—*The Grace of Christ be with your Spirit!*—I beg Leave to subscribe, dear Sir,

Your most obliged humble Servant,

______ ______

LETTER XXVII. *To* ----- -----

My very dear and honour'd Brother,

MUCH I compassionate your dear Soul, in your present Distress; and am grieved that the enemy hath got an Advantage against you in this great Trial, to make you think, or at least, apt to think, that God herein is your Enemy; and is not faithful to his Promise given you; or else to doubt, if you know any Thing of the Mind of God in his Word.—Being in the Furnace, your Dross comes up, and with *Jonah* you are ready to say, *I do well to be angry.*—But O, my Brother, will you be angry with infinite *Love?* this Affliction, is a special Fruit of God's everlasting Love to you. These bitter Waters, come streaming down to you, from the Heart of God, thro' the Blood of Christ, well sweetned with infinite Kindness. Not the least Dram of *Wrath,* is put into *your Cup*; not the least Ingredient in it, however bitter to your Taste, but was put there by *Love's* All gracious Hand. "Infinite Love, guided by unerring Wisdom, (as one well said) determines the Kind of Proportions the Degree, of the Afflictions of every Child" Not the least *Grain,* Brother, in this wisely mixed *Potion* which is given you, which is so distasteful to you, could have been *wanting,* but God would have had *less Glory* in your Salvation, and you *less Happiness,* as the Saved of the Lord. Have you forgot what is said, *Prov.* xvi. 4. *The* LORD *hath made all Things for Himself?* i. e. for his own *Glory.* And what the Apostle saith, *Jam.* v. 11. *Behold, we count them happy which endure?* If there was nothing more, Brother, concerned in this Affliction, than the *Glory of God,* it is worth while to endure it for *that,* even that *alone.* But lo, your present *Happiness,* and endless *Bliss,* are concerned therein And wou'd you have been without this Affliction upon this Condition, That God should have had *less glory* given Him by you on the Earth? Or, That you should have had *less Grace* given you in the present Time, or *less Glory* in your eternal Crown? If you would not; attempt your Duty, to say instantly in Faith and Love, *The Cup which my Father giveth me to drink, shall I not drink it?* Let *your Will,* flow complacently into the *Will of* GOD, and say with a sweet Acquiescence, *Father, glorify thy Name!* Do what thou wilt with me in the present Time; make but thy own Glory out of me, and I have enough: *Not my Will; but thine be done.*—If you should say, Brother,

Alas, I find no Addition of Grace by this Trial; I bring no Glory to God by it: Of what Advantage then can it be unto me?—I answer,

If hitherto you have been *as a Bullock unaccustomed to the Yoke, God* for *Christ's Sake forgiveth you:* And your present *Sin,* by over-ruling *Grace,* shall be the Matter of your future *Humiliation;* of that *Humility,* which precedes *Glory,* and will be your *Preparation,* for eternal *Exaltation.*—I do not say, That your *Sin* will do you *Good.* Such an assertion would be abominable in *itself;* and I believe, abhorred by *you. Shall we sin that Grace may abound? God forbid!*—But this I say, Unto us who are under Grace, *where Sin hath abounded, Grace doth much more abound:* And effects its great *Designs,* to the endless Praise of its own *Glory,* by over-ruling into a Subserviency thereto, the greatest *Contraries,* even those very *Things,* which have a native *Tendency* to dethrone Grace, and despoil it of its Glory, and to plunge its Subjects into the deepest Misery.—this as to what hath already been.—But, O *let the Time past suffice!* Say, *Once have I spoken, yea twice; but I will proceed no farther. I have heard of thee by the Hearing of the Ear; but now mine Eye seeth thee; Wherefore I abhor myself, and repent in Dust and Ashes.*—It will be *no Offence,* Brother, *nor Grief of Heart* to you, when you come to *Heaven,* that you was called to *glorify God,* by this *Trial* on the *Earth;* nor that your *Grace* was increas'd thereby, unto eternal *Glory*; but both will be the Matter of your *endless Joy.* And will you grieve *now,* for that which *shortly* and *perpetually* will be your Heart's Delight? O dry your Tears, cease Weeping, begin Rejoicing, anticipate by Faith, the Glories of Sight.—Come, my dear Brother, you are *under Grace,* that forgives your Sins, that will subdue your Iniquities, that will strengthen your Graces, and out of Weakness make you strong. *Everlasting Arms are underneath.* And *sink* you *shall not,* in *deep Waters.* Your *Shoes shall be Iron and Brass; and as your Days, your Strength.* Say then in Faith, tho' foil'd by the Adversary; *Rejoice not against me, O mine Enemy; when I fall, I shall arise: When I sit in Darkness, the* LORD *shall be a Light unto me. I will bear the Indignation of the* LORD, *because I have sinned against him, until He plead my Cause, and execute Judgment for me: He will bring me forth to the Light, and I shall behold his Righteousness.* For, *The Trial of your Faith worketh Patience, and Patience Experience, &c.*

Your former Trial, Brother, made your late Happiness more sensibly sweet and Heart-endearing.—And easily you might slide, as it were insensibly, into an Extreme of Creature-Love. Which might provoke the jealous Eyes of the Lord your Lover, to strip you of a Creature, that stole your Heart from him the Creator: To his Dishonour and Displeasure, and to your Disadvantage, present and eternal. And evident it is, that we have *exceeded* in Love to a Creature, if when the Lord takes what he gave, it must be *rent* from us. If we don't freely *resign* the Creature of Thing He *calls for;* we lov'd the same *inordinately.*—How kind then, and endearing was the *Hand,* that took away your *blooming Joy,* which robb'd Him of his *Crown of Glory,* of that Glory due from *you,* to Him your great *Lord!* And that took away that *Honey,* whereof you was like to *surfeit!* O my Brother, your *Lord's Love* is *kind.* 'Tis a *Love-Stroke* that is given you. And his Voice herein to you is, "Come, thou dear Object of my infinite Love, take up thy Delights in ME. I have took away the *Desire of thine Eyes with a Stroke;* that *I* might have thy *Heart;* that *I,* who am *All Desires,* might be to thee, *All Delights:* To my present and endless Praise, and to they present and endless Bliss. Come, taste how ineffably sweet, the uncreated eternal Fountain is, now the Creature-Stream, that transient Flow, is dry'd up and gone. *Why is thine Heart grieved? and why eatest thou not? am not I better to thee than ten Sons?*" And is this your *Beloved's Voice,* my Brother: Will you not say, returning *Love,*

"O my *Lord,* thou *Altogether lovely* One, thou *Lover* of my Soul, *Thou,* even Thou *alone,* art more *excellent* to me, than *Mountains of Prey!* Than all the Creatures, amass'd in One! Stript of that which *is not;* on which I *set* mine *Eyes;* I'll henceforth, by the Grace assisting clothe myself with THEE, whose Name *is,* I AM! And bathe my Soul in Pleasures, in THEE, thou boundless, bottomless, endless Ocean of all Delights! *Forgetting my Father's (Adam's) House,* the Creatures and Relations of this present Time, I'll henceforth fix the Intention of my Soul on THEE, my eternal LORD, my Husband-Lover, and in thine eternal Homage, will find my eternal Joy!"—If thus your dear Soul is bro't nearer to *Christ* in *Love,* by the Separation of a *Creature* from you, that us'd to divert your *Heart;* your *Gain* will be *ineffable,* by *that Loss!*—this, Brother, as to what has happen'd.—And next, to reconcile Promise with Providence: Consider,

The sudden *Loss* of your dear Companion, is no Argument against the *Promises* you had to direct and encourage you in the *Choice* of her. As the Lord gave her to you, and made you happy in her: The Event shews, that you had the Mind of God in espousing her.—And as to that Promise you particularly mention, *In blessing I will bless thee; and in multiplying I will multiply thee:* The Lord doubtless signify'd there, by, That you had and should have *his Heart* in *that Mercy,* as the *Inside* of the *Blessing.* And likewise, That in giving her to you. He would *eminently* bless you. The former, you may be well assur'd of from God's Word, That you had his Heart, in that Gift of his Hand; that he did you *Good* thereby, with his *whole Heart, and with his whole Soul.* And the latter appears from the Lord's Work: In that he made her such a *eminent Blessing* to you, while you had the Enjoyment of her.—But most surely, the Lord did not say, by that Promise, That he would give her to you for a *long Continuance of Time.* And therefore his taking her away so *soon;* is no Argument against the Truth of God's *Promise,* nor against the Truth of its *Application* to you by the *Holy Ghost.*—Your concluding from what the Lord said, That you should enjoy her *long:* Was certainly a *Mistake.* Which you easily made, by drawing out *Ways* in your own Mind, and according to your Wishes, for God to fulfill his Promise to you in.

As *Eve,* when the Lord gave the first Promise, *The Seed of the Woman shall bruise the Serpent's Head: Mistook* the Mind of God therein, from her eager Desire of its immediate Accomplishment; and tho't it must needs be her *nest* and *immediate Seed.* Whence she said upon the birth of *Cain, I have gotten a Man the* LORD, *Gen.* iv, 1. Or, the *Messiah:* As some render the Test, without the Word *from,* which is in our Translation. And I doubt not, when *Eve* saw her Mistake, she was as much *try'd* about it, as my dear *Brother* can be about *his.* And yet her Mistake, as yours, was not *total,* but only *partial.* She was not mistaken, as to the *Substance* of the Promise; but as to the particular *Way* and *Time* of its Accomplishment. She having drawn out *those* which she thought *best;* and the Lord, in his Wisdom and Goodness, having design'd *those* which were *better;* more for his Glory, for the Good of his People, and for *Eve's Joy* at last, however *trying* the present Disappointment was.

Thus the Prophet *Jeremiah,* was sorely *tried,* and knew not how to reconcile the *Promise* of God, That *Fields* should be bought and possessed in *Jerusalem;* with his *Providence,* in that the *City* was given into the Hand of the *Chaldeans,* Jer. xxxii. 15, &c. Whence he poured out his Soul before the Lord, and pleads with him, Ver. 24. *Behold the Mounts, they are come unto the City to take it, and the City is given into the Hand of the* Chaldeans, *which fight against it.*—And then follows, what he could not tell how to reconcile, *And thou hast said unto me, O Lord* GOD, *But thee the Field for Money, and take Witnesses,* Ver. 25. The *Promise,*

That Houses, Fields and Vineyards, should be again possessed in that Land; as Ver. 25. puzzled him exceedingly. He knew not how it could be fulfilled, as *Providence* seem'd directly to contradict it, and what the Lord had *said,* of the City's being given into the Hand of the *Chaldeans,* was *come to pass.* He therefore bro't this difficult Case before the Lord, *And thou, Lord,* (saith he) *seest it.* It is as if he should say, "Lord, how can these Contraries agree, with thy Truth and Faithfulness in both?" His Distress seemed to arise from his own private Tho'ts, in fixing a Time too *soon,* for the Fulfilment of the Promise: Which much perplex'd him, and put Him on thinking that it could be *fulfilled,* as it was then so *contradicted* in Providence.—Upon which the Lord, in condescending Grace to his distressed Servant, first asserts his infinite *All-sufficiency,* to fulfill his *Promise, Behold, I am the* LORD, *the God of all Flesh: Is there any Thing too hard for* ME? Ver. 27. And next informs him of the *Time* of it, that it was not to be fulfill'd *instantly,* but after their *Return* from *Captivity.* And thus he sweetly reconciled the Promise, with the present Providence: As Ver. 28, &c.

And divers such partial *Mistakes,* our Lord's Disciplines made, concerning what he said unto them, and his Promises given them. And thence, how greatly were they *tried,* when their Lord was *crucified? We trusted* (say they) *that it had been* HE *which should have redeemed* Israel, *Luke* xxiv. 21. They were so shock'd with the present *Providence,* which was so directly contrary to what they apprehended in the *Promise,* that they seemed just ready to give up their *Faith in Christ,* as the *Redeemer* of *Israel.*—Thus, some of the *Prophets* of old, before the Incarnation of our Saviour, did make some partial *Mistakes;* (as *1 Sam.* xvi.6. *1 Chron.* xvii. 2. *Jer.* xxxii. 15 &c) and some of the *Apostles* of Christ, when their Master was present with them. As inspired Men, were not always under the Spirit of Inspiration, but sometimes tho't and spoke of the Things of God, from their human Judgment. Tho' they never did so, in any Part of Divine Revelation, given either in the Old Testament, or the New, but for that, were always under immediate Inspiration.

And if those great Men of GOD, were subject to some partial Mistakes, about the Ways and Times of the Lord's fulfilling his Word: O how easy is it for such little, weak Worms as *we* to be *mistaken,* as to some *Particular* relating to the *Promises* He gives us! Let us not think it *strange,* Brother; or that the Promise *fails,* in the *Substance* of it, when we mistake as to some *Circumstances* attending it. But in Faith and Patience let us possess our Souls, and wait the Lord's Way and Time to fulfill his Word: For not a *Jot* nor *Tittle* of it shall *fall to the Ground,* or *pass away unfilled.*

And wise and gracious are the *Ends* of our great GOD, who is *great in Counsel and mighty in Work,* in permitting our little *Mistakes.* As 1. The Honour of his Power and Goodness, in supporting us *under* our Weights of Trouble, occasion'd thereby. 2. That He might shew his Grace, by ministring suitable Relief to is *in* Distress; and working glorious Deliverance for us *out* of it. 3. That *thereby* He might shew us our *own* Weakness. 4. That by the *Trial* He might exercise and increase our Graces. 5. That He might thereby *fit us* for his Service; to sympathize *with,* and speak a Word in Season *unto,* our weary Brethren, in whom the same Afflictions are accomplished. And 6. That He might thus prepare us *for,* and confer *upon us,* a more weighty Crown of Glory.—And in all these Respects, my Brother, the Lord can fulfill his *Promise* to you, *In blessing to bless you, and in multiplying to multiply you,* even by this very *Providence,* which to you appears to thwart it, and is so contrary to you Expectation.

Think not then, That your *Work for Him,* is entirely *done.* For, *out of Weakness,* you shall be *made strong:* And by these Afflictions, prepar'd to administer Consolations, to *comfort others,* by the same *Comfort* wherewith you yourself are *comforted of* GOD.

And don't be *weary of the World,* Brother. Long to be *with Christ,* which is *far better;* you may and ought. And if this Providence is blest to wean you more from present Things, it is your Mercy. But be willing to stay the *Lord's Time,* till his *whole Will* is done upon, in and by you: As his Glory and your Bliss, present and eternal, are concern'd therein. God's dear Servant's, under Pressures, may have immoderate Desires to be dissolved, and be at Rest. Which may proceed from some Degree of Impatience, or Unwillingness to endure those Trials, which must precede, and prepare for, their future Crown. As *Jon.* iv. 3. *Therefore now,*

O LORD, *take, I beseech thee, my Life from me; for it is better for me to die, than to live.*—You say, Brother,

"My Case is not like *Abraham's,* when call'd to offer up *Isaac;* He received him again. Nor like *Jacob's,* when he said, *Joseph* is not, and *Simeon* is not; *all these Things are against me:* For he had them both again. God sometimes writes Death upon the Promise for a while, to try the Faith and Patience of his Children; and then fulfills it. But He has writ Death absolutely upon mine, and laid my Glory in the Dust. I know she cannot return unto me."—I reply,

It is your *Mistake,* Brothers, That God has writ *Death* absolutely upon his *Promise.* This killing Dispensation, so cross to your Expectation, doth not *touch* the Grace of the *Promise,* nor in the least *infringe* the Truth of it; but is and shall be the *Means* of its farther Accomplishment. What if GOD'S Design, in giving you a Taste of *Creature-Sweetness,* and taking it away unto *great Bitterness:* Was to shew you more of *Creature-Emptiness,* that so He might fill you more abundantly with his *infinite Fulness?* Will not this be a farther Extension of the Promis'd Grace, *In blessing to bless, and in multiplying to multiply you?*—And what if GOD intended by the Promise, not only to bless you in your late *Relative,* but also in that *Relation,* by giving you *another* Bosom Friend, instead of *that* which you have lost? You can't receive *Her* again, in *Person.* But you may in *Value.* Is not God able to give you another that shall be as *greatly,* and more *abundantly* blest for your Comfort, while taught by the Vanity and Uncertainty of the Creature you have *lost,* you enjoy GOD in another, and in *Him* a Permanency of Bliss, that shall *never be taken from you?*—But if God should not give you another *Bosom-Companion;* if in the Want thereof, He gives you more of *Himself;* won't *that* be *better?* Tho' you can't have the joy of your deceased Relative again, in *Her* personally; may'nt you have the same Comfort in GOD transcendently? What are *Creatures,* the whole Host of them universally? Is there any Comfort to be had in them, that is suited to the Nature of an immortal, Heaven-born Soul, that is not to be enjoy'd in the *Creator* substantially and eternally?—Wherefore, Set not your *Eyes* with Grief upon that which *is not,* upon the lost Stream; but look with

Joy on HIM which *is,* and is for *you,* an Ocean of Bliss, *Yesterday, To-day, and for ever the Same!*

I should have given a Hint to your *Mistake,* "When looking on the *Parts* and *Experience* of your deceased Friend, you tho't that God had designed her for peculiar *Service,* in the Place He had set her." That this *Tho't,* being formed from the *visible Appearance of Things;* was just such as *Samuel's* was, when looking on *Eliab's* Stature, He said, *Surely the* LORD'S *Anointed is before him,* 1 Sam. xvi. 6. And the Disappointment you met with, should not be your Distress, as His was none to Him.

Once more, Tho' your Heart was enlarged to *pray* for your dear Yokefellow's *Deliverance;* which the Lord did not please to grant. He can and will answer *your Prayer,* in some *other* and *better Way.* And most graciously will the Lord accept and reward your *Faith,* in your Attempt of Duty, *Not to stagger at the Promise of* GOD *thro' Unbelief.* And some glorious *Fruit* of Faith, you shall certainly *receive.* Tho' you had it not in the *Way* you wish'd, and had devis'd in your *own Heart*; you shall find it in a *better*, contrived and prepared for you of GOD; Which you'll soon see, was more for his Glory, and your transcendant Bliss.—Wherefore, Let the *Government* of all Things rest upon your *Lord's* Almighty *Shoulder;* where the whole *Weight* of it is devolved by the *Father;* and all Things shall *end well,* to your *endless Joy, Wonder and Praise:* And what you *know not now;* you shall thus *know hereafter.*—That *the Peace of God which passeth all Understanding, may keep your Heart and Mind thro' Christ Jesus:* And *His Grace be with your Spirit:* is the hearty Desire and Prayer of, dear Sir,

Your most affectionate Friend and Servant,

——— ———

LETTER XXVIII. *To Mrs.* C.

My dear Sister,

WE may see what *Vanity and Vexation* are in every Thing here; what Thorns and Briars run thro' all the Ground; and what little Dependance is to be had on all Creatures. Happy are the Souls that have

GOD for their ALL, that Fountain of Sweetness, that Ocean of Delights! Who will cause those that love HIM, to inherit *Substance,* and never fail, nor forsake the Souls that trust in Him, thro' Time, nor to Eternity! A true Christian, in the Exercise of Faith, hath enough in GOD, to satisfy all his Desires, and need not, doth not, go out of HIM, for any Delight. Whenever we depart from the LORD our Rest, it is by an *evil Heart of Unbelief.* And oh what Fools are we, ever to stir out of the Bosom of GOD! All is Joy and Peace *there;* and nothing but Sorrow and Disquietude every where *else.* How sad is it, that those happy Souls, who have the LORD for their *Portion,* should not always live upon Him, and rejoice in Him as *such!* How do the Things of Time and Sense, thro' the Influence of Sin and Satan, divert us with their pleasing Shews, from real Pleasure; or distract us with their pinching Cares, to our real Grief? And by both rob us of that Fulness of Bliss, which is to be enjoy'd in GOD! GOD will be our *All in All* in Heaven; and the more we esteem Him *so* on Earth, and practically live upon Him as *such,* the more are we prepar'd for the Heavenly State. What would such a Soul do in *Heaven,* that can't make a Life out of GOD? And tho' there, GOD will be all to us in HIMSELF, *without* the Creatures; He is here to be enjoyed as such *in* them, by every Heaven-born Soul. In Comforts, in Crosses, in Gains, in Losses, GOD is to be enjoy'd by a Believer. Which spreads such a Glory, and Sweetness thro' all, that Strangers to GOD, neither see nor taste. Nothing in Prosperity, can make us *happy,* but what brings us to GOD, and enables us to serve Him; nor any Thing in Adversity make us *miserable,* but what separates us from GOD, and unfits us for his Service. GOD in CHRIST, is so full, so great, so substantial a Good, that if HE is not enjoy'd in Prosperity, it will prove but an empty Name, or rather, a Soul-insnaring Thing: And if GOD is enjoy'd in Adversity, it will be full of Sweetness, and much for our Souls Advantage. We should put an Estimate on both, as *true Blessings,* just so far as GOD is brought to *us,* and we to *Him* by either. And as to *enjoy,* so to *glorify Him* in both, should be our greatest *Concern.* The Glory of God in all, should be our chief Care, our constant Work; since to do us Good by all, is GOD'S Delight. If we refer all Things to *God;* God will order all Things for *us,* as shall be most for his Glory, and our Advantage.

"Fear GOD, ye Saints, and you will then
Have nothing else to fear:
Make you his Service, your Delight;
Your Wants shall be his Care."

Wishing all true Happiness in this World, and great Glory in that to come; and requesting your Prayers and Thanksgivings for us: I remain, my dear Sister,

Yours affectionately, in the LORD,

——— ———

LETTER XXIX. *To* ----- -----

My very Dear and Honour'd Brother,

BLEST be our dear Lord, that hath brought a little Ease to your Heart, by that Instance of his "accepting, and rewarding *David's* Desire to build him an House, tho' not He, but *Solomon* was the chosen Instrument for that Service." I give Thanks likewise, that any Refreshment was given you, in what the Lord sent you by me.

Far wou'd I be, my dear Brother, from positively charging you with inordinate Love to your deceased Relative. tho' I humbly tho't, you might possibly exceed. I know by sad Experience, that we are apt to exceed in Love to Creatures and Things, given us thro' Prayer, and by the Promise, and which we enjoy God in, and bless him for. And tho' we mayn't see our Excess in the Enjoyment of Mercies, yet manifest it is in the Loss of them, if when the Lord *calls* for what he gave, we don't *freely resign* to his *Will,* and bless him for *Taking,* as well as *Giving.* If we have any particular Solace in any *Creature* or *Thing* the Lord gives, that we can't find in *God,* substantially and transcendently, when it is taken from us; we certainly lov'd that Creature or Thing *inordinately,* or gave it that *Affection,* that *Attachment,* which is due unto *God alone.* We lov'd not that Creature or Thing so purely as we ought, *in God,* and *for Him,* but as a *separate Good,* or something *besides* HIM, that gave us Pleasure. For if we lov'd the LORD as we ought, as the *Summum Bonum,* the *Chief Good,* the ALL of our Bliss; whence are these *Lowings and Bleatings* of our Souls, after *Creatures?* Doth not *all Fulness* dwell in *Christ?* Is there not in HIM a Fulness of all Relations? And of the choicest and most delightful Dispositions? And is he with us, ever with us, and all that He hath, *ours:* And yet if a *Creature* is taken from us, our *Hearts* can get no *Rest?* O, if this is the Case; *that Creature,* we in some Sort, in some Degree, made *our God.* And good, good it is, that we should be stript of such Creatures, to shew us our Folly, in *forsaking* the LORD, the *Fountain of living Water,* and *hewing to* ourselves *Cisterns, broken Cisterns, that can hold no Water.* That thence, thro' trying Providences, and the efficacious Teachings of Divine Grace, we may learn more Wisdom: To drink at the *Fountain-Head,* when the *Stream of Brooks* fails us; and take our Fill more purely and abundantly from that *River of Water of Life, clear as Crystal, which preceedeth out of the Throne of* GOD *and of the* LAMB.—Be *all Obedience,* Brother; to *delight* your *Lord's Heart.* Resigning *Abraham,* in his cheerful offering up his *Isaac,* was called *The Friend of God.* Is there any Joy like this, To give your *Lord Pleasure?* Is not the *Lamb,* that bought you with his *Blood,* worthy? Worthy of yourself, and of the Whole of your Service, Love and Joy? And to please and delight him, and also to honour him, won't you give him Leave to *give and take* with you? To do any Thing and every Thing, HE *pleaseth* with you? Will you *contend* with him for taking his *own?* Will you say, "It was *mine,* Lord?" No; rather say, "Lord, *I am thine;* and all thou gavest, givest, or shalt give me, entirely at *thy Dispose.* I will call nothing *my own,* by *thy Great* SELF! And delight that *Thou,* shouldst be the sole *Proprietor* of *me* and *mine.*"—And such a Frame of Spirit, Brother, will be for your present Joy, and future Glory.

I am glad that you have a *Desire,* to have the *Will present,* tho' how to *perform,* you find not. *That* your gracious Lord accepts, and records, as *your Kindness;* and commend and reward it He will, before Men and Angels, at his appearing.—I much compassionate your dear Soul, under your present Darkness, Grief and Trouble of Mind.—Be of good Comfort: *To the Upright there ariseth Light in Darkness: Out* of Darkness: *Darkness dissipating* Light.—You *have not an High Priest that cannot be touched with a Feeling of* your *Infirmities.* And soon your Lord will *see you again, and your Heart shall rejoice; and your Joy shall no Man take from you.*—To the *Grace of Christ,* I commit you: In his sweet *Arms,* I leave you. And with a Heart full of Love and Sympathy, I am, dear Sir,

Yours in the Lord for ever,

———— ————

LETTER XXX. *To Mr. and Mrs.* W.

My Dear and Honour'd Parents,

GLADLY I received your last, and return most humble Thanks for all the Instances of your paternal Kindness. The LORD is exceeding kind to evil and unthankful *me.* Oh for a Heart to love and serve Him! My Affliction has been a Trial to me, as thereby I have been in some Measure hindred from serving the Lord as I would. But I have been sweetly resign'd into his Will, and enabled to bless Him for all his Dealings with me. I rejoice, and give Thanks, that my good God, has prolong'd my Life till now, given me such a Measure of Health hitherto, and enabled me to do *any Thing* for Him. And surely I would love and bless Him, when He takes me *off* from that Manner of serving Him, in which my Soul delighteth. I would walk with my God, in the Obedience of Faith and Love, thro' Light and Darkness, Joy and Sorrow in the present State, until He brings me into Light, Joy and Glory, perfect and eternal. I know, thro' Grace, that all Things which pass over me, are for *God's Glory,* and shall turn to *my Salvation.* And I would have *no Care,* but to *glorify God,* and to answer his *Holy Will,* in every Change of Providence. I feel my own *Inability,* that without Divine Assistance I can do *nothing.* But the *Grace* of *Christ* is *sufficient* for me. *The Eternal* GOD *is my Refuge; and underneath are the everlasting Arms.* Well then shall I be defended from all Evil, supported under all Pressures, deliver'd from all Misery, and sav'd unto all Glory. And unto the LORD *my Salvation, my Strength and my Song, by Dominion and Praise for ever and ever.* Amen.

I was delighted, my Honour'd Father, some Time ago, with the distinguishing Love of God towards *you* and *me.* In taking *you* and *yours,* to make *us* Monuments of his *Free-Grace,* when some of our *Ancestors,* as we have Reason to fear, were left among the *Strangers to God,* and unacquainted with his *special Favour*. Oh why were *we* taken, when *others* were left! Not because we were *better than they:* But because the LORD *loved us!* Wherever Electing Love ran, before the Foundation of the World, there Calling them He *justifies*, and them He will also *glorify*. Glory, my dear Father, will be the *End* of Grace. That *Grace* which has begun to save us, will save us into *Glory!* May we always rejoice in the Grace which saved *us*, and have the Joy to see Salvation brought to our nearest *Relatives!* Oh that the *Children* of my dear *Brother*, might be reach'd by *efficacious Grace*, and they also appear to belong to the *Line of Election!* That we *together* as the *saved of the* LORD, may shout *Salvation unto God, and to the Lamb for Ever!*—May the *Blessings of the everlasting Hills*, richly descend upon you, and the sensible Presence of the LORD your own GOD, be with you! I request your Prayers for me; and am with the greatest Affection, my Honour'd Parents,

Your most Obedient Child,

———— ————

LETTER XXXI. *To Mr.* T.

My dear and honour'd Brother in the Lord,

I Thank you for your kind Letter. I rejoice in the Kindness of our God, in making his own Truths, hinted in my Letters to Mr. *W.* delightful to your Soul. A *spiritual Appetite*, to relish spiritual Things, is a *distinguishing Favour*, bestow'd upon none but those that are *Christ's own. The natural Man receiveth not the Things of the Spirit of God: for they are Foolishness unto him; neither can he know them, because they are spiritually discerned.* And *spiritual Men*, that have an *Appetite*, a *Capacity* to relish spiritual Things, can have no *actual Relish* thereof, without the *actual Presence*, the immediate Influences of the *Holy Ghost*. 'Tis *He that Takes of the Things of Christ, and of the Father, and shews them unto us.* Oh did we know how much there is done for us by all the *Three Persons in God*, in every Degree of Soul-Comfort and spiritual Pleasure that is given us, we should not *count the Consolations of God small.* It is *the Spirit of Truth*, in his special Operations as the *Comforter*, that, according to our

Lord's Promise, *guides* his People *into all Truth,* John 16. 13. It is *He,* that enlightning our Minds, guides us into the Doctrinal Knowledge of every Truth; and enkindling our Souls with the Truths known, that gives us Heart-Fellowship therewith. A *Guide,* you know, that conducts another, must be *actually present* with him, or he can't be assistant to him as such. So, without the *actual Presence* of the *Holy Ghost,* going before us into any Truth, and giving us *Access, Manuduction* into it; not the least spiritual *Truth* can we know, nor the least Degree of spiritual Knowledge thereof, can we attain. Oh, it is the *actual Presence* of the *Holy Ghost* as our *Comforter,* that, by his Light and Heat, irradiates our Minds, and enflames our Souls with the Knowledge of Divine Truth. Let the Truth shine ever so brightly, or warmly *round about us;* unless the Holy Spirit shines into our *Minds,* unto the Knowledge of the *Truth* in its Glory and Efficacy; We neither *see* its Light, nor *feel* its Heat.—What need then have we to *ask* for the *Holy Spirit?* And how much are we *Debtors to Him,* as our Guide into all Truth, for every Degree of our Knowledge thereof, and Fellowship therewith! Oh the infinite *Grace* of the Holy Ghost! how much doth He *do* for us, in every Kind, and Degree of spiritual Joy, which He gives us! And lo, *He doth not speak of Himself: but whatsoever He shall Hear,* saith our Lord, *that shall he speak.* As the *Holy Ghost,* in infinite Condescension to us, has accepted the Office of *Comforter;* So in his Discharge thereof, He doth not speak to us in any Truth, nor in any Part of it, *of Himself.* That is, of Himself *merely,* and *abstractly* from the *Father* and the *Son.* But strictly regards his *Mission* from them, To shew us their Persons, their Acts and Works, their Thoughts and Words, their Glories and their Grace. Thus the Holy Ghost *hears* what the *Father,* and the *Son* say, for and about *our Consolation;* Takes all the *Particulars,* and receives all the *Grace,* to bring it *down to us. He shall receive of Mine,* saith our Lord, *and shall shew it unto you. All Things that the Father hath are mine: therefore said I, that He shall take of mine, and shall shew unto you,* ver. 14, 15. Oh this *Receiving,* this *Taking* of Christ's, and of the Father's Things, by the Holy Ghost, to *shew* them *unto us;* doth imply in it, The boundless *Love* of the *Father,* and of the *Son* towards us, their infinite *Care* of us, and the gracious *Regard* which They have for *our Consolation.* As the Holy Ghost *Receives* these Things of the Father and the Son, He receives them as *given* from both for us. And HE being GOD equal with both, in the same boundless *Love* towards us, infinite *Care* of us, and gracious *Regard* for *our Consolation,* He *Takes them* as given. And having voluntarily accepted the Office of Comforter, to *apply* all that Grace and Salvation to us, which was given us in the eternal Counsels and Covenant of the *Three-One* GOD, and which in the Dispensation of the Fulness of Times, is to be given out to us: Down He flies on the Wings of Love, as sent from the Father and the Son, and from the good Pleasure of his own Will, He *brings* the same to us.

You see then, my dear Brother, That our spiritual *Knowledge* of GOD and his *Truths,* our *Delight* in, and *Fellowship* with them; are no *casual Things,* that fall out by Hap or Chance, that might *be,* or *not* be: But are Matters of *Appointment,* and of great *Moment,* in which *Father, Son,* and *Spirit,* in boundless Grace to us, are concerned. And let us hence learn, To put a high *Value* upon, to be very *thankful* for, and to have a due *Regard* to, the *Comforts of the Holy Ghost,* and to every *Degree* of his Consolation. Since there is not the least, but springs from so *great Grace!* And let all the Comforts of the Holy Ghost, as so many *Cords,* bind our Souls, in *Love* and *Duty* to the Comforter. Oh let us beware of *Sin,* that we don't grieve Him. Let us *credit* his Testimony, *mind* his Motions, and *obey* his Dictates. And in all Manner of holy Conversation and Godliness, behave as such, that are so highly favour'd with the *in-dwelling Presence* of the *Comforter,* and with the *Consolations of* GOD!

You say, my dear Brother, "That you expect Benefit from my Correspondence; but I must expect none from yours." I hope you expect nothing from *me,* separate from *Christ;* from a *Branch,* separate from the *Root;* from a *Beam,* separate from the *Body of the Sun.* It is a great Thing, to be thoroughly sensible of the *Nothingness of the Creature,* both with respect to ourselves and others. That the Creature is *Nothing, less than Nothing, and Vanity;* And the LORD ALL, and *in All.* That all the Excellency, Comfort and Usefulness of the Creature, is wholly *derived* from, and *dependant* upon its Creator. And if thus, my dear Brother, you expect Benefit from *Me,* looking singly to the LORD for it; I am persuaded you will not be disappointed. For *none of them that trust in Him, shall be desolate.* God can supply you with all the Good you want or desire, either mediately, or immediately, which Way soever He pleaseth. And as for *Me,* mean and worthless as I am, glad shall I be, if the LORD will make *Me* a *Pipe,* to convey the Waters of Life, from *Him* the living *Fountain,* into your Soul. And this, my Brother, is all you could expect from *Me,* was I the most *excellent* of Creatures. And tho' I am the *least of Saints,* and the *chief of Sinners;* yet, even *This,* the God of all Grace, is able to do for *You,* by *Me.* God can use whom *He will,* to do what Service *He please.*—And why then mayn't I expect Benefit from *You,* that is, from *God* by *You? Is the Spirit of the* LORD *straitned?* Are any of the Members of Christ's Body useless? Verily, The Head hath appointed to every one its Place and Use; effectually worketh in every Part, unto the Edification of the other, and in the Infinity of his Grace, says concerning all, even the most *feeble,* That they are *necessary.*—I shall be glad to know the Frame of your Soul, to hear from you when you have Leisure, and to have an Interest in your Prayers.—I am, dear Sir,

Yours Affectionately in JESUS,

———— ————

LETTER XXXII. *To Mr.* R.

My dear and honour'd Brother in Christ,

AS by that dear Servant of Christ, the Rev. Mr. *W.* and our dear Friend Mr. *T.* I am inform'd that you desire a Line from me; I embrace the first Opportunity to write.—And now, my dear Brother, What shall I say? I rejoice with you, and all the Lord's People, for the glorious Things which God is doing in *Scotland.* Surely the Lord calls upon us hereby, To *arise and trim our Lamps, to go forth to meet the Bridegroom.*

Dear Sir, as to the present *Frame* of your Soul, I am entirely ignorant of it. But from the Account given me of your *State,* I feel a springing Love to *you,* and Brother *T.* and shall rejoice to have a little Talk with you on the Road, in our Way to Heaven. Oh that our JESUS would join Himself to us, and make *our Hearts burn within us, while He talketh with us by the Way!* And as God's Free-Grace, hath made *Us,* poor *Strangers,* that were once afar off, *Nigh* by the *Blood of Christ;* I would say unto *You,* as our Lord once did unto his *Disciples, Children, have you any Meat?—Come and Dine.*

Come, feast upon the Lamb of God. The Father hath given his Son, and our Lord hath given Himself, to die for us, that we might live! Oh, *Love, passing Knowledge!* A crucify'd JESUS, is our Life! What do you *want,* my Brother? Here's *All* in CHRIST; who was once dead, and now lives for *you,* that you can possibly need to crave! *Life* of all Kinds, is in Him, *Life* in its highest Perfection, and *Life* of an endless Duration! And thro' the *Death* of your glorious Lover, all his Life is made *yours!* Come by Faith daily, into the Wounds of CHRIST; and there take in all the Grace and Life your Soul wants. For all the *Grace* and *Life* of the *New Covenant,* of the GOD of the Covenant, is bestow'd upon you, and irreversibly confirmed to you in the *Lamb's Blood!* Here's a *Fulness,* that you may be *free* with! A *Fulness,* that you can neither *exhaust,* nor *Waste!* A *Well of Life,* that is *full, deep,* and *endless!* A *Sea of Glory,* that has neither *Bottom,* nor *Bound!* Oh my Brother, If all that is in GOD, the All sufficient, and Eternal GOD, is *enough* to fill you; you shall be *filled* with all Grace thro' Time, and with all Glory to Eternity! For GOD in CHRIST, is *yours!* and *You are His!* You are loved into an entire *Interest* in Him, and indissoluble *Union* to Him, and an eternal *Communion* with Him! God the *Father lov'd you,* and gave you all this Glory in *Christ,* before the Foundation of the World! *Lov'd you,* and gave his Son in the Fulness of Time, to *die* for you; to procure all this Glory for you, and to secure it to you! God the *Son lov'd you,* and gave Himself to Death, for your Life, to bring you to Glory! And God the *Holy Ghost has lov'd you,* and given you the Beginnings of all this Glory in your own Soul! HE Himself is become the *Earnest* of this your vast *Inheritance;* and by his Joys, has given you the *First fruits* of the good Land! And *He that has begun the good Work in You, will perform it,* until Grace is perfected in Glory, and *Mortality swallow'd up of Life!* Of Glory-Life, in the immediate Vision and Fruition of GOD unto Ages without End!—Oh what a firm *Foundation* then, hath your Faith to rest on! What *Encouragement* have you to Duty, since all the Fulness of CHRIST is *Yours!* And what *Obligations* are *You,* and *I,* and all the Heirs of Grace under, to give it all the *Glory,* in a *Walk worthy of* GOD, in Heart, Lip and Life!—*The Grace of Christ be with your Spirit.* Pray for, Dear Sir,

Yours in the LORD,

——— ———

LETTER XXXIII. *To Mrs.* G.

My Dear Sister in the Lord,

I Am glad, that as one of Christ's *Lambs,* you are under the *Care* of our great *Shepherd.* Verily, He will not suffer you to want any good Thing. He *lov'd you,* and gave his *Life* for you, when in his Foreview, Ungodly! *Lov'd you,* and *Quickned* you, when *dead in Sin! Lov'd you;* and took you *up,* in all your Weakness and Wants, into his own Bosom, his own Arms; into his own Fulness of Grace and Power, *to save you to the uttermost!* He *loves you,* and will never *repent* what He has done for you; never cast you off, nor forget you, leave, nor forsake you; but follow you with his *Grace,* until He has brought you to Himself in *Glory!* Oh did you *know* the infinite Tenderness of Christ's Heart towards you; you would *run* into his Bosom, in all your Times of Distress. Christ loves you as a Member of his own Body, as his *own Flesh.* And from an infinite Fulness of Sympathy with you, and Power to help you, will nourish and cherish you, succour and save you, in and from all your Griefs, and unto the uttermost of all your Desires! Yea, He will do for you, *exceeding abundantly above all you can ask or think!* Oh, our tender *Shepherd,* takes a peculiar Care of his *Lambs!* His *Bowels* yern towards them, in all their Weakness and Wandrings; and with his *Arm* will He gather them, and in his *Bosom* will He carry them: To secure them from all Deaths, and Dangers, to nourish and preserve them unto *Life Eternal!* Christ will be sure to lose none of his *Weaklings;* but *These* in a special Manner, shall be the Objects of his Care, of his infinite Tenderness! Christ hath a *tender Heart* towards the Weak and Diseased of his Flock, a *tender Eye* to look upon their Griefs, and a *tender Hand* to bind up their Wounds and relieve their Souls. His Power to help and save us, is *Infinite!* And his Compassions never fail! His Fulness we can never spend, with all our innumerable Wants! Nor will He ever wax weary of supplying us, but *rejoice over us to do us Good, with his whole Heart, and with his whole Soul!* Oh there is *none like Christ!* He is *the Chief of ten Thousand, and Altogether Lovely!* And *This,* my dear Sister, *is your Beloved!* and *This is your Friend!* Wherefore, *Trust you in the* LORD *for ever;* and, *Rejoice in Him always:* for nothing past, present, or to come, shall ever *separate you from his Love!*—Unto his Grace I commit you: And am,

Yours most Tenderly, in the

Bowels of JESUS CHRIST,

——— ———

LETTER XXXIV. *To Mrs.* A.

I Could not help sending you a Line, to tell you, That JESUS *loves you:* and that *I* love you for his Sake. Oh Dear Soul, *what great Things has the* LORD *done for you!* How sweetly has He opened your Heart by his Grace, and made you *Willing in the Day of his Power,* to be saved alone by Jesus Christ, to have Him for your *Time-Portion,* and your *eternal* ALL! Christ was first *willing* to marry *You,* to betroth you to Himself for ever; or you had never been *made willing* to give up yourself to *Him.* Christ *first desir'd you,* or you had *never desir'd Him.* It was *his* first Love to *you,* that laid *Hold* of your Heart, and *drew* your Soul to love Him. You had never seen CHRIST'S Beauty, and been *sick of Love for* HIM, the fairest of all Fairs, the *Chiefest of ten Thousand;* if HE had not reveal'd himself unto *you,* as He doth not unto the *World:* In order to allure your Soul after Him, and to satisfy and solace you with Himself for ever. Be of good Cheer, then: For CHRIST and *You* are *one!* CHRIST has given Himself to be *yours,* and taken you to be *His,* in a Marriage-Covenant. And neither Time nor Sin, Death nor Hell, shall *part you.* For *Ever,* the LORD hath *betrothed* you to *Himself;* for *Ever,* will He *love you* as his *Bride;* and for *Ever* shall you have the *Enjoyment* of Him, as your Glorious *Bridegroom!*—Into his Arms I commit you, and am,

Yours in HIM,

——— ———

LETTER XXXV. *To Mrs.* W.

My Dear Sister in Christ,

I Was much troubled to hear of your, and our Loss, in the Death of your dear Father. But, my dear Sister, be not overmuch cast down; because you have a *Father,* that can *never die.* Your dear Lord Jesus, *ever lives,* and for *You.* And, Because HE *lives, You shall live also.* So long as Christ lives, you shall never be left to go thro' the World *alone,* as an Orphan, Fatherless nd Comfortless; without One, to care for, comfort, guide and defend you. *Creatures* die, and leave you; but the LORD will never forsake you. *Death,* breaks all natural Relations: But *Christ's* Relations to *you,* can *never* be broken. And now *your Father and your Mother have forsaken you; the* LORD, in an eminent Manner, *will take you up.* You are, and shall be CHRIST'S Care. All that is in HIM, is engag'd for *you.* His Love, Grace, Mercy, Wisdom, Power and Faithfulness, are all engag'd to support you under your Distresses, to supply all your Wants, to lead you forth by a right Way, thro' a World of Trials, and to bring you safely and triumphantly Home to Himself in Glory, to that eternal Rest which remains for you. Cast, therefore, *your Burthen upon the* LORD; *and He will sustain you.* Oh, run into CHRIST'S Bosom, flee into his Arms, They stand wide open, to receive and embrace you. Come, my dear Sister, *Put* CHRIST *for a Well,* while you are *passing thro' this Valley of* Baca, this Vale of Tears. And you will find Him to be such a Well of *Life,* such an overflowing, and ever-flowing Spring of all Supply, that you shall want no good Thing. There is enough in CHRIST, to supply, solace and satisfy you, thro' Time and to Eternity. And such is his *Grace,* that it delights Him greatly, to see you come to HIM for all you want, in this your Time of *Need.* Yea, He will count Himself *Honour'd,* if *now* you will make HIM your ALL. And verily, He will not send you empty away. The strength of his Bowels, will bind Him to supply your Wants. He can no more deny *You* any Thing that He sees best for you, than He can deny *Himself.* Because He has made you *one,* inseperably and eternally *one with Him,* and *loves you as Himself.*

And as for your deceased Relative, consider, *Your Loss,* is *his Gain.* He has now done with all the scratching Thorns, and grieving Briers of the Wilderness, and is got into the Land of Rest. He is now, where He *would be,* even *with* CHRIST, *which is far, far better.* Make haste to follow him. Dispatch your Business, do all you may for CHRIST, while it is Day. And in the diligent Use of all the Means of Grace, *See that you also be ready.* For the *Lord Jesus* will *come quickly,* and take *you also* Home to Himself: *And so shall you be for Ever with the Lord.* In HIM, with dear Love, I am,

Yours for Ever,

——— ———

LETTER XXXVI. *To* ----- -----

SIR,

IT gives me Joy to hear, that you have so much of the Fear of God before your Eyes, that you will not profane the holy Sabbath, by *selling any Thing on the Lord's Day.* O that God may keep this Thing ever in your Mind, and enable you to be stedfast in this your good Resolution! For, *Whatsoever good Thing any Man doth, the same shall be received of the Lord, whether he be bond or free.* Morality, Sir, is an excellent, lovely Thing. It is excellent and lovely in the Sight of God, and of all good Men, and being full of Majesty, it strikes a Terror upon the Consciences of wicked Men. And there is no Part of moral Virtue exercis'd by and Man, but shall in this Life, in temporal Blessings, receive from God its full Reward. If you will lose any Thing for GOD, Sir, HE will make up that Loss, and bless you with double Gain.—The Town, Sir, is a most wicked Place. Ungodliness runs down the Streets thereof like a mighty Torrent; and none, alas! none there is to stem the Tide of it. Profane Cursing and Swearing, vile and beastly Drunkenness, Scoffing and Scorning of those who run not with others to the same Excess of Riot, with horrid Profanation of the Lord's Day, abound in the wretched Place.—You must therefore expect, Sir, that your Temptations to Sin, will be many. But if God helps you to withstand, your Honour and Happiness will be the greater. Satan will tempt you, Sinners will entice you; and you have no Strength to keep yourself. Flee therefore, Dear Sir, to the Strong for Strength: Make your Refuge under the Shadow of

Jehovah's Wings: Say with the Psalmist, *Hold thou me up, and I shall be safe!* God can strengthen you to resist a tempting Devil, to Non-compliance with enticing Sinners, and enable you to set your Face like a Flint, in his Service.—And what an Honour will it be, if God should have brought you to the Town, to be a Blessing to it! A Means of its Reformation, if it is but in this one single Point, as I trust you will be, if you stand fast to your Resolution, *Not to sell on the Lord's Day!*—And to this, add, a strict Watch, lay a Restraint on yourself, that you admit not *vain Company,* nor *vain Discourse,* on God's *holy Day;* but spend the Whole of it in the publick and private *Worship of God.* Give yourself to Reading and Prayer. Esteem the *Word of God* given for your Perusal, and *Liberty to* approach his *Throne,* as Privileges unspeakable; and the *Sabbath,* a choice Means of your Soul's Advantage, present and eternal: For such it is in the natural Tendency of it. Let others know by your strict Observance of the *Sabbath,* that you prize the *Gift of it,* and your happy *Lot,* that you was born in *England,* who might have been born in *India,* where the Light of the Gospel, and a Day of sacred Rest, shines not.—thus, Sir, endeavour to reform *others* by your Example. And *you* shall be blest in the present Time, and the Favourite of Divine Providence. And as to approaching Eternity, as a good Man once said, "If I thought I should be sent to Hell *hereafter,* I would beware of sinning against God *here:* Because that *Sin,* which Man doth not commit, God will not punish."

Perhaps, Sir, you will think this last, but a very inconsiderable Motive to Obedience. Nevertheless, it is great in Itself; if we consider the Greatness of that eternal Torment, which is the due Desert of every Sin, and which will be the certain Consequent thereof, unto all that die out of Christ. *The Wages of Sin is Death.* Death eternal, as well as Death spiritual and temporal. the Ungodly by *Sin,* treasure up *Wrath,* against the *Day of Wrath,* and the *Revelation* of the *righteous Judgment of God.* And the more Sin they commit, the greater Wrath will by justly inflicted upon them. Every Sin, is no other than heaping up fresh Fuel, to feed the quenchless Flame of everlasting Burnings. Hence, Those who have committed less Sin, and under less Aggravation, shall find it more *tolerable* for them in the *Day of Judgment,* than those will find it whose

Sins have been increased, and by Gospel Light aggravated. And if the least Drop of Wrath for Sin, will be inexpressibly *terrible* and absolutely *eternal* to a *Christless Soul:* O *who,* with presumptuous Sinners, would sin presumptuously, and thus provoke the heaviest Shower of Divine Vengeance and fiery Indignation, to fall on his *guilty Head!*—So that, to abstain from Sin, that a Sinner if he perish, may endure the less Wrath; is a Piece of Wisdom, and a considerable Motive it may be, to excite him to legal Performance: Tho' it be but the *Negative* of Happiness, or the *Not-suffering* of so much Misery, as otherwise he should do.

As to *Eternal Life,* that is the *Gift of God,* thro' *Jesus Christ or Lord;* and is only to be enjoy'd by *Faith in* JESUS. And in order to this, we ought to hear the Lord's Voice in the glorious Gospel, even while it is call'd *To day;* that we *harden not our Hearts,* and provoke him to *sware in his Wrath,* That we *shall not enter into his Rest.* For to the Ungodly He saith, *Let the Wicked forsake his Way, and the unrighteous Man his Thoughts; and let him return unto the* LORD, *and He will have Mercy on him, and unto our God, for He will abundantly pardon.*

But then, Sir, consider, Tho' Duty is *ours,* Power for it is GOD'S. Attempt our Duty we should, and great Encouragement for it we have: In that when we *draw nigh to God,* He hath promis'd to *draw nigh to us.* And those that diligently use the *Means* of Grace, may happily find the *Grace* of the Means descend upon them. Not because their Performances are *worthy;* but because of *God's free Mercy;* which invites Sinners to approach him in his *Son,* and makes it their bounden *Duty.* For when we have done *all* we can, in religious Performances, we must still say, *We are unprofitable Servants;* and not have the least Dependence on our own Doings, for Acceptance with God. Because such is the infinite Purity of *Jehovah's* Nature, that in Point of justifying Righteousness, He cannot accept of any Thing less than perfect Obedience to his holy Law; which we Sinners, cannot perform. We are therefore call'd to *believe in Christ for Righteousness;* who hath obey'd the Law perfectly, in every of its Commands, and fully endur'd its Penalty, even all that Curse and Wrath which our Sins deserved; who are or shall be enabled to flee by Faith unto HIM for Refuge: For the free Forgiveness of our Sins, thro' his All-attoning Blood, and for the Justification of our Persons, in his perfect

Righteousness.—thus *Christ* the *Saviour,* in his active and passive Obedience, is the *only Way* to the *Father.* For thro' Him alone it is, that we Sinners, can find Mercy with God, unto Life eternal.

And tho' we are call'd to believe in JESUS, by this great Command, and with this great Promise, *He that believeth—shall be saved:* and warned of the Danger of Unbelief, by this awful Threatning, *He that believeth not, shall be damned:* Yet is not this Faith of *ourselves;* but the *Gift of God,* to the happy Souls that experience it. For where God from the Beginning hath *chosen any Man to Salvation;* He *calls* him by his *special Grace,* at the appointed Time: Gives him his holy Spirit to dwell in his Heart, to work this saving Faith, and every Grace in his Soul. by which He gives him a new, a spiritual Nature; new Discernings, Desires, Enjoyments, and Employments. Such Discernings of his Misery as an undone *Sinner,* as he never had before. Such Desires after an Interest in, Communion with, and Conformity to, the *altogether-lovely* JESUS, as before he was unacquainted with. Such Enjoyments of *Christ,* and of *God* in Him, as before he was not blest with. And such Employments in holy and heavenly *Service,* for the *Glory* of God in Christ, as before were not delightful, but irksome and tedious to him.—Thus the happy man, in whose Heart God works Faith, flees out of Self, and Self-Dependence, unto Christ, and his Righteousness, shelters himself in this great *City of Refuge,* where he's safe from the *Wrath to come;* Enjoys the Lord as his own Saviour; And serves him in *Love,* as a *Child* doth his *Father:* Or, in a Word, is thus *passed from Death unto Life,* is blest with the *Begun-Enjoyment* of GOD in *Grace,* and a growing *Meetness* for the heavenly *Glory.*—And without this new Nature, this *new Birth,* our Lord assures us, That we *cannot see the Kingdom of God.* Without this *Faith* of the *Operation of God,* which works by *Love* to him, we *cannot please God.* And without being *found in Christ,* as having shelter'd ourselves under the Covert of the Redeemer's Righteousness, we *cannot stand* with *Acceptance* before the *Presence* of the *Father's Glory.*—And as our Destruction by Sin, is wholly of *ourselves*, and our Salvation by Grace, is wholly of GOD: How earnestly should we *seek the* LORD while he may be *found,* and *call* upon him while he is near: That *we* may be of that happy Number, who are *saved by Grace,* unto *eternal Glory!* Most heartily I wish you this ineffable bliss: and am, Sir,

Your sincere Friend and humble Servant,

——— ———

LETTER XXXVII. *To Mr.* T.

My Dear Brother in Christ,

I Thank you for your kind Letter. Blessed be our Dear Lord, that you can say, "You have felt that the Holy Ghost has taken of Christ's Things, and shewn them to you." A precious Fruit is *This,* of the rich, free, distinguishing *Love of God* An Evidence, that *Christ,* and all his *Fulness* is *yours.* And He that has *begun* to manifest Himself unto *you,* as He doth not unto the *World,* will go on to shew you more and more of his *Glory,* till that which is *perfect* shall come, and you shall see Him *Face to Face,* and *know as you are known.*

The great *Mystery of Religion,* indeed lies in *knowing* all the *Parts,* which *Father, Son,* and *Spirit,* have acted, and do act, in our *Salvation.* In *such a Knowledge thereof,* as gives the Soul *Fellowship* with the Mystery, *Communion* with the Things known. Oh! it is sweet, and the peculiar Privilege of the LORD'S *People,* to have such a *Knowledge* of the Love of God the *Father,* of the Love of his Heart, and of all its glorious Fruits, that works up the Soul into *filial* Dispositions, and a *Childlike* Carriage towards Him. To have such a *Knowledge* of the *Redeemer's* Grace, and of all the glorious Fruits of his infinite Love, that *binds* the Soul to the Redeemer, and *constrains* it to walk as the *Redeemed of the* LORD. And to have such a *Knowledge* of the Love of the *Eternal Spirit,* as an Indweller, Sanctifier and Comforter, and of all the glorious Fruits of it, in his inward, sanctifying, and comforting Operations, that *endears* the Soul to the Comforter, and makes it *obedient* to all his Dictates, fearful of Sin, that it may'nt grieve Him, and careful about Duty, that it may please Him. To have such a *Knowledge* of the Acts and Works of Father, Son and Spirit, as each hath a particular, and all have a joint Hand, in our Salvation, that brings the Soul into *Fellowship* with the Three-One

GOD, changeth it into his Image, and engageth it to dedicate itself to Him: This, my dear Brother, is *true* and *real* Religion. A *Mystery* in the Christian Religion, which is *hid* from all that are *Christless:* Whether such that are blind *Heathens,* or such that are only nominal *Christians.* And *know* it is to none but *Heaven-born Souls,* who are design'd for, and growing up into, the Glory of the *Heavenly State.*

By this we may *know* whether we are *real Christians,* and how much of *true Christianity* we have in our Souls.—To make a *Christian,* that is so *indeed,* it is necessary that the Gospel of Grace reach our Ears; that the *Knowledge* of Christ and of God in Him; be given *Doctrinally* to our Minds; that this be experienced *Influentially* upon our Hearts, and appear *Practically* in our Lives.—As to *Degrees,* there is a vast deal of Difference, between the Doctrinal Knowledge of the Things of Christ, which *one* Christian hath, and that which *another* hath; between the Heart-Influence thereof, which *one* Christian feels, and that which *another* experienceth; and between the practical Effects of known, influential Truths, which appear in the Life of *one* Christian, and in *another's.* According to that Parable of our Lord concerning the good Ground, *Those who received Seed,* the Word of the Gospel, *into good and honest Hearts:* In *all,* it was productive of *Fruit:* But *Some brought forth Thirty, some Sixty, and some an Hundred-fold.* According to the different Measures of Grace and Gifts bestow'd on them, and to their different Ages, as Babes, young Men, and Fathers in Christ.—And as it is a vain Thing for a *nominal* Christian, to think He is a Christian *indeed,* from a Knowledge of Gospel-Truths in his *Head,* without a gracious Experience of the Power thereof upon his *Heart,* and a suitable Effect in his *Life:* (Since to all that are *real* Christians, the Word of the Gospel comes not in *Word only,* but in *Power,* and brings forth *Fruit* in Holiness, unto Life Eternal) So likewise is it a great Fault in a *real* Christian, that comparatively hath but a *weak* Knowledge of the Doctrines of Faith, but *little* inward Experience, and outward Obedience; to think He is *not* a Christian indeed, because he hath not attain'd to those *Measures* of Faith. Love and Holiness, which he hears *others* speak of, and sees to be in *them.* For there is not a Soul in the World, that hath had the least Beam of the *Knowledge* of *God in Christ*, shined into his *Mind* thro' the *Word* and *Spirit* of *Jesus,* which has had any *Influence* on the *Heart,* to attract the Soul after *Christ,* and engage it to cleave to Him, *inwardly,* in the Moments of Discovery, and *outwardly,* in some Proportion therewith; but is a *true Christian,* and *really* partakes of the *Spirit of Christ:* Altho' he may be *far, far behind* many of his *Brethren.*—And so *much* of the Knowledge of the Things of God, which a Christian hath, so *much* of the inward Influence thereof as he feels, and so *much* of outward Obedience that is excited thereby; even just *so much* of *true Christianity* is in Him.

How necessary then is it, my dear Brother, that we, *Christians,* should labour after an *Increase* in true *Christianity?* To *grow in Grace, and in the Knowledge of Christ* daily, to increase in Conformity to God's First-born, and in an obediential Walk before God our Father, as his dear Children, to abound more and more unto all Pleasing? *Religion in Truth,* is a Soul-enlightning, a Heart-renewing, and a Life-reforming Thing. Oh what excellent Christians are *They,* of what an excellent *Spirit,* that cannot *rest* in present *Measures* of Knowledge, of Influence, and Practice! Nor yet in advancing *Light,* without increasing *Heat,* and a *growing Purity!* Oh how much would it be for our Lord's Honour, and for our Advantage, how much would it tend to the Increase of our Holiness here, and of our Crown of Glory hereafter, if we gave *all Diligence,* to have our *Hearts* duly *affected* with every *known Truth* and with every *Degree* of our Knowledge thereof; and to have our *Lives* continually *regulated* thereby! Oh how Happy should we be, if we minded *This,* our *every Day's Work!* And so, *forgetting the Things that are behind, prest forward towards the Mark for the Prize of the high Calling of God in Christ Jesus:* Even a perfect Knowledge of Him, Communion with Him, and Holiness to Him.—*The Grace of Christ be with your Spirit.*—Pray for *me,* who am, dear Sir,

Yours in the Lord for ever,

——— ———

LETTER XXXVIII. *To Mr.* B.

Dear Sir,

HOW it is with you as to your present Frame, I know not. But most surely, tho' in a World of *Sorrows*, you have Cause to *rejoice in the* LORD *always*. In HIM who *is*, and *has* all Things in *Himself*, and for *you;* to make you truly *happy* here, and perfectly *glorious* hereafter. Creatures and Things may fail us, a Thousand Disappointments in these attend us, and our own Heart and Flesh, in Times of Trial, and at the Time of Death, may, and will fail us. But the LORD the everlasting GOD, will *never fail* us, *nor forsake us*. And in HIM we have ALL, tho' we were stript of *every Thing*. As having *Nothing*, in *Creatures*, those Bits of Dependance, those Pieces of Self-Insufficiency; in our Self-existent, and All-sufficient JEHOVAH, we may possess *all Things*. When Wants are all around us, we may solace ourselves in infinite Fulness, lie down and rest in the Bosom of GOD in CHRIST; in those fat, *green Pastures*, by those deep, *still Waters*, which in our JESUS, have an ever-springing, an ever-flowing Glory, and will yield us a full Supply, and present, and everlasting Delight. O how *blessed is the Man that trusteth in the* LORD, *and whose Hope the* LORD *is! He shall be as a Tree planted by the Waters, and that spreadeth out her Roots by the River, and shall not see when Heat cometh, but her Leaf shall be green, and shall not be careful in the Year of Drought, neither shall cease from yielding Fruit.—Lord, increase our Faith!* What do we want, my Brother, but more *Faith*, to live continually, to live joyfully, upon, and to, our own GOD in CHRIST? And Faith is *his Gift*. Let us ask the *Spirit of Faith*, the *Holy Spirit*, for freely of his immense Goodness, our *heavenly Father* will give Him to us, as his *dear Children*. Thus we shall be enabled to walk with GOD, in the Obedience of Faith and Love; and to us that *fear Him*, there shall be *no Want*.

What think you of your *Portion*, Brother, of the LORD your *Portion?* Is it not a *goodly Heritage?* Are not the *Lines fallen unto* you *in pleasant Places?* Since all the Perfections of *Jehovah's* BEING, are made over unto you in *Christ*, for your Salvation and Bliss, present and eternal, by Grace immeasurable, in Wisdom unsearchable!—O say not in Unbelief, as God's People of old, *Wherein hast Thou loved us?* Wherein hast Thou loved me? But mark the Answer the Lord gave, and gives, to them, and you, *Was not* Esau Jacob's *Brother, saith the* LORD: *Yet I loved* Jacob, *and I hated* Esau. O this *distinguishing Love!* Which was *from Everlasting* in Commencement, which chose and blest you in Christ before the Foundation of the World; which is *to Everlasting* in Duration; and which by Calling Grace, and the Fruits of it, brightly glanceth upon you in the Limits of *Time,* as it passeth by in its *eternal Round!* O my Brother, GOD hath not *so* loved all Men. No, *Jacob* was *loved,* when *Esau* was *hated.* Will you not say, *How is it Lord, that Thou wilt manifest Thyself unto* me, *and not unto the World!* God might have made you one of the *Rich,* the *Great,* the *Honourable* of the Earth, yea, one of the *Monarchs* the *Potentates* of *this World,* and have sent you away from *Himself* forever. And had He dealt thus with you, the Riches of his common Goodness, in your Time-State, had been brightly display'd. But oh, behold, These Things he thought not good enough for *you;* These were not great enough to answer his Heart's Love to *you;* The *Inheritance,* HIMSELF in CHRIST, He hath reserved for *you,* as a *Child of Promise.*

And hath GOD thus lov'd and blest *you,* with his *whole Heart,* and with his *whole Soul:* O love and bless the LORD, give Him *your Heart, your Life, your* ALL: And follow on to *know Him,* until you are lov'd *by Him,* into a perfect Conformity *to Him,* and the full and eternal Enjoyment *of Him,* in Life and Glory, *ineffable* and *unknown!*—Live *joyfully,* Brother, as an *Heir of* GOD, and labour to *walk worthy of* Him, *unto all Pleasing.*—*The Grace of our Lord Jesus Christ be with your Spirit!* In HIM with much Affection, and hearty Thanks for all Favours, I am, Dear Sir,

Your obliged Friend and Servant,

——— ———

LETTER XXXIX. *To Mrs.* K.

My Dear Sister in Christ,

YOURS I receiv'd, and return you thanks. I rejoyce that the Lord is carrying on his good Work in your dear Soul. And since *Jesus* says to you,

Be not faithless, *but* believing: Will you not *obey his Voice?* Just when you *hear it,* and according to that Degree of *Power* with which it is attended on your *Heart?* I know you *will.* But, what, *Trust* your *Lord,* no further than you can *see him!* C*redit his Word,* no longer than just while you hear him *speak!* O the Baseness of *Unbelief!* O the *Power* of this great *Sin,* this easily-besetting *Sin,* in the *Hearts of Believers!* And yet our All-gracious Lord, pardons and pities us, under the Workings and Prevalence of this great Evil; and giveth more Grace, fresh Increases of Faith, when we are borne down by the Power of Unbelief. O his infinite Patience, and Long-suffering towards us! Who is a *God like unto Him, that pardoneth Iniquity, that passeth by the Transgression of the Remnant of his Heritage, because He delighteth in Mercy!* Doth Jesus hint to your Spirit, my dear Sister, "The Blessedness of believing without Sight:" And will you not *believe,* except you *see* as others have done? "Have you seen JESUS, the All sufficient Saviour, held out by the Gospel to your Faith, as a perishing Sinner; ventur'd to cast your Soul into the Arms of his Mercy; and heard the pleasant Whispers of his infinite Favour thro' the free Promise; unto some sweet Persuasion of Interest, and Soul-stay upon Divine Faithfulness?" 'Tis enough, my Sister, if you had no more, for you to believe your Interest in Christ upon, from henceforth, for Time's Ever; until you shall live by Sight in the Glory of endless Vision. I say, such an Experience is *enough,* for Christ's Honour and your Soul's Joy, for you to believe your *Interest* upon: Not that hereby I would deter you from *seeking* most earnestly for further and brighter *Displays* of the infinite *Love* of your own *Lord Jesus.* No; *Open your Mouth wide,* after growing Communion with Christ in Love; for HE *will fill it.* It is a little Heaven to *long* for Christ, (a great Heaven, or rather, a Foretaste of great heaven) to *enjoy* Him, in our low and little State on this Earth, until the superior Glory of the Heavenly State comes on. But in all your Breathings after Communion with Christ, my Sister, seek for more glorious Shines of his *manifestative Favour,* as believing you Interest in the *eternal Love* of his *Heart.* This I say, as pointing out your Duty; but if you can't come *at it,* vent your Desires after Christ as you *can.* If you can't come to him as a *Believer,* come as a *Sinner,* and say, "Lord Jesus, thou great Saviour, let not a Sinner perish for want of thy

Salvation, that longs for an eternal Interest in it; famish and die for Thirst, that pants after Communion with Thee in Love!" And you shall find to your unspeakable Joy, that the Saviour is full of *Bowels,* that He will not, cannot hide Himself *long,* from a Love-sick *Soul,* that *follows hard after him.*

And mean Time, my dear Sister, O that the Lord by me, would persuade you, that if you are not dandled on the Knee, and borne on the Side, kiss'd and embrac'd as *others;* yet, that you are put among the *Children,* and for ever interested in God your *Father's Love!* Aye, in the *same* Love, in which your *Brethren* stand. The love of God's Heart towards us in Christ, unto one and all, is the very *same.* An infinite *Variety* there is in the *Displays* of God's Love, cast upon various Souls; but an infinite *Sameness* in the Love of his *Heart,* in his *Love* as consider'd in *itself,* towards all the innumerable *Multitude* of the *saved Ones.* Our Lord may say to you, my Sister, under Discouragement, while some of your Brethren as to manifestative Love are more highly favour'd, as the *Father* to the *elder Brother,* is a Sort displeased, when the Prodigal was feasted; *Son* (Child) *thou art ever with me, and all that I have is thine.* And han't He spoken thus to your Soul: "*Come,* my Child, be not cast down, that thy Brethren are feasted; all my Grace is thine, *all Things* for Thee *are ready:* Come, sit down to Meat, and feast on all my Dainties prepar'd for thee, as thy own?" And further, my dear Sister, by this Word apply'd to your Heart, our Lord might hint, that tho' you had not been so richly *feasted* as others, yet all Things for you were *ready,* prepar'd for your more abundant Delight *here,* and for your everlasting Feast *hereafter.* And will you not then come by Faith, and feast upon the delicious Sweets of the *Passover-Lamb, sacrificed for you,* and drink of the *Wine* of his *Love,* which flows in his *Blood,* for *your Life;* when our Lord Himself invites you to Table, to sit and feast with him *here.* as an Earnest of that richer Feast which awaits you at the *Marriage-Supper of the* LAMB, which you shall enjoy with Him *hereafter?* The Lord perswade your Heart of his Love, and draw you by his own Hand! and then you will come freely.

Go on boldly, my dear Sister, in the Lord's Name and Strength, to *venture your Soul* in the *darkest Season,* upon *Christ,* the *Foundation* laid in *Sion;* and fear not *sinking* into *Perdition,* so long as the *Rock of Ages* endures for your *Salvation.* And be assured, that it is no *Presumption,* for a perishing *Sinner,* to rest his *Soul* on the mighty *Saviour,* and to look for that *eternal Life* thro' Him, which a GOD that cannot *lie* hath *promised:* But that true *Faith* in the Redeemer, which by the Redeemer's Gospel is *required.* It is Satan and Unbelief, my Sister, which suggest to your Mind, That your *Faith* is *Presumption:* To rob God of the *Glory,* and you of the *Joy* of its repeated *Acts.* And whenever such a Thought darts into your Mind, instead of being discourag'd by the Enemy's Voice, let it excite your gracious Resolution the more to say, *I will go in unto the King: and if I perish, I perish.* So will your Lord be glorify'd, your Joy full, and the Enemy baffled.

As to that Text, *The Harvest is past, the Summer is ended, and we are not saved:* It need strike no Terror upon *you,* who thro' the Grace of the Gospel, are saved unto *Faith in Jesus.* It only respects Those, who while they *hear* of the Saviour, and *live* under the Light of the Gospel, *neglect that great Salvation* which is proclaim'd thereby, prefer *Trifles,* and lose their *Souls:* Or, that shall at last be found among Those who are *not saved,* after all the Opportunities of saving Grace are *over.* But there is not one Soul, that is gather'd unto *Christ* by *Faith,* here in *Grace,* but shall hereafter be gather'd unto Him in *Glory;* and found among that happy Number who were *saved of the Lord,* while the *Summer* of the Gospel *lasted;* and shall enjoy to a blest *Eternity,* all that great *Salvation,* for which they were happily prepar'd in *Time.* That your Faith and Hope in Christ may be strengthned, and your Joy and Peace thro' Him be more abundant; to a rich Increase of Holiness in Heart and Life: is the sincere Desire of, my dear Sister,

Your tender Friend, and Servant in the LORD,

———— ————

LETTER XL. *To Mrs.* A. *and* M.W.

My dear Cousins,

SEEK JESUS, in your *early Days!* Exceeding great and precious, is that Declaration and Promise of his Grace, *I love them that love Me, and those that seek Me early, shall find Me,* Prov. 8. 17. Oh, *Christ's Love,* his Heart-Love, his manifestative Love, is *better than Life!* And wondrous is that Reserve of Favour, He hath in Store for them that seek Him betimes. Those that are drawn by Christ, to give *Him* their *Hearts,* their *first Love,* their *choicest Love:* in boundless Grace, shall be *loved* of *Him,* and of his *Father,* with peculiar Displays of infinite and everlasting *Kindness.* Oh my dear Children, *seek* JESUS. Seek Him, and you shall *find Him.* Find Him, and in Him you will find *Life,* of the highest Perfection, of the largest Extension, and of endless Duration.—We have *all sinned,* in our first Father *Adam,* were born Sinners, and have gone astray from the Womb. *Sin has entred, and Death by Sin: Sin hath abounded, Sin reigns unto Death.* Unto Death spiritual, unto temporal Death as a Curse, and unto Death eternal, or that cursed State of an endless Banishment from the blissful Presence of God, to *suffer the Vengeance of eternal Fire, with the Devil and his Angels.* And all must *die,* must *thus* die, but those that *find* the SAVIOUR, who is the *Sinner's Life.* And *none* find Him, but *those* that seek Him now. *Now, now,* while Gospel-Grace is proclaimed, with a *Whosoever will, let him take the Water of Life freely.* Oh take Christ, as a free Gift, every one for yourselves. The SAVIOUR holds forth Himself to the Hand of your Faith. Stretch it out, receive, embrace Him; and He is yours for ever.—Are your willing to be marri'd to the Son of God? Are you *sick of Love,* for this *altogether Lovely Lord?* Is He unto you, in your Esteem, *The Chiefest among ten Thousand?* Then will the LORD your *Maker,* your *Redeemer,* be *your Husband.* Oh give up yourselves to *Him,* to be entirely *His;* and you shall be of that happy Number, who are the *Bride, the* LAMB'S *Wife.*—Fear not he LAMB'S *Love;* He loves a Sinner *well,* that comes to Him, to be saved by Him, to be married to Him in an everlasting Covenant. And whoever, or whatever the *Sinner* be, that thus approaches the SAVIOUR'S Presence, *He will in no wise cast him out.* Not a Soul shall *die,* that is willing to *accept of Christ,* upon the Bottom of *Free Grace.* Christ was *first* willing to embrace that *Soul;* or the Soul had *not* been made willing to embrace *Christ.* And He that has loved such a One into a *Sight* of his own Beauty, and a *Desire* after Union and Communion with *Him;* will strengthen the Soul in Faith, and draw it out in Love, to give up *itself* to be the LORD'S. While He, in Grace *unknown,* in Love that passeth *Knowledge,* receives the Soul into his own Embraces, to make it *happy* in Him, yea, to be his *Love,* his *Dove,* his *Delight* for ever; and makes over *Himself* to the Soul, to be entirely its *own,* in an inviolable *Marriage Covenant,* that shall never, never be *broken.*—But oh the *Happiness* of that Soul, who is thus the LORD'S, who hath thus the LORD for his *Portion!* Neither Men, nor Angels can set it forth. It is far better experienc'd, than express'd, enjoy'd, than delineated. And in the most sweet Enjoyment of new Delights, shall the saved Ones increasingly *know,* how great, how ineffably great, their eternal *Happiness* in GOD the SAVIOUR is!

And unto you then, my dear Cousin *Elizabeth,* unto you in an especial Manner, who have *lost* your earthly Husband, let me say, Come *see* what a Husband *Jesus Christ* is! He ever *lives,* He ever *loves,* the Souls *espoused unto Him.* Oh little, little do you think, what a glorious *Husband* the SAVIOUR is, to miserable *Sinners!* What Beauties and Glories, what Grace and Love, what Wisdom and Power, what Riches and Honours, of an endless Duration, are in and with HIM! Are in and with Him for his *Bride,* to make *Her* truly *happy* in this World, and perfectly *glorious,* World without End! O come, *Taste and see how Good the* LORD *is!*

And may you all, my dear Cousins, most happily prove, how *far* the LORD our Maker, this heavenly Husband, this heavenly Lover, in his infinite Excellency, *exceeds* the best of earthly Husbands, of earthly Lovers; to your present *Joy,* and endless *Glory!* So prays

Yours Affectionately,

——— ———

LETTER XLI. *To Mr.* N.

Dear Sir,

IT is well for you, that *Christ is precious,* desirable above all Things, to *your Soul.* Not the least Ray of the infinite Beauty and Glory of *Christ,* as the only *Saviour,* hath shined into the Heart of an *Unbeliever.* No; the Soul that *sees the Glory of the* LORD, the Mediator, *and the Excellency of our* GOD, the Saviour; So as to approve of Him, as God's Way of

Salvation, and to cleave unto Him, as such; hath true, *precious Faith. The Faith of the Operation of God. Is passed from Death to Life, and shall not come into Condemnation.* The least Look of Faith to Christ, is Saving. *Look unto* ME, *all ye Ends of the Earth:*--is the Command. And, *Be ye saved:*--is the faithful Promise, the Royal Grant, that proceeding from the Heart of the Prince of Grace, is gone out of his Mouth, as a *God* that cannot *lie,* nor *repent.*—What think you of it, my dear Friend? Do you *look* to Christ for Life? And shall you indeed be *saved* by him? Do you *experience* the one, and *believe* the other? Or are you at a *Loss* about both? If you are at a Loss; what is the *Cause* of it? Do you doubt the Truth of *your Faith,* or the Truth of *Christ's Promise?* I easily think it is the former, if you doubt the latter as to yourself, as to your own Interest in, and Salvation by the Promise. But consider, If as convinc'd of your Sin-ruin'd and lost State by *Nature,* and your utter Inability to help or save *yourself,* by any Thing that *you* can *do;* You look to *Christ* as the only and All sufficient *Saviour,* for *all Salvation,* from Sin and Misery, unto Holiness and Glory: This is the *Faith of God's Elect.* Of such, and of none but such, that were from the Beginning chosen in Christ unto Salvation; and that are prepar'd by the Work of the Holy Ghost upon them in Time, for that Glory which was prepar'd for them before Time began. This is that *Faith* in *Jesus,* that *Looking* unto *Him;* unto which the *Promise* of Life and Salvation in and by him, is inseperably *annexed.* Believe it then, my dear Friend, that unto *you,* as a *Looker* unto *Christ for Life,* this *Promise,* this *Grant* of Salvation, *Be ye saved:* is made. It is *your* Promise, the Grant made to *you,* by the Prince of Life and Love, even to you in particular, as much as if your very *Name* was affix'd to it. And lo, *One* and *All the Promises of God,* are *yours* in *Christ,* are now and always, *Yea* and *Amen* in *Christ* unto *you:* To the Glory of *God* by you, in the present and future World!—Go on therefore, as a Believer in Jesus, by repeated, and stronger Acts of Faith, *to Believe on the Name of the Son of God* continually. And live joyfully as an *Heir of Promise.* For lo, God's Promise of Life in *Christ,* made to *you,* is a *free* Promise! That sought none of your Worthiness, for its Foundation; nor will fail towards you, because of your Unworthiness! It is a *full* Promise: That hath all Supplies in it, for your every Want! It is a *mighty* Promise: That is well able to bear the

Weight of the Whole of your Salvation, from Depths of Misery, unto Heights of Glory! And lo, It is an *irreversible, unchangeable, eternal* Promise! It is not only that which *cannot* be reversed, which *cannot* be alter'd, which *cannot* end, as being made by a GOD of infinite *Faithfulness,* whose Honour obligeth him to be as good as his Word: but it is also, that which God *will not* reverse, alter, or put an End to, as being made by a GOD of infinite *Love,* who is of *one* eternal *Mind,* to be thus *gracious unto you!* He lov'd you of old, He loves you still, He will love you Forever! His Love towards you is free, great, unchangeable and eternal! The *Promise* is the Expression of God's *Heart.* And for the eternal Glory of his *Grace,* and for his Heart's *Delight,* in your eternal Salvation, as an Object of his eternal Love, He will *fulfill with his Hand,* what his *Mouth hath spoken!*—Fall down therefore, my dear Brother, before the Majesty of the God of Grace, of the God of Promise! And believing in him, pour out your little Soul in *Love,* to that great HIM, who *first loved you!* And shew your Love, in having *Respect unto all his Commandments.*—So shall the Name of *Christ* be glorify'd in *you,* and your Joy and Peace in *Him* be abundant here; and your Glory *with Him* great hereafter.—*Grace be with you!* I am, Dear Sir,

Your Affectionate Friend and Servant,

In our most Precious JESUS,

——— ———

LETTER XLII. *To Mr.* W.

My dear Brother,

YOURS I receiv'd, and rejoyce to hear of your Soul's Prosperity. I should have wrote before, but thro' much Weakness of Body have been hindred. Oh my dear Brother, *work while it is Day:* The *Night* of Affliction and Death *cometh,* wherein you can do *no more* to glorify Him that hath loved you, on this Earth. I blest the Lord, for enabling , me, so weak, so vile a Worm, to do *any Thing* for Christ, while some Measure of Health and Strength was given me. I long now, to glorify my Lord, in the Weakness and Affliction I have long labour'd under: By *submitting* to his *holy Will,* by *kissing* the *Rod,* and by *loving* and *blessing Him* for *every Stroke.* I believer all my Lord's Dealings with Me, are in infinite Love, and shall be over-rul'd for his Glory, and my Advantage, present and eternal. Oh how great is our Privilege, that the LORD our *Shepherd,* our *Love,* our *Life,* is and will be *with us,* when we pass thro' the *Valley* of the *Shadow of Death!* The *bitter Waters* of Affliction and Death, are made *sweet,* so that we can comfortably *drink* of them, when our JESUS, that *Tree of Life,* that Mass of *Sweetness,* is cast into them. Since CHRIST is *ours, all Things* are *ours: Whether Life, or Death, things present, or Things to come.* We have *All,* all Things as so many *Blessings,* in Him who bore the *Curse,* in Him who is our ALL. Our vast and endless Store of all Blessings, Joys and Glories, for Time and Eternity. What can that Soul *want,* that hath CHRIST the LORD for his *Portion?* Oh, *No good Thing!* Richly replenish'd is He, with the Blessings of *Life,* of Life for *Evermore,* in the LORD *his Life;* beyond the Conception of a Mortal's Thought, or the Expression of an Angel's Tongue! The wondring Angels, may say of such a Man, *O Man greatly beloved!* But can never cast up, or tell out, the Riches of that *Love,* wherewith such a Man is *blest!* No, the Riches of JEHOVAH'S *Love,* of HIMSELF in Love, made ours in CHRIST, are *unsearchable*!

How happy then is an *Heir of* GOD! *a Joint-Heir with* CHRIST! And how joyful may he be, should he be, in his State by Grace, in every Change of Providence; all of which prepare him for the approaching State of his unchangeable and eternal Glory!—I rejoyce to think, we shall shortly meet in Heaven. To enjoy an everlasting Fellowship with each other, with all the Saints and Angels; and to be blest with the glorious and immediate Vision, of GOD and the LAMB: Where there is *Fulness of Joy,* and Rivers of *Pleasure for Evermore!—Great Grace be with you!*

Yours for Ever, most Affectionately,

In our sweet LORD JESUS,

——— ———

LETTER XLIII. *To Mr.* L.

My dear, dear Brother,

WHAT, send a Letter, and Nothing in it! It grieves me to serve you so; but I han't Time now to write. JESUS your Lord, will not send you *blank Papers.* The *Letters* of *his Love* to your *Soul,* in the Promise and Declarations of Grace, apply'd to your *Heart,* have been, and shall be, all *full* and *glorious.* Oh how *much* doth CHRIST speak to us in a *Little!* Oh how *Sweet,* how *exceeding Sweet is his Mouth! His Lips are like Lilies, dropping sweet-smelling Myrrhe!*

"His Mouth is most exceeding sweet,
All Sweetness, like an Hive.
One Word of His, like Honey is:
Oh how it doth revive!"

Go your Way, walk on in the *High Road* to *Heaven, thro' much Tribulation, rejoycing in Hope of the Glory of* GOD! JESUS *loves you.* That's *enough.* Your *Life* is in his *Love,* present and eternal! Unto the tender Care, of your own dear, loving LORD, I commit you. And with a Heart that loves you much in HIM, I remain, dear Sir,

Yours in the sweetest Bonds,

——— ———

LETTER XLVIV. *To Mr.* M.

Dear Sir,

I Hope that your Soul prospers, altho', like the *Palm-Tree,* it should be under *pressing Weights.* We must have *Pressures,* of one Kind or other, to exercise our *Faith in Christ,* and *Love to Him.* To shew us our own *Insufficiency,* and the *All-sufficiency* of Christ: While *his Strength,* in supporting us under them, is made perfect in *our Weakness.* Which Way soever the Lord leads us, it is still right, *a right Way, to the City of Habitation.* Whatever He doth with us, He is always doing us Good. He is always loving us, in all his Dispensations towards us. Tho' He don't always *smile;* yet He always *loves.* He loves in Frowns, as well as in Smiles. His Kindness flows in *Rebukes,* as well as in *Embraces.* Our God, is always shewing forth, *The exceeding Riches of his Grace, in Kindness towards us thro' Christ Jesus,* in all the Dispensations of his Providence. Altho' his Kindness therein, is not always visible to *our Sight.* But what *we know not now;* we shall *know hereafter.*—And mean Time, we are called to *believe,* when we can't *see*: To adore, what we can't comprehend, of the deep, the glorious, the unsearchable *Ways of the* LORD, in his *Mercy and Truth* towards us. And good it is for us, both to *hope, and quietly wait for the Salvation of God.* For if He should cover us with thick Darkness; *He will* again *bring us forth to the Light, and we shall behold his Righteousness.*—Wishing *all Grace may abound towards you,* and the *dear Saints* with you: I am, dear Sir,

Your obliged affectionate Friend and
Servant, in our precious LORD,

——— ———

LETTER XLV. *To Mrs.* C.

My dear Sister,

I Desire to leave all Things in the Hands of my infinitely Wise, and Gracious GOD. He cares for *Me:* What need I anxiously care for *Myself?* Why should a Soul, that is interested in GOD, be perplex'd with Fear about any Events? *Not a Hair of our Heads can fall to the Ground, without our Father.* All Things in Providence, are wrought exactly correspondent to the Counsel of *Jehovah's Will.* And done is such an Infinity of Wisdom and Goodness, that Nothing could be *better* than it is; either for the Glory of God, or the Advantage of his People! What a Shame is it then, for those happy Souls, for whose *Good, all Things work together;* to quarrel with the glorious *Worker?* Or find Fault with his glorious *Work?* As we always do, when we are anxiously careful about, or displeased with, any Events. If the Lord *brings us thro' Fire, and thro' Water,* He will *bring us thence into a wealthy Place.* Out of the *Furnace,* we shall come, *as Gold that is Seven times refined.* So that there is no Room for us to be uneasy at any Providence, with respect to our *own Good.* And if we regard the *Glory of God* in all; I am sure we have the highest Reason for a joyful

Acquiescence with his All-wise Dispose. Oh, *Who* should love and adore, think and speak well of GOD, in *every Thing,* if his *Friends* do not? Oh that the Lord, would fill my *little Soul brimful of Love to Him!* Oh that He would grant me *Grace,* to *glorify Him!* And then, Let Him do with *Me,* as HE *pleaseth.* Surely I wou'd have *no Will,* but GOD'S: *No Interest,* but *His: No Care,* but to advance *his Honour.* Oh my dear Sister, I *long* to *love* GOD. If you love me, pray, that my Love to God, may be a keen, solid, lasting *Flame!* That may nimbly run thro' all Opposition, lick up the Waters of Affliction, and ascending to Him from whence it came, join, like a *Tongue of Fire,* with *His infinite Flame!* We shall never be fully *happy,* till we are perfectly *One,* in and with GOD. *In Him,* by a Soul-satisfying *Enjoyment* of his infinite *Glories.* And *with Him,* by a perpetual and complacent *Flow,* of all the Powers of our Souls, into *His Will, Honour,* and *Interest.* The *Perfection* of this glorious *Bliss,* is reserved for the *Life to come.* But, blessed be God, it is *begun Here.* And the happy *Increase* of it, should be earnestly *sought for,* by the Favourites of Heaven, the Friends of God, continually.—That *the Love of God,* may be *shed abroad in your Heart,* more and more, *by the Holy Ghost;* and your Soul drawn thereby, to *love him, who first loved you,* is the sincere Desire of, my Dear Sister,

Yours in the Lord for Ever,

——— ———

LETTER XLVI. *To Mrs.* A. *and Mrs.* G.

My Dear Sisters in Christ,

JESUS *loves you: Believe it;* and your Hearts will be *full of Joy.* Go on to *rest* your *Souls,* and the whole Weight of your *Salvation,* upon CHRIST, *the Chief Corner-Stone, the Foundation which God has laid in Sion:* And *fear not.* For you *shall never perish, but have everlasting Life.* The *Rock of Ages,* cannot *sink* beneath you. And unless CHRIST could *fail, You* that rest on HIM, cannot sink into Perdition. *Because Christ lives, you shall live also.* Oh, doubt it *not.* You cannot wound the Heart of Christ *more,* than by *Unbelief.* It is the Joy of his Soul, to see poor, needy,

Hell-deserving *Sinners,* trust in Him, the Mighty SAVIOUR, and not be afraid. Oh stir not out of CHRIST, and the *Word of his Grace,* which he has given for *your Salvation.*—I am affectionately,

Yours in the Lord,

——— ———

LETTER XLVII. *To* ----- -----

My Dear and Honour'd Brother in Christ,

TIS enough, Dear Sir, that your *Beloved* is *yours,* and that *you* are *His.* That the *Lord of all,* is *your God.* Your *Maker,* your *Husband;* and that *You* are *His,* in an inviolable, everlasting *Covenant.* Will you not cease your excessive Grief for the Loss of a *Creature;* which casts such Dishonour upon the *Lord* your *Creator,* upon *God,* your *Saviour,* as if HE, even HIMSELF, in his vast *Infinity,* was not *enough* to satisfy and solace, your little, scanty *Soul!* Be ashamed, practically to say, That *Christ,* with all his *Fulness,* is not for *you,* a *Soul satisfying Good!* If *Christ* was *dead;* you might *grieve on,* and *refuse* to be comforted. Your Life, your Joy, your ALL were gone! But, doth JESUS *live,* and live as *your Life:* And yet your Spirit sinks into Sorrow and *Death!* How *incongruous* a Thing is this! How *unworthy* of him, how *unkind* to him, as the *Lord your God! Lovers,* among *finite Souls,* find their greatest *Pleasure,* in being ardently *loved again.* And shall the *Lord,* your infinite *Lover,* who in infinite Condescension, to make you *happy,* calls for your *Heart;* want the *Joy,* to see your *Soul* all enflamed with *Love,* to his glorious, blissful SELF! O let the *Time past suffice.* Your *Beloved* is yours. Look upon his fair Face, till you are enamour'd with his ineffable Beauty! See Him in his transcendent Fairness, as the Christ of God; in his exceeding Fitness to your every Case; in his unsearchable Riches, his inexhaustible Fulness, for the rich Supply of your every Want; and see this altogether lovely Lord, in this endearing Relation, as *your Beloved,* as entirely and eternally *yours:* And then say, with Wonder, Love and Joy, *My Lord, and my God!* Thou, Lord, art fully and forever *mine!* and *I,* beloved of Thee, and resigning to Thee, am entirely and eternally *Thine!* You have *Christ's*

Heart, Brother, you are his Love, his Dove, his fair One. Will you not give him *your Heart,* and say to Him, that matchless HIM, who is the Wonder, Love and Joy of Heaven and Earth! what is the Infinity of his Grace He speaks to you, *How fair, and how pleasant art Thou, O Love, for Delights!* Be content with your *Portion,* Brother, your wondrous *Lot,* in the *Christ of God!* Let HIM be your *exceeding Joy!* Your Ever living and exuberant *Joy!* Your Sorrow-absorping *Joy!* And give your Lord the Pleasure, to see you *His Portion,* by way of *Resignation,* and to say to *you,* melted down into Submission and Acquiescence, into all Love and Obedience, *The Lines are fallen unto Me in pleasant Places; yea, I have a goodly Heritage.*—I know, Brother, *Influence* for this, must come from *Above.* If we want *Wisdom* and *Grace,* let us *ask of God,* who giveth *liberally,* and *upbraideth not.* Duty is *ours;* Supply of Grace for it, *God's.* Exhort one another to, and attempt our Duty, *we should.* And *God* therein and thereby, doth often *speak to our Hearts,* and *strengthen* our *weak Hands.*—*The Grace of our Lord Jesus Christ be with your Spirit!* In Him, with affectionate Esteem, I am, Dear Sir,

Your sincere Friend and Servant,

——— ———

LETTER XLVIII. *To Mr.* and *Mrs.* W.

Ever Dear and Honour'd Parents,

I Long to have my *Love to God,* a pure, keen, solid, lasting *Flame:* That in Spirit, Soul and Body I might be one continual living *Sacrifice* to his *Glory.* But oh, my *little Grace,* is so press'd and annoy'd with the *Body of Sin,* with the *Body of this Death,* that I *groan* being *burdened.* I rejoice in Hope of perfect Holiness, of immortal Glory. This was very sweet to me of late: That God has *predestinated me to be conformed to the Image of his Son;* that the Work is *His;* that He has *begun,* and will *perfect it.* This Glory, my Faith sees afar off; my Loves hastes to meet it; and my Hope patiently waits for it.—And the mean Time, what long I, what wait I for? Surely it is *This:* An increasing *Knowledge of* CHRIST, *Conformity to him,* and *Service of him.* Oh pray, that I may love my Dear Lord *greatly,* in every *little Thing* I aim to do for Him. And especially, now I have so *little* Time and Strength left me to serve Him in. An Eternity of Glory, in the Enjoyment of his glorious SELF, awaits me. But oh, that I have lov'd and serv'd him *so little,* in the Days of the Years of my Life, which He hath given me; this grieves me. I know my Lord, pardons all my Unkindness.—Oh that his forgiving Love, may bind me to greater Ingenuity and Duty!

My dear and honour'd Parents, you are dear to God, and honour'd by Him. Oh may his Love, continually delight your Souls; and his Honour lie near your Hearts! He that has been your God from your *Youth up;* will be the *Stay* and *Staff* of your *Old Age:* And I trust, will make you fat and flourishing, even unto *hoar Hairs.* You have a GOD, whose *Love,* don't *decay;* whose *Mercy,* never *fails;* whose *Faithfulness,* is like the *great Mountains;* yea, firmer than the *lasting Hills. For the Mountains shall depart, and the Hills be removed: But* God's *Kindness* towards *you, shall not depart, nor the Covenant of his Peace be removed, saith the* LORD, *that hath Mercy on you.* Oh rest your dear Souls, your weary Heads, in the *sweet Bosom,* in the *kind Arms,* of the LORD your *own* GOD. There you'll find Ease in Pain, Peace in Trouble, Security in Danger, Fulness in Want, and Life in Death. Thro Life, with all its Trials, and Death, with all its Sorrows, will the LORD your Life, your Joy, your ALL be *with you,* What then can you *want?* Oh, *no good Thing!* Nothing but what is to be found in GOD, even your *own* GOD! *Delight yourselves therefore in the* LORD: *And* HE *shall give you the Desires of your Heart.—The Good Will of* HIM *that dwelt in the Bush, be with you.* I remain, my Dear and Honour'd Parents,

Yours with all Affection and Duty,

——— ———

LETTER XLIX. *To Mrs.* F.

Dear Madam,

YOU rejoice with *me,* for the Lord's Loving-kindness towards me. An Evidence this, That *You* also are one of the *Beloved of the Lord. We know that we are passed from Death unto Life, because we love the Brethren.* Not a Soul that *rejoiceth* in the *Gladness* of *God's Nation;* but is one, that is *remember'd* with *that Favour,* which He *beareth* to his *People,* and *visited* with *his Salvation.*

It gives me Joy, Madam, that you can say, "Whereas I was once blind, I now see: My lost State by Nature, and my Reconciliation thro' the Merits and Intercession of Christ." Amazing *Change!* Amazing *Grace,* that wrought it! *Alive from the Dead,* Madam: *Endless Life* is *yours! Risen with Christ:* It is to *die no more!* Your new, your spiritual Life, shall never die. The Spirit of Life from God, having quickned your dear Soul, abideth in you, as a Life-giving Flow, from Christ your living Head, to maintain, increase and perfect, his Begun-Work, till springing up, it rise to Life eternal. To a full *Perfection;* of Purity, Joy and Glory, in the Presence of *God* and of the *Lamb:* To an endless *Duration;* a blest *Eternity*! O Happy Soul! How vast is thine Inheritance! How rich art thou in Hope, as an *Heir of* GOD! And a *Joint-Heir with* CHRIST! So great a *Portion,* and so great a *Security* of its *Possession:* What a Greatness of *Joy* doth it bespeak, should it create, in every *Expectant,* of that *ineffable Bliss!* O dear Madam, this Portion is *yours!* This Portion is *mine!* As *seeing the Son,* and *believing on Him;* we *have eternal Life.* We *have it;* let Satan and Unbelief say what they will to the *contrary.* They can never *undo,* what our Lord hath *done.* They can never, by their Gainsayings, make *null* and *void*, what the All-producing Word, of a GOD *that cannot lie,* hath *spoken.* And especially, as for our *strong Consolation,* His inviolable *Oath,* who hath sworn by his great SELF, is added to his great *Word.* Let us then as *Heirs of Promise,* as such that have *fled for Refuge,* to lay *Hold* on *Christ,* the *Hope set before us;* receive the strong Consolation given us, the full and great Security, of our everlasting Salvation by JESUS. For, *Because* HE *lives; we shall live also.* Because He ever liveth, as our Intercessor, with his and our Father; we shall be saved to the uttermost. *He that believeth on the Son of God, hath Life.* And this Life is *in his Son.* We have *Christ,* my dear Sister, and Life in HIM, who is *our Life.* Had we Life in its Fulness, by Way of Grant, and had we its Perfection, in Enjoyment: If we had it in our own *single Selves,* separate and apart from *Christ,* we *might,* we *should* lose it. Perfect *Adam,* standing upon his *own Bottom,* soon *fell* from his primitive Excellency, into unknown Depths of Misery. The glorious *Angels,* that stood *alone,* soon *reeled* out of Heaven to Hell: Top heavy with their Glory, down they sunk from their first Estate, into Depths of Woe, ineffably great and endless. But *redeemed Sinners,* unto *Life by* JESUS, being *new created* after his *Image;* can *never lose* their Right to Life in its Completion; nor the Begun Enjoyment of it given, as to the Principle of Life in their Souls, Because they have Life in *Christ;* in HIM who ever liveth, to perfect and perpetuate, Life in *them.* To swallow up *Death,* in perfect endless *Life.* To bear them up, to the *Life of Glory;* and to sustain, or bear up, their *Glory-Life,* to a vast *Eternity!*

Come then, my dear Sister, Lie down and rest by *Faith,* in your *own Lord Jesus.* For, your *Beloved* is *yours,* Forever *yours.* And *you* are *His,* in an indissoluble *Union,* in an everlasting *Covenant,* that shall never be *broken.* And in Him you have *Life,* of the highest Perfection, *Life,* of an endless Duration. You have it, by an irreversible *Grant* in the Right of it; You have it in *Reversion;* You have it in the *First-Fruits* and *Earnest* thereof; And you shortly shall have it in *full Possession.* You have Life in *Christ;* A Life that cannot be *lost.* A Fulness, a Redundancy, a Transcendency of *Life.* And also a Permanency, an Immortality of *Life.* For *Life and Immortality,* are thus *brought to Light by the Gospel.* Your JESUS, is *Yesterday, To day, and Forever the same.* His Love, his Life, fixt on you, provided for you; know *no Change,* vary not with *your Frames.* Bless your Lord then, when he smiles; for He is yours in Love. Trust in Him when he frowns; for He is always yours, and always loves. Follow hard after him, when he hides and chides; He delights to see you *seek him, sorrowing,* as the *Dove* that has *lost its Mate.* And soon He will *see you again,* turn your *Sorrow into Joy,* and *your Joy* shall *no Man take from you.*—I commit you to the infinite *Love* and *Care,* of the *Lord your Life:* To be Bosom'd and Arm'd along by Him, thro' this weary Wilderness, into the Land of Rest: Where, blest with the endless *Vision* of *his,* and of his *Father's Face,* you will join in *Joy* with the *general Assembly* of Saints and Angels, to give him the eternal *Glory* of all his *Grace.* Wishing the best of Blessings: I subscribe, Dear Madam,

Your most obliged humble Servant
In our Precious Lord

_______ _______

LETTER L. *To Mr.* ----- -----

My very dear Brother in the Lord,

HAVE you lost that *Comfort* and *Sweetness*, you once enjoy'd in *Christ?* You have not lost your JESUS; you have *Him* still, an entire and eternal *Interest* in his great and glorious SELF. And shortly your *Beloved* will *turn again,* and bless you with the Vision of his Face. He will be like a *Roe,* or a young *Hart,* upon the Mountains of *Bether,* of *Division.* How great and many soever the Mountains of your Sins and Provocations may be, your *Beloved,* in the infinite Strength of his *Love,* will come *leaping* and *skipping* over them all, to bring renewed Salvation unto you. O my Brother, you are too *near* and *dear* to Christ, too nearly related to him, and too dearly bought, and affected by him, for Him to *leave,* or *forsake* you, to *disregard,* or *suffer* you to be *lost.* Your kind, tender, faithful *Shepherd,* in boundless Compassion, will gather you with his *Arm*, and carry you in his *Bosom*. Christ has an *Arm for you still,* the omnipotent Arm of his saving *Strength,* which well suits your great *Weakness,* by which he will gather you from all your Strayings. Are you like a *lost Sheep?* Your Shepherd will go *after you,* my Brother. He will as it were *leave* the *Ninety* and *Nine,* and go after *you;* He will *seek* till he has *found* you. And when he hath found you, He will lay you on his *Shoulder,* and bring you *Home rejoycing*: As if He had got some goodly Thing. For lo, He esteem you as his *Portion*; and says concerning you, *The Lines are fallen unto Me in pleasant Places, yea, I have a goodly Heritage.* Strange! That *God our Saviour*, should rejoyce over us *Sinners,* to save us from our *Sins,* our repeated, aggravated *Sins,* against his *saving Love,* notwithstanding all our Unworthiness and Provocations! But thus it is, because He is the LORD that *changeth not:* Because his Grace towards us, hath the Infinity, and Strength of the *Godhead* in it! And thence, you tender *Lamb* of Christ's Fold, your *Shepherd* hath a *Bosom* for you still.

An Immensity and Eternity of unchanging *Love,* into which he will take you, manifestatively, and in which he will carry you sweetly, to your Soul's Refreshment, Life and Growth. *The* LORD your *God in the Midst of* you *is mighty; He will save, He will rejoyce over you with Joy; He will rest in his Love, He will joy over you with Singing.* The Lord your Lover, is in the *midst* of you still. He hath erected his *Throne* in your *Heart,* and there He will dwell *for ever;* for He hath *desired it.* He is *mighty.* Mighty to *save;* to bear all the Affronts you have given him, and the Indignities done to him; and to save you from the Guilt and Filth, Power and Being of all your Sins, and unto fresh Increases of Life spiritual, which shall spring and rise into Life eternal. Yea, He *will* save. He will *rest* in his Love. He will never seek another *Object*, instead of *you*, nor cast you *off*, or *out* of his infinite Complacence, for *all that you have done.* He will rejoyce over you with *Joy,* with *exceeding great Joy;* yea, with *Singing.* Such is the Infinity of his *Heart's Delight* in *you!* He will be *silent* because of his *Love.* He will lay none of your Sins to your *Charge.* He *dy'd* to set you *free.* And were there Need, He would die *again,* rather than leave you under the Power of *Sin,* to be lost in endless *Death.*—Come then, my Brother, prostrate your guilty, filthy, diseased Soul, before the Lord your Lover. He will not condemn you, but speak Peace and Pardon to you, and thereby put Strength into you, and most graciously will He receive you as his own. *They say, If a Man put away his Wife, and she go from him and become another Man's, shall he return unto her again? Shall not that Land be greatly polluted? But thou hast played the Harlot with many Lovers, yet return again unto Me, saith the* LORD.—*I will not cause mine Anger to fall upon you, for I am merciful, saith the* LORD. O my Brother, you are, you shall be, under *forgiving Love. Grace and Peace from God our Father, and the Lord Jesus Christ,* by the *Holy Ghost the Comforter,* for your renewed Joy and increasing Holiness, unto perfect Purity and endless Glory, are and shall be *multiply'd unto you.* And this because you *stand in Grace,* have an unchangeable and eternal *Fixation* in *Grace:* Which in the Exuberance of its infinite Fulness and Freeness, will flow out upon you to your full and endless Joy, thro' Time and to Eternity.

And doubt not your *State in* Grace, because you see not your *Increase* in Grace, yea, tho' you see but *little* Grace in you. Know you not that fruitful Trees, young, thriving, growing Plants, have their Autumn, and Winter Times, as well as their Spring, and Summer Seasons: Wherein they are disrobed of their Fruit, yea, stripp'd of their very Leaves? And yet, even at such Times, they are living, fruitful, growing Trees, tho' stripp'd of the Glory of their Fruit, and of their leafy Greenness. Even so are *you,* my Brother, tho' now it's Autumn, and Winter with you, a *Tree of Righteousness,* a fruitful, growing Tree, the *Planting of the* LORD by Grace, *that He might be glorify'd.* And the Sun-like Face of your glorious Lord, in the next Spring of his infinite Favour, will look you again into a fresh Beauty and Glory, will clothe you afresh with an increasing Greenness, and more abundant Fruitfulness. And when you don't grow *upwards,* you grow *downwards,* take deeper Root by Faith into Christ, and are more grounded in Humility, by the Experience you have of Self-Nothingness and Wretchedness. And by the Condensing Cold of Winter-Dispensations, the Lord prepares you for a greater Flow of Sap, when He makes his next Approach as your Summer-Sun, with *Healing in his Wings,* with his warm and quickning Rays, to exhale your Graces into precious Fruits, to your more abundant Joy in Him, and to his more abundant Praise by you.

My kind Lord sweetly supports and comforts me, and enables me to glorify him under this *great Trial,* of the *Loss* of my *dear Yoke-fellow.* Blessed for ever be his great dear Name, He hath done all Things *well;* so well, that nothing could be *better* than it *is!* He is *mine* in this *Affliction,* and I see and receive it as a *Gift* of his infinite *Love.* And I am *His* in it, I love, adore and bless him, and as it were forget my *Pain,* in the *Pleasure,* while I count *his Glory,* my *chief Joy.—The Grace of Christ be with your Spirit!* In his Bowels, my dear Brother, I am,

Yours most Tenderly,

——— ———

LETTER LI. *To* ----- -----

My very dear and much honour'd Brother,

WHEN we parted, "Upon your speaking of the Lord's Dealing, in taking dearest Relatives *from,* whose Lives are bound up *in,* each other; while those whose Love to one another hath not those *Ardours,* are permitted to *live together:*" I tho't of what Dr. *Goodwin* says, "The Lord delights to try us in our *Isaacs.*" Else, Brother, He would not have a *Proof* of our *choicest Love.* O how did it delight the Heart of *God,* to see *Abraham* so cheerfully resign his *Isaac! Now* (says he) *I knew that thou fearest* GOD; *seeing thou hast not with held thy Son, thine only Son, from* ME. And what *Blessings* came down upon *Abraham,* as a *Reward* of this Part of *Obedience! By Myself have I sworn, saith the* LORD: *That in Blessing I will bless thee; and in Multiplying I will multiply thee.*—Our *Lord,* is an immense *Lover,* and intensely delights in *our Love,* weak s it is, when we give him *cheerfully,* our dearest Enjoyments at his *Bidding.*—Hence, Brother, whenever your late Trial returns upon your Spirit, leaning on the Strength of Jesus by Faith, attempt your Duty to him in Love: To make renewed *Resignations,* with increasing *Cheerfulness,* of what *his dear Hand,* call'd for from *yours.* It will delight your *Lord's Heart,* and bless you he will, like HIMSELF. Give him your *Pence;* He will give you *Pounds.* bless him that he hath given you an *Opportunity,* to give him any Thing so *dear* unto you; and thus to shew your *Love* to the *Lord* your *Matchless Lover!* For, To *glorify,* and *enjoy Him:* is the *chief End* of your *Being*: In *Nature,* and in *Grace,* and will be to your *endless Glory!*—That the *Joy of the Lord* may be *your Strength;* and your *Feet* made like the *Feet of Hinds;* in doing and suffering the *Will of God,* until you *inherit the Promises:* is the hearty Desire and Prayer of, dear Sir,

Your most affectionate and obliged

Friend and Servant in the Lord,

——— ———

LETTER LII. *To Mr.* F.

Dear Sir,

I Heartily thank you for your last kind Letter. The Lord by it refresh'd my Soul, made me glad in Himself, and excited my Heart to praise him. O what *Grace* is this to *me,* that my poor *Books* should be made of *Use* to *you,* and to *other Souls!* To the *Lord alone,* be the *whole Glory!* Glad am I, Brother, that you will help a weak Worm, to serve the Lord I love, by your *Prayers* for a Blessing on me, and on my weak Attempts to feed the tender Lambs, of the Lord our great Shepherd. The Lord *hear* your Prayers for *me,* and *return* an Hundred-fold, into your *own Bosom!* Well, O how well is it for us, that JESUS our *Shepherd,* hath us all, in his own Almighty and All gracious *Hand!*—You write, Brother, of the *Lion of Hell,* who goeth about, *seeking* whom he may *devour;* and sweetly bless God, that there is a *Remnant* according to the *Election of Grace,* that are put forever out of his *Reach,* out of the Reach of *final Apostasy,* under the Influence of that wicked *apostate Spirit.*—And is this *your* happy *Lot!* And is it *mine!* O let us *adore the Grace* that hath *saved us!* The rich, free, distinguishing *Grace,* that hath made *us* the Subjects of its glorious Reign, unto eternal *Life,* while *Thousands* round about us, are left under the Reign of Sin and Satan, to perish in endless *Death!* In Heart, in Lip, in Life, let us praise the Grace of *Ransom!* The Grace of *Rescue!* How great, how unsearchable are its *Wonders!* Wou'd the God and Father of our Lord Jesus Christ, display the exceeding Riches of *his Grace,* in giving his only-begotten Son, to obey and die for us Sinners, the Chief of Sinners, to save us from all Misery, and unto all Glory! Wou'd the eternal Son of God, to shew *his* boundless, matchless *Grace,* condescend to take our low Nature, and in it stoop, to take our Law-place, to bear our Sin, to be made our Curse, and to die the Death of the Cross, in our Room and Stead, to exalt us, unto his Throne of Glory! And wou'd the eternal Spirit, the Lord the Holy Ghost, in *his* unbounded *Grace,* come down into such Hearts as ours, take Possession of them for Christ, erect his Throne there, cast out Satan, and subdue Sin; and thus by *his* Almighty Energy, begin and resolve to perfect, our Deliverance from Hellish Slavery, and unto Heavenly Liberty, the *glorious Liberty of the Sons of God!* Praise to the *Father,* to the *Son,* to the *Holy Ghost,* to the *Three-One* GOD, *the God of all Grace,* who hath thus *ransom'd,* who hath thus *rescu'd* the *Vessels of Mercy,* even us who are *call'd by Grace* unto *eternal Glory!*

I was much pleas'd with what you hinted of Mr. *B.'s* Discourse from *Ps.* 23. 4. "That the Valley of the Shadow of Death, is the last Walk of a Believer. That he doth not stay, much less dwell there. And that this Walk leads a Believer unto the Presence-Chamber, the upper Court of King Jesus: To dwell for ever with the Lord; where the Wicked cease from troubling, and the Weary are at Rest."—And as a dear Servant of Christ, lately said, (preaching from *Gen* 46. 4. *I will go down with thee into* Egypt, *and* Joseph *shall put his Hand upon thine Eyes*) "That the Lord will go down with his People, into the dark Valley of the Shadow of Death:" Why then should we fear to enter upon this our last Walk? Since the *Lord* our *Light,* is and will be *with us;* the *dark Valley* shall be made safe and pleasant to us. In this lonely Walk, we shall have the choicest Company. When Christian Friends must leave us, or we rather, take Leave of them; Christ, our best Friend, will instantly and surpassingly take their Place. And by *his Light,* how safely, how joyfully, shall we *walk thro' Darkness!* The Rays of his Grace, the Shines of his Face, will make the *Darkness, Light about us.* And O! to have the *Lord* our *Life,* with us in *Death,* to *swallow up Death in Victory:* How great must be a Believer's Triumph in, and over *Death!* And beyond it, how great his *Glory!*—Let us come up therefore from the *Wilderness,* even to the last Step of it, *leaning upon our Beloved.* And the very worst to Nature, shall be best of all to Grace, and bring us to the immediate, blissful, endless Vision of our Redeemer's Face! To *see him as he is,* to *behold,* to enjoy *his Glory,* to a blest *Eternity!*—I rejoice in your Soul's Prosperity, for that Savour and Relish of the things of God, and I trust, Growth in the Knowledge of Christ, (for which I have pray'd, and) with which you are favoured. And, *That the God of our Lord Jesus Christ, the Father of Glory, may give unto you* (still greater Measures of) *the Spirit of Wisdom and Revelation in the Knowledge of* HIM: To your growing Joy, and increasing Conformity, until you are blest with immortal Glory; is the hearty Desire of, dear Sir,

Your affectionate Friend and Servant,

——— ———

LETTER LIII. *To Mr.* A.

My very dear Brother in our precious Lord,

I Thank you for your Sympathy with me in my present Affliction, and take it most kindly. Indeed my *Loss,* by the *Death* of my *dear Yoke-fellow,* is very great. but since I have not lost my *Jesus,* since *God* hath given me his *Son,* my Spirit is sweetly reconcil'd to the *Divine Will;* and delighted I am in my *Lord,* as my present and eternal ALL. HE bears *me,* and my *Burden* too: And being well *supported,* I *sink not.* Being well supply'd with spirituous *Cordials,* my Heart *faints not.* At Times, under pressing Weights, the *Archers* that hate me, *shoot at me, and sorely grieve me:* But my *Bow abides in Strength, and the Arms of my Hands are made strong by the Hands of the mighty God of* Jacob. My weak Soul hath been enabled in some Measure, to *glorify the* LORD *in the Fires:* To esteem *his Glory,* my *chief Joy;* and my Trial, a happy Mean, to that blessed End. I call my Trial a *happy Mean;* not that it is not *grieving* and *afflicting* in *Itself:* But the *bitter Waters* of Affliction, being well *sweetned* by my *Lord,* the *Tree of Life,* who is cast therein, I can *freely drink them.* While I view the present Trial, given me by infinite Wisdom and Grace, as an Opportunity to *give Glory to God,* such a Glory, as I could not *otherwise* have given him; methinks the *Bitter* of it, is lost in the *Sweet,* and well it is *relish'd* by my *spiritual Palate:* Thus kindly my dear Lord deals with me, his poor, vile, ungrateful Worm! Help me to praise him, and remember me in your Prayers.

I rejoice with you, my dear Brother, for the bright Displays of Christ's Love, with which you are highly favoured, and its All attracting Influence, of which you have the sweet Experience. An invaluable Blessing is the Love of Christ in Itself; and the Manifestation thereof an unspeakable Privilege. And blest be the Lord our Lover, our cold, dull Hearts, shan't be always in this dead, lifeless Frame. But enkindled with his infinite Love, and chang'd in our Creature-measure into its Image, our whole Souls shall ascend as a pure Flame in servant Praises, to his endless Glory. How miserable should we be, tho' the Objects of *Christ's Love,* if we were not by *Him* to be *loved into Love?* Alas, our *carnal Mind,* which is *Enmity* against *Him,* sinks us into *Death.* And nothing less than the *Love of Christ,* display'd and apply'd, by the irradiating, comforting Influence of the *Holy Ghost,* can make us *spiritual,* can raise our Hearts to *love the Lord,* which is the *Life* of our Souls. But as *our Life,* was the End of *Christ's Death,* the glorious *End* which his Love had in *View,* in giving Himself for us; So this is and shall be the blessed *Effect,* of that great *Cause.* Our dear Lord *loved us,* and *gave Himself for us,* that we *in Love* might *give ourselves to Him;* that we might live and love, love and live forever. And since an infinite Price hath been paid, and an infinite Power is engag'd for our complete Redemption, from all Misery, to all Glory; we shall shortly, *love Christ* as we *would:* With all our Powers, in perfect Service, unto endless Ages. O the *Glory,* of that *State,* when *Christ* and *we* shall be *one in Love!* When there shall be no Disunion of Hearts, nor Want of Communion between us! *Christ's Heart,* is never disunited from *us now;* but O how often are *ours* from *Him!* How little a *Part* hath *Christ* of *our Hearts?* And that little Part which he hath, how oft is it interrupted in its Flows of Love to HIM, the *Sum* of all Perfections and Delights, while our Souls are diverted by mere *Shadows* of Joys, into real Sorrows? Thus it is with us in this State of Distance and Imperfection. but when we are made perfect in Love, and at Home with Christ, no Disunion, nor Want of Communion shall be between us. We shall be fitted for the highest Communications from Christ, and abide for ever in his immediate Presence. Our Lord will not then *hide Himself* from his *own Flesh,* nor shall we wander after *other Lovers.* But under the ceaseless *Flows,* and endless *Shine* of infinite *Love,* we, to the utmost of our finite Capacity, shall *love again;* with our *whole Heart, Soul and Strength,* or *we,* with all our Powers and Faculties, shall *haste* as a swift *Stream,* into Love's *Ocean,* and *unite* as a bright *Beam* with the *Body of the Sun.* The *Lord God* and the *Lamb,* shall be our *Light* and *Life,* our *Joy* and *Glory,* to a blest *Eternity.*

And for this happy State, my dear Brother, the Lord is now preparing you. Those vast *Desires* which are wrought in your Heart, after increasing and perfect Love to Christ, under the glorious *Shine* of his infinite Love; are your *Preparation by Grace,* for that *ineffable Glory;* and the very *Bud* of that open, unfadable *Flower.* The *Lord increase you more and more,* in *Love* to *Him* and *His,* and towards *all Men:* To the *End He may stablish your Heart unblameable in Holiness, at the Coming of our Lord Jesus Christ with all his Saints!* So prays, my Dear Brother,

Yours most affectionately in our Lord the Lamb,

——— ———

LETTER LIV. *To* ----- -----

My very Dear Sister in Christ,

I Heartily thank you for your kind Letter. Blest be our dear Lord, for his great Kindness to you, and to unworthy me, that still, still, Goodness and Mercy follow us; and follow us they shall, till wafted into the Ocean of Joy and Glory: To know, and love, and serve the Lord, in the Heights of Bliss, to a blest Eternity! What manner of Love is it, that while we are in the Wilderness, our Lord cares for us! forgives our Sins, heals our Diseases, and supplies all our Wants! Feeds us with heavenly Manna, follows us with the Water of Life, clothes us with the Everlasting Robe, sustains us under pressing Weights, and out of Weakness, makes us strong! So that from blest Experience we can say, *We know that all Things work together for Good, to them that love God, to them that are the Called according to his Purpose.*—You say, my dear Sister, "there is that in Affliction, that makes the Heart rejoice." This same *That,* which you speak of, is GOD. It is GOD that makes Affliction joyful to his People. If GOD is with us sensibly in Affliction, sustains us under it, and enables us to glorify Him by it; our Hearts are exceeding joyful, when compass'd about with Sorrows. But if GOD withdraws, our Spirits sink, fail and die instantly.—And the richest Enjoyments, are not sufficient to hold our Souls in Life; if our *Beloved* withdraws, ere we aware, we fall *asleep.* As is clear by the Verse preceding those, on which you desire my Thoughts, as it stands connected with them. *viz.*

Song v. 1, 2, 3, 4. *I am come into my Garden, my Sister, my Spouse; I have gathered my Myrrh with my Spice, I have eaten my Honeycomb with my Honey, I have drunk my Wine with my Milk: Eat, O Friends, drink, yea, drink abundantly, O Beloved.*

I sleep, but my Heart waketh: it is the Voice of my Beloved that knocketh, saying, Open to me, my Sister, my Love, my Dove, my Undefiled: for my Head is filled with Dew, and my Locks with the Drops of the Night.

I have put off my Coat, how shall I put it on? I have washed my Feet, how shall I defile them?

My Beloved put in his Hand by the Hole of the Door, and by Bowels were moved for him.

Various are the Senses, that these Words may bear, and the Times and Cases, in which they are applicable to the People of God, the Spouse of Jesus. From the first of these Verses, with the Beginning of the second, we see what I have hinted, that the richest Enjoyments, are not sufficient to hold our Souls in Life, or lively for God. Tho' the *Spouse's Beloved* in answer to her Request, was *come into* his Garden, had *gather'd* his *Myrrh with* his *Spice,* had *eaten* his *Honey-comb with* his *Honey,* had *drank* his *Wine with* his *Milk,* and made a Feast for his Favourites, saying, *Eat, O Friends, drink, yea, drink abundantly, O Beloved:* Yet the very next we hear from Her is, *I sleep.* Which shews what Danger we are in of carnal Security, after we have been favoured highly: And that nothing less than renewed, and continual Influence from Christ our Life, can keep us alive for God.

Passing the various Senses, and divers Cases in which the Words you would have me write of, may be apply'd to us, I shall give a Hint only concerning *One,* which has lately been of Use to *me.*

And thus the *first* of these Verses, with the gracious Declarations and Invitations therein, which appears to be an Answer of Prayer: May respect those bright Displays of Divine Favour, which our Lord makes to his People thro' the *Promises,* in answer to their *Requests* for *desired Mercies. I am come, &c.* Which may denote, 1. The *Existence* of pray'd-for Mercies, in the *Promise.* As, *I am returned to* Jerusalem *with Mercies:* seems to be much the same with *My House* shall *be built in it.* Zech. i. 16. And 2. the real *Presence* of promis'd Mercies to *Faith.* As, *Faith is the* Substance *of Things hoped for, and the* Evidence *of Things not seen,* Heb. xi. 1.—Again, Our Lord's *Feasting* upon the *Fruits* of his *Garden,* may respect that *Delight* which He takes in the vigorous Exercise of his *Peoples Graces,* while they seek him under the quickning Influences of the *Spirit of Grace and of Supplications.* Which in one Sense may be signify'd by those Words, *Song* iv. 6. *Until the Day break, and the Shadows flee away, I will get me to the* Mountain of Myrrh, *and to the* Hill of

Frankincense: *i. e.* To *Mount Sion,* the *Church,* where *Prayers* and *Praises* are offered, which are most *sweet,* and *refreshing* unto ME. It is as if our Lord should say, "Until I and my Spouse meet, in her *gracious State,* and delight *myself* with the Fruits of *my Spirit* in her Heart and Life"—And the *Feast,* that our Lord makes for his *Favourites,* saying, *Eat, O Friends, &c.* may respect that *Fulness of Gospel-Provisions,* which is in *Himself,* and which he invites them to partake of, while He shews Himself to his *Church,* and to particular *Believers,* in the immense Glories of his Person, and in the delightful Wonders of his Atchievements, or what He hath done, doth, and will do for his People, according to the Declarations and Promises of his Grace concerning them. As *Isa.* xxv. 6, &c. *And in this* Mountain *will the* LORD *of Host make unto* all People *a* Feast *of fat Things, a* Feast *of Wines on the Lees, of fat Things full of Marrow, of Wines on the Lees well refined. And he, &c.* And O what a *marrowy Feast,* what a *delightful Banquet,* doth a Believer sometimes enjoy thro' an *applied Promise,* of a *pray'd for Mercy!*—But by and by, *Providence frowns,* the Soul *sinks* into *Discouragement!* and then, with the Spouse, says,

I sleep: □ That is, The *Vigour* of my *Graces,* Faith, Hope and Joy, is *abated.* It is as if the Spouse should say, "I am like a Person half dead: my spiritual Senses, are bound up, and restrained." In this sad Case, *Unbelief* prevails; which inclines the Soul to *depart from God,* to grow dull in its Expectations of him, and sluggish in its Supplications to him.—But yet at *Ease,* the Soul is not, cannot be, without the sought-for, promis'd Mercy. *My Heart waketh:*

i. e. some *Desires* are maintain'd and reviv'd in me, by the fresh Intimations thereof which the Lord gives me. *It is the Voice of my Beloved that knocketh, saying, Open to Me, my Sister, my Love, my Dove, my Undefiled:* As if she should say, "I know my *Beloved's Voice,* He speaks like Himself, with his endearing Language, He calls me to come forth by Faith, and let him in, that He may have a little Communion with me about his promis'd Grace." "*For,* (He says) *my Head is filled with Dew, and my Locks with the Drops of the Night.*" That is, "By thy *Unbelief,* thou reproachest my *Government,* as if I took no *Notice* of the *Petitions* of my *Subjects;* and thus thoucastest inclement, grieving *Drops* of *Shame,* upon my kind *Thoughts,* my faithful *Promises,* according to my gracious

Purposes concerning thee; in this *Night,* while my Face in *Providence,* doth not shine upon thee, but thick *Darkness* covers thee."—Doth all this prevail with the *Spouse* to open to her *Beloved?* Ah! *no.* She replies,

I have put off my Coat, how shall I put it on? I have washed my Feet, how shall I defile them? q.d. "I am *indispos'd* to Acts of Faith, and *sink* in Discouragement. If I was *my Lord's Favourite;* would *Things be thus with me?* How shall I again set my *Feet* in the *Way of Faith,* wherein I meet with so much *Difficulty?"* Oh, ungrateful Answer, she gave to her Lord's kind Call!—But doth He *leave* her in this sad Case? *No, no.* She says,

My Beloved put in his Hand by the Hole of the Door, and my Bowels were moved for him.—He touch'd her *Heart* afresh, by the *Power* of his *Holy Spirit,* thro' the *Word of his Grace:* And her *Bowels* were *moved* for him. She was *grieved* with her Unbelief and Hardness of Heart, whereby She had shew'd such Unkindness to her dear Lord, and cast such Dishonour upon him. And *quickned* She was to an holy *Resolution,* to rise up in Faith, to *open to her Beloved,* whatever Difficulties She might meet with in *Providence,* before she enjoy'd the blessed Fruit of the *Promise.*—But did She meet him *instantly?* Ah! *no.* As,

Ver. 5, 6. *I rose up to open to my Beloved, and my Hands dropped with Myrrh, and my Fingers with sweet-smelling Myrrh, upon the Handles of the Lock. I opened to my Beloved, but my Beloved had withdrawn Himself, and was gone: My Soul failed when he spake: I sought him, but I could not find him; I called him, but He gave me no Answer.*—Here, Her *Beloved* had pour'd so much of the *Oil* of his Spirit and Grace upon her unbelieving Heart, thro' some Promise or other sweetly apply'd, that her *Hands* of Faith *dropped* with *Myrrh,* and her *Fingers* with *sweet smelling Myrrh,* which He had left upon the *Handles of the Lock;* and which exceedingly delighted her spiritual Sense—But when She *opened* to her Beloved, and thought to let *Him in,* his *Promise* and the *Fulfilment* of it together: (For when our Faith is reviv'd in the Promise, we are apt straightway to expect the Accomplishment of it.) Alas! Her *Beloved* had *withdrawn Himself,* and was *gone!* She could not have that *Communion* with him in *promis'd Grace,* that She had *slighted,* nor see him in the *Performance* of the *Promise,* as She *wished.* Her *Soul failed when He spake:* In the Remembrance of his kind *Words,* of his gracious *Call,* She was *grieved* in the very *Inward* of her *Soul,* for her *Unkindness* towards him, and the *Dishonour* She had done him by her Unbelief, and ready to *fail* under his *Withdraw,* as a just *Rebuke.* She *sought him,* but She could not *find him,* She *called him,* but he gave her *no Answer.—This,* Ah! *This,* is the *Fruit* of our Unbelief. Our *Lord did not many mighty Works there,* (it is said) *because of their* Unbelief, *Mat.* xiii. 58.—But Mercy it was to the Spouse, that She was thus *quickned* and *strengthned in Faith,* to *open* to her *Beloved,* to *seek,* and *call* after him; tho' as a *Rebuke* for her *Unbelief,* and a further *Trial* of her *Faith,* He was not instantly *found* of her, He gave her *no Answer.*—But what *becomes* of this forsaken Spouse? Has her Beloved *forgotten to be gracious? Is his Mercy clean gone? Will he be favourable no more? Doth his Promise fail for Evermore? No, no:* See the *Outbreakings* of his infinite *Love,* the *Triumphs* of his *Grace, Truth* and *Faithfulness.*

Chap. vi. 4, &c. *Thou art beautiful. O my Love, as* Tirzah, *comely as* Jerusalem, *terrible as an Army with Banners. Turn away thine Eyes from me, for they have overcome me: &c.*—O strange! Is this the Voice of the Church's *Beloved,* to his ungrateful *Spouse,* who had forc'd him from her, by her *Unbelief!* O unparallel'd *Grace!* Knowledge-passing *Love! Who is a strong* LORD *like unto* Him, *and to his Faithfulness round about* him! What, was She *his Love* still, the Object of his ineffable *Delight!* And thro' his own Beauties imputed and imparted, was She still esteemed and declared, to be *beautiful* in his Eye! What, beautiful as *Tirzah,* comely as *Jerusalem,* acceptable, and desireable as a *Royal City,* the *City of Peace,* for the *King of Glory* to *dwell in!* And tho' She had been so *weak* in Faith, yet declar'd to be of such majestick *Might,* as to be *terrible* (unto all his, and her Enemies,) as an *Army with Banners!* And tho' She had look'd upon her *altogether-lovely Lord,* with such *Coldness* and *Disregard,* could He, did He say to her still, *Turn away thine Eyes from Me, for they have overcome Me! &c.* What, delighted, captivated, *overcome* by a *Look* from *Her,* who but little before, by her *unkind Looks,* had oblig'd him to *forsake her!* Did He not remember her ungrateful Treatment, and deal with her according to her Deserts? *No;* In strict Justice, in vindictive Wrath, He *remember'd* her *Sins no more!* And even his Bridegroom-Displeasure, *endur'd* but for a *Moment!* She was too *near* and *dear to Him,* to be *forsaken,* or *forgotten.* He saw her upon the Search for her *Beloved,* as quickned by his *own Love;* and instantly gives *Vent* to the *Grace* of *his Heart,* to an Immensity of unchanging *Love,* that was to run an endless *Round,* to a boundless *Eternity;* and *satisfies* the Desires of *her Heart,* in blessing her afresh with the *Vision* of his *Face,* the *Raptures* of his *Voice,* and the *Wonders* wrought by his gracious *Presence,* and bright *Appearance:* Till *full* with Blessing, She *exults* in his Praise, *I am my* Beloved's, *and his* Desire *is towards* me: *I am a* Wall, *and my* Breasts *like* Towers: *Then was* I *in his Eyes as one that found* Favour! *Ch.* vii. 10. and viii. 10.

Hence then, my dear Sister, let us learn:

1. That whenever we are favour'd with *applied Promises,* of *pray'd-for Mercies,* and blest with the Life-giving Presence of our *Beloved* therein; we ought to beware of being *lifted up* with our own *Liveliness,* and *depend* upon *inherent Grace:* Left suddenly by sad Experience we are oblig'd to say, *I sleep!*

2. Whenever our Lord gives us *Promises* of *desired Mercies;* let us beware of *Limiting Him,* as to *Ways* and *Times* of their *Performance:* As when we draw out these for *ourselves,* and the Wisdom of Providence *crosseth* our Expectations; we are thence easily beset with *Unbelief,* as to the *Performance* of the Promise.

3. When is such a Case, our dear Beloved gives us *fresh Promises,* and calls us to *open* unto Him by Faith, that He may bless us with sweet Communion with him in his promis'd Grace; O let us beware of making *Excuses,* of yielding to unbelieving *Indolence:* Whereby we give such *Displeasure* to our great Lord, and cast such *Dishonour* upon him, yea, and even *provoke him* to *withdraw* his comforting Influence from us, and *suspend* his wonderful Appearances for us.

4. When we have thus *griev'd* and *dishonour'd* our best Friend; let us *grieve* for his Dishonour by our Unbelief, and *rise up* in Faith, to *open* to our *Beloved,* by an hearty *Belief* of his *Promise,* a firm *Expectation* of its *Performance,* and an entire *Resignation* of the *Way* and *Time* of it, to his infinite *Wisdom* and *Goodness.* And

5. If our Beloved for a *While,* should be *withdrawn,* and *gone* from us; let us not sink into Discouragement, as if He would *no more* appear to us, nor for us, but meekly *kiss* the Rod, and patiently and earnestly *wait*

his Return: For, *He will see us again, and our Hearts shall rejoyce, and our Joy no Man shall take from us.*

Wishing you the Joys of your Bridegroom's Favour, the full Joys that are in his Presence, the Beauties, in the Duties, of Holiness to Him your LORD; and the Glories of his wonderful Appearances for you in Providence, according to his exceeding great and precious Promises: Till the Joy of Vision takes place of Faith, and you shall see, and say, *There hath not failed ought, of any of the good Words which the* LORD *hath spoken:* To your ineffable Bliss, and his endless Praise: I am, my Dear Sister,

Yours most affectionately in our Welbeloved,

——— ———

LETTER LV. *To Mrs.* K.

My Dear Friend,

THE Death of your Honour'd Father, is doubtless to you, a very great Loss; your own desolate Case, and additional Distress; and the great Affliction which abides one of your near Relatives; with the Concern of all, that affects another: makes your present Condition a State of *Trouble.* But JESUS *lives,* to *save them to the uttermost, that come unto God by Him. It hath pleased the Father that in* HIM *should all Fuless dwell.* Hark! All Fulness *dwells* in CHRIST; *abides* in HIM, for the full *Supply* of all *His,* thro' Time and to Eternity. When *Cisterns* of Creature-Comforts are *broken,* and fail our thirsty Souls; the LORD, the Creator of all our Bliss, who *is* our Bliss, as the *Fountain of living Waters,* is as full, free, and overflowing as *ever:* To satisfy and solace us, in all our Desires and Griefs. Come, my dear Friend, put *Christ* for a *Well,* while passing thro' *Baca's Vale:* And you shall not *want* any good Thing. How can you want *any Thing;* if you have HIM who hath *all Things,* who *is* all Things, and who is and will be ALL unto *you? Delight thyself in the* LORD: *and* HE *shall give thee the Desires of thine Heart.* In CHRIST there is a *Fulness* of *all Relation,* and a *Fullness* for *all Salvation;* to give us *all Joys,* and to deliver us from *all Griefs. The* LORD *hath his Way* (in Mercy to his own) *in the Storm, and in the Whirlwind; and the Clouds are the Dust of his Feet:*

The Forerunners and Tokens of his approaching Presence, for his People's Deliverance. For when He hath *tried us,* we shall come forth as *Gold.* Our Trials are *needful,* to purge away our *Dross,* to brighten our *Graces,* and to prepare us for future *Glory.* They are given us as subservient *Means*, to those blessed *Ends.* And that same infinite Grace, which *bestows them,* effectually *overrules* them, into a Subserviency to its glorious Designs: For its endless Praise, and our immortal Joys. And the Lord that gives us *Trouble,* gives *Himself* in it, with it, to his *People;* and thereby, abundant *Peace,* in much *Tribulation.* In the *World,* (our Lord says) ye shall have *Tribulation.* In ME *Peace:* Be of *good Cheer,* I have *overcome* the World. Our dear Lord, hath gone thro' Troubles *before us,* to overcome them for us, to take away the Curse, and make them Blessings to us. And He goes thro' Troubles *with us,* and doth and will overcome them in and by us: Or, make us *more than Conquerors, thro' Him that loved us. Thro' much Tribulation:* is the High Road to the *Kingdom.* But having such a *Companion* in Trouble, as the *Lord* our *Lover,* the *Lord* our *Saviour,* a *Friend* that *loveth* at *all Times,* a *Brother* born for *Adversity;* Yea, a Friend, in infinite *Grace,* that sticketh *closer* than a Brother, in *Nature;* who is given of God our Father, to be our glorious *Leader:* Let us not fear a safe and joyful *Passage,* thro' the most dangerous, thorny Way, not a blissful *End,* of the most rugged *Path.* Afflictions are not the Saints *Abiding-Places;* but blessed *Path ways,* to their prepared *Mansions* of eternal Glory.

Thus our dear Friend and your honour'd Father, was sweetly conducted by the *Captain of his Salvation,* thro' his late appointed *Troubles,* to his everlasting *Rest.* The *Son* hath made him *free:* and He is *free indeed!* From Sin and Sorrow, of every Kind and Degree: and is entered into Purity, Joy and Glory, full and eternal!—And can you *grieve* for his *Salvation?* No, my dear Friend, this must be Matter of your *Rejoycing.*—And let not *his* last *Trials,* be *your* lasting *Griefs.* For now, *He* remembers no more the *Sorrow,* for the *Joy:* And won't *you* rejoyce with him?) That his *light Affliction* which was but for a *Moment;* did *work* for him (as God thereby prepar'd him *for*) *a far more exceeding and eternal Weight of Glory!*—And grieve not, tho' your nearest and dearest Relatives have *forsaken* you: For now you are desolate: The LORD will *take you up.*

Cast therefore, all your *Care,* upon Him: for HE careth for you. Your *personal* Care, your *relative* Care, your *every Concern,* that *burdens* your Mind, the LORD calls for, to be cast upon HIM; and has graciously promis'd to *sustain* you. To support you *under,* and deliver you out, of all your Distresses. Wherefore, *Trust* in the LORD *forever:* for in the LORD JEHOVAH is *everlasting Strength.* And you shall see him for you, a GOD working *Wonders! The Grace of Christ be with your Spirit!* In Him, I am,

Your affectionate Friend and Servant,

——— ———

LETTER LVI. *To Mr.* F.

INDEED the Lord hath highly favour'd, and wrought Marvels for unworthy me. But ah, I have not rendred to the Lord, according to the great Things which He hath done for me! I mourn, I lament, that by reason of natural and sinful Weakness, I cannot love and serve the Lord as I would. Never did I do any good Thing of myself, but HE wrought in me, both to will and to do, of his good Pleasure. Never did I do any Thing that was good, but I some way or other, marr'd it by Sin. Never did I do any Thing worthy of my Lord's Notice. And with inward Grief and humble Shame, I freely confess, That all my *best Righteousnesses* are but *filthy Rags.*—And will my great Lord, pass by and pardon all my Transgressions, and Imperfections in his Service, and accept and reward all my little Essays, my weak Attempts to serve him, as if I had *done* Something for him; yea, *welcome me,* as you say, into endless Joy and Glory! O *Who is a God like unto* HIM, in *Grace! Grace, Grace!* is now, and ever will be my *Cry,* to the Whole of my *Salvation,* from *Foundation* to *Top Stone.* O the Sovereignty, the Immensity and Eternity of my *Lord's Grace!* Of his Inexhaustible, All-overflowing *Grace:* which follows me in various, copious *Streams,* to waft me into boundless *Bliss;* to his eternal *Glory!* O how well is it for *me,* Brother, for *you,* and for every poor *Sinner,* that flees by *Faith* to the great *Saviour,* That *Grace reigns thro' Righteousness to eternal Life, by Jesus Christ our Lord!* And unto free, rich, reigning *Grace,* which makes the Difference between those that are *saved,* and them that *perish,* be the present and endless *Praise.*

I am glad, Dear Sir, that your Heart is reconcil'd to the *Sovereignty* of GOD, in the predestinating Acts of his *Will,* respecting the *Vessels of Wrath,* fitted to *Destruction,* and the *Vessels of Mercy,* which He had afore prepared unto *Glory:* And that with pleasing Wonder and humble Adoration, at sovereign Mercy, and righteous Severity, you justify GOD in both.—You lament, as we ought, "That any of the Creatures of GOD, should tax HIM with Cruelty and Injustice, in predestinating any Man to Damnation." For such is the infinite Righteousness and Goodness of *Jehovah's Nature,* that He cannot do any Thing that is *unjust,* or be unjustly *cruel* to his *Creature.*—And however sinful Men, may now cavil against GOD'S *Decree,* as if *that* was the Cause of their Destruction: GOD will make it evident before all, at the awful Day of Judgment, that HE is *clear* from the *Blood of all Men,* that those which *perish,* have *destroy'd themselves,* that their own *Sin,* and not his *Decree,* was the procuring Cause of their *Damnation.* For *every Mouth* shall then be *stopped,* and *all the World become guilty* (and self-condemned) *before* GOD.—And one would think, it was enough to silence any poor Sinner now, if he did but duly consider:

That God's appointing any Man to *Wrath,* was only on Account of his *Sin Fore-view'd.* That to this Sin of his, he was not enforced by God's *Decree,* but sinned *freely:* As all Men did in *Adam;* and as all his Descendants do, from the mere Motion of their *own Will.* That God *destroys none,* nor *decreed* to destroy *any,* from under the Gospel-Revelation of the *Saviour,* but those who abide *impenitent* and *unbelieving,* that *go on still in their Trespasses,* and obstinately *refuse* the Calls of the Gospel, unto *Faith in Christ,* and *Repentance towards God.* That with these Vessels of Wrath, God from the Riches of his Goodness, *endures with much Long suffering.* That He never inflicts *Punishment* upon *Men,* till they by their *Obstinacy in Sin,* make the Execution of Justice absolutely *necessary.* That God *delights not* in the *Death of a Sinner,* as it is the Destruction of his *Creature.* And that, tho' the infinite Purity of God's Nature, obligeth him to have sin infinitely, and the Exactness of his Truth and Justice, to punish it severely, He exceeds not the Bounds of *Righteousness; He lays not on Man more than is meet;* not a Grain Weight of *Punishment,* more than the *Sin* of an obstinate Offender hath *deserved:* Yea, no more than is consistent with, and ever required by, the infinite *Goodness* of his *Nature.* For, Is it not a Piece of *Goodness,* in any just *Legislator,* to *punish* a capital, and irreclaimable *Offender?* And *shall not the Judge of all the Earth, do Right?* Yes verily, it is one Part of GOD'S *Goodness,* which he caus'd to pass before *Moses,* That He *will by no Means clear the Guilty,* Exod. xxxiv. 7. He will appear to be a GOD *glorious in Holiness,* in the Execution of his *strict Justice;* and for it as such, by Saints and Angels, He will be forever *glorify'd.*

And why should any be offended, That God for *Sin,* should appoint *Some* unto *Wrath;* when *all Men* as *Sinners,* had *deserved to die the Death?* And when God would have been glorious in the Execution of his strict Justice, and forever glorify'd for it by his holy Angels, had he sent *all Mankind* for *Sin,* down to *Hell,* to be punished with *everlasting Destruction,* as he did *the Angels that sinned?* Had *all perished;* it would have been an awful Display of *glorious Justice.* Are *any saved;* how bright is the Display of *free Mercy,* and *sovereign Grace!* And mayn't the sovereign Lord of all, *do what He will with his own?* Be *gracious* unto whom He *will* be *gracious,* and *shew Mercy* on whom He *will* shew *Mercy:* While in the Execution of his *Wrath for Sin,* He doth not the least *Wrong,* unto *any Man?* O what a silencing Word ought that to be, to all proud, unbelieving, cavilling Sinners, *The Wages of Sin is Death!* And what a Heart-cheering Word should that be, to all humble, believing Sinners, *The Gift of* GOD *is Eternal Life, thro' Jesus Christ our Lord!* Rom. vi. 23. *Death,* eternal *Death,* is the due *Desert* of vile, hateful *Sin.* But *Life,* eternal *Life,* is the free *Gift,* of infinite *Grace,* thro' a crudify'd JESUS!

And since the Gospel of Salvation is proclaim'd to *all,* and the *chief of Sinners* invited to *come to Christ for Life,* yea, and assured by him, That *none that come unto him, shall be cast out:* Why should any poor Soul stand disputing about, and cavilling against God's *secret Will?* Rather let him listen to, and comply with, God's *revealed Will;* for *none* shall perish from under the *Gospel,* but *those* that *disobey* the Gospel.

And let *us,* who have happily experienced the *Gospel of Christ,* to be the *Power of God* unto our Salvation; adore the *Grace* of our *Saviour*, and in all Manner of *holy Conversation,* say, *Thanks be unto* GOD *for* (CHRIST, *his unspeakable* GIFT! And the Bowels of Mercy, and in every Path of Duty, let us do our utmost to *win poor Sinners* unto *Faith in Christ,* that they with us, deliver'd from *endless Misery,* may inherit *eternal Glory! The Grace of Christ be with your Spirit!* In Him, I am, Dear Sir,

Your Affectionate Friend and Servant,

LETTER LVII. *To Mrs.* Q.

My very Dear Sister in Christ,

IT was good News to me to hear of your Soul's Prosperity, of the Lord's loving Kindness towards you, in blessing you with sweet *Communion* and daily *Fellowship* with *Himself,* as your Royal *Bridegroom:* And that now you can lay *Claim* unto Him, and all his Fulness; tho' in Times past you was apt to *doubt* your Interest. And even so, *Stand fast in the Lord,* my dear Sister: Receiving the Holy Spirit's *Witness,* borne unto your Spirit by his *Word,* that you *are a Child of God:* And thus *set to* your *Seal,* that HE is *true.* As this will be much for God's Honour, and for your exceeding Joy. To be blest with the *Knowledge* of *Interest in Christ,* is a Privilege unspeakable. And with joyful *Communion* with *Him in Love,* a choice, additional Favour.—No Wonder that such a Soul desires to *depart,* and to be *with Christ,* which is *far better.* The sweet Clusters of *Canaan's* Grapes, brought us in the Wilderness, whet our Appetite after the *Heavenly Country,* that *exceeding good Land.* Where we with all the Saints, at Home with Christ, shall feast upon HIM the *Tree of Life,* in the Variety and Perpetuity of his new and abundant *Fruits,* unto growing Joys, and endless Days. Then, O then, GOD *shall wipe away all Tears from* our *Eyes:* And *there shall be no more Death, neither Sorrow, nor Crying, neither shall there be any more Pain;* (inward or outward) *for the former Things* shall be *passed away!* Let us then, as *Heirs of* GOD, and *Joint-Heirs with* CHRIST, rejoyce now, in Hope of approaching *Glory.* Of that Glory, which awaits our Persons, which awaits our dear Fellow Members in Christ, our Brethren of the Church militant, who with us shall shortly join the Church Triumphant. Our *Lord's Joy,* as the Head of the Church, will not be *full,* till He sees all his *Seed bro't in:* Converted by Grace, and rais'd unto Glory. When He thus sees us, the whole Election of Grace, and all our ineffable Bliss, as the *Fruit* of the *Travel of his Soul;* He shall be *satisfy'd:* His Heart contented, and delighted for ever. Such is the boundless Grace, of our altogether-lovely, and infinitely loving *Lord!* And Completeness of *Joy,* it will add to the *Saints now in Glory,* to see all their Brethren *brought in;* to share with them the same Felicity, to be blest Eternity. And as for *us,* the Beloved of the Lord, appointed to Salvation by Jesus Christ, when we are *presented Faultless before the Presence of his* Glory; it will be *with exceeding Joy.* The *Joy of Glory,* to GOD, the *Father, Son* and *Spirit,* and to *Saints* and *Angels,* will be an *exceeding Joy.* A Joy far exceeding all our present Conception and Expression. So great is the *Hope* laid up for us in *Heaven!* And how great then should be our present *Joy,* in Hope of future *Glory!*

But, my dear Sister, with Patience let us wait our appointed Time, till blest Eternity comes on. Shan't *we,* so highly favour'd, to know that for us there remaineth an eternal *Rest;* be free to endure all the *Troubles* appointed for us in this present Time: Since the Glory of God and our Advantage, are jointly concern'd in our behaving well, under these light and momentary Afflictions? Not a Trouble passeth over us, but we are call'd thereby to *glorify God,* in doing and suffering *his Will,* and thus to be *Followers of them who thro' Faith and Patience inherit the Promises.*—If, like our *Lord,* we do the *Work* which the *Father* hath given us to *do,* and being meek and lowly in Heart, we *learn Obedience* by the *Things which we suffer;* we shall thereby *serve our Generation according to the Will of God,* and glorify Him upon the Earth. And doubtless, our *Labour,* is not, shall not be *in vain in the Lord:* And *our light Affliction which is but for a Moment, worketh for us a far more exceeding and eternal Weight of Glory.* Then, let us not be *weary of Well-doing; for in due Season we shall reap, if we faint not.* Shall we desire to go to Heaven, before we have done all the Work appointed us to do for the Glory of God upon the Earth? Shall we desire to shun any Cross, which is to prepare us for, and to advance our Crown? No; rather let us ask Wisdom of God, wisely to improve our every Day's Exercise, for the Glory of Him that hath loved us; which shall be unto our Glory, when Christ appears. Thus, rejoycing in, waiting for, and hastening unto, the *Coming of the Day of God;* let us spend the little Time that remains unto us: And soon our Race will be *run,* the Prize *won,* and we shall *enter into the Joy of our Lord,* to live with Him, and reign in Life by Him, to a Never-ending Eternity.—That *all Grace may abound towards you,* and you *increase with all the Increases of* GOD; till that which is in *Part,* shall be *done away,* by the Coming of that which is *Perfect:* is the sincere Desire of, my Dear Sister,

Yours most affectionately in our dear Lord,

______ _____

LETTER LVIII. *To Mrs.* H.

My Dear Sister in the Lord,

HAPPY are You, in that the Lord hath wrought such earnest Desires in your Heart, after the Building and Beauty of *Sion.* When the Lord gives the *Spirit of Supplication,* it is the Forerunner of approaching *Salvation.* And wonder not at the Darkness which now covers you; as knowing that it is *darkest,* just before *Break of Day. Hope in God;* go on to *seek him;* and you shall *yet praise him.*—The Scriptures which the Lord apply'd to your Heart, ought to be the Ground of Faith and Prayer. And that which you last mention, from which you had a Hint, that you must be brought yet lower, before Deliverance came: Should excite you to a patient Waiting for God, until He arise and have Mercy upon *Sion,* the set Time to favour her, being come. For, *In the Mount of the* LORD, *it shall be seen.* When Distresses are *greatest,* Deliverance is *nearest.* And therefore, by that Word, as apply'd unto you, *Be in Pain, and labour to bring forth, &c.* the Lord might intend, not only the *Distresses* which are now upon you, but might also point you thereby to your present *Duty* under your pressing Griefs. That you ought patiently to *endure Pain,* like a *travailing Woman,* in *Hope of Deliverance.* Because *Sion's* GOD, hath said of *Sion's Glory, Shall I bring to the* Birth, *and not cause to* bring forth? *saith the* LORD: The Self existent, All-sufficient, and Wonder-working JEHOVAH. And farther, That you should by Faith and Love wrestle with him in *Prayer;* and thereby labour to bring forth: The promis'd, long'd-for Glory of *Sion's King,* upon *Sion's Hill:* Unto whom the *first Dominion shall come.* For, *Your Heart shall live, that seek God. God shall help* you, *and that right early*—And that the Lord may grant you a great and speedy *Deliverance,* and do for you *more exceeding abundantly than you can ask or think:* to your full Joy, and his endless Glory: is the hearty Desire and Prayer of, Dear Sister,

Yours in Christ for Ever,

——— ———

LETTER LIX. *To Mrs.* H.

My very Dear Sister in Christ,

IT is your unspeakable Privilege, that your *Lord loves you.* That in his *Love,* you have *Himself,* and all his *Fulness,* in the *Right* thereof: And thence shall have the *Enjoyment* of HIM, and of all the Treasures of his *Grace* and *Glory,* for the full *Supply* of all your *Need,* thro' *Time* and to *Eternity.* If the Fulness of Christ could *decay,* if the Love of his Heart could *change,* or if your Relation to Him could be *dissolved;* you were *undone!* Your innumerable Wants, would *exhaust* his Store; your great Provocations, *alter* his Mind; and the Mis-improvement of your Bridal Relation, would snap *in sunder* your Marriage Union.—But O! *married* to the *Son of God:* In HIM you have an infinite *Fulness,* that cannot be *sunk,* unto endless Ages! In HIM you have a *Love* great enough, to bear your whole *Weight,* the Weight of your Unworthiness, the Weight of your Provocations, without the least *Warp,* or *Turn,* to the Days of Eternity! And in HIM you have a *Husband,* that Aye *sustains,* and will Forever *fill,* his Marriage-Relation to *you.* And that holds, that draws, that secures You to *Himself Forever! Having loved* you as his *Own,* as his *own Flesh,* into the nearest Relation, the closest Conjunction, He will *love* you as His, *unto the End!* Unto *Perfection,* thro' an immeasurable *Space,* of an infinite *Duration!*

Come then, Rejoyce in your *Portion.* Bosom yourself, in your great *Beloved!* Solace your Soul, in his immense, unchangeable, and eternal *Glories!* In his bottomless, boundless, endless *Fulness!* For lo, *Christ,* and his *unsearchable Riches,* are *yours,* forever *yours!* Your *Beloved* is *yours,* and *you* are *His.* Come up from the *Wilderness leaning* on his Bosom, *leaning* on his Arm. Plead Relation; your Lord will own it. Ask an increasing Display of his infinite Favour; your Lord will bestow it. Bring your empty Vessels, your unnumber'd Wants, to Salvation's Well; your Lord will grant you and exuberant Fill; and will do for you, *more exceeding abundantly than you can ask or think!* From *Love unknown!* From *Love invariable!* Unto *Bliss ineffable* and *eternal!*—O *Happy Soul! Beloved of the* LORD! *Love and serve him* increasingly, until these thou shalt do perfectly, incessantly and eternally! *The Grace of our Lord Jesus Christ be with your Spirit!* In Him, with tender Love, I am,

Your sincere Friend and Servant,

——— ———

LETTER LX. *To Mrs.* S.

My dear Sister in Christ,

THE Loss of your Relative, must nearly touch you. But tho' the Joy that you and others had in her, and her Usefulness in the Church of God below, is ceased; you have Cause of superior Joy, in that she is advanced to see the Face of *God* and of the *Lamb,* and to *serve him* in a higher *Sphere,* among the *Saints* and *Seraphs* round the *Throne.*

As to the *Fears* which seiz'd you about *your State,* from a Tho't, "That if you lov'd Christ superlatively, you would not be so unwilling to part with Creature-Comforts, nor so much cast down at the loss of them:" Consider:

That Souls who *love Christ superlatively,* are not always in the *Exercise* of *that Love:* At lease, in *that Degree* of it, which excludes *immoderate Sorrow,* for the Loss of *desirable Things* in the present Time.—The *Disciples of Christ,* lov'd his Person *superlatively,* as their Lord and Saviour: But mourn'd *excessively,* for the Loss of his *Bodily Presence,* and the sweet Enjoyments they had thereby. in his *personal Ministry,* when he told them *He must go away.* This was such heavy Tidings to them, that from a Fore-Thought of parting with their Lord,

Sorrow filled their Hearts, Joh. xvi. 6. And that this was *immoderate,* is evident, in that our Lord said unto them, *If ye loved* ME, *ye would rejoice, because I said, I go unto the Father: for my Father is greater than I,* Chap. xiv. 28. Their Sorrow, must needs be *excessive,* as it *hindred* that Joy, which they should have had in their Lord's Advancement. They lov'd their own *Enjoyments,* at *that Time,* above their *Lord's Glory,* his *personal Glory,* simply and alone consider'd. And thence, their *Sorrow* for the Loss of the former, hinder'd their present *Joy* in the latter. And yet, they lov'd their Lord's Person and Glory *superlatively;* tho' they were not then in the *Exercise* of that *Love;* at least in that *Degree* of it, which would have excluded, immoderate *Sorrow,* for their *Loss,* in their *Lord's Departure.* Our Lord by saying, *If ye loved* ME *ye would rejoice:* Did not in the least intimate, That there was *no true Love to Him* in their *Hearts,* not yet, *any superlative Love* to his *Glory:* But only signify'd thereby, that they were not then in the *Exercise* of that *Love,* and thence excited them to their Duty, to love Him and his Glory, more singly and purely, and to flow into the Will of God in his Departure from them, more fully and complacently. Which he had likewise told them was so necessary, that if *He went not away,* the *Comforter would not come;* and so much for their Advantage, that if *He departed,* He would *send Him; pray the Father,* and *He should give them another Comforter,* who should *abide with them for ever.*

Hence then, my dear Sister, whenever the Lord tries us, by taking away any Creature or Thing, below Himself, or by taking from us the Enjoyment of Himself, in this or that particular Way: Let us beware of excessive Grief, let is humble ourselves before God on account of it so far as it prevails; let us intreat the fresh Supplies of his Grace, to draw out our superlative Love to the Lord and his Glory; in such a superlative Degree, that may exclude immoderate Sorrow for our own Loss, and excite our Joy for God's Glory, accounting that our Gain, as in itself considered; and complacently flowing into the Will of God, let us believe that *all Things* do and shall *work together for our Good,* our present and eternal Advantage.

I should give a Hint to the Text you mention, *Job* xxii. 2. and *2 Cor.* v. 20. And the Lord's Voice to you in the first, *Acquaint now thyself with him, and be at Peace: thereby Good shall come unto thee:* Is this "Come now, thou dear Child of my infinite Love, now thy Heart is troubled for the Loss of a pleasant and profitable *Creature,* come to the Bosom of thy *Creator;* solace thyself in thy *God* and *Saviour,* in the Immensity and Eternity of my Love and Fulness, *acquaint thyself now with* ME, who in all my unbounded and unchanging *Glories,* am entirely and eternally *thine. Thereby Good shall come unto thee:* Thence thou shalt find ME, a superior *Bliss,* to that which thou hast lost in the *Creature;* and find thy *Loss,* under my over-ruling *Grace,* to be for thy present and eternal *Gain.*"—And by the other Text, *We pray you in Christ's Stead, be ye reconciled to God;* The Lord calls you to be *reconciled* unto *Him,* in the *present Providence,* to flow sweetly into his *dear Will,* in *this Dispensation,* who hath *reconciled* you *unto Himself by Jesus Christ,* and is in all Things to you, and in this, *The God of Peace.*

As *seeing the Son* then, and *believing in Him,* you *have eternal Life,* in the Right, and Began Enjoyment of it now: Press forward by Faith and Love, *rejoicing in Hope of the Glory of* GOD. *Faint not, but believe to see the Goodness of the* LORD *in the Land of the Living.* And soon you shall see his *Goodness,* to ineffable *Bliss,* in *eternal Life.—I commit you to Him on whom you have believed: Great Grace be with you!* And am with much Affection,

Yours in the Lord for ever,

——— ———

LETTER LXI. *To Mr.* F.

Dear Sir,

Because JESUS *lives,* you *shall live also.* Rejoice in your *Portion;* live *upon,* and *to* the *Lord,* in every Thing. You will soon live *with Him;* And glad will you be, when your *Time* is gone, and blest *Eternity* comes on, of every Word and Work, you said or did for *Christ,* while Time and Strength was *afforded.* Work *now,* for the Glory of Him that hath loved you; you will quickly enter into *Rest,* and give Him the *Praise* of *all his Grace.*—I am glad you see the Necessity of the *New Birth.* For, *without*

Holiness, of Heart and Life, by the regenerating Work, and sanctifying Influences of the Holy Ghost, *no Man shall see the Lord.* We not only must not, but *cannot* enjoy God, if our Souls are not transformed into his *Image. Like Things,* bosom *in,* as *Contraries* naturally flee *from,* each other.—It is my Joy likewise, that you *relish* the rich, free, distinguishing *Grace of God.* An Evidence this, that *you* are one of the *New-born.* For none but such, *taste that the Lord is gracious.* And this they do with ineffable Pleasure, when blest with a lively Hope, and firm Persuasion of their own *Interest,* in that sovereign *Grace of God,* which only can, and fully doth, *bring Salvation,* to all those that *believe in Jesus,* as being of old *ordained unto eternal Life.*—Then, Brother, when *Grace* hath brought us to *Glory;* we'll shout its *Praises* to a blest *Eternity:* And each, struck with sweet Surprize, with adoring Wonder strive, who shall sing loudest, *Lord, why me! Why me,* while *Thousands, Thousands* are passed by! *Even so, Father; for so it seemed good in thy Sight!* Farewel in the Lord. Dear Sir,

Your affectionate Friend in Christ,

——— ———

LETTER LXII. *To* ----- -----

My dear Friend,

IN Love to your Soul, I write a Line, to warn you of the Danger of sinning against Light: As I hear "That you are perswaded you do wrong; that you ought to forsake all, and follow the Lamb, even whithersoever He goeth; and to come out from the World of unconverted Men, and the Worship which they cleave to, lest you be a Partaker of their *Sins,* and so of their *Plagues."*—I must say, That your Case, has appear'd to me very awful, and what I could not well account for.—But it gives me fresh Hope concerning you, as the Spirit of God han't done striving with you, but convinceth your Mind that you have forsaken the Lord, and inclineth your Heart to return.—I beseech you therefore for the Lord's Sake, and for your Soul's Sake, that you regard the Dictates of the Holy Ghost to your Mind, and comply with his Motions upon your Heart. For, *To him that* knoweth to do Good, *and doth it* not, *to him it is* Sin: Aggravated *Sin: Sin* by Way of Eminence. And, *He that* knoweth his Master's Will, *and doth it* not, *shall be beaten with* many Stripes. What you State is towards God, the Searcher of Hearts knoweth: But this I think is certain, that neither you yourself, nor any other Christian, can have an Evidence at present, that you *love Chirst supremely*. And he that loves him not, *above all*, loves him not *at all*, as he ought to do, or in *Sincerity*. And you well know that awful Text, *If any Man* love not *the Lord Jesus Christ, let him be* Anathema Maran-atha, *1 Cor.* xvi. 22. Or, let him be *accursed* when the *Lord cometh*. And what Evidence, my dear Friend, have *you*, that you *do* love the Lord above all, when you *cannot* forsake all for him? You know what our Lord has taught his Disciples, as the first Lesson they are to learn, *Luke* xiv. 26, 27. *If any Man come to Me, and* hate not *his Father, and Mother, and Wife, and Children, and Brethren, and Sisters, yea, and his own Life also, he* cannot be my disciple. *And whosoever doth* not bear his Cross, *and come after Me*, cannot be my Disciple. This Hatred here spoken of, which respects our nearest and dearest Relatives, is not to be understood of an absolute Hatred of their Persons; (for these by the Law of God we are obliged to love) but of their evil Ways, when they would hinder us from following Christ. And then, we are to carry it towards them as if we hated them: That is, we are not to follow their Dictates, when they would draw us off from Christ, nor to fear their Threatnings, in cleaving to Him: but to have an Abhorence of both as evil. And this Kind of Hatred of Relations, yea, and of our own Life, when the Love of it would hinder our laying it down for Christ's Sake, if he calls for it, is required; and naturally it flows from a superlative Love to Christ in the Heart. And *without it*, and so a *Taking up the Cross*, any, and every Cross, our Lord calls us to bear; a Man *cannot be his Disciple;* Nor will be tho't *worthy of Him*, when *He appears*. If we don't *cleave* to the Truth of the Gospel, so far as we know it, in the Face of a Thousand Difficulties, Reproaches, and Oppositions; we *sell* the Truth, we *deny* the Truth, and have no Evidence, if we continue so to do, that we are *of* the Truth. We ought to follow the Lord in every Path of Duty he is pleas'd to shew us. As saith the Apostle, *Phil.* iii. 16. *Whereto we have already* attained, *let us walk by the same* Rule, *let us mind the same* Thing. And thus we are to press forward in our *Christian Race*, looking to that immortal *Crown of Glory,* which of the *freest Grace,* shall be given to *Overcomers.*

Alas, my Friend, *you did run well,* but you have been *hindred.* And what *Fruit* have you, of your forsaking the Lord? *Terror* of Conscience *now.* And how much more of that Kind of bitter Fruit you may have when *Death* approaches, you know not. God may make you a *Terror to yourself,* and to *all* about you. And how poor an *Excuse* will it be, when you appear before the *Judgment Seat of Christ,* and must give Account of the *Things done in the Body,* whether *good* or *evil,* to say, "Lord, I would have followed thee according to the Truth of thy Word, and the Light of my Conscience; if my nearest Relative had not made such great Opposition" Alas, my dear Friend, think what an awful *Reply,* our Lord would make to such a Speech. Would you lose a far more exceeding and eternal Weight of *Glory,* for a little temporal *Ease,* and Freedom from *Affliction? The Favour of God*, for *Peace with Man?* No surely. Hearken then to the Lord's Voice, *Whatsoever thy Hand findeth to do, do it with thy Might, for there is no Wisdom nor Device in the Grave, whither thou goest.* And, *Boast not thyself of To-morrow; for thou knowest not what a Day may bring forth.*

Our Lord calls you indeed to forsake all, in Heart, and to follow Him.—But then remember, HE hath promised, That *He will never leave, nor forsake you.* That your *Shoes* shall be *Iron and Brass,* and as your *Days,* your *Strength.* He doth not call you to go a *Warfare* on your *own Charges,* to conflict with Troubles in your own Strength; but hath said *His Grace is sufficient for you,* And *His Power* shall *rest upon you.* And inviting you to take his Yoke upon you, He says, *My Yoke is easy, and my Burden is light,* Mat. xi. 30. And again, He thus assures you, *Verily I say unto you, There is no Man that hath left House, or Brethren, or Sisters, or Father, or Mother, or Wife, or Children, or Lands, for my Sake, and the Gospel's, but he shall receive an Hundred fold now in this Time, Houses, and Brethren, and Sisters, and Mothers, and Children, and Lands,* (in *Value,* tho' not in *Kind:* He shall receive the *Comforts* of all these in *God,* even to an *Hundred Fold,) with Persecutions;* (as a sweet *Cross,* to prepare him for a glorious *Crown*) *and in the World to come, Eternal Life,* Mark x. 29, 30.

You see then, my dear Friend, That it is impossible for any one to be a *Loser,* in *following Christ.* The more we *lose* for *Him,* the *greater* is our *Gain.* The greater are our *Trials,* the greater and brighter will be our *Crown.*—And, believe it, if you *follow the Lord fully,* He will *appear for you greatly.* He will not *suffer you to be tempted above that you are* able to bear; *but with the* Temptation, *will make a Way to* escape. HE hath all *Hearts* in *his Hand,* and turns them as the *Rivers of Water* which Way soever *he pleaseth.* He saith to the Wrath of man, as to the raging Sea, *Hitherto shalt thou come,* and *no further,* and *here* shall thy proud Waves be *stayed.* therefore, *Fear not them that can kill the Body,* (if you was call'd to suffer even unto *Death:* for Christ would give you a *Crown of Life*) *but fear* Him, *who after He hath killed, hath Power to cast into Hell.*—That the Lord may make you wise unto Salvation: is the hearty Desire of, my dear Friend,

Yours affectionately,

——— ———

LETTER LXIII. *To Mr.* A.

My very dear Brother in Christ,

YOUR last kind Letter I receiv'd, and give Thanks to GOD, that He was pleas'd to make my poor Books of Use to many dear Souls with you; and thankful I am to you, Brother, that you told me of the Lord's Kindness therein: To *Him* the Glory is due.—I rejoice, Brother, that your Faith of Interest in Christ is strengthened, and abides firm, amidst all Shakings, by the Variation of your Frames. And that when oppressed by your spiritual Enemies, you flee to Christ for Help against them: For your Cleansing from all Sin in his precious Blood, and for the subduing of all your Iniquities by his Almighty Arm.

You *groan,* my Brother, being *burdened,* with the *Body* of *Sin*, of *Death,* that dwelleth in you: And because of that *Distance* from GOD, which by the separating Things of this World, is occasioned to you. In both you have the *Sympathy* of your *great High Priest* in *Heaven,* the infinite Sympathy of your *Beloved's Heart.* And lo, HE lives at *God's Right Hand,* HE *ever liveth,* to *save you to the uttermost.* To succour you in your

Conflicts with the Powers of Sin and Hell: To subdue your spiritual Enemies, and utterly destroy them, at his appointed, and your approaching, Time of Deliverance: And to bring you into as full Conformity to GOD, and as near Communion with Him, as your Soul can wish, unto endless Ages! And *freed from Sin,* and *bro't to* GOD, my Brother, even into his immediate *Presence,* and set, *Holy and without Blame before* HIM *in Love:* What can you *desire more?*

No, you'll say, this is the ALL of my Desire, the *Ultimate* of my hop'd-for, long'd-for, and expected *Bliss.* But O! while I abide in this Tabernacle, I *groan* being *burdened,* with *Sin* in my *Soul,* and *Distance* from GOD.

But my Brother, since your Lord's Name is called JESUS, because He shall *save his People from their Sins,* and bring them unto GOD: Let your *future Salvation,* be your *present Joy:* And press *forward* towards the *Mark,* for this *Prize* of the *High Calling of God in Christ. Follow on to know,* and love and serve the *Lord,* increasingly in this World; and in these Respects you *shall know Him. Draw nigh to* GOD, in all appointed Means of Grace; and He will *draw nigh to you,* in the Displays of his Glory. *Come up from the Wilderness,* march towards *Canaan's* Land, *leaning upon your Beloved.* His saving *Arm,* his cheering *Bosom,* are your *Joint Privilege,* your free, great *Privilege,* of distinguishing Favour, bestowed on *you,* as the *Beloved of the* LORD. And while you rest on your Mighty Lover, your Almighty Saviour, and trust your Salvation in *his Hands,* who hath laid the *Foundation,* and will bring forth the *Head Stone* thereof with *Shoutings,* crying, *Grace, Grace unto it: Rejoice* you *in Hope of the Glory of* GOD. For *now is your Salvation nearer than when you* (first) *believed.*—the Sorrows and Sufferings of this Life pass away, yea, are but for a *Moment,* if compar'd with that *Eternity* of Bliss; which awaits us in the Life to come. And while the God of all Grace works graciously upon us by these: *Our light Affliction, which is but a Moment, worketh for us a far more exceeding and eternal Weight of Glory!* Our *groaning Souls,* under present *Misery,* and after future *Glory,* are to be deliver'd from the *one,* and blest with the *other* speedily. And our *Groans* after Immortality, *that Mortality might be swallowed up of Life,* are our *Preparation by Grace,* for our *prepared Glory:* The *Appetite* given us, for that eternal *Feast* which awaits us: And are also a present *Evidence* of our future *Bliss,* or that GOD hath *wrought us for the self-same Thing.*

You long to be *dissolved,* Brother, and to be *with Christ,* which is *far better.* And soon your Desires shall be granted. But, be free to abide in the *Flesh,* your appointed Time, for the Lord's Glory in and by *you,* and for your Glory, in and with *Him,* present and eternal.—The *Canaanites* were left in the Land, to prove *Israel.* And Sin is left in our Souls, and various Sorrows must attend our Lives, to give us Opportunities to glorify our Lord, and shew the Valour of our Graces as *good Soldiers of Jesus Christ,* by watching against, and making War upon, all the Enemies of our Lord and King. Little do you think, Brother, how much you glorify Christ, and delight his Heart, when you are efficaciously taught by the *Grace* that bringeth *Salvation,* to *deny Ungodliness and worldly Lusts, and to live soberly, righteously, and godly in this present (evil) World:* Nor yet, how much your *good Conversation in Christ,* will be to his *eternal Honour and Pleasure.* Our Lord's Glory and Joy in his People, express'd before his Father, *I am glorify'd in them:* Nor will, nor can, know any *Decay.* As our *Obedience* glorifies his *Name,* and cheers his *Heart* in the *present Time;* so the Honour and Pleasure which will arise unto *Him thereby,* in the Remembrance *thereof,* will be *eternal.* And most surely, every Thing that we are enabled to do or suffer for *Christ now,* will be the Matter of our *endless Joy;* and all our Doings and Sufferings for HIM in this present Time, thro' our Lord's infinite *Grace,* shall serve as so many *Jewels,* to enrich our *Crown* of *eternal Glory.*—And who then, that *loves Christ,* his *Honour* and *Pleasure,* present and eternal; and has a due Regard to his *own Happiness* in this World, and in that which is to come; would not be heartily willing to *suffer,* and earnestly desirous to *do,* the *whole Will of God,* for these blessed *Ends!*

And tho' our Gospel Obedience, to our great Grief, is very imperfect; yet, let this be our great Joy, That *our Salvation,* from *Sin,* shall be to *God's eternal Honour.* The Forgiveness of all our Sins, to the endless Honour, of the exceeding Riches of the *Father's Grace:* The Cleansing of our Souls, from all our Uncleanness and deep-dy'd Sins, from the Guilt and Filth of all our Transgressions, to the endless Honour, of the boundless *Grace* of the dying *Saviour,* and the infinite

Merit and efficacy of his precious *Blood:* And the subduing of our Iniquity, and the Sanctification of our Nature, to the endless Honour, of the Almighty Power and Grace of the *Holy Ghost,* our *Sanctifier.*—This, my dear Brother, may be a Relief to our Spirits, under the heavy Burden of our daily Infirmities.

But as *Sin* is the greatest of *Evils* in itself; as it is the abominable *Thing* which GOD *hates;* as it casts the greatest *Dishonour* upon the LORD, *Father, Son,* and *Spirit;* and as it brings the greatest *Misery* upon *us,*and *others:* O let us in the Strength of Christ, in all Things *watch,* and *strive against Sin!* And in all Things *labour,* for GOD'S Honour, and our own and others Advantage, to be HOLINESS TO THE LORD, more than ever!—*The Grace of Christ be with your Spirit!* With affectionate Esteem, I am, my dear Brother,

Yours in the Lord for ever,

——— ———

LETTER LXIV. *To* ----- -----

My dear Sister in Christ,

I Am grieved with you, for your Loss.—But it becomes us to submit to God's holy Will. May the Lord sanctify it to you and yours, and to every of us, to whom this awful Stroke gives a loud Call, *Be ye also ready:* for at such an Hour as you *think not,* the *Son of Man cometh!* You see how suddenly, how unexpectedly, *Death* cometh; and after Death the *Judgment:* The awful Judgment, that decides our State, for a vast *Eternity!* Let this put *you* on a more earnest Concern, to be *actually ready* for your *Lord's Coming.*—And be not content to go to Heaven *alone.* Now you have but one of your nearest Relatives left, and know not how soon you may lose Him: (for when Death comes into a Family, it often strikes more than One, in a little Time.) O do your utmost, while his Health and Strength lasts, to shew him the Vanity of this World, and to perswade him to *seek a better Country,* a *City that hath Foundations,* of Bliss ineffable and eternal, whose Builder and Maker is GOD! Pray for him most earnestly and incessantly. Tell him his lost and miserable State by *Nature,* thro' original and actual *Sin.* that he must be *born again,* or can never *see the Kingdom of* GOD. And that this little Inch of *Time,* the *present* Time, is all he hath, to prepare for a blest *Eternity,* That if this is *misspent,* and the great Salvation proclaim'd in the Gospel *neglected;* his *Soul* is *lost forever! Better* far would it have been for *him,* if he had *never been born!* Tell him likewise, That God hath taken away his dear *Relative,* to warm *him,* in a very particular Manner. That he is call'd hereby, to *turn* unto GOD speedily; and that the Lord *waits to see,* if his sparing *Goodness,* will lead him to *Repentance.* Set before him the great and precious Promises of the Gospel: That those who *seek the Lord truly,* that seek him *early,* shall *find Him,* unto *Life eternal! &c.* And who knows but GOD may incline his Heart to receive Instruction?—Have you been so tender and careful of his *Body,* from the first Moment of his Birth, until now, tho' you know it must soon *perish,* and turn to its original *Dust:* And can you disregard his *Soul,* his *immortal* Soul, that is far more *precious* than the *whole World!* As our Lord saith, *What shall it profit a Man if he gain the* whole World, *and lose his own Soul?* O the *Loss* of the *Soul,* is an *irreparable* Loss! ALL is *gone,* if the *Soul* is *lost!* What if a Man could gain the Treasures, Pleasures, and Honours of the *Universe,* call Earth and Sea, Sun, Moon and Stars, *all his Own:* If CHRIST, and GOD in Him, were not his present and everlasting *Portion:* Alas for him, his *Soul* were *lost,* he were *for ever undone!* And all these his momentary Enjoyments, which only served to increase his Sins, would prove as so many Aggravations of his endless Torments! *Son, remember,* that thou in thy *Life-time* hadst *thy good Things:* Will cause a fierce *Reflection,* that will make the Furnace *glow,* and serve as fresh *Fuel* to feed the quenchless *Flame!*—O then, my dear Sister, what Care and Labour can be too much, what enough, to take your beloved Relative to prevent his *coming* into that *Place of Torment!* Should sickness seize him, and Death approach; you would fear to speak to him then, lest pensive Thoughts, should increase his Disease. Therefore, *now,* now he is in *Health,* if *ever* you do or say any Thing for his *Soul's Advantage;* Set about it *instantly,* and most *earnestly.* Don't let Trifles *divert you,* not make *him think,* That *Eternal Things,* are of *small Moment,* and not worth seeking *for,* most *ardently!*—And so far as you know the *blessed Gospel,* which has been *your Salvation;* and are satisfy'd that you hear it *clearly preach'd:* O do your utmost to bring *Him,* under the same *joyful Sound!* Who can tell but he may have the *Blessedness to know it for himself,* unto his *Joy* unspeakable here, and to his eternal *Glory* hereafter:--But perhaps you will say,

I should be glad to have my Relative attend the Worship of God with me, and to wait in the *Way* where JESUS passeth by. But the Dissenting Interest is so low and small, and there are so many that oppose and deride it; and reproach those that look towards it; I think, for the Shame and Fear of Men, he will refuse Compliance with my Request, tho' otherwise he might be so inclined.—I answer:

If upon attempting your Duty in this Regard, you find that this is *really* the *Case* with him: O *compassionate his Soul,* under those *Chains of Darkness,* in which he is *held:* And looking up to GOD for a Blessing, be *you faithful,* and tell him plainly, That the *Friendship of this World, is Emnity with* GOD: That *Whosoever is ashamed of* CHRIST, his *Words,* and *Ways,* his Gospel and Ordinances, *before Men;* Of *him,* our *Lord* will be *ashamed,* when *He cometh in his own Glory, in the Glory of his Father, and with all his holy Angels.* And that *Whosoever will come after Christ,* up to Heaven, must *deny Himself,* and *take up his Cross, and follow him:* Or he *cannot* be *his Disciple,* and will not be accounted *worthy of Him:* Whom to *know,* to possess and enjoy, is *Life eternal!*—And ask him, Which he thinks is best that a Man should chuse, Whether to suffer a *momentary Shame* for Christ's Sake, from Men *here:* Or to be raised up unto *Shame and everlasting Contempt hereafter?* Or, to be put to an *open Shame,* befire all the glorify'd *saints* and holy *Angels,* yea, to have *Christ Himself ashamed* to own him, when HE *appears*, when an *Interest* in the *Son of God,* will be apparently of more *Worth,* of infinitely more *Value,* than innumerable *Worlds*—And who can tell, GOD, by *You,* may *perswade* Japheth, and He may *dwell* in the *Tents of* Shem. And may say, to your Heart's Rejoycing, as *Ruth* to *Naomi, Thy People shall be my People, and thy God my God: Nought but Death shall part thee and me.*

As to your deceased Relative, I am glad you had *Hope* concerning him. *That,* may alleviate your *Grief* for his *Death,* and excite you to a more complacent Acquiescence with the *Will of God.* There is one *Instance* recorded in Scripture, that a dying Sinner, found Mercy; *The Thief upon the Cross:* That none should *despair,* if God is pleased to *call* them at the *eleventh Hour.* And there is but *One;* That none should *presume,* to trust to a *Death-Bed Repentance,* and put off the vast Concerns of *Eternity,* to that uncertain and afflicting Moment of *Time,* which is so very *unfit* for Things of the *greatest Importance.*—Wishing *all Grace and Peace may abound towards you,* to your abundant Growth and Fruitfulness in *this World,* and a weighty Crown of Glory in the *World to come:* I remain,

Your affectionate Friend and Servant,

——— ———

LETTER LXV. *To Mr.* F.

Dear Sir,

I Thank you for your kind Letter. It gives me Joy, that my last, with the Book sent, were acceptable and useful unto you and others. I should not have wrote so soon, but that you complain of *Darkness* and *Deadness of Spirit,* which sometimes seise you, and lament your *Heart wandrings* from the *altogether-lovely* JESUS, after *other Objects.* Whence I was induced from Sympathy with you in your Soul-Trouble, to write a Line on this Head; and especially, as while I was lifting up my Heart to God for your renewed Quickning, the following Words dropt on my Mind, which I was willing to acquaint you with : *Viz.*

Hos. 14. 7, 8. *They that dwell under his Shadow shall return, they shall revive as the Corn, and grow as the Vine: the Scent thereof shall be as the Wine of* Lebanon.

Ephraim *shall say, What have I to do any more with Idols? I have heard him and observ'd him: I am like a green Fir-Tree, from* ME *is thy Fruit found.*

Here, Dear Sir, are reviving Cordials, to raise your fainting Spirit, if the Holy Ghost your Comforter with his own Hand is pleas'd to give them.—From the 7th Verse we may observe, 1. The Description here given of the People of God: they are such that *Dwell under his Shadow.* And 2. The Privileges of those that abide under the Shadow of the Almighty: Which are 1. Restoration from all their Backslidings, from all their Wandrings: *They shall return.* 2. Renewed Quicknings, after awful

Decays: *They shall revive as the Corn.* 3. Abundant Growth and Fruit, in their Spring and Summer-Seasons: *And grow as the Vine.* And 4. The Acceptableness of their Persons, Graces and Services, to the Lord, and those that are His: *The Scent thereof shall be as the Wine of* Lebanon.

I pass, Dear Sir, from the Hints here given of the People of God, and their Privileges in general, unto You in particular. And is it your blest Experience, That *you dwell* under *Christ's Shadow?* O how *happy* is your Situation, how *great* your Security, both for Time and Eternity! O the delightful *Shade,* that GOD the *Saviour,* as a *great Rock,* affords to us poor *Sinners,* that flee by *Faith to Him,* in this *weary Land!* When weary with the Guilt of Sin, our dear Lord Jesus, our all-attoning Sacrifice, is a refreshing Shade to us, from the scorching Heat of avenging Justice, and fiery Indignation. When weary with Sin's Defilement, the cleansing Fountain of his Blood, shades us from that Displeasure which infinite Purity, must otherwise shew at our Depravity. When weary with the Power of Sin, the Shade of our Lord's promis'd Grace, the Strength of his saving Arm, engaged for us, delivers us from the Grief we feel, and the Hurt we fear, from this our killing Foe. And when our Heaven-born Souls are weary with the Inbeing of Hellish sin, O what a refreshing Shade, doth our Lord's inherent Purity, with that full Conformity thereto, we are to have in Glory, give to our Pilgrim-Souls, while seeking a better Country! Again, From Men and Devils, from the World with all its Snares, from Hell with all its Wiles and Powers, from all our Cares and Fears, our Griefs and Burthens, O what a delightful Rest, what a refreshing Shade, doth the Lord our Mighty Conqueror, our great Saviour, afford to us that come to Him, as weary, and heavy laden Sinners!—And under *his Shadow,* Sir, *you dwell,* in *Christ,* the *secret Place of the most High,* and shall abide under the *Shadow of the Almighty.*—But perhaps you will say,

If I dwell under Christ's Shadow, how is it that Deadness and Inactivity for God, that bitter Fruit of the Power of Sin, so often afflicts me? I answer:

There is a Two fold Dwelling under the Shadow of Christ, which respects Believers. As 1. *Habitual.* And 2. *Actual.* All Believers dwell under the Shadow of Christ *Habitually,* in that as they commit the

Keeping of their Souls unto Him in Well-doing; So they are under his Care, and the Habit of Faith in their Hearts, is and shall be maintain'd by his gracious Influence, in Spite of all Opposition, from within and without. And all Believers likewise, do dwell under the Shadow of Christ *Actually,* in that they actually flee repeatedly unto Him by Faith, as their Refuge, Shelter and Deliverer, from all their Foes, Griefs and Dangers whatsoever; and so are blest with his kind Protection, gracious Influence, and great Salvation. But then, in this latter Sense, they don't *always* abide in *Him,* or cleave unto *Him,* in the actual Exercise of a lively *Faith:* And so they *lose* the Sweets of those blessed Privileges, which they once *enjoy'd.*—Unbelief too often prevails, which inclines us to depart from the living GOD, from GOD our Saviour, by Heart-wandrings after other Lovers. Trifles divert our Thoughts, we lose Sight of our Beloved, and Sin getting the Ascendant of Grace, we pursue pleasing Shadows, delusive Shadows, and let go the Sum and Substance of all our Bliss: We forsake the LORD, our *Light,* our *Life,* our ALL, and depart into empty *Nothings,* vexing *Vanities,* into *Soul Darkness* and *Death.*—And never should we return unto the Lord *more,* if He did not go *after us,* seek our *lost Souls,* lay us on his *Shoulder,* and bring us *Home rejoycing.*—But O the infinite Grace of GOD our *Saviour,* towards us the *Heirs* of his *Salvation:* HE sees us in all our Misery, and in the unsearchable Depths of his Never-failing Mercy, He says concerning us, "*They shall return:* They are Mine still, tho' rebellious, beloved of Me, tho' ungrateful to Me: They dwell under *my Shadow,* they have committed the Keeping of their Souls unto ME, and as I engag'd for them in Covenant from Everlasting, when given me of my Father, and to them by my faithful Promise, when they resign'd themselves unto my Care, at the Time of their Espousals unto Me by Faith: I will not *lose them;* None of their potent *Enemies,* neither Men nor Devils, no, nor their own Sins neither, shall pluck them *out* of my All-gracious and Almighty *Hands.* I will be *merciful* to their *Unrighteousness,* and *remember* their *Sins no more.* I will *subdue* their *Iniquites,* revive and increase their *Graces,* allure their Hearts unto ME, and open to them my Heart and Arms *afresh,* to receive their *returning Souls.*"

Thus, Sir, You see how Deadness and Inactivity for GOD, at Times seiseth you, tho' as a Believer, you dwell under the Shadow of CHRIST: It is for want of a *constant* Abiding in Him by Faith. You see likewise, That tho' sad is your Case, when you *depart* from the *Lord;* yet so great is his *Grace,* that He will *restore* your *Soul:* So great is your Privilege by Promise, That you *shall return!* Dwelling under his Shadow *Habitually;* You shall again dwell under his Shadow *Actually:* and return'd from the Death of your Backslidings, you shall again increase in Life, by renewed Quicknings.—For lo, your Privilege beneath the Saviour's Shade, is not only a *Return,* to the former Vigour and Strength of your Graces, but also to a more *glorious Life*, and *abundant Fruit* and *Fragrancy*. Returning, you shall *revive as the Corn:* Which after it dies, and loseth its Beauty; as a single Grain, in the Earth, is quickned to the Glory of a springing Greenness, and of numerous Grains in one full Ear. You shall *grow as the Vine:* Which after a piercing cold Winter, by the reviving Summer-Sun speedily casts abroad its Branches, and with its tender *Grapes,* gives a *good Smell.* Yea, so fragrant shall you be in your full Fruits of Righteousness, which are by Jesus Christ, to the Glory and Praise of God, that your *Scent shall be as the Wine of* Lebanon: Refreshing to the Heart of God and Man!—But a Hint or two I wou'd give to Ver. 8.

Ephraim *shall say, What have I to do any more with Idols? I have heard him and observ'd him: I am like a green Fir-Tree, from* ME *is the Fruit found.*—In this we may observe, 1. That GOD'S *Shall,* precedes Ephraim's *I will:* Ephraim *shall say,* What have I to do *any more with Idols? I will* have *no more* to do *with Idols.* 2. The actual *Presence* of what was *future* in Itself, to the *Divine Mind: I have heard him and observ'd him:* Or, I *now hear,* and *see* with Pleasure, what *Ephraim* shall say and be *hereafter.* And 3. The *Spring* and *Cause* of *Ephraim's* Bliss, in *Christ,* his *Head of Grace: I am like a green Fir-Tree, from* ME *is thy Fruit found:* As if the Lord should say, "*I* am always green and flourishing, to represent, and refresh thee, when *thou* thro' Decay hast lost *thy* Beauty, and art weary. From ME, from *mine* immense Fulness of communicable *Grace,* is *thy Fruit found:* Both the Fruit of *my Love,* on which thou shalt feast *with Joy,* in my renewed Appearances for thee; and the Fruit of *thy Faith,* which thou shalt yield to *my Praise,* under the efficacious Influence of my All-sufficient Grace: Secur'd to *Thee,* they both are in ME."

Hence, Sir, If your poor Soul is in a lifeless, indifferent Frame God-ward, if to your Grief you have forsaken the Lord, and gone after other Lovers, and if hereby you are so weakned and wounded, that you have neither Skill nor Strength to return unto your Rest: O don't think you shall be *left* in a State of *Distance.* The Lord your mighty Saviour, will again bring you *nigh.* The Virtue of his *Blood,* and the Power of his *Arm,* most sweetly and strongly secure your *Return.* Behold, your Deliverance, your Restoration, unto full Salvation, is already engaged for, by infinite Grace and Faithfulness: The Word is gone out of his Mouth, and he will not alter it, *Ephraim,* revolting *Ephraim,* shall say, *What have I to do any more,* I will *have to do no more with Idols.* Already the Lord *hears* and *observes* you; He sees and hears with Pleasure, what you *shall say* and *be,* under the renewed Influences of his *Grace-Power.* And lo, when under sad *Decays,* the *Lord,* your *Head* and *Life,* is then for *you,* a *green Fir-tree,* an Ever green, and flourishing Beauty, to represent, and restore you; and from HIM, from his inexhaustible Fulness of Grace, *your Fruit* is and shall be *found:* To your unspeakable Joy in *Him,* and to his present, and endless Praise by *you!*

Having these *Promises* then, to encourage your Faith and Hope in God, Whenever you feel Deadness towards him, and Distance from him, attempt your *Duty* in returning to Him. For tho' the Lord must *draw us,* before we can *run to him:* Yet as God works by *Means,* and meets his People in boundless Mercy, while they wait for Him in the Paths of Duty; O stir up yourself to seek GOD. *Seek* and you shall *find; knock* and it shall be *opened unto you.* Give the Lord no Rest, until He arise and have Mercy on you. He hath promised to *increase* his People: (their Life and Joy, after Death and Sorrow:) But yet for this He will be *enquired of* by the House of *Israel,* to *do it for them:* And as the Answer of their Prayer, He will fulfill his own Promise. Hark then, my dear Brother, what the Lord says to his People, and to you, when ever you feel Deadness towards him, and Distance from him: *O* Israel, *return unto the* LORD *thy God; for thou hast fallen by thine Iniquity. Take with you Words, and turn to the* LORD, *say unto Him, Take away all Iniquity, and receive us graciously: so will we render the Calves of our Lips.* Ashur *shall not save us, we will not ride upon Horses, neither will we say any more to the Work of our Hands, Ye are our gods: for in thee the Fatherless findeth Mercy,* Ver. 1, 2, 3. Confess before the Lord, and bewail your Iniquity: Intreat his Mercy, to take it all away; and a gracious Reception, upon your Return. That so you may give him Praise, forsake Idols, and cleave unto Him alone, in whom as *Fatherless,* Friendless and Helpless, from all the Creatures, you shall *find Mercy.* And lo, unto *you,* with his *returning People,* He will say, *I will heal their Backslidings, I will love them freely: for mine Anger is turned away from Him. I will be as the Dew unto* Israel, &c. Ver. 4, 5, 6.—That the *Grace of Christ* may thus be *with your Spirit;* to make you grow and flourish in the Ways of God: is the hearty Desire of, dear Sir,

Your affectionate Friend and Servant,

LETTER LXVI. To ----- -----

My very dear Sister in our precious Lord,

GOD will *help you,* and that *right early. The Night is far spent, the Day is at Hand.* Wait but a little while longer, and *your Sorrow* shall be *turned into Joy.* You wanted to have—and so did I, and took a deal of Pleasure in hoping it would be so. But what if the Lord designs to deliver you in a better Way, and unto greater Bliss, and also unto his greater Praise? Won't you rejoice in *that?* The *Government* is upon *Christ's Shoulder:* And most surely our dear Lord hath done, and will do all Things *so well,* that we cannot wish to have any Thing *better,* than it is, and shall be. Why should we, *silly Children,* be our own Chusers? Our own Carvers? Shou'd we not thereby lessen our Portion? And wound ourselves? Since we have a *Father,* that is infinitely wise and tender, careful and faithful, whose Goodness knows no Bounds, and whose Provisions made for us, are according to his *State,* and worthy of his Great SELF; let us say in Faith and Love, in the greatest filial Duty, with an holy Cheerfulness, for his Honour and our own Joy: *Choose* THOU *our Inheritance for us.*—That *all Grace may abound towards you,* until you are filled with *all Glory:* is the sincere Desire of, my dear Sister,

Yours most affectionately,

FINIS.

ERRATA.

Index